THE PAPAL STATE IN THE
THIRTEENTH CENTURY

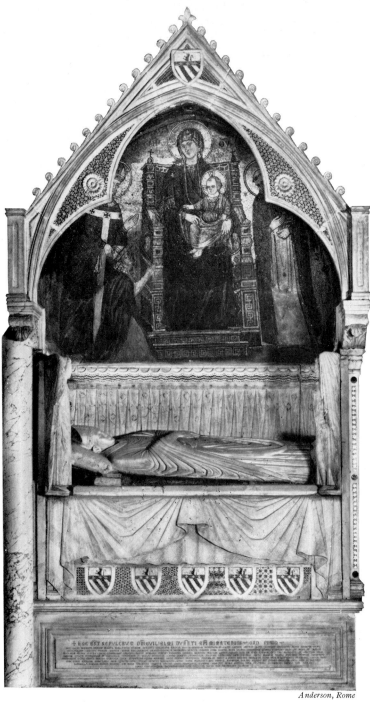

The tomb in S. Maria *sopra Minerva*, Rome, of William Durand, rector
of the Tuscan Patrimony *c.* 1277–8, of Romagna 1284–6 and 1295–6, of
the March 1295–6. By Giovanni di Cosma (1296).

THE PAPAL STATE
IN THE
THIRTEENTH CENTURY

BY

DANIEL WALEY

LONDON
MACMILLAN & CO LTD
NEW YORK · ST MARTIN'S PRESS
1961

MACMILLAN AND COMPANY LIMITED
London Bombay Calcutta Madras Melbourne

THE MACMILLAN COMPANY OF CANADA LIMITED
Toronto

ST MARTIN'S PRESS INC
New York

PRINTED IN GREAT BRITAIN

To
JOHN SIBLY

ACKNOWLEDGEMENTS

I SHOULD like to record my gratitude to King's College, Cambridge, and to the University of London for grants which made it possible for me to work in many Italian archives and libraries during the years 1952–9. I have also received much kindness in Italy from archivists, librarians and hospitable friends. Mrs. G. Cornwell typed much of the manuscript for me with great skill. For the map I am indebted to Mrs. E. Wilson of the Geography Department at the London School of Economics. The index is the work of Miss R. J. Mitchell; I am most grateful to her for undertaking this skilled and exacting task.

I have to thank the editor and publishers (Messrs. Longmans Green and Co. Ltd.) of the *English Historical Review* for permitting me to use (in Chapter IX) material which has already appeared in that journal.

Though doubtful about the appropriateness of displaying or confessing in this place a quite overwhelming domestic debt, I cannot omit to mention gratefully that my wife found time to read and criticize the whole book in manuscript.

D.P.W.

CONTENTS

CHAPTER   PAGE

INTRODUCTION   xiii

I. PAPAL CLAIMS AND PAPAL RULE IN CENTRAL ITALY BEFORE 1197   1

    Donations and claims up to the time of Barbarossa — papal rule in this period — Empire, papacy and central Italy, 1176–97.

II. INNOCENT III AND THE FOUNDATION OF THE PAPAL STATE, 1198–1216   30

    Innocent III's gains before 1202–1202–8: difficulties in Rome and the March, the parliament of Viterbo — the challenge of Otto IV — the papal recovery after 1211.

III. THE POPE'S SUBJECTS   68

    The nature of papal suzerainty — central Italy in the early thirteenth century, the economic and political development of the towns.

IV. THE INSTITUTIONS OF THE PAPAL STATE   91

    The provinces: rectors, rectors *in spiritualibus*, treasurers, judges and other officials — parliaments — central authority: papal chamber, pope and cardinals.

V. THE PAPAL STATE AND THE HOHENSTAUFEN, 1216–65   125

    Honorius III (1216–27) — Gregory IX's pontificate up to Frederick II's assault on the State (1239) — the papal-imperial struggle in central Italy, 1239–50 — the period between Frederick II and Manfred: papal disappointments — the crises of 1259–65: Manfred, Urban IV and Charles of Anjou.

VI. THE PAPAL STATE AND THE ANGEVINS, 1266–85   176

    Reconquest by Clement IV, Gregory X and their successors, 1266–77 — Nicholas III (1277–80), his family policy: Romagna and the struggle to gain power there — Martin IV (1281–85), his Angevin support: continuance of the war in Romagna.

VII. THE PAPAL STATE, THE COLONNA AND THE CAETANI, 1285–1304   209

    Honorius IV (1285–87) — Nicholas IV (1288–92), his dependence on the Colonna, his innovations in government — troubles of the long vacancy and Celestine V's pontificate — Boniface VIII (1294–1303), his innovations and governmental methods — events in the State during this pontificate — Benedict XI: the State in 1304.

CHAPTER	PAGE
VIII. THE FINANCIAL UTILITY OF THE PAPAL STATE	252

Sources of revenue — profit and loss, particularly in the period 1279–1304.

IX. THE MILITARY UTILITY OF THE PAPAL STATE   276

The obligation and its effectiveness — money-payments and mercenaries.

CONCLUSION   297

APPENDIXES:

    I. List of Parliaments   304
    II. List of Officials   307

BIBLIOGRAPHY   325

INDEX   339

ILLUSTRATIONS

The tomb in S. Maria _sopra Minerva_, Rome, of William Durand, rector of the Tuscan Patrimony _c._ 1277–8, of Romagna 1284–6 and 1295–6, of the March 1295–6. By Giovanni di Cosma (1296).   _Frontispiece_

The monument in the Duomo, Florence, of Bishop Anthony Orso, rector of the March 1302–3. By Tino di Camaino (1321).   _Facing page xiv_

Map   _at end of book_

ABBREVIATIONS

INTRODUCTION

'NEVER has dominion over great empires cost dynasties such arduous struggles as the little territory, over which they desired to rule as kings, cost the bishops of Rome. The genius of a hundred popes, the energy and property of the Church, countless wars and excommunications, oaths and concordats were expended to create and uphold the State of the Church, and almost every pope was forced to begin the work afresh and laboriously to piece together the fragments. . . . Throughout the entire Middle Ages the popes rolled the stone of Sisyphus.' In these words Ferdinand Gregorovius[1] described the theme of this book, which is the attempt of the thirteenth-century popes to found a state in central Italy. The attempt was in the main a failure and the communes continued their tradition of independence, their development relatively little affected by papal overlordship. The narrative is one, to borrow Edouard Jordan's definition, of 'a series of obscure and monotonous conflicts'.[2] To make such a story interesting may require the genius of a Gregorovius, yet no apology is needed for devoting a volume to it. Rule is no less worthy of investigation when it is unsuccessful. Moreover, papal claims were for the first time being given some sort of reality and this was the beginning of what was to remain an important and controversial feature of the European polity until Cavour crossed the Rubicon in September 1860.

My investigations have been limited to the papal attempt to rule central Italy, to the methods and policies of the popes and the reasons for their failure.[3] The theoretical justifications of this rule might well be susceptible of treatment at length but they have little direct bearing on the topic treated here in a book which is offered as a study in the *practice* of government.

There can be no claim that this work draws together the findings of many monographs, for unfortunately such studies are almost entirely lacking. The only previous attempt known to me to treat the subject

---

[1] *History of the City of Rome in the Middle Ages*, V, 1, 130.

[2] *Les Origines de la Domination Angevine en Italie*, p. 261.

[3] In order to preserve this unity of treatment I have not dealt with papal rule in the isolated papal territories of Benevento and the Comtat-Venaissin (for these, see the works of Vehse and Faure cited in the Bibliography) nor with areas, such as Ferrara and the Matildine lands, over which the popes exercised no authority in practice.

as a whole is in the pages of Sugenheim's *Geschichte der Entstehung und Ausbilding des Kirchenstaates* (1854), a good book which is based only on the few sources available in print at the time when it was written. There has been no book on the history of a single province and the only treatment of the State during a single pontificate, Seeger's short thesis on *Die Reorganisation des Kirchenstaates unter Innocenz III.*, leaves much to be desired. Few towns of the Papal State have been the subject of adequate histories, though one must except with gratitude from this generalization the writings of Dr. W. Hagemann on Fabriano, Iesi and Montolmo (now Corridonia) during the Hohenstaufen period.[1] Very considerable assistance has been derived from Professor G. Ermini's long series of publications on the institutions of the medieval Papal State, which deal with its parliaments, rectors and judges and with the status of the communes. Some errors of fact and interpretation in this book could have been avoided by waiting until more monographic studies had appeared, but the wait might have been a very long one and the author can only plead impatience and the belief that a necessarily inaccurate exploration of the ground is better than no map at all. One difficulty in writing such a work is more or less insuperable. It is concerned largely with the relations between papal authority and many dozens of communes and will inevitably be incorrect at times in its appreciation of the local implications of papal action, for it is not possible for one person to master the local political history of all these towns. Whatever inadequacies and failures of comprehension may mar the following pages it is hoped that at least the two appendixes listing the officials and the parliaments of the Papal State in the years 1198–1304 will provide solid and useful contributions to knowledge.[2]

The paucity of historical writing concerning the Papal State is all the more surprising in view of the survival of many sources for the medieval period. The archives of the provinces themselves have unfortunately disappeared almost completely, but the text of many letters to and from the provincial rectors has been preserved in municipal archives. The printed and unprinted documents of the State's numerous communes are the main source for this book. Besides letters and miscellaneous parchments, minutes of council-meetings (*riformanze*) and lists

---

[1] For details of publications mentioned in this Introduction, see Bibliography (pp. 325 ff.). In addition to the articles mentioned above, Dr. Hagemann has published many thirteenth-century documents from the archive at Gubbio.

[2] I should be grateful for additions and corrections to the Appendixes. It might be possible to print these in a sequel to this book, covering the period of the Avignon papacy, which I contemplate writing.

The monument in the Duomo, Florence, of Bishop Anthony Orso,
rector of the March 1302-3. By Tino di Camaino (1321).

of revenue and expenditure provide much information concerning papal government. Many books contain documents from these archives, or publish them in translation or summary. Among these one may mention in particular, for the March of Ancona, the many volumes of Colucci's *Antichità Picene*, Zonghi's *Carte Diplomatiche Fabrianesi*, Gianandrea's *Carte Diplomatiche Iesine*, Amiani's *Memorie istoriche della città di Fano*, Bricchi's *Annali di Cagli*, the publications by Acquacotta, Grimaldi and others from the Matelica archive, and Compagnoni's *Reggia Picena* (which is based on documents from Macerata). The other provinces can offer few printed collections of the same quality, but comparable volumes for Romagna are Tonini's *Storia di Rimini* and Fantuzzi's *Monumenti Ravennati*, for the Duchy Pellini's *Dell' Historia di Perugia*, for the Tuscan Patrimony Pinzi's *Storia di Viterbo*, and for the Campagna-Marittima Contatore's *De historia terracinensi*. These have been supplemented by visits to more than a score of municipal archives in search of unprinted materials.

The other major source of information on the Papal State is the papal registers, and these are easy of consultation, thanks to the publication by the French School at Rome of the registers for the popes from Gregory IX to Benedict XI inclusive.[1] Other important documents from the Vatican are to be found in Theiner's *Codex Diplomaticus dominii temporalis S. Sedis,* in Fabre's edition of the *Liber Censuum* and elsewhere, and use has also been made of some unprinted material from this archive.

Papal biographies of this century are on the whole disappointing. The *Gesta Innocentii III* are the best of a poor lot, but Thierri de Vaucouleurs, the biographer of Urban IV, takes a special interest in his hero's deeds in the Papal State and thus reconciles us in part to his excruciatingly bad verse. The town chronicles for the greater part of the State are also rather meagre, but with the acquisition of Romagna the papacy gained a land with superior annalistic traditions. The chroniclers of Cesena, Forlì, Faenza and in particular those of Bologna enable us to achieve a far better acquaintance with the situation in this province than is possible for the territories obtained by Innocent III. These original materials are both plentiful and varied and indeed their copiousness may explain the passing of more than a century since the appearance of the last general work on the medieval Papal State.

[1] The registers of Innocent III and Honorius III are published respectively by Migne and Pressutti. The French School's edition of the registers does not publish all letters *in extenso*, but the text of all important letters concerning the Papal State is to be found there or in Martène and Durand's *Thesaurus* or the MGH *Epistolae Selectae*.

I

Papal Claims and Papal Rule in Central Italy before 1197

Both the possession of widespread estates and an undefined claim to have succeeded to Byzantine authority within the duchy of Rome gave the popes a measure of political rule before the Carolingian donations, but since Innocent III's claim to the Papal State was based on those and later donations, it is with them that we must begin the history of this State.

The donations of Pepin (754) and of Charlemagne (774) have come down to us only in the versions of papal biographers, but is is evident that they assigned to the popes that area of central Italy which had fallen to the Lombards (the northern boundary being a line running from Luni on the Tyrrhenian through Parma, Reggio and Mantua) as well as the former exarchate of Ravenna and the provinces of Venice and Istria.[1]

For the donation of Louis the Pious to Paschal I in 817 we possess a text[2] which appears genuine in substance and is the oldest of the documents used by Innocent III. The wording of this donation is more precise, but since it names places within the area granted, instead of defining a frontier, comparison is difficult. It seems, however, that by this time[3] the Carolingians envisaged a more southerly border, running approximately through Populonia, Orvieto and Perugia, and then turning north to include Bologna and Ferrara, as well as Comacchio. Much of Tuscany and Emilia are omitted here, as well as Venetia, Istria, and the duchy of Spoleto except for the area known as Sabina,[4] but the

---

[1] *Lib. Cens.*, I, 345–6.

[2] *Lib. Cens.*, 363–5. For a discussion of the text see Ficker, *Forschungen*, II, 332–53. There is a large literature on the question of the genuineness of this document. T. Sickel, *Das Privilegium Otto I. für die römische Kirche*, pp. 50–102, has shown that the palaeographical evidence is compatible with its authenticity.

[3] Ficker, *Forschungen*, II, 346–50, shows that an agreement about this change in the area donated had probably been reached by Charlemagne and Adrian I in 781.

[4] The pope was to receive for the duchies of Tuscany and Spoleto an annual *census* equal to that previously paid for these duchies to the Lombard kings (*Lib. Cens.*, I, 364).

B

papal *patrimonia* in the south near Naples and Salerno are now included, while Sardinia and Sicily are added to Corsica, the only insular possession mentioned in the previous donations.[1]

The legal significance of these grants is uncertain, nor is it relevant to the theme of this book, but the wording of the donation of 817 makes it evident that more than a mere cession of property was intended. The lands ceded were to be held permanently by the pope and his successors *iure, principatu, atque ditione* (this formula is used twice) and the emperor expressly renounced any power of *disponendi vel iudicandi* in the area. Moreover the pope's rights in the territories now granted were equated with the powers he had hitherto exercised within Rome and its duchy.[2] Later emperors, however, were to show that they did not regard suzerainty in central Italy as having passed to the popes. As early as 824 Lothair's *Constitutio Romana* placed supreme justice in Rome itself in the hands of two *missi*, one papal, the other imperial: appeal was to lie in the first instance to the pope, but ultimately to the emperor.[3]

Before considering the effectiveness of the Carolingian donations to the popes it will be convenient to mention the confirmations of them to which Innocent III also had recourse, and to trace briefly the history of papal claims to dominion in central Italy during the four intervening centuries. The first post-Carolingian donation known to us is that of Otto I granted in 962 to John XII.[4] In this a return was made to the liberal boundary of 774, probably on the strength of an imperial grant of 875 which has not survived, yet the retention of the formula of 817 concerning the payment by the emperor of a *census* for the duchies of Tuscany and Spoleto and the proviso *salva super eosdem ducatus nostra in omnibus dominatione*, suggest that little change was now intended. The

---

[1] Ficker's contention that the addition of Sardinia and Sicily is an interpolation is not entirely convincing: see E. E. Stengel in *HZ*, CXXXIV, 233.

[2] A. Hauck, *Kirchengeschichte Deutschlands* (ed. 5), II, 493n. believes the vital passage about *disponendi vel iudicandi* to be an interpolation, but his arguments are not strong. For the duchy of Rome, see C. Diehl, *Études sur l'Administration Byzantine dans l'Exarchat de Ravenne*, pp. 63–8.

[3] MGH, Capitularia Regum Francorum, I, 322–4.

[4] *Lib. Cens.*, I, 368. For a discussion see Ficker, *Forschungen*, II, 357–65; E. E. Stengel, 'Die Entwicklung des Kaiserprivilegs für die römische Kirche 817–962', *HZ*, CXXXIV, 216–41; and M. Uhlirz, 'Die Restitution des Exarchates Ravenna durch die Ottonen' *MIÖG*, L, 1–31. Ficker's reasons for believing the return to the more northerly line an interpolation are not convincing, but the strongest argument against them is the pointlessness of interpolating the more favourable frontier without also omitting the formulae implying imperial rule in Tuscany and Spoleto, rather than Stengel's reliance on the lost terms of 875. The authenticity of the part of the *Ottonianum* referring to papal elections has been questioned by W. Ullmann in *Cambridge Historical Journal*, XI, 1 (1953), 114–28, but that of its territorial clauses is unaffected by Dr. Ullmann's thesis.

altered phrasing perhaps represents nothing more than a tactful diplomatic gesture by the emperor.[1]

The curious grant made by Otto III to Sylvester II,[2] probably in
1001, conveyed eight counties in the Pentapolis (all of which are named
in the donations of Louis the Pious and Otto I) and denied the validity
of Charles the Bald's donation of 875. It was natural that later popes
preferred to turn to the privilege of Henry II (1020),[3] which confirmed
the *Ottonianum* of 962 with a few territorial additions, the only Italian
ones being the grant of imperial domain between Narni, Terni and
Spoleto.

With the emancipation of the reformed papacy from imperial
authority in the second half of the eleventh century there is abundant
evidence of the survival of the idea of papal rule in central Italy. Thus
in 1080 a synod of Rome threatened with excommunication any
Norman daring to invade the *terras sancti Petri, videlicet* 'that part of the
March of Fermo which has not yet been occupied', the duchy of
Spoleto, the Campagna, the *Marittimas*, Sabina and the *comitatus* of
Tivoli.[4] Hildebrand's letters often speak of the *terrae sancti Petri* and
mention claims in the exarchate of Ravenna and even to Salerno and
Amalfi.[5] That these claims were based on the donation of Charlemagne
as well as the supposed donation of Constantine is made clear by the
clause in the oath sworn to Hildebrand by his anti-king Rudolf concerning the *terris vel censu quae Constantinus imperator, vel Carolus, sancto
Petro dederunt*.[6] These papal pretensions were not in general taken
seriously by the Salian emperors, who did not consider that suzerainty
in central Italy had passed to the popes; they did not adopt the phrase
terra sancti Petri, preferring to speak of the papal *regalia* and *possessiones*.[7]

[1] The suggestion made by Sickel (*Das Privilegium Otto I.*, pp. 126–7), that the Campagna,
Tivoli and other places now omitted had been granted to Rome, seems improbable. The
inclusion of Naples, Fondi, Gaeta and the Sicilian *patrimonium* and the exclusion of Sicily
and Sardinia are not relevant to the history of the later Papal State. Seven towns in the
duchy of Spoleto were also specifically ceded to the pope.

[2] MGH, Diplomata, II, 818–20.

[3] *Lib. Cens.*, I, 371–3. See Ficker, *Forschungen*, II, 365–6. The donation in the neighbourhood of Narni rounded off a grant made in the same area in 1014 (W. Kölmel, *Rom und
der Kirchenstaat im 10. und 11. Jahrhundert bis in die Anfänge der Reform*, p. 72).

[4] *Lib. Pont.*, II, 287. This was clearly an estimate of that part of central Italy claimed by
the papacy which the Normans might attempt to overrun, not a full statement of the
territory claimed by the pope, for the claim was obviously not confined to the part of the
March which happened not to be in Norman hands.

[5] For example, Lib. I, epp. 10 and 21b; Lib. VIII, ep. 1b (P.L., vol. 148, cols. 292, 304–5,
574–5).

[6] P.L., vol. 148, col. 608.

[7] Ficker, *Forschungen*, II, 303–4. This generic phrase was used by Henry V at Worms
(1122), in Lothair's coronation oath (1133) and by Barbarossa in his agreement with
Eugenius III (1153).

Yet an imperialist forgery of the late eleventh century, purporting to record the cession to Otto I by Leo VIII of the lands donated by Pepin and Charlemagne,[1] is an indication that the emperors did not regard the papal claims with complete equanimity.

The next surviving statement of papal claims dates from 1111, when an agreement was reached between the Emperor Henry V and Paschal II only after the latter had been held for several weeks as a prisoner. Henry had apparently consented before his coronation, through representatives whom he sent ahead from Tuscany, to 'restore and yield' the *patrimonia* and *possessiones beati Petri* granted by Charles, Louis, Henry *et aliis imperatoribus*.[2] Soon after Henry's departure from Rome the pope wrote to him complaining that some towns in Umbria and Roman Tuscany — among them Civita Castellana and Narni — had refused to accept his rule, but that he hoped to receive imperial support in securing the obedience of these towns, as well as the *comitatus* of Perugia, Gubbio, Todi and Bagnorea, Città di Castello, the duchy of Spoleto, the March of Ferrara *et alias beati Petri possessiones*.[3] The vagueness of the last phrase is doubtless an indication of the pope's pessimism, yet the reference to specific towns which have disavowed his rule is a sign that some action had been taken. The significance of the places named in this letter lies probably in a hope that the weak papal rule then existing in the former Roman duchy and Sabina might be extended further to the north and north-east into what is now Umbria. Only the mention of Ferrara suggests a yet more unrealistic glance beyond the Apennines.

It was more than eighty years before a pope had any possibility of achieving the scheme that may have passed briefly through the mind of Paschal II, but the persistence of the same type of traditional claim is suggested by a list of the bishops present at the Council of Pisa in 1135.[4] Here only the bishops of Rimini, Montefeltro, Urbino, Città di Castello, Gubbio, Perugia and Todi are noted as *de civitatibus beati Petri*: some other bishoprics (Spoleto, Foligno and Assisi) are described as *de ducatu*, those of the March of Fermo or Ancona are *de Marchia*, while of the other 'paper' possessions of the papacy, Toscanella, Bagnorea and Soana are *de Tuscia*.

Only under Adrian IV, the English pope, do we find another full statement of papal territorial claims, by this time increased through the

---

[1] MGH, Const., I, 674–8. The three recorded copies of this forgery are all of German origin.
[2] *Lib. Pont.*, II, 338–9.
[3] Jaffe-Löwenfeld, *Regesta Pontificum Romanorum*, n. 6295.
[4] *Zeitschrift für Kirchenrecht*, XVI (1881), 148.

will of the Countess Matilda. The terms proposed by Adrian to Frederick Barbarossa in 1159 have survived in an abbreviated form in a letter of the bishop of Bamberg.[1] In addition to the Matildine lands, which were mainly situated in western Tuscany, the Emilian Apennines and the lower Po, the principal territorial demands of the pope were the area from Acquapendente southwards to Rome, the duchy of Spoleto, Ferrara (where the papal claim to overlordship had received spasmodic recognition), Sardinia and Corsica. The struggle for the strategically important Matildine property continues throughout the second half of the twelfth century, but these areas were not destined to fall to the medieval popes and their fate is not relevant to our story.[2] The striking thing about Adrian's territorial claims in 1159 is their modesty, at least when set beside the Carolingian donations. In essence, the papacy is now hoping for a State consisting of an area little larger than the Byzantine duchy of Rome, with the duchy of Spoleto to its east. Acquapendente is proposed as the northern frontier, thus complying roughly with the line of 817. Further north the popes still hope for Ferrara and the more recently granted, but unfortunately isolated, lands of Matilda. Of the March of Ancona, the duchy of Ravenna or other claims north of the Apennines there is no word. This is the State, then, to which Barbarossa's papal opponents laid claim, and this claim is the background to the papal-imperial struggle in central Italy which lasted from 1155 until the death of Frederick's son in 1197.

*   *   *

Hitherto we have been concerned with the papacy's claims to the Papal State[3] and the basis of those claims. It is now time to turn to the reality of papal rule in the period between the Carolingian donations

---

[1] *Gesta Friderici Imperatoris*, lib. IV, c. 30 in MGH, XX, 461–2. For Ferrara *v.* P. Kehr, *Italia Pontificia*, V, 212, 235. The omission of the Campagna is probably to be explained by the opinion that the papal right to this area between Rome and the Norman kingdom was independent of imperial consent. The inclusion of Tivoli in isolation is due to Frederick's attempt in 1155 to secure the obedience of that city (*Lib. Pont.*, II, 393). The claim to Corsica and Sardinia should be seen rather as a protest against imperial intervention in these islands than as a serious statement of papal intention, although it had support from the donation of Louis the Pious (see Jordan, *L'Allemagne et l'Italie*, pp. 21 and 72–3).

[2] For the Matildine lands see A. Overmann, *Gräfin Mathilde von Tuscien*. The papal claim to these lands was strong in so far as it related to allodial territory, and the Emperor Lothair had implicitly accepted it when invested with them by Innocent II in 1133; Barbarossa, however, granted them to Duke Welf in 1152 without consulting the pope.

[3] I have preferred to use the anachronistic term 'Papal State' even for the pre-Innocentian period rather than 'Patrimony', owing to the ambiguity of the latter word, which is sometimes applied to the whole territory to which the popes laid claim, though it is generally confined to the area between Acquapendente and Ceprano. When used in the present chapter it is employed in the latter sense.

and the crisis of Barbarossa's reign. Here the contrast between what had been granted and the degree of political control achieved was striking, indeed it is difficult to exaggerate. In an age when throughout Europe political power diminished rapidly as it travelled from the place whence it was exercised, the popes were a characteristic instance of the weakness of central authority. What they lacked was less the means of conveying orders than the administrative and military strength to secure obedience to them. The resources they had were, until the era of reform, those of whichever baronial family of the Campagna was dominant, for, like sees in many other parts of Christendom, the bishopric of Rome and its temporalities became the virtual property of local secular lords. This process was naturally accelerated by the break-up of the Carolingian Empire in the ninth century.

It would be irrelevant here to trace the history of the papacy during this period, but something must be said of papal rule in the area around Rome and of the officials through whom it was exercised. In the early years of the tenth century Rome itself and the papacy were under the sway of Theophylact, duke, consul, senator, *magister militum* and papal *vestiarius*.[1] Theophylact's supremacy descended to his son-in-law Alberic and later to a grandson, Alberic II. Under the second Alberic we meet for the first time evidence that the papacy is exerting political authority in its lands: in 939 the Sabina (where popes had held large estates long before the Carolingian donations) was ruled by Ingebald *dux et rector territorii Sabinensis*. Though confronted by the powerful monastic house of Farfa, the rectorate in the Sabina seems to have survived as an annual, or almost annual, appointment, and *missi* and bishops were used in the work of administration. The office was based on that of the Frankish count and increasingly often the rectors were called *comites*. They exercised civil and criminal jurisdiction, collected the *fodrum* and perhaps other taxes. Presumably they also had military and police functions. By about the end of the tenth century they were aided by a judge, a notary and (occasionally, at least) a *vicecomes*. In 965 there was also a papal *comes* in the Campagna, Roffred of Veroli, but it is probable that this post rapidly became hereditary, for John, the *comes* or *dux Campaniae* who died in 988, was probably Roffred's son, and Roffred II, who died in 1013, his grandson.[2]

---

[1] See L. Duchesne, *The Beginnings of the Temporal Sovereignty of the Popes*, pp. 204–16: Kölmel, *op. cit.*, pp. 1–10: O. Vehse, 'Die päpstliche Herrschaft in der Sabina bis zur Mitte des 12. Jahrhunderts', *QFIA*, XXI, 129–36.

[2] Falco, 'L'amministrazione papale nella Campagna e nella Marittima dalla caduta della dominazione bisantina al sorgere dei comuni', *ASRSP*, XXXVIII, 685–8.

Under the Ottonians imperial domination in Rome alternated with that of the Crescentii, a branch of the family of Theophylact. In Sabina, too, government by an imperial *missus* who was later made Prefect of Rome and *magister imperialis militiae* alternated with the rule of members of the house of Crescentii, though there seems to have been no formal attempt to take over for the Empire the government of the Papal State.[1] From this time dates the popes' policy of strengthening their position in the vicinity of Rome by feudal grants of land in return for military and other services.[2] Velletri was granted in 977, for three generations, and Terracina, an important town which might serve as a hinge for the Papal State's southern boundary, was leased by Sylvester II to a member of a powerful local family, Count Daifer, for the same term in the year 1000. We see here already that attempt to come to terms with the possessors of local authority which runs through the whole history of the Papal State. Before 1011 the count-ship in the Campagna had passed from the family of Roffred of Veroli to that of Amatus of Ceccano, but again the holder was a member of one of the great dynasties which really ruled the 'Papal State' south of Rome.

The counts of Tusculum who won authority over the papacy in 1012 were themselves descendants of Theophylact and distant relatives of the Crescentii, but they cannot have been happy to permit this family to retain the rectorate of Sabina while Benedict VIII's brother as Prefect of the City and *consul et dux* ruled only in the immediate neighbourhood of Rome. An alliance with Farfa and the Octaviani seems to have won the day for the house of Tusculum against the Crescentii and for about twenty years (1020–40) there was again strong and undivided rule by a feudal papal family in the Papal State.[3]

Thus the earliest reforming popes were able to inherit from their 'baronial' predecessors an established tradition whereby the government of the Campagna and Sabina was the business of the papacy so long as it had the strength to make good its claims. These popes had the additional advantage of imperial support. Victor II (1054–7) was given by Henry III rule (as an imperial vassal) over the March of Ancona and the duchy of Spoleto.[4] This was probably part of a scheme for setting up a strong Papal State under the aegis of the Empire as a southerly

---

[1] Vehse, *art. cit.*, 137–49. Otto III's donation of 1001 (*v. sup.* p. 3) is an instance of the emperors' attitude to papal rights. Farfa was able to strengthen its position further by playing off against each other the two rival forces in the Sabina.

[2] See K. Jordan, 'Das Eindringen des Lehnswesens in das Rechtsleben der römischen Kurie', *Archiv für Urkundenforschung*, XII, especially pp. 37–44.

[3] See Kölmel, *op. cit.*, pp. 43–6 and 57–71, also Vehse, *art. cit.*, 137–49.

[4] Ficker, *Forschungen*, II, 322.

bastion against the now threatening power of the Normans, but the pope's judgements in these areas were pronounced *de sua parte* as well as on behalf of the emperor. The experiment might have opened up new possibilities for papal independence, but seems to have ended with Victor's brief pontificate.

Closer to Rome the reforming popes had to contend with the surviving strength of the Crescentii and counts of Tusculum.[1] War was waged against the counts, who were much weakened, but Tusculum held out. In Sabina the papacy met with little success, the Crescentii and Octaviani retaining the rectorate until at least 1066, despite the popes' persistent policy of allying themselves with Farfa and the fostering of new urban communities intended to promote colonization and to detract from baronial authority. At the same time these popes made some attempts to govern the Sabina directly from Rome and through the bishop of Sabina, in opposition to the now feudalized office of the rectorship.

The most fundamental of all the measures to strengthen the reforming popes against the baronage was the revolutionary treaty with the Normans signed at Melfi in 1059. The acquisition of Benevento (1051) had shown the development of papal interest in southern Italy, which was involved with plans for strictly ecclesiastical gains at the expense of the Greek Church. The diplomatic masterpiece of Melfi provided the papacy with a new protector who, whatever his disadvantages, was directly interested in weakening the feudatories situated on his northern border in the Roman Campagna. At the same time the popes, by the investiture of Richard of Capua and Robert Guiscard, asserted their suzerainty over all southern Italy and Sicily, a momentous claim which could be justified only by the forged donation of Constantine, for even the *Ludovicianum* had limited the papal possessions in the south to isolated *patrimonia*.

Hildebrand continued the policy of earlier reforming popes, seeking to substitute for papal-baronial control by a feudal family a new papal rule which could stand independently, supported by a paradoxical combination of military strongholds and troops with freshly won spiritual prestige. The new papacy lacked its predecessor's baronial revenues, a serious loss which could only be remedied by finding fresh sources of strength.[2] Gregory's privilege to the *castrum Albinium* near Narni per-

---

[1] For this paragraph see Vehse, *art. cit.*, 152–7, and Kölmel, *op. cit.*, pp. 125–37.

[2] D. B. Zema, 'Economic Reorganization of the Roman See during the Gregorian Reform', *Studi Gregoriani*, I, 137–68; K. Jordan, *art. cit.*, 46–8.

mitted the pope to build a fortress within the town and to garrison it, while the inhabitants owed military service as well as the usual feudal obligations of counsel and suit of court. This agreement probably resembles others which have not survived, but there were also many mercenaries among the formidable forces of Hildebrand which, in the words of Guy of Ferrara, 'within a few months overturned the enemy, won back castles and towns and put down rebellion'.[1] This policy of building up alliances with towns against powerful feudatories has, of course, many parallels — the *locus classicus* is twelfth and thirteenth-century France — and it is difficult to see where else the popes could have found support that was both powerful and close at hand. Yet it had great dangers. In Hildebrand's time Farfa, which had been granted more independence by his predecessors when needed as an ally against the Crescentii, sided with Henry IV against the pope.[2] In the same way the popes who fostered the communes of the Papal State were strengthening the future rivals of their successors.

After the death of Urban II (1099) there was a marked decline in the power of the popes within the patrimony.[3] Paschal II (1099–1118) was harassed by a series of imperialist anti-popes and spent some time in exile in France. He was driven from Rome many times and for support there seems to have been dependent on two powerful families, the Pierleoni and Frangipani, as well as his nephew Walfred the *princeps militiae*, and spasmodic Norman aid. This return to an old tradition had as its accompaniment strong baronial opposition led by the counts of Tusculum and the Colonna, an offshoot of the Tusculan house. The disorders were more or less continuous and in 1107 and 1116 the whole of the Roman duchy and Sabina were apparently lost to the pope.[4] Calixtus II (1119–24) achieved some successes against the counts of Segni and Ceccano in the Campagna and Honorius II (1124–30) was able to assert his authority in the same area, though only with the assistance of the Frangipani, who had virtually nominated him as pope. Under Anacletus II (1130–8) and Innocent II (1130–43) the position of the papacy was still weaker, for the existence of rival popes, one backed by the

[1] MGH, Libelli de Lite, I, 534.

[2] Vehse, *art. cit.*, 157. For the continuation of this policy after Gregory's time, see Velletri's privilege of 1089 granted in return for the obligation to provide military service *per Marittimam et Campaniam*, etc. (Kehr, *Italia Pontificia*, II, 104–5).

[3] Gregorovius, *History of the City of Rome in the Middle Ages*, IV, 2, 317–77; D. B. Zema, 'The Houses of Tuscany and of Pierleone in the Crisis of Rome', *Traditio*, II, 155–75; P. Brezzi, *Roma e l'impero medioevale* (774–1252), pp. 295–335.

[4] The state of the papacy is well illustrated by the actions of Ranier, a candidate as imperialist anti-pope, who offered Ninfa, Ariccia and 'Zibera' to the counts of Tusculum and the Colonna, as well as money (MGH, VI, 368–9).

Pierleoni and the other by the Frangipani, made it impossible for either to achieve territorial control.

In Sabina the papacy in effect relinquished its claims in favour of the monks of Farfa, after a lawsuit (in 1103–5) between Farfa and two counts of the Crescentii family, who were probably the last papal rectors of the area for almost a century.[1] The abbey secured a munificent privilege in reward for its fidelity to the emperor, but after 1122 Henry V renounced control over the Italian Church and Farfa ceased to be a centre of opposition to the papacy. This did not enable the popes to regain control in Sabina, nor has anything survived to suggest the continuity of even the machinery of papal government in the Campagna except the name of a single rector, and he naturally is a feudatory, Peter of Ceprano.[2]

The policy of building up an array of pro-papal towns was continued, but a development of more importance may be illustrated by the survival from this period of a rapidly increasing number of feudal documents. Yet when we read that Count Ptolemy of Tusculum took from the Abbey of Grottaferrata some land *quam dedit militibus suis*,[3] we see how the barons stood to benefit more than the pope from this tardy adoption of formal military tenure.

The Roman revolution of 1143 is an event of the first importance for the history of the popes. The Romans now asserted the right, already claimed by the major Lombard and Tuscan cities, to rule themselves instead of being ruled by their bishop. The situation was infinitely complicated by the claims of the emperor, the survival of classical titles, and the republicans' religious opposition to temporal rule by the Church, to say nothing of the *damnosa haereditas* of the past greatness of the city, but fundamentally the situation was the same as in the other great Italian towns. Just as the other communes sought control over the main routes, so the Romans aimed at securing suzerainty over Viterbo, Tivoli and Tusculum, which dominated respectively the principal northern, eastern, and southern roads from the city. If Rome had achieved rule over the duchy the history of the Papal State would have come to an end in the middle of the twelfth century, for it laid claim virtually to the same area as the popes.[4] The struggle between the popes

---

[1] Vehse, *art. cit.*, 158–65.   [2] Falco, *art. cit.*, 694 n.

[3] Document cited in K. Jordan, *art. cit.*, 52.

[4] See p. 4 above for the State claimed by the papacy in 1135. The zone claimed as its 'duchy' by the commune of Rome seems to have been the area stretching 100 miles from the city, subject in late classical times to the *praefectus urbis* (see De Boüard, *Le Régime Politique et les Institutions de Rome au Moyen Age, 1252–1347*, p. 200, and *Enciclopedia Italiana*, *s.v.* 'Roma Medievale-Storia' and 'Prefetto').

and the city was long and inconclusive, but for the survival of the Papal State the papacy was now indebted to its own baronial connections and alliances and to the weakness of the commune in the face of the feudatories, rather than to any success hitherto achieved in the task of governing its patrimony. When Rome, which had always been a doubtful factor, became a resolute enemy of the popes, it was natural that they should turn to the nobles against whom the revolution was also directed. While the new republic asserted its claims by harrying and plundering the country-side, the more distant parts of the patrimony remained under the local feudatories, in particular the Colonna and Frangipani to the south and the lords of Vico and of Anguillara in Roman Tuscany.[1]

The balance-sheet of the ten years between the revolution and the death of Eugenius III is not entirely negative, for Lucius II and Eugenius achieved some isolated gains, including the purchase of half of Tusculum with some other property of its counts.[2] Moreover the last months of Eugenius' pontificate were spent in Rome. He reached an agreement with the republic, received indignantly by its extremists, which enabled the moderate party within the city to win the upper hand through an understanding with the pope and the Frangipani.[3] The Romans, however, retained their republican constitution and their pretensions to rule the duchy or 'district' of the city.[4]

This long period of enfeeblement was ended by the energetic policy of the Englishman Adrian IV, pope from 1154 until 1159. Adrian's measures were certainly provoked to some extent by the threat of revived imperial power in Italy, but his action in refusing to recognize the Senate and placing Rome under an interdict almost immediately after his accession shows that much of the credit must go to the pope's own character. The interdict led to the expulsion of Arnold of Brescia, the

---

[1] *Lib. Pont.*, II, 387 ('civitates et castra beati Petri assiduis rapinis et gravibus guerris persequi non cessabant'); Gregorovius, IV, 2, 501–2.

[2] Theiner, dd. XVI–XVIII; Kehr, *It. Pont.*, III, 242 (Corneto, Vetralla, Radicofani). For the purchase of Tusculum see G. Digard, 'La Fin de la Seigneurie de Tusculum' in *Mélanges P. Fabre*, pp. 297–8. Tusculum had been the fortress of the most powerful baronial family of the Campagna. The division within the family which made possible the papal purchase of 1151 had already weakened the Tusculans, but that year marks the start of their downfall. The significant point is that, for a time, Tusculum was falling to the pope and not to the Roman republic.

[3] The return of the Frangipani is proved by the Frangipani witnesses to papal documents in 1153 (Gregorovius, IV, 2, 522n.). The places in the Campagna regained by Eugenius (*Lib. Pont.*, II, 387) had been held by the Frangipani (Gregorovius, 501n.) which suggests an alliance between the pope and this family.

[4] John of Salisbury states that at this period the Prefect of Rome was authorized by the Church to give justice and enjoy executive power within a radius of 100 miles (*Historia Pontificalis*, ed. Chibnall, p. 59).

religious extremist among the republicans, but not to the termination
of the commune. Pope Adrian rightly saw in the emperor a potential
ally against the Romans (as well as against a threatened Norman invasion of the patrimony), though there could be no hope of lasting
imperial support for papal rule in central Italy. Barbarossa in fact
claimed oaths of fidelity from Rome and from some of the leading
towns and barons of the patrimony, and drew *fodrum* from the towns
of the Campagna. His first expedition into central Italy ended in
retreat, but in 1158 Frederick was back with even higher claims,
demanding the *fodrum* in the Campagna and Marittima, seeking the full
revenues of the Matildine lands and claiming regalian powers throughout the patrimony. These *regalia*, as defined at the Diet of Roncaglia,
included many fiscal dues, most categories of judicial profits and the
authority to coin money, to nominate judges and receive the revenues
of vacant offices, as well as many other powers.[1] Frederick's aims, then,
were high, and if achieved they also would have led to the definitive
termination of papal rule in the patrimony. But he, too, had great difficulties to face in attempting to enforce his jurisdiction and affairs in
Germany and Lombardy so occupied him and his armies that he was
rarely able to devote much attention to central Italy.

Adrian's methods in opposing the two other contenders for the
patrimony were not novel. What was new was the vigour with which
they were employed. Their essence was the increased use of feudal con-
tracts to secure military support and the purchase of land and strong-
points for financial and strategic purposes. The process of founding new
urban communities as a counterweight against the baronage, as well as
for military reasons, was also continued. Regrettably little evidence has
survived concerning the administration of the patrimony during
Adrian's pontificate, though it is known that he twice employed
cardinals as rectors in the Campagna:[2] but many of his feudal and other
charters are extant and these merit further discussion, for they are the
relics of what was probably — we should perhaps have to except
Gregory VII — the first serious attempt by a pope to secure a firm and
permanent basis for papal rule in the patrimony.

Adrian's use of feudalism may well be connected with his origins, for
his early years had been spent in the highly feudalized England of
Henry I. Besides simple feudal agreements with barons concerning

---

[1] MGH, XX, 408 and 450; MGH, Const., I, 244–5: see also Ficker, *Forschungen*, II,
304–7.
[2] Kehr, *It. Pont.*, II, 171 (1153) and *Lib. Cens.*, I, 587–8 (1158).

fealty and military service, however, we find many compacts (in analogous terms) with towns and small urban communities, as well as purchases of land and acknowledgements of land donated. The agreements
with the larger towns, which combine feudal forms with the old traditions of a papal-municipal alliance, are of particular importance. Thus
Tivoli (after an abortive oath to the emperor against which Adrian had
protested with violence) swore an oath of fealty to the pope in 1155 and
he purchased some land here, while in 1157 the men of Orvieto swore
a similar oath and promised military service.[1] Lauri, one of the new
communities established in Sabina, owed military service and counsel
on the usual terms, and was to receive papal *nuntii* and to pay six
pounds annually as well as the *fodrum* when levied; the pope reserved to
himself the *placita de omicidiis et adulteriis*, which were to be heard by his
representatives twice yearly. It is to be remarked that such towns are
placed directly under the pope: there is no mention of a rector in the
Sabina throughout Adrian's pontificate, and the results of this centralizing policy seem to have been thoroughly satisfactory. The establishment of a series of *castra* standing to the east and west of the vital Via
Sabina gave the popes firm control over this territory, including even
the lands of Farfa.[2]

Adrian IV's gains in the Campagna and the northern patrimony were
of no less importance. Radicofani was fortified and an arc of strongholds a little to the south, Proceno, Ripesena and Orvieto, were either
partly purchased or gained as allies. Further south still the pope secured
Orchia and a number of towns and much property near the Tiber. In
the Campagna, among many other gains, Tivoli renewed its oath of
fidelity, Jonathan of Tusculum became the pope's vassal for the papal
half of Tusculum, and the powerful lords of Poli made over their lands
entirely to the pope. Adrian's was a policy of seeking small but tenable
additions to his strength. It was not spectacular, but its purpose and
effectiveness are illustrated well in the account given by his nephew and
biographer of how he went to the southern border of the patrimony to
receive the homage of his Norman vassals, accompanied by a 'splendid
army of counts and other nobles from Rome, the Campagna, and the
other neighbouring parts'.[3]

Alexander III, succeeding in 1159, was unable to maintain Adrian's

---

[1] Theiner, dd. XXI, XXIII: Kehr, *It. Pont.*, II, 80.

[2] See Vehse, *art. cit.*, 168–72, 174–5. The terms of the oath of Monte Libretti (1157) included a promise to stand with the majority of cardinals in case of a disputed papal election:
no doubt the pope had in mind the dire effects within the patrimony of papal schisms.

[3] *Lib. Pont.*, II, 393–4.

successes, but this was due to the increasing pressure of his opponents rather than to his own failings. The existence of an imperial anti-pope and Alexander's absence for four years in France led inevitably to a weakening of papal control in the patrimony, despite the vigour with which he disputed its possession with Barbarossa. For two years Alexander found sufficient support from the Frangipani and Normans to remain in the neighbourhood of Rome or occasionally in the city itself, but the pro-imperial Victor IV, who was perhaps a relative of the Crescentii and the Prefects of Vico, had the backing of the senate and most of the Roman nobles.[1] Alexander probably confirmed in office as rector of the Campagna Simon, a cardinal and Abbot of Subiaco who had occupied this position under Adrian IV, but thereafter it is difficult to trace the story of his attempts to administer the patrimony.[2] His return from France was prepared by the despatch of a cardinal who secured the submission of the Romans in 1165 and nominally took over rule in the Sabina, which however remained under imperial control.[3] Later we hear of a cardinal sent into the Campagna some time during the years 1167–9 'to organize matters there at his will to the honour of the Church',[4] but this concludes the evidence for Alexander's government in the patrimony.

It is evident that Alexander had little power in central Italy after 1161, but it is not easy to decide to what extent the emperor was the heir to Adrian IV and to what extent the beneficiary was Rome. Alexander's biographer records that in 1161 Barbarossa and the schismatics occupied the whole area of the patrimony ('from Acquapendente to Ceprano') except the towns of Orvieto, Terracina and Anagni,[5] yet the reports of a temporary imperial occupation of Latium in 1165 show that this situation was only intermittent. The gains of Rainald of Dassel in 1167 were equally transitory.[6] The only area permanently taken over from the papacy by the emperor was that northern part of the patrimony, later known as the Tuscan Patrimony, which was included in the area ruled by the imperial legates.[7] Christian of Mainz was general

[1] Gregorovius, IV, 2, 563–71 and *Lib. Pont.*, II, 399–404. For the descent of Victor IV see Hampe in *Neues Archiv*, XLVI, 53–66 and Haller, *Das Papsttum* (ed. 2, 1952), III, 147.

[2] Kehr, *It. Pont.*, II, 95 (Kehr points out the possibility that this letter should be attributed to Adrian IV, but there are no strong reasons for doing so). Several privileges and a mention of a later rector of the Campagna are undated (*v.* Kehr, II, 139 and 163).

[3] *Lib. Pont.*, II, 412.   [4] Kehr, *It. Pont.*, II, 159.

[5] *Lib. Pont.*, II, 403–4. Boso also appears to except from the rule of imperial occupation *munitionem Castri*, but a more likely reading of this passage (*munitionem castrorum*) would have the meaning that the emperor occupied fortresses as well as towns.

[6] Watterich, *Vitae Pontificum*, II, 547 and 560–70.

[7] For this area see Ficker, *Forschungen*, II, 236–8.

legate, with one interruption, from 1165 until 1177, governing Viterbo (where he built a palace) and several neighbouring towns.[1]

To the south of the territory gained by the Empire, Rome ruled as an independent state except during the brief imperial expeditions already mentioned and the two years (1165–7) of Alexander's presence in the city. Even the residence of the pope made little difference, for after the imperial retreat of 1165 it was Roman troops who occupied Latium, and in the same year Rome granted the Genoese the right to trade freely with the coastal area between Corneto and Terracina in terms suggesting a claim to control the entire patrimony.[2] A few years later Archbishop Becket's supporters were in constant fear that Henry II of England might win the support of Alexander against the archbishop by paying him a sum of money which would enable him to satisfy the Romans' extortionate demands.[3]

The pope often found protection in the Campagna, at Veroli, Tusculum or Segni, though for a time he was compelled to go to Benevento, an enclave in Norman territory. In 1169 the counts of Ceccano held the Campagna against both imperial and papal troops, and this episode suggests that the patrimony was not lost to Rome any more than to the emperor. It was rather that all central control had declined, and both barons and towns were the beneficiaries.[4] Rome itself was independent, but could not make good its wide claims, the emperor made firm gains in the northern patrimony but otherwise was content with occasional forays, while the pope — when not in a more distant place of exile — was usually content to stay in some town of the Campagna, biding his time and occasionally sending out some emissary whose powers were merely formal. From 1170 until 1173 Alexander settled at Tusculum, which stronghold he had secured in the former year and granted to his supporters the Frangipani. By an ingenious exchange the lords of Tusculum received the Frangipani lands to the southwest (Terracina, Segni, Cori and Norma). Raino of Tusculum already had possessions in this area, but it was a considerable gain to the papacy

---

[1] For Christian's privileges granted to Viterbo in 1172–3, see Böhmer, *Acta Imperii Selecta*, pp. 601–3. His legateship included at one period (1172) Tivoli. His powers were for a time delegated to Conrad of Montferrat, who after 1177 turned against the emperor and aimed at independent rule in southern Tuscany.

[2] *Codice Diplomatico del Senato Romano*, ed. F. Bartoloni (Fonti per la Storia d'Italia, vol. 87), pp. 31–6.

[3] See John of Salisbury, Letter CLXXXIII (P.L., vol. 199): 'd. papa vir sanctus et justus est. Sed eius sunt tot et tantae necessitates, tanta aviditas et improbitas Romanorum'. John of Salisbury returns to the subject in *Policraticus*, l. VIII, ch. 23.

[4] Watterich, II, 579: Gregorovius, IV, 2, 603 n. (Anagni, in the same area, was organized as a commune by 1164).

that his estates now lay further removed from those of his Colonna relatives. Tusculum, however, was too close to Rome for the Romans to be content that it should continue as a papal stronghold. They harassed the place until Alexander agreed that the walls should be lowered, possibly in return for a promise that he would be readmitted to Rome. They then destroyed the fortifications entirely, so that the pope was forced to move to Segni.[1] It is evident that Alexander's two years in Rome (1165–7) and two years at Tusculum (October 1170 to January 1173) do not constitute a real exception to the generalization that he achieved no control in the patrimony between his election in 1159 and the fateful peace negotiations with the emperor which began at Anagni in 1176.

*   *   *

The story of the popes' claims to the state granted in the Carolingian donations and of their rule within the patrimony has been related in outline up to 1176. The papal-imperial agreement of that year marks a point from which a more detailed treatment of both topics becomes necessary for an understanding of the Papal State of the thirteenth century, for the twenty-one years which intervened before the death of Henry VI saw a series of imperial attempts to reach a final agreement concerning the government of central Italy. The determination of successive popes in keeping alive their claims in the face of the overwhelming power of Frederick and Henry VI was an essential preliminary to the extraordinary gains of Innocent III. Through this period the position of the papacy was dependent on the desire of both emperors to secure the coronation of their sons in their own lifetime and that of Henry to win papal approval for his annexation of the Sicilian kingdom. The popes' resources were almost entirely diplomatic and spiritual and they had to face a number of tempting imperial offers as well as the loss of their former Lombard allies. They abode by the fundamental principles of diplomacy, keeping their claims intact and suspending action until the tide of events should flow in their favour, and they were brilliantly successful.

The terms of the preliminary peace arranged at Anagni between

---

[1] Gregorovius, IV, 2, 594–7 and Digard, 'La Fin de la Seigneurie de Tusculum, *Mélanges P. Fabre*, pp. 292–302. For the different versions of these events, *v.* Watterich, II, 414–18 and 590. The pope's biographer implies that the bad faith of the Romans lay in destroying the entire fortifications against the terms of the agreement, Romuald of Salerno that it lay in refusing to admit Alexander to Rome.

Alexander III and the representatives of Barbarossa[1] contain several clauses relating to the territory in dispute between pope and emperor. The most important required Frederick to restore to the papacy all the *regalia et alias possessiones* held by the popes since Innocent II, as well as the possession of the prefecture of Rome and of the Matildine lands. The last two of these were hedged round with conditions, for the prefecture was only granted to the papacy *quoad possessionem*, pending the statement of imperial claims to it, while the Matildine lands yielded were those held by the papacy 'in the time of Lothair, Conrad and the Emperor Frederick', in other words the allodial estates. The pontificate of Innocent II (1130–43) was probably selected for the definition of papal rights because Lothair III had on an analogous occasion sworn to maintain that pope in his *regalia*.[2] The absence of any precise definition suggests that the emperor hoped to exploit a vague frontier agreement; the territorial terms of the earlier settlement were probably uncertain. The phrase concerning the prefecture of Rome is founded on no previous donation: its inclusion as a separate clause perhaps reflects Rome's *de facto* independence as well as the retention of imperial claims, for Rome was no longer a town, but a powerful republic with political power beyond as well as within the walls. The prefect was the chief officer of the city, and in principle he was normally appointed by the pope. As recently as 1170, however, Frederick had nominated a prefect,[3] and it was of peculiar importance to the pope that the precedent should be disavowed, though the saving phrase ('quoad possessionem') meant that this was not fully effective.[4]

When definitive terms were agreed at Venice the following year,[5] Barbarossa had secured a diplomatic triumph in detaching the Lombard cities from Alexander III and this victory, which was partly the effect of the pope's 'separate peace' of 1176, is reflected in alterations in the clauses concerning the Papal State. The clause concerning the Matildine lands was now omitted, while the other two principal territorial clauses were telescoped into one, whereby the emperor was to restore *omnem* . . .

---

[1] MGH, Const., I, 350–3. See also P. Kehr, 'Der Vertag von Anagni im Jahre 1176', *Neues Archiv*, XIII (1888).

[2] Theiner, d. XIV.

[3] *Lib. Pont.*, II, 422. For the prefecture, see L. Halphen, *Études sur l'Administration de Rome au Moyen Age (751–1252)*, pp. 16–27.

[4] Ficker, *Forschungen*, II, 307–8, suggests that the clause concerning the prefecture was intended as a renunciation of imperial temporal rule within the patrimony. This is not impossible, in view of Rome's claims within the duchy of Rome, but there is no positive evidence for the hypothesis, and in any case the emperor renounced possession only, his rights remaining unaffected.

[5] MGH, Const., I, 362–5 and 371–2.

C

*possessionem et tenementum sive prefecture sive alterius rei, quam Romana
ecclesia habuit et ipse (sc.* imperator*) abstulit . . . salvo omni iure imperii.*
The generic terms in which this promise was couched were ominous
for the papacy. Not only were the Matildine estates, the Roman prefecture and all the other papal claims now thrown together in one
vague phrase, but there was no longer any indication of which claims
were recognized by the emperor or to what previous settlement a return was intended, though the words *ipse abstulit* could perhaps be taken
to imply that the papacy was to enjoy the territories it had held at the
time of Frederick's accession in 1152. Apart from all this, the emperor's
'saving' clause *(salvo omni iure imperii)* could be invoked in each case
where the pope made territorial claims. Arbiters had been appointed to
settle disputes,[1] but imperial counter-claims could at least hold up papal
claims, while the whole system of arbitration was of very doubtful value,
especially in the face of Frederick's imposing power. In reality there
had been no territorial settlement between emperor and pope, despite
the fair promise of Anagni, and Alexander was at the emperor's mercy.

Some time later Alexander wrote complaining of the imperial occupation of the March of Ancona during the course of the negotiations
at Venice, undertaken 'entirely without consulting us'.[2] But the pope's
powerlessness did not mean that no attempt would be made to imple-
ment the agreement. Frederick wanted a lasting peace and he set about
securing this in a determined manner. The duchy of Rome, so long a
No-man's-land between emperor, pope, Roman republic and a host of
other authorities feudal and municipal, was restored to the pope by the
imperial legate Christian of Mainz, in command of an army which
escorted Alexander to Rome, after the Romans had promised obedience, early in 1178. The Tuscan patrimony was retained for the
emperor, though Conrad of Montferrat disputed the area with
Frederick's legate.[3]

Outside the patrimony the pope received nothing. His biographer
suggests that he at last consented to shelve his claims to the Matildine
lands, perhaps in return for prompt restoration to the patrimony, but
that he bitterly complained of the imperial occupation of the county of
Bertinoro (in Romagna), which had been granted him as a legacy in
that very year.[4] The two areas over which the papacy might have hoped

---

[1] MGH, Const., I, 365, and *Lib. Pont.*, II, 443.   [2] MGH, Const., I, 584–5.
[3] Ficker, *Forschungen*, II, 237–8: there is certain evidence only for Acquapendente and
Montefiascone, but imperial occupation of these towns strongly suggests occupation of the
whole area. See above, p. 14–15.
[4] *Lib. Pont.*, II, 443: Kehr, *It. Pont.*, V, 136.

to assert its claims were the duchy of Spoleto and the March of Ancona, but in 1177 we find the first references to a new imperial *dux Spoletinus*, Conrad of Urslingen, and to a margrave (who later added the duchy of Ravenna to his area of administration), Conrad of Lützelhard.[1] The appointment of officials to rule over large provinces was part of Frederick's plan for setting up a semi-centralized system of imperial rule which was to cover the whole of Italy between Lombardy and the papal patrimony, but the revival of the duchy and margravate had the additional value of constituting a formal denial of papal claims. Although there was considerable opposition to these imperial officials, the weakness of their control was not such that the papacy could hope to exploit it.

Alexander murmured about the occupation of the March *nobis inconsultis* and claimed the greater part of that province as the property of the Church,[2] but this isolated and imprecise complaint is the only evidence of papal claims in the dark years that followed Venice. Not only had Alexander returned to Rome in 1178 under German protection, but the weakness of his position was emphasized by the need to request further intervention in the patrimony by imperial officials. Alexander's last two years were spent away from Rome, partly at Viterbo, where he would seem to have lived under the protection of Christian of Mainz.

Lucius III (1181–5) was able to reach an agreement with the Romans and return to the city, but he was soon forced to quit and in 1183 Christian came to his aid and undertook to defend Tusculum against the Romans.[3] The aged archbishop died soon afterwards and Barbarossa appointed a successor, Count Bertold of Künsberg, who had instructions to defend Tusculum and regain for Lucius Rocca di Papa. Bertold's intervention was doubly unsuccessful from the papal viewpoint, for he achieved little, while his very presence was a humiliating sign of dependence on imperial support.

The causes that lie behind the bitter quarrel of Rome with the popes of this period cannot be limited to rivalry within what each regarded as its natural sphere of influence, although this was the deepest source of bad relations. It had apparently become normal for the popes to make

[1] For imperial rule in these areas after 1177, *v.* Ficker, *Forschungen*, II, 241–55 and W. Lenel, 'Der Konstanzer Frieden v. 1183 und die italienische Politik Friedrichs I.', *HZ*, CXXVIII, 216–42.

[2] MGH, Const., I, 584–5 ('. . . Marchiam, que ex parte ad imperium et ex maxima parte ad ecclesiam spectat'). The request of Ascoli in the March to Lucius III in 1183 to confirm the town's *podestà* (Kehr, *It. Pont.*, IV, 154) might suggest the continuance of this claim but the authenticity of this isolated document is very questionable.

[3] For these events see Gregorovius, IV, 2, 606 ff. and H. Kauffmann, *Die Italienische Politik Kaiser Friedrichs I. nach dem Frieden von Constanz (1183–9)*, pp. 22–4.

large payments to the city in return for promises of friendly conduct. The officers of Rome were able to exploit the weakness of the papacy and its need for good relations with the city by extracting what was virtually a series of bribes on a very large scale. There may be exaggeration in Gerhoh of Reichersberg's statement that in his day the Romans would only swear fealty in return for a payment of eleven thousand talents, but John of Salisbury refers to such payments in Adrian IV's time, and the quarrel of Lucius III with Rome was apparently due to his unwillingness or inability to continue this tradition, as well as to the question of Roman expansion.[1] Lucius' refusal to pay did not solve the papacy's financial problems, since an expensive war for Tusculum raged bitterly each summer in the years 1183–5. Such was the economic plight of the pope that he sent special emissaries to Henry II of England to appeal to him and the English clergy for aid in the defence of the patrimony against the Romans.[2]

In this period such signs of long-term policy as enfeoffments and the grants of privileges are rare.[3] The fact that there is no evidence for the existence of papal rectors in the patrimony during the decade after the Treaty of Venice is suggestive of the extent to which government had passed out of the hands of the pope, and when Urban III at last appointed a representative to rule in the Campagna his nominee was a Milanese knight from whom he withheld the title of *rector*. This 'Lanterius' was a mere bailiff, who seems to have been thankful when the death of Urban III gave him an excuse for abandoning his task and returning to Milan.[4]

[1] See Wenck, 'Die Römischen Papste zwischen Alexander III. u. Innocenz III.' in *Kaisertum und Papsttum (Festschrift P. Kehr)*, pp. 418–20. John of Salisbury, *Policraticus*, VI, ch. 24 (ed. Webb, II, 71): John relates how he asked the pope '. . . quare Romanis tuis timorem non incutis et temeritate repressa eos ad fidem non revocas? At urbem vis Ecclesiae tuis muneribus conservare . . .' See also *Gesta Innocentii III* (P.L., 214, clxxix), where it is said that the Romans' aim was, 'ut, sicut soliti fuerant, a summo pontifice pecuniam extorquerent', while Innocent was 'cupiens hanc pessimam consuetudinem abolere'. At the same period English barons and clerics were paying large sums to the Crown *pro habenda benevolentia regis* and *ut rex dimittat iram suam* (J. E. A. Jolliffe, *Angevin Kingship*, pp. 96–109): the contrast brings out clearly the pope's weakness vis-à-vis those whom he claimed as subjects.

[2] Watterich, II, 651–3, 655–7, 664.

[3] Lucius III's intervention in a war between Sezze and Sermoneta (1181) and his summons of Sabina to war against Farfa are isolated instances of papal activity (Kehr, *It. Pont.*, II, 129, 55). Exceptions are the grant of Ariccia as a fief in 1178–9 (*ibid.*, 34) and of Falvaterra in 1178 (*ibid.*, 173) and Alexander III's privilege to Veroli (*ibid.*, 163). The only major papal gain of these years was the acquisition in 1179 of Lariano, the last holding of the counts of Tusculum in the Alban hills (*ibid.*, 105: see also G. Digard, *art. cit.*, in *Mélanges P. Fabre*, pp. 301–2).

[4] For this episode *v.* Watterich, II, 683. The letter of appointment of a Count of Segni as *comes sacri patrimonii* by Lucius III (Kehr, *It. Pont.*, II, 133) is a forgery and it would be rash to assume that it is based on a document appointing a count or rector at this time.

It is now necessary to return a few years in order to consider the papal-imperial negotiations of the period 1182–97 and their connection with the Papal State. Imperial power within the patrimony was often greater than the power of the pope during these years, though at times it was exercised in the pope's interest. The papacy held, however, a number of advantages, of which the most important was the need felt in turn by Frederick I and Henry VI to secure a firm settlement involving papal recognition of their territorial situation in Italy and papal coronation for their sons. Opposition to the emperor in Germany was a further source of strength to the popes, while Henry in particular had need of papal support, firstly against the rival Sicilian claimant Tancred, and then, after his victory, to carry through his plan for retaining both Sicily and the Empire in his house by making the imperial succession hereditary.

There is no need to give here a detailed account of the involved negotiations of these years and they have been well described by Wenck and Haller.[1] The Papal State plays in them a double role, as a claim put forward by the papacy to secure a territorial base in central Italy (and, after 1194, an essential bulwark against the pincers of an emperor who is also King in Palermo), and as a stake which was nominally held by the pope but at times snatched, as a diplomatic move, by his opponents. The essential importance for the history of the Papal State of the negotiations which precede the imperial *débacle* of 1197 is that through good fortune, papal determination and imperial weakness, the papal claims outlived the negotiations to flourish in that papal Golden Age, the era of the disputed imperial succession of 1197, and afterwards. The chief themes of the following pages are therefore the territorial background in central Italy to the papal-imperial negotiations and the survival of the papal claims.

The pontificate of Lucius III (1181–5) saw the first attempts by Barbarossa to secure papal consent to a settlement which would recognize imperial rule in central Italy (outside the patrimony) and imperial suzerainty in the north. The emperor sought to consolidate the gains of the Treaty of Venice by making a lasting territorial agreement with the pope, and he felt all the stronger in dealing with Lucius because Roman ambitions in Latium were now rampant and without imperial support the papacy could hardly hope to secure any temporal control. A letter from Barbarossa to Lucius III of July 1183 puts forward two distinct

---

[1] K. Wenck, article cited above p. 20 n. 1: Haller, 'Heinrich VI. u. die römische Kurie', *MIÖG*, XXXV, 385–454, 545–669.

sets of proposals and suggests a meeting to discuss them.[1] The first proposal is that the emperors shall henceforth pay one-tenth of the
revenues they derive from Italy to the pope, and one-ninth of them to
the cardinals. The second is that the Church should hold *certas possessiones* freely and without payment, except for the imperial right to
fodrum; arbiters would decide the boundaries of these possessions, but
their award would be subject to alteration, since exchanges would
be permitted if either power needed territory awarded to the other so
badly that it was prepared to offer a suitable *concambium*. Probably
Frederick had in mind to offer the pope either the patrimony itself (excluding the disputed areas in northern Latium) together with an annual
money payment, or, as an alternative, the more liberal territorial settlement which might emerge from the award of a court of arbitration, by
which the pope might gain the Tuscan patrimony and some at least
of the Matildine lands. The saving clause about exchanges was presumably designed to enable the emperor to retain the most strategically
vital of the Matildine lands, such as those controlling the Apennine
passes.

These early proposals were unacceptable to the papacy, nor were the
negotiations which took place in 1184 at Verona more fruitful, despite
the continuing weakness of the pope's temporal situation. We know
little about what occurred at Verona, though the possession of the
Matildine lands was certainly discussed, as was that of Ferrara.[2] It seems
clear that the pope was rightly adopting a 'stonewalling' policy, ap-
preciating that it could not be in the interests of the papacy to reach
terms which, at a time when the initiative lay with the emperor, would
necessarily be unsatisfactory from a papal viewpoint. The situation
could scarcely deteriorate and so long as the papacy could hold out and
the emperor continued to need a settlement, it might improve.[3] The
termination of the Verona meetings was probably unwilling on Fred-

---

[1] MGH, Const., I, 420–1. In describing the two proposals as alternative, not complementary, I am agreeing with Kauffmann, *op. cit.*, pp. 18–21, and dissenting from Lenel,
art. cit., 210–15. The strongest grounds for this are not those alleged by Kauffmann, but
the reference to the second suggestion as *alius . . . concordie modus* and the strength of
Frederick's position. It seems unlikely that he would have contemplated making large
money payments as well as the territorial cessions which an arbitration would have probably involved.

[2] Haller, *art. cit.*, 399: for Ferrara, *v.* P. Zerbi, 'Un inedito dell' Archivio Vaticano e il
convegno di Verona', *Aevum*, XXVIII (1954), 470–83.

[3] For a very good account of the papacy's delaying tactics, *v.* Wenck, *art. cit.*, *passim*.
Lucius probably knew of the lengthy negotiations which led to the engagement of Frederick's son to the Sicilian Constance, but may have used the news of this engagement as an
excuse for adjourning discussions with the emperor. There is a large literature on this
subject, evoked by Haller's belief that Lucius arranged this marriage. This view is tenta-

erick's part. His firm intention to secure an agreement and confidence that the pope would yield is illustrated by the continuance of negotiations even after the abandonment of the conference,[1] but no terms had been reached when the pope died in November 1185.

A new era began in 1186, for this was Frederick I's last year in Italy and Henry, now King of the Romans, took over the leadership of the imperialist cause south of the Alps. For the next eight years Henry was virtually the ruler of central, but not yet of southern, Italy. He was faced by a series of aged popes whose powerlessness was only a little mitigated by Clement III's agreement with Rome of May 1188. Even two Roman popes, Clement III and Celestine III, each of whom promoted members of the Roman baronage to the cardinalate, were unable to strengthen the papal position within the city; the terms of 1188 had made the senate vassals of the pope, but this could do little to remedy the pontiff's lack of temporal power. The only solid gain to the papacy from the agreement of 1188 was that Clement could take up residence in the city. All the other effective clauses of the treaty favoured the Romans, for the pope now promised to aid them in the struggle against Tusculum and to continue the traditional payments to the senators and other officials.[2] Rome remained substantially independent of the papacy and, if the popes had a home after 1188 which they had not possessed regularly since 1162, they were still faced, as they had been since 1144, with two powerful rivals to their rule in the patrimony.

Henry VI's policy in central Italy between 1186 and 1194 was to exploit papal weakness by a show of force in the patrimony; in this way he hoped to persuade the pope to agree to a final territorial settlement and (after 1189) to recognize him as King of Sicily. The terms suggested by Henry on several occasions make it evident that he made no claim to the patrimony; if he held it, it was as a stake and to remind the popes of their powerlessness, not because he wanted it as a permanent possession.

Frederick had written to Urban III on his election in friendly terms and had specifically promised to send Henry to the pope's assistance, taking the patrimony under his protection, 'as was his duty'. This

tively accepted by Wenck, but the idea that a pope might have arranged a union which could conceivably join the Sicilian kingdom to the Empire is so paradoxical that it requires stronger evidence than a solitary passage in Peter of Eboli.

[1] Haller, *art. cit.*, 437–45.

[2] For the terms *v.* Theiner, d. XXXII. For a discussion, G. Tomassetti, 'La Pace di Roma (a. 1188)', *Rivista Internazionale di Scienze Sociali*, XI (1896).

imperial promise is only known to us through Urban's letter complaining that it has not been kept,[1] but that *res in contraria versa est*. Negotiations continued through the early months of 1186, but in the spring Urban took the initiative by reversing previous papal policy concerning the disputed episcopal election at Trier and making friendly approaches to the Cremonese, Henry's principal enemies in Lombardy.[2] Henry's reply to these moves was the invasion of the patrimony which evoked the papal letter of protest quoted above. Henry marched into the Tuscan patrimony in June, bringing the stronghold of Orvieto to terms after a siege and winning round Perugia by the grant of a charter. Viterbo and Narni also fell to Henry, who then overran virtually the whole of the Campagna, ravaging the country-side and taxing the towns. Leo of Anguillara, the powerful Roman consul, was invested with Sutri and granted *regalia* and wide judicial powers; this move suggests an attempt to extend the imperial sphere of influence by installing a vassal in the area between the Tuscan patrimony and Rome, an experiment which would have limited the papal patrimony to the zone south of the city. With the pope virtually blockaded at Verona, there survived hardly a glimmer of papal rule, though Urban's bailiff in the Campagna held two castles at the time of his death in October 1187.[3] There is no evidence of continuous imperial occupation of the patrimony after 1186 and it seems unlikely, though not impossible, that Henry maintained garrisons there after the campaign of that year, except in the disputed places of the Tuscan patrimony. The support of Leo di Anguillara and the impotence of the pope probably made such an expensive policy unnecessary and the ravages of 1186 had served sufficiently to point the moral of this powerlessness both to the local population and the unyielding pope himself. But Urban died and still no agreement had been reached.

The brief pontificate of Urban's successor, Gregory VIII (21 October — 17 December 1187) saw the renewal of negotiations and the exchange of friendly letters wherein Henry spoke of his intention of restoring the pope to Rome and of enforcing the obedience of his subjects, while Gregory announced that he would give up his claims to 'imperial possessions'.[4] Nothing had come of these mutually friendly assurances when Gregory followed Urban to the grave.

Only after Clement III had reached terms with the Romans and a new series of imperial-papal negotiations had issued in the agreement

---

[1] MGH, Const., I, 441–4.
[2] Kauffmann, *op. cit.*, chapter VI, *passim*.
[3] *V. sup.*, p. 20.
[4] Kauffmann, *op. cit.*, pp. 139–41.

of Hagenau whereby Clement promised to crown Henry as emperor, was there any possibility of the patrimony returning to papal rule. The full terms of this agreement have been lost, but the survival of a letter of instructions from Henry to his nuncios makes it possible to reconstruct its territorial clauses, at least in so far as they related to the patrimony.[1] These included the return to the pope of all the cities, towns and barons of *Romania vel Campania*, as well as certain named towns, most of them (Orvieto, Viterbo, Corneto, Vetralla, Orte, Narni and Amelia) situated in the northern patrimony, though Tusculum and Terracina, also named, are further to the south. This area was restored *quoad posses-sionem*, with the proviso *salvo iure imperii tam de proprietate quam de possessione*, while the return of Tivoli was hedged round with a yet more cautious formula referring to the town's oath to Henry and his father. The places restored were released from their oaths to Henry (and, when this applied, from oaths taken to his father after 1185), they were enjoined to become obedient papal subjects, and anyone hindering their return was to be placed under the ban of the Empire. The in-structions to the nuncios show that Henry had promised to put this restitution into effect. A provisional and temporary arrangement about seisin was intended and not a judicial settlement concerning the owner-ship of the Papal State. There is a certain lack of precision in the refer-ence to *Romania vel Campania*, and Henry's unwillingness to refer to the *patrimonium beati Petri* is significant; it seems unlikely that the terms of the agreement itself defined the area concerned in more detail. If exact boundaries had been named they would presumably have been noted in the letter to the imperial nuncios.

We have no direct information about the effectiveness of the promised restitution of April 1189. There is extremely little evidence of papal rule in the patrimony in the following years. Henry's renewal of the undertaking at the time of his coronation in 1191 is not proof that the restitution of 1189 was ineffective, particularly if he now only promised the restoration of the patrimony 'si quid inde ablatum esset'.[2] It seems most probable that Henry relinquished any parts that were under his control in 1189, without them coming under the effective rule of the pope. The pope's position was so weak that such an outcome would not necessarily imply that the imperial nuncios had disregarded their instructions.[3]

[1] MGH, Const., I, 460–1. For discussion see P. Zerbi, *Papato, Impero e 'Respublica Christiana' dal 1187 al 1198*, pp. 26–7.   [2] Roger of Hoveden, *Chronica*, III, 101–2.
[3] Lenel's statement (*art. cit.*, 253) that the restitution of 1189 was never carried out is too dogmatic. See also Zerbi, *Papato, Impero e 'Respublica Christiana'*, p. 85.

What emerges most clearly from the fragmentary evidence of these years is the strength of Rome itself and the insecurity of the apparent papal success of 1188. The Romans had been dissatisfied with Clement's failure to secure Tusculum for them, but the campaign of 1190 was the last of Rome's many attempts to capture this stronghold. In 1191 the presence of imperial troops achieved what the Romans had failed to do on their own, and Tusculum was now passed on from Henry VI to Celestine III and from Celestine to Rome. At about the same time Benedict 'Carushomo' became sole senator of Rome and for some two years he held most of the Marittima and Sabina, even appointing justices in these areas. It is evident that any imperial 'restitutions' in 1191 within the patrimony can only have benefited Rome and not the papacy. The regime of a single senator lasted some half-dozen years, for Carushomo was succeeded by John Capoccio (*c.* 1195–6) and the latter by John Pierleone (*c.* 1196–7). Throughout this time there is virtually no trace of papal government in the patrimony.[1]

In June 1192 Celestine III declared his support for Tancred, Henry VI's rival for Sicily, and Henry's conquest of that kingdom in 1194 meant not merely that the papacy had backed the unsuccessful cause but that at the best it was faced by the prospect of isolation within the patrimony. So long as there had been a Norman ruler in the south, he was a counterweight to imperial pressure, while at times the emperor was useful as a balance against the Normans. Now the whole balance of power system in Italy had collapsed, leaving the pope crushed and apparently helpless. Only one element in the new situation favoured the pope, but it was an important one. Henry was faced with the task of absorbing and transmitting a vast and heterogeneous dominion, parts of which had recently been in revolt; if he was to do this, it was important to him to secure recognition as King of Sicily and vitally important to place the succession to the Empire on the same hereditary basis as the kingdom of Sicily. For both these projects the approval of the papacy was essential. The emperor would need to bid very high to secure agreement with the powerless but indispensable pope, particularly since the papacy was in no hurry and, as earlier, could afford to prolong negotiations indefinitely.

Henry's policy in attempting to bring Pope Celestine to terms consisted in a combination of force and blandishment. The former began

[1] Gregorovius, IV, 2, 626–9: Watterich, II, 709–11: P. Zerbi, 'Ebbe parte Celestino III nella consegna di Tuscolo ai Romani?', *Aevum*, XXVIII, 445–69. *Gesta Innocentii III* (P.L., vol. 214), § 8. For the emperor's ability to blockade the Papal State and prevent the entry of prelates in 1192, see *Vita Alberti Leodiensis*, MGH, XXV, 143 and 146.

with military action in the Campagna, which Henry occupied in 1194.[1] The latter led to the emperor's decision to take the crusading cross in March 1195, thereby rendering papal action against him more difficult. At the same time Henry's brother Philip, who was entrusted with the duchy of Tuscany, was permitted to extend his sphere of influence throughout the disputed towns of the 'Tuscan patrimony', as far south at least as Vetralla and possibly even further, for which action he was probably excommunicated by the pope.[2] The isolation of the patrimony was further emphasized when Conrad of Urslingen was granted the duchy of Spoleto and Markward of Anweiler Romagna, the duchy of Ravenna, the March of Ancona and the county of Abruzzi. The lands of these two powerful Germans (Conrad was also Henry's vicar in the Sicilian kingdom) lay athwart the patrimony, which in any case was now in the hands of Philip of Swabia (in the north), the Romans (around the city) and such pro-imperial families as the lords of Anguillara and the Frangipani. Henry's troops seem to have evacuated the Campagna where, however, in the words of Celestine's successor, 'the emperor was more feared than the pope'. Throughout the papal-imperial negotiations of 1196–7 there is no scintilla of papal authority in the patrimony, nor, *a fortiori*, beyond it.[3]

We are not well-informed about these negotiations between a David and a Goliath, and in particular the part played in them by the discussion of territorial disputes is unknown, though the imperialist governors of the March and the duchy of Spoleto were involved, and it is evident that territorial questions must have been debated. The emperor made an offer to the pope which he described as higher than those made by his father or any of his predecessors, but the nature of the offer is unknown. Gerald of Wales, a not very reliable authority, talks of a scheme whereby the papacy was to hold a canonry in each of the major sees in western Christendom, but there is no confirmation for this story and in any case only the offer of a territorial compact was likely to lead to the conclusion of a firm agreement.[4] The pope preferred to wait for more

---

[1] MGH, XIX, 292 (*Annales Ceccanenses*).

[2] Ficker, *Forschungen*, II, 238–9 and 313–14: Haller, *art. cit.*, 587: Innocent III, *Registrum de Negotio Imperii*, nn. 29 and 64. Innocent's claim that Philip was entitled 'dux Campanie' is one of several improbable accusations against him. Montefiascone was the southernmost of the towns named as regained in 1197 and Henry admitted in a letter that Vetralla was papal (MGH, *Const.*, I, 523). Philip's excommunication: see *Reg. de Neg. Imp.*, nn. 33, 62 and 136 (Philip's denial), *Reg. Inn. III*, P.L., vol. 214, l. I, 25 (col. 20), and *Gesta Inn. III*, col. xxxiii.

[3] Gregorovius, IV, 2, 636–7.

[4] Haller, *art. cit.*, 608 ff. (the negotiations in general): MGH, *Const.*, I, 525 (the 'highest offer'). Gerald of Wales has perhaps been taken too seriously by some writers (e.g. E.

favourable circumstances before reaching a settlement and by the spring of 1197 Henry seems to have abandoned negotiations. Before the year was out events were to justify the pope's tactics more fully than he can have dared to hope.

It is possible that the emperor made a will or an informal plan of settlement whereby the Church was to hold the patrimony and the Matildine lands, as well as enjoying suzerainty over the Sicilian kingdom, the March of Ancona and the duchy of Ravenna, together with the succession to these if Constance and Markward respectively had no heirs. Were this so-called 'will', which was cited by Innocent III in support of his claims and partly copied into the pope's *Gesta*, genuine, we should have an insight into what seemed to Henry a practicable arrangement in the dark circumstances of his last days.[1] But too much doubt surrounds this document for any confident deductions to be drawn from it. The question of its genuineness is bedevilled by the fact that we probably possess only those clauses which favoured the papacy. It is very questionable whether Henry would have suggested the wholesale cession of the Matildine lands to the papacy or even its suzerainty over the March and Ravenna, where papal claims had long been dropped. Even if Henry had been willing to continue Markward's rule over these Adriatic lands, it is unlikely that he would have proposed a papal overlord for them — indeed this suggestion seems almost absurd in the circumstances of Henry's lifetime, when the papacy was powerless, and Henry was hardly likely to foresee how fully his death would reverse these circumstances and make practicable papal suzerainty along the Adriatic. Although the will is now generally accepted as genuine, it reads so like a possible basis for negotiations between Markward and the papacy that the probability that it was faked by Markward to serve as such a basis cannot be neglected. The 'will' is certainly not a papal forgery, for it offers the papacy too little, but it may well be a fake by Markward and cannot safely be used as evidence of Henry's intentions in September 1197.[2]

Jordan, *L'Allemagne et l'Italie*, p. 163 n.): for an unfavourable estimate of his reliability see D. Knowles, *The Monastic Order in England*, p. 664. A discussion of whether Gerald's hypothetical offer was a substitute for or addition to a territorial settlement favouring the pope would take the argument too far into the realms of hypothesis, though C.-E. Perrin has attempted to reconstitute the terms of a territorial offer on the strength of the surviving fragments of Henry's dubious 'testament' (in *Mélanges L. Halphen*, pp. 565–72). Haller's theory that Henry offered to hold the Empire as a papal fief is quite untenable.

[1] *Gesta Innocentii III* (P.L., vol. 214), § 27 (the fragmentary text of the 'will'), also, for a reference to it, *Reg.*, VII, n. 228 (vol. 215).

[2] The 'will' is accepted as genuine by Hampe, *Deutsche Kaisergeschichte* (ed. Baethgen, 1945), pp. 235 n–236 n, and by Jordan, *L'Allemagne et l'Italie*, pp. 165–6; also in MGH,

Whatever the nature of these intentions, they were destined to be ineffective. To conclude the story of the Papal State before Henry's death it is necessary to return to Rome and the pope himself. It was during these years, when the papal cause seemed hopeless and the retention even of the patrimony out of the question, that the determination and faith of the Curia gave birth to a collection of documents providing a basis for papal territorial and financial claims, the *Liber Censuum*.[1] This collection was begun in 1192 by the papal chamberlain Cencius, later Pope Honorius III. Though not the first compilation of the kind, it was both more comprehensive and more orderly than its predecessors. It was not begun, as has been suggested,[2] as a reply to the emperor's implicit claim of 1189 to possess rights over central Italy. Nevertheless this silent work of preservation and compilation is evidence that the papacy was keeping alive those claims to the Papal State which came into play on Henry's death, when Pope Celestine and then Pope Innocent appealed to the Carolingian and later imperial donations as the legal basis for papal overlordship in central Italy.

Const., I, 530–1, but I understand that the document is likely to be relegated to the *spuria* in the next edition of the MGH. See also D. Clementi in *QFIA*, XXXV, 212–13. For the negotiations between Innocent III and Markward, when the latter offered to hold the March as a papal fief, see Van Cleve, *Markward of Anweiler and the Sicilian Regency*, pp. 91–2, 108–22, 205. The possibility of a forgery dating from this period is suggested by Ficker in *Forschungen*, III, 446–7 and in *Sitzungsberichte d. Phil. Hist. Classe d. K. Akad. d. Wissenschaften*, 67 (1871), especially pp. 287–95. Markward's offer to hold the March as a papal fief (*Gesta* in P.L., 214, cols. xxii–xxiv) was taken seriously as a negotiating point, for Innocent III's biographer, a prelate close to the pope and therefore well-informed, suggests that the offer was only refused because Innocent doubted whether Markward would observe the clause honestly. The case for the rejection of the 'will' is, unconsciously, put very well by Zerbi (*op. cit.*, pp. 133–4), who regards it as genuine because 'l'atto trae la sua realtà profonda di compromesso offerto alla Chiesa Romana e contrassegnato da ampie concessioni alla Chiesa stessa'. If the 'will' was forged by Markward, the 'missing' clauses (the omission of which from the *Gesta* is difficult to explain) may never have existed. The captured document would then have been passed off by Markward on a willing Innocent III as an extract.

[1] Ed. by P. Fabre and L. Duchesne, Paris, 1910–52. See also P. Fabre, *Étude sur le Liber Censuum de l'Église Romaine*.

[2] By Lenel, *art. cit.*, 254–5, but on the strength of a passage also contained in Deusdedit's eleventh-century collection (*Lib. Cens.*, pp. 58 and 363 n). The *Liber Censuum* was, as the name implies, primarily a rent-book, and rents are placed first in it: the cartulary containing the imperial donations was put last, after the *Mirabilia Urbis Romae*, the *Ordo Romanus* and the papal chronicles. For the low total value of the rents *v.* V. Pfaff, 'Die Einnahmen der römischen Kurie am Ende des 12. Jahrhunderts', *VSWG*, XL, esp. pp. 114–18.

II

Innocent III and the Foundation of the Papal State, 1198—1216

The beginnings of the first real Papal State are in a sense a negative process, for the essential factor in its origin is the 'power vacuum' in central Italy which followed Henry VI's death in September 1197. Henry's representatives in the area, his brother Philip, Conrad of Urslingen and Markward of Anweiler, were competent men with a fair control of the zones that they ruled, but the absence of an heir of suitable age brought about a rapid dissolution of Henry's empire and drew Philip at once to Germany. Within a year the position of the Empire was further weakened by a disputed succession, while the pope was claiming to decide this dispute and had secured acknowledgement of his suzerainty over the Neapolitan kingdom. Before the end of 1199 he was the guardian of Henry's son, the Sicilian heir, Conrad had abandoned Spoleto and Markward had left central Italy. Ranke's saying that 'the heir to Henry VI was Innocent III'[1] is the key to the understanding of the early years of the feeble new State, the product of imperial collapse rather than of papal resurgence.

The Carolingian donations provided legal justification for the papacy's action in plucking the 'ripe fruit'[2] of the central Italian provinces and, together with anti-German feeling, strengthened the papal hold over subjects to whom imperial weakness now left the alternatives of papal rule or independent statelessness.

The news of Henry VI's death reached Philip of Swabia at Montefiascone, in the disputed zone of the Tuscan patrimony, and there was at once a local rising against the Germans in which some of Duke Philip's men were killed.[3] Further to the north the main Tuscan towns joined in a league to secure their independence of the Empire, and the Duke

---

[1] *Weltgeschichte*, VIII (Leipzig, 1887), 274.
[2] Haller, *Das Papsttum* (ed. 2, 1952), III, 332. For the Carolingian donations as the basis for papal claims in central Italy see above, p. 1–3.
[3] BFW, n. 14a.

was hard-pressed on his journey to Germany. The rebellion in southern Tuscany probably occurred in October 1197. The Tuscan League was established in November, with the co-operation of the pope, and before the end of the year Celestine had sent out a legate and other representatives to secure oaths of fidelity from the towns of the duchy of Spoleto and March of Ancona. We have not much information about the progress of these negotiations, but when Celestine wrote to the consuls and people of Ascoli on 23 December, Perugia had submitted to the legate, Cardinal Gregory of S. Maria in Porticu, and Spoleto, Assisi, Spello, Gubbio and Amelia to his representatives. At about this time further papal *missi* were despatched into the March with instructions to gain oaths of obedience from Rimini and the towns of the March and to excommunicate anyone hindering submissions to the papacy there and in Tuscany. These directions to the bishop of Fermo and abbot of Farfa confirmed the pope's own *ipso facto* excommunication of anyone aiding Markward and other Germans 'against the patrimony of the Church'.[1] Thus the Duchy, the March and Tuscany had all been claimed, on the grounds of imperial donations, and the process of securing them to the papacy had been set firmly in motion when the aged Celestine III died on 8 January 1198.

The immediate election of Cardinal Lothair dei Conti is explicable by the need to maintain or increase the impetus of papal pressure in central Italy as well as by Lothair's outstanding talents and the necessity for forceful action in exploiting the imperial crisis. Innocent was already at grips with the problem of central Italy by the time of his consecration, which occurred on 22 February.[2] It was natural that his first efforts should be directed towards securing his position in Rome, since bad relations with the Romans had done so much to weaken his predecessors during the previous half-century. The powerful rank of his family and their lands in the Campagna, together with the absence of imperial pressure, greatly strengthened Innocent's position, and he achieved impressive success at once, for when the senator, Scottus 'Paparonis',

---

[1] Böhmer, *Acta Imperii*, 616–17: *Nachrichten v.d. Königl. Gesellschaft der Wissenschaften zu Göttingen, Phil.-Hist. Klasse*, V (1898), 43 ff. (the text of Celestine III's letters). There seems no reason to accept Ficker's view (*Forschungen*, II, § 358) that Celestine's actions must have been the execution of a long-formed plan. There is no evidence that they were so rapid that their speed could only be explained by this hypothesis, nor is the probable onset of the pope's last illness before 23 December (see Zerbi, pp. 134–5) relevant here.

[2] On the *Gesta*, the best narrative source for Innocent's Italian policy, though it is hagiographical in attitude and ends in 1208, *v.* H. Elkan, *Die Gesta Innocentii III. im Verhaltniss zu den Regesten desselben Papstes*, and Y. Lefèvre, 'Innocent III et son temps vus de Rome', *MAH*, LXI, 242–5.

resigned, the pope appointed an elector to the senatorship. This *medianus* then nominated a successor who swore fealty to Innocent.[1] The reasons for his success are not clear, but during the previous decade a regime of single senators had alternated with a plural 'college' and an individual senator such as Scottus must have had many opponents.[2] Thus a party of opposition probably helped to bring about his resignation. Although it has been stated that Innocent bribed the Romans into submission, the evidence suggests that, on the contrary, he was successful in standing out against the costly and humiliating precedent of the *donativum*.[3]

Immediately after his consecration Pope Innocent received an oath of fealty from the Roman prefect, Peter of Vico.[4] Peter had previously been the vassal of Henry VI, but the prefecture was no longer connected with power in the city itself and this fealty is not relevant to the new pope's hold over Rome. It must be considered rather in connection with the next stage in his assertion of suzerainty, its extension to the neighbouring patrimony, for the prefect's lands lay to the north of the city, around Lake Bracciano. He now swore not only to keep the peace and defend the Roman See, but to accept the submission of papal vassals only with the pope's consent, and to make no changes in the castellans and serjeants of his lordship unless the pope agreed. These terms foreshadow Innocent's next action, which was to send nuncios throughout the patrimony with instructions to secure the fealty of all towns and barons and to appoint justices, replacing those of the senator. This matter seems to have passed off smoothly and probably no opposition was encountered. Papal authority, in the absence of Roman and imperial rivalry, was likely to go unchallenged in this early stage, at least within the old patrimony around the city: the testing time would

---

[1] *Gesta Innocentii III* (P.L., vol. 214), xxii. See also F. Bartoloni, 'Per la Storia del Senato Romano nei sec. XII e XIII', *BISI*, LX, especially p. 55. The *Gesta* mention specifically only the fealty of Scottus, but that of his successor is implied.

[2] See Bartoloni's article cited above. Apart from *a priori* probability the fact that John Capoccio, who was senator *c.* 1195–6, was a leading opponent of Innocent's senator, seems to point to the existence of senatorial factions.

[3] Haller, *Papsttum*, III, 326 and A. Luchaire, *Innocent III: Rome et l'Italie*, pp. 47–8, state that Innocent bribed the Romans without giving sources (Luchaire's book cites no references, but no source is given in his 'Innocent III et le peuple romain', *Revue Historique*, LXXXI). Roger of Hoveden (R.S.,I V, 45) states that Innocent acquired great unpopularity by refusing to pay the *donativum*: his account must be based on hearsay and his version of subsequent events does not tally with the *Gesta*, but the statement of the *Gesta* (§ 133) that Innocent's Roman opponents were attempting to extort money from him while he firmly insisted on abolishing this *pessimam consuetudinem* seems more compatible with Hoveden's version than with the modern authorities.

[4] P.L., 214, cols. xviii, xxiii, 529 (also for the oath of two other barons at the same time).

come when Innocent attempted to assert his position by unpopular administrative action.[1]

The assertion of papal claims to the hitherto imperial provinces proceeded simultaneously with this domestic reconquest. The duchy of Spoleto, to the north-east of the patrimony, had been held by Conrad of Urslingen. Some towns here soon came over to papal obedience, no doubt on the orders of Innocent's emissaries, and at about the same time Conrad was excommunicated, presumably as an 'invader' of papal territory.[2] Conrad must have felt his isolated position, deprived of imperial support, to be a weak one, for soon, almost certainly before the end of March, he was engaged in negotiations with the pope for a *modus vivendi*. He offered to hold the duchy as a fief of the papacy in return for a payment of 10,000 *l*., together with an annual rent of 100 *l*. and military service within the patrimony by two hundred knights. Innocent considered the offer a tempting one, but decided to reject it because it would mean the continuation of German rule in central Italy, and indeed its acceptance would have clashed strongly both with his anti-imperial aims and with the anti-German propaganda that he was employing to reconcile his new subjects to papal domination.[3] It is likely that these negotiations were fairly prolonged, but before the middle of April they had come to an end through Conrad's decision to submit unconditionally to the pope. In theory his solemn absolution of all his former subjects from the obligation of obedience to him and transfer of their fealty to the pope, transacted at Narni in the presence of two cardinals, placed the papacy in possession of the entire duchy. In practice Conrad handed over two fortresses (Gualdo Tadino and Cesi) where he had maintained garrisons, and made an attempt, which was unsuccessful owing to local resistance, to hand over the castle at Assisi. These facts sufficiently illustrate the weak position of Conrad, whom the pope firmly ordered back to Germany. Within a few months the major towns of the duchy had acknowledged papal suzerainty.[4]

Nor was Innocent slower in trying conclusions with the more formidable personality of Markward of Anweiler, ruler of the March of Ancona and duchy of Ravenna. Immediately after his consecration he

---

[1] It is not possible to date this stage in Innocent's reconquest, but the *Gesta* (§ 22) put the dispatch of these emissaries immediately after his consecration.

[2] For the events described in this paragraph *v. Reg. Inn. III*, I, n. 88 and *Gesta*, § 22–4.

[3] Gregorovius, V, 1, 26–30, discusses this propaganda.

[4] See below pp. 36–7. The *Gesta* place the submission of Rieti, Spoleto, Assisi, Foligno, Nocera, Perugia, Gubbio, Todi and Città di Castello immediately after Conrad's oath, but it seems evident that the division here is topical and the passage does not help to establish a clear chronology for th submission of the duchy.

D

sent two cardinals into the March with the usual instructions to 'win back' the province to papal obedience. The formation of a powerful league in this area specifically directed against Markward must have encouraged papal hopes of success; this alliance between Ravenna, Rimini, Senigallia, Ancona, Fermo and Osimo was sworn on 2 February.[1] Markward, like Conrad, made a gloomy estimate of his position and sent envoys to Rome offering to negotiate. He expressed the desire to come to Rome himself for these negotiations and made a general offer to 'obey the pope's orders', while asking that the cardinals' mission should for the time be dropped. This suggestion was unpromising from a papal viewpoint, but Innocent, making a virtue of necessity, gave a promise that his representatives would only receive submissions made willingly. Markward's proposals were inadequate or too imprecise, and in any case the pope had committed himself to a policy which forbade terms with representatives of the Hohenstaufen. Innocent swept aside the offers and the negotiations went no further. Within a few weeks Markward had been excommunicated for 'invading and detaining' papal lands. Innocent realized the need to act quickly while local forces were in arms against the Germans and the Empire lacked a ruler. Soon the bishops of the March were receiving orders to excommunicate Markward's supporters, and the process whereby the towns submitted to the two cardinals moved at such a pace that Markward was stimulated to make further proposals concerning terms on which he would hold the March as a papal fief.[2]

It was customary for Innocent, when writing to his new subjects, to quote from St. Matthew the words *Jugum meum suave est, et onus meum leve*.[3] Most of them were soon able to test the accuracy of this promise, but there were some areas to which the pope laid claim without making a serious attempt to instal papal government. These were the Matildine lands, the duchy of Ravenna and Tuscany.[4] The whole of Tuscany was demanded, on the strength of the Carolingian donations. It seems possible that this claim was put forward on the bargaining principle of demanding more than one expects to receive, and with the intention of

---

[1] Tonini, *Rimini*, II, d. XCIV. For the other events of this paragraph, *v. Gesta*, § 22–4.

[2] *Reg. Inn. III*, (P.L., 214), I, n. 38. For the suggestion that Henry VI's will may have been fabricated around this time to forward Markward's policy of negotiating with the papacy *v.* above p. 28. The 'will' allots the March to Markward as a papal fief. The vagueness of the *Gesta* concerning dates makes it difficult to establish a chronology for the events described in this paragraph, but the participants in the anti-Markward league of February were among the first towns to go over to the papacy.

[3] Matthew, XI, 30 ('For my yoke is easy, and my burden is light').

[4] *Reg. Inn. III* (P.L. 214). I, n. 15 (Tuscany: see also nn. 34, 35, 88) and n. 27 (Ravenna).

at least making sure of the disputed zone of southern Tuscany which had been held by Henry VI and Philip of Swabia. Innocent was reversing papal policy when he rebuked his legates for reaching terms with the Tuscan League and insisted that the League, which Celestine III had helped to form, required his consent. Yet the claim to Tuscany was soon tacitly dropped, and while the fate of all central Italy was at stake nothing was done to pursue the Matildine claims, despite approaches made to Innocent by at least one of the towns involved.[1] The legate despatched to the duchy of Ravenna and the county of Bertinoro seems to have received no submissions, and the whole area was yielded to the archbishop of Ravenna, who was able to allege papal privileges. The pope's biographer explains that the question of the Empire and Sicily was more urgent, and this is certainly true if the 'question' is taken to include the formation of a compact, though enlarged, Papal State.

The success or failure of this attempt turned inevitably on Innocent's relations with the communes. By securing the co-operation of the towns he could at least set up a framework of papal government, whatever the attitude of intervening feudal territories owing obedience to barons. The communes were not for the most part as strong as their Lombard and Tuscan counterparts, owing mainly to the comparative economic backwardness of central Italy, but they had become used to a considerable degree of self-government, which had not diminished greatly under Henry VI.[2] They were only likely to submit to papal rule if this measure of independence was retained and in this sense papal weakness was an initial advantage in the pope's plans for achieving suzerainty in central Italy. The towns would be more willing to accept rule if it promised to be feeble and to permit them virtual autonomy. This paradoxical situation was, however, a temporary one, for the pope required not merely nominal acceptance but real subjection. He would only control central Italy in so far as municipal independence was diminished or at least subjected to an ultimate authority. Even if he hoped to deprive the Empire of land, rather than to win it for himself, his rule would only bring him financial and military advantages if the towns became truly his subjects. The test would come after the period of initial submissions.

To trace the precise chronology of Innocent III's establishment of

---

[1] *Reg. Inn. III*, I, n. 47 and *Gesta*, § 27–8. Cities attempting to come to terms with the pope over lands held by them *de facto* received no clear answer. A single grant, however, was made to the bishop of Mantua.

[2] See chapter III for a fuller treatment of the matters mentioned in this paragraph.

rule in central Italy is not possible. Certain clear gains, however, can be attributed to 1198. To the north of Rome, between the Tiber and the Tyrrhenian, opposition was soon encountered at Narni, which commune challenged papal control of the strategic fortress of Otricoli and for a time defied an interdict. Here the Roman alliance produced its first benefits, for Rome provided many of the troops which overcame the army of Narni and forced the town to pay a fine and a sum towards rebuilding the castle at Otricoli.[1] At about the same time (April or May 1198) the pope tried conclusions with Orvieto, the most important stronghold in the disputed zone of the Tuscan patrimony. Relations with Orvieto were of particular importance since this commune claimed hegemony over Acquapendente, another strategically placed fortress which dominated the road between Rome and Siena from a position closely parallel to that whence Orvieto dominated the route from Rome to Arezzo. Innocent now placed Orvieto under an interdict for usurping rule over Acquapendente. The situation was complicated by the existence of a very strong body of heretics at Orvieto, who seem to have secured control of the town for some months while the bishop took refuge at Rome. Not until the early weeks of 1199 did Orvieto yield, and receive a papal rector.[2] Montefiascone, lying rather to the south of the Orvieto-Acquapendente ridge, had sworn allegiance earlier, probably during the summer of 1198. By that time a number of barons of the same area had submitted, some of them after threatening resistance.[3] It seems probable that the process of strengthening the military defences of these parts — the *Gesta* describe new fortifications at Radicofani and Montefiascone — was well on the way by the same time. Undoubtedly these castles were envisaged as strongholds for guarding against local insurrections as well as against attack from some future imperial opponent.[4]

The pope had felt some suspicion of the Tuscan League as a rival in southern Tuscany, but the same threat was considered even more serious in the duchy of Spoleto, where the important towns of Perugia and Assisi were in particular regarded as potential recruits to the League. The people of Assisi had destroyed the castle dominating their town rather than hand it over to a papal representative, and Innocent accused

[1] *Gesta*, § 29.
[2] *Gesta*, § 27 and Legend of *S. Pietro Parenzo*, § 3–4: the Legend mentions the appointment of the papal rector in January 1199 and, by giving nine months as the length of the bishop's sojourn at Rome during the interdict, makes it possible to date the pope's quarrel with Orvieto over Acquapendente to (approximately) April 1198.
[3] *Reg. Inn. III* (P.L. 214), I, nn. 23 & 361: *Gesta*, § 29.
[4] *Gesta*, § 27–9. There was a papal castellan at Radicofani by 1200 (BFW, n. 5708).

Perugia of helping the Assisans in their defiance. But Perugia submitted by the late autumn, a little after Rieti in the extreme south of the duchy and Città di Castello on its north-western border.[1] The speed and thoroughness of the papal gains in the duchy and the lack of opposition are most striking, whatever Pope Innocent's fears. No doubt this was partly attributable to the readiness with which Conrad of Urslingen had passed on the reins of government. During the summer of 1198 the pope himself entered the duchy, an indication of his confidence that his rule there was obtaining proper acknowledgement. This progress lasted probably from mid-August till mid-October.[2] In the course of it Innocent visited Rieti, Spoleto, Perugia and Todi, returning through Amelia, Orte and Civita Castellana. Not only did he emphasize his rule by his own presence in his new province, but he used the occasion to reach agreements with these communes governing the degree of jurisdictional independence which they were to enjoy under papal rule. The powerful Perugia was granted full judicial rights, including appellate jurisdiction, while Rieti was to pay to the papacy half of the fines in certain suits and half of its revenue from tolls. When at Perugia, Innocent named Gregory, cardinal-deacon of S. Maria in Aquiro, as rector of the Duchy of Spoleto and county of Assisi, with spiritual and temporal powers, and legatine jurisdiction. This appointment, which was the first indication of the pope's design of erecting a provincial structure within his new State, governed by ecclesiastical rectors, suggests the intention of securing as much continuity as possible with the ducal administration of Conrad of Urslingen.

Further east, in the March of Ancona, the papal advance was slower. Here the problem was to convert the anti-Markward movement into a pro-papal one, and this was not easy to accomplish. The league against Markward was renewed in the summer of 1198 and Innocent's biographer suggests that all the towns in the alliance, together with others in the March, had sworn fealty to the pope.[3] Indeed the *Gesta* name Ascoli as the only town holding out against papal obedience, but unfortunately the dates of submissions are not given. In contrast with the neighbouring Duchy, the March went through 1198 without receiving a papal visit or a papal rector, and probably without exact

[1] *Reg.*, I, nn. 34, 88, 369, 375 & 401: *Gesta*, § 24–7: *Lib. Cens.*, I, 8*. Perugia probably joined the League later (Heywood, *Perugia*, p. 64).

[2] *Gesta*, § 25–6. Innocent was at Rieti (the first town he is mentioned as visiting) on 14 August: he was at Perugia on 2 October and returned to Rome about 12 October (for these dates see *Gesta* and documents cited in previous note).

[3] Martorelli, *Osimo*, pp. 72–3: *Gesta Inn. III*, § 22–4.

terms being reached governing the status of the communes. The ambiguous situation is curiously reflected in the dating clause of an alliance between Camerino and Montecchio, which was signed in May 1198 *tempore Innocentii Papae et Marcuardi Marchionis*.[1] This combination of irreconcilables suggests the caution which was the dominant note in the policy of most towns in the March. Fabriano, whose diplomacy in this period has been carefully traced by Hagemann,[2] was typical in this respect. The commune joined a large league whose members — many of them among the smaller towns — neither opposed nor supported Markward: deeds were dated noncommittally, usually by the regnal year of Philip of Swabia (throughout 1198) or (by June 1199) *vacante imperio*. Fabriano, like many other towns, was mainly concerned in using the period while the March lacked any effective overlord to extend its own rule in the surrounding country, and postponed a decision about papal claims until it became clear what these claims would entail.

During 1199 the main interest in Innocent's Italian policy shifts from the 'new' provinces to Rome itself. Despite his spectacular early successes here the pope was still faced with a powerful party of opposition prepared, in the phrase of the *Gesta*, 'since they found they could not fish in clear water, to disturb the waters and thus improve the fishing'.[3] The two chief members of this party were two former senators, John Pierleone and John Capoccio.[4] They accused the pope of robbing Rome of its property by his resumption of rule in the Campagna and Marittima and of bringing about the election of a senator favourable to himself instead of a 'common senate'. Their main aim, in the opinion of the author of the *Gesta*, was to extract money from the pontiff in return for a promise to trouble him no more.

This party of opposition achieved only moderate success, but in 1199 a dispute between the city and its powerful northern neighbour Viterbo brought to a head the issue of Innocent's relations with the Romans. This quarrel arose over Viterbo's threats to destroy the small town of Vitorchiano, which then turned to Rome for protection. The situation

---

[1] Colucci, *Treia*, d. CVI: this document has another very peculiar feature, for one of the clauses excepts 'the Emperor Henry', more than six months after Henry VI's death: there seems no reason why the deed should be a forgery and the anachronism could be due to failure to alter an earlier draft or to the unintelligent copying of a formula.

[2] W. Hagemann, 'Fabriano im Kampf zwischen Kaisertum und Papsttum bis 1272', *QFIA*, XXX, 107.

[3] *Gesta*, col. clxxvii. For the whole story of the pope's relations with Rome 1198–*c.* 1202 *v. Gesta*, § 133–5.

[4] See above p. 26. Capoccio seems to have achieved wide celebrity as an enemy of Innocent III, for Caesarius of Heisterbach has a tale about him criticizing a sermon delivered by the pope (*Dialogus Miraculorum*, II, 30).

set an awkward problem for Innocent, as his opponents undoubtedly realized. If he agreed to support Rome he could mollify his local opponents, but only at the expense of strengthening one potentially independent city and losing the fealty of another. Refusal to support the Roman cause, on the other hand, would give an ideal grievance — a *materia turbationis*, in the words of the *Gesta* — to the party of opposition in Rome. It is a sign of the weakness of Innocent's position in Rome that he chose to support the city against Viterbo; a strong Rome was against his interests, but evidently he felt unable to face the danger of a local rising.[1]

Whether the pope's policy was generally interpreted as a sign of weakness we do not know. He gave Rome support in a number of ways, placing Viterbo under an interdict for refusing to argue its case in the papal Curia, ordering the Tuscan League to desist from giving military aid to Viterbo, and instructing his own vassals to join the Roman forces. The Roman army defeated the Viterbese and returned home in triumph. In a further victorious campaign against Viterbo they had strong papal support, especially financial support from the pope's brother Richard.[2]

For a time relations between city and pope were amicable. A papal letter to a legate in Germany, written in the late autumn of 1201, boasted, perhaps a little nervously, that 'concerning Rome, we wish you to know that by the grace of God we hold it in our power' (*ad beneplacitum nostrum*).[3] Capoccio and Pierleone returned to the scene briefly when two feudal lords who were a party in a suit concerning land in the papal Curia attempted to pledge the disputed property to these opponents of the pope, no doubt in order to obtain their powerful support. But Innocent acted quickly, ravaging the lands, thus both

[1] Innocent's biographer, instead of pleading *force majeure*, gives an unconvincing legal justification of his actions. Viterbo is accused of disobeying Innocent over Vitorchiano and of helping Narni against him. But neither of these actions is referred to in the pope's letter to Viterbo about Vitorchiano (*Reg.*, II, n. 207), and the same letter seems to suggest that Innocent had already virtually taken sides before Viterbo disobeyed his summons. Since Narni quarrelled with the pope *c.* 1200 (Theiner, *Vet. Mon. Slav. Merid.*, p. 48), Viterbo's support of Narni may well also date from after its quarrel with the pope, though there had been trouble between Narni and Innocent in 1198 (see above, p. 36). The naively hagiographical attitude of the *Gesta* is nowhere more clearly shown than in the description of Innocent's Roman enemies returning from the victory over Viterbo remarking that they would 'never say another word against him'.

[2] It is not possible to date either campaign exactly. A late Viterbese chronicler attributes the first to 1199 and the second to 1200 (Ciampi, *Viterbo*, pp. 11–12). The second battle occurred on 6 January (*Gesta*, § 134): modern writers accept the date as 6 January 1200, but 1201 or even 1202 seem possible years.

[3] *Registrum de Negotio Imperii*, n. 56 (dated by the editor 'late October–early November 1201').

persuading the nobles to withdraw their pledge and depriving his enemies of another *casus belli*.[1]

Another important preoccupation in 1199 had been the invasion of the southern Campagna by Markward of Anweiler. Markward crossed from the March of Ancona into the Regno late in 1198, when the news of the Empress Constance's death and the pope's nomination as guardian of the young Frederick crystallized the possibility of Markward achieving power in the Sicilian kingdom. Throughout the spring and summer he campaigned with no great success in the Terra del Lavoro, alternating armed force with negotiations in which he attempted to persuade the pope that he was the rightful regent of Sicily. It is significant that Innocent was able to raise troops for fighting against Markward in the latter's erstwhile province of the March, as well as mercenaries from Rome, the Campagna and other parts of Italy.[2] Towards the end of 1199 Markward crossed to the island of Sicily, whereupon the pope turned to the recruitment of an invading force. The story of this invasion is irrelevant to our subject, but its effect was that in 1200, as in 1199, external campaigns took up much of the money that Innocent might have preferred to keep for domestic 'reconquest'.

In the new papal provinces the main theme of the years 1199–1202 is the continuance of disturbances in the March of Ancona. We have seen that the *Gesta* claim that only Ascoli held out against the pope, and a letter from Innocent to Iesi of March 1199 names Ascoli and Camerino as the sole opponents of the papacy.[3] Yet there was much lawlessness and the letter optimistically neglects the fact that authority was being defied by towns which had already, perhaps, officially submitted to the papacy. The archbishop of Ravenna complained of attacks on his property by Osimo as well as by Faenza in the Romagna, where there was still support for Markward towards the end of 1198.[4] The neutral league was itself a sign of mutual distrust and of the weakness of papal authority, while in the summer of 1199 Markward also invaded this province, besieging Ripatransone. With him was an imperialist count of Senigallia and Cagli and probably the Marquis Walter, to whom Markward granted a privilege confirming his fiefs, on 28 August 1199.[5] The pope's bestowal of large estates on the *vicedominus* of Fermo at

---

[1] *Gesta Inn.*, § 134. It is not possible to date this episode more exactly than *c.* 1199–1201 (its context in the *Gesta* providing these probable limits).

[2] *Reg. Inn. III*, I, n. 557.   [3] Above, p. 37: *Reg. Inn. III*, II, n. 4.

[4] BFW, n. 12179: *Reg. Inn. III*, I, n. 461.

[5] Compagnoni, *La Reggia Picena*, p. 78: for the count and Marquis see Ficker, *Forschungen*, II, § 317–18: Walter was probably the son of the Marquis Werner who had ruled in the March for Barbarossa as far back as 1164.

about the same time is symptomatic of his need of powerful allies in the March.[1]

A large number of letters of the third year of Innocent's pontificate (February 1200 to February 1201) show the pope and a series of papal officials at grips with what Innocent described, in a despairing letter, as 'dissensions and wars . . . devastations of towns, destruction of castles, burning of villages, oppression of the poor, persecution of churches, men slain and made captive, injuries, violence and rapine'.[2] It will be sufficient to give a few instances of the disorders which in 1200 faced a legate (the cardinal-priest of S. Maria in Trastevere) and two nuncios. Fermo, Ancona and Osimo had been at war and none had paid the *census* due from them to the papacy; Fermo and Ancona were under an interdict. Fano had attacked Fossombrone and occupied papal property, failed to pay its *census* and disobeyed the pope in various other ways (including making an agreement with Markward's supporter the count of Senigallia). Camerino, still in opposition, had put forward unjustified claims to various places and failed to pay its dues, while Senigallia had attempted to occupy papal property. Various other towns had merely failed to pay their *census*.[3] The only sign of papal advance during the year is the terms agreed in November with Fano, Pesaro and Iesi, which represent a very considerable achievement.[4] These towns now bound themselves to make war and peace at the request of the popes or their representatives and to give counsel. Their *podestà* or consuls were to swear fealty to the Church, appellate jurisdiction was to lie with the pope or his legate or nuncio, and the towns owed an annual *census* as well as hospitality or its financial equivalent. In return the pope recognized the 'good customs' of these communes and the jurisdiction of their consuls.

During 1201 the papal work of pacification in the March made considerable advance. By the spring five outstanding quarrels, some of several years' duration, had been submitted to the pope for arbitration and in each case truces had been arranged and preliminary awards confirmed or announced.[5] The formation of a pro-imperial alliance between

---

[1] *Reg. Inn. III*, II, n. 262.

[2] *Reg. Inn. III*, III, n. 49.

[3] *Reg. Inn. III*, III, nn. 28, 31, 48, 51–3: Theiner, *Vet. Mon. Slav. Merid.*, p. 53.

[4] *Reg. Inn. III*, III, n. 29 (further details in *Lib. Cens.*, I, 89). For the military obligations see also below pp. 276 ff. and for the financial clauses see pp. 253 ff. A papal letter to Iesi of 1201 which complains of a certain clause in Iesi's statutes as opposed to 'ecclesiastical liberty' is perhaps an indication of the practical consequences of the settlement of 1200 (Theiner, *Vet. Mon. Slav. Merid.*, p. 63).

[5] Colini-Baldeschi, *Osimo*, d. XLIV. These disputes include those involving Fermo, Ancona and Osimo mentioned above.

Camerino and Tolentino towards the end of the year was a setback, but neither town was a very powerful one.[1] In January 1202 at Polverigi (near Osimo) a really wide peace agreement was reached, involving most of the leading communes of the province: primarily this peace took the form of a settlement of long-standing disputes, which had led to much fighting, between Fermo, Osimo, Iesi and Fano on the one part and Ancona, Senigallia and Pesaro, with a number of minor allies on the other.[2] The wording of the agreement does not suggest that it was concluded under papal auspices, but general peace was likely to assist rather than hinder papal authority.

By the early months of 1202 it must have seemed that the March of Ancona could soon be added to the Duchy of Spoleto and the Tuscan Patrimony as the additional provinces of an emergent political entity. In the more southerly provinces the years 1199 to 1202 had certainly been a time of success for Innocent. Writing to Iesi in March 1199 he claimed that the Duchy of Spoleto, with Perugia, Todi and Città di Castello had 'returned' to papal obedience, together with 'a great part' of Tuscany. On the whole what is known of the history of the area bears out the optimism of this letter.[3] The Patrimony in Tuscany became a separate province within the structure of papal territorial government about the end of 1199 or in early 1200, though for a time it was joined with the Duchy of Spoleto under the charge of the cardinal-deacon of St. George *ad Velum Aureum*.[4] In 1200–2 the only serious trouble in either province appears to have been a war between Spoleto and Foligno, but this ended in 1201.[5] The years after the Rome-Viterbo war of 1199 were ones of comparative peace except in the March of Ancona, and beyond Rome Innocent III considerably streng-

[1] BFW, n. 12228: the league was concluded against all *excepto imperatore et marchione vel legato*. The *podestà* of Tolentino in 1201 was Markward's supporter the Marquis Walter (Ficker, *Forschungen*, II, 250).

[2] De Minicis, *Fermo*, pp. 536–8. The text of this agreement has been published in many other places, though some give the date as '1202', others as '1203'. I accept the verdict of BFW (n. 12233) in favour of 1202. The exclusion from the peace of Markward's supporter, the count of Senigallia, is noteworthy.

[3] *Reg. Inn. III*, II, n. 4. Civita Castellana was for a while under an interdict but the circumstances of its reconciliation with the papacy in May 1199 (*Reg.*, II, n. 78) suggest real papal control, the commune abandoning its election of a rector chosen without the pope's consent.

[4] See Appendix II. When the legate was appointed for the Duchy and Patrimony in October 1199 the inhabitants of the two provinces were informed in separate letters and the Prefect (of Vico) was appointed to assist the legate in the Patrimony only (*Reg. Inn. III*, II, nn. 202–3).

[5] *Fragmenta Fulginatis Hist.*, RIS, N.S., XXVI, 2, pp. 5–6. Both Todi (for failure to submit appeals) and Narni were out of favour for a period (Theiner, *Vet. Mon. Slav. Merid.*, pp. 48, 53), but papal letters of reproof are often a sign of increasing rather than diminishing power.

thened his southern frontier by securing the fealty of the powerful lord of Ceccano and by granting the fortress of Ninfa as a fief to his cousin James, the papal marshal.[1]

In a sense the story of Pope Innocent's struggle for central Italy is a double one, of which only one half has so far been related. While he sought to assert his authority in the old 'patrimony' and the new provinces the pope strove at the same time to secure imperial recognition of his conquests — or, to view the matter in terms of legal rights rather than practical achievements, 'reconquests'. The disputed succession between Philip of Swabia and Otto of Brunswick was of course the means which enabled the pope to make imperial recognition of the frontiers of his new state the price of his now highly valued support. For two years Innocent negotiated with both candidates. Only late in 1200 did he determine to declare for Otto, and by that time he had almost certainly received the first draft of the celebrated document whereby Otto accepted the new frontiers of the Papal State.[2] The final version of this document, the 'Promise of Neuss' of 8 June 1201, recognized papal rule over 'all the land between Radicofani and Ceprano, the exarchate of Ravenna, the Pentapolis, the March, the Duchy of Spoleto, the land of Countess Matilda and the county of Bertinoro with the other adjacent lands mentioned in many imperial privileges from the time of Louis onwards'.[3] Of the territory claimed in the early days of the pontificate, Tuscany was omitted, for the pope now demanded nothing in that area to the north of Radicofani. Doubtless he felt that he had over-reached himself in asking for all Tuscany, and indeed that claim had implicitly been disavowed as early as March 1199 when Innocent announced his hold over *magna pars Thusciae quae in nostris privilegiis continetur*,[4] *i.e.* the province of the Tuscan Patrimony from Sutri in the south to Radicofani in the north. By the terms of Neuss, Otto IV promised the pope free possession of those lands which Innocent had 'recovered' and aid in retaining them. He would also help him to regain what had not yet been secured and would restore whatever came into his own possession. He would protect and aid all papal possessions. Lest there should be any doubt concerning the political

---

[1] P.L., vol. 217, Suppl. 2, col. 286: Theiner, *Vet. Mon. Slav. Merid.*, p. 63. Ceccano dominates the Sacco valley, Ninfa the flat coastal area to the west of this.

[2] This is to accept the apparently convincing solution to the problem of the two drafts of Otto IV's promise suggested by F. Kempf, 'Die zwei Versprechen Ottos IV. an die römische Kirche, 1200–1' in *Festschrift E. E. Stengel*, pp. 359–84.

[3] *Registrum de Negotio Imperii*, n. 77.

[4] *Reg. Inn. III*, II, n. 4.

nature of papal rule, Otto promised the restoration of these lands *cum omni iurisditione, districtu et honore suo*.

With the signature of this 'birth certificate of the Papal State', Innocent's work in central Italy received the needed recognition from the only outside power whose acquiescence was essential to its success. The death late in 1202 of Markward of Anweiler, his only formidable adversary in central Italy, seemed likely to turn the scales finally in the pope's favour. His own resources were small, but his municipal and baronial adversaries rarely worked in unison. Papal rule appeared to be gaining ever-increasing acceptance. Moreover, the existence of a rival to the emperor, in Philip of Swabia, was in many ways another papal asset. Otto, who had accepted the new State, was not yet certain to succeed, but it was an advantage to the pope that Otto's own strength was tied up in Germany. The ruler of the south was a minor and Innocent's ward. His greatest undertaking, the aggrandizement of the Papal State, seemed securely founded by the end of 1202, yet many dangers had still to be faced.

$$\star \qquad \star \qquad \star$$

The second campaign between Rome and Viterbo (*c.* 1201), had been followed by papal arbitration, the terms of which were in general favourable to the Roman victors, though they included reference to papal claims to suzerainty over both combatants.[1] It is unlikely that discontent in Rome over the terms of this award played a more than casual part in the serious quarrel between pope and Romans which followed shortly after and lasted two or more years.[2] This new series of troubles seems to have arisen mainly from territorial rivalry between Innocent's family and the Orsini relatives of his predecessor, Celestine III. Such rivalries were the very stuff of Roman history, each pope of Roman origin seeking to build up the strength and wealth of his own house, and thus adding to the number of landed families competing for supremacy in the area around the city. Innocent had already embarked on such a policy to the south of Rome, and the Orsini, who had benefited from the pontificate of Celestine III, felt themselves threatened, especially in their tenure of Vicovaro and some surrounding lands. A long-standing feud between the Boboni, the family of Celestine III's

---

[1] See above, p. 39. *Gesta Innocentii III*, § 134–5: the terms of the oath sworn to Rome by the Viterbese are preserved in a document from the Archivio Comunale, Viterbo, translated in Pinzi, *Viterbo*, I, 232 n.

[2] *Gesta Inn. III*, § 135–41, is the only source for this quarrel.

father, and the Romani de Scotta, that of Innocent III's mother, served to embitter relations further. The Orsini set about the formation of a self-styled 'popular' anti-papal party in Rome and in the autumn of 1202 took advantage of the pope's absence at Velletri to attack a number of his relatives.[1] The pope hastened back to Rome and arranged that both sides should give guarantors and swear to obey his terms for peace. The senator then took over the matter, dispossessing both parties of their towers and sending the ring-leaders outside the city.

Matters came to a crisis some time in the winter of 1202–3 when relatives of the pope attacked and killed a cousin of the Orsini on the highway between Rome and S. Paolo *fuori le Mura*, where he was visiting his son-in-law, an exiled member of the hostile faction. On hearing this, the Orsini organized a popular riot, destroying several towers of the rival party. They then attempted to hold the funeral in front of the papal palace and the house of the pope's brother, in order to elicit sympathy. Although this came to nothing, disturbances continued in the spring of 1203. Once the Orsini tried to drive the pro-papal senator from his palace on the Capitol. About the end of April Innocent decided to try the effect of leaving Rome: he spent the summer at Ferentino and moved in late September to Anagni, where for a time he was seriously ill.[2]

During the pope's absence the quarrel came to centre round two other matters, the fate of the lands of the lords of Poli in Campagna, which were disputed between the senate and the pope (who wanted them for his brother), and the question of the senate itself. The Poli estates had long been held of the papacy; these lords were now in financial difficulties and Innocent's brother Richard had helped to free them from debt, at the same time negotiating for a marriage between his son and the lord's daughter, doubtless as a preliminary to acquiring the territory himself.[3] But the Poli heir had other ideas. He stirred up feeling in Rome in favour of his family, organizing quasi-religious processions to gain popular sympathy and raising a riot against a papal

[1] This attack can be dated *c.* October 1202, since the *Gesta* relates that the pope returned from Velletri on hearing the news and the last letter in his register sent from Velletri is V, n. 93, dated 6 October.

[2] The dates of Innocent's itinerary are provided by the letters of year VI in his register: the first after leaving Rome is dated 5 May, from Palestrina (n. LV), the last from Ferentino before moving to Anagni 15 September (n. CXLVIII).

[3] For this story *v. Reg. Inn. III*, VII, n. 133; and *Lib. Cens.*, I, 9*–10*: for the lands as a papal fief in the twelfth century, Kehr, *It. Pont.*, II, 80–1. It is not easy to distinguish between rioting arising from this dispute and rioting concerning the Orsini: no doubt the two discontents fused and were together responsible for Innocent's flight to the Alban hills.

procession. He then offered the lands to the Roman senate, apparently without success, for the pope granted them to his brother in 1204 and the fief was confirmed to Richard four years later.

The Poli dispute was now connected with the question of the senate, the two parties forming rival senates. The matter was complicated by the pope's illness, for Innocent had to name representatives to act for him in the senatorial election; these men appointed electors who were then browbeaten into promising to choose senators hostile to the papacy. Meanwhile the outgoing senator had handed over the Capitol to papal supporters, and there was thus a schism in the senate and anarchy in the city. There followed a succession of popular embassies inviting the pope to return and restore order to Rome, to which he eventually yielded early in March (1204).[1] Again an election took place and again it led to the formation of two rival senates.[2] By Easter preparations were well advanced for a new military insurrection, this time with Innocent's old opponent John Capoccio as the anti-papal leader. Fighting broke out, and soon besiegers with catapult machines, fire and arrows were attacking towers, many of them recently constructed. Pandulf of Suburra, the ex-senator who with Innocent's brother Richard led the pro-papal side, build a counter-castle 'on a certain old monument' close to Capoccio's tower, and the fighting of Pope Innocent's time must have played a considerable part in that destruction of ancient Rome through 'the Domestic Quarrels of the Romans', which Gibbon mentions as one of the chief causes of the disappearance of its classical buildings. Fighting continued through the summer, the Frangipani providing support for Capoccio's side and the Annibaldi for the pope. On 10 August Capoccio won important successes in several areas and captured Pandulf's *Gegenburg*. But he was unable to press home his advantage, and as time passed his supporters tended to fall away, alleging disconsolately (the author of the *Gesta* tells us) that 'the pope's money was fighting against them'. In these favourable circumstances Innocent put forward peace terms. He suggested that the two parties should elect in agreement four *boni viri* to settle the question of the senate and to reach a fuller agreement with his brother Richard and the anti-papal *boni homines de communi*. The commission was to have six months to do its work and the terms already agreed between pope and

---

[1] Last letter from Anagni (*Reg.*, VII, n. XXVIII) 6 March, first from Rome 13 March 1204 (VII, n. XX).

[2] It seems extremely unlikely that the papal *medianus* John Pierleone should be identified with Innocent's old opponent John Pierleone 'Raynerii', though several writers have thought them the same: for the strong reasons against this see Bartoloni, *art. cit.*, 65–6.

city (presumably those of 1188) were to be respected. Innocent promised to obey whatever award was made concerning the senate, for a single year only. The papal initiative was at first accepted, then for a while refused — and fighting was resumed — but at last the four arbitrators were named. Their award proposed the election of a single senator by the pope, but no individual being acceptable to both sides, they had later to suggest a return to the regime of fifty-six senators. To this the pope agreed, most reluctantly, and by the end of October 1204 peace was restored and the 'collegiate' senate installed. Innocent's prophecy that it would not meet with success was fulfilled so rapidly that before the middle of November there was again a single senator.[1] By this time the Poli lands had been granted formally by the pope to his brother.[2] Thereafter there were no serious disputes between the city and its bishop; Innocent continued to use his wealth intelligently in a manner which must have done much to win him the favour of the Romans. Instead of the initial *donativum*, a symbol of weakness rather than amity, he chose to give the city help in time of famine (as in 1201, when he apparently made over one-tenth of his revenues to Rome), and to make gifts to churches and monasteries, while his greatest single work of charity was the foundation of the hospital of Santo Spirito.[3]

The first crisis which Innocent had to face had been the result of the strength of baronial factions in the most powerful commune in his State, and the one where he stood to lose most. The second crisis arose through opposition in the most distant of the newly-won provinces, the March of Ancona, crystallized by an emissary of the imperial candidate against whom he had now declared himself, Philip of Swabia. The March, with its many small rival hill-towns, had already proved a particularly difficult area to dominate. Even the comparative peacefulness of 1202 and the following years was disturbed by minor wars between Osimo and Cingoli, Camerino and Matelica, and Ascoli and Offida: in each case a powerful town was attempting to secure the submission of a smaller one.[4] From about the end of 1204 the situation in the March was complicated by the intervention of Liupold, bishop of Worms and pro-Hohenstaufen claimant to the archbishop of Mainz. The background of Liupold's expedition is the disastrous collapse of Otto of Brunswick's cause in Germany. During 1204 Otto had been deserted by

[1] For these dates see Bartoloni, *art. cit.*, 65–7.   [2] *Reg. Inn. III*, VII, n. 133 (7 October 1204).
[3] *Gesta*, § 143, 144, 148: Theiner, *Vet. Mon. Slav. Merid.*, p. 60.
[4] Martorelli, *Osimo*, pp. 86–9: Acquacotta, *Matelica*, d. 10: Arduini, *Offida*, pp. 202–3. Another indication of papal weakness was the submission of Cagli, a town of the northern March, to Gubbio, a commune of the Duchy (*QFIA*, XXIX, 149–50).

almost all his leading supporters, and Philip of Swabia now seemed on the verge of securing unchallenged control in the Empire north of the Alps. This situation was brought home to the pope by Philip's despatch of Liupold to Italy as legate, entrusted with the task of winning back the lost provinces in central Italy and ending the papal regency in the Sicilian kingdom.

It seems likely that Liupold reached central Italy by the late autumn or early winter of 1204, for the papal legate who was despatched to oppose him excommunicated him in Fermo cathedral at Christmas that year.[1] Liupold had pressed on south and captured a number of small places close to the border of the Regno, but was halted in this area by papal troops under the legate.[2] His movements are hard to follow, but there are traces of his occupation and ravages near Fermo as well as near Teramo in the Regno. He won some local baronial support, yet the only commune known to have recognized him is Assisi, far to the west of both Fermo and Teramo. Philip of Swabia's 'privilege' to Assisi of July 1205 is virtually a treaty between the town and Liupold and provides much of the scant evidence we possess for the bishop's actions and policy.[3] This commune had resisted Innocent III strongly in 1198 and had quarrelled with him again and been placed under an interdict for appointing an excommunicate as *podestà*. It is therefore not surprising tlat Assisi should have turned to Liupold. Apart from this agreement, little is known of Liupold's activities: one story, which circulated in Germany, had it that he excommunicated the pope.[4]

Meanwhile Innocent had reacted by sending Cardinal Cinthius of S. Lorenzo in Lucina to the March as a special legate, based first on Fermo and later on Fano. An anxious papal letter to Ancona[5] asked the town to give the legate assistance and quoted Henry VI's 'will' in support of the papacy's claim to the March. Perugia, an old enemy of Assisi, certainly opposed Liupold, but the rest of the evidence is negative: probably most towns of the March and Duchy stood by the pope, for there would almost certainly be some documentary trace of any further backing for Liupold. But nothing is known of the composition of the

[1] De Minicis, *Fermo*, pp. 335 and 337–8. For Liupold's expedition *v.* Tillmann, *Papst Innocenz III.*, pp. 120–2 and the same writer's article in *Hist. Jahrbuch*, LI, 341–65: she estimates the date of his arrival in the March as October 1204, while BFW (n. 12280a) say 'March 1204', which is almost certainly too early.

[2] MGH, *Ep. Pont.*, I, 216.

[3] Ficker, *Forschungen*, IV, d. 211: *Reg. Inn. III*, VII, n. 83. Assisi was granted semi-independence and Liupold part of the commune's revenues.

[4] Caesarius of Heisterbach, *Dialogus Miraculorum*, II, 9.

[5] *Reg. Inn. III*, VII, n. 228: unfortunately the letter is only dated by the pope's regnal year (22February 1204–21 February 1205).

army of papal *familiares et amici* which trapped Liupold's army in a mountain pass and shattered it in a decisive skirmish, nor is anything known of the place of this battle or its date. It was presumably fought after the issue of Philip's privilege to Assisi in late July 1205, but before the end of that year, for by mid-February 1206 Liupold was back in his see in Germany.[1]

Liupold's failure to secure strong support in the new papal provinces is striking, though it is hard to tell to what extent this was due to the success of papal rule and to what extent to Liupold's own weakness or incompetence. One consequence of his failure was to drive Philip of Swabia back to more peaceable methods in dealing with Innocent III. Diplomatic contact had continued throughout the years of Innocent's support of Otto — indeed the pope had made use of Philip's ambassadors to threaten him with further ecclesiastical opposition at the time of Liupold's expedition[2] — and now Philip was compelled to negotiate some form of agreement with the papacy.

★   ★   ★

In the critical years 1202–5 Innocent had weathered severe troubles in Rome and Liupold's attack on the March. The following three years were a period during which he was able to work at the task of building up the organization of the new Papal State, hindered only slightly by the *volte-face* in his imperial policy necessitated by Philip of Swabia's supremacy in Germany. Some explanation of the diplomatic events of these years is a necessary background to the understanding of Innocent's actions in Italy. Relations with Philip were made easier by the slow and hesitant emergence of papal support for Otto. In 1198 Innocent had negotiated with Philip as the strongest candidate for the imperial throne.[3] Only in 1199, when the death of Constance left the way open for opposition between Philip and Innocent in the Regno and the former had declared for Markward, did the pope begin to move towards support for his weaker rival. Even then his intention was probably in part to use Otto's candidature as a means of securing a position as recognized arbiter. Towards the end of 1199 it seemed very possible that Innocent's representative, the archbishop of Mainz, might declare for Philip, but the pope averted this and late in 1200 reached an agree-

---

[1] *Chr. Reg. Col.*, MGH, XXIV, 173: BFW, n. 12292e.

[2] *Reg. Inn. III*, VIII, n. 83.

[3] For these negotiations see H. Tillmann, *Papst Innocenz III.*, pp. 91–103, an excellent account which perhaps exaggerates the pope's support of Philip in 1198–1200. There is a large literature on the subject: see also F. Kempf in *Festschrift E. E. Stengel*, pp. 359–84.

E

ment with Otto. Yet, although he now placed himself on Otto's side in Germany, he did not use the normal spiritual weapon of excommunication against Philip.[1] He and Philip remained in diplomatic contact and when Otto's cause in Germany collapsed it was still possible for the pope to seek an agreement with Philip without engineering a diplomatic revolution. At about the end of 1206 or in the first half of 1207 agreement was reached.[2] Philip was absolved and arrangements began for securing Otto's resignation. The precise terms have not survived, but Innocent's subsequent actions suggest that the territorial clauses were the same as those agreed between Otto and the pope in 1200–1. Now that Frederick had secured his claim, under papal tutelage, to the Sicilian kingdom, Philip had lost his interest in southern Italy, and the March and Duchy were no longer of importance to him as a corridor between Empire and Regno. Innocent's parliament of September 1207[3] treated the Duchy and March as part of the Papal State, and it seems unlikely that the pope made new claims or that Philip now obtained more than Otto in 1201.[4]

The agreement between Philip and Innocent was to be cemented by a marriage between Innocent's nephew, the son of his brother Richard, and Philip's daughter. The intention was that the pope's nephew should receive Tuscany as an imperial fief, thereby extending some papal influence over an area to which the direct claim of 1198 had now been dropped.[5] This scheme was well advanced, or even finally settled, when Philip of Swabia was assassinated at Bamberg on 21 June 1208.

Until 1207 Innocent III had been dependent for his central Italian achievements on skilful improvisation and the support of his family. His brother Richard had acted as his mainstay in Rome and by his acquisition of the Poli lands had been set on the road which was to lead to

---

[1] Philip may have been regarded as already excommunicated (see above, p. 27) but the ban was not made specific or repeated.

[2] Not only are many letters in Innocent's *Registrum de Negotio Imperii* undated, but the register for the years 1207–8 is misleading, since it was made after Philip's death, when the pope wished to conceal the extent of his negotiations with Philip (see the review of Kempf's edition and study by H. Grundmann in *ZSSR*, Kanon, Abt., XXXVII, 416–31).

[3] See below, pp. 52 ff.

[4] Dr. Tillmann (pp. 125–6) believes that Innocent accepted Philip's claims to the Matildine lands and the Exarchate, but there are no strong grounds for this suggestion.

[5] Rainald of Lüttich, MGH, IV, 209: Burchard of Ursburg, MGH, XXIII, 370. Burchard states that the pope's nephew was to have Tuscany, the March of Ancona and the Duchy of Spoleto. This has been shown to be improbable by H. Tillmann in *Hist. Jahrbuch*, LI, although it is still accepted by Haller (*Papsttum*, ed. 2, III, 384–5). It is conceivable that the nephew was also to be papal rector of the Duchy and March, but the two provinces were to remain papal. Frederick II knew of the plan concerning Tuscany and refers to it in a letter of 1226 (Huillard-Bréholles, II, 933).

a powerful lordship commanding the southern entry to Innocent's state. His sister's husband, Peter Annibaldi, had been another powerful Roman supporter, a cousin, James, had been papal marshal and the commander of Innocent's troops in Sicily in 1200–1, a nephew, Lando di Montelongo, had been rector of the Campagna, and another relative, 'Carzolus', rector of the Tuscan Patrimony.[1] The money of the wealthy Conti had undoubtedly played a considerable part, in facilitating the pope's philanthropy in Rome as well as Richard's very sizeable loan of 1,000 *l.* to the Romans.

With the grants of fiefs and offices to papal relations had gone an improvisatory approach to all problems of temporal government. There had, it is true, been appointments to rectorships of provinces — the Campagna-Marittima, the Tuscan Patrimony and the Duchy of Spoleto — but there was as yet no policy dedicated to constructing a firm provincial framework for the administration of the new State. Each of the three provinces named above had a rector within two years of Innocent's consecration, yet there is no surviving evidence of the government of any province by a rector between 1203 and 1207. The March of Ancona had come under a series of legates and nuncios, but in 1207 had not yet had a papal rector. The Duchy of Spoleto had had a rector, who was also a legate, and another legate had ruled the Duchy jointly with the Tuscan Patrimony. This province seems normally to have come under a rector — perhaps at one time under several[2] — between 1198 and 1203, but the only known rector of the Campagna was Lando di Montelungo, in 1199. In 1207 there was, in sum, no fixed provincial system and, as in all post-Hildebrandine papal government, much use was made of legates.

The summer and autumn of the year 1207 were devoted by the pope to the task of setting up a firmer basis for government in his newly-won lands. Innocent moved from Rome to Viterbo in June and spent the following months in the Tuscan Patrimony at Viterbo, Montefiascone, Toscanella, and Corneto, returning to Rome only in mid-November.[3] His presence doubtless served to strengthen papal control in this area and much important routine administrative work was accomplished.

---

[1] *Gesta Inn. III*, § 139 & col. xli: *Reg. Inn. III*, VI, n. 105. There are some useful remarks on the role of Innocent's family in the otherwise inadequate work of Seeger, *Die Reorganisation des Kirchenstaates unter Innocenz III.*

[2] In Innocent's fourth year — only the rubrics have survived of the letters registered in this year — a letter was sent to the *Senescallo et Rectoribus Patrimonii s. Petri in Tuscia* (Theiner, *Vet. Mon. Slav. Merid.*, p. 61). For this paragraph in general see below, p. 96 and Appendix II and Zimmermann, *Legation*, pp. 21–66.

[3] For Innocent's itinerary, *v. Gesta*, cols. clxi–clxii and clxvi–clxviii.

The Aldobrandeschine count, the leading baron of southern Tuscany, renewed his oath of vassalage. Innocent made peace between the nobles and *popolani* of Todi and devoted much time and labour to the extirpation of heresy at Viterbo. The infiltration of Patarine movements from northern Italy and Tuscany into this area represented a serious menace, since religious unorthodoxy, providing a rival organization as well as theoretical justification for opposition to secular rule by the Church, could easily serve to crystallize political antagonism to papal rule. The Cathari of Orvieto had resisted the pope for several months in 1198–9 and now Viterbo, the southernmost point of dualist advance, was a crucial centre which Innocent had to hold, for heresy at Viterbo would probably soon have infected Rome itself.[1] But the decline of Catharism in central Italy in these years was probably the consequence of the rise of the Franciscan movement rather than of papal action.

By far the most important measure of 1207 was the parliament held by Innocent at Viterbo, to which lay and ecclesiastical representatives were summoned from the March, the Duchy, and the Tuscan Patrimony with the adjacent lands *usque Romam*.[2] This parliament met on 21 September. The first day was devoted to the assertion of papal jurisdiction and the swearing of oaths of obedience by the feudatories and officers of communes. The next day the pope heard the petitions and *querelae* of his subjects. The final session on 23 September was dedicated to the publication of statutes addressed to 'all the pope's faithful subjects in the patrimony'.[3] This legislation was on a supra-provincial scale, but the emphasis in the laws themselves is on provincial organization, and they make it evident that henceforth the rectors of the provinces are to be the lynch pins of government in the Papal State. The first statute ordains that all papal subjects ('subjects' of course include subject cities) are to keep the peace, except when ordered by the rector to punish a rebel. The jurisdictional hierarchy within the State is then defined: appeal is to lie from the court of first instance to the rector or to the pope himself. The rector also has the duty of settling claims for compensation made by one subject against another. Two other clauses of considerable importance concern ecclesiastical affairs within the new State. The first forbids and automatically annuls any legislation by papal

---

[1] *Reg. Inn. III*, II, n. 1; vol. 214, cols. 529–30 (DLXXVIII), and vol. 217, cols. 298–9 (XII); X, n. 130: *Gesta*, cols. clxi–clxvi.

[2] For the Viterbo parliament *v. Gesta*, col. clxii and *Reg. Inn. III*, X, nn. 130–2.

[3] Haller takes 'patrimony' here to be an abbreviation of 'Tuscan Patrimony' (*Papsttum*, III, 544) but this is extremely unlikely. Not only is an abbreviation improbable in such a context, but the *Gesta*, which was almost certainly written in the following year, states clearly (§ 124) that representatives of the Duchy and March were present.

subjects against churches or the clergy and against canon law: here the pope is making natural use of his temporal authority to defend the Church's position in such matters as the jurisdiction of ecclesiastical courts and taxation of the clergy. The second ecclesiastical ordinance, which reflects Innocent's struggle against heresy at Viterbo, defines the measures to be taken for the repression of heresy and is issued for inclusion in the statutes of the communes of the Papal State: municipal officials are to swear annually to observe its terms.

No full code of government emerged from the Viterbo parliament, but the meeting is of the greatest importance for the history of the Papal State. The promise of Neuss had given imperial acceptance to papal rule in all central Italy, but in the intervening years the papacy had barely sketched out a system for governing this wide area — and if it was to be retained it would have to be governed, for a 'feudal' papacy would be insufficient on its own to control the city-states and barons of the March, Spoleto, and Roman Tuscany. At Viterbo the problem of governing the new state was faced for the first time. The legislative measures are not of great importance for what they ordain, but the act of summoning a parliament and the assertion of papal authority and the pope's right to hear suits and petitions mark a vital advance. The pope's subjects all owed him the duty of *parliamentum*, of coming when summoned to discuss and to give and hear counsel, but so far as is known this was the first occasion on which a pope had issued such a summons.[1]

The developments in Innocent's Italian policy in 1208 are less far-reaching than those of the previous year, but to some extent they are complementary. In 1207 he had been concerned with the new provinces and the area north of Rome. He now turned to the south and especially to the Tyrrhenian section of his frontier with the Neapolitan kingdom, prompted perhaps by the approaching majority of his ward Frederick (born in 1194) as well as by the need to round off the northern achievements of 1207.

The problems of the Campagna border were in any case brought to the pope's notice by the actions of the German castellan of three of the Regno strongholds on this frontier, Sora, Sorella and Arce.[2] Fears of a strong pope, now in agreement with a victorious imperial claimant, and apprehension of the growing authority of Frederick may well have persuaded this Conrad of Marlei to live a life of plunder while circum-

---

[1] See below, pp. 110 ff.
[2] For the events of this paragraph *v. Gesta*, § 39; Richard of S. Germano, RIS, N.S., VII, 26; MGH, XIX, 296 (*Annales Ceccanenses*) and 319 (*Ann. Casinenses*).

stances were still favourable for over-mighty subjects. He had raided
Bauco in the papal Campagna in 1204, and in the winter of 1207–8 embarked on a more serious policy of aggression in the Terra del Lavoro
and further north into the Campagna and Marittima. It is difficult to
follow the chronology of the series of campaigns waged against Conrad
by successive papal or pro-papal armies, but it is likely that the force
first sent against him was led by the rector of the Campagna and Marittima, Cardinal Peter *de Saxo*, and that a second campaign was organized
by the Abbot of Monte Cassino, possibly after Conrad had neglected
the terms of a truce. As one of the greatest landowners of the area the
abbot was naturally interested in the preservation of order; in January
1208 he gathered a large force of his own military tenants and neighbouring barons — the powerful lords of Aquino were among his allies
— and at the same time formed a plot with some relatives of his at Sora
which put his army into possession of that town. While the abbot held
Sora for the pope, Innocent sent his brother Richard and Stephen the
papal chamberlain with reinforcements from the Campagna. By this
time the rector was also in the field. The papal forces besieged Conrad
at Sorella, forced the Germans to surrender the town and took their
leader prisoner. At the end of February, Conrad was ransomed by the
surrender to the papacy of Arce, the third of his fortresses; at the same
time he gave the pope financial and other pledges for his good behaviour.

The defeat of Conrad was the negative aspect of a policy whose
positive achievements were begun during Innocent's visit to the same
area in the summer of 1208.[1] In June the pope's vassal John of Ceccano
met him at Alatri with fifty knights who escorted him through the
lord's lands and entertained him with jousting. Innocent, who now
made his brother count of Sora, passed on to the Regno, crossing the
border at Ceprano. At San Germano, in the zone recently disturbed by
the fighting with Conrad, he met the barons of the Regno at an assembly in some ways analogous to the Viterbo parliament of 1207,
made certain arrangements for public peace in the Regno, issued legislation, and received for Frederick the oaths of his vassals. He also gave
his approval to Frederick's betrothal to Constance of Aragon.[2] It was on
his way north, at Sora, that Innocent received the fateful news that
Philip of Swabia had been murdered.

---

[1] For this visit *v*. *Annales Ceccanenses* in MGH, XIX, 296–8.
[2] *V*. Tillmann, *Papst Innocenz III.*, pp. 128–9 and Luchaire, *Innocent III: Rome et l'Italie*.
pp. 194–7.

Sora lay in the territory of the Regno, and in making his brother its count the pope was exercising his powers as guardian of the Neapolitan ruler. Now that Sora, Sorella and Arce had come to him, Innocent's scheme was to set up Richard as a powerful feudatory in this key area on his southern frontier. Richard was made a count in June,[1] but the pope's plans only came to fruition in October when Richard visited Ferentino to be invested with the county of Sora and to renew his fealty for Valmontone and the former estates of the lords of Poli.[2] His oath for the Sora lands (which included Sorella, Rocca d'Arce and the smaller erstwhile holdings of Conrad of Marlei) was given 'saving his fealty to the king of Sicily' and he could not be called on to make war on Frederick by virtue of his tenure of this fief. Valmontone and Torre Piombinara (in the Sacco valley) were estates acquired by Innocent and granted by him to Richard for an annual rent. Apart from their intrinsic strategic importance they constituted a useful link with the Conti lands near Segni, Anagni and Ferentino, while the Poli castles guarded the territory around Tivoli to the east. Richard's county of Sora was merely the bulwark of an extended system of fiefs and family properties, of which it and the estates of Falvaterra near Ceprano (granted to William 'Paganus' in March 1208) and Rocca Circei on the Tyrrhenian (held by the pope's Annibaldi brother-in-law) were the forward units; behind these was dotted a multiplicity of holdings, dominated by the Conti estates but with John of Ceccano as a powerful vassal, along the Via Latina and the Alban hills, reaching back to Rome itself.[3] The years of Frederick's minority had enabled Innocent to build up a great defence in depth to the south.

From Sora the pope moved to Ferentino, where he remained far into the autumn of 1208, well after the period of his usual *villeggiatura*. This was apparently due to a renewal of unfriendly relations with the Romans, who had now elected a single senator hostile to Innocent, but at the end of October this senator was replaced and the pope yielded to the urgent request of the city that he should return for the feast of the dedication of the Lateran basilica (9 November).[4] Meanwhile he had

[1] The marriage planned between Richard's son and Philip of Swabia's daughter (see above p. 50) may have suggested the need to hasten the elevation of Richard's status.

[2] *Lib. Cens.*, I, 9*–10*: *Reg. Inn. III*, XII, n. 5.

[3] This is well treated by Seeger, *op. cit.*, pp. 42–3. For the holdings of John of Ceccano in Alatri, Frosinone, Ceprano, Piperno, Sezze, Ninfa, and many other places (including Ceccano itself) see Gregorovius, V, I, 58.

[4] William of Andres, MGH, XXIV, 744. For a discussion of the difficulties of the chronology of the senate at this point *v.* Bartoloni, *art. cit.*, 68–70: it seems probable that the senator hostile to the pope was Gregory 'Iohannis Leone Rainerii' and that he was superseded *c.* 27 October 1208 by Philip 'Lombardi'. A papal letter of the same summer,

begun to legislate for the southern province, though not on the scale of the Viterbo statutes of 1207; his first measure decreed the validity of Roman currency — *de jure* papal, but *de facto* senatorial, as the terms of the statute admit — throughout the Campagna.[1] A far more important matter lay before him, the solution of which was Innocent's most urgent problem when he returned to Rome: this was the question of his relations with Otto of Brunswick.

★   ★   ★

The removal of his opponent made Otto's position a strong one and Innocent at once set about making it still stronger. He pronounced the death of Philip, recently his candidate for the Empire, a divine punishment and organized the adherence to Otto of the German Church. The decision to revert to his earlier *protégé* was an obvious one. Indeed, Philip-Augustus of France, Otto's great enemy, gave his support to Henry of Brabant because it was so evident that Innocent would not consider the candidacy of Frederick of Hohenstaufen. Germany rallied rapidly to Otto's side and by the end of 1208 he had a strong hold in the Empire north of the Alps. It would be interesting to know something of the state of the pope's mind at this juncture. On the surface all was well concerning the *negotium imperii* and the new central Italian state. Otto owed much to Innocent, he was not a Hohenstaufen, he was not ruler in southern Italy, he had recognized the recovered lands. Yet Innocent was a realist — a mystical realist of the papal brand — and it would be surprising if he felt no occasional anxiety that Otto's new-found strength and his own comparative temporal feebleness might lead to the reopening of the Italian question in terms of a policy reminiscent of those of Barbarossa and Henry VI. However much he might stigmatize that policy as a 'Hohenstaufen' one, he must still have been uneasily aware of the essential continuity of imperial policy in Italy. Inevitably Innocent's defence against such a possibility had in the first instance to be reliance upon Otto's promises.

The first move in Otto's Italian policy was his appointment in January 1209 of Wolfger, Patriarch of Aquileia, as imperial legate in Lombardy, Tuscany, the Duchy of Spoleto, the March of Ancona and Romagna, with the right 'to concern himself with all matters pertain-

---

(*R.N.I.*, n. 153) describes risings against the pope at Rome, provoked by the bribes of Philip of Swabia: it seems likely that Innocent is here describing the events of 1202–4 and attempting to get credit from Otto (the recipient) for earlier support.

[1] *Reg. Inn. III*, XI, n. 135.

ing to imperial jurisdiction'.[1] The inclusion of papal provinces in the area of the Patriarch's legation was not necessarily a sign of Otto's intention to claim these for himself, since the legate's duties included the levying of a *fodrum* in the lands through which the emperor-elect was to pass on his way to be crowned at Rome. Nevertheless, it is characteristic of Otto's attitude to the question of Central Italy that the legate's letter of appointment makes no distinction between the papal provinces and the rest of Wolfger's sphere of authority. The case for regarding the terms of Wolfger's legation as compatible with the promise of Neuss has recently been argued with great ingenuity,[2] but its foundation is not a firm one.

Some six weeks after the Patriarch's appointment Innocent III wrote to him about the Matildine lands: this territory, he explained, was papal by the terms of the promise of Neuss, and the legate should not take possession of it except on behalf of the Church. Otto perhaps considered that the agreement of 1207 allotting these lands to Philip of Swabia strengthened his claims to them, and Wolfger's letter to the pope may have conveyed a hint of this. It is possible that Innocent was ignorant of the area of the legate's appointment, but more likely that this transpired from Wolfger's letters. Certainly the pope's letters imply recognition of his legate-ship only in the imperial territories, that is Lombardy and Tuscany.[3]

Otto's promise of 1201 was renewed at Speyer on 22 March 1209, the territorial clauses remaining virtually unchanged.[4] It must soon have been evident to the pope that Otto did not regard the new promise as an effective abdication of power in central Italy. The earliest evidence that the legate and his subordinates were continuing after Speyer to exercise rule in the area allotted to the pope seems to be provided by a comparatively trivial measure concerning trade in salt in the duchy of Ravenna. On 30 June 1209 the representatives of the count governing Romagna for King Otto and his legate Wolfger, together with the authorities of Ravenna, issued an ordinance regulating the export of salt from Cervia by sea.[5] The survival of such a document is quite

---

[1] Böhmer, *Acta Imperii*, pp. 207–8 ('de hiis omnibus se intromittat que ad imperialem spectare dinoscuntur iurisdictionem').

[2] Tillmann, *Papst Innocenz III.*, pp. 133 (n. 207) and 287–9 (Excursus 4): Dr. Tillmann argues that Otto's first formal contravention of his promises was the privilege granted to Matelica on 12 October 1209, but her thesis is more ingenious than convincing, since there is no restriction of the legate's powers in the papal lands to the levying of the *fodrum*.

[3] *R.N.I.*, nn. 185 and 186.   [4] MGH, Const., II, 36–7.

[5] Fantuzzi, *Mon. Rav.*, IV, d. XCV (this document has escaped Dr. Tillmann, whose treatment of the matter is otherwise very full). For Otto's count in the Romagna, Rudolf, *v*. Ficker, *Forschungen*, II, § 371.

fortuitous and it is evident that 30 June did not see the first exercise of authority conflicting with the territorial terms of the Speyer promise, either in the duchy of Ravenna or elsewhere. The pope had not assumed control in Romagna — though he had made a virtue of necessity by delegating his powers in the duchy of Ravenna to the archbishop — and the Patriarch, who had been in Italy since Henry VI's day, with his German count, can hardly have taken papal claims there seriously.

By August, Otto himself was in Italy and in early September, from Imola, he sent ahead of him the Marquis of Este into the March of Ancona with powers which again almost certainly conflicted with his promise made in the spring.[1] Otto himself took the Via Emilia and Via Flaminia, meeting Innocent at Viterbo late in September. The later correspondence between the two men reveals that relations between them were already bad. Innocent had discovered that Otto thought in terms of power rather than of promises, while both men knew that the pope was committed to Otto and could not now refuse him coronation. It would have been difficult enough for the pope to transfer his support to another imperial candidate at this stage, but such a change was made unthinkable by the fact that the only alternative was the already formidable Frederick. Finally, the promise of Speyer, to which there were no princely witnesses, had been given little publicity in Germany. It lacked formality, and papal condemnation of Otto's failure to observe its territorial provisions would be less effective in consequence of this. Thus Otto had strong grounds for believing that Innocent would have to crown him and scarcely less strong ones for believing that a new territorial settlement more favourable to himself might follow the coronation.[2]

Otto and Innocent were at Rome on 2 October and the coronation took place on the 4th. Thereafter feelings were so bitter that negotiations could only be conducted through representatives: though we are not acquainted with the details of these dealings we know that they concerned the *negotium terrae*, and the story that Otto demanded the Tuscan Patrimony on the day of the coronation is quite credible.[3] After

---

[1] BFW, n. 300b: see the discussion in Tillmann, *op. cit.*, pp. 287–8, where it is suggested that the Marquis' official duties may have been confined to the levying of *fodrum* and that the necessary papal consent may have been given to this: there is a heavy and unconvincing structure of hypothesis in all this, though it cannot be disproved.

[2] See the very good treatment in Tillmann, pp. 132–4: but it is not clear on what grounds Dr. Tillmann bases her belief that Otto had at first been given hopes of a final and more favourable territorial settlement at a later stage. On Speyer, *v.* also Ficker, *Forschungen*, II, § 366.

[3] *R.N.I.*, n. 194: Ficker, *Forschungen*, II, § 368.

his coronation, Otto turned north and wintered in imperial Tuscany except for one month spent at Foligno and Terni.

Almost immediately after the coronation the emperor had begun to issue privileges to towns in papal territory which were incompatible with the frontiers recognized by the promises of Neuss and Speyer. The earliest of these to have survived, a grant made to Matelica on 12 October, is connected with a scheme for establishing that town as a garrisoned centre of imperial rule: a *castrum* was to be rebuilt there for an imperial nuncio and the town was to pay an annual tax, in return for which it could retain half the revenues accruing from justice, tolls and the market.[1] Later in the same month there followed a privilege confirming the rights and possessions of the archbishopric of Ravenna in the March of Ancona and the Matildine lands. Foligno, visited by Otto in December, was another recipient of an imperial privilege. In the next two years a number of towns in the March and Duchy were wooed or rewarded by such grants, among them Camerino, Gubbio, Fermo and Fabriano, while feudal allies receiving similar favours included the Aldobrandeschi, the most powerful family in southern Tuscany and Innocent's vassals since 1207.[2]

The most straightforward declaration of Otto's intention of establishing imperial rule in the 'recovered' lands of the papacy was his appointment of governors for two of the provinces. On 20 January 1210 he named Marquis Azzo of Este as ruler of the March of Ancona, territory that he had already occupied since the previous autumn, while in February the German Dipold of Schweinspunt, count of Acerra in the Regno, was created duke of Spoleto.[3] Otto had succeeded in reconciling Azzo of Este with Salinguerra, his rival in Ferrara and the neighbouring Matildine territories, Salinguerra becoming imperial vicar in Romagna.[4] It is not easy to estimate the effectiveness of the new administration in the Duchy and March, but the few documents that survive reveal deputies ruling the March for Azzo in 1210, with judges and bailiffs at Macerata and Osimo.[5] There is no trace of government by Dipold, except that he issued at least one privilege in the Duchy and Otto con-

---

[1] Grimaldi, *Matelica*, d. XII.

[2] Fantuzzi, *Mon. Rav.*, V, n. LIV: Ficker, *Forschungen*, IV, d. 222 (Foligno: confirmed by Duke Dipold March 1210, *ibid.*, p. 277). Lilii, *Camerino*, pp. 230–2: BFW, n. 449 (Gubbio), and nn. 452–3 (Fermo): Zonghi, *Fabriano*, d. LV: Ficker, *Forschungen*, IV, d. 254: BFW, n. 441 (the Counts Aldobrandeschi: see also above, p. 52).

[3] BFW, nn. 348 (Azzo) and 350a (Dipold: the grant is confirmed and made specific only in November 1211: *ibid.*, n. 451).

[4] BFW, nn. 361a and 372.

[5] Compagnoni, *Regg. Pic.*, pp. 88–9: QFIA, XXXII, 75–6: Mazzatinti, *Archivi della Storia d'Italia*, III, 199.

sulted him before granting another.[1] The appointment of Dipold, who had experience of government in the Regno under Henry VI, and the explicit grant to him of the Duchy 'as it was held by the former Duke Conrad' and to Azzo of the March 'as it was held by Markward', all emphasize Otto's intention of returning to the traditions of Henry. There was to be no memory of the brief interlude of papal rule.

Shortly before the emperor granted the March to Azzo, Innocent came out openly against him and denounced him to the world. On 18 January 1210 he wrote to the bishop of Ratisbon that Otto had dared to plunder both Frederick II and himself. As well as denouncing Otto to the Church in Germany and northern Italy, Innocent was looking for allies; particularly humiliating was the need to approach Otto's old enemy Philip of France.[2]

Military force was first employed in the late summer of 1210 when Otto, moving south from Tuscany into the Papal State, encountered opposition from a number of towns. Radicofani, Acquapendente and Montefiascone, all in papal Tuscany, fell to him in turn before Viterbo withstood him successfully: then, bearing east, he made for Orte on the Tiber, was in the *contado* of Todi in mid-October, and besieged Rieti before entering the Kingdom early in November.[3] All this time Innocent withheld his formal condemnation, but energetic attempts were made to organize the defence of the Papal State. One instance of these was the mission of Cardinal Benedict of S. Susanna and Stephen the papal chamberlain, who in February 1210 arranged the submission of Perugia to the papacy on terms particularly favourable to the commune. This was a treaty of alliance rather than a mere renewal of fealty and Innocent bound himself to include Perugia in any peace which might be concluded with the emperor.[4] On their way back to the Curia in April the same two *missi* settled a dispute between Amelia and Lugnano. Resistance to Otto's forces[5] was probably encouraged or even organized by these papal representatives and by a legate, Cardinal Guala, who was at Perugia a little later. In August, soon after the emperor crossed into papal territory, Cardinal Guala achieved an alliance between Orvieto, Todi and Amelia:[6] the intention was presumably to attempt to hold the

[1] Ficker, *Forschungen*, IV, dd. 226, 254.

[2] Winkelmann, *Acta Imperii Inedita*, II, 676–8: Ficker, *Forschungen*, II, 401.

[3] For Otto's itinerary *v.* BFW, nn. 438a–441a.

[4] Ficker, *Forschungen*, IV, d. 225: for the Amelia-Lugnano peace see *Rivista di Storia della Chiesa in Italia*, XII, 121–5.

[5] BFW, nn. 438a–441a and Winkelmann, *Philipp v. Schwaben u. Otto v. Brunschweig*, II,239–40.

[6] Fumi, *Orvieto*, d. LXXXII. Cardinal Guala's role in England during the minority of

line of the Tiber if Otto turned east, but the general direction of Otto's delayed advance was more southerly.

The pope's ban on the emperor, though drafted late in 1210, was not published until 1211, when Otto was in the Regno. Nor were negotiations abandoned between the two sides.[1] Almost certainly Innocent was simultaneously negotiating with Azzo of Este in the hope of winning over the Marquis to the papal cause. In the light of subsequent arrangements it seems safe to suggest that the pope promised Azzo the March of Ancona as a fief if he would abandon Otto. Azzo's change of loyalty may have occurred as early as March 1211;[2] it had certainly been secured by the beginning of June, when Innocent was prepared to entrust him with the defence of Argenta and he was asking papal permission to hold a castle at Ferrara on behalf of the Church.[3] Azzo's defection marks a triumph for papal diplomacy which has hitherto undeservedly escaped notice, and it is unfortunate that we can only conjecture about the antecedents of this *volte-face* which did so much to overthrow Otto's pretensions to rule central Italy. Otto's increasing involvement from 1211 onwards in the affairs of the Regno and of Germany marks the end of a phase in the history of the Papal State, for now that Dipold was left to stand on his own it became possible for the papacy to embark on a new reconquest of what had been lost to Otto.

*   *   *

By 1212 Innocent III's support in the long drawn out *negotium imperii* was clearly being transferred to Frederick of Hohenstaufen. Soon Frederick was calling himself King of the Romans, though the pope recognized him only as 'head of the Catholic party'. But papal legates were at work in Germany winning over clergy and laity to his cause and in the autumn Frederick set out for the north, visiting Innocent at Rome on his way. In December he was elected King of the Romans and soon received Innocent's recognition.[4] The promise of Eger, issued

---

Henry III has often been described by historians who have omitted to mention his earlier services as a statesman in not dissimilar circumstances of political disturbances.

[1] Tillmann, *op. cit.*, pp. 139–40. Dr. Tillmann also shows that the suggestion that Innocent condoned Otto's invasion of the Papal State is groundless (*ibid.*, pp. 287–9). The alleged letter of Innocent to Otto blaming the latter for his seizure of the Patrimony (BFW, n. 6093) is very suspect: Ficker thought it a forgery (*MIÖG*, IV, 348–51).

[2] As suggested by BFW, n. 444b, citing no authority.

[3] *Reg. Inn. III*, XIV, nn. 77 and 80: for Azzo's tenure of the March as a papal fief from 1212 see below p. 62.

[4] On this period *v.* Tillmann, *op. cit.*, pp. 143–6.

by Frederick in July 1213, acknowledged papal authority over the same area as Otto's promises of 1201 and 1209: the Patrimony from Radicofani to Ceprano, the Duchy of Spoleto, the March of Ancona with the Duchy of Ravenna were to be papal, as well as the still unrecovered Matildine territory.[1] It seems natural to assume that this promise was one result of an agreement reached between Frederick and Innocent at Rome in the previous year regarding the conditions under which the pope was willing to support Frederick's imperial candidature. One doubts whether Innocent regarded it as a very satisfactory safeguard for his state: Otto had shown the value of such scraps of paper, and Frederick would naturally covet the March and Duchy as a corridor between imperial Italy and the Regno. Furthermore he was the son of Henry VI and the grandson of Barbarossa.

Meanwhile Azzo of Este had secured the March of Ancona as a papal fief on terms which left the papacy little more than nominal suzerainty, though the Marquis owed a really useful amount of military service — a hundred knights for a month each year, within the area between Radicofani and Ceprano and 'between sea and sea' — and the grant expired with the recipient.[2] Otto IV's retort was to assign the Matildine lands to Azzo's rival Salinguerra. The Marquis, however, did not long survive his enfeoffment by the pope. In January 1213 his son Aldobrandino received the March from Innocent on the same terms, but the break in continuity was an unfortunate one for the papal cause, since Aldobrandino's first care naturally went to the consolidation of his possessions in the Po valley, and in the meantime a supporter of Otto was gaining ground in the March. Aldobrandino became involved in war with Padua and in August 1213 Innocent wrote ordering him to enter his papal fief at once and threatening to revoke the grant.[3] Probably Aldobrandino fought clear of his Paduan entanglements soon after this, for a papal letter of early October seems more friendly to him and more convinced of his *bona fides*.[4]

Aldobrandino borrowed money from Florentine financiers — his was certainly not the last campaign fought on Florentine credit, but it

---

[1] P.L., 217, cols. 301–3.

[2] Theiner, d. LVI (the date corrected in Potthast, I, 384). The supposed grant of the March to Azzo in 1208 has the authority only of a chronicler (MGH, XIX, 44) and should almost certainly be rejected (for reasons, *v.* Salzer, *Über die Anfänge der Signorie in Oberitalien*, pp. 269–70). It is tacitly rejected by Tillmann (pp. 298–9), but accepted by Ficker (*Forschungen*, II, 382, 389) and Hagemann (*QFIA*, XXXVI, 151).

[3] Hessel, *Bologna*, p. 173: Potthast, n. 4644: *Reg. Inn. III*, XVI, n. 102: Muratori, *Antichità Estensi*, I, 410–3.

[4] *Reg. Inn. III*, XVI, n. 117.

may have been the first — and was in the March by the spring of 1214.[1]
There his principal opponent was the count of Celano who was oc-
cupying part of the Regno and southern March on behalf of Otto.
Aldobrandino recruited soldiers among his Paduan friends and in other
parts of northern Italy, but we know nothing of the military events of
his occupation. On Ascension Day (8 May) Pope Innocent preached a
sermon announcing the Marquis' entry into the March, asking for
support for him and blessing his supporters, at the same time anathe-
matizing and excommunicating their opponents.[2] Innocent gave Aldobrandino a legate as coadjutor, probably to hasten the issue of spiritual
penalties against recalcitrant vassals. At the same time (May 1214) a
series of letters in the pope's most energetic style ordered all papal subjects in the March to obey the Marquis (with particular threats to the
pro-Ottonian communes of Fano and Ancona) and asked for support
from the neighbouring province of Spoleto.[3]

While Innocent threatened interdict and excommunication, Aldobrandino was engaged in the more practical task of reaching terms with
the towns. Osimo, which in 1212 had been a member of an explicitly
Ottonian league, now received confirmation of its rights, possessions
and customs. In return for a promise by the Marquis, whose troops
were encamped nearby, that his men would help the commune to regain the rebellious Castelficardo, Osimo even risked a loan to him of
3,000 *l.* Soon afterwards Fano, hitherto an opponent, was granted
virtually independent rule in return for the promise of military service
within the March, counsel and a payment of 100 *l.* a year. Fermo and
Fabriano received similar confirmations of their jurisdiction and possessions. Fabriano was to make annual payment not exceeding the
amount paid by the town to the Marquis' father and, before him, to
Markward and Warner.[4]

Despite Aldobrandino's victory over the count of Celano his progress
in winning over the towns of the March was slow. Fabriano, which
accepted his terms in May 1214, had in October of the previous year
received a privilege from the imperialist Dipold of Acerra, and the

---

[1] For the events of this paragraph, Rolandinus Patavinus, MGH, XIX, 47 and *Annales S. Justinae, ibid.*, 151 and 186. BFW, n. 12463: G. B. Pigna, *Historia de Principi di Este*, pp. 135–6 (describes a bloody battle *ad an.* 1215, but may be imaginative).

[2] Muratori, *Antichità Estensi*, I, 417.

[3] P.L., 217, Suppl., nn. 188 (*v.* BFW, n. 6168), 189, 192, 193: Amiani, *Fano*, II, xxv.

[4] Martorelli, *Osimo*, pp. 94–100: Amiani, *Fano*, II, xxiii–xxiv: De Minicis, *Fermo*, pp. 341–2 (it is not clear whether the Marquis' grant of Fermo and Senigallia to William 'Rangonus' (BFW, n. 12463) preceded or followed this grant: if the latter, the confirmation mentioned above was not effective for long): Zonghi, *Fabriano*, d. LXIII.

town continued to date its documents by the regnal year of Otto IV as well as that of Innocent.[1] While Fabriano 'sat on the fence', other towns remained faithful to Otto. Ascoli still stood for him in September 1214, or at least Innocent regarded the town's steadfast resistance to the Marquis as inspired by fidelity to Otto.[2] As late as November 1215 Ancona, Recanati, Castelficardo (the still unsubdued enemy of Osimo), Numana and Cingoli, all towns that had long defied the Marquis, swore to a perpetual alliance, with detailed military clauses.[3] This league was primarily aimed against the pro-Este communes of Osimo, Iesi, Senigallia and Fano, but the Ottonian towns had remained linked and the deed of alliance was dated by the regnal years of both Otto and Innocent. The ripples from Bouvines, where Otto met decisive defeat, were very slow to reach central Italy, but by 1215 even Salinguerra had decided that he had better be a vassal of Innocent rather than of Otto for his Matildine lands,[4] and opposition in the March was now the result of normal municipal independence more than of any survival of loyalty to Otto.

In the Duchy of Spoleto the German Dipold had no possibility of transferring his allegiance. He struggled on under conditions that were increasingly difficult, for with Otto himself distant and enfeebled there was no reason why the towns should give him their support. In the summer of 1213 we catch a glimpse of Dipold promising to aid Spoleto by destroying the village of Trevi, but the town, which had already begun to date its deeds by the papal regnal year alone, proved capable of performing this task unassisted.[5] After 1214 Dipold, whose contribution to Innocent's difficulties in the Duchy had been insignificant, disappears from the pages of deeds, letters and chronicles. He reappears once only, disguised and riding a donkey, at Tivoli, where he fell at last into the hands of the papal authorities.[6] His province had now gone over to the papacy. When Perugia suffered severe civil disturbances in 1214 it was a papal emissary, the chamberlain Stephen, who succeeded in arranging terms between nobles and *popolo*, and by the early summer of 1215 the pope's cousin James, already rector of the Tuscan Patrimony, had become rector of the Duchy also.[7]

---

[1] Hagemann in *QFIA*, XXX, 109–117, and (for the same formulae at Iesi) in *QFIA* XXXVI, 151–5: the dating clause of deeds provides a very approximate and fallible means for ascertaining the loyalty of a town, worth using in the absence of other evidence.
[2] P.L., 217, Suppl. n. 196.   [3] Cecconi, *Castelfidardo*, d. vi.
[4] Theiner, d. LIX.
[5] Ficker, *Forschungen*, IV, d. 258: Sansi, *Spoleto*, pp. 220, 223: BFW, nn. 12444, 12451.
[6] Richard of S. Germano, RIS, N.S., VII, 73.
[7] Theiner, d. LVIII: Theiner, *Vet. Mon. Slav. Merid.*, p. 70: Potthast, nn. 5283, 5310.

The failure of Otto and Dipold did not necessarily mean success for Innocent, as is shown by the history of the pope's dealings with the town of Narni during these years.[1] Narni had been a turbulent subject from the first and the quarrel with the papacy which caused its judges to be under excommunication in 1213 was no exceptional event. In the following year the pope took more serious measures; it seems evident that he had chosen Narni for exemplary punishment. The town was deprived of its bishopric, its citizens collectively placed under excommunication and neighbouring towns instructed to take them captive. This policy of turning neighbour against neighbour was often an effective one, for boundary disputes were endemic, but in the long run it could only aggravate the problems of the papal government. For a time Narni found an ally in Orvieto, the western borderer and often the antagonist of Todi; the pope's anxiety to reconcile Todi with Orvieto[2] was probably inspired partly by the wish to deprive Narni of support. Such quarrels between pope and subject-communes were cumulative, for more grievances were felt as the dispute developed. Whatever the causes of Narni's estrangement from the papacy in 1213, by 1214 a new stage had been reached through its election of an 'outsider' as rector without consulting the pope. A whole series of further grievances had developed by the summer of 1216: Narni destroyed Otricoli and the papal castle at Stroncone, raided Amelia and other towns and the Sabina, and was now reprimanded for its treatment of ecclesiastical property, its taxation of the clergy and its attitude to heresy. When the pope demanded the rebuilding of the destroyed places and payment of a 2,000 *l.* fine Narni yielded up Stroncone, but it is not clear whether the other demands were met. The significance of this story lies not only in Narni's lengthy defiance but in the degree of anarchy within the Duchy revealed by the fulminations of Innocent's protests and demands.

Further west, in the Tuscan Patrimony, powerful towns gave rather less trouble, but in parts imperialist control was slow to disappear. Viterbo, which had resisted Otto in 1210, was consistently pro-papal, and in 1213 and again in 1214 Innocent rewarded this strong supporter with special fiscal privileges which facilitated the purchase of grain and gave general encouragement to Viterbese trade.[3] In the Patrimony Innocent's cousin James, the papal marshal, became rector by the summer of 1213 and enjoyed a comparatively long period of adminis-

---

[1] For the events of this paragraph *v. Reg. Inn. III*, XVI, nn. 94 and 116: Fumi, *Orvieto* d. XCVII: documents in *MIÖG*, XXIII, 553–4: *Lib. Cens.*, I, 456–7 and 460–1.

[2] See above, p. 60.

[3] *Reg. Inn. III*, XVI, n. 95: Pinzi, *Viterbo*, I, 261 n.

F

tration, adding the Duchy to his zone of office in 1215.[1] Yet the course of events at Radicofani shows clearly that here too what was loss to Otto was not necessarily gain for Innocent. In 1213 the castellan of this stronghold was an imperial marshal, a German named Henry; finding himself virtually deserted by Otto, he turned to Siena as the nearest likely protector, and submitted his charge to that town 'in gratitude for Siena's services to the Emperor Otto'. An agreement reached between the rector James and the citizens of Radicofani in 1215 or 1216 seems to have been ineffective, for as late as 1221 the same Henry retained a hold over Radicofani, as well as Acquapendente and Proceno.[2] The ability of an isolated German soldier to retain some of the most vital strategic positions of papal Tuscany for a number of years shows the extreme weakness of Innocent's resources. Yet there were other towns, important ones, that did go over to him. Città di Castello was a large town situated at the extreme northern limit of the Duchy of Spoleto, and therefore not at all easily amenable to papal disciplinary measures. Nevertheless, early in 1216 the citizens of Città di Castello swore fealty to the pope and confirmed that their city was papal territory.[3]

On the whole the last four years of Innocent's pontificate mark a recovery from the time of Otto's power. The decision to grant the March to the Estensi was an intelligent one which recognized the small success of the papacy in this province and by a compromise enabled Innocent to concentrate on his more southerly territories. His most impressive achievement in these years was in the extreme south. Here the frontier with the Regno was much strengthened through the co-operation of Frederick II, still partly dependent on papal goodwill and not yet ungrateful for Innocent's guardianship. In January 1212 the count of Fondi made a will granting his county, with various neighbouring baronies, to the Roman Church; three months later Frederick gave his consent to papal tenure of all this area, the pope having the right to alienate it, pledge it or grant it to any person. Innocent's southern boundary was further supported by Frederick's withdrawal of his own mesne tenancy at Sora, so that this county was now held directly of the papacy by Innocent's brother Richard, and by the grant of Aquino as a pledge for the repayment of papal expenses over Frederick's wardship.[4] The turbulent baronage of the Regno, as well as the possible threat of attacks from its rulers, made essential a strong

---

[1] *V.* App. II.
[2] BFW, n. 12429: Theiner, *Vet. Mon. Slav. Merid.*, p. 69: Huillard-Bréholles, II, 130.
[3] Muzi, *Città di Castello*, I, 33–4: BFW, n. 12493.
[4] *Lib. Cens.*, I, 257–8: P.L. 217, Suppl. 16 (col. 301): Theiner, d. LX: BFW, n. 661.

defence system in the south. In 1216 the count of Aquila conducted a large-scale raid into the Campagna, but was caught by John of Ceccano and lost seventy knights and all his loot.[1] John of Ceccano's estates were only part of a formidable defence in depth which included Richard's lands round Sora, the older Conti lands, and the papal marshal's fiefs. From 1212 these last included Ninfa, which James had hitherto held only as a pledge of the pope's intention of repaying him for his services in the campaign against Markward.[2]

On 1 July 1216 Frederick made a promise that his son Henry would reign over the Sicilian kingdom as a papal vassal and that during Henry's minority his rule would be exercised by a person acceptable and answerable to the pope.[3] The papacy, it might seem, possessed at last the fruits of its struggle of two decades and more. It had a barrier across Italy and an apparent guarantee that from the south at least there would be no pressure against that barrier. The division between Empire and Regno should also mean that the Hohenstaufen no longer desired the March and Duchy as a corridor for communication. The news of Frederick's oath never reached Innocent III, for the great pope died at Perugia on 16 July. He had been the founder of the Papal State in the form that it was to assume for three centuries. Among his many achievements his central Italian ones lasted exceptionally well. The initial victory over Rome, the imperial promise of Neuss, the State's first parliament, the strong southern frontier, the compromises with the towns of Umbria and the March were the essential preliminaries to the formation of a new state. They could only have a successful sequel if the imperial promise was kept and the communes forced within a powerful administrative structure.

[1] *Ann. Ceccanenses*, MGH, XIX, 300.   [2] *Reg. Inn. III*, XV, n. 114: see also above, p. 43.
[3] MGH, Const., II, 72.

III

The Pope's Subjects

D iscussion of the popes' prospects within the patrimony so enormously increased by Innocent III must start with a brief account of the nature of papal overlordship. In defining the juridical status of the pope's subjects it was normal to draw a distinction between those that were immediately subject (*immediate* or *nullo medio subiecti*) and the others coming under a mesne lord or city, the *terrae mediate subiectae*.[1] The latter, the fiefs of lay and ecclesiastical lords and the subject-territories of communes, were only indirectly subject to papal rule, and the ensuing pages will be concerned not with them but with the relationship between the popes and those communes, lords and rural zones that had no intervening master.

While the degree of control exercised in practice by the papal authorities varied far more in accordance with the shifting realities of political and administrative power than in obedience to the niceties of juridical subordination, something must be said of the legal status of the pope's subjects. These subjects owed fealty to the pontiff, and both barons and the representatives of towns swore oaths of obedience couched in feudal terms. Thus the *podestà* and representatives of twenty-four towns of the Duchy of Spoleto and Tuscan Patrimony took an oath in 1236 binding them to aid in maintaining papal rights and the peace in these provinces, 'saving always the fealty and orders of the pope', while feudatories swore in more generic terms 'to be faithful from henceforth to St. Peter and the Roman Church and to the lord pope and his rightful successors'.[2] A witness seeking to prove the direct sub-

---

[1] On this and the topics dealt with in the following pages *v*. Ermini 'Caratteri della sovranità pontificia', also the same author's 'Aspetti giuridici', which deals more fully with certain aspects of the same subject. When the papal authorities stated of land that 'immediate spectat ad Sanctam Romanam Ecclesiam' this was normally to deny its subjection to a commune: for a typical use of this formula, concerning the *burgum* of Monte Passillo, *v*. Ferranti, *Amandola*, III, d. 191. (Illustrative documents are here cited only when not used by Prof. Ermini.)

[2] *Lib. Cens.*, I, 481: cf. Perugia's oath of 1210 (Ficker, *Forschungen*, IV, d. 225). For a typical baronial oath *v*. *Lib. Cens.*, I, 427 (John of Ceccano, 1201). It is probable that the inhabitants of directly subject *castellanie* and bailiwicks also swore oaths of fealty, though the terms of these have not survived. For a later form of oath (Romagna, 1278), *v*. *ASI* XCI, 68–9.

jection to the papacy of the town of Ripatransone states that 'the commune and *universitas* have sworn fealty and responded and given
military service and counsel and hospitality to the general rectors of the
March for forty years'.[1]

The areas of papal domain naturally constitute an exception to the
normal nature of papal suzerainty. Not only did the pope enjoy rents
and all judicial rights here, but he usually appointed local rectors or
castellans to rule such places, which were often of considerable strategic
importance.[2] Most of this land had been papal property before 1197,
though some of it was purchased later and the popes inherited domain
rights from imperialist authorities in some fortresses and mountain villages in the Duchy.[3] Certain towns and areas were placed in a special
relationship to the pope whereby they either enjoyed particular immunities or else abdicated to an exceptional degree their independence:
an instance of the latter was Civitavecchia, which from 1224 voted the
pope powers of *plenum dominium*, one of the former was Fermo and the
other domain lands of the bishop of Fermo, wherein from the early
years of the century the bishop exercised palatine fiscal and judicial
powers.[4]

The normal terms of submission to the papacy of a commune are
perhaps most succinctly defined in Innocent III's letters to a number of
towns in the March.[5] These state that the towns' representatives have
promised fealty to the pope, that they will perform parliamentary and
military service to the extent of their powers and at their own expense
when requested by the pope or his legates, that they will pass on judicial

---

[1] Colucci, *Ant. Pic.*, XVIII, xxvii.

[2] It may be well at this point to record the names of the places figuring in a document
of 1234 as constituting papal domain in central Italy, in order to simplify later references.
These are (in Campagna) Fumone, Paliano, Serrone, Lariano; (in Marittima) Acquapuzza,
Ostia, Ariccia, Ninfa, 'Jolianum', Cori, Cisterna, Terracina; (in the Tuscan Patrimony)
Montefiascone, Orchia, Montalto, Radicofani, Proceno, Acquapendente, Bolsena, 'and
the Val del Lago'; (in the Duchy) Cesi, Gualdo, 'rocca Sacrati', 'Brusinum', 'Lorinum',
'rocca de Saxo'; (near Narni), S. Gemini, Stroncone, Miranda, Otricoli; (in Sabina)
Rocca Antica 'and all Sabina'; (in the March) Rocca 'de Plorago', Serravalle, Torre di
Palma: *v. Reg. G. IX*, n. 1715.

[3] Examples are Cesi and Gualdo Tadino; for the mountainous zone, *v.* below, p. 109.
For the acquisition of former imperial domain from the Duchy communes in 1220 *v.*
Lib. Cens., I, 10*–12*.

[4] Theiner, d. CXXXIV (Civitavecchia). The history of the bishop of Fermo's 'liberty'
can be partly followed in De Minicis, pp. 342–3, 348–9, 352–3, 542; *v.* also *Reg. Inn. III*,
P.L. 215, cols. 767–8 (the date in Potthast, II, 2048), *Reg. Hon. III*, nn. 1776, 3183, 4697;
Reg. G. IX, n. 3145, Potthast, nn. 6591, 7164, Theiner, d. CXXX, Colucci, *Ant. Pic.*,
XVIII, esp. pp. xxvi–xxxi and lxii. It is much to be hoped that Dr. W. Hagemann will
complete and publish his promised study of thirteenth-century Fermo. Papal privileges
occasionally describe towns as *filii speciales*, whom *sub apostolicae sedis protectione suscipi-
mus*: this formula appears to bear no juridical significance (*v.* Ermini, 'Caratteri', 340–3).

[5] P.L., 214, cols. 912–13.

appeals to the pope or his officials and grant all of these hospitality (*pro-curationes*). The towns will pay an annual tax (*census*). In return the pope confirms the communes' 'good customs' and the civil and criminal jurisdiction of their consuls, providing that the consuls or *podestà* 'are bound to the Roman pontiff and the Roman Church by an oath of fealty'. The communes' oath was to be renewed every ten years.

It is most significant that the pope here puts forward no claim to choose the towns' officials — nor even the direct claim that they require his approbation, though this is perhaps implied by his insistence that they must owe him fealty.[1] In dealing with some of the less powerful communes Innocent III did make such a claim. He placed Civita Castellana under interdict for electing a *podestà* without his consent, and Radicofani was forbidden to choose consuls except with his permission: moreover Città di Castello and Acquapendente, probably at his suggestion, asked him to name their *podestà*.[2] Honorius III followed this policy when he thought it necessary and feasible; he forbade Gubbio to elect from outside the State and excommunicated the officials of Ascoli for naming a *podestà* — possibly one who was suspected of pro-Hohenstaufen leanings — without his consent.[3] Yet Innocent's caution in not pressing too far his claims over the stronger towns of the March and over Perugia[4] constituted an admission of weakness in the most vital of all matters, for his ability to make a reality of papal rule depended largely upon the towns' choice of office bearers. If he could regulate this choice his overlordship was clear for all to see and he might organize a corps of officials devoted to his interests, but if he could exercise no such control the cities would form their own policies and go their own way, with the pope at best acting as an arbiter and tax-gatherer.

The latter was the process that in fact took place.[5] Its history is of such

---

[1] On the election of *podestà*, *v*. Ermini 'La libertà comunale', *ASRSP*, XLIX, 5–94: on the appointment of municipal judges, *La libertà comunale* (ii), pp. 9–16. Prof. Ermini pertinently remarks that the emperors had granted some of the stronger towns the right to choose their own consuls in the twelfth century: these towns included Perugia. Elsewhere ('Caratteri', 321), Prof. Ermini suggests that towns appointing their own *podestà* were *in demaneo* to the Church, and that only where the pope or his officials made the appointment was the town *in demaneo et dominio*: but the grounds for this hypothesis are not strong.

[2] P.L., 214, cols. 617–18, 815–16 and 215, cols. 795–6; Theiner, *Vet. Mon. Slav. Merid.*, p. 54.

[3] *QFIA*, XXIX, 156–7: *Reg. Hon. III*, n. 6179 (the nobleman Bertold chosen by Ascoli was perhaps the son of the former imperial duke of Spoleto).

[4] The terms made with Perugia in 1210 (Ficker, *Forschungen*, IV, d. 225) included a confirmation of the city's *consuetudines . . . in electione consulum seu potestatis*.

[5] See Ermini, 'La libertà comunale', 56 and 93–4. Prof. Ermini points out that it is symptomatic that whereas election by a town with papal confirmation of this choice was a privilege early in the thirteenth century, insistence on the papal right to confirm was a punishment towards the end of the century.

importance that it warrants a brief excursus which will inevitably
traverse some territory that must be revisited in subsequent narrative
chapters. In the popes' dealings with the Duchy towns, and in particular
with Assisi, one can trace a papal defeat in this trial of strength. Innocent
III quarrelled with Assisi over its choice of *podestà*, not on the grounds
that the man lacked his consent but on the never-disputed plea that he
was ineligible as an excommunicate.[1] The pope's argument in this case
suggests that he was resigned to the commune normally making its own
elections, and this position was formally accepted some thirty years
later by Gregory IX in two privileges which granted Assisi the right 'to
create freely its own *podestà* and officials like the other cities of the
Duchy of Spoleto'.[2] Thus it was now recognized that in this province all
civitates — that is, towns having an episcopal see — possessed the power
to elect their own *podestà*.

The middle years of the century saw the extension of this power, or
of its recognition, for its grant constituted a useful reward to towns
whose support was sought against the Hohenstaufen. A number of
communes, particularly in the March, received it as the reward for a
promise of future obedience.[3] Such grants, to which some additions
were made, probably for money, by Boniface VIII,[4] cannot disguise the
fact that the stronger towns continued to take no note of papal claims.[5]
Yet even after the middle of the century these claims continued to be
advanced. In 1252 a letter of Innocent IV to a number of towns in the
March asserted that these had done wrong to choose their *podestà* 'sine
consensu nostro' and the next decade saw disputes in several towns of
this province concerning papal attempts to appoint *podestà*.[6] Urban IV
still insisted that Corneto could not have a *podestà* or captain who lacked

---

[1] P.L., 215, cols. 365–6. For other instances of *podestà* being declared ineligible on similar grounds (e.g. as lying under the ban of papal authorities), *v. Reg. Urb. IV*, I, n. 150; Gianandrea, *Iesi*, d. CXCVII; Mei, *Cagli*, dd. 451–2; Ferranti, *Amandola* III, d. 228.

[2] MGH, Ep. Pont., I, 538–40 (1235; cf. *Lib. Cens.*, I, 541–2) and *Reg. G. IX*, n. 3856 (1237). At about the same period a town was granted liberties 'in praeficiendis vobis Rectoribus . . . sicut . . . civitates Campaniae', a formula which may imply possession of the same powers. For Assisi, *v. inf.*, p. 140.

[3] Sansi, I, 288–90 (Spoleto, 1247: a confirmation of the situation in 1237); *Reg. Inn. IV.* n. 4536 (Bevagna, 1249); Colini-Baldeschi, *Cingoli*, pp. xlvii–xlviii (Cingoli, 1250); QFIA, XXXVII (Montolmo, 1251, *pro hac vice*); Contatore, *Terracina*, pp. 193–4 (Terracina, 1259); AMSM, N.S., VII (1911–12), 401 (Montegiorgio, 1266). Other examples in Ermini, *art. cit.*, 11.

[4] *Reg. B. VIII*, nn. 2394 (Narni), 5206–8 (Cesena).

[5] Cagli normally chose its own *podestà* in the 1260s (Bricchi, pp. 120–1), but naturally evidence to establish this negative point is scarce.

[6] Marangoni, *Civitanova*, p. 274. For disputes in 1260s and 1270s, Bricchi, *Cagli*, pp. 120–1 and 135–7; Grimaldi, *Matelica*, dd. CCXVIb, CCXXXV, CCXXXVII; Zonghi, *Fabriano*, d. CCXVII and Fabriano, AC, Lib. Ross., ff. 122v–123.

his approbation and a new commune recognized in his time was ordered to receive its rector from the Church.[1] The result of the confused juridical situation in this period was a tendency for the papacy to recognize custom as a foundation for a claim to elect the *podestà*: thus Nicholas III appointed his chamberlain to investigate, not Fabriano's written rights, but the method hitherto adopted in choosing Fabriano's *podestà*. This was not a fixed rule, however, for only a few years later Macerata unsuccessfully pleaded usage *per tantum tempus cuius non extat memoria* in the face of new provincial statutes forbidding any commune of the March to elect its own officials.[2]

In the last two decades of the century there was a process of clarification whereby either pope or town normally came into undisputed possession of the right to elect.[3] Many communes presented the *podestà*-ship — or what amounted to the same thing, the right to appoint — to the pope himself.[4] Elsewhere, as at Viterbo, the papacy claimed the right to deprive the town of its power of choice on account of its disobedience.[5] Meanwhile Nicholas IV initiated the realistic policy of parting with the claim to appoint in exchange for an annual payment. This was applied to some dozens of towns in the March in 1289–91 and became the origin of a highly productive *census*.[6] In the interests of clear definition and peace and in return for money, the papacy thus yielded a right that it had often been unable to enforce. Sometimes a compromise proved a satisfactory solution: this was the case at Spoleto, where, by agreement with Boniface VIII, the commune presented a list of three names from which the pope or provincial rector selected the *podestà*.[7] By the end of the century this process of definition was more or less at an end, so that in 1300 the pope could legislate for the communes *que solite sunt ab antiquo ad regimen suum eligere potestates* and his rector in the

---

[1] *Reg. Urb. IV*, II, nn. 951–2; Ferranti, *Amandola*, III, d. 55 (for the effectiveness of which *v*. dd. 126, 144, 171, 228).

[2] Zonghi, *Fabriano*, d. CCXXIII. Macerata, AC, Perg. nn. 139, 145, 147–52; *AMSM*, N.S., I (1904), 334. The town protested in 1282 *a gravamine eis imposito et illato eo quod constitutum et ordinatum extitit per ipsum dominum* (*sc*. rectorem) *in generali colloquio videlicet quod nulla civitas vel comunantia eligat nominet vel assumat aliquem in potestatem capitaneum iudicem vel rectorem*, etc.; later it pleaded that it had chosen its own officials *per longum et longissumum tempus*, etc.

[3] The evidence cited by Prof. Ermini (*art. cit.*, 11–15) hardly justifies his assertion that there was in 1278–90 an 'attiva opera di riaffermazione e di riordinamento dei diritti della Chiesa sulle podestarie comunali'. But he is undoubtedly right that there was a *riordinamento*.

[4] For this process, which became common from the later 1280s, *v*. below, pp. 221 ff.

[5] *Reg. Hon. IV*, n. 485 and *Reg. N. IV*, nn. 7189–90. For another instance of this claim at Forlì in 1282) *v*. *ASI*, App., s.I, VII (1849), 36.

[6] See pp. 222 ff.

[7] Sansi, *Spoleto*, d. LXXIV. For the adoption of a similar system elsewhere in the following century *v*. Ermini, *art. cit.*, 49–55.

March for those *in quibus potestates per rectorem provincie pro ecclesia poni vel eligi solent.*[1] Custom had worked long enough to acquire the force of law and formal agreements had settled the matter in many of the towns in which the right had been contested, so that these formulae are suggestive not of evasiveness but of a generally prevailing agreement between the pope and his municipal subjects as to where the right now lay.

If the appointment of the towns' leading official was the most obvious crux of papal authority, there were other forms of intervention which were more general. The conventional feudal obligations to perform military service and to give counsel and hospitality have already been mentioned.[2] The first and last of these were to be among the bases of papal fiscality in the State, together with the payment of regular *census* and hearth-tax, tolls and money owed for the enjoyment of privileges.[3] The pope also possessed the power to legislate for his State and issued constitutions, some applicable to the State as a whole, others to particular provinces only. Provincial rectors too promulgated constitutions, frequently in parliament, for the provinces over which they were set.[4]

The pope and rectors had powers to order towns to include papal legislation in their own statutes[5] and to dictate the nature of these statutes in certain ways. They could instruct them to legislate against heresy and forbid them to make laws opposed to the interests of the Church.[6] When a commune became subject to the papacy its customs were normally confirmed, and later the pope might intervene to quash customs of which he disapproved or to confirm changes in municipal criminal codes.[7] In theory the towns were bound to submit their statutes for inspection and approbation by the papal authorities, unless they possessed the special privilege of *facultas condendi statuta.*[8] There is occasional evidence of this provision being effective, but it seems likely that on the whole it was neglected, and Boniface VIII's proposal to withdraw it in his code for the March is an instance of his realism.[9]

---

[1] Theiner, d. DXXVIII: Albornoz, *Constitutions*, l. II, c. 90 (p. 94).

[2] Above pp. 68-9: and below, pp. 276 ff. (military service) and 110 ff. (parliament).

[3] See below, pp. 252 ff. A Perugian statute of 1234 (Pellini, I, 250-1) recognized *pro facto domini papae* as one of the four grounds justifying taxation.

[4] For legislation, see below, pp. 116 ff.: also Sella, 'Costituzioni dello Stato della Chiesa,' *ASI*, LXXXV (1927).

[5] For examples *v. RSDI*, II, 303 and De Minicis, *Fermo*, p. 513.

[6] Potthast, n. 17383 (heresy). For opposition to legislation against the interests of the Church — a matter also much disputed outside the Papal State — *v. Reg. Hon. III*, nn. 3895 (Rieti, 1222) and 4771 (Osimo, 1224), etc., and in general Ermini, *art. cit.*, 97-100.

[7] E.g. *Reg. G. IX*, n. 3710 (confirmation) and *Reg. Inn. IV*, n. 7195 (custom quashed).

[8] For grants of this privilege *v.* Ermini, *art. cit.*, 115-16.

[9] For this obligation *v. Reg. Inn. IV*, n. 6068 (statutes of Civita Castellana confirmed,

The nature of papal legislation is too wide for easy definition; it extended not merely to provincial rule and relations between the towns, but to the internal affairs of the communes themselves, as instanced by Nicholas IV's decree of 1290 forbidding the re-election of officials for a period of over one year.[1] This was of course aimed at nascent *signorie*, a matter in which the pope had hitherto intervened only by occasional executive action.[2] Such intervention was characteristic of the normal role of papal authority in municipal matters, for peace-making and arbitration between warring classes in the towns was almost as common as the same type of participation in their external relations.[3]

Each town had a general obligation to keep the peace and responsibility for the maintenance of order on the highway within its sphere of influence. It might receive instructions to demolish unauthorized fortresses, but the fundamental right to hold in subjection a zone of surrounding country-side, a *contado* which was *mediate subiectus* to the papacy, was not seriously challenged.[4] Towns sometimes secured papal confirmation of this territorial subjection to them, while the papacy struggled to ensure that papal domain escaped it — often with extreme difficulty, as in the hard-fought attempt to keep the Val del Lago di Bolsena from falling to Orvieto and the fortresses of Stroncone and Otricoli from Narni.[5] The popes also sought to assist Viterbo, Velletri and the other towns in the Campagna and Patrimony threatened by Roman expansionism, and in general to stand up for small towns — the natural allies of authority — in danger of being extinguished by the powerful and lawless.[6] Some towns paid a *census* on behalf of their

1252) and Pflugk-Hartung, pp. 586-7 (Corneto pays a fine in 1302 *quia utebantur statutis non correctis*: also Theiner, d. DLXXI, clause 6).

[1] *Reg. N. IV*, n. 7245 (Patrimony): for the date of this decree and its application to the March *v*. Mei, *Cagli*, dd. 416, 418, 422. It is presumably the constitution *super electione potestatum et rectorum in terris ecclesiae* referred to in a letter to the vicar of the Campagna-Marittima (*Reg. N. IV*, n. 7273) and hence applied to the entire State. Note also Clement IV's measure forbidding alienation of certain municipal property (*Reg. Cl. IV*, n. 4).

[2] For instance at Ferentino in 1264, against Roland of Montelungo (*Reg. Urb. IV*, II, nn. 775 and 795).

[3] For typical examples of peacemaking between nobles and *popolo*, *v*. P.L., 214, clxv-clxvi (Todi, 1207); Theiner, dd. LVIII and CXXVII (Perugia 1214 and 1223) and *Reg. G. IX*, nn. 34-5 (Perugia, 1227), etc.

[4] See G. De Vergottini, 'Il papato e la comitatinanza nello Stato della Chiesa', *AMSR*, N.S. III (1951-3),73-162 and the same author's 'Contributo alla storia della comitatinanza nello Stato della Chiesa', *RSDI*, XXVI-XXVII. The following remarks, however, dissent from the findings of Prof. De Vergottini, who considers that the papacy only recognized submissions made with papal consent. On the obligation *ad custodiendas stratas v*. Ermini, 'Caratteri', 318.

[5] For papal confirmation of *contado* see, e.g., Baldassini, *Iesi*, d. xv; *TRHS*, 4th s., XXXII (1950), 121-39 (Orvieto); *Reg. Urb. IV*, II, nn. 843-4 (Narni).

[6] On Rome, De Vergottini, *art. cit.*, 83-5. Examples of papal defence of weaker towns are that of S. Gemini against Narni (*Reg. Urb. IV*, II, nn. 61 and 100), and of Trevi against

contado as well as for the city itself and, though popes might attempt to
punish refractory communes by ordering them to be deprived of their
contadi, such measures were rare and hard to make effective.[1] A town
could only become a *communantia* through papal recognition, but once
it had secured this status there was no consistent attempt to deny it the
hinterland of communal and baronial submissions achieved by all the
Italian city-states.[2]

The judicial aspects of papal rule are intricate and obscure, but of
paramount importance.[3] The pope claimed as overlord the exercise of
merum et mixtum imperium, that is to say full powers of civil and criminal
jurisdiction. Canon lawyers agreed that such powers were possessed by
the pope and exercised on his behalf by the provincial rectors in their
courts; the *podestà* of towns did not have them except *de consuetudine et
usurpatione*.[4] This phrase of the Perugian Baldus and the experienced
Durand's melancholy *usurpant sibi merum imperium* show that here too
might counted for more than right, but papal authority was willing to
contest the latter and fought at length the pretensions of any commune
claiming *merum et mixtum imperium*. In 1287–8 a long enquiry was held
by the rector of the March into Fabriano's claim to have enjoyed this
right for over a hundred years — there were eleven centenarians
among the sixty witnesses — with the consent of the provincial authorities and by virtue of papal and imperial privileges. Despite much
convincing evidence of capital punishment and other powers exercised
de facto, the rector rejected Fabriano's case.[5]

Normally the town's right to try certain criminal cases in the first
instance was recognized. The precise nature of this grant, which might
be for criminal suits according to *ordinem antiquam et approbatam consuetudinem* or for all criminal cases and civil suits involving sums of less

Foligno (*Reg. Inn. IV*, nn. 5478–9): cf. the later defence of two still smaller places against
Trevi (Sansi, *Spoleto*, d. LIX, and *Storia*, I, 103–5).

[1] De Vergottini, 'Il Papato', 103 ff. and 145 ff. and 'Contributo', *passim*.

[2] For new communes recognized by papal authority, *v. Reg. Inn. IV*, n. 6767 and
Lib. Cens., I, 563–4 (Penna S. Giovanni, 1252); Ferranti, III, d. 55 (Amandola, 1265).
In 1255 the rector of the March promulgated a constitution: *non fiat aliqua communantia
vel castrum in Marchia sine domini pape vel nostra licentia spetiali* (Grimaldi, *Matelica*, d.
CXVI).

[3] On this topic see Ermini, *La Libertà comunale* (II), *passim*.

[4] Durand and Baldus, quoted in an excellent discussion by Partner, pp. 124–5: for
merum et mixtum imperium v. also C.N.S. Woolf, *Bartolus of Sassoferrato*, pp. 134 ff. and P. J.
Jones in *EHR*, LXVII, 322–6.

[5] *QFIA*, XXXII, 81–109: a similar claim was put forward at about the same time by
Gualdo Tadino (Guerrieri, *Gualdo Tadino*, p. 64). In contrast with the invariable refusal
of *merum et mixtum imperium* to any town within the Papal State may be noted Card.
Capocci's grant of this right to Ascoli in part of the Regno in 1251 (Marcucci, *Ascoli*,
p. ccliii).

than, for instance, fifty pounds, varied enormously.[1] It was rather rare for a town to have authority to hear appeals, but such powers were held by Perugia and Todi from Innocent III's time and from a rather later period by Camerino and Spoleto.[2] Characteristically Nicholas IV and Boniface VIII acted to bring the *de jure* terms closer to reality, Nicholas by granting most towns of the March full judicial powers, except in certain major cases reserved to the rector's court, Boniface by conceding to the Patrimony's communes *usque apostolicae sedis beneplacitum* enjoyment of the papacy's cherished right of *merum et mixtum imperium*.[3]

When the situation regulating the rival jurisdiction of town and rectorial courts was fluid, it was natural that there should be much rivalry between the two, since both money and juridical control were at stake. One principle adopted in settling problems of disputed jurisdiction was that of *preventio*, whereby the first court to take cognisance of a case acquired the right to settle it. By the constitution for the Campagna and Marittima of 1295 this principle was to prevail throughout that province, but it is not clear whether the measure recorded earlier practice nor whether *preventio* applied in the other provinces.[4]

[1] *Reg. G. IX*, n. 6004 ; Colucci, *Ant., Pic.*, XVIII, d. XIII. Cf. the findings of the court of Campagna-Marittima in 1281-2 that Veroli's court had criminal powers 'prout suspendio, quandoque eructione oculorum, quandoque fustigatione, quandoque combustione, quandoque pecunialiter' (Caperna, *Veroli*, pp. 257 and 324-5). Another instance of the willingness of papal authorities to accept such claims to jurisdiction so long as they stopped short of *merum et mixtum imperium* is provided by the Vicar of the Duchy's finding in 1266 that Bevagna's officials 'consueverunt punire maleficia commissa in Mevania et eius districtu et tulerunt sententias contra malefactores et delinquentes . . . pro longo et longissimo tempore' (Alberti, *Bevagna*, pt. II, pp. 155-7).

[2] P.L., 214, cols. 355-6 and 400-1: Turchi, *Camerino*, d. XLI: Sansi, *Spoleto*, I, 288-90 (appeals below 100 *l.*).

[3] See below, pp. 222 & 234 ff. The cases reserved in the March were *lèse-majesté*, heresy, homicide, adultery, rape of a virgin, arson and certain types of robbery (*furtum* in cases where a limb might be forfeit, *latrocinium, derobatio, fractio stratarum*).

[4] On *preventio*, see Partner, pp. 125-6, and Ermini, *La libertà comunale* (II), pp. 63 ff. 1295: '. . . si potestas, capitaneus vel defensor aliquis communitatis alicuius, civitatis vel castri provinciae memoratae, in quo quidem castro potestas seu rector ad ipsius regimen hactenus eligi consuevit, aut ecclesiasticus iudex seu loci ordinarius, primo contra quemlibet ipsius provinciae incolam super delectis et excessibus quibuscumque per accusationem aut denunciationem vel inquisitionem duxerit procedendum, tunc eiusdem rector provinciae, tam in spiritualibus et temporalibus contra huiusmodi delinquentem ulterius non procedat, quantumcumque in curia rectoris praedicti super eodem delicto fuerit accusatus. Si vero praefatus rector contra huiusmodi delinquentem prius duxerit procedendum memoratus potestas, capitaneus vel defensor non procedant in aliquo contra eum' (from clause I of 'Romana Mater Ecclesia' in *Bullarium Romanum* (ed. Turin, 1857-72), IV, 629-32). For the functioning of the practice in the Campagna, *v.* Boniface VIII's privilege to Velletri, 1299 (*Reg. B. VIII*, n. 2847: discussion by Falco in *ASRSP*, XLVIII 83n). I cannot agree with Prof. Ermini that clause 2 in the March constitution 'Celestis, patrisfamilias' of 1303 necessarily implies the practice of *preventio* in that province.

I find unconvincing the contention of Prof. Ermini (*La libertà comunale*, (II), pp. 36 ff.) that the town courts won a victory over the jurisdictional claims of local papal courts, since I believe such papal judges to have existed only exceptionally and in 'domain' towns: *v.* below, p. 109.

The most promising approach to this topic is to record what cases came before the papal courts and in what circumstances. The right of appeal to the provincial court, applicable even where the city held power to hear 'first cases of appeal', was the most common and straightforward route to the rector's bench. Although towns occasionally received privileges exempting themselves and their inhabitants from the jurisdiction of external courts, only feudal courts and other town courts were envisaged in such grants, and the exemption did not apply to the provincial court.[1] In the March of Ancona the maximum period permitted before originating an appeal to the provincial rector was sixty days.[2] The three sub-provincial judges of this province were only permitted by Cardinal Napoleon Orsini to try appeals involving sums of less than 25 *l.*, more serious cases going before the rector's main bench.[3] Appeals might occasionally be taken direct from town courts to the pope, or a re-hearing in the provincial court be ordered as a first appeal from its decision, but more normally the channel of appeal was from the town via the rector to the papal curia. The last appeal, which might encounter obstacles from the provincial court, had in the opinion of Durand to be initiated within one year or, in exceptional circumstances, two years.[4] Such cases might be heard by the pope himself or they could be deputed to some specially appointed judge such as a cardinal.[5] During papal vacancies the pope's jurisdiction in these suits passed to the chamberlain and the hearings took place before that official or the *auditor* of the papal chamber; they remained in this court once incepted there, even after the election of a pope.[6] Nicholas IV appointed three papal chaplain to hear appeal suits involving sums of

[1] Many examples in Ermini, *Libertà Comunale* (II), pp. 67–77. Only Civitavecchia, by recognizing the direct jurisdiction of the papal chamber, seems to have secured full exemption from a provincial court (*Lib. Cens.* I, 597–8 (1291)).

[2] Gubbio, Sottosez AS, perg., bu. 16 (22 July 1266), a reference to a provincial statute which was repeated in 1272 (*RSDI*, II, 300). See also Partner, p. 130.

[3] Albornoz, *Constitutions*, p. 53. For these judges, see below, p. 108.

[4] For a re-hearing, *v.* Acquacotta, *Matelica*, d. 61. The complications of appellate jurisdiction may be illustrated from a suit involving S. Ginesio (Colucci, *Ant. Pic.*, XIX, 37). This town was condemned by one provincial rector and appealed to the pope. A later rector confirmed the sentence and ordered payment of a fine despite the inception of a further appeal to the papal court. Finally Innocent IV ordered a third hearing in the provincial court. For the period of appeal *v.* Durand, *Speculum Iuris*, l. II, pt. 3 (nevertheless a party in a suit in the March in 1287–8 claimed 3 months as the maximum lapse, *v.* Gianandrea, *Iesi*, d. CCXXXII). For appeal missing provincial courts, *Reg. N. IV*, nn. 7204–6, and for provincial opposition to appeals to the pope, *Bullarium Romanum*, IV, 629–32 (clause 11).

[5] For occasional appointments of a single appeal judge for the State under Martin IV and subsequently v. B. Rusch, *Die Behörden und Hofbeamten der päpstlichen Kurie des 13. Jahrhunderts*, p. 61.

[6] Examples: Gubbio, Sottosez AS, perg., bu. 10, nn. 244–252 and bu. 16 (hearings by the chamberlain, 1277–8): Rome, AS, Dipl., perg. Cagli (cass. 40), n. 2 (by general *auditor* of chamber, 1288).

under 100 *l.* in which papal claims to property were not concerned; one of these was to deal with appeals from the Patrimony and Romagna, one with the Campagna-Marittima, and the last with the March and Duchy.[1] There is no evidence that this experiment was prolonged.

The towns opposed the papal courts' appellate jurisdiction fiercely and often successfully. This opposition took many forms, the most common being the enactment of statutes forbidding such appeals and the appointment of officials (often called *exgravatores*) to hear appeals and to prevent them being made to papal courts.[2] Many a town-dweller found his attempt to appeal to papal authority opposed by a demand that he should furnish security against any such appeal being lodged and even by fines and the use of force.[3] Meanwhile some communes neglected summonses to send representatives or witnesses to these courts, while others proceed more formally by approaching the pope with the plea that custom sanctioned their attempts to prevent appeals. A stronger town would write, more bluntly, that 'you should know that there is nothing that we detest more than it being said that there should be an appeal from the decision of the *podestà* and commune of Bologna'.[4]

Much of the routine jurisdiction of the rectors' courts was in civil suits. Nicholas IV attempted to assert the principle that the litigants themselves should choose between municipal and provincial courts,[5] probably without much effect. Most of the civil cases of first instance that came to papal judges were those in which the communes them-

---

[1] *Reg. N. IV*, nn. 7204-6.

[2] Typical of such legislation is a Spoletan statute of *c.* 1296 (Spoleto, Sottosez AS, Statuti, I, f. 14v: *v. inf.*, pp. 230-1) beginning 'Item dicimus et ordinamus quod nullus appellet per se vel alium ab aliqua sententia vel processu facta vel facto contra ipsum per aliquem officialem communis Spoleti . . .' Instances of papal protests against such practices are *Reg. Hon. III*, n. 4850; *Reg. Urb. IV*, II, n. 716; *ASI*, s.l, XVI, 2, 488; Theiner, d. CCCCXXXIX: for papal legislation, Albornoz, *Constitutions*, pp. 14-16 (1262); *RSDI*, II, 301-2 (1272); *Nuovi Studi Med.*, II, 241-52 (1283).

[3] E.g. Fabriano, AC, perg. 6 June 1300.

[4] Macerata, AC, Rif. I (1287), ff. 3v-4v, 9v-12v, etc. Bologna's letter of 1293 to the rector of Romagna (Bologna, AS, Lettere del comune, Reg. 6, f. 16, n. 1) merits fuller quotation: '. . . dominationi vestre volumus non latere quod nunquam predecessores vestri appellationes aliquas de aliquibus processibus communis Bon' receperunt nec aliquatenus admiserunt et unde procedat tale per vos initium vehementissime admiramur et quidquid in litteris contineatur vix credere possumus de vestra conscientia processisse. Et cognoscatis quod nullam scimus rem quam commune et populus Bon' tam orribiliter detestarent quam dicere quod de processibus potestatis et communis Bon' debet appellatio aliqua interponi et potius nos et civitas nostra omni supponemus periculo et fortuna quam modo aliquo pateremur quod cives nostri ex civitate Bon' ad iudicium alicuivi trahentur pro appellationibus aliquibus factis vel que fient a processibus factis pro potestate et officialibus communis Bon' iuxta nostrorum continentiaque statutorum . . .'

[5] Theiner, d. CCCCLXXXIV; *Reg. N. IV*, nn. 4477-87.

selves were a party, such as disputes concerning land between towns and monastic or other ecclesiastical corporations or quarrels between neighbouring communes.[1] Typical instances of civil appeal jurisdiction in these courts concerned suits brought by officials who claimed that the communes employing them had not paid their salaries, and by towns against feudal lords for non-payment of taxes.[2] Occasionally the pope would order a civil suit to be heard in his own Curia, omitting both municipal and provincial courts, but this was probably most exceptional and a sign of great favour to one or both of the litigants.[3]

Many of the other cases — probably a high proportion of the total number heard, though the total disappearance of the provincial records makes this uncertain — were suits brought by the provincial rector himself against his municipal subjects. Communes were constantly suffering condemnation for attacking their neighbours, for causing 'disorders' and committing 'excesses' against both places and individuals (often the provincial officials or their servants), for failing to send troops or to pay taxes, for building fortifications without the rector's consent, for exporting corn illegally, or harbouring outlaws, or enacting 'illegal' constitutions, or condemning clerics to death, or failing to appear when cited by the rector or his judges, or any other of a thousand forms of disobedience. The towns of the March and Tuscan Patrimony (and probably of other provinces) had the obligation to present criminals guilty of capital and other serious offences to the provincial authorities within a certain period, and were liable to a fine if they failed to accomplish this: here was another source of many condemnations.[4] Towns which failed to preserve the security of the highway within their territories were also liable to a fine if the commission of a crime and failure to apprehend the criminal revealed deficiencies in this matter.[5] Such condemnations often involved the officials of the offending town as well, although in his codes for the Campagna-

---

[1] Examples are Gianandrea, *Iesi*, d. CCXL and Macerata, AC, Rif. I, f. 63v (towns and clergy): Grimaldi, *Matelica*, d. CCLXVIII and Marangoni, *Civitanova*, pp. 289–93 (town against town).

[2] *Reg. N. IV*, n. 7507 and Gazzera, *Sanginesio*, p. 73 (salaries: the latter concerns a municipal schoolmaster). The thirteenth century statutes of Macerata forbade the *podestà* to appeal to the provincial authorities concerning his salary (Foglietti, *Stat. Macerata sec. XIII*, p. 9). Bricchi, *Cagli*, pp. 156–7 and Pflugk-Harttung, pp. 569–70 (towns against nobles).

[3] An example is *Reg. Hon. III*, n. 4441 (involving Corneto and one of its citizens, 1223).

[4] For this obligation *v*. Gianandrea, *Iesi*, dd. CCXIX and CCXLIII; Ferranti, *Amandola*. III, d. 307; Macerata, AC, Rif. I, ff. 90v–97v: for the Tuscan Patrimony *v*. Durand, *Speculum Iuris*, IV, pt. IV (1612 edn., p. 481).

[5] On this obligation, *v*. above, p. 74: for condemnations arising from it *v*. Theiner, d. CCCCLXVIII and documents cited in the preceding footnote.

Marittima, the Patrimony and the March Boniface VIII sought to draw
a clear distinction between the responsibilities of communes and those
of their officials and citizens.[1] Finally, despite the rival claims of town
courts, many murderers, robbers and other malefactors came before the
provincial rector or his judges, charged with crimes which might
amount to nothing more than participation in inter-city warfare, but
also included conventional non-political offences.[2]

★   ★   ★

The ability of Innocent III to turn these claims into reality would
depend not only on his success in building up machinery for government and a tradition of obedience to authority, but also upon the
strength of his subjects and the extent to which they had already evolved
their own institutions for self-rule. A brief survey of the State is there-
for a necessary preliminary to recounting its history. For the most part
the trial of strength would be between pope and communes, since by the
thirteenth century central Italy was predominantly a land of towns; although there were areas under the control of feudal families, these
elements were in retreat before the advancing power of the city-states.
The towns were not centres of industry or large-scale commerce like
the greater communes of Tuscany and northern Italy, but small or
moderate-sized nuclei of population, homes of agriculturalists and
shop-keepers, situated on the defensible and healthy higher ground —
often the hilltops — of the Apennines and their outliers.

The relations of Innocent III with the city of Rome have already been
described. Potentially this was the most powerful of all the popes' subjects, a great city, proud of its unique traditions, already strongly
organized as an independent commune, possessing claims to rule a large
area in Latium, and having a prosperous banking community. Yet
Rome was often less formidable than appearances would suggest. Internal dissensions, and in particular its class of mighty noble families and
their rivalries, were one reason for this. Another was the dependence of
Rome's economic life on the presence of the papal Curia. In smaller

---

[1] Theiner, d. DXXVIII (clause 13) and DLXXI (clause 8): *Bullarium Romanum*, IV,
629–32 (clause 5). For an instance of municipal officials being condemned, Fabriano, AC,
perg. 6 June 1300 (*podestà* and seven other officials).

[2] For a 'political' condemnation for fighting against Foligno, *v.* Perugia, AS, Rif. X
(1290), f. 165v and for similar cases Gianandrea, *Iesi*, d. CCXIX, etc. For crimes, Gubbio,
Sottosez AS, Perg., bu. 16 (19 March 1266, wrongly marked '1 May'; murder); Fantuzzi,
Mon. Rav. III, n. LXXXI (1280, robbery); Colini-Baldeschi, *Cingoli*, d. xx (1300: murder),
Lombardini, *Sezze*, p. 147 (1301, murder).

towns, rents doubled when the papal court came into residence.[1] Rome
had more room, but the presence of the court and its many visitors must
have yielded a living to a multitude of shop-keepers, inn-keepers,
money-lenders and others. In particular the bankers were dependent
largely on loans to the pope and other prelates, especially those who had
come from far to do business with the court and lacked the money to
secure an expeditious hearing — or any hearing at all.[2] Thus there were
large and important elements in the Roman community which could
not afford to alienate the pope's sympathies. There was in fact a certain
common interest. Rome needed the pope and the pope needed Rome,
and hence it was often possible to attain a *modus vivendi* delimiting the
city's independence which was satisfactory to both.

Southern Latium, the papal province of Campagna-Marittima, was
a zone which at times came under the shadow of Rome's dominance,
though the papacy had long before exerted influence here, only for this
to be in turn effaced by imperial occupation in the last decade of the
twelfth century. Through this province ran the Via Appia, the Via
Labicana and the Via Prenestina, each crossing the Alban hills till it
entered the Regno some fifty miles away to the south-east. The region
was much the most strongly feudalized part of the Papal State.[3] Innocent's own family, the counts of Segni, held lands on and near the Via
Labicana, at Valmontone and closer to Rome and near Ferentino and
Anagni.[4] The more northerly Via Palestrina was dominated by the
Colonna, centred on Palestrina and around Gallicano and Olevano,
with other isolated lands further to the north, in Sabina.[5] South of the
Via Labicana the great and rising power was the house of Ceccano,
whose lord in Innocent's time could raise over four hundred horsemen,
and who inflicted defeats on the Colonna and his other neighbour,
Thomas of Supino.[6] He had much land round Ceccano itself and dominated the nearby town of Sezze. His territory spread far in the direction
of Piperno and Ninfa towards Rome, and in the north to Frosinone and

[1] Pinzi, *Viterbo*, II, 59n.

[2] For Roman bankers *v.* Brezzi, pp. 489–90: for their loans to popes and to visitors to the
Curia, P.L. 215, cols. 298–300; Potthast, n. 5779; *Chronicon Abbatiae de Evesham* (R.S.),
pp. 184 ff. (1206). Soon after this period Roman bankers were to be found at the Cham-
pagne fairs (*Reg. G. IX*, nn. 538, 1639–44, 1760–2, 2490–7, 3223).

[3] See G. Tomassetti, *La Campagna Romana*, vol. I, and his 'Feudalesimo Romano' in
Riv. Int. d. Sc. Sociali, VI (1894); Falco, 'I comuni della Campagna', *ASRSP*, XLII,
XLVIII–XLIX; Marchetti-Longhi, 'La carta feudale del Lazio', *QFIA*, XXXVI.

[4] Gregorovius, V, 1, 5–6; Maccarone, 'Innocenzo III prima del pontificato', *ASRSP*,
LXVI; Marchetti-Longhi, 'Ricerche sulla famiglia di papa Gregorio IX', *ASRSP*, LXVII.
See Map.

[5] Neumann, pp. 48–59.

[6] Gregorovius, V, 1, 57–8; see in particular *Annales Ceccanenses* (MGH, XIX 301–

Alatri. Quite separate from these baronial spheres of influence lay the zone of the Frangipani, on the Tyrrhenian coast between Astura and Terracina. A host of minor families, many of them inter-related and related to the great baronial houses, were also powers to be reckoned with in the province. They included the Papareschi or Mattia of Anagni (Gregory IX's family), the Annibaldi,[1] one of whom married a sister of Innocent III, the Rossi and the Montelungo, relatives respectively of Alexander IV and Innocent III, the lords of Supino, and the Caetani.

Despite the strength of the landed aristocracy, some of the towns of southern Latium had by the end of the twelfth century achieved a considerable degree of independence.[2] Of these, Terracina was the most economically advanced, with some traders residing in its port,[3] which served an agricultural hinterland; the commune, however, lay under the shadow of the Frangipani. Anagni on the Via Labicana, and Veroli and Alatri on the hills to the north of that road, were organized as communes in the twelfth century,[4] but the other towns, Ferentino on the Labicana, and Velletri, Sezze, Piperno and Segni to the south, were all much under the influence of baronial families who tended to monopolize the *podestà*-ship.

Like their predecessors, the popes of the thirteenth century attempted to place their control of the Campagna-Marittima on a territorial basis, the strengthening of which was with many of them a leading preoccupation, and with Boniface VIII almost a form of megalomania. Far less effort was made to rule the area through the machinery of provincial administration, probably because it was not a wealthy zone and could offer little to the tax-gatherer. Its importance was strategic, for it commanded the southern approaches to Rome and the frontier with the Regno.

To the north of Rome the Anti-Apennines present the same type of volcanic scenery. The Tuscan Patrimony was for the most part plateau land, broken here and there by lakes and gorges, with many excellent sites for castles and defensible villages. Some of the lower ground, however, was marshy and malarial. This was true of the Chiana and Paglia valleys, probably of the Tiber above the point where it was swelled by the waters of the Nera, and above all of the coastal zone. A little later

---

[1] See F. Savio, 'Gli Annibaldi di Roma nel sec. XIII', *Studi e Documenti di Storia e Diritto*, XVII (1896).

[2] See Falco's work cited above, p. 81, n. 3.

[3] There were foreign merchants at Terracina in the twelfth century: for native merchants in 1223, *Reg. Hon. III*, nn. 4465–6.

[4] Veroli had consuls as early as 1134.

Giovanni Villani remarked that 'in ancient times the coastal areas were well populated and though there was not a big population inland, in the Maremma and the Marittima towards Rome on the Campagna coast there were many cities and places which have now decayed and disappeared through the corruption of the air'.[1] There were, however, important wheat-growing areas, especially in the north, and, as in the Campagna, parts famous for their vines: one thirteenth-century rector of the Tuscan Patrimony remembered the province as 'fertile but having pestilential air'.[2]

Five principal roads ran out of Rome to the north and east, passing through either the Sabina or the Tuscan Patrimony.[3] The most easterly of these was the Tiburtino-Valeria, running through Tivoli, and soon entering the Regno. Next to this, to the north, the Via Salaria crossed the bare Sabine uplands to Rieti and led thence to Ascoli Piceno and the mouth of the Tronto, on the Marche coast. The Via Flaminia, the main route to the northern part of the March and the Romagnol coast, drove north to Otricoli and Narni. Thence there were alternative routes to Nocera in the Apennines, one passing through Terni, Spoleto, Trevi and Foligno, the other through Carsoli and Bevagna. The Via Amerina, running closer to the Tiber, linked Rome with Perugia, via a number of towns of some importance, Nepi, Orte, Amelia, Todi and Bettona. Further west the Via Cassia led into Tuscany through Viterbo, Montefiascone, Bolsena and Acquapendente.

The area immediately to the north of Rome resembled the Campagna in being periodically the victim of Rome's dreams of expansion, and in the strong hold of baronial families. The Roman prefects, the lords of Vico, controlled the zone of Lake Bracciano, with Vico, Cimino and, frequently, Civitavecchia. Further north and east were the counts of Anguillara and, around Vetralla, the Normanni. Powerful in the Sabina, an area of few towns, were the Orsini and Savelli.[4] Civita Castellana on the Via Flaminia and Nepi and Sutri (once Roman outposts against the Etruscans), respectively on the Via Amerina and the ancient Via Ciminia, were the only places of any size between Rome

---

[1] G. Villani, *Cronica*, Bk. I, ch. 50.

[2] Durand, *Speculum Iuris*, IV, pt. 1 (De lib. concept. § 14, n. 11). For the exportation of grain from this area, through Corneto, to Genoa, and the consequent presence of traders from Corneto, Orvieto and Toscanella at Genoa, *v.* V. Vitale, *Il Comune del Podestà a Genova*, pp. 87, 391, 397–9.

[3] On the Roman road system, *v.* A. von Hofmann, *Das Land Italien und seine Geschichte*, *passim*.

[4] On the lands of the Orsini, *v.* De Cupis, especially in vol. XIV, 235–88; on the Prefects of Vico, Calisse, *I Prefetti di Vico*; on the Anguillara, V. Sora, 'I conti di Anguillara', *ASRSP*, XXIX.

and Viterbo, if one excepts Civitavecchia and Corneto, both far away to the west on the coast. Civitavecchia[1] was later to have an artificial harbour and to see Stendhal as the consular representative of Louis-Philippe's France. It had in the twelfth century been attacked by Pisan galleys and sheltered the ships of Genoa and of Richard I of England, and in 1217 it was to perform the same service for Frisian crusaders. Yet it had achieved no firm municipal organization, and in the 1220s was to fall for a time under the domination of nearby Corneto, an expanding commercial centre.

Viterbo, forty miles north of Rome, marks the boundary of the area of larger towns, and of the zone which had for some decades been under firm Hohenstaufen rule: here it was that a revolt had broken out against Philip of Swabia on the news of Henry VI's death. Viterbo[2] itself was a firmly organized commune in the twelfth century, which had already experienced internal class struggles, had expanded over a large *contado* and in doing so had come into conflict with its neighbours, Corneto, Orvieto and Toscanella. Further north Orvieto[3] dominated the bridge over the Paglia from an impregnable volcanic rock. It had existed as a commune since the mid-twelfth century and by the early thirteenth had a sphere of influence which spread far in each direction except to the east, where it bounded with Todi's territory near the Tiber. Like Viterbo, it was a trading centre of some importance. Narni, Terni and Todi, the other three main towns of this region, had already started on a struggle for domination in the area to the east of the middle Tiber. Narni, once a strategically-sited colony of Rome, overlooked the bridge where the Via Flaminia crossed the Nera, and Terni a similar crossing in a wider part of the valley a few miles to the north-east. Todi,[4] yet another prominent town in classical times, was situated high above the Tiber on the Via Amerina: it had had consuls since the previous century and it also was already a prey to factional struggles.

To the west lay the wide *contado* of the Aldobrandeschi counts, extending from Montalto in the south to modern Tuscany in the north, and inland almost to Lake Bolsena. All between here and the Apennine uplands of the Sabina was a land of towns, not indeed of great commercial centres, but communes which coveted *contadi* including valuable grain-producing areas and were prepared to fight tenaciously for the inheritance of Hohenstaufen rule.

Northern Umbria came into another province, the Duchy of Spoleto.

[1] Calisse, *Storia di Civitavecchia*.   [2] Pinzi, *Storia di Viterbo*.
[3] Waley, *Mediaeval Orvieto*.   [4] Ceci, *Todi nel Medio Evo*.

The valley of Spoleto or Valtopino — both phrases are used in the thirteenth century — is a wide and clearly-marked depression, which had once been a lake, but was now drained by the river Topino: running from north to south, it divides the Apennines to the east from the lower sub-Apennine range in the western part of the province. Of the principal towns of the Duchy, Perugia, Assisi and Spoleto all dominate this valley from hills lying to its east, while Foligno is down in the valley itself at the road-junction where the Val di Chienti pass into the southern March links with the Via Flaminia. This road followed the plain between Spoleto and Foligno before climbing into the Apennines. Nocera and Gualdo lay on the Apennine stretch of the road and Gubbio high up in an isolated position away to the west of it.

For two decades this province had had a new unity imposed on it by the rule of Duke Conrad of Urslingen as duke of Spoleto, count of Assisi and count of Nocera.[1] Duke Conrad's control had been exercised largely through the occupation of a few strong fortresses, such as Assisi, Nocera and Cesi.[2] Some of the more powerful towns, such as Spoleto, Gubbio and Foligno, had been allowed to retain their *contadi* and a considerable measure of self-rule. Both the traditions of this period and the existence of communal institutions were bound to make them formidable subjects when lordship over the duchy passed to the papacy.

Perugia[3] on the Via Amerina, once an Etruscan city, was probably the most populous and wealthy town of the Papal State apart from Rome, before the acquisition of Bologna. It had had its own consuls since the early twelfth century and at the same period began an active and successful expansionist policy. Much of its *contado* lay around Lake Trasimene and to the south-west, but it had gained the submission in Barbarossa's time of Città di Castello and Gubbio in the north. Although these towns proved too strong to hold, and both acquired independent communal institutions, new acquisitions — Nocera in 1202, Gualdo Tadino in 1208 — followed the death of Henry VI, and by the Perugians this period was probably remembered rather for the gains during the disputed imperial succession than for the transfer to papal suzerainty. The ground thus won along the Via Flaminia was held with great tenacity and considerable success. In every way Perugia was a

---

[1] Ficker, *Forschungen*, II, § 316.

[2] Cesi lies away to the south in the 'Terra Arnulforum' above the Nera valley.

[3] W. Heywood, *A History of Perugia*. In the later thirteenth century (1285), Perugia had 5,529 'hearths', which probably implies a population of *c.*30,000: *v.* G. Mira, 'Il fabbisogno di cereali in Perugia e nel suo contado nei sec. XIII–XIV', *Studi in onore di A. Sapori*, I, 507–17.

fully-evolved commune of the type that flourished in Tuscany. A privilege of Henry VI (1186) had placed it on the same footing as the Tuscan cities and it had lain outside the control of Duke Conrad, coming in 1195–7 under that of Philip of Swabia, the 'duke of Tuscany'.[1] As early as 1177 Perugia had had a *podestà*. Its noble class was organized as a body in Henry VI's time and in the thirteenth century there was frequent internal strife, in which the papacy often became involved as arbiter.[2] The merchant class had its own *societas* and Perugia was a financial and commercial centre of some importance. Soon after the middle of the century it was to make a precocious, though unsuccessful, appearance among the towns striking gold coins, and a little later its bankers helped in financing the Angevin conquest of the south.[3]

Nearby Assisi was rather smaller, with a population early in the thirteenth century of about ten thousand. It also had its merchants, among them the cloth-dealer Bernardone who was father of St. Francis, and at the time of his son's birth (c. 1182) had been absent at the French fairs.[4] Here too there was class-warfare, for it was the popular element that after Henry VI's death stormed and destroyed the imperial fortress overlooking the town, while the nobles went into exile and secured the assistance of Perugia in a war of revenge. Imperial domination had probably prevented the existence of a commune, but as far back as the eleventh century Assisi's populace had been organized in opposition to its bishop,[5] and there was all the material for the pursuit of a policy of municipal independence. Foligno had a commune with a *podestà* by the first year of Innocent III's pontificate. This was another trading centre, where St. Francis came 'as was his custom', to sell his horse and his share of the cloth in his father's warehouse before abandoning his home.[6] Spoleto had been the seat of a Lombard duke from the seventh century. Its powerful fortress overlooked from the south the valley

---

[1] Ficker, *Forschungen*, II, § 314–15. The Hohenstaufen seem always to have regarded Perugia and Città di Castello as parts of Tuscany. The Perugian *contado* to the east of the Tiber, however, probably came under the duke of Spoleto.

[2] E.g. *Reg. Hon. III*, nn. 4513, 4579 (1223: in this year the Perugian nobles had joined with Città di Castello in fighting their own *popolani*, v. BFW, n. 12864).

[3] Lopez in *Econ. Hist. Rev.*, 2nd. s., IX (1956), 231; *Reg. Cl. IV*, n. 1461. For Perugian merchants at Genoa in the early thirteenth century, Vitale, *Comune del Podestà a Genova*, pp. 397–9.

[4] Sabatier, *Vie de Saint François d'Assise*, pp. 2–3; G. Pagliacci, 'Fonti archivistiche per una storia economica di Assisi', *Annali della Facoltà di Scienze politiche economiche e commerciali dell' Università degli studi di Perugia*, N.S., 4 (1955–6), 581–608 (Assisi's 2,225 'hearths' in 1232): on Assisi in general, v. Cristofani, *Delle Storie di Assisi*.

[5] H. C. Peyer, *Stadt und Stadtpatron im mittelalterlichen Italien*, pp. 31–2.

[6] Thomas of Celano, *Vita Prima S. Francisci*, § 8.

to which it gave its name and to which it held the strategic key. It had been organized as a commune since 1178 at least (possibly since the preceding century) and by Innocent's time had brought into subjection Norcia to the east in the upper Apennine, while it contested with its neighbour Foligno the smaller towns of the southern plain.[1] This rivalry between the towns was both an advantage and a disadvantage to the papacy; it meant that there was little chance of united opposition, yet it involved almost continuous warfare and sharpened each commune's awareness of its individuality and hastened its institutional development.

The March of Ancona, the Adriatic province lying east of the main Apennine ridge, was often reproached by popes as 'the fickle March'. Many of its towns did indeed turn imperialist at times in the thirteenth century, but this was merely because it lay open to Hohenstaufen invasion as the natural corridor between the Regno and the imperial lands of northern Italy. More penetratingly the March was described as the *provincia castellorum*. It is a characteristically central Italian land, its scenery a broad view of high hill-top towns, most of them not at all large. Often these are situated on the tops of the spurs, overlooking the eroded valleys around; the setting of Urbino and of Macerata is typical of this country. Some of the larger towns are on the sea, and Ancona has the best natural harbour in central Italy, but many lie on or near the main inland road, running from north to south through Macerata and Ascoli. The zone had been much divided and entrusted by the Hohenstaufen to local counts in the twelfth century: not until 1195 had the province been united under the rule of Markward of Anweiler.[2]

The March was an area of considerable agricultural wealth, trading in the thirteenth-century grain, wine, oil, cheese, salted meat and figs, with the adjoining parts of northern Italy, in particular Romagna, Lombardy and Venetia.[3] Its grain was purchased at Florence, at Ravenna, Rimini, Cervia, and Venice, and as far afield as Verona and even Genoa. The wine of the March was the principal drink of the Venetians and travelled also to the Friuli and up the Po valley to Ferrara and into Lombardy. The same areas drew on the March for their olive oil. Much of this trade was conducted by sea and river, and there was also commerce, at least as early as the twelfth century, between the Italian ports and those of the eastern shore of the Adriatic and,

---

[1] Sansi, *Storia del Comune di Spoleto*.   [2] Ficker, *Forschungen*, II, § 317–19.
[3] Luzzatto in *Nuovo Arch. Veneto*, N.S., XI (1906), 23–42.

in the case of Ancona, with the eastern Mediterranean. For all this active trade, the towns were for the most part nuclei of agriculturalists, with a handful of merchants but very little industry.[1] Already in the twelfth century the population of some towns was divided into *maiores* and *minores*; the former, the dominating element, was composed of a small class of land-owning nobles.[2]

Several coastal towns had been organized as communes and had expanded their influence into the country-side before the middle of the twelfth century; as early as 1141 this expansion had brought Fano into conflict with Pesaro and Senigallia, its neighbours to north and south. Fano had already emerged as a trading port of some standing by Innocent III's time, having a formal treaty to regulate commercial dealings with Split on the Dalmatian shore, and possessing like Pesaro that sure indication of economic activity, a Jewish community.[3] Senigallia was a place of comparable importance and housed Venetian merchants.[4] Ancona was the only port of the March that could challenge Venice's Adriatic supremacy, and more than once it was to suffer for its pretensions.[5] In the twelfth century its merchants traded already with Egypt and Constantinople, where they formed an organized colony, with their own consuls and church.[6] Ancona played a big part in shipping to the east the participants in the Fifth Crusade in Honorius III's time and continued to trade with the kingdom of Jerusalem through Acre.[7] The Anconitans also had less ambitious trading links across the Adriatic, with Trogir, Zadar and Durazzo, with the Regno ports, and with Pisa and Genoa.[8] Numana, a little to the south of Ancona, had been a flourishing port as early as 1126, but it probably ranked with Porto

[1] There seems to be no evidence of the existence of a paper-making industry at Fabriano before the early fourteenth century.

[2] See Luzzatto's brilliant article on the towns of the March, *Le Marche*, VI (1906), 114–45.

[3] Amiani, *Fano*, II, xxii–xxiii: C. Roth, *History of the Jews of Italy*, pp. 118–19.

[4] Gianandrea, *Iesi*, p. 18 and d. CLIX (1256, the port dues of Senigallia valued at 2,200 *l.* p.a.). Morozzo della Rocca and Lombardo, *Documenti del Commercio Veneziano nei sec. XI–XIII*, II, 196–7.

[5] Luzzatto, art. cited above p. 87, n. 3, 34–40: for the war between Venice and Ancona *c.* 1274–8 see below, p. 184: for that of *c.* 1290, *Reg. N. IV*, nn. 7308, 7310.

[6] Luzzatto, *art. cit.*: Heyd, *Hist. du Commerce du Levant au Moyen-Age*, I, 262 and 418–19.

[7] Theiner, *Vet. Mon. Slav. Merid.*, p. 69: Sabatier, *Vie de St. François*, pp. 258–9: Heyd, I, 157–8: *Reg. Inn. IV*, nn. 1404–6.

[8] Saracini, *Ancona*, pp. 172–3 and 175–6 (Trogir = Trau, Zadar = Zara): *Reg. Inn. IV*, n. 2861 (Durazzo): Heyd, I 237 and Herlihy, *Pisa in the early Renaissance*, p. 62 (Pisan merchants at Ancona): BFW, n. 12314 (trading agreement with Genoa, 1208). Material relating to Ancona's trade with the ports of the Regno dates from the late thirteenth century (Davidsohn, *Forschungen*, III, dd. 326, 371, 396), but its existence earlier is suggested by Venetians trading between the two areas (Morozzo della Rocca and Lombardo, I, 440–1, and II, 59).

Recanati, Civitanova and Porto S. Giorgio rather than with the four large ports in the northern part of the province.[1]

Fermo was the most powerful of the inland cities, indeed it was probably the largest town of the province. It had possessed consuls since the later twelfth century and was the recipient of privileges from all who sought power in the March; Otto IV offered it jurisdiction over the entire littoral from the Regno frontier to the mouth of the Potenza, near Recanati.[2] Its trade may well have been mainly in the hands of Venetians,[3] who, though they tended in the course of the thirteenth century to be ousted by Florentines, were still with the Jews the typical merchants and financiers of the March. Iesi was another inland town of some importance, which had been organized as a commune and had gained submissions in the late twelfth century. In Innocent III's time it was expanding further at the expense of neighbouring feudatories, fighting Ancona, its rival in the coastal part of the Esino valley, and winning territory from Senigallia.[4] Osimo, Recanati and Ascoli Piceno were towns of comparable size, and Macerata was growing to the position of importance which was to earn it a diocese and a university later in the century: it had its Florentine merchants and the *catasto* of 1268 suggests a population then of about ten thousand, most of them small land-owning families.[5] Further inland still, situated on Apennine passes, were other towns of some importance, Fabriano, which was also expanding rapidly in Innocent III's time, Matelica and Camerino.[6]

Of the smaller towns, some had scarcely emerged from the tutelage of a feudal lord, while even Urbino was under the domination of the counts of Montefeltro, and Camerino fell early to the lords of Varano. Yet the number of small independent towns is very striking, for the communes of the March were rarely strong enough to assert a lasting supremacy over a very wide area. By the end of the thirteenth century

[1] Colini-Baldeschi, *Osimo*, d. I (Numana): Leopardi, *Recanati*, II, d. 1: Marangoni *Civitanova*, pp. 263–4: De Minicis, *Fermo*, pp. 383–4 (Porto S. Giorgio).

[2] Ficker, *Forschungen*, II, § 318: BFW, n. 452.

[3] E.g. Morozzo della Rocca and Lombardo, II, 361. For Fermo's trade see also Hagemann, 'Le lettere originali dei dogi R. Zeno e L. Tiepolo conservate nell' Arch. Dipl. di Fermo', *Studia Picena*, XXV, 87–111, and 'Un Trattato del 1225 tra Fermo e Termoli finora sconosciuto' in *Studi in Onore di R. Filangieri*, I, 175–88.

[4] Hagemann in *QFIA*, XXXVI, 138–55.

[5] Davidsohn, *Forschungen*, III, d. 29: Foglietti, *Il catasto di Macerata dell' anno 1268* (of c. 1,500 property-owners recorded, only 41 owned property to the value of over 200 *l. p.a.*; about half of them held property valued at under 20 *l. p.a.*).

[6] For Fabriano, *v.* Zonghi, *Fabriano*, and Hagemann in *QFIA*, XXX and XXXII. For Matelica's Florentine and Jewish communities in the second half of the century, *v.* Luzzatto, 'I prestiti . . .', *Le Marche*, VII (1907), 249–72. For Jews at Montolmo at this time, Corridonia, AC, perg. n. 30b and Macerata, AC, perg. n. 103; for Jews at Macerata, *ibid.*, 161 (Intr. Ex. 1291), f. 1v; for Jews at Camerino, Santoni, 'Camerino', p. 60.

there were probably between one and two hundred towns in this province organized as communes.[1] This was a great contrast with the rest of the State, for the Tuscan Patrimony, the province which almost certainly had the next greatest number of towns, called under fifty communes to its parliaments in the late thirteenth century.[2] After the unsuccessful, but perhaps unavoidable, experiment of granting the March as a fief to the Estensi, the popes were to find this area of many towns the most profitable — though not the most law-abiding — of their provinces.

[1] The calculation is not easy to make. The thirty or so towns receiving privileges in 1290–1 (*v.* ch. VI) excluded the larger cities and many of the smaller communes. The *Touring Club Italiano* guide to the Marche lists some 240 places in that province: few of these are post-medieval and probably over half of them achieved communal institutions in the thirteenth century. The archival wealth of these villages, many of which have now under a thousand inhabitants, may be gauged from the 31 volumes of Colucci's *Antichità Picene* and from Filippini and Luzzatto, 'Archivi Marchigiani', *AMSM*, N.S., VII (1911–1912). 246 archives are recorded in *Gli Archivi Storici dei Comuni delle Marche* (Quaderni della Rassegna degli Archivi di Stato, n. 6), Rome, 1960.

[2] *V. inf.,* p. 113.

IV

The Institutions of the Papal State

The structure of the government set up by Innocent III in central Italy was provincial. To the provinces of the Campagna and Sabina, which were already in existence, he added three main provinces, the Patrimony of St. Peter in Tuscany, the Duchy of Spoleto and the March of Ancona. Innocent also appointed a rector in the Massa Trabaria, thus conferring on that small region a similar status. From 1278 the Romagna was added on its acquisition by Nicholas III, as the fifth major province. The small county of Sabina only intermittently attained administrative separateness; in the fourteenth century it was absorbed into the Tuscan Patrimony. It cannot be ranked with the major provinces, and among these the Campagna — normally called from Innocent III's time 'Campagna and Marittima'[1] — did not develop the same governmental energies as the others since the area was dominated by powerful feudatories.

This southernmost province, the Campagna and Marittima, had one boundary which to the south and east was that (in part following the river Liri) dividing the papal lands from the Regno. In the north it included Poli, Trevi, Alatri and Veroli, but from Tivoli to the sea the effective frontier was the limit of the zone controlled by the city of Rome. There was thus no *de facto* border with the provinces lying to the north, Sabina and the Tuscan Patrimony, though if a *de iure* frontier was ever defined it presumably allotted to the Campagna-Marittima the papal territories south of Rome.

Whereas the Campagna-Marittima had had a sporadic previous existence, though no administrative continuity, the Patrimony in Tuscany was a province created by Innocent III early in his pontificate to take in the lands to the north of Rome which had been disputed with the Empire in the previous decades, occupied by Henry VI, and now regained.[2] Its southern boundary was the undefined limit of Rome's sphere of influence, its western the Tyrrhenian. Its northern frontier was

---

[1] The province was occasionally called 'Campagna' (e.g. *Reg. Hon. III*, nn. 394, 397).
[2] See above, pp. 14, 18, 27, 30.

marked by the fortress of Radicofani from 1209, when Innocent secured imperial recognition for the addition to the State of the area between Acquapendente and Radicofani. It included the towns which had in Henry VI's time been governed by his brother Philip as Duke of Tuscany: these strong positions in the southern zone of classical Etruria were Orvieto, Bagnorea, Orte and Montefiascone, Viterbo, Toscanella, Civita Castellana, Vetralla, Sutri and Nepi towards Rome, with Corneto and Civitavecchia away to the west on the sea. In Innocent III's time it also included Narni and Amelia to the east of the Tiber, but the more normal course of an undefined and often altered boundary ran near the river itself, with the Duchy of Spoleto on the other bank in the north, and further south, around Farfa, the county of Sabina.[1]

The Duchy was no new creation, but an administrative zone inherited from the imperialist government of Conrad of Urslingen. As defined in 1198, when its first papal rector was appointed, it included the dioceses of Spoleto, Rieti, Foligno, Assisi, Gubbio, Perugia, Città di Castello and Todi.[2] Its western boundary thus took in some territory on the right bank of the Tiber, including the *dominio* of Perugia. In the north it included at times Città di Castello. From this extremity there was a frontier with the March of Ancona, running some way to the east, south of Cagli, then southwards along the spur of the Apennines to include Nocera and Norcia, but excluding Matelica, Fabriano and most of its subject lands, and Camerino. This frontier bounded with the northern limit of the Regno south of the Via Salaria, near the headwaters of the Tronto, and thence ran west, including Rieti at some periods but excluding the county of Sabina between that city and the Tiber.

The March of Ancona was an elongated region situated between the Apennine ridge and the Adriatic. Like the Duchy, it had been an imperial area of administration under Henry VI, and was treated as an entity by both Celestine III and Innocent III. Its southern boundary, with the Regno, was demarcated by the river Tronto and the southern frontier of Ascoli's *contado*. Its eastern limit was a hundred miles of seacoast, but its northern boundary, with the Romagna, starting near the mouth of the Conca between Pesaro and Rimini, was no more than a quarter of this length. Here it normally ran to the north of Urbino, and took in Cagli, high in the Apennines, whence the province marched

---

[1] P.L., 214, *Reg. Inn. III*, II, nn. 202–3. For the administrative 'no man's land' east of the upper Tiber, *v.* below, p. 94–5. The sources used for evidence concerning provincial boundaries are so numerous that no attempt has been made to list them all.

[2] *Ibid.*, I, n. 366 and *Gesta*, cols. xxv–xxvi.

with the Duchy along the central spine in a boundary that was also about a hundred miles in length.

From the pontificate of Nicholas III there was a fifth major province, the Romagna, having a short common frontier with the March to the south of Rimini and comprising the towns on the Via Emilia from Bologna to the sea, with territories extending into the hills to their south, together with Ravenna and Cervia on the Adriatic. This province had the spheres of influence of Arezzo and Florence as its southerly neighbours, with Modena on its eastern flank and Ferrara to the north. It also had formed a zone of imperialist administration.[1]

The county of Sabina, the most important of the small provinces — it would be more convenient to style them sub-provinces, for they were far smaller in size than the others and were often placed under the government of their rectors[2] — has already been mentioned. It was almost entirely papal domain, but contained no town of importance, and only two of its villages, Magliano and Montasola could raise an annual *census* of over six pounds.[3] It comprised an area of some four hundred square miles to the east of the Tiber, adjoining the territories of Narni and Terni to the north and Rieti in the east. Its boundaries appear to have been those of the diocese of Sabina.

The Massa Trabaria, another sub-province, was a small zone situated around S. Angelo in Vado and Mercatello, in the mountains to the east of the upper Tiber valley above Città di Castello.[4] This region, at the junction of Romagna, the March and Tuscany, where the pass of the Bocca Trabaria crosses the Apennines, derived its administrative unity at least in part from a common obligation to provide timber for the basilica of St. Peter in Rome. A papal outpost, it marched with Montefeltro, S. Agata and Sarsina to the north, Pesaro and Urbino to the east, Città di Castello and Borgo S. Sepolcro to the south and Arezzo in the west. Massa Trabaria had its own papal rector as early as 1205, but later in the century it was frequently placed under the jurisdiction of the rector of the March or (after 1278) the Romagna.

The county of Urbino seems only to have had a rector of its own for a few years under Boniface VIII and cannot be ranked as normally constituting a province; it was treated as a separate entity and commonly

---

[1] For a fuller treatment of Romagna see below, pp. 193 ff.

[2] For Sabina under the rector of the Tuscan Patrimony *v. Reg. Alex. IV*, n. 12 (1254), under the rector of the Duchy *v. Reg. N. IV*, n. 7316 (1291).

[3] *Lib. Cens.*, I, 377–8. For the boundaries of the diocese and county of Sabina see the map in G. Battelli, *Rationes Decimarum Italiae: Latium* (Studi e Testi, vol. 128).

[4] There is an excellent monograph by T. Codignola, 'Ricerche storico-giuridiche sulla Massa Trabaria nel XIII secolo' in *ASI*, XCVII–XCVIII (1939–40).

placed under the rector of the March, though at others it was under the rector of Romagna.[1] Various other regions are mentioned in rectors' letters of appointment in terms which suggest the survival of at least a tradition of entity, yet none can rank as papal provinces. These include the 'Terra Arnulforum', an area of papal domain lying around Cesi, to the west of Spoleto, and the former counties of Assisi and Nocera, now also incorporated in the Duchy.[2] The 'Terrae S. Agathae', adjoining Urbino and Massa Trabaria, composed part of the March, and the county of Bertinoro, donated to the papacy by its lords in the twelfth century, was part of Romagna.

A picture which presented the papal provinces as having fixed and definite frontiers would be misleading, for the very concept of a territorial boundary is an anachronism in a society where the suzerain was overlord of communes and lords, lay and ecclesiastical, who themselves in turn claimed lordship over lands which were often interspersed with those of their neighbours, and whose zone of influence ebbed and flowed with the fortunes of war, inheritance and purchase. These frontiers must therefore be visualized as ragged edges. In the north and south the frontiers between papal and imperial territory, giving the pope the lands 'from Radicofani to the bridge of Ceprano' and on the Adriatic from the Tronto to the Conca and later Ravenna, were well defined by the standards of the age, but the boundaries of the provinces themselves were the prey of continuous experiments and expedients. The most striking instance of this is provided by the towns to the east of the upper and central Tiber. Rieti, regarded in 1198 as part of the Duchy of Spoleto, was for most of the thirteenth century treated as an independent area which could be allotted to the rector of any neighbouring province, though in its last two decades it was normally joined to the Tuscan Patrimony.[3] Narni and Terni, situated further north, were allotted by Innocent III neither to the Patrimony nor Duchy, but by 1220 both were part of the Duchy; this arrangement had ended by 1264, and before the end of the century Narni was normally under the rector of the Tuscan Patrimony and Terni with the county of Sabina.[4]

[1] In 1283 this county was transferred from the March to Romagna (*Reg. M. IV*, n. 472 nn) but five years later Nicholas IV ordered that it should be permanently joined to the March (*Reg. N. IV*, nn. 7087–8). *V.* also *Reg. B. VIII*, nn. 3575–6, 4026–7, 4615–16, 5212–14.

[2] For the county of Nocera as a temporary administrative sub-region of the Duchy see below, p. 109.

[3] *Reg. Hon. III*, n. 6203; *Reg. Urb. IV*, II, n. 631; Pinzi, *Viterbo*, II, 434–5; *Reg. N. IV*, nn. 7501–6; *MAH*, VII, 180–4.

[4] P.L., 214, *Reg. Inn. III*, II, n. 202; *Reg. Hon. III*, n. 3110; *Reg. G. IX*, n. 495; *Reg. Urb. IV*, II, n. 631; Theiner, d. CCCCXLIII: *MAH*, VII, 180–4.

Todi, originally in the Duchy, was for a time with the Patrimony, then with the Duchy again; between 1272 and 1295 it struggled to obtain recognition of its independence of the rector of the Patrimony, won its case in the latter year, but in 1298–9 still appeared on the rector's lists as a city owing him taxes and *parlamentum*.[1] Perugia, which lies to the west of the Tiber and had been administered by the Hohenstaufen as part of Tuscany, was normally allotted to the Duchy, but in 1227 was joined to the zone in southern Tuscany granted to King John of Brienne.[2] Città di Castello was in the Duchy in 1198, under the rector of the Patrimony in 1273, and later in the century normally allotted to the March.[3]

In times of crisis the whole provincial system was put aside, while even under normal circumstances it was not unusual for a rector to be set over two adjoining provinces. In 1227 King John of Brienne was entrusted with 'the area from Radicofani to Rome', an enlarged Tuscan Patrimony, while three years later the bishop of Beauvais took over both the Patrimony and Duchy.[4] During the decade of Frederick II's threat to the Papal State, Cardinal Ranier acted as rector in the Patrimony, Duchy and March from 1244 until 1249, when he was succeeded by Cardinal Peter Capocci, who retained them, together with the provinces of Sabina and Campagna-Marittima, till 1252.[5] Similar measures were taken by Alexander IV, Urban IV and Clement IV in the time of Manfred's domination; the bishop-elect of Verona was rector of the Duchy and the March in 1261–4, after which the Cardinal-priest of St. Martin held these provinces with Massa Trabaria and the Tiber towns from Città di Castello to Rieti until 1268.[6] Under Boniface VIII William Durand combined the rectorship of the March with that of Romagna for several months in 1295–6 and Cardinal Napoleon Orsini those of the March and Duchy in 1300–1.[7]

The rectorship was the key institution which served to confer upon the province its identity, and the qualities of its holder determined to a

---

[1] P. L., 214, *Reg. Inn. III*, I, n. 366; *Reg. Hon. III*, n. 6203; *Reg. Urb. IV*, II, n. 631; *MAH*, cited above: for Todi's claim to exemption *v.* below, pp. 183 ff.

[2] Ficker, *Forschungen*, II, § 314; *Reg. Hon. III*, n. 6203.

[3] P.L., 214, *Reg. Inn. III*, I, n. 366; Todi, AC, perg. 20, etc.

[4] Below, p. 137.

[5] See lists in Appendix II. The bishop of Arezzo, nominal rector of the March in 1247–8, was presumably a subordinate of Cardinal Ranier. Later Innocent IV had a project for appointing three bishops as subordinate rectors of the Patrimony, the Duchy and the March, but this scheme was abandoned (*Reg. Inn. IV*, nn. 5277–8 and 5333).

[6] See Appendix II. The bishop of Osimo, rector of the March in 1267, was probably also a subordinate.

[7] Appendix II. I omit here the titular rectorate of Charles of Valois over several provinces from 1301 to 1302 or 1303.

considerable extent the success or failure of papal government. Innocent III early appointed rectors for the Duchy (1198), the Campagna (by January 1199) and the Patrimony (not later than October 1199), but the March had no rector in the period before its infeudation to the Marquis of Este in 1212.[1] Under both Innocent III and Honorius III the use of legates alternated with that of rectors. A series of legates represented Innocent in the March, while he employed legates in the Duchy in 1204, 1210 and 1215, virtually in the role of rectors, and the cardinal-deacon of S. Maria in Aquiro in 1198 and the cardinal-deacon of St. George *ad Velum Aureum* in 1199 were both legates and rectors.[2] Honorius III continued to appoint legates in the March, the Estensi acting as rectors during their tenure of that province. For a time in 1220 he used Pandulf, a papal notary and subdeacon, virtually as rector of the Duchy without conferring on him that title.[3] Later in the same year he appointed Cardinal Ranier as rector, and henceforth it became normal for each province to have its rector, the March being included from the time of the nomination of the bishop of Beauvais in 1230. After this it was by no means uncommon for the rectorship to be reinforced by legatine powers — these were held by Cardinal Ranier, Cardinal Peter Capocci, the cardinal-priest of St. Martin and the cardinal-deacon of S. Maria *in Porticu* (rector of the Patrimony in 1264), by Cardinal Napoleon Orsini, as well as by successive rectors of Massa Trabaria in 1217–26 — but with the exception of Cardinal Ranier's special rank as 'papal vicar', there was now a rector over each province.[4]

The rector was appointed by the pope *usque beneplacitum*, the appointment ending automatically with the pope's death.[5] Naturally, tenure could be confirmed by the succeeding pope. It is difficult to generalize about the duration of rectorates, but they rarely lasted less than one year or more than four. Cardinal Richard of S. Angelo held the Campagna and Marittima from 1240, or possibly a year or two

[1] Appendix II. It is possible that in 1199 the cardinal of S. Prisca bore the title of 'papal vicar' in the March (Colini-Baldeschi, *Osimo*, d. XXXIII).

[2] P.L., 214, xxii and (Reg.), Bk. I cols. 31–2; Bk. II, n. 4; III, cols. 910–12, 914–15, 936–8 and 940: P.L., 215, cols. 365–6 and 548–50: Theiner, *Vet. Mon. Slav. Merid.*, pp. 47, 53, 55: Fumi, *Orvieto*, dd. LXXXII and C: Amiani, *Fano*, II, xxv. For the use of legates in the Papal State at this period *v*. Zimmermann, *Legation*, especially pp. 142–68.

[3] *Reg. Hon. III*, nn. 811, 2551, 3110, 5092, etc.: Zimmermann, *Legation*, p. 93.

[4] As elsewhere in this chapter, references are only cited when not easily traceable in the Appendixes. For rectors of Massa Trabaria with legatine powers *v*. *Reg. Hon. III*, nn. 755, 1888, 6060, etc., and Zimmermann, *Legation*, pp. 157–60.

[5] On the rectorate *v*. Ermini, 'I rettori provinciali dello Stato della Chiesa', *RSDI*, IV. Very exceptionally an appointment might be made *pro interim*, an instance being that of the bishop of Arezzo to the rectorate of the March in 1240 for the period of his predecessor's stay at the Curia (*Reg. G. IX*, n. 5322).

earlier, until 1249; this seems to be the longest recorded tenure, while Cardinal Ranier ruled the other three main provinces for the last five years of the same period.[1] Papal letters informed the nominee and his future subjects of the appointment and enjoined these subjects to obedience. The formula normally employed in such letters gave the rector powers to 'order, arrange, dispose, ordain and do as you shall think best' (or 'whatever you consider best for the honour and convenience of the Church and the utility and prosperous state' of the faithful subjects of the province) and 'free and general power to compel any *contradictores* and rebels by spiritual and temporal compulsion (*districtio*)' — or, in the case of laymen, temporal compulsion only.[2] The pope usually stated that he would accept as valid all the rector's sentences against rebels. It was probably normal for the new rector to take a special form of oath, at least if he was at the Curia or near it at the time of his appointment. The oath sworn by three rectors in the time of Gregory X has survived;[3] for the most part this consists of conventional feudal formulae. The rector promises fealty to the pope and his legitimate successors, forswears any action that may do them harm, and promises to keep secrets and to prevent or reveal any conspiracy. He will retain and defend papal rights (*regalia*), particularly those in the province entrusted to him, and will rule that province 'well and faithfully, keeping justice in it and causing it to be kept by others to the best of my ability'. Within the province 'I shall not give, sell, lease, infeudate or in any way alienate the fortresses (*castra*), villages (*villas*), men, rights, jurisdictions, fiefs, or any other property or rights of the Church to anyone without the special order and permission of the lord pope'.[4]

---

[1] The Campagna-Marittima, as a comparatively unimportant province, lent itself to long tenures: Gregory 'de Romania' was rector there for at least six years (1225–31).

[2] Typical letters of appointment are *Reg. Inn. IV*, nn. 7775–6, *Reg. Alex. IV*, nn. 12–13, *Reg. Urb. IV*, II, nn. 308–9 and 875–8, and *Reg. B. VIII*, n. 5337 (which specifically appoints *usque beneplacitum*, this condition being implicit in the other letters). The original of the formulae translated above is 'concedentes tibi precipiendi, ordinandi, disponendi statuendi et faciendi sicut expedire videris' (or 'quicquid honori et commodo ecclesie et utilitati ac prospero statui fidelium . . . degentium expedire cognoveris') 'ac contradictores et rebelles quoslibet spirituali et temporali districtione' (or 'pena seu districtione temporali'), 'appellatione postposita, compescendi liberam potestatem . . . . Nos enim sententiam sive penam quam spiritualiter et temporaliter vite tuleris in rebelles ratam . . . observari'.

[3] *Lib. Cens.*, II, 72–3.

[4] The original of the central clauses of the oath reads: 'Papatum Romanum et regalia beati Petri que habet ubique et specialiter in ducatu' (etc., according to the province) 'predicto, adjutor ero ad retinendum et defendendum contra omnem hominem. Ducatum ipsum michi a prefato domino papa commissum bene et fideliter regam et in eo servabo justiciam et pro posse ab aliis faciam observari. Castra, villas, homines, jura, jurisdictiones, feuda seu quecumque bona vel jura ipsius ecclesie in ducatu predicto nemini dabo, vendam, locabo, infeudabo seu alias quocumque modo alienabo sine ipsius domini pape mandato et licentia speciali'.

H

He and his officials and familiars would accept no presents as bribes, exception being allowed for 'legitimate gifts of food and drink'. He recognized that his jurisdiction did not extend over the pope's own familiars, except by special order of the pope or his chamberlain. A later addition to the oath bound the rectors to hand over revenue entire to the provincial treasurer.[1] The only thirteenth-century evidence concerning the rectors' pay shows the rector of the March in 1279–80 receiving an annual salary of 3,240 *l.* (Ravenna currency) or 1,172 *l. tournois*, and a rector of Romagna *in temporalibus* three florins a day in 1289.[2] Under Benedict XI, in 1303–4, the normal salary was five florins a day, though the rectors of the March and Romagna now received eight and ten florins respectively, and the rector of the Sabina only one florin.[3] This salary and those of the other officials were paid from the provincial funds.[4]

The terms of appointment give little indication of the degree of independence of central control enjoyed by the provincial rectors, and this doubtless varied very greatly in practice. It must be assumed that the known letters from popes to rectors comprise only a small proportion of those actually written. The disappearance of the provincial archives means that such letters have only survived in copies sent to communes or through their registration in the papal chancery, and it was not the routine practice under most of the thirteenth-century popes to register such letters.[5] Nevertheless the letters that have survived make it evident that under normal circumstances the rector was left much to his own devices; it is perhaps significant that the only known collection of correspondence received by a rector — the fifty-five letters to the vicar of the Tuscan Patrimony preserved in Richard of Bury's letter-book — contains no letter from the pope.[6] Certainly there were exceptional times when a rector received frequent and detailed instructions. Between May 1265 and December 1266, at the time of the resumption of the March from Manfred after the battle of Benevento, Clement IV

---

[1] See below, p. 107.

[2] Palmieri, pp. 88, 96–7, 103: Tonduzzi, *Faenza*, p. 328 (a florin then being worth about 2 *l.* papal currency, this represents about half the amount of the March rector's salary).

[3] *Röm. Quartalschrift*, XVIII, 104.

[4] Palmieri, expenses, *passim*; *J Eccl H*, VI, 20.

[5] Much has been written about the registers of the thirteenth century popes, but little about criteria employed in registering. Prof. Fawtier says truly of the heads of the chancery (*Reg. B. VIII*, IV, c), 'leur idée de l'importance des lettres nous demeure inexplicable'. Many letters to provincial rectors were, however, registered during the pontificates of Clement IV, Nicholas IV and Boniface VIII.

[6] Richard de Bury, *Liber Epistolaris*, pp. 191–205. There is, however, one letter (n. 54) probably from the papal chamberlain. See below, p.121 n. 5.

wrote at least twenty-two letters to the cardinal of St. Martin, the rector of this province.[1] Probably a rector *in situ* normally received no written instructions, though the pope would occasionally inform him of grants made or other action taken in the province and perhaps ask him to investigate certain complaints or to act, normally as a result of a petition to the Curia. When Bertold Orsini took up the rectorship of Romagna in 1278 Nicholas III reiterated the condition that he could make no enfeoffments without consulting the pope,[2] and it seems likely that this was normally respected by rectors. The expenditure of money from their resources on matters necessary for the provincial government also lay within their responsibility,[3] though any surplus had to be paid to the papal chamber. Within the province there was naturally no constitutional check on the activities of the rector, though he called parliaments to grant taxes and on such occasions grievances could be, and were, voiced.[4] A unique charter of Annibaldo di Trasmondo, rector of the March in 1256, proclaims that he has forgiven certain towns and lords 'after taking counsel with our wise men' (*habito consilio sapientium nostrorum*),[5] but this action was entirely exceptional, and there was no body of provincial counsellors. Boniface VIII planned to compel the rector and other officials of the March to remain for ten days in the province after giving up office, so that they might be available to answer any charges of injustice or 'rapine', but this scheme was fated to remain ineffective.[6]

When the rector reached his province he would set about securing oaths of obedience from his subjects. In 1295 the rector of Romagna insisted that it was the duty of communes to send representatives to meet a newly-appointed rector at the first town that he visited within the province and to swear an oath of obedience to him on this occasion.[7]

---

[1] See below, pp. 178 ff. The letters are *Reg. Cl. IV*, nn. 888–9, 894, 907, 910–11, 940, 951, 1020, 1022, 1024, 1033, 1042, 1044, 1052, 1059, 1070, 1084, 1088, 1101, 1161 and *QFIA*, XXIX, 227. At the same period Clement wrote a number of letters to the rector of the Tuscan Patrimony (*Reg.*, nn. 900, 904, 909, 912, 921–2, 931–2, 953). Boniface VIII once claimed (*Reg.*, n. 5279) that absolution of a condemned commune by a provincial rector was invalid if it lacked papal consent, but this claim was exceptional and seems to have lacked a legal basis; it certainly contravened the spirit of the clause in rectorial letters of appointment whereby the pope agreed to accept the rector's judicial sentences (above, p. 97).

[2] *Reg. N. III*, nn. 305–8.

[3] One letter of appointment of a rector (*Reg. B. VIII*, nn. 5549–53) appears to imply that such powers were exceptional, but should probably be read as a permission to retain any surplus — and perhaps to dispense with the services of a provincial treasurer.

[4] Below, pp. 117 ff.

[5] Compagnoni, *Regg. Pic.*, pp. 121–3. The possibility that this formula refers to a provincial parliamentary assembly seems remote.

[6] Theiner, d. DLXXI: below p. 235.

[7] Fantuzzi, *Mon. Rav.*, III, n. LXXXXV (Ravenna was also to renew its oath whenever the rector visited Ravenna or a neighbouring town).

Such a demand was exceptional and was certainly not respected in this most turbulent of provinces. In the last two decades of the century, at least in Romagna, where provincial parliaments became a normal feature of papal government, it was common for the rector to hold a special parliamentary gathering at the start of his period of office. At this meeting, which included a banquet paid for by special procurations (*pro adventu novi rectoris*), the rector read his letters of appointment, received the fealty of his subjects, and published provincial constitutions. It may also be presumed that the rector would on such an occasion present his own policy and ask for counsel.[1]

No papal province had a formal 'capital' in the thirteenth century, but the extent to which the court was peripatetic varied considerably. The comparatively few documents illustrating the activity of the Campagna and Marittima suggest that, at least from the pontificate of Gregory X, the normal seat of its court was Frosinone, though in this period it is also to be found at Anagni, at Ninfa, and at Ferentino.[2] The court of the county of Sabina was situated at Tarano between 1296 and 1303 but at times the rector lived in Rome.[3] There are no clues as to the whereabouts of the court of the Tuscan Patrimony before the 1270s, but from that time the normal residence of the rector was Montefiascone, a town whose fortress, already of importance in the Hohenstaufen period, was strengthened between 1260 and 1290, especially during the rectorship of Count Taddeo of Montefeltro.[4] Yet on occasions the rector of the Patrimony is to be found elsewhere, at Orvieto, for instance, and at Valentano near Lake Bolsena.[5] The normal centre of administration for the Duchy in the earlier part of the century seems to have been Bevagna,[6] but when this province shared a rector with the March in the time of Clement IV the rector often resided at Fabriano

---

[1] See Ermini, *I Parlamenti dello Stato della Chiesa*, pp. 82–8. In 1301 the representatives of Ravenna attending such a parliament were empowered 'ad jurandum ac promittendum fidelitatem. . . . Sancte Romane Ecclesie et ipsius domini domini Rectoris . . . et de stando et parendo efficaciter mandatis ipsius domini Rectoris . . . et suorum officialium semel et pluries et quatenus (*sic*) videbitur expedire et de observandis integer (*sic*) constitutionibus quas in parlamento idem dominus Rector . . .duxerit promulgandum et ad faciendum et audiendum . . .' (Fantuzzi, *Mon. Rav.*, III, n. CIV). See also below, pp. 110 ff.

[2] Contatore, *Terracina*, pp. 76–8, 210, 212–13, 289, 291–2; Caetani, *Reg. Chart.*, I, 179–202; Pantanelli, *Sermoneta*, I, 317–26; *Reg. N. IV*, n. 6418.

[3] Terni, AS, perg. of 1296 (24 Jan., 2 June, 15 Oct.), 1297 (4 July), 1301 (24 May), 1303 (22 May).

[4] RIS, N.S., XVI, III, 35. References to the court at Montefiascone are too numerous to cite.

[5] Todi, AC, Reg. Vet. Istr., f. 106; Fumi, *Orvieto*, d. DXXVI; Pflugk-Harttung, p. 583.

[6] *Lib. Cens.*, I, 10*–12*; *BDSPU*, XXV, 14–15.

or Camerino, near the provincial boundary. Thereafter the Duchy normally had a rector of its own whose court was usually to be found at Foligno, though there were occasional migrations to Gualdo, Spello and Assisi.[1] The movements of the rectors of the Massa Trabaria are not traceable but, ominously, one of them received permission to reside in a less unsettled area, outside his province, at Peglio in the March.[2] In the two remaining provinces the government was to a far greater degree peripatetic. The rectors of the March in the last two decades of the century favoured Macerata and especially Montolmo as places of residence, but then and before the court is often to be found at Cingoli, Osimo, Fano, Montecchio and Tolentino, and at times in about a dozen other towns.[3] Circumstances forced the rector of Romagna to peram-bulate constantly; he moved between Rimini, Cesena, Forlì, Ravenna, Imola and Bologna, existing on sufferance and founding no tradition of a favourite place of residence.

Even in times of peace a visit from the provincial court was a doubt-ful honour, preceded by negotiation and bringing money but also closer supervision and intervention in municipal matters which must often have been irksome.[4] These 'courts' were certainly not elaborate affairs, even in the larger provinces. The rector would have with him a spiritual rector (if he was himself a layman), perhaps a chamberlain or treasurer, one or more judges, occasionally a marshal and a chaplain, and a mere handful of other servants of whom a few were notaries. The March had by far the largest number of notaries and other officials, owing to its judicial decentralization: twelve notaries and a clerk are mentioned in the account book for this province of 1279–80, and Cardinal Napoleon Orsini's constitutions reveal that there were also some lawyers, a few mercenary soldiers, certain general servants (*bayuli*) and butchers, bakers and vintners.[5] The notaries, who probably num-bered two or three in the other provinces, kept not only judicial deeds

[1] Gubbio, Sottosez AS, perg., bu. 16 (Gualdo, 1278: Spello, 1304): Contelori, *Cesi* pp. 25–7 (Assisi, 1281).

[2] *Reg. N. IV*, nn. 7319–20.

[3] These include Ancona, Iesi, Fermo, Pesaro, Camerino, Senigallia, Recanati and Matelica.

[4] In 1295 the rector of Romagna insisted when taking up residence at Ravenna that the city should give him its keys and reasonable rights over its custody (Fantuzzi, *Mon. Rav.*, III, n. LXXXXV). In 1287 the court of the March forbade butchers to have stalls in the *piazza* at Macerata, when resident in that town (Macerata, AC, Rif. I, f. 146v). A few years before this the authorities of the same province had had to send round messengers to various towns 'to know from them what terms they would make with us for the court's residence' (Palmieri, p. 94).

[5] Palmieri, *passim*: in 1279 the March had a salaried 'proctor and advocate' of the general court. Albornoz, *Constitutions*, pp. 71 and 75–6: *J Eccl H*, VI, 20–1 (soldiers).

and copies of the provincial constitutions, but a register of letters despatched by the rector.[1]

Many of the rectors will be discussed in later chapters of this book, but it will be convenient at this point to make some general remarks about the men who were chosen by popes to serve as rectors in the Papal State. Considerably more of them were clerics than laymen. Of some hundred and fifty identified rectors in the five major provinces between 1198 and 1304, over ninety were ecclesiastics.[2] These figures for a whole century conceal two important turning-points in the history of the rectorate. Innocent III is known to have appointed ten provincial rectors: five of these were clerics and five laymen. Thereafter, for fifty years, papal feeling very strongly favoured the appointment of clerics: between the accession of Honorius III and the death of Clement IV only seven laymen were chosen, against fifty-six churchmen. From this date, however, both the papal connection with the Angevins and an increased reliance upon relatives (normally as a basis for achieving greater independence of the Angevins) combine, somewhat paradoxically, to reverse this trend. All Gregory X's appointments were lay, and of the seventy-five rectors identifiable between 1272 and 1304 a majority (forty-four) are secular.[3]

Within the category of clerical rectors there were also significant changes in the course of the century. All those appointed by Innocent III were members of the college of cardinals and not until the papal chaplain and subdeacon Gregory 'de Romania' became rector of the Campagna-Marittima in about 1225 was any cleric of lesser rank chosen for this office in a major province. In 1230 Gregory IX appointed the bishop of Beauvais rector of the March and Duchy, and in all rather over half his rectors came from outside the college. The project for limiting eligibility for the rectorate to cardinals which probably dates

[1] For references to rectorial registers of letters *v.* (e.g.) Todi, AC, Reg. Vet. Istr., f. 100 (Patrimony, 1274); Gubbio, Sottosez AS, perg. bu. 16 (Duchy, 1278); Fantuzzi, *Mon. Rav.*, III, d. LXXXVI (Romagna, 1288); Ferranti, *Amandola*, III, d. 220 (March, 1296). For references to constitutions, *acta curie* and judicial records *v.* QFIA, XXXII, 81 ff.; Palmieri, p. 91 and De Minicis, *Fermo*, pp. 554–6 (March, 1279, 1287, 1301); *J Eccl H*, VIII, 147 (Duchy, 1297). The inclusion in Richard de Bury's letter-book (pp. 191–205) of 55 letters addressed to a rector of the Tuscan Patrimony suggests the compilation of a register of letters received, but the loss of all provincial archives makes it impossible to know whether this practice was general.

[2] The exact figures are 92 and 56 respectively: naturally rectors *in spiritualibus* are excluded here.

[3] The same trend applies to the rectors of Benevento, who were often laymen after *c.* 1271 (Vehse in QFIA, XXIII, 115–16). The rectors of the Comtat Venaissin, the first of whom was appointed in 1274, were also usually laymen in this period (Faure, p. 50).

from January 1234 was abortive.[1] Rather over one-third of Innocent
IV's appointments were cardinals, but after his death, in 1254, only
two popes, Urban IV and Boniface VIII, named cardinals as rectors.
The clerical rectors from this time were normally bishops or papal
chaplains.[2]

The lay rectors were a more miscellaneous body. Innocent III appointed four relatives and Alexander IV two (of whom one was a
cleric); other secular rectors in the first half of the century were nobles
from Rome and the Campagna, while King John of Brienne, rector of
the Patrimony from 1227, fits into no convenient category. Innocent IV
made no lay appointments, nor did Clement IV, though his predecessor
Urban had experimented with Lombard nobles as rulers of the Patrimony. From the time of Gregory X lay rectors reappear, most of them
papal relatives: Gregory himself made four appointments of this type,
Nicholas III and Honorius IV two each, and Boniface VIII six. The link
with the Angevins led to the employment of a number of Frenchmen
and Provençals, normally from the Regno; these account for all
Martin IV's five lay rectors and for three of Celestine V's, as well as for
others made by Gregory X and Boniface VIII. Nicholas IV's three
Colonna rectors almost rank as relatives, while the Orsini provided
three rectors under Boniface VIII and an Annibaldi was twice rector of
the Duchy between 1293 and 1302. Five of Benedict XI's six rectors
were laymen and these were all of north Italian origin.

The cardinal-priest of St. Praxed, rector of the March in 1233–4, had
a 'vicar' to assist him, as did his successor, the future Innocent IV. From
about this period it was not uncommon for rectors to appoint vicars to
represent or aid them, ecclesiastics naming clerical vicars and laymen
normally lay ones. Though on occasions such a vicar was merely an
assistant, he might also act in one province for a rector holding office in
two or more. It was in these circumstances that the bishop-elect of
Verona had vicars in 1261–3 in the March and Duchy, and Cardinal
Simon in the March in 1266–7. By this date important or busy men
quite often nominated substitutes to act for them. Alexander IV's
nephew, Annibaldo di Trasmondo, had been represented successively in
the March by two Romans, and the cardinals appointed by Urban IV
to rule the Campagna-Marittima and the Tuscan Patrimony both had
vicars. In the next thirty years after this a number of feudatories and

---

[1] See below, p. 139.
[2] Between 1254 and 1304, one archbishop, thirteen bishops and nineteen papal chaplains
were appointed to rectorships, as well as seven clerics of other categories.

prelates were so preoccupied by other work that they were represented by vicars for at least part of their rectorates.[1] There is no clear line of demarcation between this group and the nominal rectors, whose appointments conferred prestige and a salary while entailing no obligation to govern in person. This category can be clearly distinguished in the pontificate of Boniface VIII, when Charles of Valois was appointed titular rector of four provinces, with a vicar-general in each, and the pope's nephews Peter and Benedict had as permanent substitutes in the Patrimony and March David of Ferentino and Amatus of Anagni.[2]

The foregoing discussion of the rectorship has been confined to those rectors, ecclesiastics and laymen, who held secular powers in their provinces. In the case of clerics these were always accompanied by the right to use the spiritual weapons of interdict and excommunication, but it was not possible to grant this to laymen.[3] Thus it was necessary to appoint a cleric holding this power to assist one who could not be rector *in spiritualibus et temporalibus*, and in 1227 John of Brienne was accompanied as rector of the Patrimony by the subdeacon and papal chaplain Alatrinus, who was to use 'temporal and ecclesiastical force' against rebellious subjects in that province.[4] For some time after this there were very few secular rectors and nothing more is heard of rectors *in spiritualibus* until Annibaldo was rector of the March under Alexander IV. He was assisted first by the prior of Narni, who had powers to proceed against rebels *spiritualiter*, and later by a papal chaplain whose functions are suggested by the terms of his appointment *ad censuram ecclesiasticam in spiritualibus exercendam in Anconitana Marchia eiusdem domini* (sc. *papae*) *legatus*.[5] Five years later Guiscard of Pietrasanta was accompanied in the Patrimony by the bishop of Amelia. As the rector's *socius*, the bishop received full powers *quantum ad spiritualia*, including the right to hear lawsuits *de causis ecclesiasticis* brought before him *per querelam seu per appellationem*, to put into effect his sentences *ad spiritualia et ecclesiastica* and to use spiritual punishments against rebels. After a few months the bishop was succeeded in his post by a friar (an inquisitor)

---

[1] Examples are the count of Montefeltro in the Patrimony (1275), Bertold Orsini in Romagna (1278), the papal chamberlain in Campagna-Marittima (1279), Stephen Colonna in Romagna and Landulf Colonna in the March (1289–90), and Richard Annibaldi in the Duchy (1293).

[2] The Orsini rectors in the same pontificate, Orso and Bertold, also acted through vicars.

[3] For a full treatment of the rectors *in spiritualibus* see G. Ermini, 'Stato e Chiesa nella monarchia pontificia dei sec. XIII e XIV', *RSDI*, V, 583–629.

[4] *Reg. Hon. III*, nn. 6203 ff. (esp. n. 6216).

[5] Colucci, *Ant. Pic.*, XIX, d. XXXII; XXIX, 97.

who was to aid the rector and strengthen his rule, 'the spiritual sword bringing support to the temporal'.[1] From the 1270s onwards the appointment of a rector or vicar *in spiritualibus* became a normal feature of papal government whenever the principal rector was a layman.

Rectors *in spiritualibus* were appointed in the same way as general rectors and on the same conditions. The letter of nomination proclaimed as their purpose the 'support and aid of the temporal jurisdiction'.[2] In practice this meant mainly the proclamation of interdicts and excommunications against the rebellious, but the rector *in spiritualibus* held his own court, which probably dealt mainly with offences against provincial authority by clerics or ecclesiastical corporations.[3] He could promulgate constitutions in the provincial parliament threatening the use of the spiritual arm against rebels, and it was he who ordered the clergy to pay taxes and procurations.[4] It was natural that he should also find himself charged by the pope with miscellaneous ecclesiastical business, such as proceeding against clerics on occasions when the ordinary has proved dilatory, making grants of money to churches and asking communes to give them land.[5] Whether the theoretical subordination of the rector *in spiritualibus* to his secular colleague was fully effective in practice one cannot tell, and the situation presumably varied according to the circumstances and personalities involved. The salary of the spiritual rector was also a variable: the bishop of Grosseto drew three florins a day in 1289 as vicar in the Romagna *super spiritualibus*, but fifteen years later, under Benedict XI, the pay of the spiritual rector in each of the provinces was only one florin *per diem*. In addition to this the holder of the post was theoretically entitled to receive certain unspecified 'services' from the clergy at Easter and Christmas, at least in

---

[1] *Reg. Urb. IV*, I, n. 301; II, n. 747.   [2] *Reg. B. VIII*, n 3357.

[3] A typical instance is the condemnation in 1272 of the bishop and chapter of Viterbo by the vicar-general *in spiritualibus* of the Patrimony for not paying a tax (*BISI*, XXVII, 224). In 1279–80 the court of the rector of the March *super spiritualibus* received 650 *l*. in fines in ten months (Palmieri, *passim*). The limits of the court's jurisdiction are hard to ascertain: it is surprising that a spiritual rector in the March could fine a village for attacking a notary (Zonghi, *Fabriano*, d. CCXLIV). The court also heard civil suits in which both parties were ecclesiastics (e.g. Vogel, *Recanati*, II, 58–9: a case in 1290 between the bishop of Recanati and a monastic house). For a suit between a commune and an ecclesiastical corporation *v*. R. Sassi, 'Le pergamene dell' archivio domenicano di S. Lucia di Fabriano' (*Fonti per la Storia delle Marche*, 1939), d. 2.

[4] Ermini, *art. cit.*, 610, and constitutions issued by the rector of the March *in spiritualibus*, ibid., 180–4 (1301). Prof. Ermini's statement that the spiritual rector summoned the clergy to parliament (*Parlamenti*, pp. 20–1, 29–30) is not supported by the document that he cites.

[5] Mei, *Cagli*, dd. 359 and 395 and other documents cited by Ermini, *art. cit.*, 618–20. Any rector, if a cleric, was likely to have to perform similar tasks arising from the enforcement of excommunications etc. (for a typical instance, concerning the Duchy in 1281, Cristofani, *Assisi*, pp. 117–18).

the Duchy of Spoleto, and he presumably retained the two-thirds of the takings of his court not paid into the provincial chamber, though some of this may well have been passed on to subordinates.[1]

The men chosen by the pope as rectors *in spiritualibus* were drawn from widely separated ranks in the hierarchy. Nearly half of them were holders of canonries, but a number held bishoprics or were papal chaplains, and many occupied other miscellaneous positions.[2] When a general rector was an ecclesiastic he might appoint one vicar *super temporalibus* and another *super spiritualibus* and as the custom of appointing vicars grew a province might even find itself in the hands of the vicar of a vicar *super spiritualibus*.[3]

In the last third of the century the rectors began to have the assistance of a new official, the treasurer, who took charge of the financial administration of the province. Such matters had hitherto been the responsibility of the rectors themselves, and a letter of appointment might instruct a rector to collect 'carefully and faithfully the revenues and income of the Roman Church' in his province.[4] Some rectors, even as early as 1235, had the aid of a chamberlain, but this was rather exceptional.[5] The March of Ancona was almost certainly the most remunerative of the papal provinces and it was one in which the levying of revenue was the subject of constant innovations in technique. In 1267 Cardinal Simon, then rector in the Duchy and March, gave proctorial powers in the March to a certain Benvenuto of Foligno to receive the revenues due to the provincial court and to reach financial agreements with debtors and men who had been condemned.[6] The next move, logically, was the appointment of a permanent financial official. This was the work of Gregory X, who on 8 April 1272, only twelve days after his consecration, named Ruffino da Stradiliano of Piacenza to be papal treasurer and nuncio in the March, Massa Trabaria and Urbino, 'to seek and receive the rights, revenues and incomes of the Roman Church' in those provinces.[7] From this time there was probably no

[1] *Reg. N. IV*, n. 7220; *Röm. Quartalschrift*, XVIII, 104: *BDSPU*, XXV, 61 (when the 'services' were claimed in 1301 the clergy of the Duchy stated that they had not been rendered for ten years): for the takings of the court see above, p. 105, n. 3.

[2] Exact figures: canons, thirteen; bishops, six; papal chaplains, five; miscellaneous, ten. For sources *v.* App. II.

[3] Ferranti, *Amandola*, III, dd. 155–9 (March of Ancona, 1288).

[4] *Reg. Inn. IV*, n. 5277.

[5] Gianandrea, *Iesi*, dd. LXIII, CXXVI–CXXVII, CXXXII; Colucci, *Treia*, d. XXIII; *QFIA*, XXXVII, 131–2 (March of Ancona, 1235, 1248, 1254, 1256).

[6] Grimaldi, *Matelica*, d. CCLIII.

[7] Gianandrea, *Iesi*, d. CLXXX ('ad petendum et recipiendum iura, proventus et redditus Ecclesie romane'): Santoni, 'Camerino', 51, gives the date wrongly as '1271'.

break in the succession of treasurers in the March. The Romagna had a
treasurer from the time it became a papal province (1278), the Duchy
and Patrimony not later than 1280 and 1290 respectively, and the
Campagna-Marittima and Sabina by 1303.[1]

The treasurer was an official of the papal chamber, not a subordinate
of the provincial rector.[2] He too was appointed *usque beneplacitum*, and
the rector was asked to receive him kindly, treat him well and to hand
over to him all the revenues of the Church 'in accordance with your
oath'. Rector and treasurer were to see that books were kept recording
income and expenditure, so that they could answer fully for them when
requested to do so by the papal chamber.[3] The treasurer naturally had a
notary to assist him in keeping these accounts. In 1279–80 the treasurer
of the March and his notary both received a salary of two shillings
tournois a day; under Benedict XI, twenty-five years later, the daily pay
of all the provincial treasurers was three groats *tournois*.[4] It was in the
nature of things that the treasurer should come to acquire the right to
make sales of papal property, such as the produce of domain land.[5]
Periodically he would be called to the Curia by the papal chamberlain
for his accounts to be checked.

With only one exception, the identifiable provincial treasurers of the
thirteenth century were agents of banking firms which acted for the
papacy.[6] This meant also that they were almost invariably Tuscans;
Ruffino da Stradiliano represented the Scotti of Piacenza, but his successors came from Siena and Florence (the Pulci, Rimbertini, Spiliati,
Spini, Bardi and Cerchi), from the Chiarenti of Pistoia and the Ricciardi
of Lucca. The appointment of agents of firms with which the papacy
banked no doubt made easier the transfer of money from the provinces
to the papal chamber and vice versa, and in general served to co-

---

[1] *Reg. N. III*, n. 727; Morini, *Cascia*, d. I (Duchy); Arch. Vat., Arm. XXXV, 14, f. 85
(Patrimony); *Röm. Quartalschrift*, XVIII, 104. The advent of the treasurer did not always
mean the demise of the rector's chamberlain, who is still to be found in the March in 1277,
1280 and 1287 (Gianandrea, *Iesi*, d. CLXXXVIII; Zonghi, *Fabriano*, d. CCXXIX; Acquacotta, *Matelica*, d. 74) and in Romagna in 1295 (*Reg. B. VIII*, n. 5416).

[2] In 1280 Ugolino was 'Thesaurarius Romane Curie in Ducatu constitutus' (Morini,
Cascia, d. I) and many formulae of this sort emphasize the treasurers' link with the central
administration. For letters appointing treasurers, *v. Reg. N. IV*, n. 7094 (March, 1288) and
Reg. B. VIII, n. 5416 (Romagna, 1295). Papal instructions concerning matters which were
not purely financial were conveyed by the chamberlain to the rector, not the treasurer
(Gianandrea, *Iesi*, dd. CCXIV, CCXXV).

[3] '. . . Super receptis autem et expensis tu et ipse conscribi libros seu cartularios faciatis,
prout fieri consuevit, ut de eis nostre camere per te ac ipsum thesaurarium cum exigetur
plena ratio reddi possit' (the wording is identical in all surviving letters of appointment).

[4] Palmieri, p. 111: *Röm. Quartalschrift*, XVIII, 104.

[5] Gianandrea, *Iesi*, d. CCXXXV.

[6] See Jordan, *De Mercatoribus*, pp. 108–112. For the names of treasurers, *v.* App. II.

ordinate the provincial finances with those of the Curia. The treasurers normally performed their duties in person, though they might have to appoint a vicar to act while they were absent for the periodical checking of their accounts by the chamberlain.[1]

In their judicial functions the provincial rectors were assisted by judges, at least from the pontificate of Gregory IX.[2] At first there was one provincial judge only, but later in the century benches began to proliferate. The March had two judges-general in 1279–80 and a few years later there was a third judge, for appeal cases. In Romagna the two judges heard respectively criminal and civil suits, and by 1304 the same division of competence was made in the March and Patrimony.[3] The March, more highly organized in this as in so many ways, possessed a unique system of regional courts. The province was divided into three judgeships or *presidati*, that of S. Lorenzo in Campo, with jurisdiction from the Romagnol frontier to the river Esino, the county of Camerino in the central March with its seat at Montemilone, and in the south the Abbey of Farfa, with its bench at S. Vittoria near Fermo hearing cases for the region from the Salino, Tenna and Tennacula rivers southwards to the boundary with the Regno.[4] The judges were all subordinates of the rectors, from whom they received instructions. Very often they were natives of the Papal State. In the March in 1279–80 the three regional justices received salaries of 150 *l.* a year and the judges-general about 250 *l.*[5]

In the later years of the century there was normally a marshal in each province whose main function was to secure obedience to the orders of the court.[6] He had a few mercenaries or 'bailiffs' under his command.

---

[1] Gianandrea, *Iesi*, d. CCXXXV. For a treasurer deserting his post, see below, pp. 226–7. For the *locumtenens* of another treasurer (1304), Acquacotta, *Matelica*, d. 96.

[2] On the judges, see Ermini, 'I giudici provinciali della monarchia pontificia nel medioe vo' in *Studi Economico-Giuridici pubbl. per cura della Fac. di Giurisprudenza della R. Università di Cagliari*, XVIII–XIX (1931), 268–76, which gives full references. The Duchy and March both had judges by 1232 (for the latter province *v.* Colucci, *Ant. Pic.*, XXIX, 77–9, overlooked by Prof. Ermini), the Sabina by 1236. Romagna had judges from its start as a papal province. The earliest judges I have noted in the Patrimony and Campagna-Marittima are of 1282 (Fumi, *Orvieto*, d. DXXVI: *Reg. N. IV*, n. 6418), but the institution probably existed there before: documents for these provinces are rather rare.

[3] For the Patrimony, *v. J Eccl H*, VI, 20.

[4] On these courts *v.* Aloisi in *AMSM*, N.S., I (1904), 393–404 and Colucci, *Ant. Pic.*, XXXI, 85–93. Albornoz, *Constitutions*, p. 53. For the limits placed on their powers by Card. Napoleon Orsini, *v. sup.*, p. 77.

[5] Ermini, *art. cit.*, lists many of the judges. Salaries are calculated from Palmieri, *passim*. Rectors might also on occasion appoint special judges to hear particular suits, e.g. *BISI*, XXVII, 240 (Patrimony, 1278).

[6] The earliest reference I have noted is to Henry Visconti, marshal of the March in 1275 (Fabriano, AC, Lib. Rosso, ff. 121v–122v). There are numerous references to later

Apart from the regional courts in the March there seems to have been no territorial sub-division of the provinces except in the Duchy of Spoleto. Part of this province was allotted for some years to a 'Count' or 'judge' of Nocera, but the experiment was probably a failure; the principal towns within his sphere of jurisdiction opposed his claims strongly and had to be granted exemption.[1] At about the same time — the last decade of the century — a 'judge and captain-general' was appointed to govern the isolated part of the province in the upper Apennines. This official was normally resident at Norcia or Visso. Many traces of his activity have survived[2] and this example of decentralization, dictated by a genuine geographical division, may well have met with success.

The only other representatives of papal rule outside the provincial courts were bailiffs in areas of papal domain and in rural zones which had escaped domination by communes. In such districts many of the small centres of population — *terrae*, *loca* and *villae* — housed these officials, who were in some cases the heirs of imperialist predecessors. Their work was not of the sort to leave many traces, but they are to be found exercising fiscal and judicial functions in the Duchy and March as early as the pontificate of Honorius III.[3]

*   *   *

marshals in this province and in Romagna. At the beginning of the next century the Tuscan Patrimony had a marshal (*J Eccl H*, VI, 21).

[1] The county of Nocera had been a unit of administration in the Hohenstaufen period and references to it as a territorial entity are found in the early thirteenth century (e.g *Reg. G. IX*, n. 1715). It had been revived by 1289 (Zonghi, *Fabriano*, pp. 151, 285), and in 1291 was under a vicar (Guerrieri, *Gualdo Tadino*, pp. 70–1). For Perugia's opposition *v.* Perugia, AS, Rif. X (1297), f. 291. *V.* also *Reg. B. VIII*, n. 3493 (Nocera's exemption, 1300) and Sarti, *Gubbio*, pp. 174–7 (Gubbio's exemption, 1304).

[2] Morini, *Cascia*, d. IX (1292); Sansi, *Storia di Spoleto*, p. 123 (1294); Cascia, AC, perg. nn. 14, 17, 19 (1303–4).

[3] For early references to such bailiffs, *v.* Theiner, dd. CXV–CXVI (1222); *Lib. Cens.*, I, 534–7 (references to bailiffs of the rectors King John and the bishop of Beauvais in many eastern districts of the Duchy, 1227–32) and *Reg. G. IX*, n. 3145 (the rector of the March to withdraw 'bailiffs' and 'nuncios' from the lands of the bishop of Fermo, 1236: for a reference to the same rector's bailiff at S. Ginesio *v.* Colucci, *Ant. Pic.*, XIX, d. XXX). Their duties are best defined in the report of an enquiry into papal rights at Cervedone in 1274 (Fanciulli, *Cingoli*, II, d. LXXXIV), wherein witnesses describe how one 'reddebat ius postulantibus et perquirebat maleficia et puniebat delinquentes et portabat et perquirebat iura curie, sicut cotidie faciunt procuratores curie in aliis castris et constringebat omnes de contrata.' Cf. an account of papal rights at Castelritaldi in the Duchy (Sansi, *Spoleto*, d. LX): 'Item habuit ecclesia romana in eodem comitatu Castrum litaldi curie manuale quod est districtum, et ponebatur ibi vicecomes seu vicarius pro curia qui dominabat ibidem, et jus reddebat omnibus de contrata per judicem ipsius et fiebat ibi forum generale quolibet die martis et collegebatur ibi pedagium et salquaticum pro curia et omni apercipebat ordinabat et disponebat vicarius sicut volebat, et erat dominus in illis partibus pro Ecclesia.' The best account of these bailiffs is given by Ermini, 'Aspetti giuridici', 322–5, and *Lib. Com.* (II), pp. 16–28, but he appears to exaggerate their ubiquity, possibly through his interpretation of the statement in the document of 1274 that the rectors of the March 'in

Apart from the rectorate, the institution most characteristic of the provincial system was its parliament. The obligation to *facere parlamentum* — in feudal terms, to give counsel — was common to all the pope's subjects, but the parliament, colloquy or counsel might take many forms. The great gathering held by Innocent III at Viterbo on 21–3 September 1207 was a means of securing recognition of the recent foundation of papal rule in central Italy.[1] Prelates, feudatories and representatives of the towns of the March, Duchy and Tuscan Patrimony were present to hear the pope's claims, to swear allegiance, submit their petitions and listen to legislation concerning heresy, the protection of ecclesiastical rights and peace in the new State. Although no other general parliaments were held in the thirteenth century, popes occasionally used their power to summon representatives of their subjects to the Curia. In the summer of 1220 Honorius III sent his notary, the subdeacon Pandulf, into the Duchy to attempt to pacify that province: Pandulf called the *podestà* of almost all the Duchy towns to Bevagna and on his orders these towns later sent proctors to the pope himself, to accept papal arbitration and reiterate their recognition of papal rights.[2] Eight years later Gregory IX called another parliament of the towns of the Duchy, to form a league to oppose the Urslingen invasion of the Papal State; the pope presided over this assembly at Perugia.[3]

The period of Manfred's threat, another time of crisis, saw two such gatherings, first when Alexander IV called to Anagni ambassadors of all the towns of the Patrimony and Duchy to discuss a scheme for a general league, and later when Urban IV summoned twenty-nine major communes of the same provinces to send representatives concerning Manfred's invasion of the Papal State. Each time the towns were warned that their representatives should have 'full powers'.[4] The as-

---

eis [Cervedone and various other places] posuerunt baiulos ut in aliis castris et villis Marchiae'. But for a papal bailiff (who had to be a local man) in a non-domain town *v. Archivio Storico per le Marche e per l'Umbria*, I, 725 (Serra S. Quirico, 1265).

[1] See above, pp. 52 ff. On parliaments see Ermini, *Parlamenti*, which is a general study of parliaments in the Papal State in the later thirteenth and earlier fourteenth centuries with little emphasis on developments in the nature of parliamentary institutions within that period.

[2] See below, p. 132. Each town sent three or four proctors to the Curia at Orvieto: Perugia, Assisi, Foligno, Nocera, Terni, Spoleto, Todi, Narni and Montefalco were represented, and possibly other communes.

[3] See below, p. 136. Cristofani, *Assisi*, p. 99 (15–18 July 1228: Assisi sends its *podestà* to this parliament, held on 25 July). This gathering has escaped the attention of Prof. Ermini.

[4] See below, pp. 164–5 and 166. There is no certainty that Urban IV's summons was obeyed, no reference to the meeting itself having survived, but there is no strong reason for doubting that it took place. Alexander IV ordered representatives to have full powers to carry out his orders, Urban that they should have 'full powers to treat with us concerning these matters and to hear and execute whatever we and our brothers (the cardinals) ordain'.

sumption of suzerainty over Romagna was the occasion of a summons to the major communes of that province to Viterbo, where their proctors accepted Nicholas III's arbitration in their disputes, agreed to make a general peace, and recognized papal dominion.[1] Some eighteen years later Boniface VIII called the papacy's Romagnol subjects to the Curia to discuss peace-terms; this time the nine major towns were to send two ambassadors each, while five feudatories attended in person.[2]

The gathering at Bevagna in 1220 is the earliest recorded meeting of the subjects of a single province. Yet, in that its convenor was the provincial rector, first place in the long list of recorded provincial parliaments should perhaps be granted to the assembly of the March held by Cardinal Peter Capocci at Fano on 7 July 1249. Prelates, communal officials and at least one lay noble were present at this gathering, in which the cardinal promulgated a number of constitutions designed to win over imperialist 'rebels' and forward the invasion of the Regno.[3]

After this there is no certain evidence of provincial parliaments for a decade, but it is highly probable that assemblies of the March were held by rectors in 1252, 1253 and 1255.[4] Another parliament of the March was planned in 1266, and one was certainly held in 1272.[5] In 1260 Todi complained that the rector of the Tuscan Patrimony had called its bishop and clergy to his parliament, despite Todi's exemption from his jurisdiction: this is perhaps the earliest reference to a rector's parliament outside the March.[6] The earliest surviving evidence of rectorial parliaments in the Duchy relates to the gathering summoned to Bevagna in

[1] Below, p. 195.

[2] Below, p.236 . That towns might still at this time expect to be cited to parliament outside their own province is shown by a clause in Velletri's papal privilege of 1299 exempting that town from the obligation of parliament outside the Campagna-Marittima (*Reg. B. VIII*, n. 2844).

[3] For this parliament *v.* below, p. 149–50 and *EHR*, LXXV, 660–4: it also has not been noted by Prof. Ermini. Pandulf was perhaps *de facto* rector of the Duchy in June 1220, but did not bear this title.

[4] An oath of fealty was sworn at Tolentino on 12 August 1252 *apud Tolentinum in colloquio generali* (*Lib. Cens.*, I, 564). Constitutions were issued in this province, probably in parliaments, pre-24 August 1253 (Acquacotta, *Matelica*, d. 36) and on 7 March 1255 (Grimaldi, *Matelica*, d. CXVI).

[5] *Reg. Cl. IV*, nn. 1024 and 1033. A reference to Cardinal Simon's constitutions for this province in a letter of 1267 (Acquacotta, *Matelica*, d. 61) suggests that the cardinal held the proposed parliament and issued constitutions in it. For 1272, *v.* Sella in *RSDI*, II, 297–305.

[6] Todi, AC, Reg. Vet. Istr., f. 103v (Alexander IV writes on 7 March 1260 to the papal chaplain Ranier, rector of the Patrimony: 'Tu episcopum et clerum predictos ad parlamentum tuum . . . vocasti').

1277 by Hugh, marquis of Montemezzano, but there may well have been such assemblies before this.[1]

If a single year is to be selected as marking the transformation of the provincial assembly from an occasional into a regular feature of papal institutions, that year should certainly be 1278, the date of the assumption of rule in Romagna. Thereafter frequent meetings were held, at least in the Romagna and March, and probably in the other provinces, though the sources relating to them are very deficient: we know of at least seventeen parliaments in Romagna between that year and the death of Benedict XI, and of eleven in the March, as well as of three each in both the Patrimony and Duchy.[2] These are years in which parliamentary institutions were developing with great rapidity elsewhere, notably in England, but also in Aragon, the Sicilian kingdom (particularly in that part of it coming under Aragonese rule) and Friuli.[3] This contemporaneity should be ascribed not to the spread of ideas concerning politics and the technique of government but rather to similar developments of feudal 'counsel' by governments faced with similar fiscal and military problems. The publication of constitutions, occasionally combined with the outlawry of rebels and measures against these, played an important part in the proceedings of the provincial parliaments, but consent to taxation for the raising of troops was perhaps even more central to their purpose in these decades when a long war was being waged for control in Romagna. In the March at least six parliaments were called to approve *tallia militum* in 1278–82 alone, while the rector of Romagna was granted troops in the same way five times in the years 1287–95.[4]

[1] Knowledge of such parliaments is normally due to the survival of documents in municipal archives mentioning them, and such materials become less sparse around this period.

[2] Prof. Ermini suggests the year 1272 for this somewhat arbitrary date. For lists, see Appendix I. The compilation of these lists involves difficulties, in particular because the terms *parlamentum, parlamenta* and *colloquium* had not yet acquired a precise technical significance. Thus Bertold Orsini's citation of Bologna on 8 January 1280 (*ASI*, XCI, 72–5) at Ravenna *in publico parlamento, congregatione et contione* was accomplished with due publicity, but presumably not at what would now be called a 'parliament', since a provincial assembly was held at Faenza four days later. In January 1288 the rector Peter pronounced the ban on the lords of Polenta at Imola *in parliamento vel consilio* and repeated this in February *presente colloquio et consilio* (Fantuzzi, *Mon. Rav.*, III, n. LXXXVI). After hesitation I have excluded these from the lists of parliaments, while including the Tolentino *colloquium generale* of 1252. I have also excluded as evidence of March parliaments from *c.* 1213 the statement of a witness from Ripatransone that the town 'fecit . . . parlamentum . . . generalibus Rectoribus Marchie . . . a XL annis usque nunc' (Tanursi, *Ripatransone*, p. xxvii), though it is used as such by Ermini (*Parlamenti*, p. 14): the source is suspect and the phrase too generic. The lists could probably receive additions from unpublished archival sources.

[3] See Marongiu, *L'istituto parlamentare in Italia* (1949), pp. 128–32 and 136–8.

[4] See Appendix I and, for a fuller discussion, below, pp. 264 ff. and 291 ff.

Discussion of the nature of the fully-evolved provincial parliament of the late thirteenth century must begin with an attempt to establish who was present at these gatherings.[1] The towns sent their officials and other representatives, the number of these varying according to the status of the town. The two other elements composing the parliament, prelates and temporal lords, were for the most part summoned to appear in person, though some clerics attended as representatives of a chapter or of the clergy of a town, and feudatories sometimes did not deign to go personally but sent proctors.[2] The survival of the form of summons issued for a parliament of the Tuscan Patrimony in 1298 makes it possible to illustrate attendance at a provincial parliament from a single well-documented example.[3] To this assembly, to be held in the *palazzo* at Montefiascone on Sunday 16 November 1298, the rector, Rinaldo Malavolti bishop of Siena, summoned no less than 225 persons. About three-quarters of these were representatives of the towns, for the thirteen *civitates* (cities having bishoprics) were each to send their *podestà* with proctorial powers and four ambassadors *de melioribus dicte terre*, while thirty-six other towns, the *castra*, had to send the *podestà* or castellan as proctor with two ambassadors. There should therefore have been 173 urban representatives in all, sixty-five from the greater and one hundred and eight from the lesser towns. Twenty-eight abbots, heads of monastic houses and representatives of the lower clergy make up the next largest contingent. Three chapters of canons and the clergy of Corneto sent delegates, but the overwhelming majority of these ecclesiastics were heads of monastic and collegiate establishments. Twelve bishops and twelve temporal *domini* — these were of course rural magnates, not town-dwellers — were summoned in person and complete the list of those called. The ecclesiastical element, it will be noted, preponderates over the lay nobility, which at least in numbers is comparatively insignificant; yet both these are overshadowed by the number of town representatives. Comparison with the considerably less full evidence concerning gatherings in other provinces shows that there too parliamentary assemblies contained the same ingredients, of

[1] The following discussion relates to the four northern provinces. No references survive to parliaments of the Campagna-Marittima or Sabina, and virtually nothing is known of those of Massa Trabaria (on which *v*. Codignola, *ASI*, XCVIII, 57).

[2] E.g. *ASI*, L (1912), 338–9.

[3] Fabre, 'Un registre caméral du Card. Albornoz', *MAH*, VII, 180–4. Fabre dates this formulary '*c*. 1298', but the parliament to be held on 'Sunday the 16th instant' can be dated precisely 16 November 1298, since November 1298 is the only month during the rectorate of Rinaldo Malavolti (15 July 1298–13 June 1299: *v*. App. II) in which the 16th falls on a Sunday.

'prelates, *podestà* and nobles'.[1] It is not possible to say whether the numerical proportion between these elements was similar in all the provinces, though the proportion of *civitates* to *castra* tended to be the same. The 'feudal' nobility was more powerful in Romagna than in the Patrimony, but it may not have been more numerous. In 1301 a Romagnol parliament was attended by the count of Montefeltro as representative of Cesena and Mainardo da Susinana for Forlì, Faenza and Imola, as well as by ambassadors of these towns.[2] This was probably not the only occasion on which tyrants, nominally 'captains', appeared and thus revolutionized the effective, if not the formal, composition of a provincial assembly.

The wording of the summons to Montefiascone in 1298 illustrates well the nature of the provincial *generale parlamentum*[3] and the role of the various participants. Since the rector intends to call this meeting 'concerning the tranquil state and healthy organization of the province and whatever else we consider likely to promote the honour of the Holy Roman Church and ourselves', he summons the prelates 'to hear and devoutly receive the orders and ordinances that we shall decide to have considered and promulgated in this parliament'.[4] The formulae relating to the town representatives differ significantly, for their active share in the gathering is emphasized, together with the obligation falling on them to give publicity to the decisions of the parliament and to secure obedience to them.[5] Prelates failing to appear are threatened with spiritual punishment — specifically with excommunication, except in the case of bishops with whom a less precise form of words is employed — urban communities and lay lords with a fine of one hundred marks, or some other amount at the rector's will. The rector mentions that a copy of the summons has been entered in his register and that he will accept the word of his messenger concerning its due

---

[1] Those present at the Romagna parliament of February 1283 included an archbishop and two bishops, the *podestà* of four towns 'et multis aliis prelatis, potestatibus et nobilibus' (*Nuovi Studi Medievali*, II, 241–52).

[2] RIS, N.S., XXII, II, 58 and XXVIII, II, 95.

[3] There is no evidence of 'particular' parliaments not including some elements or localities.

[4] 'Cum . . . intendamus super statu tranquillo et dispositione salubri ejusdem provincie (*sc.* Patrimonii b. Petri in Tuscia) et super aliis que ad honorem sacrosancte Romane Ecclesie adque nostrum expedire viderimus . . . ad audiendum et devote suscipiendum mandata et ordinamenta nostra que in eodem parlamento tractanda et statuenda delibera-verimus.'

[5] '. . . provida deliberatione providimus vobiscum et cum aliis patrimonii ejusdem fidelibus . . . et ea que super dispositione prefati regiminis duxerimus ordinanda publicare et publicata injungere observari . . . (syndicum . . . et . . . ambassiatores) . . . mittere procuretis *facturos* et audituros ac efficaciter impleturos que percipere, ordinare, et tractare ntendimus . . .'

presentation to the recipient. It should be noted that there are no precise instructions concerning the form of the mandate to be given by the towns to their representatives. This may well be evidence that the communes of the Patrimony had not yet attempted to limit the authority of the parliament through granting restricted powers to their delegates. Nor does the mandate granted by Ravenna to its proctor for the Cesena parliament of November 1301 — apparently the earliest document of its nature to have survived — bear any trace of an attempt to circumscribe the representative's freedom of action.[1] Only a few years after this the towns began to have recourse to the obvious defensive technique of appointing proctors with limited — from the viewpoint of the authorities, inadequate — powers to bind those who named them.[2]

Parliamentary meetings normally took place at the town where the provincial rector was in residence, hence those of the Romagna and March are known to have been held in many different places, while the parliament of the Duchy probably met usually at Bevagna and that of the Patrimony at Montefiascone. The *palazzo comunale* was probably the customary meeting-place, though there may have been some open-air gatherings.[3] The session lasted only one day.

The main business of the provincial parliaments has been indicated above. It is not easy to assess the relative importance of their legislative, fiscal and conciliar functions, and in any case this varied considerably according to the province and the time. When meetings became more common, in the last two decades of the century, their fiscal aspect was probably the most important to both rector and subjects, and was certainly the main reason for the greater frequency of parliaments in the March and Romagna. A number of parliaments of the March seem to have been called solely to vote the *tallia militum*. In Romagna (where chroniclers have left a rather fuller account of these gatherings) military arrangements were made and the rector then granted money which would enable these to be fulfilled.[4] There is, however, no evidence that

[1] This man was to appear before the rector, swear fealty to the Church and him and promise obedience to him and his officials and full observance of the constitutions promulgated in the parliament, 'and to do and hear . . . and generally to do and accomplish *omnia et singula . . .*' (Fantuzzi, *Mon. Rav.*, III, n. CIV).

[2] Ermini, *Parlamenti*, pp. 40–4.

[3] For meeting-places *v.* App. I. For an open-air meeting in Romagna on 14 February 1301 *v.* RIS, N.S., XXII, II, 58 and XXVIII, II, 95 ('in loco ubi dicitur Canaçosia, qui locus est in confinibus districtus Faventie et districtus Ravenne').

[4] In 1288 the rector was granted 'liberum arbitrium in omnibus et per omnia' including *tallia militum*. In 1292 and 1295 he was empowered to enlist 300 cavalry, the sum needed for their pay being provided by the towns according to their wealth. In 1294 he received 'powers to take on mercenaries' (RIS, N.S., XXVIII, II, 60, 67, 76, 82).

the parliaments of the Duchy and Patrimony ever exercised fiscal functions. The formulary of the rector of the Patrimony in 1298–9 shows that *tallia militum* had then become a fixed annual payment in that province and as such presumably did not require parliamentary approval.[1]

The promulgation of constitutions or *ordinamenta* was a conspicuous function of the parliament in all the principal provinces.[2] Legislation was the main purpose of all the recorded March parliaments that were not called to vote *tallia militum*, while in Romagna it seems to have been common for the same meeting to fulfil both functions. The Romagnol parliament of March 1291 heard the letter of appointment of the new rector and his *ordinamenta*, before going on to vote him 26,000 florins for troops. In the following year and again in 1294 and 1295 there were parliaments in this province in which both taxes were voted and legislation promulgated.[3] In the Duchy and Patrimony the issue of constitutions and orders was the main *raison d'être* of the provincial assembly.[4] Constitutions were the formally recorded statutes of the province, and rectors both rehearsed with due publicity the legislation of their predecessors and added measures of their own. The abrogation of previous decrees was naturally performed with the same publicity.[5] It is not clear whether there was a sharp dividing line between *constitutiones* and *ordinamenta*. The pope occasionally issued constitutions applicable to particular provinces, and these were incorporated into the body of provincial statutes.[6] Rectors may well have issued constitutions other than in parliamentary gatherings, especially during the period before such meetings became common, but no surviving evidence for such action in the thirteenth century has been noted, and it would certainly have been rare in the age of frequent parliaments.[7]

With the issue of *ordinamenta* concerning provincial rebels one approaches the ill-defined, and indeed artificial, frontier between the legislative and 'publishing' activities of the parliament. This function is seen at its most characteristic in the recognition of a new rector, for instance of Stephen Colonna, freshly arrived in his province of

---

[1] *MAH*, VII, 187–9.
[2] See P. Sella, 'Costituzioni dello Stato della Chiesa', ASI, LXXXV.
[3] RIS, N.S., XXVIII, II, 67, 76–7; ASI, LXXXV, 5; Fantuzzi, *Mon. Rav.*, III, n. LXXXXIV; Mazzatinti, I, 161.
[4] *MAH*, VII, 180–4; Sansi, *Spoleto*, I, 124 n.
[5] Bonoli, *Forlì*, p. 109.
[6] For examples of this see below, pp. 166 and 202 n. For a copy of constitutions in the possession of a provincial court (March), *v.* Palmieri, p. 91.
[7] Rectorial constitutions of the March are mentioned in a letter of 1233 (Theiner, d. CLXXII), before the earliest recorded parliament of this province.

Romagna, at Forlì on 29 December 1289, and of the successor appointed after his capture, Aldobrandino bishop of Arezzo, in the same town on 1 March 1291.[1] Measures and negotiations concerning 'rebels' (*i.e.* those disobeying papal authority) were also a frequent feature of provincial parliaments, indeed the overwhelming majority of rectorial provisions was devoted to the problem of disobedience. In January 1280 Bertold Orsini cited recalcitrant elements among the Bolognese *in publico parlamento, congregatione et contione* in the *piazza* before the archiepiscopal palace at Ravenna; a few days later, in a formal parliament at Faenza he condemned these rebels to pay heavy fines unless they submitted within the next ten days. In February 1288 the Polenta of Ravenna were placed under the rector's ban *in parlamento vel consilio* at Imola for not paying *tallia militum*; this preceded by a week the condemnation of the same family and the Malatesta of Rimini as rebels, *presente colloquio et consilio*.[2] Such occasions well illustrate the difficulty of deciding what constitutes a provincial parliament, as does the action of the bishop of Vicenza who, says a chronicler, in 1289 recruited crusaders, and '*in suis parlamentis* he gave the cross to all who volunteered to remain' at Forlì.[3] The true *parlamentum generale* provided a yet fuller setting for the formal consideration of the same problems. Thus in February 1301 the rector met the parliament of Romagna 'and there made proposals for a general and special peace and concord in the province'. The same autumn the vicar *in temporalibus* and rector *in spiritualibus* of the March issued in a parliament at Macerata a series of constitutions threatening rebel communities with fines of up to ten thousand marks as well as with the loss of their privileges.[4] There is, in fact, no real distinction between all these activities of parliament; whether legislating, securing assent to taxation or merely giving publicity, parliament is essentially the means whereby the rector receives consent from his subjects to governmental measures.

There was of course no accepted body of constitutional doctrine defining the extent to which this consent was required, and the formulae of both summons and mandate show that there was as yet no clear idea of consent and its necessary alternative, refusal. The communes were called 'to do, hear and effectively carry out what we (the

---

[1] RIS, N.S., XXVIII, II, 60, 64.
[2] *ASI*, XCI, 72–5; RIS, N.S., XXVIII, II, 41; Fantuzzi, *Mon. Rav.*, III, n. LXXXVI. For other parliaments concerned with 'rebels' see below pp. 149–50 and (for a proposed *colloquium* in 1266) *Reg. Cl. IV*, n. 1024.
[3] RIS, N.S., XXII, II, 43.
[4] RIS, N.S., XXII, II, 58 and XXVIII, II, 95: *RSDI*, V, 180–4.

rector) order', *etcetera*, and their representatives were empowered to
swear 'to observe in their entirety the constitutions promulgated by the
rector . . . in parliament'.[1] But there is a paradox here, for the towns
who give this mandate are often powerful subjects accustomed to defy
the rector's authority. This paradox can to some extent be resolved by
considering the recorded instances of trouble arising through towns
defying the rector in parliament. One form of defiance was of course
non-attendance, but this seems to have been rare, perhaps because
strong subjects could go to the parliament with little fear of being
forced into obedience, while weak ones feared the inevitable condemnation and fine.[2] A more common and almost equally drastic form of
action was to issue before the meeting a formal statement denying the
powers of the parliament. Before the Romagnol parliament of October
1295 Bologna's proctor made a declaration that the city intended in no
way to lose its 'honour, state, liberty, privileges or customs' through
any proceedings of the parliament; and it seems to have been normal
for the city to act in this way before such gatherings.[3] The same form of
protest could be made after the parliament, should its proceedings give
a town cause for indignation. In July 1292 the rector of the Duchy
promulgated in parliament certain constitutions which were duly accepted under oath by the representatives of the towns. But Spoleto, on
hearing the terms of these constitutions, at once sent a new representative to the rector to explain that the commune's oath was given 'saving
all the rights, customs, jurisdictions and privileges which the commune
of Spoleto has and has had . . . in accordance with the indulgence and
liberty formerly granted by the supreme pontiffs to the commune of
Spoleto . . . whereby it may not be derogated in any way in its rights,
customs, jurisdictions and privileges by reason of its oath'.[4] Two years
later Ravenna remonstrated in a similar manner against constitutions
promulgated the previous day in a parliament held at Imola. The town's
representative entered a formal protest against this legislation as con-
travening its 'jurisdiction, honour, privileges and customs'. As for the
constitutions issued by the legate, especially those concerning the payment of tithes, he was told that 'you cannot make constitutions against

---

[1] Sources cited above, pp. 114–15.

[2] The following are the only cases of absenteeism I have noted. (1) 1277, Pergola
(Duchy: *v.* Gubbio, Sottosez AS, perg., bu. 10); (2) 1300, various ecclesiastical bodies
(Duchy: *v. Arch. per la St. Eccl. dell' Umbria*, IV, d. 540); (3) 1303, Amandola, Montolmo,
Monte S. Martino (March: *v.* Ferranti, *Amandola*, III, d. 340; Colucci, *Ant. Pic.*, XXIX,
d. VII; Corridonia, AC, perg., n. 48).

[3] For sources *v.* Ermini, *Parlamenti*, pp. 73–5.

[4] Sansi, *Spoleto*, I, 124 n.

the common laws nor legislate in temporal matters against laymen without their consent'.[1]

Parliamentary disputes of a more particular nature arose over fiscal and other demands made by the rectors of Romagna. In 1287 Ravenna and Rimini, controlled respectively by the Polenta and Malatesta, refused to pay a share towards the provincial army proposed at Imola by the rector Peter Stefaneschi.[2] The proctors of both communes were arrested by the rector and thrown into prison, and the defiant towns formed an anti-papal league. In subsequent years both Forlì and Bagnacavallo refused to pay the *tallia militum* demanded of them, while a statute forbidding communes to elect *podestà* and even to tax their citizens except with rectorial permission evoked many protests and was certainly ineffective.[3] All these instances illustrate the obvious fact that parliament was an institution capable of operating in the interests of an effective papal governor but not able on its own to strengthen seriously the position of a weak one.

There remains to be discussed another form of discord arising from parliaments. This was the summoning of lesser towns regarded by greater communes as their subjects. When Spoleto formally stated its reservations concerning the constitutions promulgated at Bevagna in July 1292[4] it protested also against the rector's action in calling Cerreto to this parliament. This town was *suppositus* to Spoleto, whose proctor claimed that he also represented Cerreto *tanquam pro membro et subdito ipsius communis Spoleti*. Cerreto should not be made to swear obedience to the new constitutions, nor fealty to the rector; if it had sworn such an oath, this should be revoked. Naturally cities such as Spoleto were

---

[1] Fantuzzi, *Mon. Rav.*, III, n. LXXXXIV ('. . . non possitis constitutiones aliquas contra jura communia facere nec in temporalibus contra laicos ipsis non consententibus in eorum preiudicium statuere'). The legate who issued these constitutions was 'papal vicar' in Romagna, but not rector: hence the protest may be in part against his exceeding his rights, and is not necessarily a statement of the general principle that provincial constitutions required the consent of the pope's subjects.

[2] See the (differing) accounts in Tonduzzi, *Faenza*, p. 327 and Clementini, *Rimini*, I, 494–5.

[3] RIS, N.S., XXVIII, II, 68; Tonduzzi, *Faenza*, pp. 331, 341; Bonoli, *Forlì*, p. 111. The purpose of the statute (of 1291) was presumably to ensure that towns raised troops for provincial armies and not to fight in their own interest. Bagnacavallo's protest and appeal to the pope was based on a large number of grounds. The tax was 'against justice and order of law'; Bagnacavallo had not been cited to the parliament; the parliament had not granted the rector troops 'at will' or, if it had, it had done so against the opinion of the *maior et sanior pars* of the province, and those who had consented had been the victims of deceit; so many troops were not needed; Bagnacavallo's share was too large and, finally, the rector had no authority to tax the town. This wholesale protest is summarized in Italian in *Atti e Mem. d. r. Dep. di St. Patr. per le prov. dell'Emilia*, N.S., VII (1881), 154–5: unfortunately the original is missing from the Archivio Comunale at Bagnacavallo (1959).

[4] See above, p. 118.

unwilling to accept the implication that the towns of their *contadi* were 'immediately subject' to the provincial rector, a derogation to their rights which might be used by such towns as support for claims to be independent. There was a similar dispute in 1300 between the rector of the March and both Ascoli and Fermo concerning the small town of Monte S. Pietro, and another between Gubbio and the rector of the Duchy in 1304.[1] It is noteworthy, however, that the towns called by the rector of the Patrimony in 1298 included the places of the 'Val del Lago' over which Orvieto had secured *de facto* rule; it may be that some communes were willing to allow their subjects to be summoned to parliaments so long as there was no serious threat to their control.

★   ★   ★

This discussion of the institutions of the Papal State has sought to emphasize their provincial basis, but as a description of the State's administration it is incomplete without a return to the papal Curia. From time to time the pope supplemented and to some extent superseded the provincial structure of rule by appointing special *missi* to act within the State. Such men might be instructed to decide or advise on one specific issue or might have more general powers. Their duties might be primarily judicial or — more often — fiscal; special tax-collectors were among them, such as Master Lanfranc, who undertook a mission in the Papal State and Tuscany in the spring of 1291, and Roger provost of St. Anthony's at Piacenza, who arranged *compositiones* with many towns of the March in 1296.[2]

Furthermore a considerable degree of central control was exerted over the financial aspects of provincial rule by the papal chamber, to which the rectors and treasurers were answerable concerning their

---

[1] Sarti, *Gubbio*, pp. 174–7. Gubbio, which had been involved in a long dispute with the authorities of the Duchy over its *contado*, protested successfully that Pergola, Canziano, Serra 'and certain other nobles of the *contado* and district of Gubbio' had been called 'per speciales singulares litteras ad dicta castra et loca transmissas . . . ad parlamenta et ad receptionem constitutionum'; this the commune of Gubbio regarded as a grievance 'cum sit unum corpus cum castris et personis predictis', and it should therefore answer for them. The rector agreed that the towns and lords of Gubbio's district should not be called to parliaments. See also Ermini, *Parlamenti*, pp. 34–40. Though relevant, the topic is not discussed in Prof. De Vergottini's paper on 'Il Papato e la Comitatinanza nello Stato della Chiesa', *AMSR*, N.S., III (1951–3).

[2] Master Lanfranc's takings are recorded in Arch. Vat., Arm. XXXIII, n. 33A, where he is described (f. 9) as 'Magister Lanfrancus de Scano canonicus Pergamensis, domini papae scriptor, super censibus iuribus et debitis qui debentur Ecclesie Romane in Tuscia, Ducatu Spoletanense et quibusdam aliis Ytalie partibus nuncius specialis per sedem apostolicam deputatus'. The area of his nunciature included the March and Romagna. For provost Roger see below, p. 237.

revenues and expenditure. The link with the chamber was direct in some matters, for towns purchased privileges of it, while it purchased domain, maintained fortifications and often paid troops.[1] Its authority, moreover, was not always confined to financial affairs, and the wider implications of finance gradually gave the papal chamberlain a powerful place in the government of the State. The chamberlain heard suits concerning the juridical status of communes, such as the claims to elect *podestà* made by Fabriano in 1278 and by Imola in 1291.[2] He also conveyed papal orders to provincial authorities — in 1283, for instance, a definition of the circumstances under which pardons might be granted in the court of the March — and to towns.[3] It is symptomatic of this development that Todi appealed against the 'vexations' of the rector of the Patrimony not to Nicholas III himself but to his chamberlain.[4] Only under Nicholas IV and Boniface VIII, however, did the chamberlain assume a position which did much to centralize the structure of papal rule, co-ordinating the government of the provinces and intervening directly to order (for example) the imprisonment or release of suspects.[5]

The pope's own sovereign power is seen most clearly in his legislation for the Papal State. After Innocent III's decrees for the whole State issued at Viterbo in 1207,[6] such legislation was normally specific in content and directed to a single province: thus Honorius III ordered that rebellious subjects in the Campagna-Marittima against whom troops had been summoned could only be pardoned after paying a fine and expenses, and Gregory IX forbade castle-building in Sabina except with papal consent.[7] Law-making of this sort was very spasmodic. There was a good deal of it in 1262–3 when Urban IV legislated against communes hearing appeals and issued certain special decrees for the southern provinces, then seriously threatened by Manfred.[8] After this there is almost no trace of papal legislation until a quarter of a century

---

[1] For a fuller treatment of this subject *v. J Eccl H*, VIII, 143–4.

[2] Zonghi, *Fabriano*, d. CCXXIII: Imola, AC, Mazzo IV, n. 92, letter 70.

[3] Gianandrea, *Iesi*, d. CCXIV: Ascoli Piceno, AC, Quinternone, ff. 170 and v (Nicholas IV writes on 3 November 1289 ordering the rector of the March not to transfer forcibly the population of certain villages near Ascoli: he has already given similar instructions through his chamberlain — '. . . Nos igitur . . . dilecto filio Nicolao camerario nostro mandavimus oraculo vive vocis ut tibi ex parte nostra mandaret ut mandato huiusmodi per te facto hominibus supradictis supersedere curares usque ad nostrum beneplacitum voluntatis . . .'). The *camera* also received a list of papal subjects swearing special oaths of loyalty in 1258: see below, p. 163.

[4] Todi, AC, Rif. I, ff. 5 and v.

[5] *J Eccl H*, VIII, 151–2 (imprisonment); Richard of Bury, *Liber Epistolaris*, p. 205 (release).

[6] Above, pp. 52–3.   [7] Theiner, dd. CXXXIII, CLXXVI.

[8] *Lib. Cens.* I, 568–9 (see also Jordan, *Origines*, p. 250); *Reg. Urb. IV*, I, n. 300 and II, n. 734: for a discussion, see below, p. 166.

later Nicholas IV issued his important decrees forbidding the re-election of communal officials and the formation of leagues within the State except by papal permission.[1] Boniface VIII's major reforming codes for the Campagna-Marittima, March and Patrimony are the most impressive monuments of papal legislative intervention during this period.[2]

It would, however, be misleading to depict the thirteenth-century Papal State merely as a decentralized monarchy. As contemporary lay rulers were limited in their powers by the need to keep the support of aristocratic counsellors, so the pope was tied, more formally, by the constitutional rights of the college of cardinals.[3] At the very start of our period Innocent was careful to proclaim that the terms reached in 1200 with the communes of the March were accepted by him *de fratrum nostrorum consilio*, that is after formal consultation with the cardinals in consistory.[4] The pope did well to record the consent of the cardinals to his actions since either the towns concerned or an emperor claiming them might have pleaded that their subjection was invalid if this consent was lacking. Frederick II was later to accuse both Gregory IX and Innocent IV of acting unconstitutionally in failing to consult the cardinals, and it was on these grounds that he denied that Città di Castello was papal territory.[5] The constitutional rights of the college were sufficiently precise to make such arguments plausible. Discussion of them is made difficult by uncertainty concerning the first measure concerned specifically with the cardinals' share in the government of the Papal State. In 1234 a measure was drafted by Gregory IX, the terms of which proclaimed that *de communi fratrum nostrorum consilio*, from henceforth 'some of our brothers (*i.e.* the cardinals) shall be deputed to rule the whole patrimony for a certain period . . . the pope being in charge (*ministrante*) with the counsel of his brothers'.[6] The cardinals were also

---

[1] Mei, *Cagli*, pp. 43–5; *Reg. N. IV*, n. 7245; Theiner, d. CCCCLXXXIII. Both these measures were probably applicable to the whole State, see below, pp. 219 ff. For the revocation of a statute of Martin IV which has not survived *v. Reg. B. VIII*, n. 5338 (this statute forbade the sale of land in Campagna-Marittima to Roman nobles).

[2] See below, pp. 233 ff.

[3] For the college of cardinals in the thirteenth century, *v.* Sägmuller, *Die Thätigkeit u. Stellung der Cardinäle bis Papst Bonifaz VIII.* (for the Papal State, pp. 74–6).

[4] P.L. 214, *Reg. Inn. III*, III, 29.

[5] Suetterlin, *Die Politik Kaiser Friedrichs II. und der römischen Kardinäle in den Jahren 1239 bis 1250*, p. 20: for the question of Città di Castello, Fehling, *Kaiser Friedrich II. u. die römischen Cardinäle in den Jahren 1227 bis 1239*, pp. 71–3.

[6] See *Zeitschrift für Kirchengeschichte*, XLV, 192, and for further discussion below, p. 139. The phrase *aliqui ex fratribus nostris per tempora totius patrimonii regimini deputentur* might refer to a sort of committee of cardinals concerned with the Papal State, but since the previous phrase is concerned with the unsatisfactory effects of lay appointments to provincial rectorates it is much more probable that the intention was that thenceforth all

to receive one-third of the revenues of the Papal State, half of the remainder going to the pope's chamber and the other half to the treasury of the Church 'to be applied to the common needs of the Church' as advised by the cardinals. Since the terms of this decree were not carried out, so far as is known, in any respect, it should probably be regarded as a draft which has survived, rather than a measure actually promulgated but destined to remain ineffective. It remains none the less an interesting indication of the standing of the cardinals in temporal government.

Half a century later the status of the cardinals in this matter was formally fixed by Nicholas IV's decree 'Celestis altitudo'.[1] Besides allotting to the college half the revenues of the *terrae ecclesiae*, this measure, promulgated in 1289, declared that 'we grant that the appointment and dismissal of the rectors (in the Papal State) . . . and of the collectors of these revenues . . . shall be by the counsel of the cardinals'. In practice consultation of the cardinals before making appointments to rectorates had started much earlier. When the rector of the March was captured in the spring of 1264, Urban IV did not appoint a successor until he had been able to call together the cardinals and have 'diligent and fervent discussions' with them about which cardinal was best qualified to head the papal cause in this vital province.[2]

The principle that papal territory could only be granted as a fief with the cardinals' consent was recognized from the beginning of the century, and such consent was given for Azzo of Este's enfeoffment with the March in 1212 and on similar occasions.[3] An earlier canon which forbade alienation of papal domain except by the unanimous consent of the cardinals was confirmed by Gregory IX in 1234.[4] Under Benedict XI the rôle of the cardinals in the government of the Papal State was strongly asserted in two measures revoking actions of Boniface VIII.

rectors should be cardinals. This was not carried out, nor is there evidence of the existence of a committee or of cardinals receiving a share of the income of the *terrae ecclesiae* earlier than 1289.

[1] Theiner, d. CCCLXVIII (omissions make the abbreviated version in *Reg. N. IV*, n. 2217, seriously misleading).

[2] Colucci, *Ant. Pic.*, XIX, 47 ('statim convocavimus fratres nostros . . . cardinales et cepimus tractare cum eis . . . tractatibus cum eisdem fratribus diligenter et ferventer insistimus': for the subsequent appointment of Cardinal Simon Paltanieri *de fratrum nostrorum consilio*, v. Colucci, *Treia*, d. XXXIX).

[3] Theiner, dd. LVI, LXV.

[4] *Reg. G. IX*, n. 1715; any cardinal's objection to such alienation *ex causa legitima* rendered the act invalid. Provincial rectors were expressly forbidden to alienate papal property without the pope's consent: the powers of a vice-treasurer of the March (1290) of 'alienandum res et possessiones Ecclesiae' (Gianandrea, *Iesi*, d. CCXXXV) presumably related only to agrarian produce, etc. Urban IV refused to grant certain territory in the March to various petitioners, *fratrum concordi consilio repugnante* (Martène and Durand, *Thesaurus*, II, col. 361).

The constitution 'Celestis patrisfamilias' was suspended and various financial and judicial grants to towns in the Duchy revoked, the first on the grounds that the cardinals had not consented to it, the second expressly *de fratrum nostrorum consilio*. This assertion of the cardinals' position has its importance for the constitutional history of the State, although it was not motivated by constitutional considerations.[1]

The limit placed on the pope's freedom of action in the Papal State by the need to secure the approval of the cardinals to certain measures is only one aspect of the college's ascending status, nor are constitutional gains the only sign of this development. Particularly towards the end of the century those cardinals who concerned themselves with central Italy — for the most part they were born of Italian families with lands and interests in this zone — intervened freely in the affairs of the State, forwarding the concerns of towns with which they were linked and continually writing to provincial rectors about lawsuits, appointments and other matters.[2] A number of the popes, among them Boniface VIII, had served a long apprenticeship of this sort in the affairs of the Papal State. Innocent IV had been rector of the March from 1235 to 1240 and was unique among the thirteenth century popes in having governed a major province before his elevation to the Roman See.

---

[1] *Reg. B. XI*, nn. 1147, 1206. Benedict's aim was simply to undo, in a manner that could not be challenged, certain actions of his predecessor that he found unpalatable. This shows clearly in the second reason given for the suspension of 'Celestis patrisfamilias', *i.e.* that its terms were *valde ardua*.

[2] See below, p. 224.

V

The Papal State and the Hohenstaufen, 1216 – 65

Having completed our assessment of the popes' task and the means available to them for its accomplishment, it is time to return to a chronological sketch of the development of their State. Honorius III, the successor of Innocent III, came of the family of Savelli, minor nobles from the Roman Campagna who probably descended from the Crescenzi.[1] He had served a long apprenticeship as papal chamberlain and his work as a financial administrator, of which the redaction of the *Liber Censuum* was the secure monument, had given him some familiarity with the problems of governing the State. Moreover, the period of opportunity which opened with the defeat of Otto IV continued through Honorius' pontificate and there was comparatively little imperial intervention to hinder the pope's attempts to solve these problems.

Frederick II, indeed, confirmed in 1219 his previous donation of the Papal State (adding to it the Apennine territory of Massa Trabaria): this grant was approved by the imperial princes in 1220 and Frederick issued yet another confirmation in 1221.[2] This plurality of documents suggests papal anxiety to be reassured and other evidence confirms this diagnosis. Twice in 1219 Frederick wrote to the pope insisting that he had made no attempt to grant the Duchy of Spoleto in fee: if Conrad of Urslingen's son continued to use the title 'Duke of Spoleto', this was merely German practice and had no territorial significance, and any grants of papal territory had been made in ignorance and were revoked.[3] In an attempt to allay Honorius' fears, Frederick even wrote to remind

---

[1] Clausen, *Papst Honorius III.*, pp. 1–2; Cecchelli, *I Crescenzi, i Savelli, i Cenci*, pp. 11–12.

[2] Theiner, dd. LXXVI, LXXVII, C. By this time reference is no longer made right back to the Carolingian donations. The terms of the 1221 confirmation follow those of 1213, not 1219, but it seems unlikely that this is significant: possibly the formulae of 1219 were not available to the chancery, which was on the move.

[3] Theiner, d. LXXIV: Huillard-Bréholles, I, 674.

the citizens of the March of Ancona that they were subjects of the pope.[1]

Honorius was most apprehensive about Spoleto, and rightly so, for the family of Urslingen was close to Frederick and had not resigned itself to the loss of the Duchy. When Frederick and the pope met at Veroli in the spring of 1222 the emperor asked for the Duchy, perhaps as a fief for the Urslingen.[2] Honorius vigorously turned down this request, but in conjuncture with other events it must have confirmed his fear that in Frederick's view the future of the Papal State was still an open question. At about the same period either Frederick or his representative in Tuscany, Gunzelin von Wolfenbüttel, committed the Hohenstaufen to intervention in central Italy for the first time for a quarter of a century.[3] Gunzelin secured the fealty of the Viterbese, while assisting their cause against Roman attacks, and attempted to recruit troops in the Duchy to fight on their behalf. This permeation of Hohenstaufen influence from Tuscany into the disputed zone of 'Roman Tuscany' recalls closely the situation of the 1190s. The German success at Viterbo was accompanied by considerable activity in the Duchy and March. Foligno, Gubbio, Osimo, and several other communes in these provinces, as well as a number of barons, went over to Gunzelin and his protector Bertold of Urslingen. These towns threw out papal bailiffs and accepted in their stead men named by the imperial steward. The protests and excommunications of Cardinal Ranier, the papal rector in the Duchy, were ineffective, but late in 1222 the emperor disavowed Bertold, apologized to the pope and cardinals in a series of elaborate letters, and ordered his steward to beg in person for the pope's pardon.

The gains achieved by the Germans during this episode are striking, and their control in a number of important centres in the Duchy for a period of several months was a serious blow to papal pretensions. The sincerity of Frederick's disavowal of the organizers of this exploit is questionable, but has little relevance here. It seems rather likely that the initiative was Bertold's, yet Gunzelin would hardly have supported it had he believed it to be opposed to the emperor's wishes. Frederick had

---

[1] The only actions in Honorius' early years as pope, to cast doubt on these assurances are venial intervention, not in imperial interests, at Senigallia and Fermo (with prompt apology): intervention by the Justiciar of the Regno at Rieti (boundary dispute): possible implication in a charter that Città di Castello was imperial (but no papal complaint). See Theiner, dd. LXXI, CIX; Ficker, *Forschungen*, IV, d. 288; BFW, n. 14668.

[2] *Reg. Hon. III*, n. 3949. For the possibility that Honorius III may have considered such a grant in 1217–19, see below, p. 129.

[3] For this episode see BFW, n. 12828a; *Reg. Hon. III*, nn. 3940 and 4600: *QFIA*, XXIX, 156: Theiner, dd. CXVI–CXXV (Frederick's letters): Ciampi, *Viterbo*, p. 15: *Reg. G. IX*, nn. 1592–3 (Osimo).

little to lose and was perhaps at the least willing to turn a blind eye
while papal power was submitted to a test the outcome of which was of
considerable interest to him. His unsupported word that he was opposed to the whole affair is not worth much and the Urslingen family
fell into no permanent disgrace; in fact Rainald was Frederick's legate
in Tuscany in 1224 and in 1226 legate for all imperial Italy with Bertold
as his vicar for Tuscany.[1]

Although there were no other serious inroads into the Papal State
during Honorius' pontificate, Frederick soon showed that he refused to
regard the loss of central Italy as final and complete. Requiring troops
for a Lombard campaign, he called for contingents from the towns of
the Duchy of Spoleto as well as from Viterbo and probably some communes of the March.[2] This service he claimed as an imperial right, even
in papal territory, while the demand to Viterbo was based on the town's
duty of fidelity to the emperor. When the pope protested and ordered
the towns to disobey, Frederick replied with protestations which were
compatible neither with the original summonses nor with each other.
The demands had been made without his knowledge; they concerned
service not in Lombardy, but in the Holy Land; the Papal State owed
him military service; and the papacy had attempted to deprive him
during his childhood of the exarchate of Ravenna, the March, Tuscany
and Fondi. Soon after the first apology the demand for troops was
repeated in letters to the Duchy. Honorius' replies to the emperor's list
of grievances and assertion that the status of the Papal State was defined
in Frederick's own donations made little impression.[3] Before Honorius'
death in March 1227 it had become evident that the era of Hohenstaufen withdrawal from central Italy was at an end.

When we come to consider Pope Honorius' methods of rule, we
have to deal, as far as direct rule is concerned, only with the old patrimony (including the once disputed Tuscan border) and the Duchy, for
the feudal grant of the March to the Estensi was prolonged throughout
this pontificate. Marquis Azzo VII was invested with the March in
1217, two years after the death of his elder brother Aldobrandino.
Spiritual revenues were rendered to the Church, temporal ones to the

---

[1] Ficker, *Forschungen*, IV, dd. 310 and 323–4.

[2] Huillard-Bréholles, II, 548 (for the date of this letter *v.* *QFIA*, XXIX, 157n): Richard
of S. Germano (RIS, N.S., VII), pp. 136–8: *QFIA*, XXIX, 157–8. The promise of two
men of Montecchio in 1226 to remain two months in the service of the emperor (Colucci,
Treia, d. XIII) suggests that towns in the March were also summoned.

[3] Huillard-Bréholles, II, 588–99. If the Bertold whose appointment as *podestà* of Ascoli
in 1227 was so resented by Honorius (*Reg. Hon. III*, n. 6179) was Bertold of Urslingen,
this provides another probable instance of imperial intervention.

Marquis and to his mother, on behalf of whom a proctor held the province during Azzo's minority. Azzo probably performed fealty in person when he came of age in 1225.[1] He was himself mainly concerned with the struggle against Salinguerra for Ferrara and continued to govern the March through a vicar, of whose administration very few traces have survived.[2] The system was certainly a clumsy one, as may be seen from the difficulties of the bishop of Fermo in seeking redress of certain grievances against Macerata: the bishop complained to the pope, who then approached Azzo, the nominal rector, through the Marquis' chancellor, who was also his vicar or proctor in the March.[3] Such circuitous methods cannot have made for efficiency. The impression of failure is strengthened by the attempts of Ancona to secure exemption from the Marquis' jurisdiction and the pope's indecisive attitude towards these pretensions. Honorius at first supported the claim but later wrote to the town urging it — together with a number of other 'disobedient' communes — to recognize the Marquis as its lord.[4] This tacit withdrawal of support was probably occasioned by the great difficulties of the Marquis and his vicar in ruling the province. Iesi, Recanati, Cingoli and several smaller towns were opposing Azzo at this time (1221),[5] and papal backing for one rebel might have encouraged in others the belief that exemption was the reward for successful resistance. In any case the position of the Marquis was complicated by the occasional presence of papal envoys and legates, as well as by spasmodic direct intervention by the pope himself.[6] Some of these representatives were merely prelates empowered to use spiritual weapons in support of the Marquis' authority, while others had orders to secure agreements between the Marquis and his subjects. Their very existence was a symptom of the need to fortify the position of the Marquis. Like his predecessor, Honorius sought a feudal solution to the problem of the March, but this failed to secure peace or central control.

Honorius may have considered the application of the same expedient to the Duchy of Spoleto and entered on negotiations with a potential

---

[1] Muratori, *Antichità Estensi*, II, 423–4: *Reg. Hon. III*, nn. 467, 5456, 5739.

[2] One is BFW n. 12565 (Azzo's vicar promises to observe a privilege granted to Osimo and to secure its renewal).

[3] *Reg. Hon. III*, n. 3944.

[4] *Reg. Hon. III*, nn. 3036, 3110, 3234, 3520: Theiner, d. CV: Muratori, *Antichità Estensi*, I, 426.

[5] Theiner, dd. CX, CXIV: Muratori, *loc. cit.* For a later serious dispute with the bishop of Fermo *v.* Catalani, *Fermo*, dd. LII–LIV.

[6] Theiner, d. CXXX: Compagnoni, *Regg. Pic.*, p. 95: *Reg. Hon. III*, nn. 5021 and 6179 (direct papal intervention), 5092–3 (Pandulf as legate), 5739 and 5848 (the bishop of Fossombrone and provost of Ferrara given instructions to carry out ecclesiastical censures).

vassal. Between 1217 and 1219 he was holding discussions with Rainald and Bertold, the sons of Conrad of Urslingen. The suggestion that these discussions concerned the feudal grant of the Duchy has the authority of Ficker and Winkelmann,[1] yet such a measure would have seemed a gesture of despair at a time when circumstances did not compel it, and the hypothesis should probably be rejected. The two letters that contain our only evidence for the negotiations are quite inconclusive.[2] In September 1217 Pope Honorius wrote to Rainald that the discussions begun with Bertold could go no further without Rainald's presence, but that he was prepared to carry out the terms provisionally agreed on, so far as was in his power: this mysterious phraseology could refer to an agreement about the property and rights of the family within the Duchy just as well as to discussions concerning the tenure of the province. Over a year later, in January 1219, the pope wrote both to Nocera (in the Duchy), defining the rights of Conrad of Urslingen's widow in that town, and to Rainald of Spoleto, reaffirming his readiness to carry out the terms arranged with Bertold if Rainald would ratify them. The juxtaposition of these letters suggests that the pope's discussions with the Urslingen family turned on their claims to personal rights within the Duchy rather than on a grant to them of the entire province. By the early summer of 1219 Honorius was accusing Frederick of granting the Duchy to the Urslingen in terms which suggest that his own negotiations with them, whatever their nature, had now been broken off.[3]

In the Duchy of Spoleto, as well as in the Campagna-Marittima and the outlying miniature province of Massa Trabaria, Pope Honorius appointed rectors; in the case of the larger provinces these were usually cardinals. Until the last two months of the pontificate a vacuum in the provincial structure seems to have persisted between Rome and imperial Tuscany, although Innocent had had a rector for the Tuscan Patrimony.[4] Here the pope's struggle for control was in the hands of legates and emissaries sent out from time to time with duties which were more strictly defined than those of the rectors. The presence of such envoys in the March of Ancona has already been mentioned. The missions there of the papal subdeacon and notary Pandulf in 1221 and

---

[1] BFW, n. 6249; Ficker in *MIÖG*, IV, 365.

[2] MGH, *Ep. Pont.*, I, 27: *Reg. Hon. III*, nn. 1789, 1791.

[3] Theiner, d. LXXIV. For the role of Bertold in imperial intervention in the Duchy in 1222 see above, p. 126.

[4] For the appointment of John of Brienne as rector of the Tuscan Patrimony in 1227 see below, p. 137.

1224 have many parallels. Pandulf himself had accomplished similar
pacificatory missions at Rieti in 1218 and in the Duchy in 1220,[1] while
in these years other emissaries, sometimes cardinals and sometimes papal
chaplains, some bearing legatine rank and others not, were carrying out
tasks of the same nature at Narni, Orvieto, Perugia and many other
places.[2]

In turning to Honorius' policy towards the communes we may note
his occasional insistence on his juridical rights, for example on the
principle that *podestà* required his approval, and his condemnation of
towns which punished their citizens for sueing outside the municipal
courts.[3] Such actions, however, were exceptional and normally ineffective. More characteristic are the grants of privileges to the powerful — Fermo's fiscal and jurisdictional immunities and right to a mint,
Ancona's temporary exemption from the control of the provincial
rector, Viterbo's receipt of lordship over three fortified townships in
the Tuscan Patrimony.[4] Such a policy savours of alliance more than of
rule, but there was no decision to base papal power on an alliance with
the stronger towns, nor could there be without an admission of defeat,
for in terms of the local situation the papacy would always have been
the weaker party in such an alliance. Hence the attempts to set bounds
to the strength of some larger towns by backing against them the less
powerful neighbours who were their natural enemies: such a policy
may be seen, for instance, in Honorius' promise of protection to Stroncone against the important centre of Narni.[5] Honorius had not the
means to pursue a strong policy, but his approach brought little promise
of success. Real government could never be built up on a basis of
spasmodic claims to obedience mingled with apologetic gratitude.
The small town of Spello, which had refused to submit to Gunzelin
and Bertold during their venture in the Duchy, was rewarded by
being excused from taxation.[6] These were not the tactics by which
a new state could be shaped from the intractable material of central
Italy.

Honorius, however, was more successful in Rome and the surround-

---

[1] Rieti, Arch. Cap., Arm. VIII, fasc. B, n. 2: *Reg. Hon. III*, n. 2551.

[2] E.g. *Reg. Hon. III*, nn. 750, 1861, 2967–8.

[3] For the *podestà*-ship, *v. QFIA*, XXIX, 156–7 and *Reg. Hon. III*, nn. 6179, 6258 (Gubbio, 1224; Ascoli and Camerino, 1227). The absence of letters granting papal consent to *podestà* is probably significant. For the question of external courts *v. Reg. Hon. III*, nn. 4441 and 4850 (the cancellation of the latter in the register is unlikely to represent a retraction of the decision).

[4] *Reg. Hon. III*, nn. 1776, 2840, 3183 (Fermo), 3110, 3234 (Ancona), 3818 (Viterbo).

[5] *Reg. Hon. III*, n. 5628.   [6] *Reg. Hon. III*, n. 4600.

ing region than in the new provinces.[1] Though he was driven from
Rome briefly in 1219 and 1220 by the 'molestations' of the citizens,
these periods of exile were not much more prolonged than the normal
summer *villeggiatura* and he returned, with the aid of Frederick II, for
the imperial coronation in the autumn of 1220. In 1222 a Roman attack
on Viterbo occasioned another absence, but Rome's aggression was ineffective and Honorius was able to return after only four months. His
third quarrel with the city, in 1225, was a more serious affair, for this
time the Romans installed a regime, under Parenzo Parenzo, which was
openly hostile. The original cause of this dispute was the resentment of
Count Richard, the brother of Innocent III, at the failure of the Savelli
to support his tenure of Sora, which in 1221 he had lost to the Emperor
Frederick. Count Richard intervened in the Roman factions and was
concerned in Honorius' decision to flee and in Parenzo's senatorship.
But Parenzo was overthrown after only a few months, and Honorius
returned to the city in February 1226, again assisted by the intervention
of the emperor. Despite the three *contretemps*, Honorius was in the
main successful in continuing Innocent III's policy of good relations
with Rome. The city had not extended its power and the regime,
though probably not much under his control, was normally favourable
to him.

In the province of Campagna and Marittima he also achieved a fair
degree of success: indeed good relations with Rome and the checking
of Roman 'imperialism' were the essential key to the control of the
whole area from Viterbo to the southern border. There was serious
trouble on this frontier in the first year of the pontificate, when John of
Ceccano, after repelling a raid by the count of Aquila, conducted a
private war, characteristic of this pre-eminently feudal territory,
against his neighbours the Colonna and the lords of Supino. The pacification of 1217 should almost certainly be attributed to the intervention
of the pope, who was operating in an area well known to him. Between
May and October of 1217 he made a progress in the Campagna, after
appointing as its rector Cardinal John Colonna, who could at least be
expected to defend his own family against the pretensions of John of
Ceccano.[2] There followed a remarkable period of peace in this province,
broken only in 1221 by a papal punitive campaign against the frontier
port of Terracina and its aftermath when Terracina attacked Segni in

---

[1] For Honorius' relations with Rome *v.* Gregorius, V, 1, 118–41; Gross, pp. 7–16 and
Pinzi, *Viterbo*, I, 271 ff.
[2] MGH, XIX (*Ann. Cecc.*), 300–2: *Reg. Hon. III*, nn. 394, 397.

revenge for that town's participation in the campaign. But the ability of the rector to organize a provincial force to attack a disturber of the peace is impressive, and confirms the impression of control given by the pope's success in securing agreements between Terracina and Piperno and between Ninfa and Sermoneta.[1]

To the north of Rome also, apart from the city's one war against Viterbo, Honorius' pontificate is a period of comparative peace. There is not much evidence of papal authority here, and the readiness with which Viterbo accepted the overlordship of Gunzelin is significant, but the pope's court was sufficiently powerful to attract a lawsuit between Orvieto and a neighbouring feudatory.[2] Further east, near the Tiber valley, Narni was a dissatisfied element seeking to expand at the expense of the towns around it and to ward off the advance of Terni. Local warfare here became involved with inter-communal strife in the Duchy, Narni being aided by Spoleto and Montefalco, while Todi and Foligno were drawn into the opposing party.[3] In 1220 Pandulf, the trusted papal notary, succeeded a cardinal as legate in the Duchy, called representatives of the warring towns to Bevagna, and helped to bring about effective arbitration by Honorius himself at Orvieto (June 1220). At the same time the leading towns of the Duchy acknowledged the papal succession to the fortresses and *regalia* held by Conrad of Urslingen in the time of the Hohenstaufen. Cardinal Ranier became rector of the Duchy that August and served a strenuous and instructive apprenticeship in the affairs of the Papal State. An optimistic papal report of gains in the Duchy, issued in February 1221, reveals less than does the support given at this time to Bertold of Urslingen by parties in Foligno, Gubbio and a number of other towns. Moreover Foligno took as its *podestà* Andrew Parenzo (brother of Pope Honorius' Roman opponent of 1225) who set up in open opposition to the provincial rector and perhaps plotted against his life.[4] Despite occasional intervention by Honorius, the towns of the Duchy for the most part went their own way, heedless of papal claims to suzerainty.[5]

If the condition of the Duchy was such as to explain the thesis that

[1] *Reg. Hon. III*, nn. 2203, 3470, 5036; BFW, n. 6287; Contatore, *Terracina*, pp. 183 and 286–8.

[2] *Reg. Hon. III*, n. 2132. The small fortress of Proceno near Orvieto was regained at this period and together with Acquapendente and Radicofani was placed under the (probably nominal) rule of the *podestà* of Viterbo (*Lib. Cens.*, I, 10*–12*).

[3] For this period in the history of the Duchy *v. Reg. G. IX*, nn. 1861, 2251; Terni, AS, perg. n. 12; and, in particular, *Lib. Cens.*, I, 10*–12* (papal letter of 18 February 1221).

[4] *ASRSP*, XII, 319; *QFIA*, XXIX, 156.

[5] For some instances of intervention involving Perugia, *v. Reg. Hon. III*, nn. 2967–8, 4513, 4579; (cf. BFW n. 12864).

Honorius considered granting the province to a layman as a fief, that of the March of Ancona shows that this expedient was not necessarily a solution to the problem of endemic warfare and the defiance of central authority. The history of the March, that land of comparatively small and evenly-matched hilltop towns, comes nearest to justifying Edouard Jordan's definition of the history of the medieval Papal State as 'a series of obscure and monotonous struggles'. As in the Duchy, Bertold found no difficulty here in 1222-3 in discovering towns that would turn to any intervening power for support against their neighbours. The towns formed leagues freely without reference to any superior and even committed themselves to alliances with the cities of Romagna.[1] Two of the more powerful towns, Ancona and Fermo, were at times officially exempted from the Marquis' authority, or at least granted partial immunity, but normally there can have been no need to demand such status. In 1221 six towns were stigmatized in a papal letter as rebels against the Marquis[2] and it seems probable that this was a normal state of affairs. The most dramatic example of municipal insubordination concerns the history of Fano.[3] Early in Honorius' pontificate this powerful maritime town attacked its inland neighbour Fossombrone, doing much damage to the property of its bishop. A quarrel then broke out over Fano's attempts to tax its own clergy. The *podestà* forbade any communication with the bishop and his *familia* who in consequence had to subsist for three weeks on a diet of vegetables. After the *podestà* had refused ecclesiastical arbitration, the bishop placed the town under an interdict and excommunicated the *podestà* and his leading supporters. A papal legate confirmed these sentences, whereupon the *podestà* and his men broke into the cathedral sacristy and the bishop's palace. The bishop and seven canons fled to the high altar of the cathedral, but had to give themselves up after enduring three days without food. The pope heaped on further condemnations, attempting to forbid all trade with Fano and threatening to deprive the town of its diocese, but negotiations were lengthy, for the commune was unwilling to give full compensation to the injured parties. More than five years after the original troubles the bishop arranged that the town should give financial pledges and twenty hostages *de melioribus civitatis*, and this perhaps led to a pacification, for no later reference to the affair survives.

---

[1] BFW, n. 12499.

[2] Muratori, *Antichità Estensi*, I, 426 (the towns were Ancona, Numana, Recanati, Castelficardo, Montecchio and Cingoli).

[3] *Reg. Hon. III*, nn. 729, 733, 1175-6, 4108: Amiani, *Fano*, II, xxvii-xxix (the principal document) and xxxiii. Cf. Salvemini, *Studi Storici* (1901), pp. 51-3.

The dispute at Fano was exceptional in its violence, but there were similar quarrels between lay and ecclesiastical powers in many towns of the Papal State. The most frequent *casus belli* was probably the taxation of the clergy, though papal protests refer generically to 'statutes against ecclesiastical liberty'. During Honorius' pontificate there were disputes of this nature at Viterbo, Rieti, Tivoli, Foligno, Osimo and Città di Castello.[1] They often continued for a long period and involved the excommunication of the municipal officials as well as, on occasions, an interdict on the town itself. This frequent source of discord between the pope and his subjects is a symptom of the failure of papal rule, for the Church-State quarrels in the towns of papal Italy took exactly the same form as those in the city-states of the north,[2] so powerless was the pope to shape the policies of his subject-towns.

*   *   *

The succession to the papacy of Gregory IX in March 1227 brought about a change from the pessimistic empiricism of the previous decade. Like his predecessors, the new pope was a native of the Campagna: the family held lands at Segni, Ferentino and Anagni.[3] He was a relative, probably a cousin, of Innocent III and he too had played a part in the origins of the Papal State, for he had been concerned in Innocent's negotiations with Markward of Anweiler. He held the belief that a state could be formed in central Italy and realized that strategy as well as tactics was needed to bring it into being.

In the period before the Treaty of San Germano (1230) Gregory was seriously harassed by imperial intervention. When the excommunicate Frederick II sailed on his long-postponed Crusade in June 1228 he left Rainald of Urslingen as his vicar, with heavy responsibilities to face. The pope, who was in alliance with the emperor's Lombard opponents, had freed Frederick's own subjects from the duty of obedience, while long-standing border disputes had flared up south of Rieti. At the time of his departure Frederick drafted two diplomas, one creating Rainald imperial vicar in the March of Ancona, the Matildine territories and perhaps in other lands claimed by the papacy, the other permanently

---

[1] *Reg. Hon. III*, nn. 1553, 2161, 2182, 2860-2; Muzi, *Città di Castello*, VI, 38-9; Rieti, Arch. Cap., Arm. VIII, fasc. B, nos. 2-5. For a dispute a few years later (1237) between the commune and bishop of Ascoli Piceno over the former's enfranchisement of the latter's serfs, *v.* Ascoli, AC, Perg. E., fasc. 1, n. 2.

[2] For these see Volpe, *Medio Evo Italiano* (1928), pp. 197-214 and Salvemini, *Studi Storici* (1901), pp. 39-90.

[3] For Gregory IX's family *v.* Felten, *Papst Gregor IX.*, pp. 5, 14-17: Maccarone in *ASRSP*, LXVI, and Marchetti-Longhi in *ASRSP*, LXVII.

revoking the same area to the Empire on the grounds of papal hostility
to the emperor.[1] Rainald may have been authorized to use these documents only in the eventuality of papal troops invading the Regno and
many years later the emperor claimed that in utilizing them Rainald
had acted without authority. Yet it seems highly improbable that
Frederick would have entrusted Rainald, the possessor of claims to
papal territory, with such documents if he intended them to be used
only in the event of a papal offensive. The exact nature of Rainald's
instructions cannot be ascertained, but they are in any case irrelevant
here. By the late autumn of 1228 Rainald had made public the two
diplomas and launched an attack into the border districts of the Duchy,
and was preparing the ground for an invasion of the March.[2] While
Rainald's brother Bertold moved into the Duchy and occupied the area
around Norcia, another imperial official won over the important town
of Foligno in the same province. Rainald himself advanced into the
March in 1229, gaining the support of Macerata, Montolmo, Recanati
and Osimo, and thus establishing his power in the very centre of the
province. He may have been aided by the intervention of Venice which
had established a league with these towns and many others; the Venetians, who had commercial interests in the area, were perhaps hoping
to exploit the war between Gregory and the Urslingen as a *tertium
gaudens*.[3] Rainald even opened negotiations in the hope of purchasing
the favour of Perugia, then the seat of the Curia, but these were unsuccessful.

Throughout the first half of 1229 the pope was organizing an army
under the leadership of John of Brienne and Cardinal John Colonna to
drive Rainald back to the Regno. His main strength, however, was
probably put into a counter-invasion of the Terra del Lavoro from the
Campagna, launched under the papal chaplain Pandulf of Anagni in
January, and intended to turn Rainald's flank. Towards midsummer
this army had advanced to Benevento and Capua, forcing Rainald to
retire to the Regno, where he sought to hold Sulmona. These armies
and another which had been campaigning in the Abruzzi joined and
operated together in the area of the Volturno, but Frederick's return in

---

[1] Huillard-Bréholles, III, 65–8 (the inclusion of the 'Marittima' and the 'Val del Lago'
in the text of the grant is hard to explain). On this topic *v.* Ficker in *MIÖG*, IV, 351–79
(makes the rather improbable suggestions that Rainald was also granted the Duchy of
Spoleto and that the diplomas were only to apply if the pope attacked). Good discussion
in Jordan, *L'Allemagne et l'Italie*, pp. 216–17.

[2] *Reg. G. IX*, nn. 217, 227, 332; BFW, nn. 13012, 13018, 1757–8; Colucci, *Ant. Pic.*,
XVIII, d. 9; *Vita G. IX* (*Lib. Cens.*, II), 20–1; Richard of S. Germano, p. 152.

[3] *Reg. G. IX*, n. 218; BFW, nn. 12997–8.

June 1229 led to a humiliating flight, in which Cardinal Colonna out-distanced his companions, returning to the pope 'under pretence of going to fetch money to pay the troops', as Richard of S. Germano sceptically reports. Long before the end of 1229 there were no papal troops left in the Regno: indeed Frederick and the Urslingen were again raiding papal territory by the autumn.[1]

Rainald of Urslingen's invasion had again demonstrated the extreme vulnerability of the Papal State. It had enfeebled the weak fabric of papal rule, compelled the pope for a time to divert men and money to the urgent problem of ending the incursion, and deferred any schemes for general reform. It also brought about the end of the experiment of enfeoffing the Marquises of Este with the March.[2] By the Peace of San Germano of July–August 1230 the emperor offered full restitution of the Duchy and March and promised that he would not again invade papal territory. For about nine years these terms were effective and Gregory, enjoying a return to the 'breathing-space' of Pope Honorius' time, was able to concentrate on the problems of territorial government without suffering imperial intervention. Disputes continued on the March-Abruzzi boundary, Frederick did not resign himself to the loss of Città di Castello,[3] and once (in 1236) he embarrassed Gregory by wooing the Romans. But in general the emperor's preoccupations in northern Italy made him wish to maintain friendly relations with the pope, hence his willing co-operation in the solution of frontier questions and even the despatch of a force — an inadequate one, in Gregory's opinion — to fight the rebellious Romans in 1234.[4]

Gregory's policy in central Italy is marked by energetic re-organization and by a number of experiments in rule. He himself intervened directly in the Papal State, both by legislation and administrative action, while his rectors set to work to establish lawcourts and instituted a series of enquiries into papal domanial rights in the Sabina and the Duchy, the findings of which were incorporated in the *Liber Censuum*.[5] As well as legislating against the alienation of papal property, he pursued a very active policy of purchasing strategic places, among them

[1] *Reg. G. IX*, nn. 332, 6133; Richard of S. Germano, pp. 153–64: Ficker, *art. cit.*; Böhm, *Johann v. Brienne*, pp. 84–8.
[2] See below, p. 138.
[3] On the dispute over Città di Castello in 1229–39 *v.* Fehling, pp. 71–3.
[4] *Reg. G. IX*, n. 563. See also Gregorovius, V, 1, 174–6; Gross, pp. 30 ff.; Jordan, *L'Allemagne et l'Italie*, pp. 236–7.
[5] For papal intervention, *v.* Theiner, d. CLXXVI and *Reg. G. IX*, n. 1715 (legislation); Cristofani, *Assisi*, p. 99 (parliament); *Reg. G. IX*, nn. 2715 and 4224–39 (direct orders to subjects). For the lawcourts, see above, p. 108, for the enquiries, *Lib. Cens.*, I, 377–8, 450–2, 543–5.

Gualdo Tadino and Otricoli on the Via Flaminia and Miranda, a hill-fortress above Terni.[1]

While relying upon a provincial structure for his government — no longer were there periods of vacancy between rectorships — Gregory supplemented this by the frequent use of cardinals and papal chaplains as legates and *missi*.[2] A significant development concerning the rectorate was the emergence of a small group of prelates who specialized in this office. Gregory employed by preference experienced men, especially from the Campagna. Cardinal John Colonna, who had ruled the Campagna and the Duchy under Honorius III, now became rector of the March, and Cardinal Ranier of Viterbo, rector of the Duchy for Honorius, acted as rector of the Tuscan Patrimony after 1234. There were specialists also among the papal chaplains. Gregory *de Romania* took on the rectorate of the Patrimony and the Duchy after many years of experience in the Campagna, and 'Alatrinus', a native of the Campagna, was assistant to King John in the Patrimony and then for several years legate in the March before he became rector of the Duchy.[3]

Several experiments were made with this institution in Gregory IX's time. One of these, the appointment of John of Brienne, titular King of Jerusalem, as rector of an enlarged Tuscan Patrimony, was indeed initiated by Honorius III a few weeks before his death, but the duration of this rectorship (1227–?9) falls almost entirely within Gregory's pontificate.[4] This grant has a certain resemblance to the other award of a province to a layman, the Estense tenure of the March, but the terms are different, for King John's position was not feudal. His letters of appointment contained the normal formulae, he held his own court like other rectors, indeed he differed from them only in being granted certain revenues of the territories he ruled. The immediate purpose of the appointment was probably to strengthen the pope's position *vis-à-vis* Rome by giving some unity to the area threatened by the city's policy of northerly expansion.[5] King John was above all a soldier — 'another Charlemagne', according to Salimbene — who had thrown in

---

[1] *Lib. Cens.*, I, 520–34, 537, 539–41, 546–52: the impressive list of purchases in Felten, *Papst Gregor IX.*, p. 153 is inaccurate.

[2] For some examples, *v. Reg. G. IX*, nn. 2954–5; Lilii, *Camerino*, I, 235; RIS, N.S., XV, V, 149.

[3] See App. II.

[4] See *Reg. Hon. III*, nn. 6203–4, 6209, 6216 and *Reg. G. IX*, n. 45. The area placed under King John, described as 'the patrimony of the Church in Tuscany' or 'the patrimony of the Church from Radicofani to Rome', took in Amelia, Narni, Stroncone, S. Gemini and Todi in the east as well as Perugia in the north-east. On the rectorship of King John *v.* Böhm, *Johann v. Brienne*, pp. 82 ff.

[5] As suggested by Gross, p. 15 and Böhm, p. 82. For Gregory IX and Rome see below, pp. 141 ff.

his lot with the papacy after his father-in-law Frederick II had treated him badly and tricked him out of his title.[1] He was therefore an obvious choice as a military commander when war broke out between Rainald of Urslingen and the papacy. Once engaged in this more congenial work, John never returned to rule his province. His appointment in the Tuscan Patrimony, interesting as an experiment, accomplished little in practice.

The time of King John's rectorship saw the abandonment of an earlier expedient, feudal government in the March. The exact circumstances of this forfeiture are unknown. During the summer of 1228 Marquis Azzo visited Gregory IX at Perugia and asked to leave the March, but in September the pope wrote urgently to demand his return with a cavalry force, for the province was already threatened by 'enemies of the Church'. This letter contains a veiled threat and by the autumn of 1230 Azzo had been deprived of his fief for failing to defend it against the imperialists.[2] The house of Este's greater concern with its lands in the Po valley and its failure to govern the March made the decision to withdraw its fief a logical one. It would never be easy to attract great lords to the thankless task of seeking to subdue the towns of central Italy and hence after 1230 laymen granted rule over provinces were either papal relatives or men of less standing than King John and the Marquises of Este. The experiment of the feudal grant was dropped — there was to be no parallel before the fourteenth-century vicariates *in temporalibus* — and the March from this time ranks as a normal province.

In the 'army of the keys' which opposed Rainald of Urslingen, a large French contingent had been commanded by the bishops of Beauvais and of Clermont-Ferrand.[3] The later career of Milo of Chatillon, bishop of Beauvais, suggests that he had outstanding qualities which impressed Gregory IX. In September 1230, soon after the Peace of San Germano had concluded the war that he had come to fight, Milo was appointed rector over a very large area, including the entire March and Duchy as well as Perugia, Orvieto and other towns allotted in 1227 to John of Brienne. The bishop was paid in part by financial assistance to his heavily indebted diocese.[4] His novel and powerful position doubt-

[1] Böhm, pp. 77–80: Salimbene, I, 58.
[2] *Reg. G. IX*, n. 217. BFW (n. 6738) dates the forfeiture of the fief as early as 1228, but on inadequate grounds. The latest possible date is September 1230, when the bishop of Beauvais became rector of the March: *v.* also Compagnoni, *Regg. Pic.*, p. 100.
[3] Richard of S. Germano, p. 172; *Vita G. IX*, p. 21.
[4] *Reg. G. IX*, nn. 495, 497–9, 827. Amelia, Narni and Todi were the other towns near the Tiber valley assigned to Bishop Milo.

less corresponded in Pope Gregory's mind with ambitious schemes for welding the Adriatic March, newly regained from the Estensi, to the Umbrian territories around the upper Tiber. The bishop set about this task with vigour. In the March, where the Estensi seem to have exercised no judicial powers, his judges heard many suits, while he also initiated a series of enquiries into papal fiscal rights in the Duchy.[1] Yet things did not run well for Bishop Milo. In May 1232 Ancona, Iesi, Fano, Camerino, Cagli and other towns of the March formed a league 'to the honour of the Church and the pope', promising each other aid 'against the lord bishop of Beauvais and his nuncios and followers, who are seeking to oppress the aforesaid towns dishonestly and illegally'.[2] The alliance provided for the appointment of a body of rectors to reach decisions on war and other matters. The towns of the March, unused to any superior, had reacted to the bishop's strenuous attempt to make their formal subordination a reality by resorting to open revolt. Perhaps convinced by the communes' account of Bishop Milo's rapacity, the pope decided on retreat. Before the end of 1232 the bishop was superseded and had returned to his diocese beyond the Alps.[3]

The rectorships of both John of Brienne and Bishop Milo are reflected in the decree 'Habet utilitas stimulos'[4] of January 1234, the exordium of which states that evil consequences have followed from the negligence and selfishness of 'outsiders' (*extranei*) governing the patrimony of the Church. Henceforth only cardinals were to be eligible for the rectorship. The college was always to be consulted concerning the government of the Papal State, custody of papal fortresses was to be granted only to ecclesiastics, and the profits of the State of the Church were to be divided into three equal shares, to go respectively to the papal chamber, the cardinals, and 'the treasury of the Church'. This constitution, preserved only in the *Summa Dictaminis* of Cardinal Thomas of Capua, may never have been more than a draft. In January 1234 two cardinals were appointed as rectors over four provinces, and each major province was then under the rule of a cardinal. But the new decree — if indeed it deserves this name — was effective only for a very brief period. Within four months the Duchy and the Campagna had

---

[1] BFW, nn. 13063, 13075, 13085, 13090, etc.
[2] Colucci, *Treia*, d. XIV: cf. BFW, n. 14833.
[3] *Reg. G. IX*, nn. 1030, 1591, 1594. See also below, p. 145.
[4] Printed with commentary by Hampe in *Zeitschrift für Kirchengeschichte*, XLV, 190–7. Hampe dates this document '*c.* 1233', but it is clearly contemporary with the appointment of two cardinals as rectors on 12 January 1234 (*Reg. G. IX*, nn. 1716–8) and the decree of 16 January forbidding the alienation of papal domain (*ibid.*, n. 1715). See also above, p. 122.

rectors who were not cardinals and by 1238 only the March was ruled by a member of the college.[1]

If Pope Gregory's experiments with the rectorate were more enterprising than successful, his policy towards the communes reveals him as even more restricted by the fundamental weakness of the papacy's situation. Since the initiative did not lie with him, he could not attempt to put papal relations with the towns on a new basis. His dealings with Assisi will serve to illustrate the difficulties of his situation and the manner in which realities again and again drove him towards a policy of compromise. In June 1235 he granted Assisi the right to choose its own officials 'like the other towns of the Duchy', but this choice was not to be made public until approved by the pope, if he was in the Duchy or nearby, or, in the case of his absence, by the provincial rector. If the electors could not agree, they were to leave the appointment to the pope or rector. Excommunication and other very heavy penalties were threatened in the case of any contravention.[2] The following year Assisi was one of many towns to swear an oath renewing its fealty to the pope, but an elaborate clause safeguarded the privileges and rights of the commune and there was in the oath no reference to the obligation to submit the names of officials for approbation.[3] The formation of a powerful independent league of the major towns of the Duchy[4] may help to explain Assisi's victory over the papacy in September 1237, when the commune petitioned successfully for the right to choose its own *podestà* and officials freely, 'notwithstanding the decree to the contrary confirmed by the Apostolic See'. The pope now agreed to the terms of 1235 with the omission of the clause concerning papal confirmation — and Assisi's status, symptomatically, was still that of 'the other cities of the Duchy'.[5] Grants of special immunity to powerful towns — to Ancona and Fermo,[6] for instance — tell the same story, while at times urgent need compelled yet more favourable treatment. In 1228 Gregory, in flight from the Romans, determined to instal the Curia at Perugia, a convenient point close both to the Tuscan zone

[1] See App. II.

[2] MGH, *Ep. Pont.*, I, 538–50 and (for a fuller version of the clause concerning elections) *Lib. Cens.*, I, 541–2. Contravention was to be punished by a communal fine of 1,000 *l.*, as well as individual fines on the electors: any man elected illegally was excommunicate and his acts invalid.

[3] Ficker, *Forschungen*, IV, d. 358 (also *Lib. Cens.*, I, 481, wrongly dated '*c.* 1233–4').

[4] BFW, nn. 13240, 13242–3; QFIA, XXIX, 168–77. See below, p. 144.

[5] *Reg. G. IX*, n. 3856.

[6] See in particular Theiner, d. CLXXII, a letter of Gregory to Ancona: '. . . Monetam, Comitatum, Portum et alia jura, que nullis de Marchia sunt concessa, ad nostram Curiam pertinentia, ecclesia Romana vos sustinuit hactenus habuisse'.

coveted by Rome and to that threatened by the Urslingen. Factional disputes between nobles and *popolo* had first to be quieted. The 9,000 *l.* given by Gregory 'to repair the damage caused during the troubles' and the accompanying loan of 3,000 *l.* were a humiliating bribe, in return for which Perugia consented to become the pope's headquarters and to take as its *podestà* his henchman John of Brienne.[1]

Beside all this, Gregory's intermittent struggle for the principle that submissions to papal towns required papal consent and occasional exercise of the power to review municipal statutes[2] are of little importance. At the best such insistence on papal rights aided the survival of these rights, but it was normally ineffective at the time. The only serious contribution of this period to papal authority was the erection of a system of provincial courts in the March.

That organizational change had failed to create an ordered state will be evident enough from a brief narrative of the history of the Papal State during this pontificate. Gregory was unfortunate above all in reigning during a period of Roman expansionism. The city's policy of aggrandizement caused him to spend no less than eight of the first twelve years of his rule outside Rome.[3] Made difficult at the start by Frederick II's attempts to win the sympathy of the citizens, his relations with Rome were never satisfactory from the time the city renewed its attacks on Viterbo.

In 1228 and 1229 the Romans fought campaigns against Viterbo while the pope, after brief sojourns at Rieti, Spoleto and Assisi, settled with the Curia at Perugia. The disastrous flooding of the Tiber in January 1230 was interpreted by the citizens as a judgement of God, and they recalled their bishop to take over the honourable but expensive

---

[1] *Vita G. IX*, p. 22 (not entirely accurate); Winkelmann, *Kaiser Friedrichs II.* (Jahrb.), I, 314 n.

[2] *Reg. G. IX*, n. 3710 (statutes reviewed). On submissions and papal consent *v.* De Vergottini in *AMSR*, N.S., III (1951–3), though this article fails to establish its claim that the papacy regularly regarded *contadi* as held legally only if they had papal authority, and does not cite the very relevant Theiner, d. CLXXII (re Ancona, 1233). The principle was used to bolster the independence of towns threatened by Rome and (unsuccessfully) to reclaim from Orvieto the Val del Lago (*v.* Theiner, d. CLVIII and RIS, N.S., XV, V, 149). It was also employed to punish Gubbio and Ascoli, whose *contadi* were — a least in theory — granted away by the pope (Potthast, n. 8828; *Reg. G. IX*, n. 1691; and cf. Ermini, 'Aspetti giuridici', 25 ff.

[3] On Gregory's relations with Rome *v.* Gregorovius, V, 1, 142 ff. and Gross, pp. 16 ff. and authorities cited there, particularly Richard of S. Germano. Both writers are, however, too reliant on Matthew Paris, who offers some unlikely information, such as that the Romans claimed the right to be exempt from excommunication and interdict (III, 303) and that 30,000 men were killed in their battle against the papal troops (*ibid.*, 304–5). For a very unfavourable estimate of Matthew Paris' reliability *v.* R. Vaughan, *Matthew Paris*, pp. 134–5, 140–1, 147, 151–2, 263.

task of organizing relief for the victims. The new senator was Annibaldo Annibaldi, the papal steward[1] and a relative of the pope himself, but the *rapprochement* did not last for long. In the spring of 1231 Rome renewed the assault against Viterbo and soon Gregory again made his way to Rieti. Baulked in their northerly aggression, in part by the intervention of the imperialists, the Romans turned in the late summer of 1232 to an invasion of the Campagna. The pope had now taken refuge in that area and the attack had to be bought off by a delegation of three cardinals. After appealing in vain for imperial troops, Gregory had to make a yet more humiliating request: he now asked Frederick to assist him in forcing Viterbo, his own subject, to accept the peace-terms proposed by the papal emissaries.[2] He had assured the Viterbese that their oath to the Romans was one of 'fealty, not vassalage', but the agreement ratified by Rome in July 1232 committed Viterbo to both fealty and vassalage, saving only their fealty to the Church and papacy.[3] After much persuasion by the Romans, Gregory returned to the city in November.

This second reconciliation, however, was even briefer than the first. In 1234 Rome formulated a yet more ambitious programme of ubiquitous territorial advance. By the spring of 1235 the city had secured the submission of Sutri, Nepi, Civita Castellana, Toscanella and Viterbo in the north, Corneto and Montalto to the north-west (in the Tuscan Maremma), and Orte, Amelia and Narni in the area of the Tiber valley.[4] In the east the whole Sabina seems to have sworn fealty, while Velletri, Anagni, Segni and other parts of the Campagna were attacked but perhaps not forced into submission.[5] Roman armies and officials thus took over a great deal of the two provinces of Campagna-Marittima and the Tuscan Patrimony and the entire sub-province of Sabina. 'Justiciars' from Rome moved through the whole area, demanding oaths of obedience and claiming jurisdictional rights for the Capitoline court.

The primary cause of Gregory's enmity with Rome was territorial, but inevitably this came to be complicated by other grounds of dispute such as normally arose between lay and ecclesiastical authority. The city

---

[1] Annibaldo still held this office in 1231 (*Reg. G. IX*, n. 720). See Gross, p. 21.

[2] *Reg. G. IX*, nn. 832, 924.

[3] *Reg. G. IX*, n. 6180; Pinzi, *Viterbo*, I, 322–3; *Lib. Cens.*, I, 477–8.

[4] A Perugian decree of 1234 envisages the possibility of taxation by Rome, a fact which illustrates the scope of Roman pretensions at this period (*v.* Pellini, *Perugia*, I, 250–1, and for Rome's claim to suzerainty over Perugia, De Boüard, pp. 226 ff.). For Gregory's (unfriendly) relations with Viterbo during the peaceful period of 1232–4 *v.* Signorelli, *Viterbo*, p. 184 n.

[5] *Reg. G. IX*, nn. 2435, 2454–63, 3018–19.

claimed the right to tax the clergy and ecclesiastical property, while Gregory insisted on complete exemption except by special papal permission, which was only to be granted on extraordinary occasions.[1] The jurisdiction of lay courts over clerics, the papal *familia* and pilgrims was another source of discord. During Gregory's absence the Romans occupied and looted the Lateran and some of the cardinals' palaces, took over much ecclesiastical property, and decreed that the pope might not return to the city till he had paid an indemnity of 5,000 *l.* for all 'the harm done by him to the Romans'.

Lengthy negotiations were needed before the Romans came to terms in May 1235, persuaded perhaps by the sizeable military force collected by the pope.[2] Yet the 'peace' was a truce rather than a settlement. Rome promised peace to its neighbours and an indemnity to the pope, and accepted his terms regarding clerical taxation and jurisdiction over clerks, but the question of the city's claims to its district was omitted.[3] In August the details of the treaty were being executed and the disagreements which then arose illustrate the unsatisfactory nature of the 1235 settlement. The senator protested that, though he had agreed to the destruction of the fortress built by the Romans at Montalto, 'he had not understood this as an oath to relinquish Montalto freely and absolutely to the Church, rather he had always understood that all the city's rights were to remain securely as before'.

While the city's claims were shelved but not abandoned Gregory decided against returning to Rome. For the next three years he stood aside while Frederick courted the Romans and rival factions deprived the city of the unanimity required for an expansionist policy.[4] Late in 1237 a favourable regime invited the pope to return from Viterbo, but the emperor's intrigues continued and the senator of 1238 was proimperialist. Gregory spent that summer at Anagni. He returned to Rome in October and remained there for the last three years of his life, the city becoming his base during the critical period of his struggle with Frederick II.

---

[1] *Reg. G. IX*, nn. 720, 3018–19.

[2] Huillard-Bréholles, IV, 945; *Reg. G. IX*, nn. 2633–8. Frederick II, the count of Toulouse and the bishop of Winchester had aided the recruitment of this force; Gregory had sent to France for more money and to the emperor for more troops. There are difficulties over the chronology at this point and it is hard to decide whether to accept Matthew Paris' (III, 304–5) uncorroborated story of a battle between the Roman and papal troops.

[3] *Reg. G. IX*, nn. 3019–26, 3028–34, 3037–44. The pope had intended at first to incorporate in the terms a ruling that 'men of the Patrimony shall no longer be cited to the Capitoline court', but did not insist on this claim.

[4] On this period *v.* Gregorovius, V, 1, 189–95 and Gross, pp. 40 ff.; both are based largely on Richard of S. Germano, pp. 192–8.

Pope Gregory's troubles with the Romans determined his relations with the entire zone of the old patrimony. Preoccupied by the pressing need for resistance to Rome, the Campagna and the southern part of the Tuscan Patrimony were on the whole co-operative and law-abiding, though some of Viterbo's weaker neighbours tended to make common cause with the Romans.[1] Further afield the determined efforts at organizational reform reaped a meagre harvest. In the northern Patrimony Orvieto defiantly maintained its grip on the long-disputed Val del Lago di Bolsena, while conducting an endemic frontier war against Todi, its equally unruly neighbour.[2]

Gregory IX's experiments were successful, if anywhere, in the Duchy of Spoleto, where the 1230s were a comparatively peaceful decade. The province was affected only briefly and at the periphery by Rainald of Urslingen's inroads in 1228–9 and the only serious source of disturbance during the next ten years was the lengthy quarrel between Gubbio and Cagli.[3] In the autumn of 1237 the major towns of the Duchy formed a league 'against all but the pope and Rome'.[4] Though apparently not initiated by the papal authorities, this alliance did not meet with condemnation, and was probably aimed at the organization of mutual defence against any intervention by Frederick II.

The unsubdued towns of the March continued to go their own way. The rapid shifts in their alliances are not easy to comprehend: in September 1228 the entire province was split into two systems — Fano, Osimo, Recanati and some lesser communes on one hand against Pesaro, Ancona and Iesi on the other — yet in October Gregory was attempting to break up a Venetian agreement which cut across this division.[5] Although both Rainald's invasion and Venice's diplomatic intervention were abortive, the towns were certainly not saved by their own exertions; they appear to have played no part in the campaigns

---

[1] Signorelli, *Viterbo*, p. 184 n. and *Reg. G. IX*, n. 2714 (Montefiascone): Pinzi, *Viterbo* I, 305–7 (Toscanella). For serious trouble on the Regno frontier in the summer of 1229 *v. Reg. G. IX*, n. 6130.

[2] For this war *v. Reg. G. IX*, nn. 3735, 3839–41, 4749–50; Potthast, n. 8458; *Fragm. Fulg. Hist.* (RIS, N.S., XXVI, II), 10. For the armies summoned against Todi from the March, Duchy and Tuscan Patrimony *v.* De Minicis, *Fermo*, p. 373 (1237) and *Reg. G. IX*, nn. 4224–39 (1238).

[3] Potthast, nn. 10032–9, 10046–7; BFW, n. 15104; QFIA, XXIX, 158, 160–1, 167; Bricchi, *Cagli*, pp. 91–2, 100–1. The pope intervened frequently in disputes concerning the new fortresses built by the rival communes at Pergola and Monte Vescovile respectively.

[4] BFW, nn. 13240, 13242–3; QFIA, XXIX, 168–77. See Gregorovius, V, 1, 185 n. The cities involved included Spoleto, Perugia, Foligno, Gubbio, Todi and Rocca Contrada (now Arcevia, in the March).

[5] *Reg. G. IX*, n. 218: Tonini, *Rimini*, III, 448–50. Venice's alliance involved Osimo and Recanati from the former group, Ancona from the latter.

which drove out Rainald in 1229. Except in the rare cases when papal action was in their interest, the communes were able to neglect the existence of papal officials; when Milo of Beauvais' energetic administration made such an attitude difficult, they formed a successful league against his 'dishonest oppressions'.[1] The bishop's supersession by Cardinal John Colonna did not put an end to municipal insubordination, for Ancona, Iesi and Osimo were all in rebellion against the new rector by November 1233.[2] The smaller towns seem to have welcomed the new provincial system of jurisdiction, but the large communes naturally resisted all attempts to cite their subjects and themselves before the rector's court.[3] The communes of the March rank with Rome as the powers which demonstrated the limits of Gregory IX's organizational reforms and the fundamental weakness of his position.

★   ★   ★

It is characteristic of the medieval Papal State that the year 1239 makes a break in its history through imperial, not papal, action. For eleven years, until Frederick II's death, one has to record not so much the history of a state but rather a tenacious struggle by the popes to retain their position in central Italy.

Papal support of the Lombard cities opposing Frederick had brought the two powers to a state of undeclared war some time before Gregory formally condemned and excommunicated the emperor in March 1239.[4] It was difficult for Frederick to conduct a north Italian war while the whole central part of the peninsula, dividing his base in the Regno from the Lombard theatre, remained potentially hostile: he had long realized that he needed the March and parts of the Duchy as a corridor. The pope's declaration of war helped to justify him in resuming possession of these two provinces, alleging the 'ingratitude' of the papacy towards their donor.[5] Before the end of 1239 Frederick invaded the Duchy and his son Enzo the March.

---

[1] See above, p. 139. For successful papal intervention, *v.* the peace achieved in 1229 between Pesaro and Rimini (BFW, n. 6799).

[2] These towns were threatened with interdict; their officials were already excommunicated (*Reg. G. IX*, nn. 1591–4).

[3] See above, p. 108, for these judges. For the recourse made to these courts by two small communes, Montegiorgio and S. Vittoria, *v. AMSM*, N.S., VII (1911–12), 400, 426–7.

[4] BFW, n. 7226a. But for intervention by Frederick in the March as early as May 1238, see *QFIA*, XXXVI, 172 (document from Arcevia, printed by W. Hagemann).

[5] For the Roman legal doctrine concerning 'ingratitude' and gifts, *v.* E. Kantorowicz, *Friedrich II.*, I, 442 and II, 195. Matthew Paris (III, 631–8) includes a letter of Frederick to Henry III of England on this matter, complaining *inter alia* that the pope has not permitted the towns of the Papal State to send him troops, nor Ancona to aid him against Venice. See Huillard-Bréholles, V, 707–9 for the suggestion that the emperor also took back *alias terras*: this may mean Città di Castello and perhaps the Tuscan Patrimony.

For the next decade pope and emperor disputed central Italy. There was some desultory warfare, but the devastation of a *contado* — the normal occupation of thirteenth-century soldiers — was often sufficient to win over a city whose food-supplies and subjects had suffered. To storm a town which had failed to yield was a difficult undertaking, rarely attempted. Occasionally city faction might offer a foothold to an aggressor. More often towns capitulated to threats or bribery,[1] and both sides offered privileges, exemptions and gains at the expense of neighbours.

In the altered circumstances of the 1240s the normal provincial structure of papal rule was abandoned. At the time of Frederick's assault Cardinal Sinibald (the future Innocent IV) was rector in the March, Gregory 'de Romania' in the Duchy and Tuscan Patrimony and Cardinal Richard of S. Angelo in the Campagna. In December 1240 Cardinal Sinibald was 'temporarily' replaced by the bishop of Arezzo, who was destined to remain in the March as rector until captured in battle late in 1247;[2] Frederick II executed him as a traitor in March 1248. There is little evidence of the functioning of provincial administration in the years 1240–4. Soon after becoming pope (June 1243) Innocent IV put the archpriest of Perugia over the Duchy and Patrimony, but his own experience as a rector in 1235–40 and the need for special arrangements during his absence from Italy decided him to select a single 'overlord' for the Papal State. Cardinal Ranier acquired a leading position in the papal ranks through his organization of a revolt by Viterbo against the emperor in the autumn of 1243. Innocent's arrangements at the time of his flight to Lyons in June 1244 regularized and reinforced the status of the cardinal, who now became the pope's vicar in the Tuscan Patrimony, the Duchy and the March in spiritual and temporal matters, with free powers to do whatever he thought conducive to 'the honour of the Church and the good of the inhabitants of those places'.[3] Of the other cardinals remaining in Italy, Richard of S. Angelo continued as rector of the Campagna-Marittima, Stephen of S. Maria in Trastevere became the pope's vicar in Rome, and both

---

[1] For city factions see Grimaldi, *Matelica*, d. LXXI (1241: the *popolo* turns imperialist against the nobles). For letters of Frederick relating to a plan for purchasing the support of Rieti in 1239–40, Huillard-Bréholles, V, 557–62 and 679–80.

[2] See *Reg. G. IX*, n. 5325, granting him the revenues of the diocese of Ancona, his own being lost to him through his opposition to the emperor.

[3] For this cardinal *v.* the biography by E. von Westenholz. On the probability that Ranier had earlier been made rector of the Tuscan Patrimony, *v.* Westenholz, p. 81, who suggests that Innocent wished to be able to disown him if Viterbo's revolt failed. This revolt began about 9 September 1243 and by 15 September Ranier had been appointed legate.

were assisted by Rainald bishop of Ostia, the future Alexander IV. The bishop of Arezzo, remaining in the March, became a subordinate of Cardinal Ranier.[1] These arrangements prevailed, with very little alteration, for the next five years.

Innocent, however, was not content to leave everything to the men 'on the spot'. He sometimes gave detailed instructions concerning policy to these representatives and also intervened directly in central Italian affairs in a manner that may have complicated considerably the work of the four cardinals, who were not normally informed of the pope's actions in the areas subject to their government. They were not even consulted, it appears, when the pope made grants to his supporters which may not always have been welcome to his vicars.[2]

Towards the end of 1248 Innocent had begun to show doubts about the policy of Cardinal Ranier, and in April 1249 he appointed Cardinal Peter Capocci legate and rector *in spiritualibus et temporalibus* throughout papal Italy; the modified employment of provincial machinery was now quite abandoned.[3] The unfortunate cardinal who had served the papacy so zealously spent the last months of his life in obscurity. His successor, a man of about fifty and hence ten or twenty years his junior, was thoroughly grounded in the affairs of central Italy. He came of a powerful Roman family which had intermarried with the Savelli and Colonna: his father, John, had been prominent as an opponent of Innocent III. Peter had served as a military commander against the Romans in 1231, had been promoted to the cardinalate in 1244 by his friend Innocent IV,[4] and had later served as legate in Germany. Ranier had a personal hatred of Frederick II and wrote envenomed pamphlets against him,[5] but we know nothing of Peter Capocci's feelings towards

---

[1] Although the bishop's position was now evidently a subordinate one, no letters addressed to him from Cardinal Ranier have survived. On the four cardinals, *v.* MGH, Ep. Pont., II, 561 and *Vita Inn. IV* (*ASRSP*, XXI), 87–8. For this period in the career of Cardinal Richard *v.* F. Roth, 'Cardinal Richard Annibaldi', *Augustiniana*, II (1952), 26 ff.

[2] For instructions, *v. Reg. Inn. IV*, nn. 1398, 2045–7, 2736, 2754, 3981. For intervention, *ibid.* nn., 160, 305, etc., and Potthast, nn. 11202, 17583; and for grants, *Reg. Inn. IV*, nn. 4259–62. etc. There seems no reason to doubt that the papal registers are a reliable guide to the recipients of papal letters, yet they rarely record rectors as recipients of letters concerning papal action in their own provinces.

[3] *Reg. Inn. IV*, nn. 4688–728. On Capocci see the biography by F. Reh. He was made rector of the four major provinces and Sabina, with legatine powers in exempt areas such as Rieti and various monastic lands. Cardinal Stephen remained vicar in Rome, presumably as Capocci's subordinate (*v. Reg. Inn. IV*, nn. 4697, 4703). On Innocent's waning confidence in Cardinal Ranier, shown in his refusal to confirm the terms of a privilege offered by the cardinal to Iesi, see Hagemann in *QFIA*, XXXVI, 183–4.

[4] Matthew Paris (V, 79) calls the cardinal Innocent IV's 'amicus praepotens'.

[5] Westenholz, chapter V, *passim*.

the emperor. The task set him was predominantly a military one, the organization of an invasion of the Regno.[1]

There can only be room in this work for a very brief narrative of these years, for the story of the struggle for Italy is not the history of the Papal State. By the spring of 1240, within a few months of the invasion, Enzo had won much of the March and Frederick almost all the Duchy and the Tuscan Patrimony.[2] Leaving Perugia and Assisi as potential pockets of resistance in his rear, the emperor now threatened Rome from the north. The moment looked a critical one, for Gregory IX's chances were dependent on the Romans' distrust of Frederick and on a small force of ardent crusaders, yet Frederick turned aside into the Regno without testing the city's defences. From every point of view it would suit him better for Rome to come over spontaneously, while an aged pope might prove an inconvenient captive. Perhaps there never truly was a papal crisis in 1240.

Later in 1240 Cardinal John Colonna arranged a truce, with papal permission. When Gregory decided to renounce its terms and resume the war, this veteran of Papal State administration defected to the emperor. The following year saw the imperialists gain Fano in the March, Spoleto, Gubbio and Terni in the Duchy, and Tivoli, yet the skirmishing around Rome — which now took on something of the air of a contest between imperialist Colonna and papalist Orsini — again presented no real threat to the city. In each province some towns still held out against Frederick. The citizens of these communes had in general no fixed preference between pope and emperor — each was above all a danger to municipal independence — and there were towns that managed not to commit themselves to either. Orvieto, powerful and situated in territory that was unessential to imperial strategy, lost control over its *contado*, but never came under Hohenstaufen officials: it offered little opposition to Frederick, but was never actively imperialist.[3] The formation of a neutralist league in 1242, under Roman leadership, was a natural development. Perugia, Narni and Alatri were the other powers in this alliance, which also reflects Roman hopes of resuming the city's twelfth-century role as a *tertium gaudens*.[4]

---

[1] Legatine powers were granted Capocci in the Regno as well as the Papal State.

[2] For a full narrative of these and the following campaigns, with references, *v.* Tenckhoff, chapters 1 and 2. The account here being intended only as a summary, references to sources are only given when of exceptional importance or complementary to those cited by Tenckhoff.

[3] Waley, *Orvieto*, pp. 31–3. Orvieto sent some troops to aid Viterbo in 1243.

[4] On this league see Brezzi, pp. 448 ff. and (for Alatri's participation) F. Bartoloni, 'Un Trattato d'Alleanza del sec. XIII tra Roma e Alatri', *BISI*, LXI, 125–61. The alliance is

The rebellion of Viterbo against its imperial garrison, organized by the native Cardinal Ranier, was the most striking development of 1243.[1] In June the papal vacancy, which had lasted for almost two years — Gregory IX had died in August 1241 and his successor Celestine ruled for only a fortnight — came to an end with the election of Cardinal Sinibald as Innocent IV. The new pope hesitated before supporting the Viterbese, yet these doughty enemies of Rome now defied the imperialists for three years. At the time when Innocent began his sudden flight to Lyons in June 1244 the only papal towns that had not submitted to the emperor were Ancona, Perugia, Assisi, Narni and Rieti in the March and Duchy, Viterbo, Orvieto and the fortress of Radicofani in the Patrimony, and Montasola in Sabina.[2] It is hardly surprising that Innocent made no attempt to annex the Regno to the Papal State in 1245 when he declared Frederick deprived of his crowns!

During the years 1244–7 there was some military activity, but no important change in the situation in central Italy. A papalist attempt to take the initiative in the Duchy in 1246 suffered a severe defeat near Spello and Viterbo at last yielded in January 1247. But in compensation Fano and Camerino in the March went over to the pope, thus ending Ancona's long period of isolation. Only towards the end of 1247, when Parma's defiance checked the emperor's successes in northern Italy, did the scales swing visibly, this time in favour of the pope. That winter Cardinal Ranier won over Spoleto and some of its neighbours, as well as Fermo, Iesi, Cagli and many lesser towns in the March.[3] Imperialist military successes at Terni, Osimo and Civitanova could not prevent this advance, though they checked its exploitation. When Cardinal Capocci took over the papalist leadership in April 1249, Foligno, Gubbio and Terni in the Duchy, Ascoli, Osimo, Fabriano and Macerata in the March were powerful towns which remained imperialist, but the last two of these turned coat within a year.

Capocci's task was not merely to reconquer papal territory but to utilize the March as a springboard for an invasion of the Regno. Early in July he was able to call representatives of many communes to a parliament at Fano in which he promulgated decrees condemning im-

treated by some writers as pro-papalist, but for pro-imperialists among its Roman proponents *v.* Gross, p. 66.

[1] See Westenholz, pp. 74 ff. and E. Winkelmann in *Historische Aufsätze dem Andenken an G. Waitz gewidmet*, pp. 277–305.

[2] *Vita Inn. IV (ASRSP,* XXI), 86. Minor strongholds in the Duchy still held for the pope were Stroncone and S. Gemini.

[3] These smaller places included Matelica, Recanati, Montolmo, Montefalco, S. Ginesio and S. Vittoria (Colucci, *Ant. Pic.,* XXIV, 9–10; XXIX, 90; XXI, 27).

perialist 'rebels'.[1] These were deprived of their ecclesiastical fiefs and
their property was exposed to capture by any loyal papal subject.
Other measures concerned the projected army of invasion. By the following spring the cardinal was able to organize a papalist alliance
headed by Ancona, Iesi and Fabriano, and this league was enlarged
during the summer of 1250. The province, however, was as vital to the
imperialists as it was to the pope, and its possession was tenaciously disputed. On 20 August Capocci was driven ignominiously from Cingoli,
hitherto his headquarters. In the course of an autumn campaign Fermo,
Fabriano, Macerata and many smaller towns returned to Hohenstaufen
obedience. The imperialist position in the Duchy and Tuscan Patrimony was weak, but Frederick received a steady stream of encouraging
news from the March up to the time of his sudden death in December
1250.[2]

Only in the Campagna and Marittima had papal government survived through the 1240s in much the same form as under Honorius III
and Gregory IX: there the tenor of political life was fairly peaceful,
except for a brief campaign in 1241. Elsewhere disorder, crystallized if
not produced by the struggle between pope and emperor, was the rule,
and papal attempts to retain or win back towns can be traced in a long
trail of privileges derogating from papal rights. Though on occasions
they were confirmatory, such grants had to involve new privileges if
they were to be attractive: hence they tended to include jurisdictional
and fiscal exemptions and the right to elect municipal officials. Many
towns were already in practice choosing their own *podestà* and trying
cases of first instance, but a promise that citizens should not be cited
outside the town except in appeal suits was a more substantial gain.[3]
Fiscal privileges naturally varied considerably: they might consist of
exemption from certain specified dues (such as tolls or procurations),
of the setting of an upper limit to papal demands, or — more
rarely — of total exemption from provincial taxation.[4] Similar grants

---

[1] For this parliament, *v. EHR*, LXXV, 660–4 (where the comment omits to record the
submission of Count Taddeo of Montefeltro to the pope before 6 Jan. 1249, *v. Studia
Picena*, XXIV, 80n).

[2] On this phase of the war *v.* Hagemann in *QFIA*, XXXVI, 185–7.

[3] For examples, *v. Reg. G. IX*, n. 6004 (Ascoli); *Reg. Inn. IV*, n. 4536 (Bevagna); Gianandrea, *Iesi*, d. XCII; Colini-Baldeschi, *Cingoli*, pp. xlvii–xlviii; Turchi, *Camerino*, d. XLI.
A clause insisting that the *podestà* had to be faithful to the Church could still be used to
justify intervention by a sufficiently powerful pope. It will be noted also that rectors could
still build up papal jurisdiction through cases of appeal.

[4] Examples are *Reg. G. IX*, n. 6033, *Reg. Inn. IV*, n. 4083, and Gianandrea, *Iesi, loc. cit.*
(specific exemptions); Turchi, *Camerino, loc. cit.*, and Colini-Baldeschi, *Cingoli, loc. cit.*
(upper limits); *Reg. G. IX*, n. 6005 (total).

included trading privileges and the occasional award to a town of revenue due to the papacy from its *contado*.[1] Sometimes towns were wooed over to the papal cause by a reduction of their military obligations.[2]

Cardinal Ranier's privilege to Spoleto of 13 November 1247 illustrates the type of grant that papal authorities were prepared to make to win over a vitally important commune.[3] Spoleto was excused all past offences and confirmed in the possession of lands which included the previously papal territory of the Terra Arnulforum and two abbeys, as well as the rights held by Foligno at Trevi. It received the power to make its own statutes, to elect its own officials and to try all suits of first instance and appeals involving a penalty of less than 100 *l*. Its military obligation was reduced to one week's service, within the Duchy. The Church promised to build no new fortifications at Spoleto and to garrison the castle only with the commune's consent. Only if the commune agreed would it readmit to its obedience those who had been 'traitors against the Church and Spoleto'. No other grant was so generous, though some towns gained a great deal piecemeal: Montolmo was the recipient of four privileges between February 1248 and May 1250.[4] Like two other towns in the March, Iesi and Cingoli, this commune's support was highly valued and it acquired both fiscal and judicial advantages.[5]

There were other types of grant which probably did more to destroy the chances of making papal rule a reality after the emperor's death. It was natural that pro-papal towns and individuals should be granted immunity concerning actions against their imperialist enemies,[6] but the practice of benefiting one town at the expense of another was a dangerous one indeed. The papacy had so little of its own that it was almost forced to show its generosity at the expense of others, and in times of crisis a day-to-day policy was inevitable, yet such expedients could only serve to intensify strife between the towns. One practice was to deprive a hostile town of its diocese and to confer this on a papalist commune. In 1240 the see of Osimo was transferred to Recanati and part of its

---

[1] *Reg. Inn. IV*, n. 1404 (trading privilege to Ancona). For grants of revenue from *contado*, *Reg. G. IX*, n. 5292 (Spoleto), *Reg. Inn. IV*, nn. 166 (Assisi) and 4537 (Bevagna).

[2] Turchi, *Camerino, loc. cit.*; Sansi, *Spoleto*, pp. 288–90.

[3] Sansi, *Spoleto, loc. cit.* For Innocent IV's confirmation, *ibid.*, pp. 291–2.

[4] *QFIA*, XXXVII, 122–6.

[5] Gianandrea, *Iesi, loc. cit.*; Colini-Baldeschi, *Cingoli, loc. cit.* Iesi loaned Cardinal Capocci 3,300 *l*. and Cingoli housed his headquarters.

[6] Examples are *Reg. Inn. IV*, nn. 165 (to Assisi, against Foligno and Spello), 618 (Narni against Terni), 4243 (Bevagna against Foligno).

revenues granted to the neighbouring bishopric of Numana.[1] Two friendly towns were thus gratified at the expense of an enemy one, but the cost in subsequent disputes and disorder, both temporal and ecclesiastical, was considerable. Moreover the whole episode reflects very ill on papal administration. The bishop of Numana was informed of the measure five months later than the town of Recanati and by this time the original financial scheme had been modified. The affair was to have a long and involved aftermath in the 1260s which is recounted below.[2] A similar expedient was to grant one town part of the subject-territory of another: thus Cardinal Capocci granted Cagli those parts of the *contado* of the rebellious city of Gubbio which lay *citra montes* (*i.e.* to the east of the main Apennine peaks) and in the diocese of Nocera.[3] Grants to supporters might also be made at the expense of the papal chamber, as witness the handsome award of domain to two citizens of Camerino who had presumably played a large part in the *volte-face* which brought that town over to the papacy late in 1247.[4]

During the ten years when all semblance of a central Italian state under papal control had vanished, even pro-papalists must have doubted whether the Church's claim to the area would ever resume any reality. A significant clause in a grant to Montecchio by a rector of the March promised that the town would be excluded from any restitution of the province by the papacy to the Empire.[5] Doubtless the commune insisted on this clause in the face of disclaimers from the rector, but only a few years later Frederick II proposed that the pope should hold the Duchy and March as a fief or, alternatively, should retain in them only the right to military service and *fodrum*.[6] Rumours of negotiations on such lines may well have circulated in central Italy.

For a decade the pope's subjects had tasted virtual autonomy. This had meant at the worst freedom to decide whether or not to submit to the Hohenstaufen, at the best — for the Romans — ten years as an independent and highly-valued ally of the papacy. The Hohenstaufen set up an administration in central Italy largely based on the provincial pattern of papal rule, but they in turn achieved no firm control, struggled

---

[1] For this matter *v.* Potthast, nn. 10899–900; *Reg. G. IX*, nn. 5240, 5309, 5330; Compagnoni, *Regg. Pic.*, pp. 104–5.

[2] Below, p. 171.

[3] Bricchi, *Cagli*, pp. 107–12. At the same time the bishop of Cagli received the diocese of Gubbio as an addition to his own.

[4] Theiner, d. CCXXXII.

[5] Colucci, *Treia*, p. 69. A month earlier a grant from King Enzo to Iesi (Gianandrea, d. LXXXV) had envisaged the possibility that 'the March might be restored to the pope'.

[6] See Jordan, *L'Allemagne et l'Italie*, p. 268.

to win the friendship of towns, and allowed virtual independence to their supporters.[1] Everything came back in the end to the powerlessness of central authority against the communes and when Frederick died there was no legacy of hegemony to which to succeed.

*   *   *

The papacy's attempt to impose its rule on central Italy in the years after the emperor's death must be seen against the background of the wider schemes of that period, in particular those involving the Regno.[2] Frederick's death and the absence of a legitimate heir in Italy appeared to give the Church an opportunity to assert its suzerainty over the Sicilian kingdom and to put an end to its dreaded union with the Empire. After the failure of Cardinal Capocci's invasion in 1251, Innocent IV soon resigned his schemes for direct rule in the south. When negotiations with both Conrad IV and the illegitimate claimant Manfred failed, he turned to France and England in the search for a conqueror to rid him of the Hohenstaufen. Conrad made himself master of the entire kingdom, but died in May 1254, and the pope now sought and for a time achieved an understanding with Manfred. A second papal invasion of the Regno followed, but almost at once Manfred turned against Innocent and defeated his troops decisively. The pope had time to renew his negotiations with Henry III of England before his death at Naples in December 1254. Alexander IV, the successor, was driven out with his army by Manfred, and achieved an agreement for an English expedition to gain the Regno for Henry's son Edmund: this plan never came near accomplishment and had later to be abandoned. Meanwhile Manfred had himself crowned (1258), and soon claimed the March and Duchy, as his father had done on more substantial grounds. That summer he began the conquest of the March, putting an end to papal Italy's brief immunity from external intervention.

There is a striking contrast between Innocent IV's administrative methods in the Papal State during his years of exile and his arrangements after the return from Lyons (1251). Cardinals Ranier and Capocci were granted wide powers and were not expected to have recourse to the pope except for general instructions on policy. When Cardinal Capocci received from Innocent letters appointing three bishops as his subordinates (they were to be rectors of the March, Duchy and Patri-

---

[1] For this imperial administration *v.* Ficker, *Forschungen*, II, § XXVI and XXXI.
[2] See Jordan, *L'Allemagne et l'Italie*, pp. 317 ff.

mony), he decided against this scheme and did not forward the letters to the intended recipients. Far from objecting, Innocent applauded the cardinal's initiative.[1]

The three bishops, however, had they become rectors, would have been markedly more dependent on papal supervision than their predecessors. Innocent's instructions empowered them to receive back formerly pro-imperial towns (on obtaining pledges for their good conduct) but past offences were not to be pardoned nor punishments inflicted or revoked, *quia ista nostro arbitrio reservamus*.[2] This letter sets the tone for the status of the rectors who followed Capocci after his return to the Curia at the end of 1251. It is significant that of the nine provincial rectors known to have been appointed by Innocent during the remainder of his pontificate seven were papal familiars.[3] The pope continued to intervene directly in the affairs of the Papal State as readily as before, but he now supplemented this by sending a stream of directions to his rectors. It was he who initiated policy, and the rectors became mere administrators.[4] Moreover he continued to deal with matters in the Papal State without informing the rector of the province concerned: the exceptions to this were usually cases when further action was deputed to the rector. In July 1253 the rector of the Campagna-Marittima was notified that all concessions of papal rights and revenues in his province were now automatically revoked. It seems unlikely that he had even been consulted about this highly important measure.[5]

Deprived of the power of initiative, the rectors now tended to wait for papal orders and to act upon these cautiously and deliberately.[6] Another cause of slowness in administration and a serious element in sapping the position of the rectors was the readiness with which the towns appealed to the Curia against the decisions of officials whose diminished status they must soon have observed. Apart from normal

---

[1] *Reg. Inn. IV*, nn. 5277–8, 5333. This episode also has a certain interest for the light it throws on the deficiencies of the papal registers as historical sources. Only the letter appointing the rector of the March (n. 5277) was registered, although rectors were named at the same time for the other two provinces. Moreover the fact that nn. 5277–8 never reached the intended recipients is only known to us through the fortunate registration of n. 5333.

[2] *Reg. Inn. IV*, n. 5277.   [3] See App. II.

[4] An instance of this may be cited from May 1253. Innocent IV then took under his protection the town of Rocca di Foce (dioc. Fermo) and confirmed its liberties and possessions. The rector of the March was merely told to act as *conservator*, *i.e.* to see that the terms of the grant were observed (*Reg. Inn. IV*, n. 6557: MGH, *Ep. Pont.*, III, 169).

[5] *Reg. Inn. IV*, n. 7754.

[6] For an instance *v.* Grimaldi, *Matelica*, dd. CXI, CXIV (the pope writes to the rector of the March on 15 May 1254, but only on 25 August does the rector pass on to Camerino orders not to build a new fortress).

appeals from the decisions of provincial courts to the Curia, it became common for towns to complain that the provincial rector was treating them unjustly. In 1254 we find Innocent IV ordering the rector in the March to instruct his provincial judge to reconsider the sentences recently passed respectively on S. Ginesio and Iesi.[1] The dangerous aspect of this tendency to appeal, and to listen to appellants, is obvious. Rectors could have little confidence when a powerful and prosperous town was likely to react to any unfavourable treatment by the prompt dispatch of an embassy to the Curia. Above all, to act on the statements of such petitioners was a dubious way of conducting policy. One cannot be sure that the rectors went unconsulted on such occasions — this seems probable, but such an *argumentum ex silentio* is inconclusive — but more and more papal letters concerning the Papal State seem to be the outcome of petitions.[2] A commune that could send an embassy well provided with money had a good chance of a sympathetic hearing, and this centralizing development in the government of the Papal State must be regarded as a harmful one. Supervision of powerful rectors should have been the aim rather than the supersession of weak ones.

The history of the process whereby the hitherto pro-imperialist towns of the March and Duchy abandoned the Hohenstaufen and came to terms with Innocent IV is an involved one, but fundamentally the situation was simple and there is no purpose in following the fortunes of individual communes. It seems unlikely that Conrad IV ever claimed these provinces and Manfred did not do so until much later. Since there was no longer a crystallizing point for opposition to the papacy the towns came round to at least nominal obedience. By the end of 1251 all the towns of the March had reached terms with the papal authorities and the following summer they were joined by a belated imperialist element among the barons and by Foligno and Terni, the last strongholds of imperialism in the Duchy.[3]

More important than the principle of reconciliation with the papacy is the question of the terms on which this was achieved. The normal arrangement was the confirmation of the commune's existing rights and privileges; no doubt imperial privileges were regarded as invalid, but in any case these had usually merely confirmed earlier papal grants.

---

[1] Colucci, *Ant. Pic.*, XIX, 37: Gianandrea, *Iesi*, d. CXXVIII. The implication in these letters that the provincial judicature is normally independent of the executive is striking and may be a further indication of the rector's new standing: see below, p. 158 n.

[2] Some examples are *Reg. Inn. IV*, nn. 5900, 5909, 6280; Acquacotta, *Matelica*, dd. 36–8; Colucci, *Treia*, dd. XXVIII–XXIX, and *Ant. Pic.*, XXX, 15 and d. VI.

[3] *Reg. Inn. IV*, nn. 5864, 5886, 5894. See Reh, pp. 111–22 and Tenckhoff, pp. 65–7.

The conferment of additional rights was rare. Ascoli secured exemption from all tolls and certain other special privileges, but this was unique among the towns that had gone over to Frederick, and its explanation is undoubtedly Ascoli's position near the frontier and importance as a base for Innocent's schemes in the Regno.[1] Assisi and Perugia now received new jurisdictional privileges — neither was to be cited to courts outside the city — but both these communes had been pro-papal, while Assisi's grant was a temporary one made when the papal Curia was in residence.[2]

The pope, though he gave little away, was able to exact little from the 'rebels' of the 1240s. Money was badly needed for the Neapolitan projects, yet Innocent's position was too weak for him to make heavy fines for past misdeeds the rule. A few towns were punished in this way, but there would perhaps have been no submissions if all had been threatened with punishment. Even the fines successfully exacted were less productive than had been hoped — unless the amounts originally named were merely bases for bargaining. Terni, for example, was fined 10,000 *l.* and then pardoned after paying half that sum, while Civitanova was absolved on payment of one-fifth of its 5,000 *l.* fine.[3]

Even if the towns came back because it was convenient to strike a compromise with the papal authorities, rather than as suppliants, the unwonted peace of these years in the March must have been welcome to Innocent.[4] This was perhaps the peace of exhaustion after the turbulent 1240s, but it was only seriously troubled by the disputes of Iesi and Montalboddo.[5] To the west there was less willingness to forget the hatreds of the past, Todi and Orvieto continued their endless frontier warfare and Perugia fought a long but successful war of revenge against its old imperialist rival Foligno.[6]

Orvieto had benefited greatly from the emperor's death, more by

---

[1] *Reg. Inn. IV*, nn. 5900, 5909; BFW, n. 8509; Theiner, d. CCXLIV.

[2] *Reg. Inn. IV*, n. 6001; Fortini, *Assisi*, p. 210.

[3] Fines paid by Macerata and Fabriano (1251), Civitanova and Terni (1252) totalled about 10,000 *l.* V. Compagnoni, *Regg. Pic.*, pp. 117–18 (Macerata); Marangoni, *Civitanova*, pp. 273–4, 277–8; *Reg. Inn. IV*, n. 5886 (Terni); Zonghi, *Fabriano*, dd. CLXVI–CLXVIII, CLXIX–CLXX.

[4] In December 1252 the Marquis of Este asked Innocent IV to renew the grant of the March in fee to his family, but the pope firmly refused (*Reg.*, n. 6781). The marquises long continued to employ the title of 'Marquis of Ancona'.

[5] These disputes concerned the *podestà*-ship; there was fighting against an exiled faction which had taken refuge at Montalboddo (Gianandrea, *Iesi*, dd. CXXVI–CXXIX, CXXXII–CXXXIV).

[6] RIS, N.S., XV, V, 152 and XXVI, II, 12–13; BDSPU, X, 479–84. In 1253 the pope warned Gubbio, Terni and Viterbo not to become involved in fighting (*QFIA*, XXIX, 200–1).

chance than through its own exertions. Manfred Lancia, nephew of one of Frederick's mistresses and King Manfred's cousin, had been administering as his father's vicar the lands 'from Amelia to Corneto' when the news arrived of the emperor's death. He at once entered into negotiations with Orvieto and Siena, the two cities nearest to the Aldo-brandeschine fiefs which made up much of the western half of his province. Realizing that the Hohenstaufen were likely and the Lancia certain to forfeit all authority in the area, he attempted to salvage what he could for himself. A bribe to an Orvietan official secured him a settlement whereby he became a prosperous citizen of the town while Orvieto was able to resume its suzerainty over much of the Aldobrandeschine territory together with Acquapendente and the Val del Lago di Bolsena. All this happened before Innocent could assert the papal claim to Acquapendente and the Val del Lago.[1]

Rome's exploitation of the emperor's death was less spectacular but scarcely less thorough. The city was Innocent IV's rival as the potential beneficiary by the new power-vacuum in central Italy, at a time when the pope was handicapped by his residence in far-off Lyons, yet almost two years elapsed before the Romans installed an aggressive regime bent on a return to the expansionist tradition. Innocent by then had returned to Italy, but his debts made him shy of the city and its bankers, and he was forced to watch from Umbria the early stages of Branca-leone's rule.[2] In August 1252 the Romans asked Bologna to send them a senator, and three months later there arrived Brancaleone degli Andalò, a Bolognese who had served in the armies of Frederick II. The 'popular' nature of his support was soon confirmed by his appointment as Captain of the Popolo, and he duly embarked on an imperialist policy, claiming for the city suzerainty over towns as distant as Terracina and Viterbo.[3] The pope at last returned to Rome late in 1253, to a humiliating situation in which he had to be defended against his creditors by the anti-papal senator,[4] and when Brancaleone regained for the Romans suzerainty over Tivoli, Innocent left for Assisi, never

---

[1] For this episode *v.* esp. Fumi, *Orvieto*, dd. CCLXXXIV–CCXCI, CCCI, CCCXVIII–CCCXIX, CCCLXXV, CCCLXXXVI–CCCLXXXVII, CCCXCII and RIS, N.S., XV, V, 144–5 and 151; Ficker, *Forschungen*, IV, d. 416; *Libr. Entr. Usc.* (Siena), XI, 64: also Jordan, *Origines*, p. 252 n. and Waley, *Orvieto*, pp. 34–5. Acquapendente appealed to Siena, in vain since Siena joined in partitioning the Aldobrandeschine lands. 'From Amelia to Corneto' was the imperialist version of the papal province of the Patrimony in Tuscany.

[2] On Rome at this period *v.* Gross, Ch. VII, *passim*; Gregorovius, V, 1, Ch. VII, *passim*; Dupré-Theseider, *Rome*, pp. 10–37.

[3] Contatore, *Terracina*, pp. 59–68 and 191–3; Pinzi, *Viterbo*, II, 42.

[4] Brancaleone later forbade the Romans to serve as papal troops, to send food to the Curia when it was at Anagni, and to lend Innocent money.

to resume residence in his see, for he quitted Umbria only to accompany his armies on the ill-fated invasion that followed the death of Conrad IV. At the time of his death Rome had not succeeded in resuming its sway over the wide territory intermittently controlled under Honorius III and Gregory IX, but the slow pace of the city's advance was not due to the opposition of the papacy.

Alexander IV, the last of the Conti popes, possessed the advantage of having served Innocent IV in Rome and in his native territory, the Campagna, during the time of the Lyons exile.[1] As an administrator in the Papal State he now followed closely the methods of Innocent's last years. The dispatch of an embassy to the Curia was the way to success for discontented towns, since it was clear that the rector's word was not final.[2] Even the executive actions of the rectors could be overturned, with consequences that must at times have been disastrous: in 1255 the rector of the Duchy leased to the commune of Gubbio its own *contado*, but the pope quashed this grant and substituted for it a lease of the same area to the rival city of Perugia.[3] This was opportunism at its worst, and it follows from such an attitude that papal orders were at times transmitted direct to provincial judges,[4] who seem to have played an increasing part in administration, while rectors went unconsulted. Rectors who failed to report promptly on what action they had taken were now ordered in threatening terms to reply by return of post.[5]

As in the preceding years, rectors were chosen almost entirely from the papal chaplains. The sole exception is, however, an interesting one. The rector of the Duchy in 1253–4 had been a papal chaplain who was also the pope's nephew, Boniface of Fogliano. In May 1256 Alexander moved further in the same direction by appointing as rector of the March a certain Annibaldo di Trasmondo who was his nephew and a layman. There had been no lay provincial rector since 1230. It has often

---

[1] For Alexander IV's relations with the Papal State *v.* Tenckhoff, *Papst Alexander IV.*, pp. 75–87, 111–16, 127–32. For his dealings in the State before his pontificate, including the Rome-Viterbo peace of 1232, *ibid.*, pp. 5–6.

[2] In 1256 Amelia, which wanted Castel Foce, also claimed by Narni, petitioned the pope: Alexander then ordered the rector of the Patrimony to grant the disputed fortress to Amelia (Amelia, AC, perg. n. 6). The same year Fabriano appealed against heavy fiscal burdens — and indeed they were heavy if the cost of an embassy was thought lighter — and the pope duly instructed the rector of the Duchy to modify his demands (Zonghi, *Fabriano*, d. CXC).

[3] *QFIA*, XXIX, 201–2; Theiner, dd. CCLX–CCLXI; Ficker, *Forschungen*, IV, d. 428; *ASI*, XVI, 2, 483–4. The papacy claimed domanial rights in the *contado* of Gubbio in succession to those held by the Hohenstaufen (*v. Lib. Cens.*, I, 544–5 and *Reg. G. IX*, n. 1691).

[4] For an instance of this *v.* Potthast, n. 16290.

[5] *Reg. Alex. IV*, n. 557. An isolated reference to the existence of a 'council' of the rector of the March (*supra*, p. 99) may also reflect the diminished status of the rectors.

been argued that the popes could trust their relatives better than anyone else to preserve papal interests, but Annibaldo's slowness in taking up his post — he was represented successively by two Roman laymen[1] — suggests that this consideration was not the principal reason for his appointment. Certain other actions of Alexander IV confirm that nomination to a position of authority in the Papal State was now becoming a recognized method for making a financial award to papal relatives.[2] It is not easy to plot the course of the slow and insidious process whereby responsibilities became transformed into rewards, but the appointment of Annibaldo is a significant point in this disastrous development.

Alexander IV's officials had moreover to face a considerable deterioration in the tranquillity of the Papal State. This was particularly marked in the March of Ancona. The year 1255 saw the formation of a number of alliances in this province,[3] a sinister symptom of the restlessness which resolved into widespread warfare in the course of 1256. Camerino was in rebellion in that year, Fano renewed the old struggle against Fossombrone, and Ascoli and Offida, sending troops to the rector's assistance, found themselves treacherously attacked by the militia of Fermo, which took this excellent opportunity to effect a murderous ambush.[4] This was the situation when Alexander IV relieved the papal chaplain Roland 'de Campania' of his post and replaced him by Annibaldo di Trasmondo. By September the new rector had patched up a general truce,[5] but this was quite ineffective in checking the anarchy of the March. In 1257 Macerata, Civitanova, S. Ginesio, Camerino and Fermo were all under rectorial condemnation for attacks on their neighbours, while Fermo's defiance was continued into 1258 with no shortage of allies.[6] Here was ideal territory for Manfred's intervention in the Papal State. He was probably in touch with Fermo, which had a long pro-Hohenstaufen tradition, as early as 1257,[7] but his invasion of the province began in earnest only with the capture of Camerino in August 1258. Papal fears of his winning over Ascoli, the

---

[1] BFW, n. 14894; Compagnoni, *Regg. Pic.*, p. 124. Annibaldo was given a vicar *in spiritualibus* who became his successor.

[2] E.g., the grant to a nephew of all papal revenues from Terni, notwithstanding any grants of the same by provincial rectors (Angeloni, *Terni*, 1878 edn., dd. XII–XIV).

[3] BFW, nn. 13958, 13974, 13979, 15131; Grimaldi, *Matelica*, d. CXXVII.

[4] Zonghi, *Fabriano*, d. CLXXXV; Amiani, *Fano*, II, lii; Marcucci, *Ascoli*, p. cclxvi and De Minicis, *Fermo*, p. 415 (on the ambush see also below, p. 286 n.). For other local wars of this period, involving Macerata, S. Ginesio, Tolentino, Montolmo and Ripatransone *v.* Compagnoni, *Regg. Pic.*, p. 123 and Colucci, *Ant. Pic.*, XIX, d. XXX.

[5] Compagnoni, *Regg. Pic.*, pp. 121–3.

[6] Marangoni, *Civitanova*, pp. 279–80; Acquacotta, *Matelica*, d. 45; De Minicis, *Fermo*, pp. 416, 419; Colucci, *Ant. Pic.*, XIX, dd. XXXII, XXXV.

[7] De Minicis, *Fermo*, p. 416.

key town near the border, are reflected in a series of generous privileges to this commune, one of which bestowed on it part of the revenue due to the pope from its *contado*; this money was to be expended on the upkeep of four frontier fortresses.[1]

Meanwhile the Duchy had been almost equally bellicose. All the old rivalries broke out again, Terni fought Narni, Todi fought Orvieto, Perugia fought Gubbio, Spoleto and the provincial rector.[2] Gubbio was both a perpetual enemy of Perugia and a town with strong imperialist traditions, and it was here that Alexander IV perpetrated a courageous but questionable *coup* by granting the town's *contado* to its oldest rival.[3] The policy of robbing Peter to pay Paul could not have have been adopted in a more decisive manner. If the papacy was to be merely one power among many in central Italy, with its own allies, enemies and opportunistic policy, such actions could be condoned or even praised, but there is a note of defeatism in their adoption in the 1250s, when the Church seemed to have a chance of asserting a suzerainty to which it should at least have been laying claim.

In the Tuscan Patrimony the scene was more peaceful, and Alexander even reopened, though without effect, the question of papal claims against Orvieto.[4] But in much of this zone, and indeed in the Duchy and Campagna also, the main factor in the situation was the re-emergence of the power of Rome.[5] Alexander spent little of his pontificate in the city, particularly after the popular revolt of 1257, led by that enigmatic figure the English baker Matthew Belvoir, which brought about the recall of Brancaleone, who had lost power eighteen months earlier. Tivoli now submitted again to Rome and Sezze in the Campagna was under pressure.[6] In the spring of 1258 the city even intervened to force peace terms on Narni and Terni.[7] Evidence concerning the collusion of the new regime with Manfred is inconclusive, but its policy was of undoubted assistance to him, for Brancaleone, while

[1] Ascoli P., AC, Perg. A, Fasc. 1, n. 1 (privilege mentioned in text): for the relations of Ascoli with Alexander IV, *v.* also Perg. E, fasc. 1, nn. 3–4; Perg. R, fasc. 1, n. 2; Quinternone, ff. 163–164 v (f. 163 for privilege renewing Ascoli's exemption from external suits 'cum ad rectorem Marchie super huiusmodis causis propter capitales inimicitias et alia impedimenta legitima non poterit haberi recursus').

[2] Terni, AS, perg. 16 June 1255 (uncatalogued) and n. 160: Todi, AC, perg. nn. 12, 14: RIS, N.S., XXVI, II, 14: *ASI*, XVI, 2, 483. Foligno also fought Gubbio and Gualdo Tadino the rector at this time.

[3] See above, p. 158.

[4] *Reg. Alex. IV*, nn. 531, 557.

[5] See Dupré-Theseider, *Rome*, pp. 39 ff.

[6] *Cod. Dipl. Tivoli* (ed. Pacifici), pp. 9–16; Lombardini, *Sezze*, p. 48.

[7] Terni, AS, perg. n. 160 (*v.* Gregorovius, V, 1, 326 n.). Brancaleone now became titular Capitano del Popolo at Terni, another gain for Roman power.

opposed to all noble houses and prelates connected with them, naturally concentrated on opposition to papal relatives such as the Annibaldi. When Alexander, who had fled at first to Viterbo, moved to Anagni, Brancaleone threatened to attack the town and the pope was compelled to beg him to spare it. Brancaleone died suddenly in 1258, while besieging Corneto, but his policy was for a time continued by his uncle.

Rome's successes provide the clearest evidence of the papal failure in the 1250s, but relations with all the communes tell the same story. Alexander legislated against towns appointing officials to hear appeals, but without securing obedience, towns which illegally appointed their own *podestà* were upbraided but not fined, while fines for disobedience were spasmodic and rarely paid in full.[1] Requests for military service too were often ineffective.[2] In the active functioning of administration in the March there is some evidence of energetic government, but the authorities were constantly in the position of having to compromise with those whom they wished to regard as their subjects. Particularly eloquent is the understanding reached by Annibaldo, on taking up his rectorship in the March, with the commune of Iesi.[3] By the terms of this agreement the town promised him military service (for the duration of his rectorate) and help against S. Severino. The rector for his part made three promises to his subject commune: he would forgive their past offences, accept their outlawries as valid and — like Iesi — would make no separate peace with S. Severino. The document is in fact a treaty of alliance against S. Severino. There could be no clearer demonstration of the tendency of struggling papal authority to become a participant in the turbulent play of inter-city struggles which it was supposed to regulate.

In the 1250s a policy of compromises and alliances might look like a *pis-aller*, less satisfactory than assertions of authority, but productive of some obedience and destined to lead to a slow tactical recovery in happier circumstances. Indeed it is possible that this view was correct, that the pope held so few cards in his hand that no other approach to the problem of government in central Italy was then practicable. But such policy was not rule, compromises easily broke down under pressure,

---

[1] For Alexander's legislation *v.* Jordan, *Origines*, p. 250. For examples of fines not paid in full, Macerata, AC, perg. III, 11 (300 *l.* instead of 6,000 *l.*, 1256); Gianandrea, *Iesi*, dd. CXXVI–CXXVII, CXXXVI–CXXXIX, CXLII, CXLV–CXLVIII (3,500 *l.*, in place of 10,000 *l.*, 1254–5);Colucci, *Treia*, d. XXXIV (Montecchio, 750 *l.* for 1,000 *l.*, 1254).

[2] See below, pp. 279 ff.

[3] Gianandrea, *Iesi*, d. CLXII: see also below, p. 286.

and the necessary happier circumstances were not forthcoming. Concentration on the question of the Regno must provide part of the explanation of the failure of the 1250s, but from a papal viewpoint the results of a return to the conditions of Honorius III's pontificate were bitterly disappointing, and this time less than eight years were vouchsafed before the renewal of the Hohenstaufen attempt to dominate central Italy.

* * *

The anti-papal towns of the March were almost certainly in touch with Manfred before he began his invasion of the province in the late summer of 1258.[1] Fermo was the first commune to receive a Manfredian privilege, in October, after Manfred had laid claim — on no clear legal principle — to the March, the Duchy and Romagna, and had appointed his relative Percival Doria as his vicar-general.[2] Thereafter the issue of a steady stream of privileges attests d'Oria's rapid progress in the March. Iesi, Recanati and Cingoli formed a Manfredian league in the central March before the end of the year, and by the following summer a number of towns were paying him taxes.[3] Camerino held out for a long while, but in August 1259 the *podestà*, a local baron, overcame the popular party which had favoured resistance, and d'Oria burned the town as a lesson to the 'yokels' who had attempted to defy him.[4] Ancona, as in the 1240s, held out against the Hohenstaufen, and Manfred suffered a serious check early in 1260 when d'Oria fell into the hands of Gentile da Varano, another feudatory, at Camerino.[5] The general impression is of endemic local warfare now partly directed, but not wholly polarized, by the struggle of two overriding external powers, which themselves have little independent military potential to contribute and are consequently dependent upon local allies and local rivalries. Under d'Oria's successor, Henry of Ventimiglia, Manfred's cause continued to make some progress in the March, but achieved no real penetration into the Duchy, where Gubbio alone had gone over late in 1258 or early in 1259, and was neutralized for

---

[1] Potthast, n. 17430; BFW, n. 4681; Malaspina, pp. 223–4 (mentions Manfred's contacts with the March, but may exaggerate the extent to which the towns took the initiative in these negotiations).

[2] BFW, nn. 4681–2, 14068a.

[3] BFW, n. 14074: Grimaldi, *Matelica*, d. CLVII: *QFIA*, XXXII, 79 (Fabriano).

[4] BFW, nn. 14000a, 14108: Malaspina, pp. 223–4 (Manfred's opponents at Camerino described as 'archipopulares' and 'protorusticos'): *Fragm. Fulg. Hist.*, p. 14: Compagnoni, *Regg. Pic.*, p. 125 (gives year wrongly as '1258').

[5] Potthast, n. 17789: BFW, n. 14121b.

some months by war with Perugia.[1] It would be unprofitable to attempt to trace the course of the campaigns. The towns that recognized
Manfred's rule normally received from him privileges confirming the
rights and possessions that they had enjoyed under the papacy. It is
sometimes stated that the communes of central Italy were able to gain
in strength by 'playing off' against each other the two rivals who
claimed their allegiance,[2] but the periods during which both pope and
Hohenstaufen actively sought this allegiance as rivals were brief, and
even within them the two powers were rarely equally balanced in any
province. A real competition for support would have been reflected in
generous additional clauses in the charters of privileges, but the rarity of
such clauses in Manfred's grants at this time[3] confirms that most towns
won little in constitutional status by the papal-Hohenstaufen struggle,
however much they gained indirectly by the periodical erasure of papal
authority.

While Alexander sought to direct the opposition to Manfred from
Viterbo and Anagni, the Romans continued to assert their supremacy
in the city's 'district' in spite of changes of regime. One of the joint
senators replacing Castellano degli Andalò after the rising of May 1259
was a papal relative, Richard Annibaldi. Nevertheless the city secured
the re-submission of Tivoli and threatened military aggression against
Terracina. Almost the last blow to Alexander IV was the disputed
senatorial election of 1261: one party was for Richard of Cornwall, the
English claimant to the Empire, the other for Manfred![4]

Alexander's policy was not entirely a vacillating and negative one.
At the time of Manfred's initial invasion he ordered his subjects in the
zones bordering on the Regno to renew in person their oaths of fealty:[5]
this measure perhaps suggests an exaggerated trustfulness, but the calling of a parliament in the Tuscan Patrimony[6] — still an abnormal

---

[1] BFW, nn. 14085, 14121b: *ASI*, XVI, 2, 485–6: *QFIA*, XXIX, 210–14.

[2] E.g. by Jordan, *Origines*, p. cxxx.

[3] For examples, BFW, nn. 4682–4, 4689a, 4702–3, 4724, 14071, 14073, 14080–5, 14119,
14130: an exception is n. 14078, whereby Fano's military obligation is limited to a thirty
mile radius.

[4] Contatore, *Terracina*, pp. 69–71, 193–4: *Cod. Dipl. Tivoli*, pp. 17–27. For the paragraph *v.* also Gregorovius, V, 1, 328–31 and V, 2, 344 ff., and Jordan, *L'Allemagne et
l'Italie*, pp. 343–4.

[5] This measure applied to the dioceses of Rieti and Ascoli Piceno. *V.* Rieti, Arch. Cap.,
Arm. VIII, fasc. D (not C, as in Mazzatinti, IV, 255), n. 7 (to communes in dioc. Rieti,
18 August 1258) and Ascoli P., AC, Perg. E., fasc. 1, n. 6 (Alexander IV to bishop of
Ascoli, 31 August 1258). Municipal officials and feudatories were to take the oath in
person, communities both *communiter per sindicum* and, in the case of male citizens aged
from fourteen to seventy, in person. The bishop of Ascoli was ordered to send a list of
jurors to the papal chamber.

[6] See App. I.

expedient — points to an attempt to organize the defence of this province and the Duchy against Manfred. So too does the appointment as rector and captain-general in both provinces of Manfred de' Roberti, bishop-elect of Verona, a capable and energetic administrator from a powerful family of Reggio Emilia, who was to play an extremely important role in the Duchy and March during the next pontificate.[1] But undoubtedly Pope Alexander's serious application to this problem shows most clearly in his attempt in the winter of 1260–1 to organize a pro-papal military alliance in the Patrimony and Duchy.[2] The implications of the formation by the pope of a league of his own subjects may pass for the present: the practical utility of the league might well outweigh the constitutional embarrassments. On 28 November 1260 Alexander wrote to the towns of the two provinces asking them to send at once ambassadors with full powers to make a general peace. Some towns sent representatives with an insufficient mandate — a very old gambit — and thus the whole matter had to be postponed till after Christmas. In January most of the communes sent ambassadors with proper powers. They were now requested to agree to the alliance, the terms of which provided for mutual assistance in the case of Manfred invading the lands of the Church: towns were to send troops 'wherever they were ordered to go by the captain or captains of the Church'. The representative of Viterbo refused to swear to these terms, stating that his commune was unwilling to send soldiers into the Duchy.[3] On 26 January Alexander wrote to the town again, insisting that this refusal cut across the whole scheme for collective security; they were to give their ambassador instructions to take the oath as it stood, or send a new man. The letter implies that Viterbo was holding up the plan for an alliance, but since nothing seems to have come of the scheme one must assume that the other communes were equally unco-operative. Probably the towns of the Duchy favoured the league more than those of the Patrimony, to which there was no immediate threat; Viterbo, for instance, would certainly have shown more interest in an alliance against Rome. Lack of common interests and lack of papal authority combined to doom this ambitious

---

[1] It is important to note that this appointment was made by Alexander IV, since Jordan (*L'Allemagne et l'Italie*, p. 345) ascribes it to Urban IV and uses it as an instance of Urban's superior insight, a point which he emphasizes and perhaps exaggerates: cf. his *Origines*, pp. 312 ff. The mistake is repeated by Y. Azais in *La Chrétienté Romaine (1198–1274)*, (Histoire de l'Église, ed. Fliche and Martin, vol. 10), p. 436.

[2] Pinzi, *Viterbo*, II, 79–85 (unfortunately this Viterbese source provides, so far as I am aware, the only evidence concerning the episode).

[3] For the principle that towns owed military service only within their own province see below, p. 276.

scheme to failure. Soon after (May 1261) Alexander died and — despite the fears of the cardinals — Manfred did not exploit the four-month vacancy which followed by attempting a sortie into the Duchy.[1]

The Frenchman Urban IV (elected 29 August 1261) was the first thirteenth-century pope who had to face the problems of the Papal State without previous experience of the political condition of central Italy. His achievement is a reminder that inexperience might aid a return to first principles. The character of the new pope was well described by a Sienese merchant, who wrote of him that 'he does what he wishes and no one dares contradict him; he acts more like a temporal lord than a pope and he wants to make the land submit to him as much as he can; no pope since Alexander III has been so constant in his deeds and words.'[2] Although the situation made a great advance in papal authority an impossibility, Urban IV showed how the problems of temporal government should be approached. He made use of the law to insist on his rights, he gave his officials real authority and support, while insisting on proper service from them, above all he displayed admirable persistence.

It was no easy task to serve in Urban IV's time as a provincial rector, and he chose men with courage and previous political experience. The bishop-elect of Verona, hitherto rector in the Patrimony and the Duchy of Spoleto, was now made responsible for a more easterly zone which included the Duchy together with the main theatre of war, the March of Ancona. Here Bishop Manfred carried on the struggle against his namesake with great tenacity until he was captured in battle in the spring of 1264.[3] Urban's most original appointment was Guiscard of Pietrasanta, a layman from Milan with much experience as an administrator in the anti-imperialist cause, who became rector of the Tuscan Patrimony in July 1263.[4] Guiscard was murdered in February 1264,[5] but was succeeded for several months by his brother Pipio, also a layman, who served the pope for some time as a military commander. Urban's later appointments were more conventional, though it is interesting to see him following, thirty years late, the counsels of 1234. Bishop Manfred was succeeded by Cardinal Simon of S. Martin, Pipio of Pietrasanta by Cardinal Matthew of S. Maria in Porticu: by the

---

[1] For this period, *v.* Mazzatinti, IV, 168 (Manfred's threat to Spoleto, June) and *ASI*, XVI, 2, 486–7 (cardinals' letter to Perugia, July).

[2] Document published by F. Schneider in *QFIA*, XV, 50–1. The writer says of Urban's actions in the March, 'et totum hoc per se solum facit, non petito consilio'.

[3] Colucci, *Ant. Pic.*, XIX, 47.   [4] See Jordan, *Origines*, pp. 313 ff.

[5] See below, p. 170.

autumn of 1264 all the four major provinces and even the Sabina and Massa Trabaria were under cardinals.[1]

Urban IV's rectors were given plenty of responsible work, though papal chaplains continued to be used for missions of minor importance. The pope gave the rectors support by issuing statutes for particular provinces and at least once by summoning the towns of the Duchy and Patrimony to a parliament,[2] but the clearest sign of his backing is a negative one, the absence of a stream of papal letters initiated by petitioning embassies. Communes did not cease appealing to the pope, but the prospects for a successful appeal against a provincial rector had now deteriorated. In September 1263 Cagli appealed to Urban against its condemnation by Bishop Manfred. The pope's reply denounced the appeal as frivolous and warned the town to obey the rector's orders promptly in future; if the rector had cause to complain again, Urban would re-impose his original punishment with additional temporal and spiritual penalties. The phrasing of this letter shows how anxious was the pope to stand by his subordinates, though he did on this occasion excuse Cagli its condemnation, while insisting on its future good behaviour.[3]

His firmness in dealing with the towns is the most notable aspect of Urban's temporal administration. He opposed the communes' exercise of appellate jurisdiction by legislating against the appointment of officials whose function it was to hear appeals.[4] Most towns of the March, Duchy and Patrimony possessed such captains or *exgravatores* and the struggle for their removal was a bitter one. Probably it rarely achieved ultimate success; Rieti, for instance, dismissed its captain in the autumn of 1263, but appointed another the following February.[5] Over the principle that *podestà* required papal approval Urban fought another, and probably a more effective, battle. Towns were now cited to the Curia over this matter and ordered to send a proctor or, occasionally, the *podestà* himself.[6] Cagli, after the affair mentioned above, was told by the pope the name of its *podestà* for the next year, and

---

[1] *V.* App. II.

[2] *Reg. Urb. IV*, I, n. 300 (legislation for Patrimony and Sabina, August 1263, concerning outlawries by rectors); II, nn. 734–5 (for Campagna-Marittima, December 1263, against sale of land to outsiders: for its effectiveness, nn. 782, 793–4, 864); II, 858 (parliament).

[3] Bricchi, *Cagli*, pp. 135–7.

[4] *Lib. Cens.*, I, 568–9 (14 Dec. 1262): also incorporated in Albornoz, *Constitutions* (pp. 14–16), Lib. I, cap. 7 ('De non habendo judicem appellationum vel exgravatores sine licentia sedis apostolice').

[5] *Reg. Urb. IV*, I, nn. 89–91, 94–6, 147–9; II, nn. 716–27: Rieti, Arch. Cap., Arm. I, fasc. D, nn. 1–2; Arm. VIII, fasc. B, n. 8.

[6] *Reg. Urb. IV*, I, n. 197; MGH, *Ep. Pont.*, III, 501; etc.

accepted him. This is not an instance of routine administration, but it illustrates Urban's approach and Gubbio's appeal in 1265 to Clement IV to name a *podestà* for the town shows the sort of success that this approach might achieve.[1]

Urban was willing to intervene in the towns to achieve such ends as dissolving factious *societates*, checking an incipient tyranny or securing the just payment of a *podestà*,[2] but naturally his interventions were usually made in defence of papal rights. He was willing to challenge communes and barons in defence of papal domain and revenues, as witness his struggles with Orvieto over Acquapendente and the Val del Lago, with Narni over the fortresses of S. Gemini, Otricoli and Stroncone, and especially with Spoleto over the 'Terra Arnulforum', Miranda, and other lands in the same locality.[3] Even when there was some danger that such an attitude might drive a town into negotiations with Manfred, Urban stood by his rights.

What these were he usually knew well, and if he wished to have them established more surely he appointed a commission of enquiry, such as those which investigated papal rights in the Terra Arnulforum, at Marta (on Lake Bolsena), in the lands of Peter di Vico, and at Acquapendente.[4] The firmness of his tactics is no less striking than the sureness of his strategy. The story of Urban's relations with Spoleto in 1262–4 provides a good examplar of this tenacity.[5] In the summer of 1262 a papal enquiry concluded that the Terra Arnulforum, a large lordship lying around Cesi and Acquasparta (to the west of Spoleto), was papal domain but had been usurped by Spoleto for a period of about fourteen years.[6] Soon the pope appointed a castellan at Cesi and warned Spoleto to give up the Terra Arnulforum, while giving the town an opportunity to appear at the Curia with charters which might authenticate its claims. Spoleto, which was by this time under interdict, sent transcripts of various privileges granted by Cardinal Ranier, Innocent IV and Alexander IV. The pope characteristically, and rightly, refused to

---

[1] *QFIA*, XXIX, 223–4; *Reg. Cl. IV*, n. 959. For routine approval of a *podestà* (at Corneto), *Reg. Urb. IV*, II, nn. 951–2.

[2] E.g. *Reg. Urb. IV*, II, nn. 282, 775, 795; Narni, AC, perg. (uncatalogued) 10 November 1262 (payment of *podestà*).

[3] See below, pp. 168 ff.

[4] *Carsoli Rediviva*, pp. 167–72 and MGH, *Ep. Pont.*, III, 501 (Terra Arnulforum, 1262): *Reg. Urb. IV*, I, nn. 197 and 199–200 (Marta, 1262), n. 237 (Vico lands, 1263): Theiner, d. CLXXIII (Acquapendente, 1263).

[5] Sources: *Reg. Urb. IV*, I, nn. 59, 198; II, nn. 192, 275, 310–15, 329, 339–41, 370, 528, 717, 772–4, 879–80 (twenty-two letters carefully registered concerning this matter); *Vita Urb. IV* (RIS, O.S., III, 2), cols. 412 ff.: *Carsoli Rediviva*, pp. 167–72.

[6] For the grant of this area to Spoleto in 1247, see above, p. 151.

accept the evidence of the transcripts and demanded to see the originals. When Spoleto at length sent new representatives — apparently without the originals, which may have been disappointing in comparison with the 'transcripts', for we hear no more of them — the pope and cardinals gave them a full hearing, but decreed that the Terra Arnulforum must be yielded to the Church. By the summer of 1263 Spoleto had tentatively offered obedience but failed to send ambassadors with full powers. Urban now set about regaining various other areas of papal domain around Spoleto which had been usurped or threatened by the Spoletans, and the rector Guiscard of Pietrasanta commanded in person two punitive campaigns. In July the town was fined 1,000 marks, to be paid within two weeks, but this was ineffective for in August Urban attempted to organize an alliance including the threatened feudatories and some communes, among them Terni, a neighbour and always a rival of Spoleto. These and other measures achieved little. In August 1264 the rector of the Tuscan Patrimony at last received powers to absolve Spoleto from interdict; the town was granted Perocchio, one of the disputed fortresses, but presumably not the Terra Arnulforum. This is not the end of the story; Clement IV had trouble with Spoleto again, though the town seems at last to have come over to papal obedience by July 1265.[1] What is striking is Urban's extraordinary persistence in standing on his rights and in employing judicial methods.

Edouard Jordan remarks that Urban IV's life by Thierri of Vaucouleurs reads like a cartulary: he aptly describes it as 'a versified list of the castles, fiefs and rights reintegrated by the pope into the Church's direct domain'.[2] The implementation of this policy cannot here be followed in detail. Its objects were partly military and fiscal, yet behind these aims undoubtedly lay a more general scheme for the assertion of the papacy's temporal authority. The struggle with Narni for control over S. Gemini, and with a baron, Offreduccio, for Miranda, provide instances of military objectives; S. Gemini was among the many fortresses strengthened at this time.[3] Both these fortresses, overlooking the valley of the Nera, would have had a part to play had Manfred broken into the Duchy from the east. Each cost the pope a long dispute with a commune, for Offreduccio had the support of Rieti, of which town he was *podestà*.[4] Not only were papal fiefs resumed, if necessary at

---

[1] BFW, n. 9485; *Reg. Cl. IV*, nn. 740, 909.

[2] *L'Allemagne et l'Italie*, p. 345: *v. Vita*, in RIS, O.S., III, 2, 409 ff.

[3] *Reg. Urb. IV*, II, nn. 61, 100, 198, 328 (S. Gemini): *ibid.*, I, nn. 147–9 and Rieti, Arch. Cap., Arm. I, fasc. D., nn. 1–2 (Miranda): for Miranda, *Vita*, col. 413.

[4] See above, p. 166.

the expense of powerful communes and feudatories; even prelates were to find that the custody of such fiefs was no sinecure. Trevi, near Anagni, was one of the many papal fortresses in the Campagna which had come into the possession of Rainald 'Rosso' of Genna, a baron of the Conti family. After citing Rainald to the Curia in vain, Urban attacked him, forced him into obedience, and placed Trevi under custody of the abbot of Subiaco. Within a year, the pope ordered the abbot to yield Trevi to a papal familiar, and to pay to this Templar compensation for having diminished the value of Trevi by cutting down trees, leaving land uncultivated and removing armaments from the fortress. The abbot was probably surprised to find that the conventional appropriation of 'perquisites' now led to energetic papal condemnation.[1]

Urban concentrated on this work of recovering lands and rights in three areas, the zone around Spoleto and to its west in the Duchy, the environs of Lake Bolsena and the Vico territory further south in the Tuscan Patrimony, and those parts of the Campagna which were threatened by the relatives of Alexander IV. The quarrel with Spoleto, which has already been described, concerned Manfred's probable route through the Apennine range into the Duchy. In the Patrimony Urban's chief 'recuperations' were Marta on Lake Bolsena and its homonymous island, another island formerly called Isola Bisentina and now renamed Isola Urbana, Valentano, and *castrum Arsi* near Castro. These gains were made mainly at the expense of Viterbo, the lords of Bisenzio, and Orvieto, though the attempt to win Acquapendente from the last of these towns was unsuccessful.[2] Further south Urban tried conclusions with Peter di Vico who had gained possession by force of Bieda, Civitavecchia and other lands previously held by his relative and namesake Peter III. Urban cited Peter to prove his rights in the Curia, alleging the need to ensure that no lordship in the Papal State fell into the hands of a rebel or one not devoted to the Church. After repeated refusals, Peter sent a proctor and the pope and cardinals appointed a commission to enquire into the matter, but apparently Urban was not able to press any further this projected confiscatory action against a powerful opponent who in 1264 rendered much assistance to Manfred.[3] Indeed Urban's policy in the Patrimony was the least successful aspect of his work in the Papal State. Peter di Vico kept his lands, Orvieto kept Acquapen-

---

[1] *Reg. Urb. IV*, I, n. 127 and II, nn. 78–9; *Vita*, col. 409. The abbot, who had offered Brother Martin 10 *l.* was ordered to pay him 60 *l.* within a week, on pain of ecclesiastical censure, and to pay the rent outstanding to lay lords.

[2] *Reg. Urb. IV*, II, nn. 140, 155, 197, 199–200; *Vita*, cols. 409–13; Theiner, d. CLXXIII.

[3] *Reg. Urb. IV*, I, nn. 201, 237: *Vita*, cols. 413–19.

dente, and a rector, Guiscard of Pietrasanta, paid with his life for the enmity of the lords of Bisenzio. Three brothers of this family attacked Guiscard when he was on a routine journey from Montefiascone to Canino: they killed him, then mutilated his body, cutting out the tongue and heart. Orvieto, which had provided Urban with a safe residence for two years, failed to punish the surviving lords of Bisenzio for their murder, and the pope also held it responsible for the loss of the castle of Bisenzio to Ghibelline supporters.[1] It was for these reasons that he left Orvieto in September 1264, near the end of his life. Even in the southern Patrimony he had achieved partial success in building up a *bloc* of papal lands, but the repulsive murder of Guiscard of Pietrasanta is a reminder of the difficulty of securing orderly government.

In the Campagna the baronial relatives of former popes were more menacing to Urban than the rather indecisive threats of Manfred. The accumulation of lands by Rainald of Anagni in the area of Ferentino has already been mentioned.[2] After Rainald's defeat Roland of Montelungo, who was probably another distant connection of the Conti, attempted to take over Ferentino itself as *signore*.[3] Meanwhile Richard Annibaldi, also a relative of Alexander IV, sought to occupy Ostia, Alexander's former see, and set himself up for a time as lord of Tivoli, while Matthew of Anagni, a Conti, tried conclusions with the township of Frosinone.[4] In this land of barons the best that a 'foreign' pope could do was to attempt to check the feudatories in their municipal ambitions and to retain a grip on his own isolated domains.

Although firmness is the dominating note in Urban IV's methods, he could at times — perhaps not always at the right ones — make use of the alliances and compromise that were characteristic of his predecessors. In 1262–3 he used Gubbio against Cagli, which had gone over to Manfred, granting Gubbio privileges and giving the town permission to fight 'a hard and bitter war' against this old enemy.[5] Another expedient threatened against Cagli, though not put into practice, was the removal of its bishopric. Under Urban the disadvantages of this type of action

---

[1] *Vita*, col. 419; and *v.* Waley, *Orvieto*, pp. 45–6 (A. Lazzarini in *ASI*, CX, 210–11, states incorrectly that Nicholas of Bisenzio was executed. It is clear both from the biography and from *Reg.*, II, nn. 757 and 764 that this brother was killed in the scuffle when the murder was committed. Nor is Dr. Lazzarini convincing when he argues that the lords suffered confiscation of their lands).

[2] Above, p. 169: *v.* also *Reg. Urb. IV*, I, n. 84.

[3] *Reg. Urb. IV*, II, nn. 775, 795: for the suggestion that the Montelungo were relatives of the Conti, see Falco in *ASRSP*, XLVII, 138–9.

[4] *Reg. Urb. IV*, I, nn. 229, 508; II, nn. 755, 763.

[5] *QFIA*, XXIX, 214–16 and 220–1. Gubbio was also granted the power to harm the persons of the people of Cagli and their property.

became manifest, for as Recanati, which had gained the see taken from
Osimo in Frederick II's time, hesitated between Manfred and the
papacy, so the pope hesitated between restoring the see to Osimo and
permitting Recanati to retain it. These oscillations were so frequent
that the people of the towns concerned may well have been puzzled as
to whether or not they had a bishop.[1] The transference of dioceses as a
punitive measure was both clumsy to administer and unsatisfactory in
its ecclesiastical consequences, and it did not end with Urban IV.
Clement IV gave Recanati a bishop again, or at least planned to do so,
only a year after Urban's last deprivation.[2]

Urban's strenuous struggle with Narni for the fortress of S. Gemini
has been mentioned above. This was solved by an uncharacteristic
diplomatic compromise, S. Gemini being yielded in June 1264, at the
same time as Urban insisted that the two other strongholds coveted by
Narni, Stroncone and Otricoli, should owe military service to the
papacy only. A loan made to the Church by Narni later in the year may
have been part of the same bargain.[3] In the face of the strength of the
communes it was inevitable that even Urban IV should sometimes have
to prefer the unpalatable policy of compromise to an insistence upon
legal rights that he often lacked the means to enforce. Spoleto had felt
his power and learnt to respect it, but to many towns, particularly in the
March, papal authority was a fiction. Some statutes of the town of
Macerata survive from about this period. They include only one
reference to the authorities of the Papal State, which occurs in a clause
in the oath to be taken by the *podestà* on assuming office: he swears 'not
to seek letters from the rector of the March or his judges which order
my salary to be paid other than according to the dispositions of this
statute of Macerata'.[4] In the eyes of the commune of Macerata papal
authority is nothing more than a potential judicial loophole.

[1] For this episode *v.* in particular *Reg. Urb. IV*, II, nn. 335, 416, 522, 744. In July 1263
Recanati was deprived of its see, which was presumably to be restored to Osimo, but by
December of that year Recanati was pro-papal and the transfer had not yet taken place.
Less then three months after this the town had again gone over to Manfred and Osimo
got its bishop back. Recanati was thus deprived of a bishopric which officially it no longer
possessed.
[2] *Reg. Cl. IV*, nn. 222–3. The first of these orders the restitution, the second — which
was presumably intended to be kept secret from Recanati — orders the same recipient, a
legate, not to act at once but to consider the circumstances, since the pope still feels unsure
of Recanati.
[3] *Reg. Urb. IV*, II, nn. 843–4, 849: S. Gemini submitted to Narni on 9 June, a week after
the letter concerning Stroncone and Otricoli and five days before the papal grant of S.
Gemini. *V.* Mazzatinti, IV, 168 and, for the loan of 1,500 *l.*, Narni, AC, perg. (uncatalogued) 7 December 1264.
[4] Foglietti, *Statuti di Macerata*, p. 9.

The history of Manfred's struggle with Urban IV and Clement IV in 1261–5 falls only in part within the scope of this work, though much of the campaigning was done in the Papal State and is relevant to papal control there.[1] The critical points in 1261–3 were Rome and the March.[2] The Romans had tasted dictatorial rule under the Andalò, and their 'popular' party regarded the regime of a powerful man as a strong asset against both pope and nobility. Thus in 1261 rival factions had stood for Manfred and Richard of Cornwall, while in 1263 Manfred again and his son-in-law Peter of Aragon were under discussion as senators, though the choice went eventually to Charles of Anjou. Manfred did not abandon hopes of gaining the senatorship, but Charles' election was joyous news for the pope, mitigated only by the unwelcome knowledge that the Romans wished to have Charles as senator for life. After prolonged bargaining Charles promised Urban not to retain the senatorship for more than three years after conquering the Regno. Early in 1264 his vicar took up office in the Capitol and the city, though even now not entirely abandoning expansionist ambitions,[3] became a centre of the Angevin-papal alliance.

In the March the struggle continued to alternate, as is well attested by Recanati's rapid changes of allegiance. Manfred's nephew, Conrad 'of Antioch', succeeded Henry of Ventimiglia as vicar-general in 1262, but in the same year was captured in humiliating circumstances by the township of Montecchio. While Galvano Lancia spent the remainder of 1262 in an unsuccessful attempt to reduce Montecchio, Bishop Manfred was pouring out money in the hope of winning over his valuable captive. Eventually Conrad was able to escape, and soon after the papal rector was himself taken prisoner.[4] Urban's constant fear of inroads into the Duchy[5] was natural, but probably he overrated the strength of the Manfredian army in the March.

The critical year was 1264, when Manfred had his last chance of subduing central Italy before the arrival of Charles of Anjou.[6] His purpose was almost certainly to capture the pope himself at Orvieto. He had the

---

[1] On the papal crisis of these years and its influence on the popes' bargaining position and hence on the terms on which they received Angevin aid see the brilliant chapters in Jordan's *Origines* (Bk. II, chs. V–VII: Bk. III).

[2] Hampe, *Urban IV. u. Manfred*; Tenckhoff, ch. 4, *passim*; Gregorovius, V, 2, 335 ff. (not entirely satisfactory).

[3] For fiscal schemes involving Terracina in January 1264, *v.* Contatore, *Terracina*, pp. 195–6.

[4] *Vita* (RIS, O.S., III, 2), 411–12, 417: S. Malaspina, p. 231: *Reg. Urb. IV*, II, n. 1827: *v.* Tenckhoff, pp. 89–90.   [5] E.g. *Reg. Urb. IV*, II, n. 736.

[6] For a masterly account of the military events of this year *v.* Hampe, *Urban IV. u. Manfred*, pp. 44–60.

assistance of Peter di Vico, who in the spring attempted unsuccessfully to take Sutri with the object of separating the two papalist strongholds of Rome and Orvieto. Around the beginning of June Manfred initiated operations on a larger scale by threatening Rome from the south and the north-east. Count Richard Filangieri's push into the Campagna was perhaps not intended as a serious penetration, but d'Oria made considerable headway in the Duchy, and the Romans, possibly perturbed by Manfred's skilful diplomatic activities within the city, withdrew their troops from Vico. Doria's force now turned north-east into the Duchy again, with the intention of marching on Orvieto from the upper Tiber, but their leader was drowned when fording the Nera near Spoleto towards the middle of July, at the same time as Urban was planning a hasty parliament[1] and issuing urgent appeals for crusaders to supplement his three thousand mercenaries. The troops that had been under d'Oria's command fled without giving battle when confronted by an untried papal army near Terni, and thus the immediate threat to Orvieto passed in a manner which suggests that Manfred's men lacked the quality to accomplish their apparently easy tasks.[2] A later success for Hohenstaufen Germans and Di Vico's Italians north of Rome was not exploited. Before the end of the autumn (2 October) Urban IV died at Perugia, but there were no operations during the papal vacancy, which fell at an unfortunate time of year for Manfred.

1265 was a slightly less difficult year for the papacy. Although Charles of Anjou only reached Italy in May, and the bulk of his army at the end of the year, his advent was expected and Manfred now had less support within the Papal State. In the March the pope's position improved considerably, although a large number of towns still stood by Manfred.[3] The conversion to the papal-Angevin cause in July of Peter di Vico was another important development.[4] Manfred himself led a raid at about this time to the neighbourhood of Tivoli, but a Sienese attempt to break through to the south from Tuscany was a more serious threat to the pope at Perugia.[5] However, this Ghibelline army fled when the

---

[1] *Reg. Urb. IV*, II, n. 858. This may also be the period of a rumour that Terni had gone over to Manfred, mentioned in an undated letter of Urban IV (printed by F. Bock in *Miscellanea Archivistica A. Mercati*, pp. 106–7).

[2] Hampe blames Manfred's weak strategy for his failure, and links this with defects in his character: the results of these perhaps appear more clearly in his failure to acquire able and devoted supporters.

[3] Zonghi, *Fabriano*, d. CCIII; *Reg. Cl. IV*, n. 740 (Fabriano and Camerino now pro-papal). For the campaigning and two engagements *v.* QFIA, XVIII, 242–3 and *Reg. Cl. IV*, n. 907.

[4] *Reg. Cl. IV*, n. 904.

[5] *Reg. Cl. IV*, n. 945; Waley, *Orvieto*, p. 46 (for other sources for the Sienese campaign).

Orvietan and Sienese Guelf troops opposed to it received reinforcements from Charles' Frenchmen, and this episode of August 1265 marks the end of Manfred's threat to the Papal State, though he still had supporters in the March. Urban IV had secured the agreement which brought Charles of Anjou to Italy and now his successor Clement, though constantly bemoaning his poverty,[1] had the consolation of seeing that French troops could be effective in clearing central Italy of the Hohenstaufen and their supporters.

The special circumstances of the year 1265 cannot provide a sound basis for an evaluation of Clement IV's policy in the Papal State, which will be considered later. At a time when the papal cause stood or fell by Angevin support, it was essential not to antagonize the man who was about to invade the Regno. It was inevitable that Charles' presence in Rome with a considerable force should win him a certain authority in neighbouring parts of the Papal State: this had been foreseen by Urban IV.[2] It was none the less an ominous sign for the papacy, and a sign of a tendency that was to dominate its history for more than a century, that Charles, presuming at the expense of a pope whom he remembered as a layman in his brother's service, occupied Clement's palace on the Lateran without asking permission. When the pope protested, Charles arranged to move elsewhere.[3] There were more substantial causes of grievance, such as Charles' attempts to tax Viterbo, Toscanella, Orvieto and Perugia, and to appoint officials to rule several towns in the southern part of the Tuscan Patrimony.[4]

The Angevin victory over Manfred near Benevento on 26 February 1266, and Manfred's death, mark the end of an era in Italian history. For the pope it meant the end of the Hohenstaufen attempts to dominate Italy. The terms agreed between Charles of Anjou and Urban IV included an acceptance of the Papal State — not merely the Duchy, the March and the old patrimony, but undefined *aliae terrae*, which could leave room for future claims[5] — and Charles could consent to this with a sincerity which no descendent of Barbarossa could have felt. Moreover he took an oath whereby he renounced all rights in this State other than those he held as Roman senator.[6] He was a better neighbour for

[1] E.g. *Reg. Cl. IV*, nn. 951, 953.

[2] In a letter of Christmas Day 1263 (Martène and Durand, II, 30) he had written that tenure of the Roman senatorship with the Regno would tend 'quantum saltem ad temporalia pertinet, Romani pontificis potestatem deprimere'.

[3] *Reg. Cl. IV*, n. 892; and *v.* Gregorovius, V, 2, 368.

[4] *Reg. Cl. IV*, n. 912; BFW, n. 9623; see below for Charles' oath that he would claim no rights in the Papal State except as senator.　　　[5] *Reg. Urb. IV*, II, n. 269.

[6] For this oath *v.* the document printed by F. Bock in *BISI*, LXVI, 105–6.

the papacy than any Hohenstaufen could be, yet his power would inevitably detract from the popes' independence. As a potent ally he was bound to demand a say in the affairs of central Italy. The Hohenstaufen had been overthrown, says Gregorovius, 'at an incalculably high price'.[1] To suggest this is perhaps to compare the situation after 1266 with an imaginary one in which the pope is left alone to face his ecclesiastical and temporal problems, among them that of governing his central Italian subjects. Such a comparison lacks reality, since but for the support of Charles of Anjou the popes might well have had no Italian subjects to govern.

[1] Gregorovius, V, 2, 343.

VI

The Papal State and the Angevins, 1266 – 85

The battle of Benevento was decisive for the history of the Papal State during the rest of the century and even far beyond. After it the popes were faced with an entirely new situation and the main problem of territorial policy was that of deciding between full acceptance of an Angevin alliance and reliance upon the strength of the pope's own family as a counterweight and source of independence.

During the first twelve years after Benevento no pope had strong support from his own family and the period is characterized by Angevin predominance, which shows most clearly in the long Roman senatorship of Charles I. There are parallels between the situation after 1266 and that after the death of Frederick II; in each case the disappearance of the Hohenstaufen challenge to the existence of a central Italian papal state revealed weaknesses in the papal position more fundamental than the counter-claims of a rival ruler. The unfavourable circumstances are sufficiently evident. For six years the March had passed out of papal control, while Manfred's threats had been felt further west, in the Duchy and Tuscan Patrimony. Behind the six years of Manfred lay ten years of struggle against Rome and other cities, and beyond that the decade of Frederick II's power in central Italy. No tradition of obedience to papal government had been established. In addition, the popes' financial support of the Angevin expedition had brought them heavily into debt, a situation which was doubly disadvantageous, for policy in the Papal State was affected by fiscal needs, while Roman bankers were foremost among the popes' creditors and this made difficult a return to the city.[1] Certainly the popes now had an ally, but he was a powerful one who would be able to enforce his own will not only at the expense of the pope's enemies. Concessions would have to be made to him, in

[1] For papal debts to Roman bankers v. Reg. Cl. IV, nn. 1037, 1050 (a letter of 24 April 1266 in which the pope explains that his debts prevent him from going to Rome), 1486, 1494. For the connection between these debts and policy in the March see below p. 178.

particular in the critical circumstances of 1267–8, when Frederick II's grandson Conradin briefly challenged Angevin-papal dominance in Italy. The interests of the Angevins were quite distinct from those of the popes; and beside control in the Regno they sought power and alliances in Tuscany and northern Italy to link their new lands with France. Hence they occupied the place of the Hohenstaufen nutcracker against which the popes had striven since the days of Henry VI.

Just as failure in their dealings with Rome had marked the testing-time of Innocent IV and Alexander IV in the 1250s, so now again papal control was most lacking in the very area that should have been its centre. To Charles of Anjou continued rule in Rome, over which there had been much debate during the negotiations which preceded the expedition, meant security for his lines of communication and for the northern frontier of the Regno. To the popes, it must have seemed in some ways like the installation in their capital of a new emperor, who yet stood to lose nothing by the affirmation of Roman claims in the Campagna and Tuscan Patrimony. Before Benevento, in January, Clement had complained that Charles' officials were progressing through the Campagna and other papal lands, taking over control, and even appointing an official to rule a commune in the Sabina.[1] Soon afterwards the King's vicar in Rome was sending instructions to Viterbo to render help against a fortress which was resisting Rome, and to Rieti, over which Rome had no possible claims to jurisdiction, to assist in rounding up supporters of Manfred. A month before this, Rieti, as a strong and independent commune, had discussed whether or not the pope should be allowed to enter the town; the battle of Benevento had given it a master, but he was not the pope.[2] Though Clement might grumble in a letter to a cardinal about the ill-treatment of 'our people' by Charles' officials in Rome, when it came to the test he made a humiliating withdrawal at the expense of the rector of the Tuscan Patrimony. This rector had received an oath of obedience from certain towns, and had made them abjure their oaths to Rome. On 12 May Clement informed the royal vicar and the Roman council that he had absolved these places from their oaths to the papacy and revoked the abjurations. The rector's actions might be defensible on the grounds of justice, he wrote, a little pathetically, but he had now been told not to take aggressive action except with special papal consent.[3] At the same

[1] *Reg. Cl. IV*, nn. 1004–5.
[2] Pinzi, *Viterbo*, II, 181–3: Michaeli, *Rieti*, III, dd. VII–VIII.
[3] *Reg. Cl. IV*, nn. 1050, 1055.

N

period Rome was seeking expansion to the south as well as north. In May Charles of Anjou resigned his senatorship, as the terms of his agreement with Urban IV compelled him, but the pope still kept away from Rome and the regime which followed showed itself no more submissive.[1]

Later in 1266 Clement had a further grievance against Charles; the king, he complained, had failed to prevent aid from the Regno reaching the rebellious town of Fermo in the March.[2] In this province the pope had to meet his most serious difficulties and, thanks to the registration of a large number of his letters to his legate, Cardinal Simon Paltanieri, we are able to observe his policy there in some detail.[3] It was essential to win the support of the towns, almost all of which had supported or at least recognized Manfred, yet their friendship must not be achieved at the expense of papal authority, and fines had to be collected from former rebels wherever this was possible. The pope's debts made this essential and money gathered in the March was transferred at once to the bankers who were his creditors.[4] Thus papal policy trod a tightrope, with the prospect on one side of friendly subjects but no authority and no money from fines, and on the other of a correct insistence on rights meeting defiance and gaining neither authority nor fines. In these circumstances it is not surprising that Clement should have supervised very closely the work of his legate, who many times referred to him questions of policy that would normally have been settled by a provincial rector without consultation. The tone of the letters suggests, moreover, that Clement was a suspicious man and did not enjoy delegating authority.[5] The essential thing, he emphasized, was that towns which had been favourable to the Church should not 'grow fat' at the expense of the Church or of their less worthy neighbours, as Fano was attempting to do with Fossombrone. As for the many towns who pleaded *force majeure* in excusing their past misconduct, the legate should beware of committing himself to them. His policy should be at first to

---

[1] Theiner, d. CCCXIII; *Reg. Cl. IV*, n. 1087: Gregorovius, V, 2, 401 ff.

[2] *Reg. Cl. IV*, n. 1279. For Fermo's relations with the papacy at this period *v.* U. Cameli, 'Un episodio di storia Fermana dei tempi di Manfredi e Corradino', *Studia Picena*, XI, 173–80.

[3] *Reg. Cl. IV*, nn. 1020, 1022, 1024, 1033, 1042, 1044, 1052, 1059, 1070, 1084, 1088, 1101, 1161, 1196, 1279, 1290 (full text of these letters in Martène and Durand, cols. 286 ff.); unregistered letters in *QFIA*, XXIX, 227. This cardinal should not be confused with Simon de Brie, the future Martin IV (as he is by Bock in *ASRSP*, LXXVIII, 91). He is the subject of a biographical article by A. Main in *Nuovo Archivio Veneto*, n.s., XXII (1920), 65–141.

[4] *Reg. Cl. IV*, n. 788.

[5] E.g. *Reg. Cl. IV*, n. 1070, in which he tells the cardinal that the bishop of Albano has absolved Conrad of Antioch, but that he wishes to have further information about Conrad's damage to papal interests.

annul all unauthorized leagues, to make no grants, and to withhold all privileges from towns that had not sworn obedience; later, if things went well, it might be time to order the destruction of the walls and fortifications of erstwhile rebels. The pope admitted that his information was defective through the contradictory statements made by the many emissaries of March communes at the Curia, though he assured Cardinal Simon that he need not fear the results of such embassies.

The major obstacle throughout 1266 was the continued defiance of Fermo, a city with a long Ghibelline tradition whose resistance was encouraged late in the year by the news of Conradin's election as King of the Romans. In 1267 Fermo took as its *podestà* Lorenzo Tiepolo, a Venetian who had already given it assistance against papal authority. Urbino also remained defiant, but the treatment of towns that had submitted set even more difficult problems of policy. In April the pope ordered Cardinal Simon — whom he ruefully described as one who had 'learnt the conditions of men and places in the school of experience' — to make the all-important decision concerning the treatment of Ancona, the main city of the province. But this did not prevent him from returning to the topic in June and again in July. Finally he advised that the town should pay 10,000 *l.*, the rest of its fine being suspended. The pope's close supervision of his legate in the March went against the traditions of government in the Papal State, but its results were on the whole promising. Ancona and even Fermo were paying taxes by early 1267,[1] while the less powerful towns came to heel with greater promptitude. Matelica was in revolt in February 1266, but paid its dues early in April, sued in the rector's court in July and in October began payment of the 6,000 *l.* fine to which it had been condemned. In December it accepted a *podestà* named by the provincial vicar and in July 1267 received a general absolution after paying 5,000 *l.* of the fine.[2] It is not possible to tell whether the financial successes achieved at Ancona and Matelica are typical, but this seems improbable, although other towns submitted and the rector's court was active.[3]

On balance Clement was perhaps not disappointed with the achievements of 1266. Some headway had been made in the March, and the pope's letters were full of plans to be attempted later *in tempore opportuno*. The Duchy and Tuscan Patrimony had not been seriously

[1] De Minicis, *Fermo*, p. 432.
[2] Acquacotta, *Matelica*, dd. 58–60; Grimaldi, *Matelica*, dd. CCXXVI, CCXXIX, CCXXXI, CCXXXV, CCXXXVII, CCXL, CCXLIV, CCXLIX–CCLI, CCLVII.
[3] *BDSPU*, XXV, 36–8; Zonghi, *Fabriano*, d. CCV; Fabriano, AC, Rivendicazioni Comunali, vol. I, fasc. IV.

affected by Manfred's invasion, and the energetic rector of the latter, Guy *de Pileo*, archdeacon of Soissons, had gained recognition in various northern parts of his province to set against his losses to Rome in the south. Todi, which had often claimed exemption from provincial rule, submitted in January 1267, and the towns of the Val del Lago of Bolsena, claimed by the commune of Orvieto, swore fealty to him in the same year.[1]

Throughout 1267 the most serious sign of papal weakness in central Italy was the attitude of Rome, where a series of changes of regime brought no tendency towards agreement with the pope.[2] The senatorship of the nobles Conrad Monaldeschi and Luca Savelli was followed by the popular rule of Angelo Capocci and this in turn by that of Henry of Castile, an adventurous son of Ferdinand III, whose choice may have owed something to the support of Charles of Anjou and Clement. Yet Henry, whose wealth and renown presumably recommended him principally to the Romans, was soon following in the footsteps of Brancaleone and others who had found Roman ambitions conveniently reconcilable with their own. By July 1267 Clement was warning his subjects in the Patrimony not to recognize the usurped jurisdiction of the senator and people of Rome; a little later, Henry had entered into alliance with the Tuscan Ghibellines and was styling himself 'captain-general of Tuscany'. Soon he declared openly for Conradin (who was now at Verona), imprisoning a number of relatives of cardinals of Roman birth. In December Clement found himself compelled to call in Charles of Anjou. He was willing to overlook the terms of the king's oath, he said, if only Charles could succeed in acquiring the Roman senatorship for himself.[3] The threat of a new Hohenstaufen invasion had thrown the papacy back on that very abdication to the Angevin which Urban and Clement had striven to avoid.

Yet as a whole the pope's subjects did not rally to Conradin. Città di Castello, a border territory and one always more amenable to Tuscan pressure than papal claims, went over, but to its south both Perugia and Assisi sent military contingents to resist the expedition.[4] 1268, the last year of Clement's pontificate, was not entirely a dark one. The continued resistance of Fermo, overshadowed though it was by the threat

---

[1] Theiner, d. CCCXVII; *Lib. Cens.*, I, 569; Arch. Vat., Arm. XXXV, 14, ff. 59v–61; RIS, N.S., XV, V, 157.

[2] For Rome in these years *v.* Gregorovius, V, 2, 401–26 and Dupré-Theseider, pp. 146–50.

[3] *Reg. Cl. IV*, nn. 1238, 1247, 1275, 1312, 1314–15.

[4] *Reg. Cl. IV*, nn. 698, 1383, 1393; *Lib. Cens.*, I, 587; Ficker, *Forschungen*, IV, d. 454: Perugia, AS, Rif. VI, ff. 187, 217–18.

of Conradin, was the only serious sign of trouble within the Papal State. The city was now placed under interdict and deprived of all privileges and jurisdiction and of the right to be ruled by a *podestà*. By May Fermo had sent emissaries to begin negotiations with the pope at Viterbo, but Clement thought it probable that they were playing for time and waiting to see how things went for Conradin.[1] The problem of Fermo illustrates well the difficulty of living up to the pope's warning against benefiting the towns at the expense of papal enemies, for Ripatransone, a neighbour and opponent of Fermo which sought greater independence, was now pardoned for its support of Manfred.[2]

The question of Fermo, as Clement remarked, would have to wait till the greater matter of Conradin was settled. On 23 August 1268 the victory of Tagliacozzo resolved the last Hohenstaufen challenge, but its aftermath was the restoration of the Angevin senatorship at Rome. Some months earlier the pope had offered Charles this office for ten years unless Rome withdrew at once its support of Conradin: immediately after his victory Charles styled himself senator, though he was not formally installed till he came to the city in September.[3] The Angevin senatorship symbolized more than papal dependence on an ally, for it was a working agreement relying upon the goodwill of the Romans, who had in practice, as Clement admitted in a letter to Charles, the *possessio ordinandi senatum*. Thus Charles' senatorship combined the *de facto* independence of papal rule of the greatest central Italian commune with a specially privileged status within the State for the prince who had defeated the Hohenstaufen.

Clement IV, who died on 29 November 1268, had never been in Rome as pope. For the next ten years the city remained under the government of a succession of Provençal vicars of Charles of Anjou while only Gregory X, for a few months in 1272, resumed residence in a See which had rarely seen its pastor since the distant days of Gregory IX. Yet the two-year vacancy which followed Clement's death was on the whole a period of peace in the Papal State. The only serious exception to this was a war in the Duchy between Assisi and Bettona, in

---

[1] *Reg. Cl. IV*, nn. 697, 1362, 1382. Fermo was also threatened with the loss of its See. The statement of De Minicis (*Fermo*, p. 435) that the city was absolved on 5 May 1268 seems to be incorrect.

[2] *Reg. Cl. IV*, n. 620. Cardinal Simon was now succeeded in the March by the bishop-elect of Verona, but Clement found difficulty in maintaining contact with the new rector, whom he reprimanded severely for deserting his province (*Reg.*, nn. 1404, 1413).

[3] Gregorovius, V, 2, 426–47: Dupré-Theseider, pp. 139, 182–3. Charles appears to have been elected for life, but to have reached a secret agreement with the pope that he would hold the office for ten years only (see Jordan, *L'Allemagne et l'Italie*, p. 401).

which Perugia and Orvieto became involved, though one should note
also the disgraceful intervention of the Viterbese in the papal conclave.[1] Rome dominated a large zone — it even had a 'province' named
Campagna and Marittima, under a royal vicar — but at least it co-
operated with papal troops in opposing the revolt of an Annibaldi baron
in the Campagna.[2] It is impressive to see the framework of provincial
rule continuing to function, with rectors receiving support and instructions from the college of cardinals, and to find Perugia and a number of
other towns responding when called by the cardinals to undertake a
punitive expedition against Orvieto.[3]

The election in December 1271 of Tebaldo Visconti of Piacenza
brought to the papal throne a man who had no experience of the problems of the Papal State and whose dearest projects were concerned with
the Holy Land. His schemes for a crusade were not easily reconcilable
with Charles of Anjou's Byzantine ambitions and in part explain his
attempt to become more independent of the king who, as senator in
Rome and imperial vicar in Tuscany, stood astride his central Italian
possessions. For much of his pontificate Gregory was outside Italy, at
Lyons, and few of his letters — or few of those that were registered —
are concerned with the Papal State, but in his choice of provincial
rectors can be seen a family policy which looks back to that of many of
his Italian predecessors, in particular Innocent IV, and also foreshadows
the more drastic methods of Nicholas III, Nicholas IV and Boniface
VIII. Not that Gregory, who had no lordship in the Campagna behind
him, was in a position to abandon the Angevin connection, or that he
sought to do so. Most prominent among the rectors of his pontificate
was the Provençal Fulk of Puyricard, who had previously served
Charles as counsellor, justiciar of the Principato and royal vicar in
Sicily, and from 1272 to 1276 was rector of the 'fickle' March.[4] The
other provinces, however, were entrusted to papal relatives, the Campagna-Marittima to Uberto Visconti, the Patrimony to Visconte Visconti, and the Duchy first to William Visconti and then to Uberto.

---

[1] Pellini, *Perugia*, I, 280–1; Perugia, AS, Rif. VI, ff. 286, 290: BFW, nn. 9956, 9961–2,
9965 (conclave).

[2] *ASRSP*, XXXVI, 448–56; Dupré-Theseider, pp. 184–5. For Rome's 'provinces', *v.*
also Dupré-Theseider, pp. 243–4.

[3] Orvieto's chronicler (RIS, N.S., XV, V, 158) reports troops from Rome and the
Campagna, the March and Duchy, as well as Perugia, 'the Patrimony', Toscanella and
Viterbo.

[4] Saba Malaspina, p. 268. Fulk was probably known to the pope through one of the
latter's nephews who had been a judge in Provence and archbishop of Aix (Runciman,
Sicilian Vespers, pp. 150–1): for his career in the Regno *v.* P. Durrieu, *Les Archives Ange-
vines de Naples*, II, 369.

Even Fulk in the March was accompanied as marshal and for a time as vicar by yet another member of the family, Henry Visconti.[1]

The period of comparative peacefulness in central Italy extended throughout Gregory X's time, the pope himself helping to achieve this through the important innovation of provincial treasurerships and through enquiries into papal rights and revenues.[2] Surviving evidence concerning the activities of the provincial authorities also suggests that much judicial and administrative business was being conducted and, in some provinces at least, a degree of control achieved over the towns greater than at any time in the past.

These gains by papal authority were accomplished in the face of opposition, and there was no general crisis of municipal power. To talk of 'success' may seem an exaggeration, but in comparison with the earlier decades of the Papal State there is an advance in the routine activities of rectors and their courts and in the compliance of the communes.[3] Even disputes between towns and papal authorities show that papal claims were felt to be worth disputing, hence Todi's long drawn-out case concerning its claim to be exempt from the authority of the Tuscan Patrimony is to be seen as a sign of the rector's rather than the town's strength. This suit, first brought forward in 1272, was not settled for a quarter of a century.[4] The most serious problem in the Duchy of Spoleto was a product of the policy of Urban IV and concerned the grant to Perugia of the *contado* of Gubbio: Perugia's claim to Gubbio, Gualdo and Nocera Umbra was now challenged by the authorities of the Duchy, supported by the pope. This multilateral dispute was in the hands of the rector of the Duchy by May 1273. He sentenced Perugia to a fine of 1,600 *l.* and the pope added excommunications, but this matter also was unsettled at the time of Gregory X's death.[5] Elsewhere papal complaints refer to attempts by Rome, normally quiescent at this period under Angevin

---

[1] See App. II.

[2] For the treasurership, see above, p. 106: for an enquiry (October 1272) into papal 'civitates, castra, ville, canalia, feuda, libertates, census, affictus, redditus' etc. in the March, Duchy, Campagna and Benevento by Guy of Zena, canon of Mantua, *v.* Theiner, dd. CCCXXIV–CCCXXV.

[3] It would be otiose to cite references for this impression, drawn from a multiplicity of sources. The *riformanze* of Perugia for 1275 (vols. I, II, III and VIII) show that city in constant negotiation with the rector of the Duchy (mainly concerning its condemnation for not paying the *podestà* of Gualdo Tadino, who had been appointed by the rector) and reveal the rector's court at work summoning minor places within Perugia's sphere of influence. For fines and taxation in the March at this time *v.* (e.g.) Gianandrea, *Iesi*, d. CCLXXX; Lilii, *Camerino*, II, 41–2, 44–5; Fabriano, AC, Lib. Ross., f. 92v.

[4] Todi, AC, perg. nn. 20–1, 24–5 and Reg. Vet. Istr., ff. 90–2, 94–8, 100, 102, 105v–106, 155v–156, etc.

[5] Pellini ,*Perugia*, I, 283–5; Perugia, AS, Rif. VII, ff. 8, 10v–12, 24, 35v, 46–8, 73–6, 81, 89, 91–2, 96, 110, 161, 163, etc. Discussion in Ermini, 'Aspetti giuridici', pp. 25–7.

vicars, to extend its power to the south in 1272 at the expense of Piperno, Sezze, Acquapuzza and even Terracina,[1] while the prolonged but unsuccessful attempt by Venice to enforce her commercial monopoly in the Adriatic by naval and military campaigns against Ancona may also have begun during Gregory's pontificate.[2]

Although the government of the Papal State was not one of the principal preoccupations of Gregory X, it was he who opened the negotiations with Rudolf of Hapsburg which were to lead to the acquisition of a new province. Undoubtedly his intention was to solve the problem of the imperial *interregnum* and at the same time to instal a counterweight to Angevin influence in Italy. The plan was not wholly successful in either respect, but Rudolf's need of papal support was such that he was willing to purchase it by ceding Romagna. It is not quite clear at what stage the decision was made on the papal side to demand this very considerable price. The popes had already played with the idea of acquiring Romagna, for Innocent III had claimed it and then tacitly withdrawn his claim, while Innocent IV had persuaded his puppet William of Holland to grant the province (ineffectively) to a papal nephew, Thomas of Fogliano.[3] Clement IV had found the frontier between the March and Romagna an embarrassment, in that aid for rebels in the March was often forthcoming from Romagna; his gifts to his ally Malatesta of Verucchio are the first sign of a serious papal policy in Romagna and foreshadow later events.[4] This problem of Romagnol support for rebels, together with the pope's strong bargaining position and the achievements of papal rule during the preceding decade, must have been responsible for the temerarious decision to attempt the acquisition of a very large and unruly territory. In any case rulers are normally quicker to see the advantages than the disadvantages of gaining land.

In June 1274 Rudolf, who had been elected King of the Romans the year before and now gained papal recognition, accepted the Papal State as defined in the donations of his predecessors. It was probably not till

---

[1] Contatore, *Terracina*, pp. 198–9; Lombardini, *Sezze*, pp. 48–9.

[2] Peruzzi, *Ancona*, II, 13: see below p. 186.

[3] See above, p. 35. Ficker (*Forschungen*, II, 449 ff.) suggests that the inclusion of the word 'Pentapolis' and 'Exarchate' instead of 'Romagna' in the imperial donations of Innocent III's time is indicative of Innocent's unwillingness to press this claim, but this is clearly incorrect, since the same formula was used in the confirmation of Rudolf (Theiner, d. CCCLXII).

[4] On Malatesta's relations with the Church up to 1278, *v.* P. J. Jones, 'The Malatesta of Rimini', pp. 87 ff. The marriage of Malatesta in 1266 to a niece of Cardinal Paltanieri, then rector of the March, was connected with the papal alliance (*v. Nuovo Archivio Veneto*, n.s., XXII (1920), 108–10).

the end of the following year that he became aware that Gregory now intended to take the cession of the Pentapolis and Exarchate, included in these donations, *au pied de la lettre*.[1] The negotiations between Gregory and Rudolf, which related also to Charles of Anjou's abandonment of his imperial vicariate in Tuscany, were slow and painstaking. Bitter experience taught the pope not merely to insist on confirmation of Rudolf's promises by the German princes, but to add a clause to Rudolf's oath concerning the Papal State binding him to accept 'no office or dignity or any power whatsoever in these lands, and expecially in the city of Rome'.[2] A precise understanding between Gregory and Rudolf's representatives concerning Romagna was achieved during the pope's visit to Bologna in the second week in December 1275, for on 12 December he complained that a petition from Rudolf's nuncios appeared to conflict with the agreement reached by him with them at Bologna *super statu partium Romaniole*.[3] It is impossible to say whether earlier discussions may have taken place, but this appears to be the first written reference to the agreement to cede the Romagna *de facto* as well as *de jure*.

The rôle of Gregory X's short-lived successors, Innocent V (January–June 1276), Adrian V (July–August 1276) and John XXI (September 1276–May 1277) was limited to standing by the position adopted by Gregory. Thus Innocent in March 1276 and John in November protested against alleged attempts by Rudolf's officials to intervene in Romagna and receive oaths of fealty from its towns. Innocent's letter to Rudolf, after recalling Gregory X's protests, asked that the king's representatives 'should act more cautiously, carefully abstaining from deeds of this sort in the lands of the Church and especially in the Exarchate and Pentapolis, and in no way intervening again except on special orders from us'; the king was to tell the communes that their oaths of fealty had been received in error, and that they were to obey the pope. John XXI wrote in similar terms, rebuking Rudolf for not obeying Innocent's request and asking that the papal nuncio who was carrying this letter should bear a reply stating explicitly that these oaths had been

---

[1] It is not clear on what evidence Haller (*Papsttum*, V, 40–1) bases his statement that Gregory sent representatives to accompany those of Rudolf assuming suzerainty over the Romagnol towns and thereby accepted his rule by implication.

[2] Theiner, d. CCCXXX (see also d. CCCXLV).

[3] Theiner, d. CCCXLVIII. This document provides clear evidence that the agreement over Romagna dates from Gregory's pontificate and is confirmed by d. CCCLII. Ficker (*Forschungen*, II, 453) is in error in stating that the first reference to this agreement occurs only in March 1276. Gregory was at Parma on 6 December, at Bologna on the 11th and at Pianoro on the 12th. (for his itinerary *v.* Potthast, p. 1701).

received in error. Both these popes ordered Rudolf not to come to Italy for coronation until he had satisfied them on this and other points, and after John XXI's death the cardinals wrote in the same strain.[1] It was partly due to the brevity of these three pontificates that final agreement over Romagna was only achieved in 1278, by Nicholas III.

While these momentous negotiations went on their dignified way, the papal provinces continued in a state of comparative passivity. Fulk of Puyricard remained as rector of the March under Gregory's successors and this long tenure by an able man, together with some Angevin military support, helps to explain the improved condition of what had hitherto been the most disturbed of all the provinces. But the notorious 'fickleness' of the March had arisen largely from the interest taken in it by Frederick and Manfred. Now that it could no longer be a Hohenstaufen corridor its governor would meet no problems more threatening than the powerful communes and feudatories to be found in all the papal provinces, and in fact few of the March cities could muster the same resources as the strongest towns of the western provinces, Rome, Viterbo, Orvieto and Perugia. For the most part it was a land of small communes, who were often checked in their desire for expansion by powerful neighbouring lords. The most serious disturbance to the March in these years was the Venetian assault on Ancona of 1276–7, an attack by sea and land against which the cardinals protested in vain.[2] In this attempt to subdue their only mercantile rival in the Adriatic the Venetians sought unsuccessfully for support from the other towns of the March. They abandoned the war in 1277 after the failure of a fifth attack, made with twenty-four galleys. The stronger towns and barons of the March were not entirely quiescent, for Fulk experienced defiance from Fermo, Ascoli, and the powerful Rainald of Brunforte,[3] but there were also achievements which are the more impressive in view of the lack of continuous papal backing. Iesi, a town of considerable strength, paid its regular hearth-tax and *tallia militum* in 1276–7, as well as almost 8,000 *l.* to secure absolution from a series of fines, some of which went back ten years to the time of Cardinal Simon. These belated payments were made in accordance with an award pronounced by the Provençal James Ganteaulme, who in the early summer of 1276 commanded a corps sent into the March by Charles of Anjou

[1] Theiner, dd. CCCLII–CCCLVI.

[2] For this war see esp. Raynaldus, *Ann. Eccl., ad* 1277, § 43–5.

[3] De Minicis, *Fermo*, pp. 457–60; Raynaldus, *Ann. Eccl., loc. cit.*; Colucci, *Ant. Pic.*, XIX, dd. XXXVIII–XXXIX.

to give assistance to the Savoyard Innocent V.[1] Salimbene quotes in his chronicle[2] some 'prophetic' verses which confirm the impression that this province was now providing the popes with considerable funds. 'The March of Ancona', says the poet, 'will remain under the Roman Church, which will shear its wool daily'.

The Perugian council-minutes show the town in constant communication with the rector of the Duchy in 1276–7 and illustrate this official's considerable power. In 1276 the Perugians suggested that the rector should arbitrate in a dispute between themselves and Spello: soon afterwards he excommunicated Spello's *podestà*.[3] Early in the following year a new rector, Hugh Marquis of Monte Mezzano, a powerful feudatory whose family owned much property at Perugia, held a parliament to inaugurate his period of office. He intervened effectively in the affairs of Perugia, confiscating some animals acquired by robbery, deciding disputes with Assisi and Nocera, and attempting to call the town to arms against the people of Torgiano.[4]

Though John XXI acted in support of this rector, it was normally only the more fundamental disputes involving papal sovereignty that went to the papal Curia. The question of Perugia's claim to Gubbio's *contado* was still under discussion there throughout these years. In 1276 the Perugian council concluded that the best method might be to seek advice from a number of 'defenders' within the Curia, and agreed that 800 florins each should be offered to six cardinals, Richard Annibaldi, Matthew 'Rosso' Orsini, Ottobuono, William and James Savelli, and Uberto de Coconato: the decision is instructive both for the methods of the Curia and for Perugia's determination to achieve success.[5] This was a three-sided debate and 1277 saw the beginning of a controversy between Gubbio and the papal authorities over the

---

[1] Gianandrea, *Iesi*, dd. CLXXXIV–CLXXXVIII. The records of Iesi for these years happen to have survived: there is no reason to suppose that this was an isolated case and at the same period Fabriano paid 1,000 *l.* fine and 150 *l. tallia militum* (Fabriano, AC, Lib. Ross., ff. 93 and 122v–123). For the troops sent in April 1276 *de mandato summi pontificis contra rebelles S.R.E.* (with Ganteaulme as captain and James de Sénacourt as marshal) *v.* Laurent, *Innocent V*, pp. 410–11, 475.

[2] II, 254.

[3] Perugia, AS, Rif. III, f. 57v; Rif. IX, ff. 35v–36.

[4] *Ibid.*, Rif. VIII, ff. 128, 144, 177v, 183–7, 193v–194v, 196; Rif. IX, ff. 167v–168v, 172–3; Rif. 177, ff. 9v, 26v–27. The same rector acted to quell a dispute between Spoleto and the papal castellan of Cesi in the Terra Arnulforum (Contelori, *Cesi*, pp. 24–5; Sansi, *Spoleto*, d. LXV). In 1285 Hugh Marquis of Monte Mezzano and his brothers held between them property in Perugia assessed at 8,000 *l.* (Mira, 'L'estimo di Perugia', p. 403).

[5] *Ibid.*, Rif. VIII, ff. 6–7, 12, 20–1, 122, 140; IX, f. 140v. The letter is mentioned by Davidsohn, *Geschichte von Florenz*, II, 2, 128n.

right to tax the disputed area, which was not settled for at least twenty years.[1]

The power of papal authority to make itself felt even in the unpromising circumstances of 1276-7 shows most clearly in a success further south, in the Tuscan Patrimony. During the vacancy after the death of John XXI, Narni built a fortified tower at Monte S. Angelo close to the papal fortress of Miranda. At the request of the cardinals, Raymond 'de Nogeriis', the rector of the Patrimony, went to the new stronghold, talked to Narni's representatives and troops there, and gave them formal warning that if they continued building they would be excommunicated and fined 2,000 marks. Only twelve days later Narni's ambassadors went to Viterbo, where the cardinals were in conclave, to report that the tower had now been destroyed and to receive absolution from the interdict and excommunications imposed, on giving pledges and swearing an oath of obedience.[2]

The period between the battle of Benevento and the acquisition of Romagna twelve years later marks the first positive achievements in erecting a system of papal government in central Italy. Owing to the loss of the provincial archives that government can be glimpsed only in the occasional references of receipts, municipal council-minutes and other documents, but it is evident from these that at least in the March and Duchy provincial rectors, treasurers and judges were capable of exerting pressure on towns and securing obedience in performing a routine task of supra-municipal administration. The comparative lack of inter-town warfare in these years was of course due in part to the absence of prolonged Hohenstaufen influence and to successful Angevin rule in Rome, though the latter was a humiliation to these popes, none of whom took up permanent residence in the city.[3] By 1278 there was no determined resistance to papal authority, even from Fermo and the formerly Manfredian communes of the March whose defiance had so haunted Clement IV in 1266-7. Certainly there had been no universal acceptance of the rectors' power, but a sort of balance or *modus vivendi* had been achieved which might lead to the formation of a state comparable with the Angevin kingdom of Naples. The popes had communes on their hands, whereas in the south the Normans had long

---

[1] Gubbio, Sottosez AS, perg., bu. 10, nn. 244-50 and bu. 16; some of the documents concerning this case are summarized in *BDSPU*, XXV, 42-7, 49-50, 54-5, 57-8. The places in dispute were Pergola, Canziano, Serra S. Abondio and Collestazaro.

[2] Terni, AS, perg. (10-22 Aug. 1277).

[3] Gregory X was consecrated at Rome, but spent the years 1273-5 at Lyons and died in Tuscany on his return journey. Innocent V moved to Rome and died there, but both Adrian V and John XXI ruled from Viterbo.

since ended serious claims to municipal independence, but the achievements of these twelve years had been considerable and explain the decision to accept a new province.

*   *   *

On 25 November 1277, six months after the death of John XXI, the cardinals chose as his successor John Gaetan Orsini, who had long been prominent as a leader of the non-French element in the Curia. The rôle of the Orsini in crystallizing and commanding the opposition to the French and Provençal cardinals who had enjoyed a powerful position since the pontificate of Urban IV has never been disputed, though it rests on little precise evidence.[1] Of the under-currents of bitter feeling between French and Italian in the Curia at the time there is clear evidence in a satirical poem composed at Viterbo during the conclave of 1269–71, in which a French cleric mocks the rustic clownish ways of the 'stony Campagna', and the 'hairy shoes' worn by those whom 'impoverished Anagni' breeds: now both *regnum* and *sacerdotium* have been transferred from the Romans to the French, with whom they shall remain *stabiliter . . . in eternum*.[2] Nicholas III, a Roman aristocrat by birth, was well fitted to lead the reaction against the Franks, and to undertake a pontificate gaining from, if not resting on, the physical and psychological support of a landed family of the Campagna, a pontificate in the tradition of the highly respectable Innocent III, not to mention the more extreme 'local' popes of the era before the Hildebrandine reform. The Orsini had come to the fore as 'Boboni' or 'Boveschi' in the late twelfth century and Pope Celestine III was of the family, which held considerable land in the city itself, at Vicovaro and elsewhere in the Campagna, and in the adjoining part of the Regno.[3] But there was an unspiritual zeal about Nicholas III's family policy — immortalized in the Dantesque pun which defined it as the wish to 'avanzar gli orsatti'[4] — which had the flavour more of what was to follow than of what had come before. Dante himself hints at this when he makes Nicholas proclaim prophetically that he will have to move further down among the simoniacs to make room for Boniface VIII, and a recent writer has justly remarked that 'he seems at times a precursor of the popes of the Renaissance'.[5]

---

[1] See Morghen in *ASRSP*, XLVI, 298–9 and Previté-Orton in *Cambridge Medieval History*, VI, 194. For Charles of Anjou's indignation of Nicholas' election *v.* F. Baethgen, 'Ein Pamphlet Karls I. v. Anjou zur, Wahl Papst Nikolaus III., *Bayerische Akad. d. Wissenschaften, Phil-Hist kl., Sitzungsberichte*, Jahr. 1960, Hft. 7.

[2] *Archivio per la Storia della Pietà*, I (1951), 347–8.

[3] *Inferno*, XIX, l. 71.   [4] De Cupis, XIV, 129–52.

[5] *Inf.*, XIX ll. 76–8: Dupré-Theseider, p. 208.

Nicholas III's Roman provenance was of great assistance to him in his dealings with the city. When he came to the papal throne Charles of Anjou's ten year tenure of the senatorship had rather less than a year to run. To end the Angevin regime and instal one which was both favourable to the papacy and acceptable to the Romans was an obvious aim which stood a far better chance of accomplishment by a Roman pope than by an outsider. This may indeed have been in the mind of the cardinals when they elected Nicholas, though his choice should undoubtedly be interpreted as a victory of the non-French 'party'. To prepare his way in his dealings with Charles and the Romans, Nicholas ordered the compilation of a register of papal documents concerned with the Roman senatorship and in particular with its tenure by the Angevin.[1] Armed with this material, he went to Rome to negotiate an agreement with Charles and was so successful that on 18 July he was able to issue from Viterbo his fundamental *Constitutio super electione senatoris Urbis*.[2] The main outlines of this document, decreed with the advice of the cardinals, and valid in perpetuity, were simple. No emperor, king, prince, marquis, duke, count, baron, or close relative of any of these could become senator or ruler of Rome, nor could any other man hold the office for more than a single year; any exceptions to this rule would require papal consent. Any election to the contrary would be void and those responsible for it would suffer severe penalties. There was one significant exception: Romans might be chosen (for not more than one year), even if they had relatives in the forbidden categories and held positions — though not as lay nobles — outside Rome. These terms make it evident that the pope had it in mind to take over the senatorship himself, and indeed he may already have reached an agreement with the Romans to this effect.[3] A week after issuing this constitution Nicholas sent two recently created cardinals, both nephews of his, to Rome with instructions to arrange the city's *regimen* for the period after Charles' officials had left the city. They were to be careful not to give the impression of intervening in the senatorial election, 'for we do not desire your proceedings to be such that it may be thought that we wish to concern ourselves (*nos intromittere*) with this election in

---

[1] See F. Bock, 'Il Registrum super senatoria Urbis di papa Nicolò III', *BISI*, LXVI, 79–113, which, however, fails to relate the compilation to Nicholas' negotiations with Charles in 1278. See also Gregorovius, V, 2, 484 ff.

[2] *Reg. N. III*, n. 296.

[3] The clause limiting tenure to one year requires some explanation in view of its apparent incompatibility with Nicholas' intention to hold office himself. Either he originally intended to seek election for a single year only in the first place or alternately he may have regarded a reference to life tenure as too revelatory.

any way'. Meanwhile the pope agreed that Charles should remain senator until 16 September. In that month the Romans duly invited Nicholas to accept the senatorship, presumably in his capacity as a private person and a Roman.[1]

For the pope the Roman settlement of 1278 was a triumph, a glorious end to a decade of humiliation. But how did it appear to the Romans? The proscription of foreign senators, designed to prevent a repetition of the episodes which had brought Spaniards, Frenchmen and even an Englishman to the Capitol, was certainly flattering to the pride of the proudest of all municipalities. The arrangement was anti-Angevin but in no way anti-Roman. It gave the city a Roman senator again and founded a new epoch of aristocratic power and rivalry which, however fatal for its future history, ensured for the settlement a strong body of support. It was a check to democratic hopes, never at any time strong in the absence of individual leadership, but the Romans could be united in welcoming the new Roman senator so long as there seemed no serious prospect of his power as pope diminishing the city's virtual independence within the Papal State.

Nicholas III naturally delegated the senatorship to a series of vicars, thereby continuing the Angevin tradition, though Roman nobles replaced Provençal officials. The vicariate was held first by the pope's brother Matthew 'Rosso' Orsini, then jointly by John Colonna and Pandulf Savelli. Nicholas' building achievements at the Lateran and St. Peter's were as near as he could come to offering the Romans circuses, but the frequent presence of the Curia in the city must have brought to many the means of buying more bread. There is little evidence concerning the degree of his control over Rome, but some angry papal letters of 1278 show that the city was retaining Piperno, Sezze and Terracina, all far to the south, within its sphere of influence, citing their men to its court and compelling them to export to it their grain and wine.[2]

The family basis of Nicholas III's policy is to be seen in his dealings with the rest of the Papal State as clearly as in his Roman settlement. The rectorship of the Tuscan Patrimony he entrusted to Orso Orsini, the great undertaking of the assumption of rule in Romagna to two other nephews, Cardinal Latino Malabranca and Bertold Orsini. Papal

---

[1] *Reg. N. III*, nn. 703–5, 712. The terms of the election are unknown and it is not clear whether Nicholas was now made senator for life: see Gregorovius, V, 2, 487 ff. and Dupré-Theseider, p. 215.

[2] *Reg. N. III*, nn. 998–9. For Nicholas' building operations *v.* Saba Malaspina, p. 316.

nepotism was no novelty, and the justification that can be offered for it has often been stated: a later pope, Clement V, put the case well when he appointed to an office a relative 'whose merit and virtues are through familiar experience not unknown to us'.[1] Moreover Cardinal Latino was a capable man who had held posts of responsibility under Urban IV and had already been used in a pacificatory rôle at Florence and Bologna. Nicholas III's reputation has suffered from the general acceptance of the story, which rests solely upon the hearsay of a later writer, Ptolemy of Lucca, that he planned an Orsini kingdom in northern Italy. Yet he shocked Dante and many of his contemporaries, and when we encounter the tone of his views as expressed in his letters — 'no public character has ever stood the revelation of private utterance and correspondence' — we see the justice of their condemnation. Early in March 1280 Nicholas prepared two 'memorials', which he entrusted to a friar minor, brother Bartholomew of S. Gemini, respectively for Cardinal Latino and Bertold Orsini, his two representatives in Romagna.[2] There is much emphasis in these instructions on the need for family solidarity; evidently the two nephews had been unhappy in their collaboration. The pope is shocked at the dilemma with which he is faced as a result of this. He must have an ecclesiastical legate in Romagna, and if Cardinal Latino insists on withdrawing he will have to put Bertold under a different prelate, not a relative: 'would this befit his family, would it befit the honour of the papacy, that his nephew, and such a man, should serve as a marshal under another?' Bertold was threatened that if his attitude made co-operation impossible he might return to Rome as he had set out from it ('*talis redeat, qualis ivit*'). Bertold's remark, quoted in the same letter, that 'he would abandon Guy of Montefeltro only when Mary Magdalene was divided from Christ' suggests a secular approach to his duties, yet the pope himself had advised the legate in the same matter to make full use of dissimulation.[3]

Nicholas had procured for himself a country house at Soriano, near Viterbo — perhaps no true Roman could relish Viterbo itself as a summer residence — after securing the condemnation of its owners on a charge of heresy, and this transaction too met with the criticism of contemporaries.[4] But he was no advocate of a general policy of insouci-

---

[1] *Reg. Cl. V*, n. 364. For a defence of Nicholas' nepotistic policy *v*. Haller, *Papsttum*, V, 56–7.

[2] Full text in F. Kaltenbrunner, *Actenstücke zur Geschichte des Deutschen Reiches*, pp. 218–25.

[3] *Reg. N. III*, n. 727 ('in istis tractatibus dissimulanda suntmulta, palp anda sunt aliqua, tacenda sunt plura').

[4] *Reg. N. III*, n. 702: for this episode *v*. Pinzi, *Viterbo*, II, 372–8.

ance, and in two interesting letters of August 1279 he upbraided the rectors of the March and Duchy for financial scandals in their respective provinces which had been brought to his notice. The former was told that his marshal and his vicar *in spiritualibus* were accepting bribes, perverting justice and extorting money illegally, the latter that his brother had also been taking bribes in return for promises of judicial favours to towns cited to court or summoned for military service, 'taking on himself the position of a mediator'. These letters throw a vivid light on the failings of provincial administration.[1]

Nicholas III's achievement in Italy would stand or fall by the Romagna, where Innocent III had failed. This was one of the most fertile and wealthy provinces of Italy, with several flourishing towns, among them Bologna, a great mercantile and educational centre. Romagna, which in Dante's view[2] had never known peace and would never know it, was a corn-growing land, whose towns were strung close together along the Via Emilia, near to the sharply contrasting Apennine area which was the home of the lawless feudal lords who so often became their masters. Bologna, Imola, Faenza, Forlì, Cesena and Rimini lay on this road: only Ravenna of the leading towns, some twenty miles north-east of Faenza, on the Adriatic, failed to conform to the pattern. Bologna probably had a population at this time of sixty thousand;[3] certainly it was considerably larger than any commune of the March, Duchy or Tuscan Patrimony, and ranked with the great cities of Lombardy and Tuscany. To its east the plain of Romagna was dominated by the feudatories of the mountain zone, worthy precursors of the terrible *innominato* of Manzoni. The greatest of these, Guy of Montefeltro, controlled Urbino and the surrounding area in the hilly part of south-eastern Romagna. The Malatesta had their origin in the adjoining lands and presumably drew their retinues from them. By the middle of the century they were emerging as the leading family in Rimini, in rivalry with the Parcitadi. At about the same time the Polenta were gaining ascendancy in Ravenna. Further west Forlì changed hands a number of times and Faenza was still in dispute between the Manfredi and Mainardo dei Pagani, a powerful lord with

---

[1] *Reg. N. III*, nn. 776–7. A curious and illuminating transaction of this time is the grant of absolution to Fabriano by Annibaldo di Trasmondo, who had been rector of the March some twenty years earlier (Zonghi, *Fabriano*, d. CCXXVIII). Fabriano paid 100 florins in lieu of fines totalling 21,000 *l.* and 17,000 gold oz., presumably in the hope of slowing up the judicial processes whereby the papal authorities sought to enforce their heavy demands.

[2] *Inferno*, XXVII, ll. 37–8.

[3] Peyer, *Zur Getreidepolitik Oberitalienischer Städte*, p. 18 (for grain production in Romagna see this work, *passim*).

lands around the upper valleys of the Senio and Lamone. The Alidosi, another feudal family from the mountains, often dominated Imola, while Bologna was the prey of more conventional city factions, led by the Geremei and Lambertazzi.[1]

Imperial rule had never achieved much hold in this inflammable and quintessentially unrulable province, though it had served to crystallize its unceasing factionalism around rival 'Ghibelline' and 'Guelf' loyalties. After the death of Frederick II Romagna was left to a 'free for all' among the leading families, though the rough alliances continued to dignify themselves with the name of 'Guelf' and 'Ghibelline' in honour of their earlier traditions, and the latter contributed something to the causes of both Manfred and Conradin. King Rudolf presumably knew of the anarchical condition of the province and may well have thought that the popes were welcome to see if they could govern in such unpromising territory.

The imperial vacancy had led to a deterioration, if this were possible, in the state of Romagna. Count Guy of Montefeltro, a 'Ghibelline' who had acted as Roman senator for Henry of Castile in 1267 and supported Conradin before Tagliacozzo, was the leader of a party which had gained ascendancy by the mid-1270s. In alliance with Mainardo he gained Forlì, Faenza and Cesena and in June 1275 won a great victory at S. Procolo over the Bolognese, now dominated by the 'Guelf' Geremei. The leaders of the discomfited alliance included Taddeo of Pietrarubbia, head of a cadet branch of the Montefeltreschi, Malatesta of Rimini, Guy da Polenta of Ravenna and the Manfredi of Faenza. Of these, the first two at least had important papal and Angevin connections, for Taddeo had served Charles as his *podestà* at Lucca, Florence and Siena (1270–2) before becoming rector of the Tuscan Patrimony (1273–5), while Malatesta had aided Urban IV against Manfred and preceded Taddeo as royal vicar at Florence.[2]

Hence the party in Romagna which had pro-papal traditions was in need of help at the very time when the popes were claiming the cession of the province. Undoubtedly negotiations between its leaders and the Curia preceded Nicholas III's attempted assumption of control, but

---

[1] This sketch of Romagna in the period before 1278 is mainly dependent on the following works: G. Fasoli, 'Guelfi e Ghibellini di Romagna nel 1280–1', *ASI*, XCIV; R. Honig, *Guido da Montefeltro*; G. Franceschini, 'La Signoria dei Conti di Montefeltro a Cesena', *Studi Romagnoli*, V, and 'Un caduto del "sanguinoso mucchio" ', *ibid.*, VII; P. J. Jones, 'The Malatesta of Rimini', chapters I and II. (I wish to thank the author for a long loan of a copy of this thesis.)

[2] *Studi Romagnoli*, VII, 51; P. J. Jones, *op. cit.*, pp. 87 ff.

their date and the form that they took cannot be ascertained.[1] A contemporary poem refers to the secret visit to Rome of one of the leaders — probably Guy da Polenta — disguised as a pilgrim, while a hostile chronicler roundly states that the chiefs of the 'Church' party 'all went off together to Rome and, in so far as they were able, yielded the province of Romagna to the Roman Church'. At about the same time Nicholas completed the work of his predecessors in securing agreement with Rudolf. In June 1278 he at last achieved full ratification of the king's promise to cancel the oaths of fealty taken by the Romagnol towns. The communes were at once informed of this, though the matter was only concluded in March 1279 when final confirmation of the cession came from the German princes, almost six years after negotiations had begun between Rudolf and Gregory X.[2]

Nicholas' first moves to take over Romagna date from the summer of 1278 and thus coincide with his Roman settlement.[3] On 20 June he dispatched Geoffrey of Anagni, a papal chaplain, and John of Viterbo, a Dominican, to receive oaths of fealty from the Romagnol towns. They were to take particular care to ensure that all such transactions were formally recorded by notaries. By August this mission had been strengthened by the addition of another Dominican and of William Durand, a papal chaplain and distinguished canonist who had recently served briefly as rector of the Tuscan Patrimony. Cardinal Latino had been appointed as legate in Romagna by early June, but apparently did not reach the province until August. Papal action took a double form, for as these emissaries toured Romagna to secure recognition from the resident authorities they also instructed the towns to send embassies to the Curia at Viterbo. In July all the leading towns had representatives negotiating at Viterbo, the two Bolognese factions sending independent envoys.[4] The chronology of these events is a little difficult to establish,

---

[1] The sources are RIS, O.S., XIV, cc. 1104–5 (Cesena annals); RIS, N.S., XVI, III, 14 and 'Il serventese romagnolo del 1277', printed by A. F. Massèra in *ASI*, LXXII, 3–17. If the date of this mission could be ascertained it would be clear whether it can have played any part in the papal decision to attempt the annexation of the province. This is very improbable, since the decision goes back to 1275 or earlier, while the Cesena annals date the mission 'a year or two after the capture of Roversano' (Sept. 1275). If the embassy was literally 'to Rome', as the other two sources state, it was probably made to Nicholas III, not before December 1277, though Innocent V was in Rome during the first half of 1276: in any case, 'Rome' is often carelessly used as a synonym for 'the papal Curia'.

[2] Theiner, dd. CCCLVIII, CCCLX–CCCLXIII, CCCLXV–CCCLXIX, CCCLXXXI, CCCLXXXIII–CCCLXXXV, CCCLXXXVII–CCCLXXXVIII, CCCXCIII. At the pope's request, Rudolf's letter of June 1278 named individually each town that was ceded.

[3] *Reg. N. III*, nn. 253–9, 265–72, 305–8, 942, 958–60.

[4] For Nicholas' relations with Bologna in 1278–9 *v.* Fasoli, 'La Pace del 1279 tra i partiti bolognesi', *ASI*, XCI, 49–75, and sources cited there.

but it seems that the communes' representatives negotiated with Cardinal Matthew 'Rosso' Orsini before agreeing to accept the pope's own arbitration concerning their status and to recognize papal rule. The second pair of emissaries was perhaps sent at this stage to inform the first of these developments and to aid them in securing confirmation of the new settlement. Rimini's representatives agreed on 27 July in the presence of John of Viterbo that they were subjects of the pope, as formerly of the emperor: only on 18 September did they take an oath of fealty before the later emissaries and they now added a *protestatio* that their rights should not be prejudiced. Meanwhile Bologna's mission at Viterbo had also recognized papal suzerainty (29 July), but with a similar clause saving their rights in Bologna and its district.[1]

Towards the end of September the first step was taken to put the government of the province on a normal basis when Bertold Orsini was appointed its rector *in temporalibus*.[2] He was to co-operate with the cardinal-legate in peace-making, and both the towns and the Angevin troops in the province were instructed to obey him. Bertold, however, was not given the full freedom of action of a normal rector. He was not to enfeoff any person with papal territory, nor even to ratify or confirm any such grant, without consulting the pope in each case, informing him at the same time of the full circumstances. Later instructions added that any layman or cleric might petition concerning lands or rights of the Church which had come into his possession, but Bertold was to forward such petitions, accompanied by the relevant privileges, to the pope.[3] He was also to inform the pope of any rights he had failed to recover. Though later the legate was warned by Nicholas not to expect advice over details,[4] such a warning is itself indicative of much papal supervision, and he was ordered to send frequent reports. Apart from three long 'memorials', two addressed to the legate and one to Bertold, these officials were given special advice to avoid extreme sentences in settling peace-terms at Bologna, while at times their actions — for instance in placing Forlì under an interdict — were actually reversed.[5]

The three 'memorials' are interesting for the information they give concerning Pope Nicholas' approach to the problem of securing control in the Romagna and the difficulties with which he was faced, them-

---

[1] Tonini, *Rimini*, III, 602–5; *ASI*, XCI, 52–3, 68–9. For Imola's promise, on 4 July, to send representatives to the Curia *v*. Theiner, d. CCCLXV.
[2] *Reg. N. III*, nn. 601–2. [3] *Reg. N. III*, nn. 305–8.
[4] *Ibid.*, n. 727.
[5] *Ibid.*, nn. 506–7, 751–2: for the *aide-mémoires* see above, p. 192.

selves due in part to the failings of his incompetent relatives. The rector's terms of appointment had naturally emphasized the need to lay claim to all the rights of the Church and to establish a sort of *quo warranto* procedure in investigating these rights. The first set of instructions to the legate dwelt on the need for cautious tactics, especially in dealing with powerful Bologna. Direct conflict was to be avoided and hence direct refusals: a policy of gentle delay might avoid exasperating the Bolognese into an attitude of defiance. Yet, as the rector was reminded in his letter, this was not equivalent to 'peace at any price'; in particular he was to be careful to exact pledges whenever appropriate. Much of this letter is devoted to what sounds like a well-merited castigation of Bertold Orsini's short-comings. When troubles broke out at Bologna he had withdrawn his own household from the city and had later disregarded the pope's order to return there. He had shown obvious partiality towards the Lambertazzi faction, had fraternized with men notorious for their openness to corruption and their anti-papal views, and had failed to give support to the pro-papal group in the city's council. The general charge of *incuria* seems justified. It would not have been an easy time to dismiss the rector of the Romagna, but had he not been an Orsini he might well have gone. In addition to all this, Nicholas had a legate who stubbornly remained at Florence, pleading ill-health, when the pope wanted him to be at Bologna.[1]

Papal letters to legate and rector also make frequent references to financial difficulties; both are reminded to seek money wherever possible. Nicholas realized from the start that an army would be required in Romagna and asked his representatives to give estimates of the total number of soldiers needed and of the number that could be recruited locally. The military potential of the March and Duchy was also investigated but the main armies were in fact provided by Charles of Anjou, an arrangement facilitated by the assistance that he was already rendering to Guelf Bologna.[2] As early as July 1278 a corps was at Bologna under Count John de Montfort though Nicholas protested to Charles about the reported presence among them of the count's namesake Guy, the son of Earl Simon and murderer of Henry of Almaine.[3] Bologna agreed to assist in paying these Angevin troops, but the first body was insufficient and the archbishop of Ravenna was sent to

[1] *Ibid.*, nn. 794–6, 834.

[2] *ASI*, XCI, 51 (Bologna takes its *podestà* from Charles in 1276 and has the assistance of French troops). For the fiscal exploitation of the March at this period (mainly to assist in financing wars fought in that province), *v.* below, pp. 261 ff.

[3] *Reg. N. III*, n. 259 (Nicholas suspected Guy of seeking political control at Bologna).

Charles to ask for more men. By September another corps of 300 cavalry had arrived, led by William Estendart de Beynes, one of Charles' most trusted officials, who had served as marshal of the Regno, seneschal of Provence and royal vicar in Sicily, and was later to be royal vicar at Rome. Though Nicholas soon spoke hopefully of dispensing with these costly troops, he had to write to Charles for more at least twice before the spring of 1280.[1]

If he had had an abundance of money, the pope explained, not Bertold Orsini but the lowest of men could have taken on the arduous task and been sure of achieving his aim.[2] Yet the difficulties encountered by the rector make one wonder whether even a considerable garrison in each town could have won control for the papacy. Bertold's perambulations through the province in 1278–80 and the constant defiance which he met are recounted at length in the contemporary annals of Faenza and Forlì,[3] but this is not the place to repeat a detailed narrative. The rector reached Rimini in October 1278, but was taken ill and for a time had to be replaced by his son Gentile, who visited Imola and Bologna, and on 1 December held a provincial parliament at Cesena which was attended by representatives of all the towns. Constitutions for the province were proclaimed at this assembly. The great problem of the rival factions at Bologna had not yet been tackled and no progress was made before Bertold reached Romagna. Attempting to assume a position above the fray, Nicholas had withdrawn his previous condemnation of the Ghibellines and in May 1279 proclaimed an 'award' decreeing the terms on which the exiled faction was to be re-admitted. Bologna's rector was to be appointed by the pope and the city had to provide three hundred cavalry 'to keep peace in the whole province'. This arbitration was accepted in June and a 'general peace' at Bologna confirmed in August: before the end of September the Ghibelline Lambertazzi were at last able to return from their five-year exile.[4] For a time all seemed well, though the rector had to keep constantly on the move, calming troubles at Ravenna and Imola, while the legate achieved a peace between the latter town and Faenza.[5] Two days before

---

[1] *Ibid.*, nn. 308, 723, 727, 795, 820. For Estendart *v*. Léonard, pp. 127–8 and Malaspina, pp. 286 and 331–2. In connection with relations between Nicholas III and Charles of Anjou, mention should be made of a boundary dispute between the rector of the March and the justiciar of the Abruzzi concerning Monte Calvo (Ascoli P., AC, Perg. H., fasc. 2, n. 2).

[2] Kaltenbrunner, *op. cit.*, p. 225.

[3] RIS, N.S., XXII, II, 32–3 and XXVIII, II, 28–45; *v.* also Prof. Fasoli's articles in *ASI*, XCI and XCIV for Romagna in 1278–81.

[4] For a full account of the peace *v. ASI*, XCI, 49–75.

[5] RIS, N.S., XXVIII, III, clxiii.

Christmas the storm burst. After bitter fighting the Lambertazzi were again driven from Bologna, then from Imola. In revenge the Ghibellines drove the Guelfs from Faenza, while there was rioting at Forlì. The rector, coming in haste from Rimini, was unable to enter Imola. Two weeks later he held a parliament at Faenza — apparently it was well attended — at which the Geremei and their supporters were condemned. Cited before the rector, they sent representatives with insufficient powers, refused to renew their oath of fealty and were ordered to pay 10,000 *l.* for the maintenance of papal troops. This was the period when the pope was complaining of the legate's absence and Bertold's irresponsibility! The Geremei made a formal submission in March 1280, but only two days later Imola declined to open its gates to the rector and he failed to make new terms between the Bolognese factions. Much of that summer was spent in an inconclusive and inessential campaign in the mountains south of Forlì. When Nicholas III died on the 22 August the new province was in its customary anarchical condition and Bertold's departure a few weeks later was the signal for a full-scale Ghibelline revolt under Guy of Montefeltro, now commanding the forces of Forlì and a large body of exiles. Bertold's action in taking with him Lambertazzi hostages and a large money caution from the Geremei was entirely ineffective. It is significant that we possess virtually no indication of routine judicial or administrative activity in Romagna during Nicholas III's pontificate.[1]

The later stages of the struggle in Romagna are dealt with below. It is now time to return to the fortunes of Nicholas III in his dealings with the remaining provinces. Here the promising achievements of the previous decade were for the most part continued, though the March in particular was not without its troubles. The great success of this time was in financial administration. The survival of a large number of documents from some of the March towns — Fermo, Macerata, Fabriano and Iesi, as well as some smaller places — show that in the years 1278–80 at least 5,000 *l.* was drawn from these towns alone in taxation and fines.[2] Both the amount gathered and the regularity with which the *fictus* and *tallia militum* were rendered point to a time of firm papal control, and this impression is confirmed by the survival of many deeds referring to routine activities of provincial administration. Macerata's account-book for 1280 shows that town in constant negotiation with papal officials,

[1] Exceptions are the suit between Rimini and the archbishop of Ravenna, Jan.–Aug. 1280 (*v.* Torre in *Studi Romagnoli*, II, 350–1) and an outlawry pronounced in the provincial court at Imola in June 1280 (Fantuzzi, *Mon. Rav.*, III, d. LXXXI).

[2] For a fuller treatment with references *v.* below, pp. 261 ff.

and communes which continued to flout the rector's claim to appoint or approve their *podestà* could no longer do so without being fined or prosecuting their claims to independence in the papal Curia.[1] But the March was certainly not subservient. During 1280 Ascoli was at war with Macerata, Fermo (which was also fighting Iesi) and a number of neighbouring *castra*.[2] The money and troops raised in the province at this time were required locally and could not be spared for Romagna.[3] Moreover, soon after Pope Nicholas' death the March became involved in the troubles of Romagna, for in 1280 a bloodthirsty *coup* by Guy of Montefeltro won Senigallia as a new Ghibelline stronghold.[4]

In the more southerly provinces disputes tended to take judicial rather than military form. Gubbio and Todi pursued their seemingly eternal lawsuits, the latter perhaps with a greater feeling of urgency since it had incurred an interdict and been threatened with a punitive campaign: *riformanze* reveal the town considering both the offer of an annual payment to secure exemption from the control of the Patrimony and the possibility of maintaining a permanent proctor at the papal court.[5]

Nicholas III's death was also the occasion of outbreaks of violence at Rome and Viterbo. A family policy, especially in a city context, inevitably entailed rivalries, and in Rome there had emerged as leaders of the opposition to the Orsini the Annibaldi, who already owned much land in the city itself as well as estates in the Alban hills.[6] A *coup* now brought the Annibaldi party to power not only at the Capitol but in the whole area around which had been subject to the vicars of Pope Nicholas.[7] The Annibaldi also acted rapidly at Viterbo, where the cardinals met in conclave. A rising engineered by Richard Annibaldi removed Orso Orsini, the papal nephew who had been rector of the Patrimony and titular *podestà* of Viterbo. Richard himself replaced Orso as *podestà*,

---

[1] Macerata, AC, 160, ff. 8–10, 25v, 26v, 28v, 38v, 41. For condemnations for illegal appointments of *podestà* v. Gianandrea, *Iesi*, d. CXCVII; Palmieri, pp. 67 and 89 (S. Ginesio). For Fabriano's suit in the papal Curia, Zonghi, d. CCXXIII.

[2] Macerata, AC, 160, ff. 8 and 38v; De Minicis, *Fermo*, pp. 106–7 and 470.

[3] See Luzzatto, 'Matelica', p. 94; Gianandrea, dd. CXCVII, CXCIX; Zonghi, d. CCXXIX; Macerata, AC, 160, f. 41; and above, p. 197.

[4] *Ann Plac. Gib.* (MGH, XVIII), 572; Salimbene, II, 209 ('1,500 killed'): v. also *Reg. N. IV*, n. 7127.

[5] Gubbio, Sottosez AS, 'Liber Oblongus', ff. 1–5. Todi, AC, Rif. I, ff. 1–10, 13v, 22, 28, 42v, 55v–57, 65; perg., nn. 24–5; Reg. Vet. Istr., ff. 97v–98; Todi chronicle (*Studi di Filologia Italiana*, XIII), 90–1.

[6] On the Annibaldi v. the rather tentative article by F. Savio in *Studi e Doc. di. Storia e Diritto*, XVII, 355–63 and the remarks by Falco, in *Rivista Storica Italiana*, N.S., VI (1928), 227, 230–1, 248–52, 272–3.

[7] *Lib. Pont.*, II, 458–9: v. also Gregorovius, V, 2, 491–2.

attacked the Orsini villa at Soriano and seized two Orsini cardinals in an attempt to extort promises from them concerning the papal election. It seems probable that this renewal of the disgraceful scenes of 1269–71 had the approval, if not the active support, of Charles of Anjou. Precisely six months after Nicholas' death a French pope was duly elected, but especially around Viterbo the events of the vacancy had left a bitter legacy. Fighting continued between Viterbo and some of the Orsini and the town was long under an interdict. The Annibaldi and Orsini made their peace in 1284, but Viterbo only gained pardon many years later for its rôle in this conclave.[1]

*   *   *

Simon de Brie, Pope Martin IV, had, like Clement IV, been a councillor of Louis IX and had later as papal legate in France played a leading part in Urban IV's negotiations which preceded Charles of Anjou's conquest of the Regno. 'He disturbed the Church of God through his love of his own people and wanted to rule the whole world in the French manner,' says a contemporary.[2] The rapid collapse of the Orsini's position on Nicholas III's death shows how fragile were bound to be the achievements of a policy based on family support. The erection of a formidable counterpoise to Angevin power could only be carried out by methods involving both dubious friendships and bitter enmities. Martin IV's return to the Angevin alliance had therefore much to recommend it, though it marks a sudden reversal of papal policy which it is hard to reconcile with the recent dictum of a distinguished historian that each pope should be seen 'as merely one link in a long chain', not 'as an individual with his own personal programme, method and aims'.[3] The close connection with the Angevins led to papal support of Charles' ambitions in the east at the expense of Michael Palaeologus and even to the grant of the Aragonese throne to a Capetian, but our concern is with its effects in central Italy only.

[1] On the conclave and its aftermath *v.* Morghen in *ASRSP*, XLVI, 308–13; documents in Pinzi, *Viterbo*, II, 397 and 410; Arch. Vat., Arm. XXXV, 4, ff. 54v–55v, 287. For the attitude of Charles of Anjou, Léonard, pp. 130–1.

[2] Alexander of Roes, 'Notitia saeculi', *MIÖG*, XIX, 670 (quoted by Haller, *Papsttum*, VI, 343).

[3] W. Ullmann in *EHR*, LXXII, 155–6. But cf. the same writer's opinion that if *Hostiensis* had become pope 'relations between England and the papacy might have taken a different turn' and that if Cardinal Stefaneschi had been elected in 1305 'the history of the fourteenth-century papacy would have been a little different' (*Medieval Papalism*, pp. 4–5; *J Eccl H*, VI, 28n). One is reminded of Acton's remark that 'the human element in ecclesiastical administration endeavours to keep itself out of sight, and to deny its own existence, in order that it may serve the unquestioning submission which authority naturally desires' (from 'Conflicts with Rome', reprinted in *The History of Freedom and other Essays*).

Charles of Anjou had left for the Regno shortly before Martin's election, but many of his household remained with the pope at Orvieto and Martin proceeded, doubtless with the king's consent, to nominate various Angevin courtiers to positions in the papal provinces. Adam Fourrier, a councillor, became rector of the Patrimony, Jean de May-rolles, 'knight and familiar', rector of the Duchy, Amiel d'Angoult, lord of Courban, rector of the March and Massa Trabaria. Another French 'familiar', Geoffrey de Sommersot, took over the Campagna-Marittima. Jean d'Eppe, formerly seneschal of the Regno, was made commander of the forces in Romagna and, a little later, temporal rector of that province. His vicar *in spiritualibus* was the Provençal canonist Durand who had already served as a papal emissary in Romagna and had been rector of the Tuscan Patrimony.[1] Since a 'crusading' tenth was levied in France to help finance the Romagnol war, there is no exaggeration in the remark that Martin IV's pontificate provides 'a foretaste of Avignon'.[2]

Immediately after his election Martin sent two cardinals to treat with the new authorities in Rome; they negotiated an agreement with the city whereby the then senators became 'electors', who proceeded to grant to Martin the *regimen senatus*. This position he received for life, as a private individual, together with the right to appoint a senator or senators to act in his place. After Martin's death the Romans were to resume their normal powers. The pope admitted that the scheme possibly contravened the 'constitution' of Nicholas III, though it made the gesture of describing him as a 'Roman'. Like his predecessor, Martin passed on the senatorship to another, but his choice went directly against the terms of 1278. On 29 April 1281 he wrote to Charles of Anjou offering him the senatorship, for the duration of his (Martin's) life, unless the grant should be expressly revoked earlier.[3] It would be of great interest to know why the Romans accepted a settlement which installed a new series of unpopular Angevin vicars. Perhaps the party which had assumed power on driving out the Orsini regarded this as the only practicable alternative to an Orsini *signoria*; it seems very unlikely that they were tricked into the 'election'

---

[1] For these names *v.* App. II. To them may be added that of Robert de Richeville, marshal of the papal court under Martin IV. For Durand's career, *v. Dict. de Droit Canonique*, V, cols. 1015–29.

[2] Previté-Orton in *Cambridge Medieval History*, VI, 197.

[3] Potthast, n. 21737; Theiner, d. CCCXCV. Martin's statute forbidding the sale of land in Campagna-Marittima to Roman nobles (ref. in *Reg. B. VIII*, n. 5338) is another aspect of co-operation with Angevin power at Rome. For the events described in this paragraph *v.* also Gregorovius, V, 2, 493–5 and Dupré-Theseider, pp. 224–6.

of Martin as senator without understanding the implications of their choice.

By setting up his court permanently in Umbria, Martin left a free hand to the Angevins at Rome, which became as under Clement a sort of extension to the Regno, while he himself was conveniently situated nearer to the main trouble-centre of the Papal State, the Romagna. He never visited Rome as pope, but remained first at Orvieto, where he was accompanied by a French garrison, and after the summer of 1284 at Perugia.

After the Roman settlement, the situation in Romagna was undoubtedly the most pressing of Martin's Italian preoccupations. In the spring of 1281 Guy of Montefeltro's Ghibelline party, now under pressure from Bologna, sent representatives for negotiations at the papal Curia. These were carefully watched by a rival Guelf delegation and no agreement was reached.[1] Martin then appointed d'Eppe to the military command in Romagna, with Taddeo of Montefeltro as a subordinate to take charge of the Italian troops.[2] For the next few years the pope had on his pay-roll a very large army, comprising the Angevin forces, French troops recruited both in France and Italy, and mercenaries from the Papal State and a number of Tuscan and other cities. Some aid was given by towns of the March while Romagnol Guelfs, mainly from Bologna, Imola, Faenza and Rimini played a prominent and continuous part in the civil warfare which ensued. Charles of Anjou furnished men on the strict understanding that the pope would pay their wages, but consented to provide pay for the period of their return journey from Romagna to the Regno.[3] Philip III of France could afford to be more open-handed than this and in 1282 agreed to make available 100,000 *l.* of the sum which had been collected as a crusading tenth and was held by the Templars at Paris.[4]

D'Eppe conducted his first campaign on reaching Romagna in the summer of 1281.[5] With assistance from Bologna, Imola and Ravenna, he took Faenza, but an attack on Forlì failed and S. Leo and Monte-

---

[1] Fasoli in *ASI*, XCIV, 171.

[2] Potthast, n. 21760; Theiner, d. CCCXCVIII. For Taddeo *v.* above, p. 194, and Franceschini's biographical article in *Studi Romagnoli*, VII, 45–81. For a fuller account of these armies *v.* below, pp. 289 ff.

[3] Document printed in *ASI*, XCIV, 176: Theiner, d. CCCCV.

[4] *Reg. M. IV*, nn. 271–4: Theiner, d. CCCCXVIII. It is not clear whether the whole sum was paid, but Italian bankers accepted it as security for an advance of 20,000 *l.*

[5] The military events of these years are described in many contemporary annals, and in great detail by those of Romagna, e.g. Cantinelli (RIS, N.S., XXVIII, II), 50 ff.; *Annales Caesenates* (RIS, O.S., XIV), cc. 1105 ff.; RIS, N.S., XVIII, I, 211 ff.; RIS, N.S., XXII, II (*Ann. Forliv.*), 35 ff. *V.* also Franceschini in *Studi Romagnoli*, VII, 57 ff.

feltro in the mountains held out against Count Taddeo. The following spring, while the 'rebels' again negotiated unsuccessfully with the pope, d'Eppe won over Cervia (possibly with money)[1] and the lords of Castrochiaro before mounting a new assault on Forlì. This time he forced his way into the city on 1 May, only to be driven out in a bloody counter-attack which cost the French heavily.[2] D'Eppe was still strong enough to besiege Meldola for the remainder of the summer,[3] but without success, though he had received reinforcements under Guy de Montfort.

In 1283, the fourth year of the war, the tide at last turned in favour of the pope. D'Eppe held a parliament at Imola in February, issuing forty constitutions, many of which were concerned with the punishment of rebels; this legislation was revoked by Martin IV a month later on the grounds that it was too severe.[4] Under Montfort, now acting as captain-general, a successful attack was made on Cesena, and in May Forlì also submitted, accepting papal terms whereby the Lambertazzi and other Ghibellines went into exile. The walls of both Forlì and Cesena were rased to the ground. Guy of Montefeltro, the rebel leader, was still at large and most of the rest of 1283 was devoted to an unsuccessful attempt to capture him at Meldola, the new headquarters of revolt. Hearing rumours of unauthorized approaches by Montfort to the rebels, the pope sent the cardinal-bishop of Porto as legate with instructions to take over peace negotiations.[5] The rebellion had been driven out of the plain, but resistance continued in the mountains; not only did Meldola hold out for the remainder of 1283, but Urbino had become another Ghibelline stronghold. This town was the main centre of operations in 1284, French troops and men from the March being employed against it. Montfort withdrew from his command in July to defend his newly acquired lands in southern Tuscany and his French successor was killed in a rash assault. In March 1285, only a fortnight before his death, Martin IV had again to call the March communes to arms against Urbino.[6] He was denied the satisfaction of receiving the submission of Guy of Montefeltro.

---

[1] Villani, *Cronica*, VII, ch. 82.

[2] 'La terra che fe già la lunga prova / E dei Franceschi sanguinoso mucchio' (*Inferno*, XXVII, ll. 43–4).
Estimates of casualties in this battle vary so widely that it is not worth quoting them.

[3] As late as 18 November d'Eppe wrote to Bologna asking for a loan to pay the troops still besieging Meldola (Bologna, AS, Reg. nuovo, f. 375v).

[4] *Nuovi Studi Medievali*, II, 241–52.

[5] *Reg. M. IV*, n. 472jj.

[6] *Reg. M. IV*, nn. 472 mm and nn; Tonini, *Rimini*, III, d. CXLVIII; Acquacotta, *Matelica*, d. 77; RIS, N.S., XVIII, I, 221; Theiner, d. CCCCXLI.

Although the towns of the March played some direct part in the later stages of the Romagna war, their rôle was in the main a financial one. In 1281 and again in 1282 they were called on to pay a double *tallia militum*.[1] A list drawn up in May 1283 recorded the towns in part of the province paying annual *census* and *affictus potestariarum*.[2] The amount actually rendered was over 4,000 *l.*, but a number of small places paid nothing because they were under the sway of powerful communes and there were also entries of *rebellat*, of *usurpavit potestariam*, and of *nihil dat*. A month later the rector received instructions that express papal consent was required for 'compositions' granted for fines of over 300 *l.* This ruling strongly suggests the popes' dependence on the revenue of the March — at a time when Macerata and twelve other towns had a mutual compact to co-operate against the fiscal demands of the rector and his officials.[3]

Macerata also conducted a long struggle for recognition of its right to appoint its own *podestà*, while Ancona, Fermo, Ascoli and other towns clashed with papal authority over the question of appellate jurisdiction.[4] Some of the towns and nobles of the March were said, no doubt justly, to have furnished food and other necessaries to the Romagnol rebels.[5] More serious was Iesi's action in receiving a band of Montefeltro's supporters, who wrought much damage in the neighbourhood.[6] This episode led to a lengthy interdict. Although the town submitted early in 1281 and paid 5,000 marks in the next two years, in 1288 the full amount of the fine had not yet been rendered. One sees here how the anarchy of the Papal State was cumulative. Such episodes, the results of the disturbances in the neighbouring provinces, became themselves the source of further disputes between towns and papal authority, for Fabriano and Amandola were condemned for refusing to attack Iesi, and Matelica itself attacked by papal forces for not paying *tallia militum*.[7]

Meanwhile Perugia and Foligno, old rivals, fought a two-year war in

---

[1] Gianandrea, *Iesi*, dd. CCIII, CCV–CCVII; Fabriano, AC, Lib. Rosso, ff. 91–92v; etc.
[2] Theiner, d. CCCCXXVII.
[3] Gianandrea, d. CCXIV. For the compact, *v.* Macerata, AC, perg. n. 138 (other towns involved included Montolmo, Civitanova, Montecchio, Tolentino, S. Elpidio, Montemilone).
[4] Macerata, AC, perg. nn. 139, 145, 147–52. For an oath by towns of the March at this time accepting rectorial appointments of *podestà*, *v. Reg. N. IV*, n. 4477. For disputes over appeals, Theiner, d. CCCCXXXIX and *Reg. B. XI*, n. 592 (Matelica).
[5] *Reg. M. IV*, nn. 284, 309.
[6] Gianandrea, *Iesi*, dd. CCI, CCIV, CCVII, CCIX, CCXV–CCXVI, CCXXIII, CCXXX. Iesi perhaps used these troops in a war against Cagli (Bricchi, *Cagli*, p. 149).
[7] Zonghi, *Fabriano*, d. CCXXX; Ferranti, *Amandola*, III, d. 129; Mazzatinti, 2nd. s., II, 208.

the Duchy. Spoleto had drawn on itself an attack by papal troops in 1281, but the serious troubles only began in the spring of the following year. In April 1282 the Perugians launched an offensive under the command of a specially employed *capitano della guerra*, Gonzolino of Osimo, with the support of Spoleto, Assisi, and a number of other towns of the Valle Spoletana.[1] The towns were all placed under an interdict and Perugians forbidden to hold office in the Papal State; to this they retorted by burning the pope and cardinals in effigy.[2] The gesture may in part have been provoked by the lack of success of the 1282 campaign, which achieved nothing except destruction in Foligno's *contado*. In 1283 the attack was renewed, but met with defeat. That summer Perugia withdrew from the war and the commune secured papal absolution just before the pope moved his court there from Orvieto — probably at the price of 40,000 florins or more.[3] It is noteworthy that Perugia had in February 1282 received a papal privilege confirming its judicial exemptions and that it sent troops to fight for the pope in Romagna in the same year.[4] There is irony in the presence of a Perugian contingent in a papal army while other Perugians were burning the pope and cardinals in effigy, yet there is no real paradox here, since the war against Foligno, though condemned as rebellion by the papacy, was in Perugian eyes merely a war against a rival city.

Further south Martin IV had less bellicose subjects, but intermittent warfare continued between Viterbo and the Orsini, and Radicofani on the northern boundary of the Tuscan Patrimony revolted in 1284.[5] Narni's deafness to the papal order that Perugians should hold no municipal office also suggests lack of firm control in the Patrimony, but some surviving accounts from the Sabina show regular payments of dues by Terni and a number of neighbouring towns.[6] Minor disturbances in the

---

[1] The war began after 27 February (*Reg. M. IV*, n. 106) and before 16 April (Potthast, n. 21889). The main authorities for it are *Fragm. Fulg. Hist.* (RIS, N.S., XXVI, II), 16 and *Reg. M. IV*, nn. 280–3, 470, 484. The other towns involved were Nocera, Spello, Gualdo, Bevagna, Visso, Cascia (for Perugia); and Norcia (for Foligno).

[2] Narni, AC, perg. 6 November 1282. For the burning episode, *v.* in particular Salimbene, II, 214–15, who describes the Perugians exclaiming 'Iste est talis cardinalis et iste est talis'.

[3] *Reg. M. IV*, nn. 477, 492, 575. On 23 October 1284, after discussing a proposal that 20,000 florins be given to the pope, Perugia voted 'that 10,000 be paid on 1 November' (Perugia, AS, Rif. X, ff. 4v–5). In November 1288 Perugia still owed 10,000 florins of 40,000 due through condemnations (*Reg. N. IV*, n. 7212) but this may include subsequent offences. The last absolutions of towns involved in this war are *Reg. Hon. IV*, nn. 23, 835. Perugia was excused payment of the last instalment of this fine in 1296 (*Reg. B. VIII*, n. 1123).

[4] *Reg. M. IV*, n. 106.

[5] *Ibid.*, nn. 474–6; Theiner, d. CCCCXXXIV.

[6] Narni, AC, perg. 6 November 1282: Theiner, d. CCCCXLIII.

Campagna were a baronial rising which secured temporary control of Frosinone and raiding by Conrad of Antioch, a survivor of Hohenstaufen times and supporter of Peter of Aragon.[1]

His link with the Angevins was to bring Martin his most severe trials as well as his military successes. In Rome the Angevin vicars, particularly Estendart, were intensely unpopular. Their difficulties were certainly increased by the activities of Aragonese agents in searching for Roman and other sympathizers during the period when Peter III's conquest of Sicily was in gestation.[2] Moreover Martin found, as had so many of his predecessors, that Rome under a friendly power was not necessarily a Rome confined within what the popes regarded as the bounds of its own territory. He had soon to complain to the Angevin vicar that the city was again molesting Velletri.[3] Orvieto, with a French garrison and at times an Angevin court, presented the same xenophobic dangers, and there was serious anti-French rioting in this town in the spring of 1281.[4]

The situation became yet more difficult after the outbreak of the 'Sicilian Vespers' in the spring of 1282, for the Angevins were now fully committed elsewhere, their power was seen to be facing a crisis, and opposition to them had a leader and cause around which it could crystallize.[5] During the same year the Orsini, presumably suspected of anti-Angevin sentiments, were driven from Rome, perhaps with the assistance of their factional rivals. The harvest of 1283 was a poor one and early that winter there were serious signs of discontent. On 22 January the Orsini led a rising in Rome, stormed the Capitol, killed a number of Angevin soldiers and imprisoned the royal vicar and many of his officials. John Malabranca, a relative of the Orsini, became captain of the city. The new regime, however, felt its position to be weak and entered into negotiations with the pope. A compromise was arranged, whereby the new captain was put aside and Martin nominated as his senatorial vicars Annibaldo Annibaldi and Pandulf Savelli. Malaspina thinks very poorly of the papal vicars, who were partial and ruled badly,

---

[1] Theiner, dd. CCCCXXV, CCCCXXIX, CCCCXXXIII, CCCCXXXV, CCCXLVI. For Conrad of Antioch *v.* Gregorovius, V, 2, 498–9.

[2] Malaspina, pp. 331–2: his stigmatization of the vicars' policy as 'Ghibelline' is vague' but he is more precise in branding Estendart as 'inexpertus . . . in regimine civitatum'. For Aragonese activity *v.* Theiner, d. CCCCXII and Haller, *Papsttum*, V, 69–70.

[3] Borgia, *Velletri*, pp. 291–2. In 1282 Rome was fighting Corneto, probably in pursuit of a monopoly of grain exports (Dupré-Theseider, pp. 229–30).

[4] Waley, *Orvieto*, pp. 53–6.

[5] Nevertheless it seems impossible to accept M. Léonard's suggestion (p. 149) that the Romagnol and Umbrian 'rebellions' were directly connected with the Sicilian Vespers.

but the pope had at least emerged with little damage from the collapse of Angevin power in Rome.[1] In Orvieto, however, he was faced by the formidable opposition of Neri della Greca, the leader of a popular anti-Guelf party and the city's Capitano del Popolo in 1280–1 and 1284.[2] This man made life so uncomfortable for the Curia that in the summer of 1284 Martin decided on a migration to the recently defiant Perugia. The wisdom of the move was shown when Della Greca attempted an anti-Guelf *coup* at Orvieto in October.

After — perhaps on account of — the Vespers, Martin relied less on Frenchmen as provincial rectors: d'Angoult in the March and Sommersot in Campagna-Marittima were replaced by Italians in 1282 and 1283 respectively and d'Eppe by Durand in the following year. The part played in the events of this time by anti-French feeling is most striking; the Orvietan rioters of 1281 rose to the cry of 'Death to the French!' and the tone of Malaspina's chronicle shows the same spirit. Martin IV's reliance on Angevin and French support clearly did much to sharpen that intrinsically negative sentiment, national feeling. After the Vespers the ally on whose power he had based his policy became too preoccupied with the Sicilian war to be able to spare much of his strength for papal ends. The boot was now on the other foot, for in the last year of Martin's life Charles of Anjou is to be found asking the rector of the Tuscan Patrimony to order towns of this province to provide troops or money for the war.[3] Charles also had recruiting agents in the March, acting with papal support, and Martin declared the war a crusade.[4] In his most important Italian undertaking, the subjugation of Romagna, Angevin co-operation had brought him some success, but his achievement there was military and not administrative and hence it was superficial and impermanent. Elsewhere Martin's pontificate exemplified the perils of a French alliance with the same clarity as Nicholas III's had exemplified those of a policy based on nepotism.

---

[1] Gregorovius, V, 2, 498–500; Dupré-Theseider, pp. 229–31, 246. The main sources are Malaspina, pp. 388–9 and *Ann.Plac. Gib.* (MGH, XVIII), 577. On Malaspina see the article by A. Nitschke, *Deutsches Archiv*, XII, 160–86.

[2] Waley, *Orvieto*, pp. 53–8.

[3] Document printed in Calisse, *Prefetti di Vico*, pp. 47–8.

[4] Amiani, *Fano*, II, lxiv–lxv; *Reg. M. IV*, n. 570.

VII

The Papal State, the Colonna and the Caetani, 1285–1304

Cardinal James Savelli was at once chosen to succeed on Martin IV's death in March 1285. The Savelli, a Roman family probably descended from the Crescenzi, had a palace on the Aventine and estates in the Sabina and at Castel Gandolfo, Savello, Albano and Ariccia in the Alban hills.[1] They had already given Rome one bishop, Honorius III, in whose honour James took the style of Honorius IV. His Roman origins were useful to him from the first, for on his election (2 April 1285) the city offered him life tenure of its senatorship.[2] In his letter of acceptance the pope announced his intention of going to Rome, and he in fact settled in the city for most of his two-year pontificate. The senatorship he conferred on his brother Pandulf, who had already acted as vicar under Martin IV's settlement of the previous year, while his nephew Luca became papal marshal and rector of the Tuscan Patrimony.[3] The preoccupation of the Angevins with the Sicilian war now compelled the popes to seek some sort of family support for their rule in the Papal State, whatever their attitude to the Angevins might be. During the next twenty years the only pope not to adopt such a policy was the ill-fated Celestine V.

Despite his firm Roman basis and his reliance upon Italian officials,[4] Honorius' pontificate saw an increasing degree of anarchy in the Papal State. Though he had broken with Martin IV's methods there was continuity in this lawlessness, which seemed subject to what Henry Adams might have diagnosed as a 'law of acceleration'. This did not apply to

---

[1] Tomassetti, *Campagna Romana*, II, 141, 153; Cecchelli, *I Crescenzi, i Savelli, i Cenci*, pp. 23–5.

[2] *Reg. Hon. IV*, n. 825. Honorius was elected at Perugia on 2 April. His letter accepting the senatorship is dated 5 April. As Perugia was at least a full day's ride from Rome, this suggests an immediate decision by the Romans on hearing the news of Honorius' elevation.

[3] For papal relatives in office as *podestà* in the Papal State, *v.* Corridonia, AC, Perg. n. 35 (Montolmo, 1285).

[4] In the Duchy a French rector (Robert de Lavène, formerly justiciar of Terra di Lavoro and royal pro-senator at Rome) was replaced on Martin IV's death by his rector *in spiritualibus*, Roland of Ferentino (Sansi, *Storia di Spoleto*, p. 216).

P

Campagna-Marittima, nor to the Tuscan Patrimony (where Honorius' administration achieved the pacification of Viterbo),[1] but elsewhere papal control was on the decrease. The towns of the Duchy, in particular Perugia, continued to assert their *de facto* independence. In October 1286 a remarkable treaty was made between Gubbio, Assisi and Spoleto.[2] This alliance was concluded 'to the honour of God, the Virgin Mary, the Roman Church, Pope Honorius IV and the college of cardinals', in the interests of peace and obedience to the Church in the Duchy, and for mutual support in those interests. Its principal clause, however, provides that if any of the contracting towns quarrels with the provincial rector 'on account of his oppressions' none of them is to reach a separate agreement with him. Later in the same year Perugia made an alliance with Spoleto, Todi and Narni in preparation for new assaults on Foligno in 1287 and 1288.[3] During the vacancy after Honorius' death Perugia assumed a position in Umbria that should have belonged to the provincial rector. In a way the alliance of 1286 bears witness to the rector's formidability, but in the next two years Perugia was acting as arbiter of internal and external disputes at Terni, Narni and Todi, had fortified Gualdo in defiance of the rector's orders, and had drawn Cagli and Camerino into its system of alliances.[4]

The March under Honorius IV presents the more paradoxical spectacle of a much-governed yet unruly province. At Iesi in 1285 three brothers made an attempt to instal a dictatorial regime, threw out the Roman *podestà* sent by the pope and committed many acts of violence in the neighbourhood.[5] Fermo, Ascoli and Ripatransone were also engaged in wars at this time: by May 1286 the last of these had run up a list of debts in fines to the papal authorities which totalled around 64,000 *l*.[6]

Yet both the attempts of towns to secure some exemption from his jurisdiction and the many surviving references to his routine activity

[1] For Viterbo, *Reg. Hon. IV*, nn. 485–7, 927; Pinzi, *Viterbo*, II, 434–5, 437–40, 442. There was some trouble at Terracina (*Reg. Hon. IV*, n. 931) in 1286.

[2] Summary by Hagemann in *QFIA*, XXXIV, 116.

[3] *Fragm. Fulg. Hist.* (RIS, N.S., XXVI, II), 18; Todi, AC, perg., nn. 28–30.

[4] Raynaldus *ad* 1287, § 10; Pellini, *Perugia*, I, 300; *ASI*, XVI, 2, 490; Bricchi, *Cagli*, p. 162; Mei, *Cagli*, pp. 18–19.

[5] *Reg. Hon. IV*, nn. 839 (where 'Ianuensibus' is surely a misreading for 'Fanensibus'), 840, 896; De Minicis, *Fermo*, pp. 487–8.

[6] De Minicis, *Fermo*, pp. 489–90; Theiner, d. CCCCLI; *Reg. N. IV*, n. 7289; Ascoli P., AC, Quinternone, ff. 167–8. Ripatransone's absolution in 1290 in fact cost the commune 7,000 *l*. The same 'oriental' tactics in bargaining concerning fines was often used with other towns: for another instance v. Macerata, AC, Rif. I (1287), ff. 14–19, 25, 29, 34, 118v, 124v, 128v (300 *l*. reduced to 50 *l*.).

show that the rector of the March was a power to be reckoned with. For a year, from February 1287 to February 1288, Fabriano fought a decision of the rector, reached after a long and careful enquiry, that the town did not possess *merum et mixtum imperium*.[1] This was essentially a dispute over judicial power, and by no means a theoretical one. At the same time Macerata was opposing the right of the provincial court to hear appeals from the commune's court in cases involving fines of less than 40s. and asserting its liberty to choose its own *podestà*.[2] The judicial, fiscal and administrative activity of the rector during the years 1286–8 was ceaseless. Macerata now kept a permanent proctor at the provincial court, felt sufficiently confident of securing justice in it to threaten to sue an abbot there, and even secured the services of the Judge-general to arbitrate in an internal dispute concerning the tax to be levied to build the Palazzo del Comune.[3]

By far the most serious signs of deterioration in papal control came from Romagna, where the events of Honorius's time proved the papal military achievement to be as fragile as it had looked. Though Guy of Montefeltro soon submitted to Honorius and was compelled to give two sons as hostages and to go into exile in Piedmont,[4] the loss of a leader made no difference to an anarchy which was essentially endemic. Durand, who had succeeded d'Eppe as general rector, arranged that Faenza's Ghibelline exiles should be allowed to return. When they did so, many of them were murdered, whereupon the rector sentenced those guilty of this outrage and sent into exile their party, the Manfredi. They then came under the leadership of the powerful feudatory Mainardo of Susinana, and with his aid made attacks on Imola and Forlì in the summer of 1286.[5] The rector's troops foiled both these attempts, but were overcome in November, when Mainardo gained Faenza and later Forlì. In the following year a new rector, Honorius' cousin Peter, exiled leaders of both factions, but the Faentine exiles, among them Mainardo, returned defiantly and set up a league against the rector which was joined by Ravenna, under Guy of Polenta, and

[1] Fabriano, AC, Rivendicazioni Comunali, n. 2, partly printed by W. Hagemann in *QFIA*, XXXII, 81–109.

[2] Macerata, AC, Rif. I, ff. 9v–12v, 133v–135v.

[3] *Ibid.*, ff. 44, 63v, 101–112v. Evidence for the activity of provincial administration at this period may be found in the same volume, *passim*, and in Mei, *Cagli*, pp. 11–19. It may be noted that the papal judge quite rightly declared for democratic fiscal methods 'according to wealth' (*secundum. . . facultates cuiuslibet*) against the hearth-tax (*per fumantem*).

[4] Villani, VII, ch. 108.

[5] There is a well-documented account of Mainardo's career in G. Zaccagnini, 'Maghinardo da Susinana ed il comune di Bologna', *AMSR*, s. IV, VIII (1918), 52–145. The fullest primary source for this period is Cantinelli (RIS, N.S., XXVIII, II), 54–7.

Rimini, under Malatesta. The erstwhile 'Guelfs' had thus become the leaders in rebellion. The 'rebel' towns naturally refused requests for *tallia militum*, but in spite of this the rector's troops inflicted a sharp defeat on the forces of Rimini in June. Honorius had already died (April 1287) and when his successor was elected Cesena, Rimini, Ravenna, Faenza, Forlì, Cervia, Bertinoro and Forlimpopoli were all in revolt or in the hands of the rebels. In fact the only towns of any size not under the rector's ban were Imola and Bologna.[1]

Outside Romagna the ten-month vacancy between Honorius IV's death and the election of a successor was not a time of major disturbances, though the towns of the March were called to arms against 'rebellious' Pesaro, two communes in the Patrimony joined in a raid on a neighbouring castle and the rector of the Duchy fell for a time into the hands of Norcia when attempting to mediate between that town and Monte S. Martino.[2]

Jerome of Ascoli, who became pope as Nicholas IV in February 1288, was the first mendicant to rise to the pontificate. He was also the only pope before the sixteenth century whose origins lay in the new papal provinces and his derivation from papal territory is reflected in a particular interest in the government of the State, to whose problems he dedicated himself with an energy and originality to which justice has never been done. Since Urban IV — certainly since Clement IV — the popes had given little thought to policy; rather, the search for a basis of power in the State had taken the place of thinking on the fundamental questions of the attitude to be adopted to the communes and measures to be taken to check endemic lawlessness and warfare. With Nicholas IV this drift comes to an end; he had ideas about the Papal State and he was responsible for a number of innovations. His correspondence itself bears witness to this interest, for a much higher proportion of letters concerning the State was entered in the registers.

Nicholas's local ties led him to take a special interest in the welfare of his native Ascoli. Very soon after becoming pope he assumed the rectorate of the city *auctoritate apostolica*, which was later confirmed for life. He even insisted that a provincial rector should remain at Ascoli for over a month to deal with internal discords and the city received a

---

[1] For the rebels' condemnation in parliament at Imola (Feb. 1288), *v.* Fantuzzi, *Mon. Rav.*, III, 138–47 and Tonini, *Rimini*, III, 648–51. An indication of Mainardo's control at Faenza was his success in influencing the choice of a new bishop there in 1287.

[2] Compagnoni, *Regg. Pic.*, pp. 147, 150; Macerata, AC, Rif. I, ff. 86–7: Arch. Vat., Arm. XXXV, 4, ff. 287v–288v. ('castrum Geczi' burnt by Toscanella and Castro): *Fragm. Fulg. Hist.* (RIS, N.S., XXVI, II), 17; *Reg. N. IV*, n. 7275.

papal privilege exempting its citizens from the jurisdiction of the sub-provincial courts of the March.[1]

To pacify municipal factions was to play a rôle familiar to the mendicants since their foundation, but Nicholas' special tenderness for the March is clearly attributable to local patriotism. He added to it Urbino, hitherto often administered with Romagna, in June 1288, and a few days later wrote to the provincial rector to advise a general reduction of the fines imposed on rebels.[2] Men from the March now had a better chance of achieving office in the Papal State and one can perhaps detect a preference for natives of the other provinces also: Orvieto, where Nicholas passed much of the year 1290, provided general rectors of Romagna and Campagna-Marittima as well as a spiritual rector in the latter province.[3]

Although Nicholas was willing to do occasional favours to his own family,[4] he realized that they could give him no substantial backing: for that he turned to the Colonna. Possibly he had judged the backing of the Savelli as inadequate for Honorius IV, and Boniface VIII's pontificate was again to show the disadvantages of seeking support from a family which had only a moderate baronial position. Nicholas' family had not even this rank, whereas the Colonna drew their origins from the counts of Tusculum and thus from the family which had dominated the degraded papacy of the pre-Hildebrandine era.[5] The original Colonna castle was situated near Tusculum; in the twelfth century the family added to this Palestrina on the Via Prenestina and lands in Sabina, and by the later thirteenth they held a powerful lordship reaching across the Alban, Volscian and Sabine hills and much property in Rome itself in the region of the present Palazzo Colonna on the western slope of the Quirinal. The several branches of the family were not always on friendly terms, but, with lands extending in a crescent from Genezzano in Sabina right round to the river Sacco in the south, the Colonna were

[1] For Nicholas' relations with Ascoli *v. Reg. N. IV*, nn. 830, 2413, 6961–5, 6982, 6995, 7006, 7025, 7027, 7030, 7036–7, 7082–3, 7098–7100, 7122, 7149, 7236: also Ascoli P., AC, Quinternone, ff. 165v–170v and Perg. A, fasc. 1, n. 3; G, fasc. 1, n. 3; H, fasc. 2, nn. 1–2; R, fasc. 1, n. 4. He once lowered a fine on the commune and he favoured local men in making appointments in the Papal State. Nicholas made Stephen Colonna his first vicar as rector or *podestà* of Ascoli. For Nicholas' action in ending Ascoli's interdict, restoring confiscated fortresses etc. *v.* Quinternone, ff. 165v–166 (19 Jan. 1291).

[2] *Reg. N. IV*, nn. 7087–8, 7093, 7336.

[3] *V.* App. II.

[4] Acquacotta, *Matelica*, d. 82 (Nicholas' nephew Robert appointed *podestà*).

[5] A good account of the origins and possessions of the Colonna is to be found in Neumann, *Die Colonna*, pp. 48–59. See also the map of 'feudal Latium' in *QFIA*, XXXVI.

placed astride the routes leading out of Rome to the east and south-east, besides holding many other isolated territories.[1]

The links between Nicholas and the Colonna go back to the time before his pontificate, since he became bishop of Palestrina under Martin IV and probably Cardinal James Colonna played some part in his elevation. He at once proclaimed his intention to rely on the Colonna for the government of the Papal State, appointing Landulf rector of the Duchy a week after his consecration and John Colonna rector of the March some four months later. The following year Stephen, a member of the branch deriving its title from Genezzano in Sabina, became rector of Romagna.[2] The family also received many more strictly ecclesiastical favours. A contemporary cartoon depicts Nicholas as a scarcely visible figure between two substantial columns,[3] and his vicarious nepotism was naturally considered more humiliating than the dependence of those popes whose support came from their own kin. Yet his success and that of Honorius IV in retaining the friendship of Rome, after the collapse of Martin IV's policy, suggest the necessity of support from one of the great baronial families. Like his predecessors, Nicholas received the life senatorship of Rome and, though he took himself to various Umbrian towns as summer residences, he spent the remainder of each year in the city itself.[4] The difficulty was to retain power in Rome and the Campagna without making enemies. The Colonna were now threatened with opposition from the Orsini, just as the Orsini had aroused the hatred of the Annibaldi in Nicholas III's time.

Nicholas IV's friendly relations with Rome, however, were not evidence of complete success in his dealings with the southern papal provinces. The disturbed condition of the State continued throughout his pontificate, without any remarkable deterioration: his achievement lies in sketching out a policy, not in installing peace. In the Campagna-Marittima, indeed, there were now more serious troubles, due to the ambitions of certain feudal families in the southern part of the province, where war between the lords of Ceccano and those of Supino raged in the early months of the pontificate, involving the commune of Ferentino. Then Terracina, threatened by both the Annibaldi and Ceccanesi, turned to Nicholas, making him its *podestà*. The pope was compelled to

---

[1] For example: round Nepi, to the north of Rome; Ninfa (Campagna); Melice (Duchy); Civitella and Montevecchio (Romagna).

[2] When John Colonna took up the Roman senatorship (in which he was later succeeded by Stephen Colonna) his son Agapito became his vicar in the March.

[3] Gregorovius, V, 2, 514–15.

[4] With the exception of a prolonged stay at Orvieto from June 1290 to October 1291.

ask Rome to come to Terracina's defence, but the Romans could never be a disinterested party in the affairs of the Campagna.[1]

Under a series of Colonna senators and others friendly to the pope, Rome now enjoyed a period of papal acceptance of its domination, Nicholas reverting to the policy of Gregory IX in supporting a temporarily friendly Rome at the expense of papal authority — and of the Viterbese. In the summer of 1290 Rome was able to use Viterbo's refusal of military aid to the pope against Todi as a pretext for attacking the city. For a time Nicholas protested, but when Viterbo was compelled to accept humiliating terms of submission the following spring he made no further move. Viterbo had to pay 17,000 florins and John Colonna, as senator, received the town's oath of vassalage, while his brother James and another cardinal provided a loan to facilitate the payment of this heavy indemnity.[2]

This acceptance of Roman overlordship in the southern Patrimony was a juridical withdrawal, but papal authority in the area had never been strong. Despite occasional complaints,[3] the province was comparatively peaceful in Nicholas IV's time, and some surviving accounts for 1291 and the following years[4] give evidence of a considerable degree of papal control. The regular payments then being made by the often recalcitrant larger communes are significant; among these are Orvieto, Corneto and Viterbo, and the inclusion of the last two shows that papal submission to Rome's imperialism was not necessarily accompanied by fiscal withdrawal. Viterbo, in fact, defeated by a Roman-papal alliance, rendered its dues to both victors and thus paid twice over.

The Duchy and March continued under Nicholas disturbed, bellicose, and yet profitable and by no means entirely anarchic. To detail the petty disturbances would be intolerably tedious. By far the most serious war in the Duchy was the prolonged Perugian attempt to overcome Foligno. This was renewed in the spring of 1288, and a special mission of two cardinals, Matthew 'Rosso' Orsini and Benedict Caetani, failed to accomplish a pacification.[5] Papal troops were called against Perugia and the town declared a rebel, but it secured the support of Todi and Spello,

[1] *Reg. N. IV*, nn. 6996–7, 7097, 7264–5; Contatore, *Terracina*, pp. 79–80, 206.

[2] *Reg. N. IV*, nn. 7252, 7257–9; Pinzi, *Viterbo*, II, 462–4, 467–70, 474–84.

[3] *Reg. N. IV*, nn. 7257–61, 7316 (revolt at Pereta; expansionist moves by Todi and Narni).

[4] Theiner, pp. 317–21; Arch. Vat., Arm. XXXV, 14, f. 85.

[5] For this war *v. Reg. N. IV*, nn. 584–93, 645–7, 2168–9, 2179–80, 2262, 3109, 3680, 4750, 7017–24, 7026, 7028, 7197–8, 7212; *ASI*, XVI, 2, 490. For Todi's rôle, Ceci, *Todi*, p. 183; Mazzatinti, III, 107; Todi, AC, Reg. Vet. Istr., f. 136v. *V.* also Morghen, 'Una legazione di B. Caetani', *ASRSP*, LII, 485–90.

and launched a new campaign against Foligno in 1289. Todi withdrew from the war in July 1289 and Spello the following April, yet the Perugians achieved some success and made no submission to papal authority in Nicholas IV's time.[1] Of the minor wars in the Duchy, those involving Cascia, Nocera, Gualdo and Sassoferrato were probably connected with the major struggle between Perugia and Foligno, while others — Norcia's attack on Monte S. Martino, Assisi's on Cannaria, Spoleto's capture of Arrone — were independent of it.[2] In spite of all this, this province also was yielding a quite handsome profit during the later part of the pontificate, providing a revenue of some 8,000 florins — of which rather over 2,600 florins was profit — in a ten months' period in 1290–1.[3]

The Apennine zone extending through much of the eastern part of the Duchy and western March was one of the most turbulent areas of all, and disturbances in one province were naturally linked with those in the other. Men from Camerino and Fabriano in the March fought Nocera, Gualdo and Sassoferrato in the Duchy, while the pope attempted to call towns of the March to war against Perugia.[4] Nor did the March lack wars of its own, though here there was no major issue to crystallize them. Macerata fought Montemilone, there was a baronial revolt at Monte Calvo, Amandola fought surrounding castles with the assistance of the lords of Brunforte and their retinue, while Fermo and Fabriano too threatened their neighbours.[5] The provincial authorities also intervened to check internal disputes at Cagli, Fabriano and Ripatransone, as well as those already mentioned at Ascoli.[6] Nevertheless the routine activity of the provincial court continued unabated, Macerata even attempting legislation to forbid recourse to it. Moreover revenues from the March continued at a respectable level.[7]

[1] The submission of Foligno to Perugia in Aug. 1289 (reported by Pellini, *Perugia*, I, 304) lacks confirmation. Perugia was in bad odour with the pope in June 1291 (*Reg.*, nn. 7329–30).

[2] *Reg. N. IV*, nn. 6727–8, 7275, 7332, 7380; Lilii, *Camerino*, II, 49–50; Zonghi, *Fabriano*, d. CCXLIX; Arch. Vat., Arm. XXXV, 4, ff. 56v–57v.

[3] Theiner, p. 321. For an isolated payment of 1,165 florins by Cascia in 1293 *v.* Morini, *Cascia*, d. VI.

[4] *Reg. N. IV*, n. 7026; Compagnoni, *Regg. Pic.*, p. 150; Lilii, *Camerino*, II, 49–50, 52–3; Zonghi, *Fabriano*, d. CCXLIX; Macerata, AC, perg., nn. 243, 247, 252.

[5] *Reg. N. IV*, nn. 7120, 7123, 7288, 7290, 7337; Ferranti, *Amandola*, III, d. 169; Zonghi, *Fabriano*, d. CCLIV; Ascoli P., Perg. H, fasc. 2, n. 2.

[6] *Reg. N. IV*, nn. 7171–2, 7174, 7176, 7331; Mei, *Cagli*, pp. 30–1; Mazzatinti, 2nd. s., II, 229; Zonghi, *Fabriano*, dd. CCXLVII–CCXLVIII. For Ascoli *v. sup.*, p. 212.

[7] Macerata sent representatives to the Judge-general of the March 'occasione inquisitionis quam facere intendebat contra dictum commune et dictum iudicem super eo quod dicebatur ipsum commune fecisse constitutiones quod homines Maceratae non irent ad causandum ad curiam domini Marchionis' (Macerata, AC, Intr. Ex. 1291, f. 8v). For a discussion of revenue from the March at this period, *v.* below, pp. 269 ff.

The March also became involved in the fighting in Romagna, in this case at the insistence of papal authority. Its military service played a large part in some stages of the war, having become concerned in it first through Pope Nicholas's action in joining to the March Urbino, an important centre of the Romagnol rebels.[1] When Nicholas came to the papal throne almost the whole of Romagna was in revolt and the frenzied tempo of its history was maintained throughout the four years of his pontificate.[2] In 1288 the rector's main military effort was concentrated against the rebels at Urbino, but papal troops also took part in the war which followed Malatesta's expulsion from Rimini, supporting the erstwhile lord against the town.[3] Urbino was now held against the pope and Malatesta by the sons of Count Taddeo, but at last fell to an assault by John Colonna, rector of the March, on 23 September 1289.

Pope Nicholas' first rector in Romagna had been the Orvietan Ermanno Monaldeschi, who had already served as *podestà* at Lucca and Florence. In the summer of 1289 Monaldeschi was succeeded by Stephen Colonna,[4] but the new rector was at first represented by a vicar and only reached his province shortly before Christmas. He succeeded to no fund of goodwill or even of resigned acceptance. Bologna, which was perhaps his least disobedient subject, had in the previous month issued a formal assertion of its 'ancient and wonted freedom, jurisdiction, power, authority and custom' which could in no way be derogated by rectorial constitutions, and this statement conveniently defines the outlook of both lords and cities in Romagna.[5] Early in 1290 the new rector made peace with Rimini, but this was short-lived, the town's *podestà* (an Orsini) having confessed to a plot against Colonna.[6] Ravenna was another city to show some support for papal rule, while Bologna rendered military assistance but took the precaution of concluding an alliance with Mainardo of Susinana.[7]

[1] *Reg. N. IV*, n. 7294; Fabriano, AC, perg. n. 299 (Fabriano's troops fighting at Urbino, 1289).

[2] The main source for the history of Romagna under Nicholas IV is Cantinelli (RIS, N.S., XXVIII, II), 57–73: *v.* also *Ann. Caes.* (RIS, O.S., XIV), cols. 1107–8; *Ann. Forliv.* (RIS, N.S., XXII, II), 40–1.

[3] *Reg. N. IV*, nn. 7150–1, 7192–3; Tonini, *Rimini*, III, 654–60: for Urbino *v. Studi Romagnoli*, VII, 65 and Arch. Vat., Instr. Misc., n. 246.

[4] On Stephen Colonna (an exile in France and England after Boniface VIII's condemnation of the Colonna) *v.* Petrarch, *Ep. Fam.*, II, 3 and E. Martin-Chabot in *Annuaire-Bulletin de la Société de l'Histoire de France*, LVII (1920), 137–90. On Monaldeschi, Waley, *Orvieto*, p. 50n.

[5] *Nuovi Studi Medievali*, II, 231–2. It is also significant that the Bolognese statutes of 1288 (ed. Fasoli and Sella, *Studi e Testi*, vol. 73) contain no mention of papal authority.

[6] Tonini, *Rimini*, III, 663–7; Clementini, *Rimini*, I, 497–8.

[7] Bologna, AS, Rif. 1289, ff. 32, 411v, 413v (200 cavalry sent to the rector). Bagnacavallo, in Bologna's sphere of influence, now paid *tallia* and fines and chose the rector as

The climax of Romagnol defiance occurred in November 1290. When Colonna went to Ravenna to claim that city as a subject, its *podestà* — the son of Guy of Polenta, *de facto* lord of Ravenna — not only refused to take an oath of submission, but imprisoned the rector, his marshal (who was also his son-in-law) and his bodyguard.[1] During this time of humiliation for papal rule Faenza fell first to the Manfredi, then to a Polenta-Susinana alliance, while Malatesta regained Rimini. The bereaved officials of the provincial court fled from Cesena to Forlì, but within a few days — shortly before Christmas — that city also yielded to the league of rebels. They now held all but the most westerly part of the province, where Bologna had come into possession of Imola. It was in these circumstances that the pope turned to the March for help.[2]

Nicholas at once appointed a successor to his captive rector in the person of Aldobrandino bishop of Arezzo, whose qualifications combined high clerical rank with derivation from a great baronial family of the Romagnol-Tuscan border, the Counts Guidi of Romena.[3] In a crisis the pope did not hesitate to make use of a feudal family against its rivals and Bishop Aldobrandino was accompanied by a brother, Count Alexander, who was to act as his military commander. During 1291 a certain recovery was achieved in the papal position. Ravenna released Stephen Colonna and paid a fine of 3,000 florins in exchange for a pardon.[4] After holding a parliament at which he was granted some taxes, the new rector was able to subdue troubles at Cesena and Imola, but he did not dare to enter Faenza and in June his forces were checked at Ghiaggiolo by Galasso of Montefeltro.[5] Bologna had greeted him in a letter which offered him homage and troops, but reminded him that his predecessors had been content with these and with 'peaceable and honourable words'; the city did not intend to pay *tallia* or to accept any constitutions contrary to its interests. A subsequent letter reaffirmed that Bologna would yield no jurisdiction over its own territory and

its *podestà* (*Atti e Mem. Dep. St. Patr. Emilia*, N.S., VII (1881), 151–2) while Imola sent delegates to promise obedience to the rector's legislation forbidding the export of grain (Imola, AC, mazzo IV, n. 57). For Bologna's alliance with Mainardo *v.* Zaccagnini, 'Maghinardo', 135.

[1] *Reg. N. IV*, nn. 7294–7303.

[2] *Ibid.*, nn. 7317–18.

[3] There is a genealogical table of this family in Paget Toynbee, *Dante Dictionary*, p. 586.

[4] Fantuzzi, *Mon. Rav.*, III, n. LXXXX. On 26 January Colonna wrote to Bologna to announce that he had been released 3 days before, thanks to the pope, the bishop of Arezzo 'and your help'. Bologna wrote on the 29th to congratulate him on his release (Bologna, AS, Lettere del Comune, Reg. 4, ff. 6 (n. 3) and 6v (n. 1)). For Bologna's rôle in this release *v.* also document in Zaccagnini, 'Maghinardo', 83.

[5] See Franceschini in *Studi Romagnoli*, VII, 66.

advised the rector to send no more letters 'disturbing the peace' be-tween them.[1] The following spring this rector was driven from Forlì (where he had held his 1291 parliament) with the loss of his brother and nephew as prisoners of war and he was also dispossed of Imola. Apart from the dubious support of independent Bologna, he how only held Castrochiaro and Bertinoro in the hills, with Cesena 'tra 'l piano e 'l monte'. The plain to the east of Imola was entirely in the hands of the coalition of *signori*, Mainardo of Susinana, Guy of Polenta and Mala-testa and their captain-general, Bandino of Modigliana.[2]

Against this disorderly background Nicholas IV's attempts at inno-vation in the Papal State, though energetic and many-sided, seem 'mere shadows, insubstantial things'. They could not conjure up papal control in the absence of adequate papal temporal means, but they did define the lines along which Nicholas and several of his successors approached the problems of governing and exploiting the State within these limita-tions.

Nicholas IV's willingness to face such problems is perhaps most evi-dent in his legislation against tyrannies. The lordship, or *signoria*, was not a new phenomenon in the Papal State in Nicholas' time. Ferentino in the Campagna had fallen to the control of a local baron as early as 1264, while many of the small communes of the March existed pre-cariously, never fully enfranchised by a feudatory who continued often to overshadow their counsels.[3] A number of unsuccessful attempts were made to instal *signorie* in the March — at Iesi in 1285, at Senigallia in 1288, at Ripatransone in 1291 — and in most cases the would-be tyrants were evidently precocious *condottieri* with military retinues.[4] Nicholas might well expect such situations to occur in the Duchy also; Perugia had employed a *condottiere* for the war against Foligno in Martin IV's time.[5] The acquisition of Romagna, where the *signoria* was

---

[1] *Nuovi Studi Medievali*, II, 230–1; Bologna, AS, Lettere del Comune, Reg. 4, f. 11v, nn. 1–2. Bologna's many surviving letters of this year show how a powerful city could follow its own neutral policy, at the same time protesting friendship with Mainardo and with the provincial authorities (e.g. Reg. 3, f. 7v, n. 2; Reg. 4, f. 10v, n. 1; f. 27v, n. 2; f. 29).

[2] This league now held its own formal parliaments: *v.* Ghirardacci, *Bologna*, pp. 282–6.

[3] For Ferentino (a brief episode) *v. Reg. Urb. IV*, II, n. 775. An instance of a March com-mune dominated by a feudal lord is Penna S. Giovanni (*v.* Colucci, *Ant. Pic.*, XXX): this type of commune would repay further investigation.
The assertion that the lords of Varano became *signori* of Camerino soon after the middle of the thirteenth century, though repeated by recent authorities (e.g. *Enciclopedia Italiana*, *s.v.* 'Camerino' and 'Varano') rests on the uncritical seventeenth century historian Lilii and seems to have no firm corroboration from contemporary documents.

[4] *Reg. Hon. IV*, nn. 839–40: *Reg. N. IV*, nn. 7127, 7331.

[5] See above p. 206.

already installed as a normal form of government, first brought the papacy face to face with this new type of subject on a large scale. For more than one reason they were less acceptable as subjects than the republican communes. Their juridical status was dubious and, what was more serious, they were particularly liable to arouse violent opposition and hence to add to the tale of turbulence with which provincial rectors were faced. The history of Romagna in 1288–92 illustrates adequately the precarious and shifting position of the early *signori*. Nor was there much more to be said for them if they did reinforce their position, since the pope would then have a 'monolithic' *signoria* to deal with in place of a commune weakened by the normal divisions of political controversy.

It is therefore not surprising that Nicholas should have issued in February 1290 a constitution nullifying all elections to municipal rule when prolonged beyond one year.[1] The preamble of this measure states that some nobles have gained control of towns at the Church's expense, using 'honeyed words and superstitious threats' to persuade the citizens to re-elect them as rectors for year after year. The operation of the constitution was intended to be retrospective — but tyrannies are not overturned by legislation unsupported by power. There was certainly no general policy of backing the communes against the feudatories. It is interesting, for example, to see Nicholas taking into his service the lords of Brunforte, a particularly turbulent baronial family from his native province. After fighting against Innocent IV and Alexander IV, supporting Manfred and later tyrannizing the zone between Fermo and Camerino, they now became provincial rectors and *podestà* of papal towns.[2]

Another statute for the Papal State issued by Nicholas IV prohibited the formation of alliances except with the knowledge and consent of the pope, but this merely reiterated a principle that had long been formulated.[3] Of greater practical importance was the experiment, made

[1] For the issue of this statute to the March, *v.* Mei, *Cagli*, dd. 416, 418, 422 (which provides the date). For its issue to the 'Patrimony' (perhaps the Tuscan Patrimony only), *v.* *Reg. N. IV*, n. 7245 (dated in Nicholas' 'third year', *i.e.* 22 Feb. 1290–21 Feb. 1291). It is probable that the measure was applied to all provinces.

[2] The lords of Brunforte were strong at Montefortino and Amandola, within ten miles of Nicholas IV's birthplace. For the early history of these local tyrants, *v. inter alia* De Minicis, *Fermo*, pp. 420, 545, 548–9; Ferranti, *Amandola*, III, dd. 55, 169; Colucci, *Ant. Pic.*, XIX, dd. XXXVIII–XXXIX; Potthast, 14930. For their position under Nicholas IV, *v.* Contatore, *Terracina*, p. 206 (Ottaviano of Brunforte rector of Campagna-Marittima and *podestà* of Terracina) and *Reg. N. IV*, nn. 7236 (Rainald of Brunforte *podestà* of Viterbo), 1988 and 2580 (confirmation of Brunforte lands).

[3] Mei, *Cagli*, d. 456 (18 Nov. 1290): the same statute is mentioned by De Minicis (*Fermo*, pp. 493–4), but wrongly attributed to Nicholas IV's 'second year' (Feb. 1289–Feb. 1290). For an instance of the earlier functioning of this principle *v. Reg. G. IX*, n. 218 (quashing of March towns' alliance with Venice, 1228).

in December 1288, of appointing three papal chaplains as special judges for routine appeal suits from the Papal State. One of these was to hear appeals from the Tuscan Patrimony and from Romagna, a second those from the Campagna and Marittima, the other those from the Duchy and March.[1]

The most significant changes in the practice of government in Pope Nicholas' time were those concerned with appointments as *podestà*. These took two different forms. In the first place, it now became increasingly common for the pope to accept the *podestà*-ship for himself and to occupy it through a vicar. The constitutional basis of this practice was of course the pope's right to appoint the *podestà*: when a town offered its *regimen* to the pope or his local representative, the provincial vicar, it was referring back the power of appointment to the centre from which the power was originally derived. This right had been allowed to lapse in the case of many of the larger towns, but it could only be alienated legally by the pope, and such alienation was not regarded as final. Nicholas IV assumed the *podestà*-ship of Ascoli in a time of internal dissensions *auctoritate apostolica*, as mentioned above, and before this Urban IV had taken similar action at Cagli and Honorius IV had deprived Viterbo of its power to appoint, as punishment for disturbing a conclave[2] Moreover the right of appointing was far from universal, even among the larger communes; Nicholas IV granted it to a new town, S. Angelo Papale, in May 1290, but a few months later denied it to Civitavecchia when placing that town's status on a formal basis.[3] Since the popes invariably appointed vicars to act in their place as *podestà* there was little practical difference between the situation in a commune where the pope had retained the power of appointment and that in a commune which had chosen the pope as its *podestà*.

To choose the pope as *podestà* was both to make a gesture of fidelity and to pass on the responsibility of selecting the commune's leading official. The circumstances under which such action might seem appropriate were manifold, but in particular the pope was a possible 'compromise candidate' at a time of deadlock between rival factions and a possible defender when a town was threatened from without. The most frequent of such contingencies was a threat to a commune's

---

[1] *Reg. N. IV*, nn. 7204–6: these judges were not empowered to hear suits involving the papacy as a party or those for which the punishment was a fine exceeding 100 *l.* The only subsequent reference to these judges noted is in October 1291 and concerns the judge of appeals for the Duchy and March (Macerata, AC, perg., n. 316).

[2] *V. sup.*, p. 212; Bricchi, *Cagli*, pp. 120–1; *Reg. Hon. IV*, n. 485.

[3] *Reg. N. IV*, n. 2699; *Lib. Cens.*, I, 597–8.

independence from a would-be tyrant — and this is in part the explanation of the rapid extension of the practice in the decade when an increasing number of towns were threatened by *signori*.[1] Terracina,
typically, turned to the pope and made him its *podestà* for life in 1289,
when two local baronial families menaced the commune's independence.[2] But long before this became a conventional move other towns
had turned to the pope or provincial rector: the rector of the Patrimony
had been *podestà* of Perugia in 1228 and the vicar of the March *podestà*
of Ripatransone in 1234. Gubbio had asked Clement IV to find it a
podestà in 1265, Matelica had made the rector of the March its *podestà* in
1272, and Fabriano offered the post to Gregory X's nephew two years
later.[3] These occasions all foreshadow the election of the pope himself
to the *podestà*-ship, the first recorded instance of which seems to have
been the choice of Martin IV at Orvieto in 1284.[4] Such an arrangement
may also have brought financial advantages to the papacy, since the
pope may not have passed on to his vicar the full amount of the salary.
The assumption of the *podestà*'s office by the pope only began to become a regular arrangement under Nicholas IV,[5] but within a few
years, under Boniface VIII, it was widespread.

Nicholas IV's other innovation concerning the *podestà*-ship was the
sale to a number of towns in the March of Ancona of the right to elect
their own *podestà*, together with judicial powers of first instance in
minor cases.[6] Many of the stronger communes had already acquired
this right by grant or custom[7] and Nicholas now sold it to forty towns
or more. This was not merely to exchange rights for money but also to
accept payment for juridical recognition of a situation which often prevailed already, for papal appointments of *podestà* in the March had been

---

[1] Note the comments of Dr. Jones in *EHR*, LXVII, 321: 'By the end of the thirteenth
century the office of *podestà* was already an office for sale, and the papacy was beginning
to enter into strenuous rivalry for the legacy of communal independence with a new
power, no less hostile, which had arisen upon it, that of the *signori*, the *tiranni*, the petty
despots.'

[2] Above, p. 214.

[3] Above, p. 141; Colucci, *Ant. Pic.*, XVIII, d. X; Sarti, *Gubbio*, pp. 156–7; Acquacotta,
Matelica, p. 129; Zonghi, *Fabriano*, d. CCXV.

[4] Waley, *Orvieto*, p. 57.

[5] E.g. at Ascoli and Terracina, at Orvieto (Waley, p. 59) and Fermo (*Reg. N. IV*, nn.
7114–18).

[6] Criminal cases reserved to the papal courts were those involving *lèse-majesté*, heresy,
homicide, adultery, rape of a virgin, arson, robbery when the punishment might involve
the loss of a limb, and all misdeeds on the highway.

[7] See above, pp. 70 ff. Some towns of the March had been paying *affictus potestariarum*
in 1283 (Theiner, d. CCCCXXVII: although this may have been an annual sum rendered
in return for the right to elect, the communes are defined as those *que solvunt salaria
potestatibus ipsarum*).

spasmodic at the best. The reason for the restriction of this innovation to a single province is mysterious. The intention may have been to strengthen and conciliate towns in an area where the danger of *signorie* was particularly strong.[1] Moreover the March was *par excellence* a region of small towns, some of which were expanding and seeking rights already enjoyed by communes which they had now eclipsed in size.[2]

These grants were all made between September 1290 and September 1291.[3] The number of recorded recipients is forty. Naturally the size of the towns varied considerably and hence the amount of the *census* promised.[4] The omission of all the larger towns of the province, to the number of a dozen or so, is presumably explained by their prior posses-sion of these rights, but not all the smaller towns were included.[5] As the sum due is not always recorded it is impossible to estimate accurately the amount that should have accrued to the papal chamber, but a dozen years later, under Boniface VIII, revenues from this source amounted to about 2,700 *l. per annum*.[6]

The other major innovation of Nicholas IV's pontificate also con-cerns finance, but does not relate to the Papal State only. This is the decree *Celestis altitudo potentie* of 18 July 1289, which allotted to the cardinals half of the pope's revenues derived from 'Sicily, England, other kingdoms, Sardinia, Corsica, and other islands, the March, Romagna, the Duchy and Terra Arnulforum, the Tuscan Patrimony, Campagna and Marittima, Sabina, Massa Trabaria, Garfagnana, the Comtat Venaissin, Benevento, and the other lands of the Church'.[7] This measure certainly reflects both the rising status of the college of cardinals[8] and the dynastic background to papal history in this period.

---

[1] Thus Prof. Seidlmayer (*Hist. Jahrbuch*, LX, 81) sees this measure as 'support of com-munal institutions'.

[2] Macerata provides a typical instance of such a place: for its growth in the thirteenth century see above, p. 89. Another explanation of this innovation being confined to the March is that it may have derived from the initiative of a provincial official, but this is made less likely by the fact that the rector, John Colonna, was represented by a series of vicars.

[3] *Reg. N. IV*, nn. 3187, 3545–70, 4477–87, 5411–12.

[4] Thus Macerata owed 150 *l. per annum* and Rotelle a mere 16 *l.* The amount owed is not always recorded in *Reg. N. IV*, but supplementary information on this point can be found elsewhere, e.g. in Theiner, pp. 312–13; Arch. Vat., Arm. XXXV, 5, ff. 268, 271, 273; Colucci, *Ant. Pic.*, XXIX, 134–6, XXX, 8–9, and *Treia*, d. LI; Marangoni, *Civitanova*, pp. 287–8. There are a few minor discrepancies between these sources, e.g. *Reg. N. IV* records Cosignano as owing 30 *l.*, while Arch. Vat., Arm. XXXV, 5, f. 273 has '40'.

[5] Matelica provides an instance of a town which continued to receive its *podestà* from the provincial rector. Of the newly privileged towns only Numana was the seat of a bishop.

[6] See below p.269.

[7] Theiner, d. CCCLXVIII: see also above, pp. 123 ff.

[8] On which *v*. Sägmuller, *Die Thätigkeit u. Stellung der Cardinäle bis Papst Bonifaz VIII*.

There were now two Colonna and two Orsini cardinals; soon there would be Caetani cardinals as well. To grant revenues to the cardinals was to give money to powerful supporters and potential opponents; possibly Nicholas thought, or the Colonna suggested, that their need of money was as great as his.

A similar and connected development was the growing importance of individual cardinals within the Papal State. Many towns had their own protectors in the college, to whom they had recourse when they wanted favours at the Curia: Todi, for instance, turned to Matthew of Acquasparta and Benedict Caetani, each of whom had local connections, and Orvieto, rather later, to the papal chamberlain Theoderic.[1] In some circumstances it might be necessary to gain the support of a wider circle in the college; Perugia decided in 1276 to make payments to six cardinals and in 1291 Bologna petitioned no less than ten to intercede with Nicholas IV concerning an onerous salt-tax.[2] The cardinals for their part intervened in the affairs of the State when their own interests were involved or when a petitioner could persuade them to take up his case. A lot of money was to be made in this way, as Bologna came to realize in 1289 when it made a gift of 1,000 florins to Cardinal Benedict Caetani in connection with an arbitration which also committed the commune to pay 3,500 florins to a former rector of Romagna, Bertold Orsini.[3] Cardinals sometimes merely urged communes to pardon an outlaw, but intervention could take forms which were more harmful to papal authority, as when Cardinal Napoleon Orsini, citing no justification, boldly ordered the vicar of Sabina to erase from his books the condemnation of Terni and one of its citizens, 'the dispute being now settled'.[4] The cardinals were in fact beginning to conduct independent policies, a development accentuated by the very long duration of the cardinalates of such prelates as Matthew 'Rosso' and Napoleon Orsini (1262–1305 and 1288–1342 respectively). The international diplomatic manifestations of this situation have been vividly described by Canon Mollat.[5] Besides all this *Celestis altitudo* gave the cardinals a more official interest in the welfare, or at least the productivity, of the Papal State.

★   ★   ★

[1] Todi, AC, Rif. II, ff. 38v–42, 47–48v; Rif. III, ff. 72v–73: Waley, *Orvieto*, pp. 72–3, 156–7.

[2] *Supra*, p. 187: Bologna, AS, Lettere del Comune, Reg. 4, f. 25, nn. 1–4 (those approached included James and Peter Colonna, Benedict Caetani and Cardinal Latino).

[3] Bologna, AS, Lettere del Comune, Reg. 2, f. 2v, n. 1; f. 23, n. 3.

[4] Todi, AC, Rif. I, ff. 66–67v: Terni, AS, perg. 4 February 1302.

[5] In *Mélanges L. Halphen*, pp. 511–12.

The death of Nicholas IV on 4 April 1292 was followed by a papal vacancy which endured for some two years and a half, while Colonna and Orsini cardinals manoeuvred for position in a crucial conclave.[1] There was considerable lawlessness in the State during these years, but neither in its intensity nor its location did this differ sharply from the disturbances of Nicholas' time. It is tempting to see in acts of defiance committed during a papal vacancy attempts to exploit a temporary advantage, but the success of such acts must always have depended as much upon the tenure of the rectorship as on the papacy, and in the most disturbed provinces, the March and Romagna, there was no change of rector after Nicholas' death. There is perhaps a slight deterioration in the papal position — only in the northern part of the Tuscan Patrimony is it at all marked — but this is of the nature of a continuing trend, predictable from the previous decade.

Unrest in Rome[2] reflected the rivalry of Colonna and Orsini, but for over a year these two families shared the senatorship, while an Annibaldi continued as rector of the Duchy. Thus no single dynasty dominated the city and the surrounding zone. Orsini and Caetani intrigued for the hand of the Aldobrandeschine heiress, Countess Margherita,[3] but this and many other manifestations of a territorial struggle for power did not disrupt provincial government and there seems to have been no diminution in receipts from the Tuscan Patrimony in these years. Warfare in the middle Tiber — Todi and Orvieto were both fighting Amelia in 1293 — was endemic anyway, but two episodes do suggest the intention of exploiting the papal vacancy. These are Narni's renewed attack on the papal fortress of Stroncone and Orvieto's on the disputed zone of the Val del Lago di Bolsena. Narni was repulsed by the firm action of Cardinal Matthew of Acquasparta, supported by troops under the Justiciar of Abruzzi sent by Charles II of Sicily, who was anxious to impress the electors.[4] The cardinals also acted promptly in

---

[1] For the conclave *v.* Boase, *Boniface VIII*, pp. 29–41; on its connection with events in central Italy in 1292–4 *v.* Digard, *Philippe le Bel et le Saint-Siège*, I, 158 ff. and Baethgen, 'Beiträge zur Geschichte Cölestins V.'.

[2] For the involved history of Rome in 1292–4 *v.* Gregorovius, V, 2, 516 ff.; Dupré-Theseider, pp. 271 ff. and works cited in preceding note. An important primary source is the chronicle of Bartholomew Cotton (R.S.), pp. 251–2.

[3] For Countess Margherita *v.* my paper in *TRHS*, s. 4, XXXII, 121–39. For revenues from the Tuscan Patrimony, *infra*, p. 270.

[4] RIS, O.S., III, 1, 622 ff. (Stefaneschi's life of Celestine V); *Reg. B. VIII*, n. 2394; Pellini, *Perugia*, I, 312. For the probability that the Colonna cardinals, then linked with the Aragonese against Charles II, gave support to Narni, *v.* Baethgen, *art. cit.*, 289–90. Narni was compelled to swear an oath of obedience to the Church (significantly this was valid only for the duration of the vacancy and three months beyond), to make good the value

turning to Rome, Viterbo and many barons and other towns of the Patrimony for aid against the threat to the Val del Lago and again a force was mustered, though its defence of Bolsena was unsuccessful, and within two months all the disputed towns except Acquapendente were in Orvietan hands.[1]

The many requests for military assistance received by Perugia during 1293 mirror the quandaries of a papal town. Narni wanted its aid against Stroncone, Camerino against Matelica, and Todi against Amelia; simultaneously there came a demand from the rector of the Duchy for service *against* Todi, as an aggressor. Perugia's first decisions could not have been worse from the papal viewpoint, for the council determined to support Narni, Camerino and Todi. Two weeks later, after receiving a letter from the cardinals describing their formidable array, Perugia reversed this decision and agreed that the cavalry chosen for service with Narni should now be sent to aid Cardinal Matthew against that city![2]

The Duchy was not an easy province to rule in these years. The rector held a parliament at Bevagna in July 1292, but Spoleto withdrew its representative's consent to the new constitutions.[3] The following year Gubbio attempted to end the protracted dispute over its *contado* by capturing the judge of the Duchy then dealing with the matter and taking his law-books. Though the judge was released, Gubbio's condemnation for this exploit and failure to pay the fine served to complicate and prolong the suit yet further.[4] The difficulties of this time are also well illustrated by the irresponsible action of the treasurer Berto 'de Scivinictis', a Florentine, who in July 1293 quitted his post, apparently without the rector's consent, and handed over his powers to two merchants of Foligno.[5] The finances of the province thus came into the hands of two local men, apparently at the whim of an official whom

of the damage caused to Stroncone and to give guarantees for future good behaviour (summary of documents of 16–18 July 1293 in *BDSPU*, I, 133–5).

[1] To the sources cited in my *Orvieto*, pp. 64–5, should be added Raynaldus, *ad* 1294, § 1–2; Cotton, *loc. cit.*; and letters printed by Baethgen, *art. cit.*, 303–5 and 315–17. Of the recipients of the cardinals' pleas for help, Bagnorea had already sent troops to aid Orvieto, while one feudatory could not be found by the cardinals' messenger 'pro eo quod dictus Raynerius in exercitu Urbevetanorum esse dicebatur'. The same was true of Orsello Orsini, Orvieto's general, who received a special appeal from Cardinal Matthew. Excommunicated, he pleaded that Orvieto had forced him to give his services.

[2] Pellini, *Perugia*, I, 312; Perugia, AS, Rif. X, ff. 192v–194. Perugia's change of heart occurred only three days before Narni's submission and may have been too late to be effective.

[3] See above, p. 118.

[4] *BDSPU*, XXV, 54–5, 58; Guerrieri, *Gualdo Tadino*, p. 74.

[5] This deed is perg. n. 321 (Busta V, n. 235) in AC, Fabriano. It reads: 'Bertus de Scivinictis de Florentia Thesaurarius Romane Ecclesie in Ducatu Spoleti quia propter quedam iminentia se in dicto Ducatu personaliter interesse non potest ad presens immo

'imminent affairs' 'called home' to Tuscany and who could not be compelled to stay.

The state of the March again presented no considerable change. Local systems of alliance and local warfare were the dominant elements in the political life of the province. Fermo, Ancona, Iesi and Recanati formed one powerful league, which warred with Osimo, Civitanova and other less powerful neighbours, while a minor alliance, comprising Matelica, Tolentino and S. Severino, challenged Camerino and S. Ginesio. A number of other towns conducted subsidiary wars or had been condemned for 'rebellions'. There was, however, no abandonment of the attempt to govern. The rector, the bishop of Valencia, condemned towns for failing to provide military service and for other forms of disobedience, sought to intervene as peacemaker — normally without success — and continued to hold his court. Moreover some towns fulfilled their military obligations, and revenue was still forthcoming in the form of fines and payments in lieu of military service.[1]

The end of Nicholas IV's pontificate had seen the power of the rector of the Romagna confined to the mountainous district in the southeastern corner of the province. The circumstances of the vacancy made any firm recovery impossible, but something might yet be achieved by enterprising diplomacy. The rector correctly saw Bologna as a potential

necessitatis causa presentialiter opporteat eidem repatriare, fecit constituit et ordinavit Anestaxium domini Hermanni presentem et Corradum domini Anestaxii absentem mercatores de Fulgineo et utrumque ipsorum in solidum ita quod non sit melior condictio occupantis suos veros et legitimos procuratores actores factores et nunctios speciales ad petendum confitendum et recipiendum omnes denarios et introitus qui pervenirent sive intrarent in curia generali Ducatus, tam ex condempnationibus, compositionibus, afflictu, scriptura penne notariorum generalium, quam ex quacumque alia causa modo et iure vice et nomine Romane Ecclesie et pro ipsa, et ad faciendum nomine dicte Romane Ecclesie et pro ipsa finem et quietationem perpetuo valituram de hiis que receperint sicut et quomodo occurrerit faciende (*sic*). Commictens eis et cuilibet eorum vicem suam et plenam et liberam potestatem faciendi exercendi et procurandi in predictis et quolibet predictorum et aliis quibuscumque et quecunque fuerint opportuna et que dictus Bertus facere posset si personaliter interesset et ad faciendum omnes expensas que videbitur domino vicario Ducatus vel que idem dominus vicarius eis vel alicui ipsorum mandaverit faciendas. Promictens dictus Bertus per se et suos heredes ratum gratum et firmum habere et tenere perpetuo quicquid dicti pro se vel altero ipsorum fecerint in predictis circa predicta et quelibet predictorum sub pena et obligatione bonorum et rerum Romane Ecclesie.' The deed was drawn up at Foligno and the Judge General of the Duchy was a witness.

[1] De Minicis, *Fermo*, pp. 499–501, 505; Acquacotta, *Matelica*, dd. 83, 85, 87–9; Marangoni, *Civitanova*, pp. 289–93; Lilii, *Camerino*, II, 62–3; Gianandrea, *Iesi*, dd. CCL–CCLI; Zonghi, *Fabriano*, dd. CCLV–CCLVII, CCLX, CCLXII (for Fabriano's other wars, against Serra S. Quirico and S. Ginesio, *v.* Serra S. Quirico, AC, perg., II, f. 45 and Colucci, *Ant. Pic.*, XIX, dd. XLI–XLII). Serra S. Quirico, AC, perg. I, ff. 56–85 (suit in provincial court, Sept.–Oct. 1292). For military service *v.* also *AMSM*, N.S., VII (1911–1912), 403 (Montegiorgio, Apr. 1294); Mazzatinti, 2nd. s., II, 240; Ferranti, *Amandola*, III, dd. 177b, 183; Gucci, 'Compendio delle Memorie della Città di Cagli' (MS in Bibl. Com., Cagli), II, f. 46v.

ally, since its zone of influence abutted on the area dominated by the league of *signori*, with which it disputed Imola. He therefore made an alliance with Bologna in the summer of 1292 on terms which were favourable to the city and allotted to it rule over Imola and Medicina.[1] This abdication of papal rights he no doubt regarded as a temporary move justified by drastic circumstances. The league held most of eastern Romagna, but the rector raised a force, which clashed with its troops near Imola. Meanwhile Guy of Montefeltro had reappeared, in an interval between acting as commander of the Pisan forces, and had again occupied Urbino.[2]

Guy of Montefeltro's resurgence was a threat to the league as well as to the rector, and in consequence the late summer of 1293 saw a diplomatic revolution in Romagna. The rector came to terms with the league of *signori* and at the same time condemned Bologna, with whom he was already in dispute over appellate jurisdiction and that city's war against the Alidosi. Bologna was now ordered to restore Imola and Medicina.[3] In 1294 Riminese troops took part in the papal campaign against Urbino and Rimini acquired the right — quite incompatible with its status as a subject — to fight campaigns in Romagna and elsewhere 'whenever it thinks fit'.[4] The change of alliance brought no rapid success, for in August Guy of Montefeltro captured Pesaro from Malatesta, while the league itself split and Calboli and Ordelaffi fought for the possession of Forlì. The rector may well have felt proud of the strenuous achievement that had at least given him a certain influence in his province, but this had been accomplished solely through diplomacy; he had in effect resigned the claim to rule.

The four-month pontificate of Celestine V (August–December 1294) made little impact on the Papal State. Celestine was a subject of Charles of Anjou and his relationship to the Kingdom (in which he spent the whole of his pontificate) renewed briefly the traditions of Urban IV, Clement IV and Martin IV. He created eight French cardinals, 'Ange-

---

[1] Imola, AC, Mazzo IV, n. 117 (condemnation of Imola, 31 May 1292); Ghirardacci, *Bologna*, pp. 301–2 (grant of Imola and Medicina, 26 June); Bologna, AS, Reg. Gross., ff. 395–9 (Bologna takes over Imola and receives exemption from tolls throughout Romagna, 10–17 July): RIS, N.S., XVIII, I, 236–7 and XXVIII, II, 67–73.

[2] RIS, N.S., XXVIII, II, 73–4. For Guy at Pisa *v.* Honig, *Guido da Montefeltro*, pp. 60 ff., but this inadequate biography misses altogether Guy's return to Urbino in 1292–4.

[3] Ghiradacci, *Bologna*, p. 310 (Bologna condemned, 14 Aug. 1293). Bologna, AS, Lettere del Comune, Reg. 6, f. 4v, n. 1 (17 Aug., Bologna to pass on hearth-tax registers for Imola and Medicina to provincial officials): *ibid.*, f. 2v, n. 2; f. 4, n. 3; f. 8v, n. 2; f. 10, n. 1; f. 12, n. 3; f. 14, n. 2; f. 14v, n. 1 (dispute concerning Alidosi prisoners); *ibid.*, ff. 15v, n. 2 and 16, n. 1 (appellate jurisdiction).

[4] RIS, O.S., XIV, cc. 1109–10; Tonini, *Rimini*, III, 677–89.

vin' officials or barons were appointed to at least three of the provincial rectorships and Count Thomas of Sanseverino became Roman senator, probably as Charles II's vicar.[1]

In the provinces the routine struggle persisted.[2] The ageing warrior Guy of Montefeltro at last submitted to Pope Celestine and set out to repair in his few remaining years a long life of opposition to the Guelf and papal cause. Guy's repentance and the pope's own temperament serve to explain the advice given to the new rector of Romagna that he should modify the heavy sentences hitherto imposed in that province.[3] Cornay held a parliament at Imola in November, ended Faenza's interdict on payment of 2,000 florins and made preparations for the absolution of Imola itself.[4] The parliament granted him powers to take on troops and Bologna sent some, but Ravenna protested against his constitutions, which threatened to deprive the city of its rights and *praedicta de jure facere non possitis*.[5] In the wording of this protest one sees common sense revolting at claims which bore no relation to reality. The background to it is provided by Cesena's chronicler when he says of Robert de Cornay that he 'stayed for a few months' (in Romagna) 'was ill-obeyed, and went away again (*repedavit*). The whole province was then in revolt'.

★   ★   ★

[1] The rectors were 'Oderisius', a feudatory from the Abruzzi (Tuscan Patrimony); Gentile of Sangro, formerly Justiciar in the Regno (March); and Robert of Cornay (or Gournay), formerly Justiciar of Basilicata (Romagna). It is not possible to determine whether Charles II became nominal senator during Celestine's pontificate: for differing views *v.* Baethgen, *Engelpapst*, pp. 126–7 and Boase, *Boniface VIII*, p. 50 (both think Charles was senator), Gregorovius, V, 2, 523 and Dupré-Theseider, p. 278 (both deny this). The only relevant document, printed (but misdated and misinterpreted) by Cantèra, *S. Pier Celestino*, p. 110, is a bull of 13 October 1294 which makes Charles and his successors eligible for the senatorship, *non obstante* Nicholas III's decree. During the papal vacancy there had been a party favouring the election to the senatorship of Frederick of Aragon (*v.* Finke, *Acta Aragonensia*, I, 16–17).

[2] The rector of the Duchy had to outlaw Perugia's *Capitano del Popolo* and papal bankers sent the rector of the March 2,000 florins, presumably to pay troops (Perugia, AS, Rif. X, ff. 280v–281: Potthast, n. 23949).

[3] RIS, O.S., XIV, c. 1110. Celestine's letter (Ghirardacci, *Bologna*, p. 318) of 9 September runs, in its essential passages: '. . . Sicut accepimus . . . officiales diversis rectoriatus temporibus condemnationes fecerunt et penas inflixere diversas, ad quarum satisfactionem seu solutionem ipsorum condemnatorum non sufficiunt facultates. Nos . . . volumus super huiusmodi penis et condemnationibus illam meditationem et temperantiam debitam observari . . . mandamus quatenus pensatis attentius et diligenter consideratis . . . condemnationes easdem moderari . . . iuxta tuae discretionis arbitrium videris faciendum, super quibus plenam et liberam tibi auctoritatem . . . concedimus facultatem . . .'

[4] RIS, N.S., XXVIII, II, 74–6: Imola, AC, Mazzo IV, n. 55 (25 Nov. 1294: the vicar-general of Romagna *in spiritualibus* orders the clergy of Imola to end the interdict on Imola and its district after receiving the usual oath of obedience).

[5] Ghirardacci, *Bologna*, p. 320: Fantuzzi, *Mon. Rav.*, III, n. LXXXXIV (*v.* also above, pp. 118–19).

In December 1294 Celestine resigned and was soon replaced by
Cardinal Benedict Caetani, pope Boniface VIII. Much has been written
concerning Boniface's Italian policy during his nine year pontificate.
Emphasis has naturally been placed on the territorial aggrandizement
of his family and the quarrel with the Colonna, but these cannot be
treated in isolation from his government in the Papal State.[1] Boniface's
attitude towards the towns and his technique as a temporal administrator deserve study in their own right, while an assessment of his
achievement in central Italy is an essential preliminary to judgements
concerning the papal move to Avignon.

The most striking aspect of Boniface's policy is his realistic approach
to the problem of the communes and his eagerness to achieve practicable agreements with them. It may be well to consider this policy in
action before discussing Boniface's methods of rule and attempting an
estimate of his success in the Papal State. An early settlement with
Spoleto[2] goes far beyond the terms of Nicholas IV's grants in the March
and well illustrates the pope's willingness to compromise. In June 1295
he granted this city full jurisdiction in all cases, with *merum et mixtum
imperium*; all suits concerning Spoleto's subjects were to be heard in the
podestà's court in the first instance, and the right to appoint a judge of
appeals was also recognized.

Spoleto was to present twice a year to the pope or the rector of the
Duchy a list of three nominees as *podestà* and three as 'captain' of appeals, one of whom would then be appointed to each office. If the pope
or rector had made no nomination within a month, Spoleto might
make its own choice.[3] These terms, it may be noted, bear some resem-

---

[1] On Boniface VIII see the life by T. S. R. Boase: for his family policy *v.* G. Caetani,
Domus Caietana and *Regesta Chartarum*; Falco, 'Sulla formazione e la costituzione della
signoria dei Caetani', *Riv. Stor. It.*, XLV, 225–78; G. Digard, *Philippe le Bel et le Saint-
Siège*. For the Papal State, *v.* Seidlmayer, 'Bonifaz VIII. u. der Kirchenstaat' *Hist. Jahr-
buch*, LX (brief and mainly concerned with the new constitutions for the Patrimony and
March).

[2] Sansi, *Spoleto*, d. LXXIV. This grant is stated to have been made in answer to Spoleto's
petition, but its terms no doubt reflect negotiation between the commune and the pope.
For Boniface VIII's later relations with Spoleto *v.* below, p. 245.

[3] The clause permitting the city to submit its lists to *either* pope *or* rector seems to provide
a possible 'loophole', since each of these might believe that they had been presented to the
other.

Spoleto maintained its hold over appellate jurisdiction by forbidding its citizens to
appeal, as is revealed by the following clause in its statutes (*c.* 1296): '41. *Quod nullus
appellet a sententia lata per privilegia papalia.* Item dicimus et ordinamus quod nullus appellet
per se vel alium ab aliqua sententia vel processu facta vel facto contra ipsum per aliquem
officialem communis Spoleti per privilegia papalia et quod qui contrafecerit puniatur a
potestate in tota quantitate de qua appellaverit vel plus suo arbitrio in persona vel rebus
et nichilominus ipsam pecuniam de qua appellatum fuerit teneatur de facto exsecutioni
mandare, omni exceptioni vel appellationi remota. Et teneatur procedere non solum contra

blance to the compromise reached with Orvieto a year later over the Val del Lago towns; there the Church retained its power to appoint *podestà*, its choice being restricted in alternate years to a list of four Orvietan nominees for each post.[1]

The handsome privilege to Spoleto had no immediate successors, but in 1298 Boniface reached analogous agreements regulating the status of a number of communes, and a few others follow in later years.[2] Most of the settlements of 1298–9 concern towns in the March. Some of these merely defined the terms on which absolution was given to communes that had failed to pay fines,[3] but those regarding Ascoli, Ancona and Iesi are both more important in their implications and more difficult to interpret. On the surface nothing could be plainer than Pope Boniface's grant to Iesi on 1 June 1299, recorded in his register,[4] whereby the town received jurisdiction over its subjects in 'principal' cases and cases of first appeal *tam in civilibus quam in criminalibus*, with complementary exemptions from the jurisdiction of the provincial court. The issue of this privilege was motivated by 'the sincere devotion which you have had in former and recent times and have now towards the Roman Church and the services that you have rendered and propose to continue against the Colonna, those schismatics and rebels against us and the Roman Church'. All would be quite clear but for the survival, in the Iesi municipal archive,[5] of the deliberations of various communal councils on the 8th, 9th, and 10th of October of the same year, in which the topic debated was whether or not to purchase this privilege at a price of three thousand florins. These discussions make it evident that the letter issued on 1 June was no more than a draft designed to inform Iesi of the terms of a privilege which it might buy. This *pro forma* was then brought back to Iesi by a certain citizen, Manente, who was acting as go-between. For some reason the matter lapsed for several months, but

appellantem sed etiam contra propinquiores appellantis ut sibi videbitur et potestas et quilibet eius officialis de omni eo quod faceret de praedictis vel aliquibus praedictorum non valeat sindicari ab aliquo nec molestari a commune vel speciali persona, omni appellationi et exceptione remota de quibus exgravator nullam habeat contradictionem et ipse capitaneus de praefatis non possit ab aliquo sindicari et potestas servetur indempnis et alii officiales conserventur indempnes de praedictis' (Spoleto, Sottosez AS, Statuti, I, f. 14v).

[1] Fumi, *Orvieto*, dd. DLXI–DLXII.

[2] *Reg. B. VIII*, nn. 2394 (Narni, 1298: right to elect *podestà*), 2844–7 (Velletri, 1299: jurisdiction in cases of first instance), 5206–8 (Cesena, 1303: right to elect *podestà*).

[3] *Ibid.*, nn. 2399, 2552, 2555 (Fermo and Recanati).

[4] *Ibid.*, n. 3153 (the date misprinted as '1298').

[5] Iesi, AC, perg. n. 168 (also gives the full text of the letter summarized in *Reg. B. VIII*, n. 3153). The mention of future aid against the Colonna is of course a euphemistic reference to the need to purchase this privilege.

in October these councils were debating the question of 'whether the privilege is valid only for the lifetime of the present pope'. One citizen suggested that it might be worth paying more for a grant *imperpetuum*, but finally Iesi decided in favour of purchase for whichever period the pope had in mind, with payment in three instalments.[1]

Iesi, then, presumably bought its privilege, some months after the date under which its terms had been misleadingly recorded in the pope's register. Narni's privilege of 1 February 1298, Ascoli's of the same day and Ancona's of 20 February 1298 (the latter conferring exemptions in cases of first instance) should perhaps also be regarded not as valid charters but as statements of terms open to purchase.[2]

The matter of the Iesi privilege provides a good instance of how misleading a 'document' may be, but the probable financial motive for these grants does not invalidate the statement that Pope Boniface wanted settlements with his towns and was willing to enter into special negotiations to obtain them.[3] Such settlements might merely regulate fiscal matters — typical of these was the substitution of 'block' payments from some communes for one-third of certain receipts[4] — but even this was calculated, by giving more precision, to diminish the number of disputes between towns and provincial rectors. The special missions of men despatched to achieve *compositiones* with towns in certain provinces[5]

---

[1] It was decided to pay 3 *l.* a day to Manente, Iesi's agent in this matter, for the duration of his next visit to the Curia, bearing these proposals: his mission was expected to last a month (Iesi, AC, *loc. cit.*).

[2] *Reg. B. VIII*, nn. 2394–6, 2409. These 'grants' contain a clause referring to services rendered against the Colonna, but not to future services. Ascoli entered its grant in the register of municipal privileges (Ascoli P., AC, Quinternone, ff. 171v–172) which suggests that it achieved validity: furthermore the pope wrote on 28 April 1298 to the rector of the March announcing that Ascoli was pardoned all outstanding condemnations on account of services rendered 'especially against the Colonna' (*ibid.*, f. 171: these condemnations were to be 'crossed out' in the rector's books and not 'erased').

[3] Mention should however be made of what was possibly an attempt to over-ride these privileges by a *non obstantibus* clause in the terms of appointment of some later rectors of the March. For this see Iesi, AC, perg., n. 181 (the full clause is: '. . . Non obstantibus quibuscumque privilegiis indulgentiis et litteris apostolicis quibuscumque personis et locis ecclesiasticis vel secularibus aut ordinibus ab eadem sede concessis seu eorumdem ordinum constitutionibus contrariis etiam si fuerint confirmati auctoritate sedis eiusdem per que tue iurisdictionis executio posset in hac parte quomodolibet impediri sive si aliquibus generaliter vel specialiter ab eadem sede indultum existat quod excomunicari vel interdici nequeant aut suspendi nisi de indulto huiusmodi plena et expressa seu de verbo ad verbum in eisdem nostris litteris fieret mentio specialis'). These are included in the terms of appointment of Cardinal Napoleon Orsini on 27 May 1300. There is a very similar clause in Benedict XI's appointment of Rambaldo as rector of the March on 1 December 1303 (*ibid.*, perg., n. 200).

[4] *Reg. B. VIII*, nn. 3198, 5498 (Foligno and Bettona).

[5] Typical of these was the mission in the March (1296) of Roger, provost of St. Anthony's, Piacenza (*inf.*, p. 237). Communes paying *compositiones* recouped from individuals condemned by demanding payment of a proportion of the original fine. Thus

testify to the same zeal for reaching precise and practicable terms, preferably with a return in money, and often at the expense of papal rights which had remained theoretical through powerlessness to enforce them. With this was certainly combined the intention to make the towns, often threatened by *signori*, regard the pope as their ally. In keeping with this policy was the increasingly frequent choice of the pope as *podestà*, sometimes for life.[1]

The major monuments of Pope Boniface's policy in the Papal State are the three reforming constitutions issued for the Campagna-Marittima in 1295, the Tuscan Patrimony in 1300 and the March in 1303. These were not complete codes but lengthy and thorough revisions affecting the constitutional status of his subjects and above all the methods of provincial justice and administration. It is well to note the order in which they were issued: the emphasis on the territories around Rome — reflected also in the list of towns that made Boniface their *podestà* — reveals the close link between his dynastic schemes and his government in the papal provinces.

Romana mater ecclesia, Boniface's constitution for Campagna and Marittima, was promulgated at Anagni on 28 September 1295.[2] After a preamble praising this province, *praedilictus et delitiosus ortus Ecclesiae in quo ipsa . . . percipit dulces fructus*, there follow fifteen substantial clauses. The first of these lays down the judicial principle of *preventio*: precedence between the rectorial and communal courts is given to whichever acts first.[3] The other clauses are all concerned with the abolition of abuses by provincial officials — in appeal cases, in demanding pledges, in misinterpreting the principle of joint responsibility for certain crimes (*custodia stratarum*), in exercising pressure on would-be

Spoleto *c.* 1290 (after a *compositio* with Landulf Colonna, rector of the Duchy) ordered payment of 1*s.* in the pound on condemnations below 1,000 *l.* (Spoleto, Sottosez AS, Statuti, I, f. 29v).

[1] For this development in the time of Nicholas IV, *v. supra*, pp. 221 ff. Among the towns granting office to Boniface were Terracina, Velletri, Toscanella, Viterbo, Corneto, Orvieto, Todi and Rieti (Contatore, *Terracina*, pp. 208–9; Theiner, dd. DIX, DXVII, DXXXV, DXLIV; *Reg. B. VIII*, n. 4051; Todi, AC, Rif. V, ff. 120v–121; Rieti, Sottosez AS, perg. 11 May 1298). Terracina provides a well-documented instance of the circumstances under which the pope might become *podestà*. Originally Boniface was made *podestà* there for life, but later this term was extended, in the sense that if he died within ten years he was to be succeeded automatically by the rector of Campagna-Marittima. Terracina was threatened by both the Annibaldi and the lords of Ceccano. One of Boniface's actions was to deprive both these houses of any *dominium* or *regimen* at Terracina. The lord of Ceccano (who was later among the Anagni conspirators) was also forbidden to hold any property there. *V.* Contatore, *Terracina*, pp. 80–90, 208–9; *Reg. B. VIII*, nn. 5508–9.

[2] *Bullarium Romanum* (Turin, 1858), IV, 629–32: preamble only in Contatore, *Terracina*, pp. 74–5 (Potthast, n. 24194).

[3] See above, p. 76.

appellants to the papal court, and so on. Particularly to be avoided are financial exactions practised by the rector's court at the expense of communities when litigants are overcharged and too many witnesses called. A final clause reassures the barons of the province and their vassals: their rights are to be respected and in no way diminished.

Licet merum,[1] the constitution for the Tuscan Patrimony issued on 20 January 1300, in many ways resembled *Romana mater*, but contained one more radical provision. It granted judicial authority (*merum et mixtum imperium*) *usque beneplacitum* to those towns which by custom possessed the right to choose their own *podestà* and officials, six grave offences only being excepted.[2] Another clause — there are sixteen in all — regulates the obligation of *custodia stratarum* in accordance with the principle formulated for Campagna-Marittima; a town may only be punished for genuine negligence. Again most sections are concerned with the methods of the rector's court and in particular seek to regulate its gaol procedure and its use of guarantors and pledges, while others are directed against fiscal innovations.[3] The principle that foodstuffs should not be exported from the province is reasserted, but exceptions are permitted for supplying the residence of the papal Curia and, *de gratia speciali*, for the city of Rome. Essentially *Licet merum* is an attempt to find a practicable solution to the problem of the relation of the towns to provincial authority, by defining reasonable frontiers. The communes are granted the jurisdictional powers which it had never been possible in practice to deny them and limits are put to the financial demands that may be made on them. The clauses concerned with the rector's court are again intended mainly to make procedure there less expensive. In return the towns are to become reconciled to the rector's appellate jurisdiction and the final clause insists that they should not carry out sentences when an appeal to the rector's court is pending.

Celestis patrisfamilias, the constitution for the March[4] issued on 6 September 1303, bears a general resemblance to its two predecessors in its aims, but again differs very considerably in its provisions. This time there is no general grant of *merum et mixtum imperium*; instead the towns receive an acknowledgement of their right to try such cases as are theirs

---

[1] Theiner, d. DXXVIII (the date given incorrectly as '1299').

[2] These were heresy; schism; *lèse-majesté*; the forgery of money, papal bulls or letters; rape against a virgin; and treason.

[3] The hearth-tax was to be levied 'in accordance with ancient custom' and procurations according to the custom of the last thirty or forty years (and only in the case of a visit by the provincial rector in person).

[4] Theiner, d. DLXXI.

'by law or custom' (*de iure vel consuetudine*).[1] This noncommittal phrase at least recognizes that the communes are hearing suits of first instance, but *Celestis patrisfamilias* resembles *Romana mater* in that it is concerned mainly with the settlement of specific grievances. Six of its twenty-one clauses are designed to check abuses in rectorial justice, in particular those concerning the taking of pledges and costly methods of procedure. Two clauses relate to grievances over military service; money received as scutage is to be returned if not used for military expenditure, and if the rector orders one town to be guarded by troops from another the expense is to be borne by the town thus garrisoned. Obligations of *custodia stratarum* are defined in terms similar to those of *Romana mater* and *Licet merum*. The rector's right to inspect town constitutions is severely restricted, and there are measures to check infringement on municipal jurisdiction. The pope also quashes certain of the recent provincial constitutions issued by the rector, and prohibits their enforcement by the use of interdict.[2] The last clause returns to financial grievances against papal government: henceforth officials must remain in the province for ten days after their period of office, in order to answer any charges of 'rapine' or injustice that may be brought against them. The disavowal in *Celestis patrisfamilias* of previous statutes and its implicit condemnation of methods hitherto in use is striking, as is the removal of the rector's regular right to inspect town statutes. The rectors who were thus disowned included Cardinal Napoleon Orsini, who may well have played a part in securing the abrogation of the entire constitution in the following pontificate.[3]

It is now time to turn from Boniface VIII's approach to the problems of rule to his administrative methods. The pope's temperament, his family policy in central Italy and his links with both the Tuscan Patrimony and the Campagna prepare us for his very large personal rôle in the affairs of the Papal State. He was probably born at Anagni, had spent much of his youth at Todi, and during his twenty years at the

---

[1] It is puzzling that a letter of Benedict XII to the rector of the March (Theiner, II, d. XXIII: 23 April 1336) refers to a measure of Boniface VIII for that province providing 'ne aliquis extra suam civitatem et diocesim ad iudicium evocetur', etc. *Celestis patrisfamilias* contains no clause to this effect and is hardly compatible with it. I cannot suggest a solution to this mystery.

[2] This clause is reminiscent of Boniface's decree *Provvide attendentes* (Theiner, d. DLXII) ordering that no district or place should be subjected to interdict 'pro pecuniario debito'. This measure was not restricted to the Papal State. Its aim was to prevent interdicts on communities on account of the debts of their citizens (for an instance of these, *v. Reg. B. VIII*, n. 4656), not to prevent the use of this weapon in enforcing rights in the State: it has been misinterpreted by Prof. Seidlmayer (*art. cit.*, 84).

[3] See below, p. 250; and *v.* Boase, p. 342.

Curia as notary and in other official positions and later as cardinal he had come to know many of the towns of central Italy.[1] It was natural that his interventions should continue when he became pope and his register, like Nicholas IV's, reflects his interest in the affairs of the State. A few instances will suffice to indicate the nature of his rôle. In 1295 he orders the rector of the March to absolve various towns from interdict. In the following year he not only gives detailed instructions to a new rector in the March, but summons to the Curia representatives of the principal towns of Romagna and the province's leading nobles in order that he may make a peace settlement. A little later Todi is ordered to send ambassadors so that the pope may lay down terms for an internal pacification and the commune decides that its affairs are so dependent on the Curia that it must keep a permanent representative there. Towns in the Duchy and March receive direct instructions about their territorial disputes, alliances in the Patrimony and Duchy are dissolved, Rieti is cited to the Curia for building an unauthorized castle, Ascoli and later Uguccione della Faggiuola are absolved after periods of rebellion.[2] Boniface even stated the principle — it would have been hard to maintain it consistently — that an agreement reached between a provincial rector and a commune was invalid if it lacked papal assent.[3]

Another aspect of Pope Boniface's centralizing method was the despatch of specially empowered envoys on missions that contrasted with the normal provincial structure of papal rule. An early instance of this was the mission entrusted to the papal chaplain Richard of Ferentino in March 1295. His task, which was pacificatory, extended over the three provinces of the Duchy, March and Romagna. In Romagna Richard's work was soon disowned, for the following winter the bishop of Pavia was sent with instructions to make a full enquiry to the unauthorized actions of Richard of Ferentino and his officials, particularly his nephew. Richard was said to have effected absolutions and restitutions 'at the expense of us and the Church', and town officials appointed by him were to be removed. Richard and his nephew, together with a former rector whose administration was also under investigation, were informed that they might appear before the bishop in Romagna, in

---

[1] Boase, pp. 6–26; for intervention by Boniface in the State during his cardinalate see above, p. 224 n.

[2] *Reg. B. VIII*, nn. 943–4, 1556–8, 1589, 3358, 4188, 4321, 4663–4, 4668–9, 5409–12: Todi, AC, Rif. V, f. 19; *QFIA*, XXXIV, 117–18 and Gubbio, Sottosez AS, perg., bu. 10, n. 236.

[3] *Reg. B. VIII*, n. 5279.

person or by proctor, 'should they judge this to be in their interest'.[1]
The need of one *missus* for the sole purpose of enquiring into the mal-
administration of another may seem unpromising, but Boniface did not
abandon this technique. A few months after the bishop of Pavia set out
for Romagna, Roger provost of St. Anthony's, Piacenza (another papal
chaplain), was on his way to the March, with the task of bringing the
condemned towns and communities of that province to terms.[2]

Control from the centre was not confined to the interventions of the
pope himself and his special *missi*, for an important part in the work of
governing the State was now played by the papal chamberlain.[3] Since
the chamber received the profits of the provinces, together with
revenue from domain and many other dues and fines, the chamberlain
was necessarily closely involved with the State's financial administration. By the 1270s this rôle was increasing and he was concerned in
other aspects of territorial government, both administrative and judicial.
Nicholas IV's chamberlain, Nicholas of Trevi, was probably a figure of
some significance in the affairs of the papal provinces.[4] He was a native
of the State, as were Theoderic of Orvieto, chamberlain from 1295 to
1300, and Theoderic's successor, John of Anagni. Since Theoderic was
one of Boniface's most trusted advisers and was raised to the cardinalate
in 1298 there is nothing surprising in the supervisory rôle allotted to
him over the administration of the State. This development filled a gap
in what was otherwise a dangerously decentralized structure, for it was
impossible for the pope himself to maintain personal control over the
routine government of his provinces.

One letter to the vicar of the Patrimony,[5] characteristic of many

---

[1] *Reg. B. VIII*, nn. 735–7, 740, 836–42, 1569–70: Ghirardacci (*Bologna*, p. 332) makes the
rather unlikely statement that Richard of Ferentino was originally an emissary of Celestine
V.

[2] Iesi, AC, perg., n. 146 (17 Nov. 1296: summary in Santoni, 'Camerino', p. 57). Roger
was to use temporal and spiritual penalties, if necessary, to persuade the refractory to
agree to satisfactory financial terms. When such terms had been settled he was to grant
absolution.

[3] See above, pp. 120 ff. and, for a fuller treatment of this topic, my paper in *J Eccl H*,
VIII, 141–52.

[4] Examples of his intervention are mentioned in *Reg. B. VIII*, n. 2148 (he sentences
Spoleto to a fine of 14,000 marks); Zonghi, *Fabriano*, d. CCLIV; Todi, AC, perg. n. 117;
Ascoli P., AC, Quinternone, f. 170; Imola, AC, Mazzo IV, n. 92, letter 70 (for the last
two references see above, p. 121).

[5] Richard of Bury, *Liber Epistolaris*, p. 205 (letter 55: the name of the writer is omitted
but by the nature of the instructions given it can only have been Theoderic). See *ibid.*,
p. 191 (letter 2) for a reference to another letter from Theoderic to the same vicar. It may
be suggested that Theoderic's position was connected with the large number of provinces
under vicarial control. For similar letters see his register in *J Eccl H*, VIII (letters 5, 7, 11,
17, 19, 26, 28).

written by Theoderic to provincial rectors and vicars very much as to subordinates, must suffice to indicate the nature of his control. In it he complains that provincial officials have arrested representatives of the small town of S. Gemini 'for light and almost frivolous reasons', alleging statutes in derogation of the Church's rights or of ecclesiastical liberty: these men are to be released unless there is particularly good reason for holding them. In 1300 Theoderic became rector of the Tuscan Patrimony and was succeeded as chamberlain by John of Anagni, but it is not certain that John continued to exercise the same very full powers of superintendence over temporal administration.[1]

The names of Pope Boniface's provincial rectors are of great interest for the study of his family policy and temporal alliances, but of much less significance for the nature of his government in the State, since they were normally nominal appointments, the work being performed by vicars. All the provinces except Romagna came at some time under the titular rule of his nephews or great-nephews, and the Tuscan Patrimony was successively under Peter, Roffred, and Benedict Caetani. Peter was at another time rector of the March, Roffred of the Campagna-Marittima, and Benedict of the Duchy, while James Caetani — the only other recorded nephew of Boniface who was not a cleric — acted as rector of the Sabina. The rectorship of Rostand de Ganteaulme in the Campagna-Marittima in 1297 reflects the pope's Angevin alliance during the war of the Vespers, just as Corso Donati's appointment as rector of Massa Trabaria in 1300 arose from the alliance with the Florentine Blacks.[2] Boniface's dependence on the Orsini family shows in the rectorships of Orso in the Patrimony, Bertold in the Duchy, and Cardinal Napoleon in both Duchy and March. Lastly, Charles of Valois' adoption in 1301 in a sort of neo-Angevin rôle as a temporal ally led to his nomination as rector of Romagna, the March, the Duchy and Massa Trabaria, as well as captain-general throughout the Papal State.[3]

Though Orso Orsini, Cardinal Napoleon, and Rostand de Ganteaulme performed their duties in person, and Bertold Orsini may have

---

[1] Evidence on this point is defective. Examples of John's intervention in the State are to be found in Orvieto, Sottosez AS, Rif. 1301, f. 49v (orders Orvieto to be absolved from interdict); Pinzi, *Viterbo*, III, 49–50 (orders investigation into heresy at Viterbo); G. Baldassini, *Iesi*, pp. 85–7 and Fabriano, AC, perg. nn. 380–1 (arbitrates in dispute between these two communes).

[2] App. II and *Reg. B. VIII*, n. 3480. Rostand later became senator of Rome (Dupré-Theseider, p. 357).

[3] Charles, whose main mission was to fight the Aragonese in Sicily, received authority to appoint vicars in the rectorships: *v. Reg. B. VIII*, nn. 4392, 4394, 4398–9.

done so for a time, Charles of Valois and the papal nephews were no more than figureheads who held the title of rector and presumably derived from it some salary or revenues.[1] Thus several provinces were normally ruled by vicars, and this depression of the status of his officials fitted well into Boniface's centralizing policy. It had disadvantages, among them the degree of pressure exercised on the vicars by men who ranked above them in position and power. Amatus of Anagni, vicar in the Tuscan Patrimony, received a constant flow of letters from papal relatives, cardinals and members of the pro-papal Roman baronage asking mercy or favours for communes and individuals with which they were connected.[2] Moreover the nominal rector himself retained the power to intervene and such intervention might conflict with the policy being followed by his vicar. Thus in 1301–2 Charles of Valois and his vicar, the bishop of Rieti, were directly opposed in their attitudes to Mainardo da Susinana and the rebellious towns of Romagna. Mainardo and representatives of the towns made contact with Charles at Florence and persuaded him to annul their sentences, after the bishop had failed to do so on Charles' orders. The consequence was that the vicar had to be replaced, though he had certainly been in a better position to judge the situation in Romagna.[3] The arrangement whereby a vicar could clash with and be over-ruled by an absentee rector was most unsatisfactory. How one such rector regarded his office we can learn from the conduct of Peter Caetani, who took to his bed in indignation on hearing that the Ghibellines' capture of Gubbio had led to his replacement as rector by an active legate, Cardinal Napoleon Orsini.[4] But the most serious aspect of such appointments was the attitude that they implied. Boniface VIII considered the government of the Papal State a matter of the highest importance, worthy of much of his own time and energy, yet the assignment of rectorial titles without corresponding duties to papal relatives and temporal allies must have served to suggest that such offices deserved to rank only as honorific sinecures. This evil example was soon to be followed and surpassed by Clement V.

---

[1] Charles of Valois was permitted to retain the revenues of the March (*QFIA*, XX, 189–90) and it seems unlikely that Boniface granted his nephews titles without financial benefits.

[2] Of the 55 letters to Amatus contained in Richard of Bury's *Liber Epistolaris* (pp. 191–205), thirteen are of this description. Ten of these are from eight different cardinals and others from James Caetani, Peter Savelli and Matthew 'Rosso' Orsini.

[3] RIS, N.S., XXVIII, III, 185–7; Ghirardacci, *Bologna*, p. 439. Charles had passed through Bologna on his way to Tuscany (J. Petit, *Charles de Valois*, p. 63) but can have had no opportunity to study the involved situation in Romagna.

[4] Finke, *Acta Aragonensia*, I, 85–6.

The Roman and Campagnol basis of Boniface's Papal State policy also requires emphasis. Early in his pontificate he received the now conventional power, for life, of appointing senators. Those whom he appointed normally came from a few leading families whom he made his allies, the Savelli, Annibaldi and Orsini: in the later part of the pontificate this last family was able to assume a preponderant position in Rome.[1] His tactics were to keep the baronial houses divided and to maintain good relations with the city by supporting its expansionist aims. The conquest of Toscanella in 1300 appears to have evoked no papal protest, though the town had made Boniface *podestà* for life, presumably in the hope of winning his protection. The clergy of Tivoli even received exemption from the terms of *Clericis laicos* to enable them to pay their share of the town's dues to the Romans.[2] The pope's officials also actively assisted Rome's in making compulsory purchases of grain in the neighbouring provinces, a matter in which the city's interests coincided with the Curia's.[3] The Jubilee of 1300 must have brought much wealth to the Romans and it is no surprise to find Boniface at that time intervening in legal decisions and firmly in control of the city.

Through their involvement with his family territorial policy the towns and people of the Campagna were also of great importance to Boniface. Handsome privileges went to Anagni and Velletri, and men from these and neighbouring towns received grants of papal fiefs and held manifold offices in the Papal State, as chamberlain and *missi*, as provincial rectors, vicars and treasurers, as *podestà* and castellans.[4]

*   *   *

Before judging Boniface's achievement as ruler of the Papal State a narrative account of its history during his pontificate must be attempted. In the anarchic and ill-ruled Romagna the war between Bologna and the league of Ghibelline tyrants continued unabated until 1297.[5] During

---

[1] *Reg. B. VIII*, nn. 2334, 5545–6; Campanari, *Toscanella*, II, 189; and discussion in Dupré-Theseider, p. 356 and Boase, p. 288, of Boniface's ill-documented relations with Rome. Rostand de Ganteaulme's senatorship was an Angevin interlude and Charles of Valois was at one time intended to assume this office. A saying attributed to Boniface at his posthumous trial was: 'Unless there is discord between the *magnates* of Rome, the pope cannot be a real pope or dominate the city and the lands of the Church' (Dupuy, p. 344).

[2] *Reg. B. VIII*, n. 3248. An attack on Tolfa in 1301 (Theiner, d. DLVI) is further evidence of Roman expansionism at this time.

[3] *J Eccl H*, VIII, 147–8: above, p. 234 (clause in *Licet merum*).

[4] Some examples: *Reg. B. VIII*, nn. 403, 1383–6, 2844–7 (privileges); nn. 5413, 5425, 5446–7, 5482 (fiefs); n. 5543 (cast llanship). See also App. II.

[5] A provincial constitution promulgated in parliament at Imola on 27 February 1295 by the rector Robert de Cornay and the vicar-general *in spiritualibus* throws a vivid light on the chaotic administration of Romagna at this time. The preamble describes the loss 'propter guerrarum discrimina et turbationes status provintie Romaniole' of certain 'libros

the summer of 1295 the archbishop of Monreale (Cornay's successor as rector) and Richard of Ferentino came to terms with the rebels, but Boniface was suspicious of what appeared to be a capitulation.[1] In September he dismissed the archbishop, appointing in his place the rector of the March, William Durand, who had already served in Romagna under Martin IV and Honorius IV. Durand reached his new province in October, bringing with him mercenaries from the March, and he soon reported unfavourably on the pacificatory moves of his predecessors, most of which were now annulled.[2] Though he held a parliament at Cesena, he met with general defiance and was even compelled to avoid the main roads when moving between towns. When he attempted to cite representatives of Faenza to his court at Rimini, Faenza (again under Mainardo) protested that it dared not send men to a town ruled by its deadly enemies, the Malatesta; the rector's safe-conduct was useless for 'even if he wished he could not protect them against the great force and power' of the Malatesta, with whom the rector had 'notoriously and manifestly allied himself'.[3] In January 1296 Boniface sought a new approach by calling representatives of the communes to the papal Curia, apparently ineffectively, and a little later the bishop of

rationum . . . libros processuum, condemnationum et bannorum ad . . . Romanam Ecclesiam spectantium' (*sic*: ? for 'spectantes'). The two rectors therefore decree 'quod nulla persona ecclesiastica vel secularis . . . audeat vel presumat scripturas predictas vel libros sive ratione officii quod alias gessit seu alia quacunque de causa dicte scripture vel libri ad ipsos quoquo modo pervenerint vel illos qui eos habent vel sciverint tenere vel occulte per se vel alium. Immo ipsas scripturas vel libros infra quindecim dies postquam huiusmodi nostra constitutio ad notitiam eorum pervenerit, sive autentica sint sive non, assignare et tradere teneantur Thesaurario in dicta provincia pro Romana Ecclesia commoranti vel officialibus Ecclesie. Denuntiatione pena contrafacientibus imminere (*sic*). Si clericus fuerit cuicunque gradus ordinis et conditionis existeat excommunicationis et suspensionis dignitatis quam haberet. Si laycus excommunicationis necnon quingentarum marcharum argenti, penis imminentibus eisdem quas ex nunc ipsos et ipsorum quemlibet prout ad cuiusque nostrum spectat officium determinamus incurrere ipso facto. Adiicentes constitutioni predicte quod si processus aliquis quocunque nomine censeatur factus vel promulgatus temporibus retrohactis per quoscumque offitiales Romane Ecclesie in dicta provintia, tam contra communia quam singulares personas ipsius provintie vel alterum ipsorum, non cancellatus apparuerit in futurum qui cancellari debuerint propter compositiones et pacta inter nos nomine Romane Ecclesie et communia et singulares personas dicte provintie seu alterum ipsorum factas quantum ad unumquemque in compositionibus predictis comprehensum tangeret, ex nunc eos cassamus et annullamus et iuribus carere determinamus' (Imola, AC, Mazzo V, n. 61: hitherto unpublished).

[1] The main chronicle sources for the history of Romagna in these years are RIS, O.S., XIV, cc. 1111–16 and RIS, N.S., XXII, II, 55–6 and XXVIII, II, 77–8. *V.* also RIS, N.S., XXVIII, III, clix and 218–23; Fantuzzi, *Mon. Rav.*, III, nn. LXXXXIII (dated '1294' for '1295'), LXXXXV, LXXXXVIII, IC.

[2] Durand's report can be inferred from the mission of the bishop of Pavia. For his mercenaries *v.* Colucci, *Ant. Pic.*, XXIII, 252–3: *v.* also Franceschini in *Studi Romagnoli*, V, 320.

[3] For the many attempts to cite Faenza and her allies between December 1295 and November 1296 *v.* Tonduzzi, *Faenza*, pp. 341–6, 350–2 and Tonini, *Rimini*, III, d. CLXVII.

Pavia set out on his mission to investigate the work of Richard of
Ferentino and the archbishop of Monreale, who were presumably suspected of having taken bribes from the rebels.[1] A great 'Ghibelline'
coalition captured Imola from the Bolognese in April, at about the
time when Boniface was writing gloomily to his legates in France of the
state of the lands of the Church, 'full of discord, exposed to the blasts
of war and in parts to grave devastation'.[2] As well as Bologna, Durand
had some support from Rimini (where the Malatesta had now secured
a firm *signoria*)[3] and Ravenna. That autumn, however, the elderly rector
had to be relieved and he died at Rome on 1 November. His successor,
Maximus of Piperno, resided for three weeks at Faenza, but then had to
leave suddenly 'without greeting his host, and saying that he was going
hunting'. Later in the year he held a well-attended parliament at
Ravenna; even Mainardo made an appearance.[4] Bologna was now
engaged in a conflict on two fronts, since the Estensi had attacked it
from the north; in consequence it began to play a smaller part in
Romagna.[5] The war was less fierce in 1297 and that October the two
sides at last accepted papal arbitration.[6] Throughout the struggle the
provincial rectors had been the dependents rather than the allies of the
'Guelf' party: still less had they been rulers.

Meanwhile things had gone less badly for the pope in the other provinces. In the March local warfare was plentiful as ever; in 1295–6
Senigallia was at war with Fossombrone, Cagli with Gubbio, Montecchio with Cingoli, and Pesaro with Conrad of Montefeltro, while
Fermo, Iesi, Recanati and a number of other towns had been condemned for defying papal authority.[7] Yet some progress was made
against lawlessness here. Ancona, Fermo, Iesi, Recanati and some smaller
communes came to terms and were absolved from interdict in the
spring of 1295, though their payments were slow and incomplete.[8]

To move south was to enter less disturbed territory, though even
here Perugia only determined to defer to the rector of the Duchy in a
dispute over S. Ercolano and Torgiano because 'he is a special friend of

[1] See above, pp. 236–7.   [2] *Reg. B. VIII*, n. 1585.
[3] Jones, 'The Malatesta', pp. 99–104.   [4] Ghirardacci, *Bologna*, p. 339.
[5] On this war *v*. Gorreta, *La Lotta fra il comune bolognese e la signoria estense*. On the
negotiations of Cardinal Peter of Piperno with Bologna, RIS, O.S., XIV, c. 1115 and
N.S., XVIII, I, 248–9. This cardinal was half-brother of the rector Maximus (Boase, p. 87).
[6] *Reg. B. VIII*, n. 3299.
[7] *Ibid*., nn. 524, 736–7, 896, 946–7, 1064; Colucci, *Treia*, d. LIV; De Minicis, *Fermo*,
pp. 514, 518; Iesi, AC, perg. n. 152.
[8] *Reg. B. VIII*, nn. 2399, 5409–12, 5486–7, 5501–2; Iesi, AC, perg. n. 146. Another sign
of increasing control was the dislodgment of Iesi from Staffolo (*v*. documents printed by
Gianandrea in *Arch. Stor. per le Marche e per l'Umbria*, III, 291–5).

the commune of Perugia'.[1] But Perugia and Todi were at last pardoned for the wars they had fought against Foligno in the 1280s and early 1290s, and Todi, the home of Boniface's youth, received the long sought exemption from the authority of the Tuscan Patrimony.[2] Meanwhile Orvieto had become a papal ally on receiving the Val del Lago in return for the Aldobrandeschine *contado*, in accordance with the agreement made with Boniface before his pontificate.[3]

In May 1297 Pope Boniface's dealings with the Papal State were revolutionized by the outbreak of the war against the Colonna. The origins of this quarrel are linked with the pope's acquisitions of territory for his family, and this is not the place for a full treatment of his territorial policy or of the Colonna war; besides, they have been well described elsewhere.[4] The story begins with the Caetani's first attempts, in the 1280s, to build up a landed base for their power in an area in which greater feudal families, in particular the Colonna,[5] were already securely entrenched. After Roffred Caetani, the brother of the future pope, had secured the county of Caserta in the Regno, the aim of the family was to acquire estates along the Via Appia and Via Latina, the main roads linking the western Regno with Rome. When Boniface became pope he had already purchased Calvi, Selvamolle and Norma and soon Count Roffred's son Peter acquired Torre, overlooking the route which joined the Via Latina to the more easterly Via Tiburtino-Valeria. After this Peter secured Sermoneta, Bassiano and S. Donato, all previously possessions of the Annibaldi. His next aim was known to be Ninfa, which was the property of Cardinal Peter Colonna. At this stage, on 2 May 1297, Stephen, the man of action among the Colonna, set an ambush near the tomb of Cecilia Metella on the Via Appia and was able to capture much of the purchase-money for Sermoneta.

The war that followed was the result of a rivalry that extended back over some time, although the Colonna cardinals had apparently voted for Boniface in 1294. The campaigns lasted three years, but were brief and localised. In consequence they had little direct influence on the condition of the State. Nepi, the main property of the Colonna to the north

---

[1] Perugia, AS, Rif. X, ff. 291, 296v–297.

[2] *Reg. B. VIII*, nn. 831, 835, 1123. The pope settled internal disputes at Todi in 1296–7 by personal arbitration (*Reg.*, n. 1589: Todi, AC, perg. n. 130).

[3] *TRHS*, 4th s., XXXII, 121–32: see above, p. 225.

[4] See in particular, G. Caetani, *Domus Caietana* and *Regesta Chartarum*; Falco, 'Sulla formazione e la costituzione della signoria dei Caetani', *Rivista Stor. Italiana*, N.S., VI, 225–78; Boase, esp. pp. 159–85; and Marchetti-Longhi, 'La carta feudale del Lazio', *QFIA*, XXXVI, 324–7 and map.

[5] For the Colonna lands *v.* above, pp. 213–14.

of Rome, fell to papal forces in 1297. The following summer fighting centred around the strongholds of Ninfa, Colonna, Palestrina and Zagarolo, of which the last alone held out after the general submission of September 1298. In June 1299 John of Ceccano, the would-be *signore* of Terracina and the Colonna's only powerful baronial supporter, was captured after a short final campaign.

This war rendered great returns in the form of confiscated estates, most of which went to repay supporters. In particular they were used to secure the benevolence of the Orsini,[1] for a coalition of Colonna and Orsini might well have overturned the upstart Caetani. There were pickings too for the Annibaldi and for Spoleto, as well as for relatives of Cardinal Theoderic, who became the first cardinal-bishop of Città Papale, the new town which was to supersede destroyed Palestrina.[2] The Caetani themselves were careful not to take over confiscated land. A little later, however, Peter purchased from its inhabitants the former Colonna stronghold of Ninfa and the acquisition of Sgurgola ('donated' by Adinulf of Supino), Collemezzo and Carpineto, together with Trevi, Filettino and Vallepietra on the Via Tiburtino-Valeria, gave him an immensely powerful situation, which he was able to fortify still further in the first years of the new century.[3]

The aid furnished by the Papal State to Boniface during the Colonna war is impressive. Many towns in the Patrimony, Duchy and March sent troops in 1297 and probably again in 1298.[4] Their support was given at a certain cost, for several communes received privileges granting them judicial exemptions as a reward, but we have seen that these charters sometimes had an additional purchase price.[5] Such grants indicate the impact on the State of the Colonna war, but to part with rights that could not normally be enforced was entirely in keeping with the main tendencies of Boniface's policy. That the war in some ways served to tighten rather than weaken the pope's hold over the State is suggested by the extremely handsome profit declared by the bishop of Siena after his rectorship of the Tuscan Patrimony in 1298-9, while

---

[1] *Reg. B. VIII*, nn. 2264, 3911–15, 4747, 4911.

[2] *Ibid.*, nn. 2561 and 5517–18 (Spoleto: the lords of nearby Arrone were condemned as supporters of the Colonna); 5490 (Richard Annibaldi); 5510–1 (Cardinal Theoderic's nephew).

[3] *Regesta Chartarum*, I, 115, 144–5, 163, 165, 177 ff.: *v.* also Falco, *art. cit.*, 252 ff. For later purchases *v.* below, p. 246.

[4] Orvieto, Todi, Perugia, Ascoli and Matelica sent troops in 1297; so probably did many other towns (RIS, N.S., XV, V, 170; *Cronaca Todina*, 94–5; Perugia, AS, Rif. X, ff. 295v–324v; Mazzatinti, 2nd s., II, 259 and III, 84). For 1298 *v. Reg. B. VIII*, n. 5499 and Mazzatinti, IV, 173.

[5] Above, pp. 231 ff.

only two months later some nobles of Alatri and Bauco in the Campagna paid the enormous sum of 11,900 florins as a fine for having disturbed the peace.[1] Even in Romagna the long war, continued throughout 1298, came to a temporary end in the spring of 1299, when peace terms were agreed between Bologna and the league through the arbitration of Florence and the prior of the Dominican house at Faenza. That summer 'all the merchants of Bologna were able to go to these towns and return in safety with their wares'.[2]

Boniface was unable to maintain his successes in the State in the new century. The first crisis was a *coup* by the Romagnol Ghibellines in the Duchy, the capture of Gubbio in May 1300. Uguccione della Faggiuola became *signore* of this defiant community, a menacing extension of Ghibellinism to the south which so disturbed the pope that he at once despatched Cardinal Napoleon Orsini as legate and rector in the Duchy and March, with the special task of reducing Gubbio.[3] Before the end of June the cardinal had achieved this with the support of the Perugians, old opponents of Gubbio who doubtless hoped to benefit from their share in the town's recapture. When disappointed in this expectation, Perugia refused to receive the legate and he was compelled to find a different headquarters, at Spoleto, whose hospitality now justified the privilege of 1295 and subsequent grants of confiscated land.[4] Orsini set to work strenuously in 1300–1, particularly in the March, promulgating constitutions, granting privileges, pacifying quarrels, hearing lawsuits and attempting to check the expansionism of Fermo.[5] In September 1301, however, a new vicar in the March had to issue a

[1] *Reg. B. VIII*, nn. 3192, 3408, 5541, 5549: for a discussion of the declared profit, which cannot be accepted literally, *v.* below, p. 270. For possibly adverse influence of the Colonna war on papal rule in the Patrimony one may note the story that Corneto could not be punished for attacking its castellan and killing two of his men because it might, if alienated, have supported the Colonna. The source, however, is a late one (*ASRSP*, XVIII, 460: *c.* 1320).

[2] RIS, O.S., XIV, cc. 1116–18; N.S., XXVIII, II, 89–92; Clementini, *Rimini*, I, 519; Villani, VIII, ch. 28. The Romagnol Ghibellines played a part in the final stages of the war against the Colonna, capturing their fortress at Montevecchio.

[3] The main sources for this episode are RIS, O.S., XIV, cc. 1120–1 (*Ann. Caes.*) and N.S., XXVI, II, 19 (*Fragm. Fulg. Hist.*); *Reg. B. VIII*, nn. 3886–91; Finke, *Acta Aragonensia*, I, 85–6. *V.* also Willemsen, *Kard. N. Orsini*, pp. 8–10, though this biography ignores the cardinal's activities in the March.

[4] Spoleto had to be absolved from an interdict which had been incurred over a territorial dispute. *V. Reg. B. VIII*, nn. 3727, 3729–31, 3904, 3958.

[5] Four of Cardinal Orsini's statutes survive in Albornoz, *Constitutions* (pp. 53, 71, 75–6, 94): these respectively threaten towns illegally electing their own officials; regulate which papal judges may hear appeals; define the legal immunities of provincial *curiales*; and provide that the *advocati fisci* must act for the poor without payment. For privileges (to Macerata and Civitanova) and the dispute between Osimo and Recanati, *v.* Compagnoni, *Regg. Pic.*, pp. 157–8; Leopardi, *Recanati*, II, 380; Colucci, *Ant. Pic.*, XXIV, 65–7. For judicial activity, Iesi, AC, perg., nn. 172–3, 185.

special statute threatening fines up to 10,000 marks for rebels; Fermo, Ascoli, Camerino, Recanati, Osimo, Cagli, Iesi, Fano and Ancona — the chief communes of the province — were all named as cities 'threatening commotion'.[1]

At about the same time Boniface's schemes for securing a Caetani zone of influence to the north of Rome led to the outbreak of serious trouble in the Tuscan Patrimony. In September 1296 Roffred Caetani, already rector of the Patrimony, had married Countess Margherita degli Aldobrandeschi and come into possession of her lands, which were the pope's share of the bargain whereby Bolsena, Acquapendente and the Val del Lago had been ceded to Orvieto.[2] Two years later this marriage was dissolved on the grounds that a previous husband of the countess was still alive and the county was placed under the custody of Cardinal Theoderic. Margherita, however, turned for support to her cousin, Count Guy of S. Fiora, and defied the pope's attempt to deprive her of her land. In October 1300 control of the Patrimony and leadership in this war were granted to Orso and Gentile Orsini, whose family had a claim to inherit from the countess.[3] As in Campagna, however, the Caetani and not the Orsini were intended to be the principal legatees. In March 1303 Boniface declared the countess' lands confiscated and granted them to Roffred's younger brother Benedict, who now in his turn became rector of the Patrimony.

Count Roffred, after the dissolution of his marriage to Margherita, was at once betrothed to the heiress to the county of Fondi on the border of the Regno and was thus brought into the pope's schemes for extending the Caetani lands in the south. Here his father, Peter, acquired in 1301 the coastal sites of Astura from the Frangipani and Rocca Circea and S. Felice from the Annibaldi.[4] With the papal fortresses of Fumone, Serrone, Lariano and Castro dei Volsci, the Caetani now had strongholds on all the three main routes and on the subsidiary roads joining them. With the chief branches of the Colonna eliminated and the provincial administration of Campagna-Marittima entirely in their hands,[5]

---

[1] *V.* document published by Ermini in *RSDI*, V, 180–4. For the continued defiance of Fermo *v.* De Minicis, pp. 552–6 and *AMSM*, 3rd s., I (1916), 248–9.

[2] For this affair *v.* *TRHS*, 4th s., XXXII (1950), 121–39, esp. 130–7.

[3] The countess had married Orsello Orsini and her daughter by yet another marriage was the wife of Gentile's son Romano.

[4] *Regesta Chartarum*, I, 226 ff.: *v.* Digard, *Philippe le Bel et le Saint-Siège*, II, 147–51 and Falco, *art. cit.*, 271.

[5] Clear evidence of this is provided by some letters of Peter Caetani (father of the provincial rector) to the vicar of Campagna-Marittima. These show the Caetani using the provincial court to force two brothers to yield their rights at Sgurgola (Feb.–Apr. 1300: *Regesta Chartarum*, I, 179, 181–2, 185–202, 204–5; *v.* also Falco, *art. cit.*, 263–9).

they may have felt invulnerable. But to expand, especially in feudal territory, is to make enemies. When Nogaret came to Italy in 1303 on behalf of Philip IV to convoke Boniface before a General Council he was already co-operating with the dispossessed Colonna, and he soon made other allies, who were to play the major part in the subsequent 'outrage'.[1] Nogaret and the Colonna rode into Anagni on 7 September 1303 accompanied by a large contingent led by Rainald of Supino, captain of Ferentino, whose sister had been divorced by Francis Caetani, Peter's brother, in order that he might take up a cardinalate. Other members of the conspiracy were the sons of John of Ceccano, who had lost his lands and liberty fighting in alliance with the Colonna in 1297–1299,[2] and Nicholas and Adenulf dei Conti, members of a branch of the pope's own family which had lost Sgurgola to Peter Caetani. For two days the pope and his nephews were in the power of the Colonna. The Campagnol enemies of the Caetani had taken the initiative from the hands of Nogaret, but on 9 September, after much hesitation, the people of Anagni rose in arms and drove the conspirators from the town with heavy losses. A week later the shattered old man returned to Rome, to spend the last month of his pontificate under the protection of the citizens and his Orsini allies.

The war for the Aldobrandeschine county, then the outrage of Anagni and Orvieto's consequent assault in the Patrimony,[3] all suggest that Boniface's family policy weakened papal control in central Italy during the last years of the pontificate. Moreover Romagna returned to its normal warlike condition.[4] The old alliances there were re-formed and for a time the Ghibellines extended their sphere of influence into the Duchy. Cardinal Matthew of Acquasparta, legate and rector in 1300–1, worked hard but unsuccessfully for a general pacification. He was followed in this task by the bishop of Sabina and a friar, Ranier of Bologna, but 1302 found the authorities in two minds, with Charles of Valois issuing pardons while the bishop of Rieti, rector *in spiritualibus*,

---

[1] For the 'outrage of Anagni' *v.* Boase, pp. 344–50 and Fawtier in *MAH*, LX, 153–79 (too exculpatory of Nogaret: for a criticism *v.* M. Melville in *Revue d'Histoire de l'Église de France*, XXXVI, 56–66). It may be noted in passing that the constitution for the March *Celestis patrisfamilias* (*sup.*, pp. 234 ff.) had been promulgated just one day before the attack.

[2] See above, pp. 233 n. and 244: also *Reg. B. VIII*, nn. 3417, 3898, 5226. Peter Caetani was married to a member of this family and was perhaps intended by the pope to inherit most of John of Ceccano's lands, though some had been granted to Richard Annibaldi.

[3] On hearing a report of the pope's capture, Orvieto attacked and overran Countess Margherita's lands: this was at a time when Boniface was Orvieto's titular Capitano del Popolo (*v.* Waley, *Orvieto*, pp. 74–5).

[4] For Romagna in 1300–3 *v.* esp. RIS, O.S., XIV, cc. 1120–4; N.S., XXII, II, 58–9; N.S., XXVIII, II, 94: also Theiner, d. DLI; *Reg. B. VIII*, nn. 4663–4, 4668–9, 5001, 5206–8, 5374.

refused them.[1] This rector was then dismissed by the pope, presumably for insubordination. The death without heirs of Mainardo — still lord of Faenza and Imola — occurred in the same year but brought no relief, and the submission of Uguccione della Faggiuola was short-lived and probably insincere. Schemes for a general peace came to nothing and a papal letter of July 1303 describes a situation which had now become normal; Cesena, Forlì, Faenza and Imola are 'rebels', and there is danger of Bologna joining them.[2] A new rector, the bishop of Vicenza, attacked Forlì, but was repulsed by the Ordelaffi and wounded, perhaps fatally.[3]

Boniface's temporal position had certainly deteriorated since 1299, but the Aldobrandeschine war, like the Colonna war of 1297–9, was local in its effects, and the outrage of Anagni, for all its dramatic nature and its close connection with the pope's territorial policy, seems to have had no immediate effect on the Papal State except in unleashing the attack of Orvieto. The enemy was repulsed, many felt indignant who had little sympathy for Boniface otherwise,[4] and at the time the pope lost no possessions except the lands of Countess Margherita. His death only a month later came before the fuller effects of the episode could be felt. There was no general collapse of authority in the Papal State and the Duchy and March were unaffected by disturbances in the other provinces.

Haller acclaimed Boniface as one who strengthened papal rule and 'possessed more power in the provinces of his State than any pope since Innocent III'. Professor Mollat, on the other hand, holds that papal authority in central Italy had become so feeble by the early years of the fourteenth century that 'the insecurity of Italy' explains and justifies the long residence of the papacy at Avignon.[5] The latter opinion postulates a decline which is in contradiction with the evidence: it is not convincing. Boniface sketched out a policy of compromise with the communes, in particular with certain strategically placed towns, and he probably regarded the rewards of such a policy as satisfactory.[6] In

---

[1] RIS., N.S. XXVIII, III, 185–7: see also above, p. 238.

[2] In 1303 the league continued to hold formal parliaments, which were attended by Bolognese delegates (Ghirardacci, *Bologna*, pp. 451, 453).

[3] The mortal wounding of the rector is described by *Ann. Caes.* (RIS, O.S., XIV, c. 1123) and there attributed to 1 September 1302. It is confirmed by Ghirardacci (p. 445). Yet this rector was still in office in December, 1303 (*v.* App. II). The date is clearly wrong: possibly the Cesena annals of this period are misdated and require to be put forward one year (their chronology presents other difficulties at this time). The story of the rector's death is perhaps 'greatly exaggerated'.

[4] *Purgatorio*, XX, ll. 86–7.

[5] Haller, *Papsttum*, V, 101–2; Mollat, *Les Papes d'Avignon* (ed. 9), p. 22 (*v.* also p. 540).

[6] For example when Spoleto gave hospitality to Cardinal Orsini in 1300 (*v. sup.*, p. 245).

circumstances where there were no means for setting up really strong government he had probably done as well as was possible. The fundamental problem was the strong town or baron facing a rector with little money and virtually no soldiers in territory which had no tradition of abiding by the law. We see such a situation in the Duchy of 1300 when Perugia first joined the rector in fighting Gubbio, then turned on him and refused him entry.[1] In the March, moreover, there was still the legacy of the Hohenstaufen occupations. As late as 1296 the pope was claiming papal fortresses taken by Camerino in Manfred's day and never relinquished, and Numana was still demanding money due from Recanati since the same period through the loss of its bishopric.[2] Even the attempt to secure appellate jurisdiction for the provincial court was bound to meet powerful opposition. Fabriano in the early years of the fourteenth century followed a stubborn policy of forbidding appeals to the rector's court, sometimes by exacting pledges, and of systematically ignoring the court and its decisions. Notaries were ordered not to record appeals and witnesses not to appear. Citizens who nevertheless attempted to have recourse to it were fined.[3]

Yet this was not a period of deterioration. The ill-effects of the Caetani's family feuds, though potentially dangerous, were only local. The situation in October 1303 was not unlike that at the end of Nicholas III's pontificate. Some sort of solution had been found to the problems arising from the time of Orsini lordship and the same might be achieved after that of the Caetani.

The nine months of Benedict XI's reign (October 1303 to July 1304) are a strange postlude to the pontificate of Boniface, during which a harassed pope made no clear choice between defending and disowning the policy and memory of his predecessor. The Colonna were restored in part, yet the Caetani lost none of their possessions. Meanwhile the case against the French was taken up, but tepidly. The Caetani and Colonna had not yet begun their armed struggle in the Campagna,[4] and for the time the consequences of Boniface's actions were implicit in the situation rather than actively effective.

---

[1] Above, p. 245. Equally typical of the communes' attitude to rectorial authority is another contemporary episode: S. Ginesio pleaded that its atack on Fermo had the approval of the rector, Fermo then being in rebellion, and that in any case the question was no longer outstanding since it had paid a fine of 30 florins (*Reg. B. VIII*, n. 5279; Colucci, *Ant. Pic.*, XIX, d. XLVI). The rector then attempted to levy a fine of 42,000 florins (*Ant. Pic.*, XXIV, 68–9).

[2] *Reg. B. VIII*, nn. 896, 1064: for the question of the bishopric see above, p. 171.

[3] Fabriano, AC, perg. of 6 June 1300 and 4 September 1303 (n. 362).

[4] On which *v.* Falco in *ASRSP*, XLIX, 132–48.

Hence the pope's indecisiveness had no serious consequences in the Papal State.

Benedict was Nicholas Boccasini, a north Italian, from Treviso. His local loyalties show strongly in his choice of provincial rectors, for his advent brought about a clean sweep of officials. Soon Romagna was under a Brescian, Tebaldo Brusciati (a former *podestà* of Treviso),[1] the March under Rambaldo of Collalto, count of Treviso, the Duchy under a Bolognese, the Patrimony under a Venetian, and a Parmesan ruled the Campagna-Marittima. Benedict himself wintered in Rome, where the Orsini now shared the senatorship with the Savelli, but moved north to Umbria in the spring.[2]

The one important action taken by Benedict in the Papal State was the abrogation, in January 1304, of Boniface's constitution for the March, *Celestis patrisfamilias*.[3] Later he hoped to provide new statutes for the province; meanwhile *Celestis patrisfamilias* was suspended, since its terms were *valde ardua* and it had been promulgated without the consent of the cardinals. There is something unconvincing about giving two reasons for the revocation when each should have been strong enough on its own. The constitution was essentially a check upon the powers of the provincial authorities and its abrogation had probably been urged by those who opposed limitations on the rectors' freedom of action. The promised new statutes for the March were not forthcoming in Pope Benedict's time.

In the Duchy also Benedict set out to disavow some of the work of his predecessor. Here he revoked grants of certain revenues made by Boniface to several towns and ended Nocera's right of exemption from the rector's jurisdiction. This looks like an abandonment of the policy of reaching reasonable compromises with the towns, but it would be misleading to deduce a 'policy' for a vacillating man from such thin evidence.[4]

The situation within the Papal State as a whole in Benedict's time bore a strong resemblance to that prevailing before the outrage of Anagni. There was no rector who had not his troubles. In Romagna Bologna and Forlì were defiant. Forlì had as its principal opponent the Malatesta, who were themselves involved in warfare with the chief

---

[1] *V.* Dupré-Theseider, p. 378.   [2] Gregorovius, V, 2, 602.

[3] *Reg. B. XI*, n. 1147. For the constitution, *supra*, pp. 234 ff. For discussion of this abrogation as a precedent in canon law *v.* Tierney, *Foundations of the Conciliar Theory*, p. 187.

[4] *Reg. B. XI*, n. 1206. The towns whose grants were revoked were Assisi, Foligno and Bettona. That Benedict intended no radical change in policy is suggested by his sale to Matelica of the right to elect its own officials, with certain jurisdictional powers (*Reg.*, n. 592).

towns of the northern March, Fano, Pesaro, Senigallia and Fossombrone.[1] Meanwhile the rector was concerned in a bitter legal struggle with Rimini over the possession of certain places once disputed between that town and the archbishop of Ravenna.[2] In the March Benedict's rector inherited a good deal of trouble from his predecessor, the bishop of Fiesole, who had become involved in a war between Iesi and Fabriano and had levied fines with more enthusiasm than judgement. The lawsuit between the two communes outlasted Benedict's pontificate, but the war was not resumed.[3] The threat of Gerard of Imola, 'count of Nocera', to the independence of Gubbio was the chief disturbance in the Duchy, while further south Viterbo menaced Montefiascone, seat of the Patrimony.[4] The degree of lawlessness suggested by this survey is not at all unusual. On the other hand revenues from the State were very low during Benedict's pontificate and all his provincial rectors had to resort to bankers for loans.[5]

Despite the bitter Romagnol wars of two decades, the Colonna war and the outrage of Anagni, the situation was still fundamentally the same as it had been — except during the periods of Hohenstaufen control in the 1240s and 1260s — throughout the preceding century. Papal officials were everywhere at grips with strong towns and feudatories, subjects who defied them and yet at times had recourse to their justice and yielded them considerable though irregular revenues. There had not been such deterioration in the position of papal authority that this struggle for control could only be conducted from a base outside Italy. The situation in the Papal State was not in itself sufficient to justify Clement V's failure to come south of the Alps. Yet Avignon was not an obviously bad choice as a base for territorial rule: proximity was not a solution to its problems and distance would not necessarily be a disadvantage.

---

[1] *Reg. B. XI*, n. 712; Bonoli, *Forlì*, p. 125; Vernarecci, *Fossombrone*, I, 284; RIS, O.S., XIV, c. 1125: *v.* Jones, 'The Malatesta', pp. 125–6.

[2] For this dispute *v.* De Vergottini in *AMSR*, N.S., V (1953–4), 105–14 (but for the earlier history of this quarrel, not discussed by Prof. De Vergottini, *v.* A. Torre in *Studi Romagnoli*, II, 333–55).

[3] For the fines, *v.* p. 249 n. 1: for the lawsuit, G. Baldassini, *Iesi*, pp. 85–7; Iesi, AC, perg. nn. 198, 202, 206–7; Fabriano, AC, perg. nn. 380–1. For another commune (Montolmo) under condemnation at the same period for failing both to send troops and to attend parliament *v.* Corridonia, AC, perg. n. 48.

[4] Gubbio, Sottosez AS, perg. (20 March 1304), bu. 16; *Reg. B. XI*, n. 1277.

[5] On the revenues *v.* QFIA, XX, 167 and *J Eccl H*, VI, 18–25. For the loans, *Reg. B. XI*, nn. 1238, 1243: the sums involved were not very large (the total was 9,650 florins, of which 6,000 were for the rector of Romagna). During the preceding century the papal registers record no other occasion on which more than one province needed a loan: but loans may have taken place of which no evidence survives.

VIII

The Financial Utility of the Papal State

The purpose of this chapter is to attempt an answer to two questions to which, owing to the paucity of the sources, no satisfactory answers can be given: what financial advantage was derived by the papacy from its territorial possessions in central Italy and what proportion of the pope's total income did they provide?

A short survey of the sources is an essential preliminary. The surviving series of account-books of papal revenue and expenditure relates for the most part to the Avignon period and later.[1] There is however an isolated account-book for the March of Ancona which chronicles the receipts and expenses of that province between 1 May 1279 and 1 March 1280.[2] This volume is of great interest because it is unique, but knowledge of a single province in an isolated period of less than a year cannot safely be used to illustrate the condition of the State as a whole throughout the thirteenth century. There are no other full provincial accounts before those which relate to the Tuscan Patrimony in a period which begins a month after the death of Benedict XI, but there are some summaries of revenue and expenditure for the Tuscan Patrimony in 1290–4 and for the Duchy of Spoleto and Sabina in 1290–1.[3] The general lists of papal receipts and expenses in 1299–1300 and in 1302 also contain a number of items concerning the Papal State.[4] Apart from this there is a list of revenues of the Sabina in 1284–6,[5] and many single items recording receipt of taxes and fines in municipal archives, particularly in the March. Finally, there are lists of revenues due from the State, in the *Liber Censuum*, in the valuable formulary of Rinaldo Malavolti (rector

---

[1] For these see de Loye, *Les Archives de la Chambre Apostolique au XIVe siècle*.

[2] Palmieri (ed.), *Introiti ed Esiti di papa Niccolò III, 1279–80*.

[3] Theiner, pp. 317–21 and Arch. Vat., Arm. XXXV, 14, f. 85 (unpublished fragment for the Patrimony, 1290). For the Patrimony accounts of 1304–6 v. *J Eccl H*, VI, 18–25.

[4] Arch. Vat., Coll. n. 446 and Intr. Ex. 5: discussed and printed in part by Baethgen in *QFIA*, XX, 114–237.

[5] Theiner, d. CCCCXLIII. Some receipts of the chamber of the college of cardinals are also useful for the period after 1294: v. Baumgarten, *Untersuchungen u. Urkunden über die Camera Collegii Cardinalium* and Kirsch, *Finanzverwaltung des Kardinalkollegiums*.

of the Tuscan Patrimony in 1298–9)[1] and elsewhere, but these are not of much assistance in calculating money actually received.

It is necessary also to list the various forms in which the popes drew money from their lands, the object being to present a general survey of these rather than to attempt a technical discussion of the often intricate distinctions between them. For this purpose it will be convenient to subdivide the types of revenue into taxes, the proceeds of justice, and other payments, such as domain profits, which come into neither of these principal categories.

Regular direct taxation was a considerable source of revenue in the Papal State, and it took many different forms. The most common of all was the annual payment to the chamber — originally direct, or to a provincial rector, but from the later thirteenth century normally through the provincial treasurer — of a fixed *census* or *affictus*. These terms were almost interchangeable, and where contemporaries were content to refer to *fictum seu fumantem vel censum*, and so on, there is danger in seeking subtle classification.[2] *Census* implied a fixed annual due in money, but its *raisons-d'être* were various: it might be a sum due from a commune in recognition of papal suzerainty — the *census* owed by the towns of the March from Innocent III's time was of this sort and it was common obligation of towns in other provinces — or it might be a regular payment in return for a privilege such as a town's right to choose its own *podestà*.[3]

The *castellania* was the farm paid by a castellan for the tenure of a *castrum* directly subject to papal rule; *castellaniae* were regularly ceded each year in the Tuscan Patrimony towards the end of the century, but there is very little evidence concerning them in the other provinces. The farming-out of the *podestà*-ship produced an analogous form of revenue, *potesteria*.[4] In the March a number of the smaller communes paid *affictus potestariarum*, a due owed by towns paying their own *podestà* which should perhaps be regarded as the equivalent of the *census* of the large communes; its payment did not confer on the town the right to choose its own *podestà*.[5]

[1] *MAH*, VII, 177–80, 185–95.

[2] For this formula *v.* Colucci, *Ant. Pic.*, XXIX, 96–7: for similar ones, Theiner, d. CCCCXLIII; Colini-Baldeschi, *Cingoli*, pp. xlvii–xlviii; Ferranti, *Amandola*, III, d. 55. But *affictus* and *census* cannot be regarded as synonyms: *v.* Partner, p. 117.

[3] For annual payments of this privilege, *v. supra*, pp. 222 ff. For payments of *census* outside the March *v.* (e.g.) *Reg. Urb. IV*, I, nn. 215–6 (Rieti); *Lib. Cens.*, I, 597–8 (Civitavecchia); Theiner, d. CCXLVII (Montasola, Sabina). *Census* was also used to describe rents from papal vassals and tenants of papal domain.

[4] Theiner, d. CCCXCI; *MAH*, VII, 177–80; Palmieri, p. 74 (March, 1280).

[5] Theiner, d. CCCXXXVII.

It is characteristic of the lack of fiscal definition in the Papal State that the *census* payable by the towns of the March is in one official receipt styled as *affictus fumantie*.[1] A real hearth-tax (*focaticum*) was levied on certain communes in this province, in Romagna and in the Duchy of Spoleto, but is found most frequently in the Patrimony, where thirty-seven towns appear on the rector's list in 1298 as owing *focaticum*.[2] The normal due was 26*d*. per hearth, though this was frequently commuted — the commune then paying an agreed total sum.

Another regular fiscal source of revenue was the *procuratio*, the money payment made in lieu of hospitality to the overlord. The provincial rector was regarded as the lord and *procurationes* rendered to him, in particular by the pope's spiritual subjects. The formulae of 1298 show that in the Patrimony many towns as well as bishops, abbots and other ecclesiastical persons and institutions owed a fixed annual *procuratio*, but the constitution of 1300 ruled that this should only be levied on the occasion of a rectorial visitation.[3] In the March *procuratio* was probably a regular and sizable revenue; although in theory an obligation on both laity and clergy it seems to have been paid only by the latter.[4] The only surviving reference to *procurationes* in the Duchy of Spoleto defines them as due when a new rector took up office, a contrast which illustrates well how the fiscal arrangements differed in the various provinces.[5]

Certain regular dues in kind were also owed by various communities, such as game, grain and timber in the Patrimony, and sausages in the March.[6]

Owing to differences between the provinces there is no clearly-defined division between regular and irregular sources of revenue. Just as *procuratio*, an irregular tax by its nature, had become a regular obligation in the Patrimony, so the payment of *tallia militum*, the money commutation of military service, had been converted into a fixed annual

---

[1] Gianandrea, *Iesi*, d. CLXXXIV (1276).

[2] For the March, *v*. Ferranti, *Amandola*, III, d. 55; for the Duchy, *Reg. B. VIII*, n. 3198 (Bettona); for Romagna, Bologna, AS, Lettere del Comune, Reg. 6, ff. 4v–15v (Imola and Medicina). Patrimony; *MAH*, VII, 185–7 and earlier references, e.g. Angeloni, *Terni*, dd. XIII–XIV (1259). For the figure of 26*d*. per hearth *v*. Theiner, dd. CLXXIII, CCCCLXVII; *Reg. Cl. IV*, n. 805; Ferranti and Angeloni, *loc. cit.*

[3] *MAH*, VII, 190–3: Theiner, dd. CCCXCI, DXXVIII (clause 8) and Pflugk-Harttung, pp. 571–2.

[4] For payment by clergy only *v*. Palmieri, *passim*, and Colucci, *Ant. Pic.*, XXIX, 94–5: for *procuratio* as a lay obligation, Turchi, *Camerino*, d. XLI.

[5] *Reg. B. XI*, n. 1206. The obligation of hospitality is occasionally described as *fodrum*, e.g. in *Annales Ceccanenses* (MGH, XIX), 296–8 (clergy and bishop of Ferentino, 1206) and *Reg. Hon. III*, n. 4600 (Spello, 1223).

[6] *MAH*, VII, 189–90, 193–4; Ferranti, *Amandola*, III, d.55; *Reg. Cl. IV*, n. 805.

tax in the same province before the end of the century, whereas it continued elsewhere to be levied at irregular intervals under the pressure of military necessity. *Tallia militum* was first levied in the March soon after the middle of the century, and was extended to Romagna on the acquisition of that province. Although it was an important source of income in both the northern provinces and the Patrimony, there is no evidence that it was paid in the Duchy or in the Campagna and Marittima.[1]

Last among the direct taxes, mention must be made of certain miscellaneous payments and services rendered irregularly by towns, such as the grain provided by Perugia and Todi in 1288.[2] *Corvées* might also be demanded, to carry grain, or even to assist in building a church.[3]

Indirect taxation existed in the form of tolls, some of which were farmed, and of agreed sums paid by certain communes in commutation of this and other dues. The three tolls in the Patrimony, Sutri, Montefiascone and Acquapendente, and that at Terni were all farmed by Boniface VIII's time.[4] The total produce of a farmed toll was not necessarily the pope's; at Acquapendente and Rieti half the proceeds were the property of the commune, while at Foligno the town retained two-thirds.[5] The pope also held rights of toll at Assisi, Gualdo Tadino and Bettona in the Duchy, in the Terra Arnulforum and possibly in other places, but they were not a substantial source of revenue.[6] Nor is it likely that monopolies yet played an important part in papal finance, though the salines of Cervia in Romagna were farmed out by Nicholas IV's time and there was a general toll on salt in the same province.[7]

Grazing-rights in the south-western part of the Tuscan Patrimony, also a valuable monopoly later, were farmed in the late thirteenth century, when they perhaps belonged rather to the category of papal

---

[1] For a fuller treatment of *tallia militum*, *v.* below pp. 291 ff.

[2] Todi, AC, Rif. II, ff. 4, 24v–25v, 40v. The Christmas presents given by Perugia to the pope and cardinals (1265–6) and by Macerata to the rector of the March were presumably personal gifts (Perugia, AS, Rif. VI, ff. 17, 135v–137; Macerata, AC, Rif. I, f. 152v).

[3] Pflugk-Harttung, pp. 564–5 (Corneto, grain); Macerata, AC, Rif. I, ff. 61–3 etc. (labour and materials for church-building). The rector *in spiritualibus* of the Duchy claimed certain unspecified services at Easter and Christmas (*BDSPU*, XXV, 61).

[4] Theiner, d. CCCCXLIII; *MAH*, VII, 194–5; Pinzi, *Viterbo*, III, 33 (Montefiascone toll in Innocent III's time).

[5] Theiner, d. CLXXIII; *Lib. Cens.*, I, 8*; *Reg. B. VIII*, n. 5498.

[6] Theiner, CCCCXLIII; Angeloni, *Terni*, dd. XIII–XIV; Terni, AS, perg., 2 June 1296 etc.; *Reg. B. VIII*, nn. 2981, 3198; *Lib. Cens.*, I, 452.

[7] *Reg. N. IV*, nn. 7251, 7253, 7256, 7334; Ghirardacci, *Bologna*, pp. 302–3. In 1291 a Bolognese merchant farmed the right to provide salt to that city, as a means of paying the *datium salis*: it was agreed with the rector of Romagna that he should pay 30s. per *centenarium*, but the city complained that he was being made to pay 65s. (Bologna, AS, Lettere del Comune, Reg. 4, f. 25 and v.).

domain.[1] Here again definition is difficult, since before the thirteenth century the popes had drawn profits from domain lands which under Innocent III came under the provincial structure of rule, and whose revenues were thus incorporated with non-domanial income. The *Liber Censuum* recorded a complex mass of *iura et consuetudines* in Rieti, Terni, the zone around Narni and Amelia, the county of Sabina, the Terra Arnulforum and elsewhere, embodying rents, a share of judicial profits and tolls, *fodra* in money and *adiutoria* in money, grain, hens and pepper.[2] The papacy also had widespread property in the form of fortresses, dwellings, mills, fields, woodland, meadows, vineyards, fisheries and so on, for which rents were owed in money and kind.[3] In the thirteenth century many additions were made, chiefly by the purchase of strategically sited *castra*, to this domain territory. Paliano and Serrone in the Campagna, Stroncone and Miranda near the upper Tiber valley, are typical of the fortresses owned by the papacy, while between them lay many holdings in land, often small and usually leased out to favoured tenants — members of the papal *familia* and their relatives, or relations of highly-placed prelates for the most part — at a more or less nominal rent. Such possessions were thus both a convenient fund for providing *douceurs* and presents and a source of revenue. The form of tenure adopted was often feudal, but the *census* asked was never great; the only vassals within the State to owe a rent of any considerable size were the Estensi during the years when they held the March, but even their hundred pounds *per annum*[4] was an insignificant item in the pope's receipts. The comparatively small rôle of the domain in the finances of the State is well illustrated by the accounts for the Patrimony — a province containing much papal domain — in 1304–6: over a period of twenty months the revenue from this source, including sales of grain, amounted to only 73 *l.*, less than 1% of the total.[5] The March accounts of 1279–80 record no receipts from domain land at all.

The profits of justice rank high among the resources of the State, though, perhaps even more than taxes, their size was dependent upon the reality of papal control and thus varied greatly. This requires fuller discussion later, when an attempt will be made to turn from a qualitative to a volumetric analysis. For the present it will suffice to divide judicial

---

[1] Theiner, d. CCCXCI. Excellent discussion of later arrangements in Partner, pp. 118–22.

[2] *Lib. Cens.*, I, 8*, 377–8, 452.

[3] For Adrian IV's purchases of such property *v.* pp. 12 ff.: for a typical example of these holdings *v.* Theiner, d. DLXXXVI (at Marta in the Tuscan Patrimony).

[4] Theiner, d. I.VI.   [5] *J Eccl H*, VI, 19.

revenues into their various components. The most important single source was normally fines imposed on either communities or individuals. Towns often paid large sums for having rebelled or supported the pope's enemies, for evading military service, exporting grain illegally, or failing to detect or punish crime. A characteristic form of payment was the *compositio*, a 'lump sum' agreed on to secure the cancellation of all fines due to the papal authorities from a commune under these various headings. Although the *compositio* was normally an amount far less than the total theoretically due, such payments were among the provinces' chief sources of revenue. Routine fines on individuals produced profits in the rector's own court and in the courts held by the spiritual rector and (in the March only) by the regional judges; these, however, were normally much less considerable. As already mentioned, a share of the profits of justice in town courts might be due to the papacy. This was most commonly either one-half (as at Rieti, Acquapendente and Frosinone) or one-third (as at Foligno and Bettona); it was not one of the more important sources of revenue.[1] To the fines in money must be added the quite valuable proceeds of confiscations of condemned men's property. The other judicial source of profit was the due known as *caposoldi*, the payment made by litigants in civil suits 'towards the salaries of the judges': this provided some 8% of the revenues of the March in 1279, the total share of judicial profits being 57% of the whole.[2]

A few sources of revenue remain to be mentioned which can be classed neither as taxation, domain profits nor the profits of justice. Payments made to provincial chanceries were not altogether negligible.[3] More irregular were the 'lump' payments made by towns to secure privileges — such as that made by Iesi to Boniface VIII — and the proceeds of papal punitive action, for example the grant of the *contado* of Gubbio to Perugia by Alexander IV at a rent of 200 *l. per annum*.[4] These last examples are a reminder that the finances of the State cannot be treated solely in terms of its provincial structure. Administrative and judicial intervention by the pope's Curia both brought revenue from the State and caused expenditure on it, but the nature of the sources makes this even more difficult to assess than provincial finance.

---

[1] *Lib. Cens.*, I, 8*, Theiner, d. CLXXIII; *Reg. M. IV*, n. 506; *Reg. B. VIII*, nn. 3198, 5498: but note the payment of over 100*l.* from Otricoli in 1285 (Theiner, d. CCCCXLIII).
[2] Calculations from Palmieri, *passim*: see below, pp. 261 ff.
[3] They provided *c.* 3% of the total revenues of the Tuscan Patrimony in 1304–6 (*J Eccl H*, VI, 19).
[4] See above, p. 160.

Nor can the financial utility of the State be measured only by outright payments, for loans were made by communes, sometimes under pressure, to the papal chamber, to members of the Curia and to provincial rectors.[1]

*   *   *

It will be convenient to turn from this list of papal resources to a chronological discussion of the State as a source of revenue, before finally attempting an estimate of its financial advantages and disadvantages: the last will naturally necessitate treatment of papal expenditure on the State. The first question which presents itself is the financial implications of Innocent III's territorial gains. To judge whether much money came from the State to the popes in the period between these acquisitions and Frederick II's counter-attack is extremely difficult owing to the scarcity of evidence for these decades. The terms reached by Innocent with a number of towns in the March allowed for the payment of an annual *fictus*, normally of 50 *l.*; surviving receipts and occasional complaints concerning non-payment suggest that these dues were normally rendered, but their total cannot have been sufficient to alter the pope's finances at all materially, while presumably they were not owed during the years 1212 to 1230 when the Marquises of Este held the March in fee.[2] Innocent III's biographer states that the early rectors of the Tuscan Patrimony succeeding in drawing from the communes of that province the *fodrum*, a payment in lieu of hospitality which had hitherto been due to the emperor.[3] There is no evidence that provincial courts heard lawsuits during most of this period and it is impossible to tell whether justice brought money from the State to the popes; on the whole it seems probable that a share of the profits of municipal courts rendered something, but provincial courts very little.[4] Altogether it is very unlikely that between 1198 and 1239 the papacy drew more from the State than it spent on it. Armies had to be raised, administrators paid, Perugia given a present of 9,000 *l.* to reconcile it to Gregory IX's presence, Rome then bribed to abandon the war

---

[1] For examples of loans *v.* Gianandrea, *Iesi*, pp. 105–9 (1248); Colucci, *Treia*, d. XXIII; *Lib. Cens.*, I, 596–7; Narni, AC, perg. 7 December 1264.

[2] 50 *l.* was due from Fermo, Fano, Pesaro and Camerino, 40 *l.* from Iesi, 25 *l.* from Matelica: Ancona, Osimo and probably other towns also owed *fictus* (P.L., 214, *Reg. Inn. III*, III, 28, 52–3; Theiner, *Vet. Mon. Slav. Merid.*, p. 57; Grimaldi, *Matelica*, d. LXVIII).

[3] P.L. 214, *Gesta Inn. III*, xxix: for other references to this due, *supra*, p. 254.

[4] For early references to provincial courts (March, 1230s), *v. supra*, p. 108 n.

against Viterbo.[1] The March of Ancona, potentially the richest province, was for almost twenty years granted at a nominal feudal rent. In the 1230s, after its resumption, this province became a financial asset, the wealthy bishop of Fermo alone probably providing 6,000 *l.* in 1231-6,[2] but even in these years the State as a whole may well have cost more than it rendered.

A few special fiscal agreements with communes made in 1239-41 as a result of imperial pressure provide the last indication of papal taxation before a decade dominated by Frederick II.[3] In the period when Cardinal Ranier struggled to retain a hold in the papal provinces, military expenditure was heavy. Innocent IV, according to his biographer, spent over 200,000 marks in seven years on the conflict with Frederick, an average of about 20,000 *l.* a year.[4] Another expensive measure much employed at this time was the grant of fiscal exemptions to towns and pensions to individuals who were either allies of the papacy or coveted as such.[5] In the early months of 1248 Cardinal Ranier raised a forced loan, to pay troops, from the communes of the March which had recently deserted the imperialists. This loan probably secured him several thousand pounds in a time of crisis,[6] but the absence of any indication of fiscal or judicial revenues in the State — if indeed it can be styled a state during this decade — suggests very strongly that it remained a financial liability throughout the period during which its possession was disputed with Frederick.

When communes that had supported the emperor returned to papal obedience, even after Frederick's death, their fiscal obligations were not increased.[7] This is symptomatic of the policy followed by the papal authorities in circumstances which were less favourable than they appeared on the surface. The focus of opposition vanished when Frederick died, but each town was a potential opponent which could only be overawed by a real re-conquest: the provincial machinery of rule had

---

[1] *Lib. Cens.*, II, 22 (*Vita Gregorii IX*); Richard of S. Germano, pp. 181-2.

[2] Catalani, *Fermo*, dd. LIX-LX.

[3] Colucci, *Treia*, p. 69 (Nov. 1239); Turchi, *Camerino*, d. XLI (Jan. 1240); *Reg. G. IX*, nn. 6032-3 (Castelficardo, May 1241).

[4] *ASRSP*, XXI, 103: this cannot be more than an estimate and it is not easy in any case to see how this type of expenditure could be separated from other papal expenses. For military expenditure in the 1240s, note Theiner d. CCVI (Innocent IV sends Card. Ranier 2,500 gold oz.) and *Reg. Inn. IV*, n. 4702 (Card. Capocci empowered to borrow 10,000 gold oz.).

[5] For examples *v. Reg. G. IX*, n. 5292; *Reg. Inn. IV*, nn. 166, 305, 4083, 4537; Theiner, d. CCXXXI.

[6] Gianandrea, *Iesi*, d. XCIX; Colucci, *Treia*, d. XXIII; Acquacotta, *Matelica*, d. 27. There were probably loans from other towns.

[7] See (e.g.) Colucci, *Ant. Pic.*, XVIII, xxiv-xxv and *Treia*, d. XXV.

to be re-installed and nurtured till it inspired respect. This was only possible with compliant subjects and hence each town had to be won back on terms which placed the minimum strain on the pope's weak resources. It had to be offered the prospect of peaceable conditions and economic well-being, otherwise it would reject papal rule, and yet that rule could only be made a reality with the aid of money which must come from taxation and, for a time, from fines punishing the 'dis-obedience' of the last decade. To shirk such fines entirely would not only be to neglect the most likely source of revenue but by implication to withdraw papal claims of suzerainty. The papacy, in other words, could only fine these subjects in so far as its temporal and spiritual strength put the towns in fear. Thus the communes were upbraided for having elected their own *podestà*, yet none of them was fined for this blatant declaration of independence, while strong towns continued to receive fiscal exemptions.[1] Although Terni had paid 5,000 *l.*, Fabriano 2,000 *l.*, Civitanova 1,000 *l.* and Macerata an unknown sum by the sum-mer of 1252, other towns probably managed to make their peace without condemnation.[2]

It is only an apparent paradox that disobedience produced more fines when it became less general, and under Alexander IV this situation was beginning to come about, both in the March and the adjoining lands. In 1254–6 3,000 *l.* was extracted in fines from Fano, 2,000 *l.* from Iesi, and smaller sums from Matelica, Macerata, Fabriano (concerning its territory in the Duchy) and Perugia.[3] It is symptomatic of the stronger papal position that Alexander himself tried to mulct Civitanova of the full 5,000 *l.* fine to which it had earlier been sentenced, despite the town's full absolution in January 1252 on payment of 1,000 *l.*[4] At the same period the confiscation of Gubbio's *contado* had begun to bring in 200 *l. per annum* and a few scraps of evidence suggest that regular taxes were being paid now in the March, the Duchy and the upper Tiber.[5]

[1] Marangoni, *Civitanova*, p. 274; *Reg. Inn. IV*, n. 5900 (Ascoli exempted from tolls in same year, 1252).

[2] This is suggested by the fact that only Terni and Macerata were fined on the grounds that they had supported the emperor (*Reg. Inn. IV*, n. 5886; Compagnoni, *Regg. Pic.*, pp. 117–18: cf. Zonghi, *Fabriano*, d. CLXVI–CLXIX, and Marangoni, *Civitanova, loc. cit.*) and by the terms on which Card. Capocci received back many towns in 1249–51, quashing all outstanding condemnations (BFW, nn. 13730, 13753, etc.).

[3] Amiani, *Fano*, II, lii; Gianandrea, *Iesi*, dd. CXXXVI–CXXXVII; Acquacotta, *Matelica*, d. 45 (350 *l.*); Macerata, AC, perg., III, 11 and Compagnoni, *Regg. Pic.*, p. 123 (800 *l.*, some of which is taxation); Zonghi, *Fabriano*, dd. CLXX, CXCI (600 *l.*); *ASI*, XVI, 2, 483 (Perugia: fine of 50 marks for each cavalryman and 25 for each infantryman sent to aid Fano). [4] Marangoni, *Civitanova*, pp. 273–4, 277–8.

[5] Above, p. 160. For tax payments in March and Duchy (1256), Macerata, AC, perg. III, 11 and Zonghi, *Fabriano*, d. CXC; for Terni's payments (1259), Angeloni, *Terni*, dd. XIII–XIV.

Manfred's attack on central Italy, however, came before the structure of fiscal and judicial administration could achieve solidity. Between 1259 and 1266 much of the State was under Hohenstaufen control, while the proximity of the enemy meant that subjects had to be treated with caution and often with tenderness. This did not signify that the State entirely ceased to be a source of revenue. Rieti and Camerino continued to pay their *census*,[1] and so probably did other towns in the area not over-run. Fines were levied in the Duchy and the Campagna-Marittima, but it is impossible to know whether Urban IV's reassertion of papal rights in the Duchy and Tuscan Patrimony brought in more money than it cost.[2] Earlier evidence suggests, though it is too scanty to prove, that before Manfred's day the March may well have yielded more money for the papacy than the other three provinces combined: now almost all of it was occupied by the Hohenstaufen. Moreover these were years, like the 1240s, when low revenue went with high expenditure, especially on troops and diplomacy. Urban IV's well-informed biographer has it that Manfred bishop-elect of Verona, rector of the March and Duchy from 1261 or 1262, spent at least 30,000 *l.*, yet his soldiers' pay was in arrears when he was captured in 1264.[3] Until Benevento the papacy was never granted the opportunity to undertake the financial exploitation of central Italy.

The topic of this chapter calls for different treatment in the period after the Hohenstaufen defeat, both because the papacy was now better able to exploit its resources and because the surviving evidence is a little less fragmentary. Among these sources the unique March account-book of 1279–80 is paramount, and any attempt to investigate the finances of that province in the two decades after Benevento must begin with an analysis of its contents.

The receipt section of this book, which covers the period from 1 May 1279 to 1 March 1280 (inclusive), records revenue to the value of 5,556 *l.*, in the currency of Ravenna.[4] Rather over half this total — 57% — was provided by judicial sources. The most important of these were fines which, including the proceeds of confiscated property, were

---

[1] *Reg. Urb. IV*, I, nn. 215–16; Santoni, 'Camerino', 48.

[2] *Reg. Urb. IV*, I, n. 84 and II, n. 683; RIS, O.S., III, 2, 411 (Spoleto fined 1,000 marks): see also above, p. 168 ff.

[3] RIS, O.S., III, 2, 411–12: *Reg. Urb. IV*, II, n. 683. A German chronicler states that Urban was spending 1,000 marks a week on mercenaries (MGH, XXIV, 203: not '4,000', as in Dupré-Theseider, p. 82). Urban himself claimed that by mid-July 1264 his campaigning in that year had already cost him 200,000 *l.* (Martène and Durand, *Thesaurus*, II, 82).

[4] For the following passage *v.* Palmieri, *passim*. I have relied on my own calculations, which vary slightly from those of the compiler of the accounts.

responsible for 2,005 *l.*, or approximately 36% of all revenues. To this should be added the payment of one-third of the takings of the courts of all the provincial judges, including that of the rector *in spiritualibus*; these were paid over separately and presumably were composed of smaller fines, such as those for non-attendance. They brought in a further 732 *l.* and with this addition the profits of justice accounted for 49% of the revenue. The other 8% (450 *l.*) came from the *caposoldi* paid in civil suits. Most of the remaining revenue was provided by the *fictus*, the direct tax paid by the communes; this accounted for 1,661 *l.*, about 30% of the total. *Procurationes* paid by the clergy amounted to 443 *l.*, almost exactly the same amount as the *caposoldi*. The last 5% was a single 'lump' payment of 305 *l.* 10s. made by the town of Fermo for the castellan-ship of nearby Moresco 'and for some other small things'.

The expenditure recorded in the account-book amounts to 4,221 *l.*, leaving a balance of 1,334 *l.*; or approximately one-fifth of the revenue. Almost the whole of this expenditure (93%) was on the salaries of the rector, treasurer, judges and notaries. The remainder is accounted for by small payments to messengers and an unexplained repayment to Fermo.

The compiler noted that he had omitted 'my own payments, because I do not know what these amount to'.[1] Unfortunately these are far from being the only omissions in what we certainly cannot regard as a full financial statement for these months. The most obvious gap is the absence from the recorded revenue of *tallia militum*. Iesi paid the treasurer 200 *l.* for *tallia* on 17 August 1279,[2] and no doubt similar payments were made by other communes but there is no record of them here. There may well also have been some military expenditure.

Despite these missing elements the account-book provides a far better guide to the finances of the State than anything surviving from an earlier period. Above all it makes it clear that regular taxation and judicial profits were yielding a considerable sum in the March, but that this did little more than cover the salaries due to the administrators and judges who were the essential agents in this process. Scarcely any profit remained for the papacy, even supposing an ideally peaceful situation necessitating no military expenditure, a situation which can rarely have

---

[1] Palmieri, pp. 107, 111. The compiler of the account-book (which is in the vernacular) was perhaps not the provincial treasurer Roger of Florence, for he notes separately payments to 'my notary' and to 'the treasurer's notary' (pp. 106, 111). A possible candidate is William *de Monte Desiderio* who in July 1280 was chamberlain to the abbot of Montmajour, rector of the March 1278–82 (Zonghi, *Fabriano*, d. CCXXIX).

[2] Gianandrea, *Iesi*, d. CXCVI.

prevailed. The period covered by the accounts was in fact an unusually quiet one, but the later months of 1280 saw a full-scale war in the March between Fermo and Ascoli.[1]

Receipts and other evidence from the March for the years 1266–88 can be used to assess the degree to which 1279–80 is typical. It is convenient to begin with direct taxation. The account-book suggests that most towns of the March were paying *fictus*, for it records its payment by nearly one hundred communes, while others may have paid more or less regularly although making no payment during the ten months covered by the accounts. A fragmentary document of a few years later[2] lists some hundred towns in the March owing an annual *census* or *fictus*, though nearly half of these are noted as not now paying, either because they have lost their independence to a larger town (this is by far the most common reason) or in a few instances because the place 'is in rebellion' or 'is empty'. Fifty-eight towns remain as normally rendering the tax and the names of forty-one of these duly appear in the account-book of 1279–80 as paying *fictus*. The document of 1283 relates only to five dioceses, but in some of these the correspondence with the payments of 1279–80 is quite close. Thus nineteen towns in the diocese of Fermo were expected to pay and in fact nineteen had done so in 1279–80, while seven towns out of eleven paid in the diocese of Camerino and ten out of seventeen in that of Ascoli. The amounts paid are always below those recorded as due, but are frequently an exact fraction of that sum, varying between a half and one-tenth. One-sixth is the proportion most commonly paid and the total rendered is approximately one-fifth of that due.[3] It is clear that the small towns recorded in this register paid only a quota of the *fictus* theoretically due from them, and that they did so regularly; S. Vittoria, for example, theoretically liable for 100 *l.*, paid 15 *l. per annum* year after year.[4] The large towns, however, tended to pay the full amount due, which was normally no greater than the sum agreed with Innocent III and was often smaller than that due from far less wealthy communes. Fermo and Camerino still paid the 50 *l.* they had owed since Innocent's time and Iesi's liability had only been raised from 40 *l.* to 50 *l.*[5]

Other evidence confirms that *fictus* was a regular and productive due

---

[1] De Minicis, *Fermo*, pp. 106–7.

[2] Theiner, d. CCCCXXVII (a copy dated 1 May 1283 from an older register, but with annotations referring to 1283).

[3] The towns whose dues and payments are both recorded owed between them 3,750 *l.* and paid 714 *l.*

[4] *V. inf.*, p. 264 n.

[5] See above, p. 258 and (for Iesi) below, p. 264 n.

in the March after 1266. Several towns paid *fictus* in 1279–80 for more than one year, and were thus presumably making good past non-payments; Fano, for example, paid for two years.[1] But most conclusive of all are the receipts surviving in certain archives to prove that some towns paid year after year. Iesi paid *fictus* for at least thirteen years in the period 1270–90, S. Vittoria at least fourteen times in the years 1278–98, and Amandola fourteen times in 1278–99.[2] These payments were not always made promptly by the day on which they were due (normally 1 May)[3] but the important thing is that they were normally made. It seems clear that the impressive productivity of direct taxation in 1279–1280 should be regarded as typical of the March in the years after Benevento.

The implications of the *tallia militum* as a liability will be discussed in the next chapter, but it is essential here to attempt an estimate of its importance as a source of revenue. In this case it is not possible to deal with the period 1266–88 as a whole, for it is striking that the evidence for *tallia militum* as a heavy obligation in the March relates only to the years 1277–84. It is most unlikely that this is due to the fortuitous survival of material from these years, for the figures are overwhelming in their effect. Iesi paid at least 2,800 *l.* in *tallia militum* in 1277–82 and Fabriano 1,600 *l.* during the same period, while Fermo subscribed 1,350 *l.* between 1278 and 1284. Macerata paid rather over 300 *l.* in 1280 alone.[4] There is no record of Fabriano paying *tallia* again till 1289 and then, characteristically, the sum disbursed was a mere 50 florins.[5] After 1284 the *tallia* survived in the March, but only as a minor and irregular due.[6] It may also be significant that the well-preserved archives of several minor towns bear no trace of this brief heyday of scutage. The burden seems to have fallen on the larger communes, whose

---

[1] Palmieri, p. 31.

[2] Gianandrea, *Iesi*, dd. CLXXX, CLXXXIV, CXC, CXCIV, CXCIX, CCII, CCVIII, CCXIII, CCXXXI, CCXXXVIII; *AMSM*, N.S., VII (1911–12), 419–20; Ferranti, *Amandola*, III, dd. 117, 120, 124, 133, 138, 153, 164, 166, 177, 182, 198, 216, 259, 267. Iesi paid 50 *l.* a year, S. Vittoria 15, Amandola 10. Undoubtedly most towns paid these small sums conscientiously: for another example (Serra S. Quirico, which paid 8 *l.* only) *v.* *Archivio Storico per le Marche e per l'Umbria*, II, 294–5.

[3] For a characteristic story of delay and of payment made three months late after many threats from the provincial authorities *v.* Macerata, AC, Rif. I, ff. 25, 34, 58–9, 64, 93v–94, 99–100.

[4] Gianandrea, *Iesi*, dd. CLXXXVIII, CXCI, CXCIII, CXCVI, CXCIX–CC, CCIII, CCV, CCXIX; Zonghi, *Fabriano*, d. CCXXIX and Fabriano, AC, Lib. Ross., ff. 89v–93; De Minicis, *Fermo*, pp. 462–3, 473, 487; Macerata, AC, 160 (Intr. Ex. 1280), ff. 12v, 37 and v, 39v–40, 41v–42.

[5] Fabriano, AC, perg. n. 299.

[6] Thus Amandola paid 140 *l.* in 1293 (Ferranti, III, d. 183) and Camerino 50 *l.* in 1294 (Santoni, p. 56).

wealth was for a few years tapped with great success, to provide a sum far exceeding the proceeds of the *fictus*. In 1280 alone Iesi probably paid 600 *l.* in *tallia*, Fabriano 400 *l.*, and Macerata rather over 300 *l.*;[1] besides such sums as these — to which should almost certainly be added comparable payments by other large communes — the 1,600 *l.* raised from the *fictus* of the whole province in 1279–80 seems almost insignificant. But the papal authorities were perhaps over-reaching themselves, for they do not appear to have attempted to continue their triumphant employment of *tallia militum* in the March after the major victories had been won in the great war in Romagna.

There is almost certainly another way in which the accounts of 1279–80 understate the average provincial revenues for this period. Among the fines recorded are only two appreciable sums levied on towns, amounting between them to about 700 *l.*, or roughly one-third of the money received from fines.[2] A number of surviving documents suggest that this amount is untypical. During the years 1280–90 inclusive nearly 35,000 *l.* was paid in fines to the authorities of the March by the communes of Camerino, Fabriano, Iesi, Ascoli, Ripatransone and Macerata alone.[3] There is no reason to suppose that these six towns were exceptional or to doubt the payment of similar sums by other communes which, by flouting the law in various ways — most often by fighting neighbouring towns, or by refusing to fight others — had earned the condemnation of authorities whose strength they were eventually unable to withstand. Since these six communes alone paid between them an annual average of rather over 3,000 *l.* during the decade 1280–90, it is likely that receipts from fines were normally far greater than the 700 *l.* of 1279–80. Had the provincial authorities succeeded in extracting from the communes the full amounts of the condemnations, the revenue would have been far higher still, but the usual procedure was for each town to compound periodically for all outstanding fines. These debts piled up in an extraordinary fashion — in April 1280 a former rector of the March claimed from Fabriano 21,000 *l.* and 17,000 oz. of gold in unpaid fines and taxes[4] — and normally a certain amount of bargaining ensued before a *compositio* was

---

[1] For references *v.* above, p. 264 n. 4.

[2] Palmieri, pp. 67 and 74 (Iesi paid 500 *l.* for taking an outlaw as *podestà*, Macerata 209 *l.* for not sending troops against Ascoli).

[3] Gianandrea, *Iesi*, dd. CCI, CCIV, CCVII, CCIX, CCXV; *Reg. Hon. IV*, n. 896; *Reg. N. IV*, nn. 7046, 7100, 7289; Zonghi, *Fabriano*, dd. CCXXX, CCXLIV, CCXLVIII; Compagnoni, *Regg. Pic.*, p. 150. These receipts are not always absolutely explicit and it is not impossible that the same payment may have been counted more than once.

[4] Fabriano, AC, Lib. Rosso, ff. 39v–40.

agreed.[1] At one time Martin IV forbade the rector to compound with cities without consulting him in all cases when the dues involved amounted to over 300 *l.*, but one cannot be certain that these instructions were obeyed.[2]

Although the decade 1280–90 has been chosen for treatment here because the evidence is more plentiful, 'compositions' were already an extremely important source of revenue in the preceding years. There had been a cautious tendency to refrain from fining towns after Benevento for support given to Manfred,[3] but throughout the 1270s condemnations of communes were frequent and rewarding. It is thus clear that, both through the omission of *tallia militum* and through a fortuitous absence of large *compositiones*, the accounts of 1279–80 give a quite misleading impression of the total revenues of the March at this period. To their 5,500 *l.* should be added (to employ only the recorded figures from the few towns whose archives have survived) some 3,000 *l.* in fines and — at least between 1278 and 1284 — some 1,000 *l.* from *tallia militum*. This alone would almost double the recorded revenues, but it is highly probable that other towns paid corresponding sums. The total receipts may be estimated at well over 10,000 *l.* a year and when *tallia militum* was at its height they may well have reached 20,000 *l.* or even more, in this province of many communes.

It has already been remarked that the annual expenditure of the province must also normally have amounted to more than the 4,200 *l.* of the account-book. Military expenditure may not have been high, and the absence of any reference to a permanent nucleus of provincial troops suggests that there was nothing beyond the rector's small *familia*, paid from his own salary. The towns themselves provided and paid troops on many occasions, but the *tallia* must at times have been expended on mercenaries employed within the province. Yet, even if the expenses recorded for 1279–80 were abnormally low, a good profit was probably expected from the March. That this was so is perhaps confirmed by a letter of Clement IV promising that a loan made by some Sienese bankers would be repaid 'from the fines or other revenues

---

[1] E.g. Macerata, AC, Rif. I (1287), ff. 49–50v, 52v, 54v, 55v–56v.

[2] Gianandrea, *Iesi*, d. CCXIV. A typical 'composition' was that arranged between Fabriano and the rector of the March in 1289: the commune owed 13 fines totalling 7,350 *l.*, but was absolved on paying 1,800 *l.* (Zonghi, *Fabriano*, d. CCXLVIII). The same technique is reflected in the accounts of 1279–80, for the *c.* 2,000 *l.* received in fines would have been *c.* 3,500 *l.* had payment always been made in full (Palmieri, p. 109).

[3] See above, pp. 178 ff. Exceptions I have noted are Ancona (Martène and Durand, *Thesaurus*, II, c. 361: 10,000 *l.*) and Matelica (Grimaldi, dd. CCXXXIII, CCXLIV, CCLI: 5,000 *l.*).

of the March'.[1] This letter was written in the summer of 1266, when the province was only beginning to fall under papal control. However much of the March's wealth finished in the hands of unscrupulous officials,[2] it could still provide the pope with a handsome surplus.

The fact that the March did not absorb all its revenues did not mean that this favourable balance was part of a general profit obtained from the Papal State as a whole: it is quite possible that they were swallowed up by the expense of governing the other provinces. This must certainly have been the case during the great Romagnol war of the early 1280s, when armies of several thousand men were raised each year, and at one time over 75,000 florins were spent in a few months on French mercenaries alone.[3]

It is time to turn from the March to the other provinces in an attempt to decide whether the flourishing conditions of its finances may be regarded as typical. Any answer to this question must be a hesitant one, for the sources are exiguous indeed. One may begin, however, by postulating that routine administration would cost approximately the same in each province, since the officials received similar salaries; the March may have cost rather more than the others since it had a larger body of judges. Concerning other expenditure there are no data except the certainty that after 1278 vast sums had to be spent on the subjugation of the Romagna. In the other provinces expenditure apart from that involved by normal administration was probably low. On turning to revenue, however, one receives the impression that the returns of the March were in this period far greater than those of any other province. In the other provinces there was almost certainly less recourse to the courts and the routine profits of justice must have been much lower. Occasionally a large fine is recorded, and it is noteworthy that Perugia alone appears to have paid in 1284–8 the enormous sum of 40,000 florins — equivalent perhaps to the total revenues of the March in these years — to secure papal absolution after its condemnation for attacking Foligno in 1282–4.[4] This is a reminder that large payments made by wealthy communities under strong pressure could have the effect of increasing papal revenues in an extraordinary way, and that receipts probably varied very greatly from year to year. Other recorded payments of fines outside the March in these years are the 1,000 mark fine paid by Rieti in 1280 and Spoleto's 550 florins paid *c.* 1288–90: it is

[1] *Reg. Cl. IV*, n. 782.   [2] For complaints of this in 1279 *v. Reg. N. III*, n. 776.
[3] Theiner, d. CCCCXL. Note also the bribe of 1,600 florins paid to Cervia in 1282 (Villani, l. VII, c. 82).   [4] See above, p. 206 n.

probable that other large fines were paid by towns both in the March and elsewhere.[1] There is little evidence, however, of any attempt to fine the rebellious communities of Romagna; such a policy would probably have been unrealistic, and the normal procedure was simply for the rector to place the offending town under a ban.[2]

It is also probable that taxation was more productive in the March than elsewhere. Despite a preliminary attempt to levy money for troops from Bologna in 1280, *tallia militum* was only drawn from Romagna for the first time in 1287.[3] The earliest extant reference to this tax in the Patrimony dates from 1290 and it seems not to have existed in the other provinces in the thirteenth century.[4] Some fragmentary lists of revenues drawn from Terni and the neighbouring fortress of Otricoli in the 1280s[5] show that such towns were then paying a small *census* — Terni paid 200 *l.* in four years — while the toll at Terni was farmed at a mere 25 *l.* a year. The proceeds of justice were not inconsiderable and at Otricoli seem to have amounted to some 200 *l.* in a single year. Rents from domain would have provided some revenue in those zones — particularly the Campagna and the Patrimony and upper Tiber — where the Church had for long held lands and fortresses. Yet even these, together with the proceeds of tolls and a share of the profits of town courts, would not have compensated for the absence of that regular process of taxation and fining to which many of the wealthier towns of the March had to submit. The enormous fine paid by Perugia is a reminder that with insufficient evidence it would be much safer to make no guess at all; but if a guess must be made it would be to put the revenues of the other provinces a long way behind those of the March. In any case it is unlikely that the yield of the entire State could normally do much more than cover administrative and military expenses. It was certainly inadequate for this in the early 1280s, but the papacy then had special assistance in the form of a very large crusading tenth from France.[6] The heavy revenue and expenditure of these years serve as a

---

[1] Rieti, Sottosez AS, perg., 17 October 1280; Spoleto, Sottosez AS, Statuti, I, f. 29v. While other fines were certainly paid of which no evidence has survived, it would be misleading to suggest that such survivals are entirely fortuitous: for instance, Perugia's payments to Nicholas IV were presumably noted in his register because his chamberlain regarded them as important.

[2] For an exception *v.* RIS, N.S., XXVIII, II, 54 (1285): but there is no evidence that Faenza's exiles paid these fines.

[3] Ghirardacci, *Bologna*, pp. 252–5; RIS, N.S., XXVIII, II, 55.

[4] Arch. Vat., Arm. XXXV, 14, f. 85. *Tallia* was paid in the Duchy during the fourteenth century, but in the fifteenth century was still not due in Campagna-Marittima (Partner, p. 114).

[5] Theiner, d. CCCCXLIII.   [6] *Ibid.*, d. CCCCXVIII.

reminder of the dangers of discussing a 'normal situation', when there were violent fluctuations in papal finance and generalizations cannot be applied even to so brief a period as the two decades discussed in the foregoing pages.

The nature of the surviving evidence, although this remains quite fragmentary, makes it possible to treat the fifteen years from Nicholas IV's election to Boniface VIII's death in terms of the State as a whole, without using the finances of one province as a starting-point. This period includes one striking innovation, for it was in 1289 that the college of cardinals was allotted a half share of the papacy's temporal revenues. This measure may not have been fully effective,[1] but it indicates that both the cardinals and the pope were now coming to regard the revenues from the Papal State as an appreciable and regular element in papal finance. Whatever setbacks there may have been, the revenues of the pope's territories must have tended to increase quite considerably after 1266. It seems likely that the measure of 1289 should be associated with the realization of this fact, although the abortive legislation of 1233[2] suggests that the cardinals had already begun to covet the profits of the State in the epoch before the Hohenstaufen inroads.

The evidence from Nicholas IV and Boniface VIII's time tends to support this picture of increasingly successful fiscality. The March — still on the whole the best documented province — acquired a new regular source of revenue with the grant in 1290–1 to many towns of jurisdictional privileges in return for an annual payment.[3] This *census*, which was entirely independent of the *fictus* already owed by many communes of the March, was paid with great regularity.[4] Under Boniface VIII it yielded some 2,700 *l.* a year.[5] Meanwhile fines continued to be demanded and compounded for to much the same extent as before.[6] *Tallia militum* was now assessed at a much lower level; but the new *census* must have at least compensated for this. In any case military expenditure in the State as a whole was not as high as before except during the very brief episode of the Colonna war. The assignment in 1301–2 of the revenues of the March to Charles of Valois, the

---

[1] For its effect in a later period *v.* Partner, pp. 138–40.
[2] See above, p. 139.
[3] Above, pp. 222 ff.
[4] For an example *v.* Ferranti, *Amandola*, III, dd. 222, 232, 240, 257, 290.
[5] Arch. Vat., Coll. n. 446, f. 2v and Intr. Ex. 5, f. 2: *v.* also *QFIA*, XX, 155 and Baumgarten, p. 161.
[6] Some examples: Santoni, 'Camerino', 56 and 59–60 (3,000 florins in 1294, 300 in 1300): *Reg. B. VIII*, n. 2399 (Recanati: 2,800 florins in 1298).

province's nominal rector,[1] tends to confirm that the March was then running at a profit.

The finances of the Tuscan Patrimony can be traced more closely in the 1290s than in the preceding period, thanks mainly to the survival in the Vatican of some fragmentary accounts for the years 1290–4.[2] The total sum due from the hearth-tax in this province was then 1,427 *l.*, while *tallia militum* — now apparently a regular tax — should have yielded 2,040 *l.* The accounts show that in 1290–2 a number of the major towns were paying both these dues in full and suggest that they may well have produced 3,000 *l.* a year between them.[3] The farmed-out *castellaniae* and *potestarie* were also handsome sources of profit; Acquapendente was farmed regularly at 350 *l. per annum*, for instance, and Orchia (near Viterbo) at 240 *l. Procurationes* produced at least 250 *l.* in 1291 and the grazing-rights at Montebello were leased each year for 80 *l.* These accounts are quite insufficient for a calculation of the 'profit-ability' of the Patrimony, but they can be supplemented by receipts for some considerable fines, such as the sums amounting to over 2,000 *l.* paid by Corneto between 1296 and 1303.[4] The bishop of Siena was rector of the Tuscan Patrimony from July 1298 until June 1299, when he paid over, and the pope acknowledged, exactly 10,000 *l.* as the 'profit' of his period of tenure.[5] The possibility that this sum in fact represents the exact amount of the surplus of revenue over expenditure in that period seems remote, but this puzzling transaction may conceal the grant of the rectorate for a period of one year in return for a payment of 10,000 *l.*, the balance being retained by the bishop. Such an agreement would not be incompatible with the arrangement whereby the next rector was permitted to retain all the revenues[6] — presumably as a source of profit to himself. If this interpretation is correct it is clear evidence for what in any case seems probable, a large profit from the Patrimony in the last years of the century. Yet the accounts for 1304–6,[7]

---

[1] Arch. Vat., Intr. Ex. 5, f. 6v: cf. *QFIA*, XX, 189–90.

[2] Arch. Vat., Arm. XXXV, 14, f. 85 and v (1290–1); Theiner, d. CCCXCI (1291–4). The preservation of these accounts is perhaps a symptom of greater productivity, but might be wholly fortuitous.

[3] For amounts due *v. MAH*, VII, 185–9. That the *focaticum* due was not always paid in full is shown by the case of Montalto which owed 105 *l.*, but paid only 50 *l.* in both 1292 and 1305 (Arch. Vat., Coll., n. 241, f. 22v), while Viterbo was exempted from payment of *tallia militum* after 1298 (Pinzi, III, 33). Payments by larger towns such as Viterbo may usually be taken as indications that the less formidable small towns paid too: *v. J Eccl H*, VI, 20.

[4] Note also the payment of *procurationes* (100 *l.*) by Corneto in both 1295 and 1296. For these and fines *v.* Pflugk-Harttung, pp. 570–3, 584, 586–8.

[5] *V. J Eccl H*, VI, 25.   [6] *Reg. B. VIII*, nn. 5549–53.

[7] *J Eccl H*, VI, 18–25.

with revenue for twenty months at around 8,000 *l.* and expenditure (much of it military) at about 9,500 *l.*, show a serious loss and remind one that the fiscal situation of the State could change with extreme rapidity. Already under Benedict XI revenues in the Duchy were shrinking and rectors of all provinces needed loans.[1]

With this reminder that it is dangerous to guess the financial situation of any year from its predecessor or successor and that the whole foundation of this chapter is quite unsure, we may turn to the Duchy of Spoleto, which at least has a statement for 1290–1 purporting to give the total of revenue and expenditure for a period of ten months.[2] These accounts (which include the county of Sabina) give the revenues as about 7,760 florins,[3] and expenditure on salaries 'and other necessary costs' as about 5,150, so that the resulting profit works out at about one-third of the revenue. The figure is not an improbable one in a period when some towns were paying handsome fines. Spoleto paid 550 florins *c.* 1288–90, Cascia 1,165 florins in 1291 and 1,000 in 1303, Terni disbursed 780 florins in 1296 and Perugia was once again mulcted, in 1301, of 10,000 florins[4] — and others were paying recently agreed fixed annual sums in lieu of multifarious dues.[5]

The finances of Romagna remain extremely problematical, but *tallia militum* was now periodically sought, and on occasions paid.[6] Moreover there was a certain revenue from fines in this period of less constant warfare. One can perhaps trace the rising graph of this source in the dealings of the provincial authorities with Faenza, for this commune defied a condemnation in 1288, paid a nominal fine of 25 marks in 1290, and in 1294 regained its privileges on expending the handsome sum of 2,000 florins; by 1300 Faenza and Forlì were jointly paying a fine of 5,000 *l.*[7] As elsewhere, to render taxes and fines was a sign of weakness: the small town of Bagnacavallo had paid 4,000 *l.* as early as 1291, while four years later Bologna paid a mere 126 florins — nominally in chancery dues — to secure absolution from interdict and a 10,000 mark fine.[8]

[1] *Supra*, p. 251.   [2] Theiner, p. 321.

[3] For equivalents *v. infra*, p. 272 n.

[4] Spoleto, Sottosez AS, Statuti, I, f. 29v; Morini, *Cascia*, d. VI; Cascia, AC, perg. n. 15; Terni, AS, perg. 24 Jan., 15 Oct. and 7 Dec. 1296; Baumgarten, p. 177.

[5] E.g. *Reg. B. VIII*, nn. 3198 (Bettona, 100 *l.* p. a.), 5498 (Foligno, 100 florins): for payments *v.* fragmentary accounts printed in *QFIA*, XX, 211–17.

[6] Ravenna paid in 1295 (Fantuzzi, III, n. LXXXXIII). For more typical defiance (by Bologna in 1291) *v. Nuovi Studi Med.*, II, 230–1.

[7] *Reg. N. IV*, nn. 7150–1; Theiner, dd. CCCCLXVIII, DLI; RIS, N.S., XXVIII, II, 76.

[8] *Reg. N. IV*, nn. 7321–2; Ghirardacci, *Bologna*, p. 324.

Finally, the Campagna and Marittima, the poorest province and presumably the one that normally yielded least, provides in Boniface VIII's time yet another reminder of the unreliable nature of generalizations made from scanty sources. In August 1299 the vicar-general of this province acknowledged receipt of the sum of 11,900 florins as a fine from certain lords of Alatri and Bauco who had been condemned for causing civil disorders.[1] One may wonder how the pope was able to secure payment of this enormous sum and reflect too that it may well be involved with his policies in the area and hence not rank truly as a fine. If it disguises a bribe of some sort, it still illustrates the surprisingly large sums that even the poorer zones of central Italy might yield to the papacy.

When one remembers the existence of large individual payments such as this, and the far larger ones made at the same period by Perugia, it is difficult to agree with Prof. Baethgen, who would put the average revenue of the State in Boniface's time at between fifteen and twenty thousand florins a year.[2] This estimate may well be a good deal too low. The revenue of the March in a rather earlier period has already been estimated[3] at between ten and twenty thousand pounds; since then the fall in *tallia militum* had been compensated for by the new *census*. The Tuscan Patrimony was normally bringing in far more than the 5,000 *l. per annum* average of the 1304–6 accounts. If the 10,000 *l.* paid by the rector of 1298–9 as 'profit' represents approximately the revenue minus salaries, the yield of this province was around fifteen thousand pounds, though this might be setting it too high. The revenues of the Duchy and Sabina, with some adjoining territories, were about nine thousand florins *per annum* in the early 1290s. Thus these three provinces between them were almost certainly producing a revenue of over twenty thousand florins. To this should be added the proceeds of the Romagna and Campagna-Marittima. The probability of most years producing some really large payment from a big commune or other wealthy subject — something to rank with Perugia's thirty thousand florins or the twelve thousand of the Campagna barons of 1299 — must also be remembered. Altogether twenty-five thousand florins or even thirty seems a more likely guess than Prof. Baethgen's.

---

[1] *Reg. B. VIII*, n. 3408.
[2] *QFIA*, XX, 166–9. The following rates of exchange between pounds and florins may be useful. 1302: 1 florin=35s. of Ravenna (normal currency in Romagna and March). 1299: 1 florin=32s. 6d. papal currency (much used in Patrimony and Campagna). 1304–6: 1 florin=43s. 4d. papal currency. *V.* Arch. Vat., Intr. Ex. 5, f. 2; Coll. n. 446, f. 2v; Coll. n. 241, f. 66v.
[3] Above, p. 266.

To estimate expenditure is yet more difficult, largely because there can be no clear distinction between what did and what did not concern the Papal State. It would be futile to debate whether or not the cost of the Colonna war should rank as money spent on the State. But the total outlay on administration, as well as on the military and diplomatic aspects of papal territorial policy must always have been very high. If purchases of property for St. Peter or for the pope's own family is added, one can well understand the certainty of Nicholas IV's chamberlain, Nicholas of Trevi, that any provincial profits had to go 'to diminish the debts owed in common by the (papal) chamber and cardinals by reason of the finances (*pecuniarum*) of the lands of the Church, from which less is received than is expended'.[1] The system of accountancy prevailing cannot have made it possible for the papal chamberlain to base such a statement on calculations, even if one were to accept his definition of what constituted 'expenditure on the lands of the Church'. Nevertheless his pronouncement is of great importance as bearing witness that the man who was in the best position to know confidently believed that even in the fertile years of Nicholas IV the State cost more than it brought in.

Clearly such generalizations as are made in this chapter are quite provisional ones. Only the wide variations between province and province and between year and year seem certain, the relative sterility of the Campagna under its feudatories, the lean periods of Frederick II and Manfred's greatness, and the rapid financial decline after the fat years of Nicholas IV and Boniface VIII. The consideration of money on its own cannot make possible a full assessment of the State's utility to the papacy: when *tallia militum* became a heavy financial burden in the March, for example, military service by the communes for a while declined and thus a price had to be paid for increased revenues. Moreover the yield of the State was not equivalent to the direct gain of the pope, for many of its sources of revenue — in particular the domain lands — were alienated to members of the Curia and other ecclesiastics, to other papal supporters, or to relatives or familiars of these.

To discover why some provinces were so much more fruitful than others is extremely difficult in view of the lack of economic and administrative information about each zone. Not enough can be known about the personality of any rector to make possible an estimate of the rôle of individual administrators in building up the lucrative structure of rule in the March. There were busy papal courts in that province as

[1] Theiner, p. 321.

T

early as the 1230s, but the great period of its fiscality probably dates only from the Angevin era, and its achievement should probably be ascribed to four assiduous rectors, Fulk of Puyricard (1272–6), Bernard abbot of Montmajour (1278–81), Geoffrey of Anagni (1282–5), and Frederick bishop-elect of Ivrea (1285–8). None of these was a sinecurist, indeed all have left manifold records of their energetic government, and between them they provided a continuous tradition of hard-working administration covering a period of sixteen years. Yet it is possible that the explanation of the March's fiscal fertility lies mainly in its economic wealth and in its great number of towns. Some of these, such as Macerata, grew considerably during the century, some bene-fited from commercial relations with Venice, Florence and Pisa, and some from the capital of local Jewish communities.[1] The principal source of riches, however, continued to be agriculture and in the present state of knowledge it is not possible to estimate the relative agricultural wealth of the various provinces. The March and the Duchy had much comparatively unproductive soil high in the Apennines and the Tuscan Patrimony included the barren and malarial Maremma. The Romagna had fertile lands in the plain as well as sterile soil in the Apennine, but its towns were never sufficiently under papal control to yield much of their wealth to anyone but the war-lords of the mountainous zone. It is also doubtful whether the March can be safely described as by far the most productive province when the ill-documented Duchy can show such large revenues for the single year 1290–1.[2]

Whereas chaos and disobedience tended to mean poverty for the papal chamber,[3] there was a period in the later part of the century when much lawlessness and defiance of authority were yet compatible, at least in the March and Duchy, with fiscal productiveness. There were many times when Perugia and the towns of the March preferred to make the considerable payments of which they were capable, rather than face the inconveniences of defiance. It was not that they were overawed by the strength of the papacy, for the administrators of the State never had the military means to make this possible, but to lie under an interdict and to have incurred the pope's disapproval was a real inconvenience.

---

[1] See above pp. 87 ff. For the heavy fiscal dues of the March in the early fifteenth century *v*. Partner, pp. 115–16.

[2] See above, p. 271.

[3] One may note that a Bolognese merchant farmed a toll in 1291 on the condition — or so Bologna claimed — that he had to pay the agreed farm only if there was no *turbatio* or rebellion in Romagna. It was realized that during warfare the toll would be less productive. *V*. Bologna, AS, Lettere del Comune, Reg. 4, ff. 25, n. 4 and 25v, n. 1a.

In 1262–3 Urban IV had won over many of the Tuscan bankers by threatening to free their debtors from the liability of repayment.[1] The merchants of the Papal State were never wooed in the same style, so far as is known, but there must have been many who preferred peace with the higher power and access to church, even at a price. Although it was never a strong tradition, and could soon become enfeebled — one can trace this process in the rapid diminution of the revenues of the Tuscan Patrimony after Boniface VIII's time — there were periods when to pay taxes and fines was the conventional course. This situation could never last for long owing to the impuissance of provincial government, the cause in turn both of lower revenues and higher expenditure. In such circumstances the pope had to turn to those other sources of income which had assisted the growth and survival of the State at a time when the proceeds of the patrimony had been insignificant. Even at the end of the century income from the State probably accounted for only about one-tenth of the papacy's total revenues.[2]

[1] See Jordan, *Origines*, pp. 336–55.
[2] Pfaff, 'Die Einnahmen der röm. Kurie am Ende des 12. Jahrh.', *VSWG*, XL, 97–118; Baethgen in *QFIA*, XX, 166–9. Bauer, 'Die Epochen der Papstfinanz', *HZ*, CXXXVIII, has nothing to say about the topic of this chapter.

IX

The Military Utility of the Papal State

I t is natural to turn from the State's financial productivity to its contribution in manpower. The performance of military service at the request of the papal authorities was a normal obligation of the communes. A typical formula (in a letter of Innocent III to Fano) defined a town's duties as follows: *Ecclesiae Romanae fidelitatem curabitis universaliter exibere, expeditionem, parlamentum, pacem et guerram ad mandatum nostrum et legatorum et nunciorum nostrorum per totam Marchiam bona fide iuxta proprias facultates vestris expensis facere sine fraude.*[1] Occasionally the terms employed are slightly different (some communes are to *facere exercitum, facere exercitum et cavalcatam, facere hostem*, and so on), but the substance is always the same. Terracina seems to have been unique in claiming exemption from military service, but this privilege, although admitted by the provincial authorities, was not always effective.[2] Lay feudatories owed military service on similar terms to the towns.[3]

The stipulation that Fano owed military service only within its own province, the March, was characteristic, though this was not a fixed rule. Popes found much difficulty in persuading their subjects to fight further afield; the refusal of Viterbo in 1260-1 to enter an alliance which might commit it to warfare in Umbria is typical of this attitude.[4] Before the provincial divisions of the State were firmly fixed some other form of boundary might be named as the limit: thus Perugia agreed, in

---

[1] Amiani, *Fano*, II, xvii: these terms were confirmed in 1200 (Theiner, d. XLIII), 1247 (Amiani, II, i), and 1251 (Theiner, d. CCXXXVIII). The same terms applied to Pesaro and Iesi (P.L., vol. 214, cols. 912-13).

[2] Contatore, *Terracina*, pp. 75-8. At Montefiascone (P.L., vol. 214, col. 339) and Civita Castellana (Theiner, d. CLXXXII) the commune received a share of the profits of a toll in return for garrison and campaign duties, but such special arrangements constitute no real derogation of the principle of a universal obligation of military service.

[3] See K. Jordan, 'Das Eindringen des Lehnswesens in das Rechtsleben der römischen Kurie', *Archiv für Urkundenforschung*, XII (1932). The usual obligation was to *guerram et pacem facere contra omnes homines*, but the terms of fealty might include no specifically military clause: see for example a grant by Boniface VIII in return for the *consueta servitia que alii feudatarii eiusdem ecclesie in patrimonio beati Petri in Tuscia exhibere tenentur* (*Reg. B. VIII*, n. 1845).

[4] See above, p. 164.

1210, to provide troops for the pope *a civitate Perusii infra usque ad urbem Romanam.*[1]

Although most towns were held merely to *facere exercitum* or to provide *tam equites quam pedites habiles ad pugnandum,*[2] there were a few whose obligations were defined more precisely. In the terms fixed with Camerino in 1240 and with the new town of Città Papale in 1299 the amount of service due varied according to the locality in which it was rendered. Camerino was to provide its full *posse* for service within its own *contado*, five cavalrymen in the case of a summons to serve elsewhere in the March, and two cavalrymen only for duty farther afield.[3] Città Papale owed six days service, at its own expense, if near at hand, but only three in *Campanie ac aliis remotioribus partibus.*[4] An agreement made in 1247 between Spoleto and Cardinal Ranier bound the commune to provide military assistance within the Duchy for a period of not longer than eight days, except by the town's express consent.[5] Such arrangements as this were the outcome of bargaining between the papacy and individual towns at times when pope and emperor were contending for the allegiance of the communes. In 1226 Fabriano promised the rector of the Duchy service by its *posse* for three days only in a year, together with service for eight days from a much smaller force of two cavalrymen and three mounted crossbowmen: this obligation, however, related only to Fabriano's lands in the Duchy — the town itself and much of its *contado* was in the March — and is therefore quite exceptional.[6]

The terms of the summonses to arms sent by the pope or provincial rector to towns were also somewhat general. Typical of them is the call of Martin IV to the towns of the March in 1285, against Urbino, in which the communes are ordered that *vos potenter et viriliter accingatis ad dictum exercitum decenter muniti equis et armis predicto termino accessuri.*[7] This is an instance of a *generalis exercitus*, involving the whole military strength of the province, but in less serious troubles a few towns, or one only, might be summoned. It was common for the pope himself to

---

[1] Ficker, *Forschungen*, IV, d. 225. In the twelfth century Orvieto had owed military service between Tintinanno in the north and Sutri in the south (*Lib. Cens.*, I, 391).

[2] Borgia, *Velletri*, p. 276.

[3] Compagnoni, *Regg. Pic.*, p. 104: the previous year the imperialist authorities had fixed Camerino's *servitium debitum* at three cavalrymen within the March, for two weeks (*ibid.*, pp. 103–4).

[4] Theiner, d. DXXIV: these terms are interesting in that they may well reflect the practice of the last years of the thirteenth century in this province.

[5] Sansi, *Spoleto*, pp. 288–90: see above, p. 151.

[6] Document printed by W. Hagemann in *QFIA*, XXXII, 76–7.

[7] Theiner, d. CCCCXLI.

initiate such calls to arms, either by warning the towns that the provincial rector was likely to write to them soon demanding military
service or, frequently, by himself sending a definitive summons. A
papal summons was no doubt considered more impressive and more
likely to be effective than a rectorial one, and it was natural that the
pope should write himself when troops were to be called from more
than one province.[1] But it was also a normal practice for rectors to call
troops without any preliminary papal warning, and indeed the delays
in gathering an army would have been enormous had such a warning
been essential, particularly during the quite lengthy periods when the
pope was at Lyons.

It was normal to summon the full *posse* of the town, but a considerable number of letters have survived which specify the troops to be
sent and thereby throw much light on the militia of the communes and
on thirteenth-century warfare. A particularly interesting summons to
Macerata from the rector of the March in 1287 demanded ten cavalrymen, each with two horses, 500 infantrymen, twenty-five cross-bowmen specially chosen (*electos*) all properly equipped with armour,
shields, lances, cross-bows and *aliis opportunis et condecendentibus armis*,
as well as 100 sappers (*guastatores*) *cum ferris opportunis ad guastum*. This
force was to report at Fano within five days of the receipt of the rector's
letter, for ten days' service against Pesaro, which was 'in revolt'.
Macerata was threatened with a fine of 10,000 marks if its troops failed
to appear, and since the letter refers to a *generalis exercitus* we must suppose that the other towns of the March received similar calls to arms.[2]
A number of similar precise demands required at times a mixed force
(once a body of fifteen cavalrymen and 600 infantry, once three cavalrymen, ten cross-bowmen and sixty infantry),[3] on other occasions a
uniform one (for instance of 100 or 200 heavy infantry or of ten or
fifteen horsemen).[4]

The normal terms of military obligation make no mention of the
frequency with which service could be demanded, but the commune of
Amandola, newly recognized in 1265, was to serve 'as often and whenever it is ordered',[5] and this was certainly the usual understanding. In
times of emergency the papal authorities made calls at very short

---

[1] For an instance of this in 1280 *v. Reg. N. III*, n. 821.
[2] Compagnoni, *Regg. Pic.*, p. 147.
[3] Arch. Vat., Arm. XXXV, vol. 4, ff. 56v–57v (summons to Bevagna): Luzzatto,
'Matelica', p. 95.
[4] Colini-Baldeschi, *Osimo*, dd. CXXIV–CXXVII: Gianandrea, *Iesi*, d. CCXIX: *Reg.
Cl. IV*, n. 991: *Reg. B. VIII*, n. 5499.
[5] Ferranti, *Amandola*, III, d. 55.

intervals. Thus Cagli received three demands for military assistance from the vicar-general of the March in the summer of 1299, within a period of less than two months: on 29 May the town was asked to provide pay for twenty-five serjeants who were to garrison Senigallia for a month, on 1 June orders were received to prepare troops for a *generalis exercitus* against Osimo, and on 28 July it had to send soldiers against Fabriano.[1] Such frequent demands may have met with many refusals, but the refusals could in turn be a source of revenue to the papacy if the offending town was fined for non-fulfilment of military service, and in fact much of our knowledge of papal armies is derived from condemnations of this sort.

More important than the terms of the obligation to provide military service is the question of the effectiveness of papal summonses. This is perhaps best approached from a statistical standpoint and through taking as examples a few well-documented towns, after which we may bring in further evidence in discussing the attitude of the towns towards military service and the utility to the popes of this obligation.

I have noted one hundred and thirteen summonses to towns to provide troops, falling between the years 1234 and 1303. The sources are for the most part chronicles, records of payments made to those on service, and condemnations of towns for not sending soldiers: the last category is an important one, and may exaggerate the proportion of ineffective summonses. Of these one hundred and thirteen calls to arms, forty-nine were effective, while twenty-three met with refusals; we do not know the outcome of the remaining forty-one. This high proportion of uncertain responses is a warning of the very impressionistic nature of these 'statistics'; should the 'unknowns' happen to conceal many more ineffective summonses than effective ones, the weight of the evidence would shift in such a manner as to suggest that more calls were refused than obeyed. Nevertheless these numbers at least establish that there was no overwhelming tradition one way or the other; it was not unconventional for a commune to respond to a summons, nor was it unconventional to flout it.

These figures on their own necessarily appear somewhat abstract and to consider the records of some towns of various sizes and in different provinces may do something to remedy this. Unfortunately the evidence comes entirely from the second half of the century, for the earliest extant summonses are random survivals and there are not many

[1] Cagli, AC, 'F^a Lettere', uncatalogued.

from any one town. The table which follows summarizes the evidence
from the towns about which we have most information.

Response to demands for military service[1]

	Summonses	Effective	Ineffective	Not known
Perugia (1256–1300)				
troops	17	10	1	6
money	nil	—	—	—
Macerata (1256–90)				
troops	4	2	—	2
money	5	5	—	—
Fabriano (1255–94)				
troops	8	2	6	—
money	14	14	—	—
Iesi (1277–85)				
troops	6	—	5	1
money	9	8	1	—
Cagli (1265–99)				
troops	9	2	2	5
money	5	4	—	1
Matelica (1257–1302)				
troops	5	4	1	—
money	4	3	1	—

The city about which we possess most information is Perugia, whose
response to papal demands should be symptomatic of the attitude of the
larger communes. The number of occasions on which Perugia sent
troops is impressive, though there is a regrettably large figure for 'unknowns' here. The size of the force sent is sometimes recorded and is
never the full *posse*; obviously such a city would be unwilling to expose
itself to attack by sending a large proportion of its army, and it is not
surprising that it preferred to send a body of 100 cavalry or, less frequently, 200. In compensation for the rather small force supplied,
Perugia was willing to pay these troops, occasionally for quite a long
period, and to send them beyond the boundaries of its own province:
since it lay near the frontiers of the Tuscan Patrimony and the March
and not very distant from Romagna, the despatch of soldiers to the
latter province in 1282 and 1283 and to the Patrimony in 1269 and the
March in 1287 is not evidence of extraordinary devotion to the papacy.
The period of service is rarely recorded, but the troops sent for ten
days in August 1268 at the request of Clement IV, and paid by Perugia,

---

[1] For the sources on which these figures are based see the following footnotes.

were needed for a period of a month in all and the town was asked to pay their wages for the whole period. The cavalry provided for the war against the Colonna in 1297 was sent for three months.[1]

This information about Perugia is particularly valuable as comparative material because all the other towns concerning which we have a relatively large amount of evidence lie in a different province, the March, where town archives have survived more intact than in the other parts of the Papal State. In consequence we are well-informed about Macerata, Fabriano, Iesi, Matelica, and Cagli. None of these communes could rival Perugia in strength and the last two were small towns. Unlike Perugia, they were frequently asked for money in lieu of troops and nearly all of these demands were effective, though sometimes only after great delay. Since these requests for money were far more likely to meet with success than requests for men, it is not surprising that they were more numerous. When troops were provided they served within the boundaries of the province, except that Matelica and Cagli sent men to Urbino, which bordered on the March's northern frontier. The force supplied was often larger than Perugia's usual contribution — Macerata sent no less than 600 cavalrymen in 1287 — and it was a common practice to send a mixed body of cavalry, infantry and cross-bowmen.

Macerata[2] and Fabriano[3] were both fairly large towns, but the former was often the seat of the provincial government, whereas the latter was

[1] 'Regesta Reformationum Comunis Perusii, 1256-60', *BDSPU*, XXV, 253, 278, 286 (1256, requests); Ficker, *Forschungen*, IV, 441-2 and 447-8 (1259 and 1261, requests); Perugia, Rif. VI, f. 60 (1266, request); Potthast, n. 20391 (June 1268, request); Perugia, AS, Rif. VI, ff. 217-18 (August 1268, troops sent: probably 200, see Pellini, *Perugia*, I, 279); Perugia, AS, Rif. VI, ff. 289-90 and *Annales Urbevetani* in *Ephemerides Urbevetanae* (RIS, N.S.), XV, V, 158 (100 cavalry against Orvieto, 1269); Pellini, I, 295-6 (two paid cavalry forces to Romagna, 1281); Cronica A in *Corpus Chronicorum Bononensium* (RIS, N.S.), XVIII, I, 213 (fifty cavalry, Romagna, 1282); Perugia, AS, Rif. X, f. 44v (aid to Cagli, March 1287); *ibid.*, ff. 192v-3 (request refused, June 1293); *ibid.*, ff. 193v-4 (cavalry against Narni, July 1293); *ibid.*, ff. 295v-324v (100 paid cavalry for three months against Colonna, 1297); *Cronaca di Benevenuto* in *Fragmenta Fulginatis Historiae* (RIS, N.S., XXVI, II) 19 (against Gubbio, 1300).

[2] Macerata, AC, perg. III, 11 (1256, money payments): *ibid.*, 160 (Intr. Ex. 1280), f. 12v (Apr. 1280, money) and ff. 37-42 (Oct.-Nov. 1280: money) and f. 41 (Nov. 1280, request for troops); *ibid.*, Rif. I, ff. 86-7 (July 1287, request for troops: partly printed in Compagnoni, *Regg. Pic.*, p. 147) and f. 122v (Sep. 1287, 600 cavalry to Iesi: see also perg. XI, 12, 14, 16); *ibid.*, perg. XIII, 20, 24, 29 (1290, troops sent to Tolentino).

[3] Zonghi, *Fabriano*, dd. CLXXXI (1255, money), CCVII (March 1267, money, twice), CCVIII (August 1267, troops sent), CCXXVI (Oct. 1287, cavalry, infantry and cross-bowmen sent against Fermo), CCXXIX (July 1280, money), CCXXX (June 1282, ineffective demand for troops), CCLXII (July 1294, reference to four ineffective demands for troops): Fabriano, AC, Libro Rosso, f. 92v (1275, money), f. 93 (1277, money), f. 89v (Oct. 1278, money: repeated f. 101v), f. 90 (1279, money), f. 90 and v (March 1280, money), f. 91 (March 1281, money), *ibid.* (July 1281, money), f. 91 (Dec. 1281, money), f. 91v (Feb. 1282, money); *ibid.*, perg. V, n. 219 (1289, money).

situated close to the boundary of the March. It is therefore not surprising that Macerata has a better record of obedience, but the figures may be misleading since condemnations for evading military service are one of our main sources of information in the case of Fabriano.

It should be noted that all the surviving evidence about Iesi[1] relates to an eight-year period between 1277 and 1285. Within that time our information is fairly full and, although this was a particularly bellicose decade in the Papal State, a total of six military summonses and nine demands for money in lieu suggests that the figures for the other towns omit a great deal.

Cagli and Matelica, the last two towns, were small and distant from the centre of the province; the former, indeed, lay on its northern boundary, separated from the usual centres of provincial administration (Montolmo or Macerata) by a mountain range as well as by a distance of some fifty miles. Cagli, comparatively weak but far from the seat of government, has a record rather similar to Macerata, which was more powerful but more accessible to the representative of papal rule.[2] Matelica, smaller and closer to the provincial court, has an impressive record of military service rendered to the papacy, but it seems likely that this is in part a reflection of the survival of many thirteenth-century accounts for this commune.[3] The accounts mention payments made to troops serving the papal authorities; those sources which most frequently provide evidence of evasion of military service, papal and rectorial letters, are rare for Matelica.

These examples will at least have established the point that there was much evasion of military service. Fabriano was fined 300 *l.* in 1294 for failing to send troops on four different occasions, having been condemned for similar offences in 1278 and 1282; in 1278 the rector of the

---

[1] Gianandrea, *Iesi*, dd. CLXXXVIII (1277, money), CXCI (1278, money), CXCIII (Jan. 1279, money), CXCVI (Aug. 1279, money), CXCVII (Jan. 1280, troops refused), CXCIX (Aug. 1280, money), CC (Jan. 1281, money), CCIII (Aug. 1281, money), CCV (1282, money), CCXIX (1284: four refusals of military service, one of money, mentioned): Theiner, d. CCCCXLI (1285, demand for troops).

[2] *Reg. Cl. IV*, n. 991 (1265, call for ten cavalry); Bricchi, *Cagli*, pp. 135–7 (1263: call for troops, result unknown), 143–4 (1274, call for troops), p. 147 (*c.* 1277–9, same), p. 148 (1279, troops sent), p. 150 (1282, troops against Iesi refused), p. 193 (1283, troops against Urbino refused); Theiner, d. CCCCXLI (March 1285, demand for troops against Urbino); A. Gucci, 'Compendio delle Memorie della Città di Cagli' (MS. in Biblioteca Comunale, Cagli), II, f. 46v (1293, money paid, thrice); Cagli, AC, 'Fᵃ Lettere', uncatalogued (three letters of May, June, July 1299, one demanding money and the other two troops).

[3] Acquacotta, *Matelica*, pp. 97–8 (*c.* 1257, refusal); Luzzatto, 'Matelica', pp. 75 (1274, mixed force sent to Iesi) and 95 (1284, mixed force against Urbino); Mazzatinti, 2nd. ser., II, 208 (1281, failure to provide money), 229 (1288, troops sent to Cagli), 240 (1292, money payment), 259–60 (1298, troops against Senigallia), 276 (1302, troops sent to Arcevia in August and to Cingoli in September).

March had attempted to make the commune pay 12,000 ounces of gold, being the wages of the cavalry employed to attack the place when it defaulted in its military obligations.[1] Although little evidence has survived from the early part of the century — the earliest known instance of a town performing service seems to date from 1221[2] — it is clear that our findings concerning the later period are at least partly applicable to that time. As early as 1199 communes were asking the papacy to order out the troops of neighbouring towns in their defence, and six years later Innocent III threatened to call the surrounding towns against Viterbo.[3]

The gaps in the evidence concerning service rendered are so considerable that information about the feelings of the townsmen themselves is extremely valuable. Fortunately the attitude of the communes on the subject is illuminated both by the terms in which demands for service were phrased and by those in which city councils discussed them. There was sometimes an almost pleading tone in the apologetic words with which provincial rectors asked towns for military assistance, which contrasts strongly with the confident — though not always justifiably confident — formulae of the papal chancery. When the rector of the Duchy asked the Perugians for aid in June 1293 against Todi he reminded them of their long tradition of fidelity to the papal cause and 'implored' them to send help, invoking both their love of the Church and their friendship with himself and his family.[4] A few years later the accounts of the Patrimony reveal the same anxious attitude in the phrasing of an entry which concerns the payment of a messenger sent to Amelia 'to find out whether its help might make it possible to take action against the outlaws of Orte and S. Gemini'.[5] The little that we know of proceedings in the council meetings of the communes confirms that requests for military service were not treated as commands, but considered 'on their merits'. The *riformanze* for the year 1256 are extant at Perugia;

---

[1] For references, see above, footnote 3 on p. 281.

[2] Theiner, d. CVIII (service by Segni against Terracina).

[3] Theiner, d. XL (Città di Castello asks Innocent III to call Perugia and Massa Trabaria against Arezzo): P.L., vol. 215, cols. 673–4.

[4] Perugia, AS, Rif. X, ff. 192v–193: 'cum dictus dux (=Rector) memorie reducat devotionem et fidelitatem Perusinorum circa matrem eorum ecclesiam Romanam et quod nunquam defuerunt a servitio ecclesie pro eius parte imploratur ut verius ipso devocio pareat quatenus placeat tum ob reverentiam ecclesie tum propter amorem quem habet ipse dominus Dux ad commune Perusii et commune Perusii ad ipsum dominum Ducem et domum suam suscidium ordinari fieri per commune Perusii ipsi ecclesie et domino Duci ad resistendum exercitui et obsidioni quod si intendit per commune Tud. contra terram ecclesie...'

[5] Arch. Vat., Coll. 241, f. 36: '...ad sciendum ab eo si suo adiutorio posset fieri executio contra illos de civitate ortana et castri S. Iemini exbannitos curiae'.

they mention the discussion of three requests for military service, and twice the request is called a *petitio*. On one occasion it was decided that the rector of the Duchy should appear in person before the major council of the commune *et ibi debeat proponere peticionem suam*, after which the *podestà* and Captain with certain specially appointed *sapientes* were to debate the question and decide 'what action would be in the best interests of the commune' (*quicquid fuerit melius pro commune*).[1] Macerata's refusal to send troops on the fantastic grounds that it owed no service beyond the Potenza (a river running immediately to the north of the town)[2] shows a similar attitude to papal authority.

There were times when the pope or rector could be sure of a hearing, and this was when they urged one town to attack another which was already its enemy. Since warfare was endemic within the State such circumstances were frequent. In some cases they were so notorious that the letter of summons was couched in a special form appropriate to the occasion. In February and again in April 1263 Urban IV wrote to Gubbio giving that commune permission to capture and hold the territory and inhabitants of Cagli, with their possessions, and to do Cagli all possible harm without fear of incurring punishment. Gubbio had old scores to repay with Cagli, which had been granted its *contado* by the papacy only a few years earlier. In this and many similar instances the pope was merely unleashing a hound whose barking had already proclaimed its appetite for flesh.[3] Sometimes it is difficult to know whether or not to class such a campaign as warfare on behalf of the papacy. Gregory IX called many towns to aid Orvieto against its old rival Todi in 1238, but at the end of this war the Orvietans paid the rector of the Patrimony compensation and a sum equal to his expenses: in their eyes this had been an Orvietan, not a papal, campaign.[4]

Further evidence of the authorities' pessimism about the response to their calls for military service is supplied by a number of negative demands, asking towns not to oppose the papal cause, or to give no help

[1] 'Regesta Reformationum Comunis Perusii, 1256–60,' *BDSPU*, XXV, 253, 278, 286.
[2] Macerata, AC, Rif. I, f. 87 (1287).
[3] Gubbio, Sottosez AS, Libro Rosso, ff. 43–46v: the letter of 2 February concludes: 'personas et bona eorumdem civium tanquam Romane Ecclesie proditorum universis exponamus libere capienda, dantes vobis spetialiter impune capiendi eis in personis et rebus faciendi quoque ipsis per vos et amicos vestros duram guerram et asperam ipsos quibuscumque modis poteritis impugnandi plenam et liberam auctoritate presentium facultatem'. For a similar letter to Spoleto, concerning Trevi (*c.* 1273), *v.* Sansi, *Spoleto*, pp. 104n–105n. For Cagli and Gubbio's *contado*, see above, p. 152.
[4] Fumi, *Orvieto*, d. CCXLII: for the war, *Reg. G. IX*, nn. 4224–39, etc. For another instance of Orvieto fighting Todi (in 1274) at the request of the authorities of the Patrimony, *v. Ephemerides Urbevetanae* (RIS, N.S., XV, V) 158, and on the rivalry of these two towns Waley, *Orvieto*, pp. 16, 19, 40, 70, etc.

to its enemies. Thus the towns of the Duchy are asked by Honorius III in 1222 to send no troops to Viterbo and to offer no recruits to the imperial seneschal then recruiting in the towns of the Duchy or to any other imperial envoy.[1] In 1258 Fermo was in revolt; Alexander IV's letters to S. Ginesio and Perugia did not request aid, but told them of the rector's campaign against the rebels and asked them not to hinder the papal forces (*ut nullum praebant impedimentum*).[2] That such a pessimistic attitude was sometimes justified is shown by the events of 1282 in the Duchy. Perugia attacked Foligno and was excommunicated for this attack by Martin IV; Spoleto, though merely requested to 'give no aid to the Perugians', joined in on their side and was condemned in its turn by the pope.[3] Negative demands were no more certain than positive ones to be obeyed, but their very existence is a commentary on the difficulties facing the papal authorities in the enforcement of military service. Had the system been consistently effective we might expect to find a number of appeals from towns asking the papacy to provide protection for them, but such requests are extremely rare.[4]

It is not easy to give a general estimate of the effectiveness of the obligation to perform military service. Often aid was sent willingly when there is no evidence that it was requested; a community of interests must have put many towns within the Papal State at the side of the pontiff in much the same way as towns of Lombardy or Tuscany, while a commune was often sent by the pope to the aid of another to which it was in any case bound by the terms of an alliance. Such military assistance still illustrates the working of the obligation to serve the pope with troops, but it is a reminder that aid is not always proof of the efficient functioning of the machinery of government, and that where these inducements were lacking service was frequently evaded. Sometimes we have no evidence of a call to arms being refused, simply because the papacy made no call, there being no hope of enforcing it. Again, troops were often sent which were inadequate in quality or quantity, or with orders that enabled them to return home without rendering effective assistance.[5] Nor was obedience invariably

[1] Ficker, *Forschungen*, IV, d. 301. [2] *Ibid.*, d. 429: Potthast, n. 17280. [3] *Reg. M. IV*, n. 281.
[4] I have noted three instances only. One is from Città di Castello in 1199 (see above, p. 283 n.), one from S. Ginesio in 1250 (Potthast, n. 14110), the last from Bologna in 1299 (Ghirardacci, *Bologna*, p. 379).
[5] For instances of this, see Winkelmann, *Acta Imperii Inedita saec. XIII*, I, 549 and 553–4 for the troops sent by Rome to help Viterbo against Frederick II in 1243, which turned back at Sutri without accomplishing anything, and *Fragmenta Fulginatis Historiae* (RIS, N.S., XXVI, II), 17 for the army which accompanied the rector of the Duchy against Norcia in 1287, but put up such a poor showing against this small town that the rector was defeated and captured.

the safest policy, for on at least one occasion an enemy town accepted the tempting opportunity to ambush troops camping in the open at the *rendezvous* appointed by the provincial rector. The cardinals' attempt to raise a force against Orvieto in 1294 met with difficulties which were probably typical.[1] At least six towns and five baronial families received letters asking them to defend the Val del Lago that summer, but of these one commune and two barons were already engaged in the campaign-on Orvieto's side. Viterbo promised troops, as did Orte 'in accordance with its means, but not without other subjects of the Church', and the lords of Vico *pro viribus*, but in the end the cardinals seem to have received no aid whatsoever.

Naturally the situation regarding military service varied very greatly from time to time and from province to province. Almost entirely ineffective during the period of Frederick II's power, when the towns that fought for the papacy were its allies rather than its subjects, the system survived to have a very considerable impact during the last three decades of the century, particularly in the March. At its best it was adequate for the maintenance of an internal police force, each town being prepared to act against rebels in its own province. This situation is reflected in the agreement reached between Iesi and the rector of the March in August 1256. In return for the renewal of its privileges, and with the addition of a few detailed stipulations, the commune promised 'to serve me, the lord Annibaldo, for the whole period of my rectorate in good faith and without fraud, in *exercitus* and *cavalcate* generally and specially against all who rebel against me in the said March of Ancona, at my request and to the capacity (*posse*) of the city'.[2] It is to be noted that Iesi promises for the rector's period of office only a service which should have been a perpetual obligation requiring no special agreement, and that warfare against 'rebels' is specifically mentioned as the normal form of service. Iesi was already exempt, as were many other towns, from service beyond the bounds of its own province.[3] It was natural, however, that in times of crisis, and especially when virtually a whole province was in revolt, the papacy should look to the neighbouring provinces for military assistance. When the serious troubles began at Bologna and in Romagna early in 1280 Nicholas III wrote to the rectors of the March and the Duchy asking each to hold at once a secret enquiry

---

[1] See above, p. 226. For Fermo's treacherous attack on the troops of Ascoli and Offida in 1256 see Marcucci, *Ascoli*, p. cclvii; Colucci, *Ant. Pic.*, XIX, 40 and De Minicis, *Fermo*, pp. 349–50 (based on Ascoli Piceno, AC, Perg. R., fasc. 1, n. 2 and Quinternone, f. 164).

[2] Gianandrea, *Iesi*, dd. CLX–CLXII: *v. supra*, p. 161.

[3] See above, p. 276.

into the total force in cavalry and infantry owed him by the *civibus, baronibus, nobilibus, terris et locis* of his province, and the duration for which service was due: they were to send in this information at once to enable the pope to decide whether to ask for help in Romagna from these provinces and, if he did so, how much and of whom.[1] If we possessed the returns they would tell us as much about the subject of this chapter as all the other sources combined, but they have not survived. Whatever the result of the enquiries, the two provinces concerned played virtually no part in the ensuing war in Romagna, though they entered it in the very last phase, the operations at Urbino in 1284–5.[2] Hence this apparent exception to the rule that the communes gave little aid outside their own province in fact supports the rule.

A request for military service against rebels was a possible solution to internal unrest, but it was also a way of converting one rebellion into two, if the request was refused, and at the worst of making confusion worse confounded by spreading civil war from one province into the next. This is what happened, to some extent at least, as a result of the papal attempts to get aid from the other provinces for the war of 1280–5 against Guy of Montefeltro and his allies in Romagna. A *tallia* was levied in the March, in lieu of military service, possibly because the rector's report on military service there had been discouraging. Matelica failed to pay this tax and the rector took on some mercenaries to attack the defaulting commune.[3] Such a situation was unsatisfactory indeed, but scarcely as humiliating for the papacy as the obligations assumed on occasions by communes of the Papal State towards other powers. It was natural that the emperor should demand military service from the State while he occupied it, and Frederick II claimed this as a right,[4] but engagements to city-states were a different matter, and the promise made by Massa Trabaria in 1257 to perform military service at the request of Arezzo[5] is an indication of extreme papal weakness. If the capital of a sub-province — albeit an outlying one — could thus commit itself to a Tuscan city, what hope can there have been in such times of a satisfactory system of military service in the State as a whole?

*　　　*　　　*

In this discussion of the effectiveness of the obligation to provide

[1] *Reg. N. III*, nn. 821–2. [2] See above, p. 204: Theiner, d. CCCCXLI.
[3] Mazzatinti, 2nd ser., II, 208. [4] Huillard-Bréholles, VI, 1, 218.
[5] Pasqui, *Documenti per la Storia della Città di Arezzo*, II, n. 605.

military service it has been necessary to refer to the occasional substitution of troops by money payments. The change from unpaid feudal
armies to professional ones is characteristic of the thirteenth century in
many parts of Europe, and in northern and central Italy the cavalry
element in the communal forces was increasingly composed of mercenary soldiers rather than town-dwelling nobles or wealthy trades-
men.[1] Papal armies provide much evidence of this increase in the use of
paid troops, and we must now consider the extent to which they were
recruited within the Papal State and the effects of the change on
demands for military service.

Before the acquisition of Romagna the popes drew most of their
professional soldiers from outside the State, in particular from northern
Italy and France. Innocent III, however, had raised men in Rome and
the Campagna to fight Markward,[2] and Gregory IX and Innocent IV
recruited both here and elsewhere in the State during their wars with
Frederick II.[3] Troops from all parts of the State were in the army that
invaded the Regno in 1254, and mercenaries from the Campagna
fought against Manfred and Conradin.[4]

The Angevin conquest of the south added to the floating population
of professional soldiers; between Tagliacozzo and the Sicilian Vespers
many members of the victorious army must have been available for
fighting elsewhere in Italy. In 1276 a corps from the Regno raised and
paid by Charles of Anjou served Innocent V in the March of Ancona.
The army which fought for Nicholas III in Romagna in 1278–9 contained a large French element recruited in Italy, as well as men from
France, and troops enrolled locally, at Bologna and elsewhere, and in
Rome and the Patrimony.[5] In Martin IV's campaign in Romagna the
basic elements were French mercenaries and local troops, with some
additions from other parts of Italy, including the Campagna. Of the

---

[1] For a fuller treatment of this topic and of papal use of mercenaries from outside the
State, *v. EHR*, LXXII, 15–21. The smaller demands made on Camerino by both emperor
and pope (above, p. 277) may reflect this change.

[2] P.L., vol. 214, cols. xli–xliii and Reg., n. DLVII.

[3] Richard of S. Germano, pp. 152–61 (1228–9, troops from Campagna); Winkelmann,
'Kaiser Friedrichs II. Kampf um Viterbo', (1243, from Papal State); Huillard-Bréholles,
VI, 1, 125–6 and Böhmer, *Fontes Rerum Germanicarum*, IV, 711 (1245, from around
Viterbo); Gianandrea, *Iesi*, d. LXXXIX (1247, Romans); *Reg. Inn. IV*, n. 4698 (1249,
Papal State); *QFIA*, XVIII, 240–1 (c. 1249–50, Rome and Campagna); for measures
regarding recruitment in the March in 1249, *v. EHR*, LXXV, 660–4.

[4] *Vita Inn. IV*, p. 116 and Saba Malaspina, pp. 215–16 (1254, Campagna, Patrimony,
Duchy, March); Saba Malaspina, pp. 232–41 and Martène and Durand, II, 82 (1264,
Campagna); *Reg. Cl. IV*, nn. 1141 (1266, Peter Colonna and mercenaries from Campagna)
and 1327 (1268, Campagna).

[5] Laurent, *Innocent V*, pp. 410–11, 475: *Reg. N. III*, n. 308: *ASI*, XXXVI, 430–1:
Petrus Cantinelli (RIS, N.S., XXVIII, II), 29.

3,500 men put into the field under d'Eppe in 1282, 1,300 were from Bologna, 150 from elsewhere in Romagna and at least 350 from other towns of the Papal State.[1]

From the outbreak of the War of the Sicilian Vespers the papal troops in Romagna were for the most part local men, the French no longer being available. During the 1290s the rector required a regular campaigning force each summer, and on occasions this was very large; in 1292 it possibly attained 1000 cavalry and 30,000 infantry.[2] This standing army of the Romagna was not the only regular force maintained by the papacy, although the disturbed conditions of the province and the possibilities of local recruitment had combined to make it by far the strongest. The pope himself retained a small bodyguard; during the pontificate of Boniface VIII this force usually numbered thirty or forty horsemen, though its size fluctuated considerably according to circumstances.[3] In the Tuscan Patrimony the rector had at his disposal early in the fourteenth century a very small nucleus of cavalrymen, never exceeding ten in number or falling below four, under the command of a marshal. Apart from these headquarters troops, the province then had permanent garrisons in two fortresses; each of these numbered about a dozen, only very few of whom were mounted.[4]

The larger towns of the Papal State were themselves recruiting mercenaries early in the thirteenth century. While such recruitment continued for the most part to be local in scope, Bologna in 1277 hired 600 French cavalry, and in the 1290s the towns of the March took on men in Lombardy and the Regno. Around the same time outside powers, such as Manfred and Charles of Anjou and even Philip IV of France, themselves sought mercenaries within the Papal State.[5] By the

---

[1] Cronica A in *Corpus Chron. Bonon.* (RIS, N.S., XVIII, I), 213: there are slightly differing versions in Cronaca di Villola, *ibid.*, 213-14 and in Villani, VII, LXXX; to this force should probably be added 300 mercenaries sent by the towns of the March for three months (Theiner, d. CCCCVII).

[2] *Annales Forolivienses* (RIS, N.S., XXII, II), 40-54. Such a figure, for a brief campaign, is not incredible, in view of the number of Romagnol communes capable of providing a large force: Bologna alone put 800 cavalry and 7,000 infantry into the field in 1295 (Cantinelli, RIS, N.S., XXVIII, II, 55-72). Moreover the opponent of these armies, Guy of Montefeltro, was employing a similar force on a slightly smaller scale.

[3] Arch. Vat., Coll. 446, *passim* (1299) and Intr. et Exit. 5, *passim* (1302). The force was strengthened when the pope was on the move and required a large escort.

[4] *J Eccl H*, VI, 20-1.

[5] P.L., vol. 214, col. clxxxii (Rome and Viterbo recruit mercenaries, 1203) and Cristofani, *Assisi*, pp. 85-6 (1215). For local recruiting later, note Perugia's force in 1297 raised largely from Todi and Arezzo (Perugia, AS, Rif. X, ff. 295v-324v), *Corpus Chron. Bon.* (RIS, N.S., XVIII, I), 197 (Bologna, 1277) and De Minicis, *Fermo*, pp. 500 and 518 (March). The earliest extant agreement by a papal town to employ a regularly organized

u

last decade of the century the employment of paid troops was so normal that papal requests for military service began to specify that the troops sent were to be mercenaries; Fabriano was fined in 1294 *quia non misit stipendiarios sibi impositos*.[1]

This great change in the composition of armies meant that the popes found warfare far more expensive by the end of the thirteenth century than at its start; in their State, as elsewhere, the increased cost of war is undoubtedly one of the reasons for the fiscal innovations of the period.[2] There is a good deal of evidence to suggest that the communes had normally to pay their own troops when sending them to fight on behalf of the papal authorities.[3] The logical alternative to this system was that the towns should provide the pay but not the troops, while the pope or his representatives found the soldiers where they wished. Such a change would have a number of obvious advantages. Towns were on the whole less reluctant to send money, while mercenary troops were likely to be more experienced and formidable than a heterogeneous force collected from a number of communes.

A forced loan was imposed in the March to pay mercenaries in 1248, but the earliest recorded example of the provision of money-payments as a substitute for military service is not found until seven years later, when Alexander IV ordered a number of towns in the same province to furnish troops *vel opportuna pro eis stipendia* to the bishop of Faenza.[4] The army was required for service in the Regno, and the wording suggests that the choice between men and money was to be made by the bishop, not by the communes. Within a few years scutage was quite common, at least in this province. In an early form, the town paid the mercenaries employed by the papacy; this is an intermediate stage between the commune sending troops and paying them, and the final

mercenary band seems to be Matelica's employment of John 'Bayese' and his twenty-five *socii* as horsemen for three months in 1293 (Luzzatto, 'Matelica', 95n.). For recruiting in the Papal State by Manfred *v. Reg. Urb. IV*, nn. 758–9; by the Angevins, Martène and Durand, II, 178 and Amiani, *Fano*, II, lxiv–lxv (which implies that some papal communes had legislated against their citizens taking service as mercenaries).

[1] Zonghi, *Fabriano*, d. CCLXII.

[2] *V.* Lunt, *Papal Revenues in the Middle Ages*, I, 10–12.

[3] E.g. Tonini, *Rimini*, III, d. CXLIV; Pellini, *Perugia*, I, 295; Mazzatinti, 2nd s., II, 229 and 259–60; Theiner, d. DXXXIV; Macerata, AC, Rif. I, f. 122v and Perg., nn. 179, 243, 247, 252.

[4] Gianandrea, *Iesi*, dd. XCV–XCVI, XCVIII–XCIX and Colucci, *Treia*, d. XXIII (the forced loan). Acquacotta, *Matelica*, d. 39; Colucci, *Treia*, d. XXXVIII; *QFIA*, XXXVII, 129 (Montolmo); BFW, 8926 (Macerata and Fermo): the version of this letter in Compagnoni, *Regg. Pic.* (pp. 120–1) misleadingly has '*et* opportuna', etc., instead of *vel*. This letter dates from 28 January 1255: by July Fabriano had made a money-payment (Zonghi, d. CLXXXI).

method, whereby the town merely sent money and had no concern with the troops. In this perfected system of scutage the payment was known as *stipendia militum* and the number of troops for whom pay was required was specified as well as the campaign or garrison-duty for which they were needed. Thus on 20 December 1289 the treasurer of the March acknowledged the receipt from Fabriano of fifty florins *pro paga quinque militum morantium in civitate Urbini*.[1] The number of soldiers for whom pay was to be provided varied greatly; it might be for one man only, or it might be for twenty-five or even more.[2] Boniface VIII's statutes for the March provided that sums of money paid as scutage by communities of the province were to be repaid to them if the campaign for which they had been required was cancelled;[3] this suggests that rectors had been known to abuse the obligation by calling for *stipendia militum* and then employing the money for other purposes.

The amount due from each town, when more than one was asked for money, was the *tallia* of that particular commune: this can be rendered as the 'share' due from the town, and the word was in common use in contemporary Tuscany to describe the number of troops due from the members of a league to its military force, or the money due to pay mercenaries.[4] From the late 1270s it became usual, at least in the March of Ancona, to refer to the payment itself as *tallia militum*. The earliest reference to it under this name seems to date from 1277,[5] and within a few years it had become almost an annual obligation in this province; it was levied on a number of towns each year between 1277 and 1284, at the time of the great war in Romagna, and during this period was an extremely heavy liability. Iesi made a payment every year between 1277 and 1282, including two in 1281, and these payments totalled 2,800 *l.*; as the 400 *l.* paid in February 1282 are described as a double *tallia* for a three-monthly period, and another payment of 300 *l.* was made for the following quarter it would seem that the obligation had been converted in a very few years into a regular and onerous one.[6] Fabriano paid 1,600 *l.* as *tallia militum* between 1277 and 1282,

---

[1] Fabriano, AC, perg. n. 299.

[2] Ferranti, *Amandola*, III, 177b; Cagli, AC, Fᵃ Lettere, 1 June 1299; Zonghi, *Fabriano*, d. CCVII. An early example of *stipendia militum* is Montelparo's payment for 40 infantrymen in 1273 (Cicconi, *Montelparo*, d. XXXIV).

[3] Theiner, d. DLXXI.

[4] In 1267 Fabriano paid 300 *l.* 'pro stipendiis militum . . . occasione taliae impositae communi et hominibus dictae terrae pro stipendiariis domini cardinalis' (Zonghi, d. CCVII). For the *tallia* in Tuscany, see L. Naldini in *ASI*, LXXVIII.

[5] Fabriano, AC, Libro Rosso, f. 93.

[6] Giannandrea, *Iesi*, dd. CLXXXVIII, CXCI, CXCIII, CXCVI, CXCIX–CC, CCIII, CCV. See above, p. 264.

so that Iesi was not alone in bearing the burden: further evidence from
Macerata and Fermo[1] shows that the other towns were making
frequent payments of *tallia* in the same years, though the provincial
rectors were unable after this formidable start to retain the tax as a
regular due.

The change from *stipendia militum* to *tallia militum* is clearly connected
with a system of levying scutage on the whole province at one time,
and is part of a provincial reorganization achieved in the March under
the pressure of military necessity in Romagna. By 1280 the tax was
being farmed out and the first definite statement that it was being levied
on a provincial basis dates from 1281, when Martin IV wrote to the
rector telling him to make his province provide sufficient money for
the pay of 100 not 200, cavalrymen.[2] The new nomenclature and
system in the March achieved more than a convenient technique for
calling a fiscal *generalis exercitus*. By putting scutage on a new basis it
seems also to have made it easier to draw from the towns at short
intervals aid that could be either military or financial according to the
circumstances: that there was no rule that *tallia militum* absolved a commune from service in men within the same year is shown by Macerata's
provision of both in November 1280 and the requests for both made
within three days to Cagli in 1299.[3] This great change was only made,
or at least consolidated, with the consent of the towns, for after 1280
the rector of the March only levied *tallia militum* after calling a provincial parliament at which his subjects gave their formal consent.[4]

The new system soon spread to other provinces and especially to
Romagna, where the military tasks of the papacy were heaviest. By
1283 Urbino had to include in its statutes a clause stating its obligation
to contribute to *collectas pro stipendiariis tenendis* in Romagna when it
was included in that province, and the earliest definite reference to
tallia militum in Romagna dates from 1287, when the rector is reported
to have asked Forlì for the fantastic sum of 30,000 *l.*, which was refused.
At about this time Ravenna and Rimini, under their respective lords,
held out in a parliament at Imola against paying *tallia*, but a sum of
20,000 florins was levied in 1290. In 1294 and 1295 provincial parliaments consented to the levying of *talliae* to pay, respectively, 300 and

---

[1] Fabriano, AC, Lib. Rosso, ff. 90–91v, 92v–93, 101v; Macerata, AC, 160 (Intr. Ex.
1280), ff. 12v, 21, 37 and v, 39v–40, 41v–42; De Minicis, *Fermo*, pp. 462–3 and 487.

[2] Macerata, AC, 160 (Intr. Ex. 1280), f. 21: Theiner, d. CCCCIII.

[3] Macerata, AC, 160, ff. 37–42: Cagli, AC, Fª Lettere, 29 May and 1 June 1299.

[4] Fabriano, AC, Lib. Rosso, ff. 90–1; Gianandrea, *Iesi*, dd. CXCIX, CCIII, etc. For
parliaments and *tallia* see above, pp. 115 ff.

400 men. Faenza's share on one of these occasions, for a period of only four months, was 1,400 *l.*, so that here too the obligation was exceedingly burdensome.[1]

The alternative to occasional very heavy demands was a system for the regular payment of lighter *talliae*; we have seen that the regular and heavy *talliae* of the March lasted for a few years only. This alternative prevailed in the Tuscan Patrimony by the end of the thirteenth century. A list dating from about 1298 records the payment due annually from each town of the province as *tallia militum*: the amount totals 2,020 *l.* A few years later only about half of this sum was being paid, yet it was then the second biggest source of revenue in the province (ranking after the profits of justice) and accounted for almost a quarter of the total.[2] The rector's formulary of *c.* 1298 describes *tallia* as the tallage due 'for the mercenaries which the rector of the Patrimony keeps for the safe custody of the roads'. It is unlikely that the money obtained from the tax was set aside for the province's small permanent force and there is no evidence of this in the accounts: the significance of the formula is that *tallia militum* paid thus was due under the oath taken by the papacy's subject-towns *ad custodiendas stratas*,[3] not under the obligation to provide military service. Hence the situation was regularized whereby the authorities demanded both *tallia militum* and service in troops. It seems unlikely that this regular tax had to be voted by the parliament of the Patrimony. As in the March it could be doubled in times of crisis.[4] No reference has survived to *tallia* in the Duchy or Campagna-Marittima, and it seems unlikely that it was levied in these provinces.

There were soldiers also who accepted spiritual wages for their services, the crusaders. Unfortunately it is rarely clear whether such troops received worldly payment as well,[5] but numerous popes thought it worth while to offer crusading privileges to encourage recruitment. Innocent III granted them to the men who fought Markward, Gregory IX to the defenders of Rome in 1240 and Innocent IV to those of

---

[1] Theiner, d. CCCCXXIII; Cantinelli (RIS, N.S., XXVIII, II) 55, 76–7 and 82; *Annales Forolivienses* (RIS, N.S., XXII, II) 49 and 52; Tonduzzi, *Faenza*, pp. 327, 331, 341; Clementini, *Rimini*, I, 494–5. Bagnacavallo paid *tallia* in 1289, 1295, 1296 and 1302 (and was asked to pay in 1301 also): see *Atti e Mem. Dep. St. Patr. Emilia*, N.S., VII (1881), 152–5.

[2] *MAH*, VII, 187–9; *J Eccl H*, VI, 20.

[3] For this phrase, which was part of the general obligation on papal subjects to keep the peace, etc., see in particular Ermini, 'Caratteri', p. 318.

[4] For the *tallia militum duplicata* see Gianandrea Iesi, d. CCIII and *J Eccl H*, VI, 19.

[5] The topic is treated more fully in *EHR*, LXXII, 24–6.

Viterbo in 1243.[1] Alexander IV took many crusaders with him when he invaded the Regno in 1255, and in the fateful summer weeks of 1264 Urban raised a crusading force in the Duchy and Tuscany.[2] Clement IV too made use of this weapon and it had not lost favour by the end of the century; in 1289 the defenders of Forlì against rebellious Romagnol subjects received the cross, and later still Boniface VIII proclaimed a crusade against the Colonna.[3]

The obligation of military service on the towns of central Italy did not play a major part in the great papal struggle against the Hohenstaufen. In comparatively peaceful times it might provide a force capable of performing police duties, but when the contest for the control of Italy was at its height in the 1240s the Papal State was no more than a shadow and the communes that fought for the pope did so virtually as allies, though nominally they were subjects. In such a situation they fought primarily because to many of them, as to the cities of the north, the prospect of imperial control was distasteful; it is hard to analyse motives in such circumstances, but these towns were obedient subjects to the pope through coincidence of interests, not through any tradition of obedience. Moreover, despite the part played by men from the Campagna in 1228–9 and the more important rôle of local papal subjects at Rome in 1240 and Viterbo a little later, the main armies involved in the war with Frederick II were not the popes', but those of the Lombards, sometimes helped by papal money. In 1264 Urban IV had a really large force in the field, of some 3,000 mercenaries, besides many crusaders, the troops of Rome and the count of Anguillara with many other friendly towns and barons.[4] That year, however, was quite exceptional and a large army was always felt by both the popes themselves and those whom they taxed to represent an intolerable financial burden. One echo of the big armies of the 1240s may be found in the scheme, indignantly reported by Matthew Paris — though the idea was never put into practice — for making various English prelates liable for the entire pay and equipment of five, ten or fifteen cavalrymen respectively, for a whole year.[5]

---

[1] MGH, XXII, 540: *Reg. Inn. IV*, nn. 170, 2945, 4097; Huillard-Bréholles, VI, 647.

[2] Jamsilla, p. 191; Hampe, *Urban IV. und Manfred* pp. 44–60 (1264).

[3] *Reg. Cl. IV*, n. 175; BFW, n. 9582; RIS, N.S., XXII, II, 43; *Reg. B. VIII*, nn. 2273, 2352, 2375, 2383, 2878, etc.

[4] See Hampe, *Urban IV. und Manfred*, loc. cit.

[5] Matthew Paris (R.S.), IV, 536–7. According to Paris the intended victims of the scheme were ordered by papal envoys to reveal it to no one for six months, on pain of excommunication. It all makes a good story, which probably loses nothing in the telling. Cf. the similar tale, current in French circles, that Boniface VIII drew enough money to pay 3,000

Since pitched battles were a rarity in the thirteenth century, the popes required troops mainly for manoeuvring and garrison duties, in which amateurish forces of the communal militia were at no very serious disadvantage. The commanders in major campaigns, such as those in Romagna, were often 'regulars', but prelates sometimes acted as generals in the field; Cardinal John Colonna did so in 1229, Cardinal Ranier in 1243 and Cardinal William of St. Eustace in 1254–5. Durand says in the *Speculum Iuris* that as rector in Romagna he was responsible for the administration of his armies but did not command 'men of blood'.[1] The distinction may not have been easy to draw in practice, but this arrangement was probably the best from a military as well as a theological viewpoint. No thirteenth-century pope accompanied his men into action.[2]

Though central Italy, in particular the Campagna, was a favoured zone for recruitment, this might well have been the case even without the papacy's new territorial ambitions. In one way, however, the new State did serve as a distinct military advantage to the popes: it gave them more room. After 1198 a larger territorial barrier protected them from their opponents, and in an age when the melting-point of armies was low this form of protection was an important one. In 1264 it was perhaps the distance between the Regno frontier and his own residence at Orvieto which saved Urban IV from becoming a prisoner, for the zeal of Manfred's invading army languished in the Umbrian hills and thus his schemes came to nothing. This was the last great triumph of papal troops and papal distances: it had been an immensely expensive and a necessarily brief effort.[3] Thereafter military duties and their concomitant power passed to the Angevins. Only after the start of the war of the Sicilian Vespers, and especially during Boniface's campaigns against the Colonna, do we find again those mixed armies of papal mercenaries, papal subjects and crusaders which characterize the pre-Angevin era. Drawing up a final balance sheet, the advantages of the papacy's new

cavalry and 20,000 infantry for the Colonna war from French prelates alone (Dupuy, *Hist. du différend*, p. 343).

[1] Lib. I, pt. 1 (p. 66 of Frankfurt edn., 1668). The entire passage is of interest: 'Clericus ergo non debet praeponi bellis, nec retiariis, nec balistariis, nec huiusmodi viris sanguinum; ... tamen justo bello, quod non ad occidendum, sed ad defendendum, seu recuperandum sua geritur, praeponi potest ... ut respondeat militibus et sumptus ministret, tractatus teneat, sententias proferat, et negotia cuncta disponat, prout nos huiusmodi officium gessimus in guerra quam Ecclesia Romana contra civitates sibi rebelles in provincia Romaniolae gessit'.

[2] The description in Digard, I, 357–8, of Boniface VIII watching his troops go into action from the ramparts of Rome is the picturesque product of a misinterpretation of a passage in a contemporary letter (printed in P.L., vol. 185, col. 1858).

[3] See above, p. 261, for expenditure at this period.

status in central Italy to its military strength must be accounted as dubious indeed. Its strength was entirely consumed in attempting to make good the new claims and was insufficient to accomplish this. Hence the unceasing conflict with papal subjects, seen in its most concentrated form in the long and unsuccessful struggle to absorb the powerful tyrants of Romagna. The conclusion must be that in a military as in a financial sense there were few periods in the thirteenth century when the new State could declare a profit, and at the best it could do little more than produce the money and men required for its own consumption.

Conclusion

After recounting the tale of the papacy's attempts to govern central Italy it is natural to turn to the question of the influence of these efforts on general papal policy and papal prestige. This is exceedingly difficult to assess, since no genuine distinction can be made between rule in the Papal State and other aspects of the papacy's Italian policy. In the middle of the twelfth century the popes had made the decision to withstand Barbarossa's attempt to dominate the peninsula. That they should do so was the natural result of the traditions of the Church — which had from the start accepted land and the territorial authority which went with it and which was not committed to pacifistic non-resistance. Characteristically, a favourite quotation of Gregory VII had been 'Cursed be he that keepeth back his sword from blood' (*Jeremiah*, XLVIII, 10). From the decision to resist the Hohenstaufen there is a complete continuity of tradition into the thirteenth century, when the situation only differed in degree — not in kind — through the further decision to seek practical overlordship in the Duchy and March in 1197. This was clearly preferable to the alternative of a settlement with Markward of Anweiler and Conrad of Urslingen and thereafter no satisfactory circumstances offered themselves for laying down the burden of central Italian rule. The Angevin alliance and the acquisition of Romagna represent the continuation of the same attitude to Italian commitments.

If one attempts to visualize the consequences of a decision not to exploit Henry VI's death by claiming the Duchy and March, one must set against the picture of what actually ensued not a vision of a papacy freed from all territorial entanglements but one of a smaller patrimony of St. Peter corresponding to the Campagna-Marittima and Sabina (possibly with the Tuscan Patrimony). There would still have been the problem of Rome itself, of baronial rivalries and much more besides. Such a patrimony might have left the papacy no poorer and little weaker in military potentialities, but it would not have left the popes free of temporal preoccupations. The enlarged State was indeed invaded by Frederick II and by Manfred and these invasions were a source of grievance and condemnation, but what the popes feared was Hohen-

staufen domination in central Italy rather than trespass on their territories. Later the State served as something of a base for Charles of
Anjou, or at least its institutions provided the means for Angevin permeation. Again, however, Angevin control would have expressed
itself in different forms had the State been smaller, and was in no way
the product of the State itself. As for nepotism, the alternative to
Angevin power, this too would have existed without the State, as it had
in earlier times, though the State did much to determine its nature and
certainly increased the popes' need to have recourse to it. In Boniface VIII's family policy in the Campagna and Tuscan Patrimony there is
an indivisible fabric of territorial control achieved both through purchases
nd inheritance of land and through the tenure of provincial offices.

The thirteenth-century Papal State was in no significant sense a
theocracy, for many of its rulers were laymen. Nevertheless it took up
much of the time and energies of popes, cardinals and other clerics and
in this way it affected the 'tone' of the Church and played a part in the
slow decline in spirituality which marked the age between St. Francis'
reform and Luther's.

To estimate the effect of the State on papal prestige is even harder for
'prestige' is an intensely difficult concept to handle. Everything depends
on whose opinion is in question and the very nature of public opinion
changes radically during the thirteenth century, particularly in Italy,
through the appearance of a large class of articulate and educated laymen. If 'opinion' seems to change, this may be the result of alterations
in the holders of opinion as well as in the institutions concerning which
opinions are held. Prestige is thus essentially evasive and in constant
motion. Moreover, assessments of prestige are particularly the prey of
individual prejudice, for it is difficult not to equate 'what people thought
at the time' with 'what I think I would have thought at the time'.
Judgements on the papacy are specially open to unconscious anachronism of this sort; it is not easy for Protestants to go back into a
climate in which there was rarely a respectable alternative creed to
Catholicism.[1] Yet another difficulty is provided by the need to distinguish between prestige and popularity. What we are seeking here is

[1] Some of the striking remarks of A. L. Smith in his Ford Lectures on the thirteenth
century papacy are perhaps open to this criticism. He says 'the Papal States were a very
body of death to the spiritual life of the greatest institution in human history': Innocent IV
had launched the Church 'irretrievably upon a downward course . . . In ruining the
Empire, he had ruined also the future of the Papacy . . . the papacy of the thirteenth century
. . . bartered spiritual leadership for temporal rule' (*Church and State in the Middle Ages*,
pp. 210, 245).

the view of the serious-minded rather than general opinion. There have always been men like the Sienese poet who would have enjoyed being pope because he would have been able to 'embroil' the whole of Christendom[1] and the Florentines who welcomed the prompt but salacious retort of a friar with: *Benedicatur ipse, quia de nostris est,*[2] but these are not the people we are now consulting.

Even these preliminaries do not dispose of the difficulties in assessing contemporary views of the Papal State. It was of course taken for granted that the Church should be an institution which possessed territory and hence secular power. If St. Edmund had his hundreds, why should not St. Peter have his patrimony? Monastic comforts and Roman avarice were fair game for the satirists, but even these never attacked ecclesiastical lands as an institution; Anabaptist proposals of this sort come only from such an extreme religious radical as Arnold of Brescia. When Matthew Paris was indignant about Innocent IV's armies it was not the armies as such that he objected to but the suggestion that the English clergy should help to finance them.[3] It was only when such commitments seemed pre-eminent over spiritual ones that they met with criticism from men like Caesarius of Heisterbach, who complained of the German bishops that 'since they make wars they are compelled to be more anxious about the pay of their soldiers than the welfare of the souls committed to their care'.[4] Dante went further and deplored the donation of Constantine. He believed that the Church had 'fallen in the mud' and 'sullied itself and its burden' by combining temporal with spiritual rule, but he also wrote of papal policy generally, not specifically of the State.[5]

One result of all this was that, the *terrae ecclesiae* being taken for granted, not much attention was paid to their great extension in the thirteenth century or to the profound alterations in the nature of their rule. It has to be confessed, in fact, that there is little evidence that contemporaries recognized the existence of a 'Papal State' and if they did not know it existed it is no use asking what they thought of it. Outside

---

[1] S'i' fosse papa sare' allor giocondo,/che tutt'i cristiani imbrigherei' (Cecco Angiolieri in *Sonetti burleschi e realistici*, p. 112).

[2] Salimbene, I, 110.

[3] See above, p. 294.

[4] *Dialogus Miraculorum*, Bk. II, ch. 27. Caesarius seems to have believed that the Church outside Germany had no military obligations.

[5] *Purgatorio*, XVI, 127 ff. These views were expressed and to some extent formed several years after the period covered by this volume. For the date of the *Divina Commedia v.* Cosmo, *A Handbook to Dante Studies*, pp. 139 ff. and D'Entreves, *Dante as a Political Thinker*, pp. 59 ff. The *Purgatorio* was certainly not written before 1313, for VI, 107 refers to events of that year.

Italy men judged the papacy by its emissaries and its fiscality rather than by reports of its policy in the peninsula, but the lack of comment from central Italy itself is most striking. No doubt this in part reflects the popes' failure to make their subjects aware of their overlordship, but it can also be explained by a lack of the sort of literature in which such comment might be sought: there is very little in the way of satire and of political writings, chroniclers tend to limit themselves to narrative and there are as yet no diaries and virtually no biographies, even of a hagiographical nature.

In this general silence an occasional voice may be heard raised in complaint. The action of the Perugians in burning the pope and cardinals in effigy[1] must be accounted the outstanding example of papal overlordship diminishing papal prestige. Such an expression of indignation was, however, quite exceptional. Romagnol poets complain about the omnipresence of Frenchmen and one satirist thinks that 'Charles has become God's messenger on earth',[2] but these criticisms of papal dependence arise from an Angevin dominance which is not essentially a product of the Papal State. Discontent with the papacy might be expected to express itself in heresy, especially in an age when religious argument was often *ab homine* if not *ad hominem*: Bologna had a number of heretics in 1299, most of whom based their beliefs on the view that Boniface VIII was 'malus homo' and could not be pope in the lifetime of Celestine V.[3] Heresy was very strong in the Tuscan Patrimony in the early thirteenth century,[4] but this was merely the southern outcrop of the powerful dualism of Lombardy and imperial Tuscany, whence its teachers came. It was not a protest against papal rule and in any case it soon yielded before the mendicants' Catholic reconquest. The many Bolognese heretics at the end of the century, though they spoke 'multa mala de domino papa de cardinalibus et clericis et de fratribus', had not a word to say against the pope's temporal power. They also had been converted by men from further north. Altogether heretical movements were not strong in the Papal State in the period covered by this book, though dissident Franciscans and Fraticelli were to found many strongholds in Umbria and the Marches during the following century.

Since contemporaries were, justifiably, barely aware that the popes

---

[1] See above, p. 206.

[2] *Poesie Provenzali storiche relative all' Italia* (ed. De Bartholomaeis), II, 215–21 and 288: but there are also pro-Angevin poems. *Sonetti burleschi e realistici*, pp. 52–3 (anonymous Florentine poem against Charles of Anjou).

[3] Dupré-Theseider, 'L'Eresia a Bologna nei Tempi di Dante' in *Studi Storici in onore di G. Volpe*, I, 381–444. The passages quoted here are from pp. 416 ff.

[4] Above, pp. 36 and 52.

of the thirteenth century were working at the foundation of a new state, it is not surprising that the most explicit discussion and criticism of the state should come from an interested party. This was the French monarchy. Philip III's representatives suggested to Gregory X in 1273 that the Church in Italy might be rescued from its perennial disturbances and afflictions 'if it was governed in temporal things by some (lay) prince'. The pope made a cautious reply to the effect that he would favour such an arrangement if the decision lay with him, but that there many arguments against the change and it was not a practicable one in prevailing circumstances.[1] Nothing more was heard of this proposal for a time, though at some periods Charles of Anjou's relationship with the papacy was such as to give it a trial in a modified form, *de facto* though not *de jure*. It reappears, however, in the writings of Pierre Dubois, the Norman legist and pamphleteer. In his *Summaria*, written *c.* 1300, Dubois deplores the fact that the popes have never been able to enjoy full control over their lands, owing to the wickedness of their subjects. They are usually too old and unwarlike to overcome this difficulty and lack the necessary friends and relatives to suppress rebellion by force of arms. In any case, what pope is to be found capable of undertaking this task and yet suitable to hold spiritual office? The only solution is that the King of France should be senator of Rome (appointing a vicar) and should hold the entire Papal State as a fief, paying the pope an amount equal to the revenues at present derived from temporal possessions.[2]

---

[1] '... l'esglise de outre mons qui mout se deveroit esjoïr se elle estoit governée quant à sa temporalité par tel prince, et déliverée seroit et à seur de turbations et des aversités qu'el a soffert longuement au tens des autres princes'. The papal reply, as reported, included the words: 'quant estoit de sa volenté, il vouroit mout que la chose se feit' (document printed in Champollion-Figeac, *Documents historiques inédits*, I, 653–4).

[2] Petrus de Bosco, *Summaria brevis.*, (ed. H. Kämpf), pp. 12–13. The relevant passage reads as follows: (the French king) 'poterit procurare ab ecclesia Romana quod de cetero quicumque rex Francorum sit senator urbis Rome per alium hoc excercens, et quod ab ecclesia Romana tenet totum patrimonium ecclesie Romane. Ita quod estimatis omnibus obvencionibus eiusdem patrimonii ad papam spectantibus, tam de urbe Romana Tucia maritimis et montanis quam de regnis Sicilie Anglie et Aragonie et aliis; per manum vestram habeat papa tantum quantum habere consuevit, vos autem homagia regum et aliorum principum ac omnes obediencias civitatum castrorum villarum habeatis cum proventibus universis quos papa percipere consuevit. Quod autem hunc tractatum facere sic mondum regere uterque parti expediat, declarari potest in hunc modum: Licet enim papa in regno Sicilie, Urbe romana, Tucia maritimis et montanis aliisque terris quas habuit ex donacione primi catholici imperatoris Constantini . . . tamen propter maliciam et caliditatem et fraudem huiusmodi locorum gaudere nunquam potuit nec potest super hiis pleno iure, ymmo quia non timebant eum eo quod bellicosus non erat nec esse debet, multe guerre orte fuerunt, multi fuerunt ab ecclesia condempnati principes cum adherentibus. Item in Romanos pontifices non eliguntur . . . nisi senes aut ectiam decrepiti, plerumque non nobiles genere, in armis non experti nec assueti. Quomodo autem talis, qui non habet amicos bellicosos, affeccione sanguinis sibi conjunctos, talium subdictorum . . . superbias in modico tempore quo vivet tantum tot rebelliones et insidias poterit superare? Non est

Dubois returned to this scheme in his longer work, the *De Recuperatione Terre Sancte*, which was written early in the pontificate of Clement
V (*c.* 1305–7). Again he deplored the perils of temporal rule for papal
spirituality. The only conclusion possible was that the pope must secure
exemption from his secular responsibilities by granting his lands in fee
to a ruler or rulers; he would still receive their revenues, after the
deduction of expenses, or a fixed annual payment in lieu. The monarch
suggested is, of course, the King of France, who should obtain 'rule,
possession and governmental powers over the pope's temporals in
perpetuity.' The King would pass on the work of government to his
brothers or sons, as he saw fit. One of these should be senator of Rome
and, in the King's absence, 'supreme justiciar of the patrimony', but
final appellate jurisdiction might lie with the pope. One advantage of
all this would be that the popes could live in France. The Roman prelates would lose their rich livings and, thanks to the climate, their
conduct would improve.[1]

Dubois was a zealous and naive nationalist, more concerned for the
welfare of the French monarchy than for that of the Holy See. More
relevant to the theme of this book than his proposals is the information
adduced to justify them. The Angevin connection and Philip the Fair's
dealings with Boniface VIII are sufficient explanation of the familiarity
shown by this Frenchman with the political condition of central Italy.
In some ways his viewpoint was perhaps shared by Clement V and his
Avignonese successors — no native of Europe north of the Alps could
resign himself easily to Italy's peculiar municipal traditions — though
they never proposed that rule over their state should pass to the French
royal family. They saw its anarchic condition as the cause of their exile
and, if this was not truly such as to make the sojourn at Avignon inevitable, they were entirely justified in devoting much energy to it. They

racioni consonum nec verosimile quod hoc possit evenire, et, quia vix aut nunquam evenit
temporibus retroactis juxta legis consilium presumi non debet quod eveniet in futurum
. . . etsi ipse possit habere commodum solitum sine honere et impedimento cure animarum
sibi commisse, terrenas occupaciones et occasiones malorum victando, et hoc recusare
presumit et audet, quis eum a cupiditate, superbia et presumpcione temeraria poterit
excusare? Quis ille qui se possit et audeat estimare sufficientem ac ydoneum ad utriusque
gladii tante rei publice potestatem! Quomodo gravissimum superbie vicium poterit
evitare? Tot enim et tam cogentes raciones ad hoc possent induci, maxime perhibentes
factorum illarum terrarum experienciam . . .' These suggestions may be related to the
powers conferred in 1301 on Charles of Valois (see above, p. 238). For the dating of this
work *v.* Dubois, *The Recovery of the Holy Land* (ed. and trans. W. Brandt), p. 48.

[1] *De Recuperatione Terre Sancte* (ed. Langlois), pp. 25, 33, 98–102, 105. Dubois believed
that it would be for the general good if the whole world was subject to France: 'propter
tocius rei publice salutem expediret totum mundum subiectum esse regno Francorum'
(*Summaria*, p. 11).

had to work hard to bring about a situation favourable for a return to Italy, and in the Avignon period the Papal State provides, as it were, the framework within which the papacy has an Italian policy: it thus plays a much greater part in papal policy as a whole. For the period of the struggle against the Hohenstaufen any such division would be misleading, but the situation in 1266–1304, when pro-Angevin and family policies alternated, resembles much more closely that of the Avignonese papacy. The abandonment in 1303 of an Italian strategy based on the territorial power of the Roman noble families was in part a result of the inability of thirteenth-century popes to dominate their central Italian State, but Dubois' writings are a reminder of the strong external forces with which these pontiffs were confronted. In their government of the Papal State both Nicholas IV and Boniface VIII acted wisely. Moreover many earlier popes had sought a similar basis of temporal power, and neither the policies of the thirteenth-century pontiffs nor the circumstances which determined their failure were essentially the product of the new and ambitious state. Although the setting of provincial government pitted against communal independence is a unique one, this story of central weakness and local strength is a characteristic medieval tale. The popes had no particular cause to reproach themselves for failure in the impossible task of ruling the towns: at this time constant warfare prevailed in northern as well as central Italy. But critics, when they became aware of the State, would not always be willing to make allowance for its difficulties and the papacy was liable to be judged by special standards. There were cardinals who realized this already at the time of Benedict XI's death and asked: 'How can we rule in other lands if we cannot dominate and pacify our own?'[1]

---

[1] Finke, *Acta Aragonensia*, I, 177.

Appendix I

LIST OF PARLIAMENTS

Note: When parliaments have been discussed in the text, a page reference to the relevant passage is given. In other cases, a source is cited.

General Parliaments

1. 21–23 September 1207. Viterbo. See pp. 52–3.
2. *c.* December 1260. Rome. (Tuscan Patrimony and Duchy). See p. 164.
3. *c.* July 1264. Orvieto. (Tuscan Patrimony and Duchy). See p. 173.

Campagna and Marittima

None recorded.

Tuscan Patrimony

1. Before 1260 (probable) (reference in Todi, AC, Reg. Vet. Istr., f. 103v).
2. After 25 May 1281. Montefiascone. (Todi, AC, Reg. Vet. Istr., ff. 105v–106.)
3. 1288–92 (*temp.* Nicholas IV) (probable). See ref. *MAH*, VII, 181.
4. 16 November 1298. Montefiascone. See pp. 113–15.

Duchy of Spoleto

1. *c.* mid-June 1220. Bevagna. See p. 132.
2. *c.* 29 June 1220. Orvieto. See p. 132.
3. After 25 July 1228 (probable). Perugia. See p. 110.
4. Between 17 February and 1 June 1277. Bevagna. (Perugia, AS, Rif. X, ff. 182v–183 : Gubbio, Sottosez AS, perg., bu. 16.)
5. 6 July 1292 (and preceding days). Bevagna. (Sansi, *Storia del Comune di Spoleto*, I, 124 n.)
6. 8 November 1300. Bevagna. (Fausti in *Archivio per la Storia Ecclesiastica dell' Umbria*, IV, d. 540.)
7. Between 18 December 1303 and 20 March 1304 (probable). (Gubbio, Sottosez AS, perg., bu. 16.)

March of Ancona

1. 7 July 1249. Fano. See pp. 149–50.
2. 12 August 1252. Tolentino. (*Lib. Cens.*, I, 564.)
3. 7 March 1255 (probable). Tolentino. (Grimaldi, *Matelica*, d. CXVI.)
4. After 28 March 1266 (planned, but possibly not held). (Martène and Durand, *Thesaurus*, II, cols. 286–7, 293–4.)

5. 24 May (*or* 24 June *or* 24 July) 1272. Macerata. (*RSDI*, II, 297–305.)
6. Between 20 April and 25 December 1278 (probable). Iesi. (Vernarecci, *Fossombrone*, I, 268.)
7. Before 11 March 1280. Iesi. (Fabriano, AC, Lib. Ross., f. 102.)
8. Before 15 January 1281 (probable). Fano. (Gianandrea, *Iesi*, d. CC; Fabriano, AC, Lib. Ross., f. 91.)
9. Before 8 July 1281. Tolentino. (Fabriano, AC, Lib. Ross., f. 91; Gianandrea, *Iesi*, d. CCIII.)
10. Before 5 December 1281. Cingoli. (Fabriano, AC, Lib. Ross., f. 92v; Gianandrea, *Iesi*, d. CCV.)
11. Before 20 February 1282. Iesi. (Fabriano, AC, Lib. Ross., f. 91v; Gianandrea, *Iesi*, d. CCVI.)
12. Between 23 May and 2 July 1282. (Macerata, AC, perg. n. 139.)
13. Before 3 June 1291. (Macerata, AC, 161 (Intr. Ex. 1291), f. 8.)
14. 27 September 1301. Macerata. (*RSDI*, V, 180–4.)
15. Between 2 January 1302 and 30 November 1303 (probable). (Theiner, d. DLXXI.)
16. *c.* July 1304. (Ferranti, *Amandola*, III, d. 340; Corridonia, AC, perg. n. 48.)

Romagna

1. 1 December 1278. Cesena. (RIS, N.S., XXVIII, II, 30.)
2. 12 January 1280. Faenza. (RIS, N.S., XXVIII, II, 41; Ghirardacci, *Bologna*, p. 251.)
3. 13 February 1283. Imola. (*Nuovi Studi Medievali*, II, 241–52.)
4. Between 5 April and 30 December 1287. Imola. (Tonduzzi, *Faenza*, p. 327; Clementini, *Rimini*, I, 494–5; Ghirardacci, *Bologna*, p. 269.)
5. 16 May 1288. Forlì. (RIS, N.S., XXVIII, II, 57.)
6. 25 June 1289. Cesena. (*ASI*, LXXXIII, 246–50.)
7. 29 December 1289. Forlì. (RIS, N.S., XXII, II, 43 and XXVIII, II, 59; Ghirardacci, *Bologna*, p. 289.)
8. 1 March 1291. Forlì. (RIS, N.S., XXII, II, 44 and XXVIII, II, 63–7.)
9. Before 14 December 1291. Cesena. (Imola, AC, Mazzo IV, n. 92.)
10. 28 December 1291 (planned: probable). Forlì. (Imola, AC, Mazzo IV, n.92.)
11. 1292 (but perhaps identical with previous entry). Forlì. (*ASI*, LXXXV, 6–7.)
12. 1292 (probable). Faenza. (RIS, N.S., XXVIII, II, 67; Bonoli, *Forlì*, pp. 112–13.)
13. Between January and September 1294. Imola. (Ghirardacci, *Bologna*, p. 317.)
14. 10–11 November 1294. Imola. (RIS, N.S., XXVIII, II, 76; Fantuzzi, *Mon. Rav.*, III, n. LXXXXIV.)
15. 24 April 1295. Imola. (RIS, N.S., XXII, II, 49 and XXVIII, II, 77; Ghirardacci, *Bologna*, p. 325.)

16. 27 October 1295. Cesena. (*Nuovi Studi Medievali*, II, 233; RIS, N.S., XXII, II, 52 and XXVIII, II, 82–3; RIS, O.S., XIV, col. 1112, with incorrect date, '26 October'.)

17. Before 1 March 1296. Rome (representatives called to papal Curia). (See p. 241.)

18. 7 November 1296 (probable date). Ravenna. (Ghirardacci, *Bologna*, p. 339; *AMSR*, s. IV, VIII (1918), 111.)

19. 14 February 1301. 'Canacosia' (between Ravenna and Faenza). (RIS, N.S., XXII, II, 58 and XXVIII, II, 95; Tonduzzi, *Faenza*, pp. 357–8, with incorrect date.)

20. Between 1 November and 25 November 1301. Cesena. (Tonduzzi, *Faenza*, p. 359; Fantuzzi, *Mon. Rav.*, III, n. CIV; *Atti e Mem. St. Patr. Emilia*, N.S., VII (1881), 154–5.)

21. 8 April 1302. Cesena. (RIS, O.S., XIV, cols. 1122–3; *ASI*, L, 338–9.)

Appendix II

LIST OF OFFICIALS

Note: *n.* = date of nomination to office.

    f.r. = first reference noted to tenure of office when date of nomination is not recorded.

    l.r. = last reference noted to tenure of office (given only when date of successor's nomination is not recorded and when a long gap suggests a possible intermediate tenant).

A. RECTORS

This list includes rectors *in spiritualibus et temporalibus* and rectors *in temporalibus*. It includes a few officials who exercised the normal functions of provincial rectors without holding that title, but omits other legates etc. Vicars *in temporalibus* are also noted.

Campagna and Marittima

1. Lando da Montelungo, *f.r. c.* Jan. 1199 (*Gesta Inn. III*, P.L., 214, col. xli).

2. Peter 'de Sasso', cardinal-priest of S. Pudenziana, *f.r. c.* spring 1208 (*Gesta Inn. III*, cols. lxx–lxxiii; MGH, XIX, 296; *v.* Maccarone in *Rivista di Storia della Chiesa in Italia*, X, 175, suggesting 'late 1208').

3. John, cardinal-priest of S. Praxed, *n.* 5 March 1217 (*Reg. Hon. III*, nn. 394, 397).

4. Romanus, cardinal-deacon of S. Angelo, *f.r.* 6 March 1220 (*Reg. Hon. III*, n. 2350), *l.r.* 24 March 1222 (*ibid.*, n. 3888).

5. Gregory 'de Romania', subdeacon and papal chaplain, *f.r.* 16 Sept. 1225 (*Reg. Hon. III*, n. 5645), *l.r.* 22 July 1231 (Theiner, d. CLXI).

6. Stephen, cardinal-priest of S. Maria *Transtiberim*, *n.* 12 Jan. 1234 (*Reg. G. IX.*, nn. 1716–18).

7. Anthony (a cleric), *f.r.* 15 May 1234 (Marangoni, *Civitanova*, pp. 263–4).

8. 'Donus', *f.r.* 8 Aug. 1235 (*Reg. G. IX*, nn. 3039–40), *l.r.* 21 Jan. 1236 (*ibid.*, n. 2919).

9. Stephen, papal chaplain, *n.* 5 June 1237 (Borgia, *Velletri*, pp. 274–5), superseded before 12 Apr. 1239 (*Reg. G. IX*, n. 4830).

10. John 'Judicis', Roman: before 13 July 1240 (*Reg. G. IX*, n. 5254).

11. Richard, cardinal-deacon of S. Angelo, *f.r.* 13 July 1240 (*Reg. G. IX*, n. 5254), *l.r.* 22 Oct. 1248 (Contatore, *Terracina*, pp. 188–9).

12. Peter, cardinal-deacon of S. George *ad Velum Aureum*, *n.* 7 Apr. 1249 (*Reg. Inn. IV*, nn. 4688–94).

13. Jordan, subdeacon and papal notary, *f.r.* 2 July 1253 (*Reg. Inn. IV*, n. 7754): later papal vice-chancellor, then cardinal-deacon of SS. Cosma and Damian: 27 Nov. 1263 (*Reg. Urb. IV*, I, n. 508) his vicar is his nephew John 'Pirunti': for another vicar, a bishop, *v.* Batzer, *Zur Kenntnis der Formularsammlung des Richard v. Pofi*, p. 69: *l.r.* 1 May 1264 (*Reg. Urb. IV* II, n. 795).

14. Hubert 'Niger' Visconti, *n.* 9 June 1272 (*Reg. G. X*, n. 181), *l.r.* 24 May 1273 (Contatore, *Terracina*, pp. 75–6).

15. Guy 'Codeporcus', *f.r.* 27 Aug. 1274 (Contatore, *Terracina*, pp. 76–8: his vicar-general then Philip 'de Sartinano').

16. James 'Confarenerius' (between 27 March 1272 and 10 Jan. 1276: possibly before previous entry: *Lib. Cens.*, II, 72–3).

17. Benedict, papal chamberlain, *f.r.* 22 July 1279 (vicar-general then James of Ripatransone: Theiner, d. CCCXCII).

18. Nicolino 'de Camilla', *f.r.* 14 July 1280 (*Reg. N. III*, n. 854).

19. Geoffrey of 'Sommersot', *n.* 29 Apr. 1281 (*Studi Romagnoli*, V, 309).

20. Andrew Spiliati, papal chaplain and canon of Cambrai, *f.r.* 7 Nov. 1283 (Theiner, d. CCCCXXIX: then has vicar 'Bonogarzo' of Ripatransone), *l.r.* 18 March 1284 (Potthast, n. 22117).

21. Frederick, bishop-elect of Ivrea, *f.r.* 15 Oct. 1284 (Potthast, n. 22181): probably superseded on becoming rector of the March in 1285 (see below).

22. Deodatus of Rome, probably before 3 Apr. 1288 (ref. *Reg. N. IV*, n. 7097).

23. Cittadino 'Episcopi' of Orvieto, *n.* 3 Apr. 1288 (*Reg. N. IV*, nn. 6967–8).

24. Ottaviano da Brunforte, *f.r.* 22 July 1289 (Contatore, *Terracina*, p. 206), *l.r.* after 4 Apr. 1292 and before 5 July 1294 (*Reg. B. VIII*, n. 3417).

25. Nicholas dei Boccamazzi, *f.r.* 16 July 1295 (*Reg. B. VIII*, n. 5426), *l.r.* 26 June 1296 (Contatore, *Terracina*, p. 210).

26. Rostand de Ganteaulme, *f.r.* 9 March 1297 (Contatore, *Terracina*, pp. 210–212), *l.r.* 30 May 1297 (*ASRSP*, LXVII, 306).

27. Count Roffred Caetani, *f.r.* 20 Jan. 1298 (*Reg. B. VIII*, nn. 5508–9): vicars-general *in temporalibus* James 'de Ranzano' (21 Aug. 1299: *ibid.*, n. 3408) and Walter of Offida (15 May 1303; *ibid.*, n. 5226: this is also *l.r.* to Count Roffred, but he probably held office till Boniface VIII's death on 11 Oct. 1303).

28. Thomasinus 'de Inzola' of Parma, *n.* 4 Feb. 1304 (*Reg. B. XI*, n. 276), *l.r.* 19 March 1304 (*ibid.*, n. 1238).

County of Sabina

1. Stephen, cardinal-priest of S. Maria *Transtiberim* (with Campagna-Marittima, *q.v.* n. 6 *ad* 12 Jan. 1234).

2. Crescentius, *f.r.* 13 July 1234 (*Lib. Cens.*, I, 520 ff.), *l.r.* 27 Feb. 1236 (*ibid.*, 555-7).

3. Peter, cardinal-deacon of S. George *ad Velum Aureum* (with Campagna-Marittima, *q.v.* n. 12 *ad* 7 Apr. 1249, and other provinces).

4. Guy 'de Pilleo', papal chaplain, *n.* 17 Dec. 1253 (*Reg. Inn. IV*, nn. 7778-9).

5. Leo 'de Romania', canon of Bayeux, *n.* 28 Dec. 1254 (*Reg. Alex. IV*, nn. 12-13), *l.r.* (for Sabina) 13 June 1256 (Amelia, AC, perg. n. 6).

6. John Gaietani Orsini, cardinal-deacon of S. Nicholas *in Carcere Tulliano* (later Pope Nicholas III), *f.r.* 31 Oct. 1263 (*Reg. Urb. IV*, II, n. 726).

7. Ingeramus 'de Savolis', noble (? of Arezzo: *v.* Sperandio, *Sabina Sagra e Profana*, p. 108), ref. 1284 (Theiner, d. CCCCXLIII).

8. James of Velletri, *f.r.* Aug. 1285, *l.r.* Aug. 1286 (Theiner, d. CCCCXLIII).

9. Ranier of Pisa, papal notary, *f.r.* 5 March 1291 (*Reg. N. IV*, n. 7316), *l.r.* 27 June 1291 (*ibid.*, n. 7332).

10. Nicholas, bishop of Todi, *f.r.* 18 Oct. 1291 (*BDSPU*, XXV, 51).

11. James Caetani, *f.r.* 4 May 1295 (*Reg. B. VIII*, nn. 5414-5).

12. Guarnazonus of Anagni, *n.* 13 Dec. 1295 (*Reg. B. VIII*, nn. 5434-7): has vicar, on 4 July 1297 (Terni, AS, perg. 4.vii.1297) and 24 May 1301 (which is *l.r.*: *ibid.*, 24.v.1301) this is Nicholas Caetani of Pisa.

13. Napoleon Orsini, cardinal-deacon of S. Adrian, *n.* 6 July 1301 (*Reg. B. VIII*, nn. 4377-8).

14. Peter, cardinal-bishop of Sabina, *n.* 3 Jan. 1302 (*Reg. B. VIII*, nn. 5077-8): has vicars, James of Civitella 4 Feb. 1302 (Terni, AS, perg. 4.ii.1302), Bernard 'de Iordanis' of Parma 22 May 1303 (*ibid.*, 22.v.1303, which is *l.r.*).

15. John, bishop of Rieti, *n.* 4 Dec. 1303 (*Reg. B. XI*, nn. 1133-4).

Patrimony of Tuscany

1. 'G. Centii' (Cenci ?), noble of Rome, *f.r.* between 22 Feb. 1199 and 21 Feb. 1200 (*Reg. Inn. III*, P.L. 214, II, cols. 755-6).

2. Gregory, cardinal-deacon of S. George *ad Velum Aureum* (aided by Peter di Vico, Prefect of Rome), *n.* 15 Oct. 1199 (and therefore possibly preceding entry above: *Reg. Inn. III*, II, cols. 750-2).

3. 'S. Roman. Carzoli' (?Stephen Carzolus), relative of Innocent III, *f.r.* 30 June 1203 (*Reg. Inn. III*, P.L. 214, VI, col. 112: *v.* also P.L. 217, Suppl. 12, col. 299).

4. James (count of Andria), papal marshal, cousin of Innocent III, *f.r.* 21 Aug. 1213 (*Reg. Inn. III*, P.L. 216, XVI, col. 894), *l.r.* 7 June 1215 (*BDSPU*, I, 131-3).

5. King John (Brienne) of Jerusalem, *n.* 27 Jan. 1227 (*Reg. Hon. III*, n. 6203: see pp. 137 ff.).

6. Romanus, cardinal-bishop elect of Porto, *n.* 12 Jan. 1234 (*Reg. G. IX*, nn. 1716-18).

7. Ranier, cardinal-deacon of S. Maria *in Cosmedin*, *n.* 1 Aug. 1234 (BFW, n. 7033).

8. Godfrey dei Prefetti, papal chaplain, *f.r.* 1 Apr. 1238 (*Reg. G. IX*, n. 4226), *l.r.* 26 July 1239 (Fumi, *Orvieto*, d. CCXLII, but possibly incorrect, *v.* next entry).

9. Gregory 'de Romania', subdeacon and papal chaplain, *f.r.* 14 June 1239 (*QFIA*, XXIX, 177–9: but cf. previous entry).

10. Archpriest of Perugia, papal chaplain, *n.* 26 Aug. 1243 (*Reg. Inn. IV*, nn. 65–8).

11. Philip, bishop of Camerino, jointly with abbot of S. Severo (Orvieto), between n. 10 and n. 12 (reference in *Reg. Inn. IV*, nn. 85–7).

12. Ranier, cardinal-deacon of S. Maria *in Cosmedin* (see n. 7 above), *n.* 28 June 1244 ('papal vicar': BFW, n. 7479).

13. Peter, cardinal-deacon of S. George *ad Velum Aureum* (with Campagna-Marittima, *q.v.* n. 12 *ad* 7 Apr. 1249, and other provinces).

14. Zoen, bishop of Avignon, *f.r.* 6 July 1252 (Narni, AC, perg. 6.vii.1252), *l.r* 1 Aug. 1252 (Fumi, *Orvieto*, p. 56: *v.* BFW, n. 8502).

15. Ranier of Viterbo, papal chaplain (nephew of n. 7 above), *n.* 3 Jan. 1254 (*Reg. Inn. IV*, nn. 7775–6).

16. Leo 'de Romania' (with Sabina, *q.v.* n. 5 *ad* 28 Dec. 1254), *l.r.* 1 May 1259 (Todi, AC, Reg. Vet. Istr., f. 102).

17. Ranier of Viterbo (see n. 15 above), *f.r.* 5 March 1260 (Potthast, n. 17801), *l.r.* 12 Jan. 1261 (*ibid.*, n. 18010).

18. Manfred, bishop-elect of Verona, *f.r.* 8 May 1261 (*QFIA*, XXIX, 214): probably relinquished this office before 29 Aug. 1262 (BFW, nn. 14190–2).

19. Guiscard of Pietrasanta ('rector and captain'), *n.* 14 July 1263 (*Reg. Urb. IV*, II, nn. 308–9): killed 3 Feb. 1264 (Pinzi, *Viterbo*, II, 104).

20. Pipio of Pietrasanta (brother of above), *f.r.* 2 Apr. 1264 (*Reg. Urb. IV*, III, n. 2515), *l.r.* 5 July 1264 (*ibid.*, n. 2669).

21. Matthew, cardinal-deacon of S. Maria *in Porticu*, *n.* 9 Aug. 1264 (*Reg. Urb. IV*, II, nn. 875–6: but n. 879 of 6 Aug. already calls him 'rector'): has bishop of Penna as vicar 19 March 1265 (Fumi, *Orvieto*, d. CCCXCVI), 'Bertold' on 30 June 1265 (*Reg. Cl. IV*, n. 900): *l.r.* 5 Sept. 1265 (*ibid.*, n. 953).

22. Guy 'de Pilleo', archdeacon of Soissons (*v. ad* Sabina, n. 4), *f.r.* 12 May 1266 (*Reg. Cl. IV*, n. 1055), *l.r.* '1267' (RIS, N.S., XV, V, 157).

23. Visconte dei Visconti of Piacenza, *n.* 5 June 1272 (*Reg. G. X*, n. 180).

24. Taddeo, count of Montefeltro, *f.r.* 10 July 1273 (Todi, AC, perg. n. 20), *l.r.* 15 Oct. 1275 (*ibid.*, Reg. Vet. Istr., ff. 91v–92: then has a vicar, Buonsignore 'de Castello').

25. Raymond 'de Nuceriis', papal chaplain, *f.r.* 30 Jan. 1277 (Todi, AC, Reg. Vet. Istr., f. 96), *l.r.* 22 Aug. 1277 (Terni, AS, perg. 22.viii.1277: the ref. *ad* 23 June 1278 in BISI, XXVII, 240, is probably misdated, *v.* next entry).

26. William Durand, papal chaplain, held office between n. 25 above and n. 27 below (for references *v. Dict. de Droit Canonique*, V, cols. 1022–3).

27. Orso Orsini, papal marshal (nephew of Nicholas III), *f.r.* 24 July 1278 (*Reg. N. III*, n. 702), *l.r.* 23 July 1280 (*ibid.*, n. 853: probably held office till Nicholas III's death on 22 Aug. 1280): on 19 Jan. 1280 he had a vicar-general, Malabranca dei Tedaldini (Todi, AC, Reg. Vet. Istr., f. 98).

28. Adam Fourrier, knight and familiar of Charles of Anjou, *n.* soon after Martin IV's election on 22 March 1281 (*Studi Romagnoli*, V, 309), *l.r.* 4 June 1284 (Theiner, d. CCCCXXXIV).

29. 'Giles', in office 1285 (Pinzi, *Viterbo*, II, 434–5; Signorelli, *Viterbo*, pp. 296 n–297 n).

30. Luca Savelli, papal marshal (nephew of Honorius IV), *f.r.* 19 Feb. 1286 (Pinzi, *Viterbo*, II, 434–5: then has vicar, Peter 'de Manganella'), *l.r.* 5 Aug. 1287 (Orvieto, Sottosez AS, Dipl. 1287).

31. Niccolino 'de Camilla', papal chaplain and canon of Amiens (*v.* Campagna-Marittima, n. 18), *n.* 1 June 1288 (*Reg. N. IV*, nn. 7051–6), *l.r.* '1289' (Signorelli, *Viterbo*, pp. 301–2).

32. 'Magister Raynucinus de Murro', *f.r.* 14 Aug. 1290 (Arch. Vat., Arm. XXXV, 14, f. 85v), *l.r.* 23 Aug. 1290 (*Reg. N. IV*, nn. 7260–1).

33. William Cibo of Genoa, *n.* 27 Sept. 1290 (*Reg. N. IV*, nn. 7266–7), *l.r.* 20 Oct. 1290 (Arch. Vat., Arm. XXXV, 14, f. 85: but probably still in office 23 Oct. 1290, *v. Reg. N. IV*, nn. 7278–9).

34. Peter of Piperno, papal chaplain and canon of Rheims, *f.r.* '1291' (Theiner, d. CCCCXCI), *l.r.* 3 July 1293 (Pflugk-Harttung, pp. 564–5).

35. Odonisius (*or* Oderisius) of Aversa, *f.r. c.* Aug. 1294 (Baethgen, *Engelpapst*, pp. 126–7: cf. Bury, *Liber Epistolaris*, p. 192).

36. Peter Caetani, *f.r.* 27 March 1295 (Pflugk-Harttung, pp. 571–2), Amatus of Anagni his vicar in Jan. 1296 (*ibid.*, pp. 572–3).

37. Count Roffred Caetani, *n.* 31 March 1296 (*Reg. B. VIII*, nn. 5452–4): Amatus remains as vicar (*ibid.*, n. 1845, etc.).

38. Rainald, bishop of Siena, *n.* 15 July 1298 (*Reg. B. VIII*, nn. 5541–2).

39. Theoderic, cardinal-bishop of Città Papale (Palestrina) and papal chamberlain, *n.* 13 June 1299 (*Reg. B. VIII*, nn. 5549–53): his vicar in May 1300 and later is Peter, provost of S. Fortunato, Corneto (Pflugk-Harttung, p. 583, etc.).

40. Orso Orsini (see n. 26 above), *n.* 23 Oct. 1300 (*Reg. B. VIII*, nn. 3905–7). His vicar on 5 Oct. 1301 is 'Alamannus Galganus' (Pflugk-Harttung, p. 584), on 12 May 1302 the knight, judge and doctor of laws Paparonus of Rome (*ibid.*, pp. 586–7).

41. Benedict Caetani, *n.* 10 Apr. 1303 (*Reg. B. VIII*, n. 5337): on 26 Oct. 1303 his vicar is Amatus (Pflugk-Harttung, pp. 587–8: see nn. 35–6 above).

42. James 'Quirini' of Venice, *f.r.* 19 March 1304 (*Reg. B. XI*, n. 1238), *l.r.* 21 Apr. 1304 (*ibid.*, n. 1243).

Duchy of Spoleto

1. Gregory, cardinal-deacon of S. Maria *in Aquiro*, summer 1198 (P.L. 214, *Reg. Inn. III*, I, cols. 331-2 and *Gesta*, cols. xxv-xxvi).

2. Gregory, cardinal-deacon of S. George *ad Velum Aureum* (aided by Peter di Vico, Prefect of Rome), *n.* 15 Oct. 1199 (*v.* Patrimony in Tuscany, n. 2).

3. Ranier, cardinal-deacon of S. Maria *in Cosmedin* (*v.* Patrimony in Tuscany, nn. 7 and 12), *n.* 3 Aug. 1220 (*Reg. Hon. III*, n. 2595), *l.r.* 13 Apr. 1223 (*QFIA*, XXIX, 156).

4. John, cardinal-priest of S. Praxed (*v.* Campagna-Marittima, n. 3), *f.r.* 21 Dec. 1225 (BFW, n. 12925). *l.r.* 16 Apr. 1227 (*Reg. G. IX*, n. 34).

5. Milo, bishop of Beauvais, *n.* 25 Sept. 1230 (*Reg. G. IX*, nn. 495-8).

6. Romanus, cardinal-bishop elect of Porto, *n.* 12 Jan. 1234 (*v.* Patrimony in Tuscany, n. 6).

7. Alatrinus, subdeacon and papal chaplain, *f.r.* 4 Apr. 1234 (*Lib. Cens.*, I, 537), *l.r.* as rector 18 Dec. 1235 (*BDSPU*, IX, 126), but in Duchy as papal nuncio Nov.-Dec. 1236 (*QFIA*, XXIX, 167-8; *Lib. Cens.*, I, 481).

8. Rainald of Supino, *f.r.* 16 Jan. 1238 (*Reg. G. IX*, n. 4032), *l.r.* 1 Apr. 1238 (*ibid.*, n. 4224). On 25 March 1237 'S. magistri Iohannis' is vicar (*BDSPU*, XXV, 14-15), possibly for Rainald.

9. Gregory 'de Romania' (*v.* Patrimony in Tuscany, n. 9, for *f.r.* 14 June 1239).

10. Archpriest of Perugia (*v.* Patrimony in Tuscany, n. 10, for *n.* 26 Aug. 1243).

11. Philip, bishop of Camerino, jointly with the abbot of S. Severo (Orvieto) (*v.* Patrimony in Tuscany, n. 11).

12. Alexander, papal chaplain, *f.r.* 3 May 1244 (Theiner, d. CCIX).

13. Ranier, cardinal-deacon of S. Maria *in Cosmedin* (see above, n. 3, and Patrimony in Tuscany, n. 12 for *n.* 28 June 1244).

14. Peter, cardinal-deacon of S. George *ad Velum Aureum* (*v.* Campagna-Marittima, n. 12, and other provinces *ad* 7 Apr. 1249).

15. Boniface of Fogliano, papal chaplain (nephew of Innocent IV), *f.r.* 13 March 1252 (Zonghi, *Fabriano*, d. CLIX; cf. BFW, n. 15124), *l.r.* 5 Feb. 1254 (Zonghi, *Fabriano*, d. CLXX).

16. John 'Compater', papal chaplain, *n.* 20 Jan. 1255 (*QFIA*, XXIX, 201), *l.r.* 15 May 1257 (*ibid.*, 207-8) and has relinquished office by 2 Jan. 1258 (Theiner, dd. CCLX-CCLXI).

17. Roland of Ferentino, papal chaplain (cousin of Alexander IV), *f.r.* 11 Jan. 1259 (Ficker, *Forschungen*, IV, d. 430).

18. Manfred, bishop-elect of Verona (*v.* Patrimony in Tuscany, n. 18, for *f.r.* 8 May 1261: his vicar in Duchy then 'Guy', and in Dec. 1262 Giles, a judge, *v.* BFW, nn. 14190-2): is made prisoner of war *c.* late Apr. 1264 (Colucci, *Ant. Pic.*, XIX, 47).

19. Simon, cardinal-priest of S. Martin, *n.* 20 May 1264 (*Reg. Urb. IV*, II, nn. 631, 640). 9 Oct. 1266, has vicar-general, Bartholomew 'de Palatio'

(Alberti, *Bevagna*, II, 155-7): *l.r.* 5 Apr. 1268 (*Reg. Cl. IV*, n. 697), but probably holds office till death of Clement IV (29 Nov. 1268).

20. Ubertino Visconti, nephew of Gregory X, *f.r.* 21 March 1273 (Sansi, *Spoleto*, d. LIX), *l.r.* 14 May 1273 (Perugia, AS, Rif. VII, f. 8). (Apparently not identical with the almost homonymous rector of Campagna-Marittima, n. 14.)

21. William Visconti, *f.r.* 16 June 1273 (Perugia, AS, Rif. VII, f. 24: and *ibid.*, ff. 24-112v for many other references in 1273).

22. Hugh 'marquis of Montemezzano', papal chaplain, *f.r.* 21 May 1277 (Contelori, *Cesi*, pp. 24-5), several later refs. and probably held office till after election of Nicholas III (25 Nov. 1277).

23. Philip of Naples, papal chaplain, *f.r.* 14 May 1278 (Gubbio, Sottosez AS, perg., bu. 16), *l.r.* 8 Jan. 1281 (Cristofani, *Assisi*, p. 117).

24. Jean de Mayrolles, *n.* soon after 22 Feb. 1281 (*Studi Romagnoli*, V, 309), *f.r.* 11 Apr. 1281 (Sansi, *Spoleto*, pp. 368 n-369 n).

25. Roland of Ferentino, papal chaplain (*v.* n. 17 above), *f.r.* 13 June 1285 (*Reg. Hon. IV*, n. 23), *l.r.* 18 Sept. 1287 (Sansi, *Storia del comune di Spoleto*, I, 125).

26. Landulf Colonna, *n.* 1 March 1288 (*Reg. N. IV*, nn. 6955-60), *l.r.* 29 Apr. 1289 (Arch. Vat., Arm. XXXV, 4, ff. 56v-57v).

27. Ranier of Pisa, papal notary (*v.* Sabina, n. 9), *f.r.* 2 Sept. 1290 (Zonghi, *Fabriano*, d. CCLIV), *l.r.* 10 Aug. 1291 (*Reg. N. IV*, n. 7380).

28. Nicholas, bishop of Todi, *f.r.* 18 Oct. 1291 (*v.* Sabina, n. 10).

29. Richard Annibaldi, *f.r.* 6 July 1292 (Sansi, *Storia del comune di Spoleto*, I, 124n), *l.r.* 29 May 1294 (*ibid.*, 123).

30. Blaise of Anagni, papal chaplain and canon of Cambrai, *f.r.* 17 Sept. 1295 (*BDSPU*, XXV, 55), *l.r.* 6 Sept. 1296 (*Reg. B. VIII*, n. 1341).

31. Bertold Orsini, *f.r.* 27 Jan. *or* 8 Feb. 1297 (when he is represented by a vicar: *J Eccl H*, VIII, 147), *l.r.* 6 Oct. 1299 (Sansi, *Spoleto*, d. LXXX). Other vicars (1299): Angelo of Rieti and Peter 'Vaiani' of Rome (Sansi, *Spoleto*, dd. LXXIX-LXXX).

32. Napoleon Orsini, cardinal-deacon of S. Adrian (*v.* Sabina, n. 13), *n.* 27 May 1300 (*Reg. B. VIII*, nn. 3886-91), *l.r.* 13 Feb. 1301 (*ibid.*, n. 3958).

33. Charles of Valois, *n.* (and to other provinces) 22 Apr. 1301 (*Reg. B. VIII*, n. 4394).

34. Benedict Caetani (*v.* Patrimony in Tuscany, n. 41), *n.* 18 June 1301 (*Reg. B. VIII*, nn. 4375-6). Anthony, bishop-elect of Fiesole, is *n.* as vicar-general 23 Sept. 1301 (*ibid.*, nn. 4398-9).

35. Richard Annibaldi (see above, n. 28), *n.* 2 Jan. 1302 (*Reg. B. VIII*, nn. 5083-4), *l.r.* 23 July 1303 (Cascia, AC, perg. n. 18: his vicar-general then Andrew of Cesi) but probably in office till death of Boniface VIII on 11 Oct. 1303.

36. Deoteclerius of Loiano, *n.* 1 Dec. 1303 (*Reg. B. XI*, n. 1142), *l.r.* 20 March 1304 (Sarti, *Gubbio*, pp. 174-7: he then has a vicar-general, Jobensius 'de Azoguidis', noble of Bologna and doctor of law).

March of Ancona

1. John, cardinal-priest of S. Prisca, legate in the March 1198–9, with Cinthius, cardinal-priest of S. Lorenzo *in Lucina* (P.L. 214, *Gesta*, col. xxii, and *Reg. Inn. III*, I, cols. 31–2 and II, n. 4) is perhaps styled 'papal vicar *in spiritualibus et temporalibus*' (Colini-Baldeschi, *Osimo*, d. XXXIII) on 17 Nov. 1199.

   [1212–c. 1230: this province is held as a fief by the Estensi and no rectors are appointed.]

2. Milo, bishop of Beauvais, *n.* 25 Sept. 1230 (with Duchy of Spoleto, *q.v. ad* n. 5), *l.r.* 15 May 1232 (Colucci, *Treia*, d. XIV).

3. John, cardinal-priest of S. Praxed (*v.* Campagna-Marittima, n. 5, and Duchy of Spoleto, n. 4), *f.r.* 23 Oct. 1232 (*Reg. G. IX*, n. 928), his vicar 1233–4 is '*magister* Caesarius', who in Apr. 1233 is accompanied by another vicar, Gentile 'de Popleto' (Mazzatinti, s.1, III, 199): *l.r.* is 5 Dec. 1234 (Colucci, *Ant. Pic.*, XVIII, 15).

4. Sinibald, cardinal-priest of S. Lorenzo *in Lucina* (later Pope Innocent IV), *f.r.* 12 Feb. 1235 (Amiani, *Fano*, II, xlvii), *l.r.* 15 Nov. 1240 (Compagnoni, *Regg. Pic.*, pp. 104–5): has vicar, Manente, Aug.–Oct. 1235 (*AMSM*, N.S. VII (1911–12), 400: Potthast, nn. 10032–7).

5. Marcellinus, bishop of Arezzo, *n.* 12 Dec. 1240 (*Reg. G. IX*, n. 5322) as temporary measure during absence of n. 4 at papal Curia, but retains office at least till 26 Aug. 1243 (*Reg. Inn. IV*, nn. 72–6) and probably until *n.* of n. 6 below (*q.v.* for vicariate).

6. Ranier, cardinal-deacon of S. Maria *in Cosmedin*, *n.* 28 June 1244 (*v.* Patrimony in Tuscany, n. 12, and Duchy of Spoleto, n. 13): is represented in the March by n. 5 above, *f.r.* 15 May 1247 (*Reg. Inn. IV*, n. 2736) and probably until his execution on 8 March 1248: in 1248 his 'captain-general' is Ugolini 'Rainerii' (Zonghi, *Fabriano*, d. CLII) and on 30 Apr. 1248 his vicar is his chaplain, *magister* Deutacomandus (Bricchi, *Cagli*, pp. 102–6).

7. Peter, cardinal-deacon of S. George *ad Velum Aureum*, *n.* 7 Apr. 1249 (*v.* Campagna-Marittima, n. 12; Patrimony in Tuscany, n. 13; Duchy of Spoleto, n. 14): in Oct. 1251 he has a vicar-general in the March, Philip abbot of Rambona (dioc. Camerino: *v.* Zonghi, *Fabriano*, dd. CLXVI, CLXVIII and Colini-Baldeschi, 'Macerata', d. I). The appointment as vicar of the bishop of Fano on 25 Jan. 1251 was ineffective (see pp. 153–4).

8. Walter, archdeacon of Luni, *f.r.* 13 March 1252 (Zonghi, *Fabriano*, d. CLIX: cf. BFW, n. 15124), *l.r.* 29 Nov. 1252 (BFW, n. 8543): on 11 May he has as vicar-general Thomas, a judge (*AMSM*, N.S., VII (1911–12), 401). He has relinquished office before 2 June 1253 (Serra S. Quirico, AC, tomo II, Cl. IX, perg. n. 2, where he is referred to as archbishop of Genoa: he was promoted to this archbishopric on 23 Apr. 1253 (Eubel, I, 292)).

9. Gerard Coxadoca, papal chaplain, *f.r.* 24 Aug. 1253 (Acquacotta, *Matelica*, d. 36), *l.r.* 6 Dec. 1254 (Colucci, *Treia*, d. XXXIV).

10. Roland 'de Campania', papal chaplain (possibly identical with Duchy of Spoleto, nn. 17 and 25), *n.* 18 Jan. 1255 (*Reg. Alex. IV*, n. 44): holds office until succeeded by n. 11.

11. Annibaldo 'Transmundi' (nephew of Alexander IV), *n.* 6 May 1256 (BFW, nn. 9056, 14894), has as vicars (Romans) Oddecinus (a cousin) and Matthew of S. Alberto (*ibid.* and Compagnoni, *Regg. Pic.*, p. 124): probably still in office 1260 (De Minicis, *Fermo*, p. 422).

12. Andrew Spiliati, subdeacon and papal chaplain (*v.* Campagna-Marittima, n. 20), *f.r.* between 20 Dec. 1260 and 12 Jan. 1261 (Amiani, *Fano*, II, lvi).

13. Manfred, bishop-elect of Verona (*v.* Patrimony in Tuscany, n. 18, and Duchy of Spoleto, n. 18), *f.r.* 29 Aug. 1262 (Cecconi, *Osimo*, p. 7): in Dec. 1262 has judge, Giles, as vicar (BFW, nn. 14190–2): for capture *c.* Apr. 1264 see above, *loc. cit.*).

14. Simon, cardinal-priest of S. Martin, *n.* 20 May 1264 (see Duchy of Spoleto, n. 19). Vicars in the March: Guy, archpriest of Sasso, Dec. 1266 – May 1267 (Grimaldi, *Matelica*, dd. CCXXXV, CCXLIII), Clerecattius 'de Monte' Aug. 1267 (Zonghi, *Fabriano*, d. CCVIII). *L.r.* 5 Apr. 1268 (*Reg. Cl. IV*, n. 697).

15. Manfred, bishop-elect of Verona (see above, n. 13), *f.r.* before the end of Apr. 1268 (Grimaldi, *Matelica*, d. CCLXX), *l.r.* 18 Sept. 1268 (*Reg. Cl. IV*, n. 1413).

16. Benvenutus, bishop of Osimo (possibly not rector *in temporalibus*, but there are a number of references to this bishop as rector in the March which are difficult to reconcile with the dates of other tenures): *v.* Grimaldi, *Matelica*, d. CCLIX (4 Sept. 1267) and Colucci, *Ant. Pic.*, XXII, 32–3 (18 Apr. 1272 and 25 Sept. 1274).

17. Fulk of Puyricard, *n.* 6 May 1272, to hold office 20 May (*Reg. G. X*, nn. 168–79). Vicars: William of S. Lawrence (18 Sept. 1272: Grimaldi, *Matelica*, d. CCCXXXIII) and Henry Visconti, nephew of Gregory X (5 Apr. 1275: Compagnoni, *Regg. Pic.*, p. 140). *L.r.* 15 May 1276 (Gianandrea, *Iesi*, d. CLXXXV).

18. Hugh 'the Red', provost of Rheims, *f.r.* 20 March 1277 (Fabriano, AC, Lib. Ross, f. 93), still in office '1278' (De Minicis, *Fermo*, pp. 462, 487). On 19 Apr. 1278 Peter 'Alafredi', a cleric, is vicar-general, for Hugh or his successor (Compagnoni, *Regg. Pic.*, p. 141).

19. Bernard, abbot of Montmajour (dioc. Arles), *f.r.* 8 May 1278 (Macerata, AC, perg. n. 108), *l.r.* 24 March 1281 (Fabriano, AC, Lib. Ross., f. 91).

20. Amiel d'Angoult of the lords of Courbon, *n. c.* March 1281 (*Studi Romagnoli*, V, 309), *l.r.* 14 Feb. 1282 (Gianandrea, *Iesi*, d. CCV).

21. Geoffrey of Anagni, papal chaplain and *auditor contradictarum*, *n.* 23 May 1282 (Potthast, n. 21903), *l.r.* 23 July 1285 (*Reg. Hon. IV*, n. 839).

22. Frederick, bishop-elect of Ivrea, *f.r.* 5 Dec. 1285 (Gianandrea, *Iesi*, d. CCXXII), *l.r.* 22 June 1288 (*Reg. N. IV*, nn. 7078–81).

23. John Colonna, *n.* 27 June 1288 (*Reg. N. IV*, nn. 7089–90): his son Agapitus his vicar 9 Apr. 1290 (Mei, *Cagli*, n. 422) to 15 Dec. 1290 (Compagnoni, *Regg. Pic.*, p. 150), which is perhaps *l.r.*, but on 27 June 1291 Andrew '*dictus* Vetulus', a noble, is vicar (*Reg. N. IV*, n. 7331), probably for John Colonna.

24. Rainald, bishop of Valencia, *f.r.* 27 July 1291 (*Reg. N. IV*, n. 7336): vicar-general Oct. 1291 – Jan. 1292 is Raymond 'Caprarii', canon of Lerida (Ascoli P., AC, Quinternone, ff. 66–67v): *l.r.* 7 Aug. 1294 (Acquacotta, *Matelica*, d. 85).

25. Gentile da Sangro, *f.r.* before 28 Aug. 1294 (Potthast, n. 23949): vicar is *dominus* Bernard 'de Podio' on 2 Dec. 1294 (Iesi, AC, perg. n. 152) and 8 Jan. 1295 (Colini-Baldeschi, *Cingoli*, d. XIX), which is *l.r.*

26. Frederick, bishop of Ferrara (identical with n. 22 above), *f.r.* 23 March 1295 (*Reg. B. VIII*, n. 740), *l.r.* 18 Aug. 1295 (Colucci, *Ant. Pic.*, XIX, d. XLIII), but successor had then already been *n.* (see n. 27).

27. William Durand, papal chaplain (see Patrimony in Tuscany, n. 26), *f.r.* 11 Aug. 1295 (Potthast, n. 24163): holds office till *n.* of n. 28 .

28. Peter Caetani, *n.* 20 Apr. 1296 (*Reg. B. VIII*, nn. 5455–6): his vicar is David 'Paparone' of Ferentino, probably throughout his rectorate: holds office till *n.* of n. 29.

29. Napoleon Orsini, cardinal-deacon of S. Adrian, *n.* 27 May 1300 (*v.* Duchy of Spoleto, n. 32).

30. Charles of Valois, *n.* 22 Apr. 1301 (*v.* Duchy of Spoleto, n. 33).

31. Peter Caetani (see n. 28 above), *n.* 18 June 1301 (*Reg. B. VIII*, nn. 4375–6): James 'de Renzano' *n.* 23 Sept. 1301 (*ibid.*, nn. 4398–9) as vicar and is still vicar on 9 Feb. 1303 (*QFIA*, XX, 211–17), but is apparently acting for n. 30 above, while Peter Caetani's vicar is Amatus 'di Giovanni' (*f.r.* 27 Sept. 1301, *v. RSDI*, V, 180–4: *l.r.* 5 Apr. 1302, *v.* Colucci, *Ant. Pic.*, XXIX, 46). This is also *l.r.*, but see n. 32.

32. Anthony, bishop of Fiesole, *n.* 2 Jan. 1302 (*Reg. B. VIII*, nn. 5085–6), *l.r.* 27 Sept. 1303 (Martorelli, *Osimo*, pp. 138–9).

33. Count Rambaldus of Collalto, Trevisan, *n.* 1 Dec. 1303 (*Reg. B. XI*, nn. 1114–8), *l.r.* 19 March 1304 (*ibid.*, n. 1238).

Massa Trabaria

The list only includes rectors who held this province separately: the periods during which it was joined with other provinces in joint rectorates are omitted.

1. Peter 'Iudicis', canon of S. Peter's, Rome, *n.* 30 Aug. 1216 (*Reg. Hon. III*, n. 755).

2. Nicholas 'Falconis', subdeacon and papal chaplain, *n.* 22 Feb. 1219 (*Reg. Hon. III*, n. 1888), *l.r.* 22 Nov. 1226 (*ibid.*, n. 6060).

3. Rainald, subdeacon and papal chaplain, *f.r.* 25 Oct. 1232 (Theiner, d. CLXIII).

4. Jaquintus, papal chaplain, *f.r.* 3 Jan. 1234 (*Reg. G. IX*, nn. 1683, 1687), *l.r.* 14 June 1240 (*ibid.*, n. 5242).

5. Hugh 'the marquis', papal chaplain (perhaps identical with Duchy of Spoleto, n. 22), *n.* 14 July 1253 (*Reg. Inn. IV*, nn. 6937–8); no longer in office by 1264, when the province was joined with the Duchy of Spoleto and March of Ancona (*v.* Duchy, n. 19).

6. Robert, papal chaplain, *f.r.* 19 Oct. 1288 (*Reg. N. IV*, n. 7175), *l.r.* 20 Dec. 1288 (*ibid.*, nn. 7207–10).

7. Ubertus, papal chaplain and canon of Reggio, *f.r.* 10 March 1289 (Mei, *Cagli*, n. 382): but possibly identical with n. 6 above.

8. 'Rancerus' de Robertis, *f.r.* 18 March 1291 (*Reg. N. IV*, nn. 7319–20).

9. 'Guenzolus de Pusio', *n.* 6 March 1295 (*Reg. B. VIII*, nn. 5418–9).

10. Berard da Varano, of Camerino, *n.* 9 June 1298 (*Reg. B. VIII*, nn. 5532–3).

11. Corso Donati, of Florence, *n.* 9 Feb. 1300 (*Reg. B. VIII*, n. 3480): on 22 Apr. 1301 the province was joined with several others and Donati cannot have been rector after this date (*v.* Duchy, n. 33, etc.).

12. Giles '*domini* Blaise' of Todi, papal familiar, *n.* 29 Apr. 1303 (*Reg. B. VIII*, nn. 5212–14): by Jan. 1304 the province has been joined with the March of Ancona (Colucci, *Ant. Pic.*, XXIV, 68–9).

Urbino

When a separate province.

1. 'Salcius Grappavingie' of Todi, *n.* 31 March 1296 (*Reg. B. VIII*, nn. 5450–1).

2. Gerardinus of Todi, papal familiar, *n.* 12 May 1300 (*Reg. B. VIII*, n. 3575).

3. Mathiolus of Todi, papal familiar, *n.* (to succeed n. 2) 13 Apr. 1301 (*Reg. B. VIII*, n. 4026).

4. Richard Annibaldi, noble of Rome (son of Theobald and apparently not identical with Duchy of Spoleto n. 29, whose father was named Matthew), *n.* 8 Apr. 1302 (*Reg. B. VIII*, n. 4615).

5. James (son of John) of Todi, *n.* 28 Apr. 1303 (*Reg. B. VIII*, n. 5212).

Romagna

1. Bertold Orsini (see Duchy of Spoleto, n. 31), *n.* 24 Sept. 1278 (*Reg. N. III*, nn. 305–8): on 28 Oct. 1278 has vicar, Manente of Spoleto (Tonini, *Rimini*, III, 605–6): many refs. summer 1280 and probably holds office till death of Nicholas III (22 Aug. 1280).

2. John d'Eppe, *n. c.* Apr. 1281 (*v. Studi Romagnoli*, V, 309): probably holds office till end of 1283.

3. William Durand (see Patrimony in Tuscany, n. 26 and March of Ancona, n. 27), *f.r.* 29 Feb. 1284 (RIS, N.S., XXVIII, III, 101–2), *l.r.* 23 Feb. 1286, (*Reg. Hon. IV*, n. 301). Vicar, the (? French) knight William 'de Alba', *v. Studia Picena, XXIV*, 86n., letter of 31 Oct. 1286, when Durand is probably still rector.

4. Peter Stefaneschi, Roman proconsul, cousin of Honorius IV, *f.r.* before the end of 1286 (RIS, N.S., XXVIII, II, 55), almost certainly holds office till *n.* of n. 5 (though last definite reference 25 Jan. 1288: Tonini, *Rimini*, III, 648–51).

5. Ermanno Monaldeschi of Orvieto, *n.* 5 Apr. 1288 (*Reg. N. IV*, nn. 6979–80: also n. 6966 for temporary vicariate of the bishop of Tripoli): held office until succeeded by n. 6 in Aug. 1289.

6. Stephen Colonna, succeeds Aug. 1289, with Richard of Alatri as temporary vicar (RIS, N.S., XXVIII, II, 59); effective tenure ends on capture at Ravenna, Nov. 1290 (see p. 218), after which time Lorenzo of S. Alberto acts as vicar (*AMSR*, s. IV, VIII (1918), 83).

7. Aldobrandino da Romena, bishop of Arezzo, *n.* 22 Dec. 1290 (*Reg. N. IV*, nn. 7535, 7582), *l.r.* '1294' (Ghirardacci, *Bologna*, p. 317) and probably holds office till *n.* of n. 8.

8. Robert de Cornay, *n.* 9 Sept. 1294 (Ghirardacci, *Bologna*, pp. 317–18), holds office at least until Apr. 1295, when succeeded by n. 9 (*ibid.*, p. 325).

9. Peter, archbishop of Monreale, *n.* before 14 Apr. 1295 (RIS, N.S., XXVIII, II, 77: but n. 8 is still effective rector on 24 Apr., see previous entry), *l.r.* 18 Sept. 1295 (Fantuzzi, *Mon. Rav.*, III, n. LXXXXVI).

10. William Durand (see above, n. 3, and other references there), *f.r.* 25 Sept. 1295 (*Reg. B. VIII*, n. 524): succeeded between 15 July and 2 Oct. 1296 by n. 11 (RIS, N.S., XXVIII, II, 83–7).

11. Maximus of Piperno, brother of cardinal Peter 'of Piperno' (*v.* Patrimony, n. 34): (possibly at first nominally as vicar for his brother: *v.* Tonduzzi, *Faenza*, pp. 350–2): for date of succession see n. 10: probably holds office till succeeded by n. 12.

12. Matthew 'of Acquasparta', cardinal-bishop of Porto, *n.* 19 July 1300 (*Reg. B. VIII*, n. 3900, which grants permission to appoint a vicar): *l.r.* as effectively in office June 1301 (RIS, O.S., XIV, c. 1122), though already nominally succeeded by n. 13.

13. Charles of Valois (*v.* Duchy of Spoleto, n. 33), *n.* 22 Apr. 1301; 23 Sept. 1301, James, bishop of Rieti is *n.* his vicar (*Reg. B. VIII*, nn. 4398–9). Both hold office till succeeded by n. 14 (*q.v.*).

14. Rainald, bishop of Vicenza (rector, but also referred to occasionally as vicar for n. 13); *n.* 4 March 1302 (*Reg. B. VIII*, nn. 5006–7), *l.r.* 14 Dec. 1303 (Fantuzzi, *Mon. Rav.*, IV, n. CXXXXVII), but probably holds office till succeeded by n. 15.

15. Theobald Brusciati, *n.* 13 Jan. 1304 (*Reg. B. XI*, n. 243).

B. Rectors (and Vicars) in Spiritualibus

This list records officials known to have held spiritual powers only.

Campagna and Marittima

1. James of Parma, clerk of papal chamber, vicar-general *in spiritualibus, f.r.* (and *l.r.*) 22 July 1279 (Theiner, d. CCCXCII).
2. James 'Johannis', clerk of S. Apostoli, Orvieto, rector *in spiritualibus, n.* 13 Apr. 1288 (*Reg. N. IV*, nn. 6993–4).
3. Lambertinus of Tolentino, canon of Bologna, rector *in spiritualibus, n.* 23 May 1289 (*Reg. N. IV*, nn. 7230–1).
4. Andrew of Gubbio, canon of Tricarico, rector *in spiritualibus, f.r.* (and *l.r.*) between 4 Apr. 1292 and 5 July 1294 (*Reg. B. VIII*, n. 3417).
5. James 'de Bargiaco', sacrist of Evreux, rector *in spiritualibus, n.* 11 May 1297 (*Reg. B. VIII*, n. 2345), *l.r.* 15 May 1303 (*ibid.*, n. 5226), but probably holds office till *n.* of n. 6.
6. 'Comes de Cercaldo', canon of S. Appiano (dioc. Florence), rector *in spiritualibus, n.* 10 Nov. 1303 (*Reg. B. XI*, n. 6).
7. Gaspar 'de Montasia', canon of Cumae, rector *in spiritualibus, n.* 16 Feb. 1304 (*Reg. B. XI*, n. 349).

County of Sabina

1. James 'de Porclano', clerk of S. Angelo 'de Palan'. (dioc. Anagni), rector *in spiritualibus, f.r.* 2 Oct. 1296 (Terni, AS, perg. *ad annum*), *l.r.* 15 Oct. 1296 (*ibid.*).

Patrimony in Tuscany

1. 'Alatrinus', subdeacon and papal chaplain (see temporal rectors, Duchy of Spoleto, n. 7), *n.* 27 Jan. 1227 and probably holds office until *c.* 1230: see p. 137.
2. Walter, bishop of Amelia ('cura . . . quantum ad spiritualia'), *n.* 7 Aug. 1263 (*Reg. Urb. IV*, I, n. 301).
3. Brother Bartholomew of Amelia (inquisitor), (as n. 2), *n.* 10 Jan. 1264 (*Reg. Urb. IV*, II, n. 747).
4. Armannus, canon of Piacenza, vicar-general *in spiritualibus, f.r.* (and *l.r.*) 9 Sept. 1272 (*BISI*, XXVII, 224).
5. Peter, prior of S. Ippolito, vicar-general *in spiritualibus*, reference '1274' (Signorelli, *Viterbo*, p. 271 n.).
6. Angelo 'de Malliano', vicar *in spiritualibus, f.r.* 17 Oct. 1280 (Rieti, Sottosez AS, perg. *ad annum*: also, undated, *Reg. Hon. IV*, n. 496).
7. Simon, bishop of Bagnorea, vicar *super spiritualibus*, reference between 2 Apr. 1285 and early 1286 (*Reg. N. IV*, n. 479).
8. Lituardus, bishop of Nepi, vicar *in spiritualibus, n.* late in 1285 or early 1286, *l.r.* 19 Nov. 1287 (Signorelli, *Viterbo*, pp. 289 n – 299 n).

9. Peregrinus, papal chaplain and provost of 'Vancis' (dioc. Padua), rector *in spiritualibus, n.* 23 Oct. 1290 (*Reg. N. IV*, nn. 7278–9).

10. 'Rannus Raynaldi', rector *in spiritualibus, n.* 15 May 1295 (*Reg. B. VIII*, nn. 5420–1).

11. Andrew of Gubbio (possibly identical with Campagna-Marittima, n. 4), *plebanus* of S. Stephen's *di Loreto* (dioc. Gubbio), *f.r.* (and *l.r.*) 21 March 1298 (*Reg. B. VIII*, n. 2449), superseded 15 July 1298 (*v.* temporal rectors, n. 38).

12. Henry 'Manentis', canon of Spoleto, rector *in spiritualibus, n.* 28 Oct. 1300 (*Reg. B. VIII*, n. 3908).

13. John of Guarcino, rector *super spiritualibus, f.r.* (and *l.r.*) 26 Oct. 1303 (Pflugk-Harttung, pp. 587–8).

14. Henry, *plebanus* of S. Stephens *de Campis* (dioc. Florence), rector *in spiritualibus, n.* 22 Dec. 1303 (*Reg. B. XI*, n. 1143).

Duchy of Spoleto

1. Moricus, canon of Assisi, vicar-general *super spiritualibus*, reference 3 July 1276 (Perugia, AS, Rif. III, f. 56).

2. Roland Taverna, bishop of Spoleto, rector *in spiritualibus*, early part of Martin IV's pontificate, i.e. 1281– (Sansi, *Spoleto*, p. 120): dies in office, 3 Apr. 1285 (Eubel, p. 485).

3. Roland of Ferentino, papal chaplain (see Duchy temporal rectors, nn. 17 and 25) succeeds n. 2 as rector *in spiritualibus*, becoming rector *in spiritualibus et temporalibus* on 13 June 1285 (Sansi, *Spoleto*, p. 120).

4. John 'Angeli', canon of Narni, rector *in spiritualibus, n.* 1 March 1288 (*Reg. N. IV*, nn. 6955–60).

5. Jordan 'di Labbro', vicar *in spiritualibus, f.r.* 18 Feb. 1301, *l.r.* 16 May 1301 (*Archivio per la storia ecclesiastica dell' Umbria*, IV, 367).

6. John of Guarcino, canon of Albano (see Patrimony in Tuscany, n. 13) rector *in spiritualibus, n.* 18 June 1301 (*Reg. B. VIII*, nn. 4375–6).

7. John 'Guallati', canon of S. Theodore's, Rome, rector *in spiritualibus, n.* 2 Jan. 1302 (*Reg. B. VIII*, nn. 5083–4).

8. John of Guarcino, canon of Albano (see n. 6), rector *in spiritualibus, n.* 18 Dec. 1303 (*Reg. B. XI*, n. 1144).

March of Ancona

1. 'Nicholas', vicar *super spiritualibus*, ref. 21 Sept. 1236 (Gianandrea, *Iesi*, d. LXXIV).

2. Prior of Narni, (probably vicar: to proceed *spiritualiter*, etc.), ref. 1 Feb. 1258 (Colucci, *Ant. Pic.*, XIX, d. XXXII).

3. Guy, papal chaplain and abbot of S. Anastasius ('*ad censuram ecclesiasticam in spiritualibus exercendam*', etc.), ref. 18 Sept. 1258 (Colucci, *Ant. Pic.*, XXIX, 97–9).

4. William of S. Lorenzo, papal chaplain and provost of S. Antoninus, Piacenza, vicar *in spiritualibus, n.* 6 May 1272 (*Reg. G. X*, nn. 168–79).

5. Thomas, provost of Fano, vicar-general *super spiritualibus*, ref. 26 May 1273 (Turchi, *Camerino*, d. LIX).

6. Bernard, papal chaplain and archdeacon of Narbonne, vicar *in spiritualibus*, *f.r.* 15 March 1274 (*Reg. G. X*, n. 333), *l.r.* 1 Feb. 1276, when Bernard is archbishop-elect of Genoa (Colini-Baldeschi, *Cingoli*, d. vi).

7. Peter 'Alafredi', vicar *super spiritualibus*, *f.r.* 6 Jan. 1280 (Gianandrea, *Iesi*, d. CXCVII), *l.r.* 15 May 1280 (Colucci, *Ant. Pic.*, XXX, 37–8): there are also some earlier references to him as vicar *super spiritualibus et temporalibus*.

8. Martin 'Mayxonen.', canon of Narni, vicar *in spiritualibus*, ref. '1282' (Leopardi, *Series Rectorum Anconitane Marchiae*, p. 18): probably before 23 May 1282 (see temporal rectors, n. 21).

9. Stephen, canon of S. Peter's 'da Torrice', vicar-general *in spiritualibus*, ref. 31 Aug. 1283 (the year not absolutely certain, however) (Compagnoni, *Regg. Pic.*, pp. 143–4).

10. John 'Bellus' of Milan, vicar *in spiritualibus*, *f.r.* 27 Sept. 1286 (Acquacotta, *Matelica*, d. 73), *l.r.* 17 June 1288 (Zonghi, *Fabriano*, d. CCXLIV: before 19 May 1288 this vicar was himself represented by a vicar, Gerard *plebanus* of S. John 'de Penna', *v.* Ferranti, *Amandola*, III, dd. 155–9).

11. Matthew, canon of Assisi and chaplain of the cardinal of S.M. *in Via Lata*, rector *in spiritualibus*, n. 20 July 1288 (*Reg. N. IV*, nn. 7091–2), *l.r.* 27 Sept. 1290 (Vogel, *Recanati*, II, 58–9).

12. James of Foligno, vicar *in spiritualibus*, ref. 20 Feb. 1291 (Ferranti, *Amandola*, III, d. 171).

13. Bernard, canon of Ferrara, vicar-general *super spiritualibus*, ref. 23 June 1293 (Serra S. Quirico, AC, perg., II, f. 45).

14. Constantinus, canon of Adria, rector *super spiritualibus*, ref. 2 Dec. 1294 (Colucci, *Ant. Pic.*, XXXI, 40–1).

15. William Durand, archdeacon of Mende (nephew of his namesake, for whom *v.* Romagna, n. 1, etc.), vicar-general *in spiritualibus*, *f.r.* 9 March 1295 (Ferranti, *Amandola*, III, d. 220), *l.r.* 5 July 1296 (Acquacotta, *Matelica*, d. 92), thus apparently overlapping with n. 16.

16. Matthew of Rieti, canon of S. Croce 'de Luniano', rector *in spiritualibus*, *f.r.* 10 March 1296 (Ferranti, *Amandola*, III, d. 220: 'Martin' is probably a misreading), *l.r.* 11 May 1300 (Santoni, 'Camerino', p. 60): probably superseded on 27 May 1300, *v.* temporal rectors, n. 29.

17. Andrew of Gubbio, canon of Châlons-sur-Marne (*v.* Campagna-Marittima, n. 4, who is perhaps identical) rector *in spiritualibus*, n. 18 June 1301 (*Reg. B. VIII*, nn. 4375–6), *l.r.* 27 Sept. 1301 (*RSDI*, V, 180–4): probably superseded on 2 Jan. 1302 (*v.* temporal rectors, n. 32).

18. Gabriel 'de Patientibus', clerk and doctor of laws, rector *in spiritualibus*, n. 5 Jan. 1304 (*Reg. B. XI*, n. 1145).

Massa Trabaria

1. Collus, canon of Pieve S. Lazzaro (dioc. Florence), rector *in spiritualibus*, *n.* 24 May 1300 (*Reg. B. VIII*, n. 3695).

Romagna

1. William Durand, papal chaplain (*v.* temporal rectors, Patrimony in Tuscany n. 26; Duchy, n. 28; Romagna, nn. 3 and 10), rector *in spiritualibus*, *n.* 30 May 1281 (Potthast, n. 21761): holds office until he becomes rector *in spiritualibus et temporalibus c.* Feb. 1284.

2. Bartholomew, bishop of Grosseto, vicar *in spiritualibus*, *n.* 26 Feb. 1289 (*Reg. N. IV*, n. 7220), *l.r.* 25 June 1289 (*ASI*, LXXXIII, 246–50).

3. Peter 'Saraceni', bishop of Vicenza, vicar-general *in spiritualibus*, *f.r.* 29 Dec. 1289 (RIS, N.S., XXII, II, 43), *l.r.* 28 March 1290 (Tonini, *Rimini*, III, 663–7).

4. Peter 'de Buclano', archpriest (dioc. Chieti), rector *in spiritualibus*, *n.* 11 Sept. 1294 (Ghirardacci, *Bologna*, pp. 318–19), *l.r.* 24 Apr. 1295 (*ibid.*, p. 325).

5. Hubert 'de Notis' of Milan, canon of Milan, doctor of canon law, vicar *in spiritualibus* before 14 Dec. 1303 (Fantuzzi, *Mon. Rav.*, IV, n. CXXXXVII and V, n. LXXIII), *n.* rector *in spiritualibus* 20 Jan. 1304 (*Reg. B. XI*, n. 244).

C. Treasurers
Campagna and Marittima

1. Rainald 'de Basciano', ref. 21 Aug. 1299 (*Reg. B. VIII*, n. 3408).

Patrimony in Tuscany

1. 'Bernard', ref. 20 Oct. 1290 (Arch. Vat., Arm. XXXV, 14, f. 185).
2. Bonsignore 'Gregorii' of Siena, ref. '1291' (Theiner, p. 317).
3. Nicholas 'Guarcini' of Anagni, ref. 26 Oct. 1303 (Pflugk-Harttung, pp. 587–8).

Duchy of Spoleto

1. 'Ugolino', ref. 22 July 1280 (Morini, *Cascia*, d. I).
2. Maynectus 'de Puliti' of Florence, ref. 11 Dec. 1291 (Morini, *Cascia*, pp. 23–5).
3. Bertus 'de Scivinictis' of Florence, ref. 8 July 1293 (Fabriano, AC, perg. n. 321).
4. Avogadus Gherardi of Florence (in Duchy and March of Ancona), *f.r.* 30 Apr. 1302 (Colucci, *Ant. Pic.*, XXIX, 143), *l.r.* 4 Sept. 1302 (Fabriano, AC, perg. n. 362): see also March of Ancona, n. 20.
5. Dinus of Florence, ref. 23 July 1303 (Cascia, AC, perg. n. 18).

March of Ancona

1. Ruffinus da Stradiliano, *n.* 8 Apr. 1272 (Santoni, 'Camerino', p. 51), *l.r.* 5 March 1273 (Gianandrea, *Iesi*, d. CLXXX).

2. Hugo 'Montan'., ref. 23 Dec. 1277 (Macerata, AC, perg. n. 103).

3. Henry of Florence, *f.r.* 13 May 1278 (Ferranti, *Amandola*, III, d. 117), *l.r.* 24 Jan. 1279 (Gianandrea, *Iesi*, d. CXCIII).

4. Roger of Florence, *f.r.* 5 June 1279 (Gianandrea, *Iesi*, d. CXCIV), *l.r.* 11 March 1280 (Fabriano, AC, Lib. Ross., f. 90).

5. Rimbertinus 'Piovanelli', *f.r.* 2 Aug. 1280 (Gianandrea, *Iesi*, d. CXCIX), *l.r.* 24 March 1281 (Fabriano, AC, Lib. Ross., f. 91).

6. Philip 'Hugonis Spine' of Florence, *f.r.* 17 June 1281 (Gianandrea, *Iesi*, d. CCII), *l.r.* 14 Feb. 1282 (Jordan, *De mercatoribus camerae apostolicae*, p. 109).

7. Rainald 'Campane' of Florence, *f.r.* 20 Feb. 1282 (Fabriano, AC, Lib. Ross., f. 91v), *l.r.* 17 June 1283 (Gianandrea, *Iesi*, d. CCXV): but *c.* July 1282 Clarus 'Sagine' of Florence appears to be acting as treasurer (*ibid.*, d. CCXIX).

8. Philip 'Hugonis Spine' of Florence (n. 6 above), *f.r.* 11 Jan. 1284 (Gianandrea, *Iesi*, p. 262), *l.r.* Feb. 1284 (Grimaldi, 'Il nonno di Petrarca nelle Marche', p. 88).

9. Clarus 'Sagine' of Florence (see *ad* n. 7), *f.r.* 28 June 1284, *l.r.* 26 June 1285 (Grimaldi, *op. cit.*, pp. 88, 91–2).

10. Manfredo di Rainuzio of Siena, ref. 17 Jan. 1286 (Grimaldi, *op. cit.*, p. 88).

11. Bindus 'Deotavive' of Siena, ref. 13 May 1287 (Mei, *Cagli*, nn. 334–5).

12. Altovitus Bartholomei of Siena, *f.r.* 22 Aug. 1287 (Macerata, AC, perg. n. 171), *l.r.* 2 July 1288 (Zonghi, *Fabriano*, d. CCXLIV).

13. Simon 'q. Bonaccursi' of Pistoia (of the firm of Chiarenti), *n.* 18 July 1288 (*Reg. N. IV*, n. 7094), *l.r.* 27 Nov. 1288 (Macerata, AC, perg.).

14. Ranier de Ranieri of Lucca (of the firm of Ricciardi), ref. 25 March 1289 (Mei, *Cagli*, p. 31).

15. Roland 'Paganelli' of Lucca (of Ricciardi), *f.r.* 3 Apr. 1289 (Fabriano, AC, Lib. Ross., f. 169v), *l.r.* 8 Aug. 1294 (Santoni, 'Camerino', p. 56): his vicar on 14 Aug. 1290 and 21 May 1291 is 'Cecius Dentis' of Lucca (Macerata, AC, perg. nn. 265, 294).

16. Bertus 'Simonicti' of Florence (identical with Duchy of Spoleto, n. 3), ref. 3 Feb. 1295 (Ferranti, *Amandola*, III, d. 216).

17. Nicholas 'Giandonati' of Pistoia (of Chiarenti), *f.r.* 15 Jan. 1296 (Ferranti, *Amandola*, III, d. 232), *l.r.* 26 June 1296 (Santoni, 'Camerino', p. 57).

18. Nicholas 'Gualterii' of Anagni (possibly identical with Patrimony in Tuscany, n. 3), *f.r.* 4 May 1297 (Iesi, AC, perg. n. 161), *l.r.* 26 May 1300 (Santoni, 'Camerino', p. 60; which has 'of Ancona' in error).

19. Baldus 'Rembein. de Sum.' (*sic*), ref. 6 Jan. 1301 (Ferranti, *Amandola*, III, d. 286).

20. Avogadus Gherardi of Florence (for tenure of treasurership of Duchy and March, *v*. Duchy, n. 4). In March only: *f.r.* 1 Jan. 1303 (Ferranti, *Amandola*, III, d. 307), *l.r.* 21 March 1303 (*v*. n. 21).

21. Nellus Paganelli of Florence (of the firm of Spini), *f.r.* 21 March 1303 (as vicar for n. 20), *l.r.* 2 Sept. 1303 (Colucci, *Ant. Pic.*, XXIII, 114–15).

22. Buonconte and Francis 'Bernardi' of Florence, jointly (of the firm of 'Eculor' (? = Cerchi), ref. 19 Jan. 1304 (Ferranti, *Amandola*, III, d. 320).

Romagna

1. Ranuccinus Bonacolti, ref. 1285 (Theiner, p. 280).

2. 'Pinus olim d. Loteringii', ref. 26 March 1291 (Arch. Vat., Arm. XXXIII, n. 33a, f. 51).

3. Clarus 'Montalti' (or 'Metaltissimi') of Pistoia, ref. 14 July 1294 (Tonini, *Rimini*, III, 681–90; Balduzzi, 'Bagnacavallo', p. 153).

4. Thomas 'Lapi Diedi' of Florence (of the firm of Mozzi), *n*. 11 May 1295 (*Reg. B. VIII*, n. 5416), but possibly holds office a few weeks earlier, *v*. Ghirardacci, *Bologna*, p. 325.

5. Lottus 'Falconieri', vice-treasurer, ref. 3 Feb. 1296 (Balduzzi, 'Bagnacavallo', p. 154).

BIBLIOGRAPHY

This is not intended to serve as a full bibliography of the subject. It is a list of the books and articles cited in this volume, omitting those not directly concerned with the subject of this book to which isolated reference has been made. Hence most works cited in the first chapter only are not included.

When a work is cited in an abbreviated form in the footnotes this is noted in brackets after the entry.

The division between 'Documentary Sources' and 'Secondary Works' is to some extent arbitrary, since many books and articles include documents as well as a commentary on them. I have attempted to distinguish between works valuable primarily for the documents they publish and those in which the discussion is of more importance than the materials printed.

I. Sources

A. *Narrative*

Annales Caesenates, RIS, O.S., XIV.

Annales Casinenses, MGH, XIX.

Annales Ceccanenses, MGH, XIX.

Annales Forolivienses, RIS, N.S., XXII, II.

Annales Placentini Ghibellini, MGH, XVIII.

Bartholomew Cotton, *Historia Anglicana*, R.S.

Burchard of Ursburg, *Chronicon*, MGH, XXIII.

Caesarius of Heisterbach, *Dialogus Miraculorum*, ed. J. Strange (Cologne, 1851).

Chronica Breviora aliaque monumenta faventina a Bernardino Azzurinio collecta, RIS, N.S., XXVIII, III.

Cobelli, L., 'Fatto d'armi tra Guido da Montefeltro il vecchio, Giovanni d'Appia e il Conte di Monforte' in *ASI*, Appendices, VII (1849).

Corpus Chronicorum Bononensium, RIS, N.S., XVIII, I.

Cronaca Todina di Ioan Fabrizio degli Atti, ed. F. Mancini in *Studi di Filologia Italiana*, XIII (1955). (*Cronaca Todina*.)

Cronache e Statuti della Città di Viterbo, ed. I. Ciampi (Florence, 1872). (Ciampi, *Viterbo*).

Ephemerides Urbevetanae, RIS, N.S., XV, V.

Fragmenta Fulginatis Historiae, RIS, N.S., XXVI, II.

Gesta Innocentii III, P.L., vol. 214.

Liber Pontificalis, ed. L. Duchesne (Paris, 1886–92). (*Lib. Pont.*)

Marcha di Marco Battagli da Rimini, RIS, N.S., XVI, III.

Matthew Paris, *Chronica Majora*, R.S.

Nicolaus de Jamsilla, *Historia de rebus gestis Friderici II eiusque filiorum*, ed. Del Re (*Cronisti e scrittori napoletani*, vol. II), (Naples, 1868).

Petri Cantinelli Chronicon, RIS, N.S., XXVIII, II.

Richard of San Germano, *Chronica*, RIS, N.S., VII, II.

Roger of Hoveden, *Chronica*, R.S.

Rolandinus Patavinus, *Cronica*, MGH, XIX.

Saba Malaspina, *Rerum sicularum*, ed. Del Re (*Cronisti e scrittori napoletani*, vol. II), (Naples, 1868).

Salimbene, *Cronica*, ed. F. Bernini (Bari, 1942). (Salimbene.)

S. Pietro Parenzo. La Leggenda scritta dal Maestro Giovanni, ed. A. Natalini (Rome, 1936).

Stefaneschi, Jacopo Gaetano, *Opus Metricum*, ed. F. X. Seppelt in *Monumenta Coelestiniana* (Paderborn, 1921).

Thomas of Celano, *Vita Prima S. Francisci* (Quaracchi, 1926).

Villani, G., *Cronica*, ed. F. G. Dragomanni (Florence, 1844-5). (Villani.)

Vita Gregorii IX in *Liber Censuum*, vol. II.

Vita Innocentii IV, ed. Pagnotti in *ASRSP*, XXI (1898).

Vita Urbani IV, RIS, O.S., III, 2.

Watterich, J. M. (ed.), *Pontificum Romanorum Vitae* (Leipzig, 1862 ff.). (Watterich.)

B. *Documentary*

Acquacotta, C., *Memorie di Matelica* (Ancona, 1838). (Acquacotta, *Matelica*.)

Amiani, P. M., *Memorie istoriche della città di Fano* (Fano, 1751). (Amiani, *Fano*.)

Angeloni, F., *Historia di Terni* (ed. 2, Pisa, 1878). (Angeloni, *Terni*.)

Ansidei, V. and Giannantoni, L., 'I codici delle sommissioni al comune di Perugia', *BDSPU*, I–IX (1895-1903).

Baethgen, F., 'Ein Pamphlet Karls I.v. Anjou zur Wahl Papst Nikolaus III.' *Bayerische Akad. d. Wissenschaften, Phil.-Hist. Kl., Sitzungsberichte*, Jahr. 1960, Hft. 7.

Baldassini, G., *Memorie istoriche della città di Iesi* (Iesi, 1765). (Baldassini, *Iesi*.)

Balduzzi, L., 'Sugli archivi di Bagnacavallo', *Atti e Memorie della R. Deputazione di Storia Patria per le provincie dell'Emilia*, N.S., VII (1881). (Balduzzi, 'Bagnacavallo'.)

Baumgarten, P. M., *Untersuchungen und Urkunden über die Camera Collegii Cardinalium von 1294 bis 1478* (Leipzig, 1898.)

Bock, F., 'Annotationes zu den Registern Urbans IV.', in *Miscellanea Archivistica A. Mercati* (Vatican City, 1952).

Böhmer, J. F., *Regesta Imperii, V: 1198-1272* (ed. Ficker and Winkelmann, Innsbruck, 1881-1901). (BFW.)

Böhmer, J. F., *Acta Imperii Selecta* (Innsbruck, 1870).

Borgia, A., *Istoria della chiesa e città di Velletri* (Nocera, 1723). (Borgia, *Velletri*.)

Bullarium Romanum (Turin, 1857-72).

Caetani, G., *Regesta Chartarum* (in *Documenti dell' Archivio Caetani*) (Perugia, 1922-32).

Carsoli Rediviva ovvero storiche ricerche intorno all'antichissima città di Carsoli nell' Umbria (Macerata, 1800).

Catalani, M., *De Ecclesia Firmana* (Fermo, 1783). (Catalani, *Fermo.*)

Cecconi, G., *Carte Diplomatiche Osimane* (Ancona, 1878). (Cecconi, *Osimo.*)

Cecconi, G., *Storia di Castelfidardo* (Osimo, 1879). (Cecconi, *Castelfidardo.*)

Cenci, P., 'Regesto delle pergamene della Sperelliana di Gubbio', *BDSPU*, XXV (1922).

Cicconi, G., *Le pergamene dell'archivio municipale di Montelparo* in *Fonti per la Storia delle Marche* (Ancona, 1939). (Cicconi, *Montelparo.*)

Clementini, C., *Raccolto istorico della fondatione di Rimino* (Rimini, 1617). (Clementini, *Rimini.*)

Colini-Baldeschi, L., *Il libro rosso del comune di Osimo* (Macerata, 1909). (Colini-Baldeschi, *Osimo.*)

Colini-Baldeschi, L., *Il riordinamento dell'antico archivio di Cingoli* (Cingoli, 1909). (Colini-Baldeschi, *Cingoli.*)

Colini-Baldeschi, L., 'Le "Constitutiones Romandiole" di Giovanni d'Appia', *Nuovi Studi Medievali*, II (1925).

Colucci, G., *Treja oggi Montecchio illustrata* (Macerata, 1780). (Colucci, *Treia.*)

Colucci, G., *Antichità Picene* (31 vols.) (Fermo, 1786–96). (Colucci, *Ant. Pic.*)

Compagnoni, P., *La Reggia Picena* (Macerata, 1661). (Compagnoni, *Regg. Pic.*)

Contatore, D. A., *De historia terracinensi* (Rome, 1706). (Contatore, *Terracina.*)

Costituzioni Egidiane, ed. P. Sella (Rome, 1912). (Albornoz, *Constitutions.*)

Davidsohn, R., 'Un parlamento di Carlo di Valois per le cose di Romagna', *ASI*, L (1912).

De Cupis, C., 'Regesto degli Orsini e dei conti Anguillara', *Bollettino della Società di storia patria A.L. Antinori negli Abruzzi*, XIV–XVI (1902–04). (De Cupis.)

De Minicis, G., *Cronache della Città di Fermo (colla giunta di un sommario cronologico di carte fermane)* (Florence, 1870). (De Minicis, *Fermo.*)

Dubois, P., *De Recuperatione Terre Sancte* (ed. Langlois, Paris, 1891).

Dubois, P., *Summaria brevis et compendiosa doctrina felicis expedicionis et abreviacionis guerrarum ac litium regni francorum* (ed. Kämpf, Leipzig-Berlin, 1936).

Dupuy, P., *Histoire du Différand entre le pape Boniface VIII et Philippe le Bel* (Paris, 1655). (Dupuy.)

Durand, G., *Speculum Iuris* (Frankfurt, 1668).

Egidi, P., 'L'archivio storico della cattedrale di Viterbo', *BISI*, XXVII (1906).

Ermini, G., 'Costituzioni per la provincia della Marca Anconitana del 1301', *RSDI*, V (1932).

Fabre, P., 'Un registre caméral du Card. Albornoz en 1364', *MAH*, VII (1887).

Fanciulli, L., *Osservazioni critiche sopra le antichità cristiane di Cingoli* (Osimo, 1769). (Fanciulli, *Cingoli.*)

Fantuzzi, M., *Monumenti Ravennati* (Venice, 1801–4). (Fantuzzi, *Mon. Rav.*)

Fausti, L., 'Le pergamene dell'archivio del duomo di Spoleto', *Archivio per la storia ecclesiastica dell' Umbria*, IV (1917–19).

Ferranti, P., *Memorie storiche della città di Amandola* (Ascoli Piceno, 1891–2). (Ferranti, *Amandola*.)

Ficker, J. F., *Forschungen zur Reichs- und Rechtsgeschichte Italiens*, vol. IV (Innsbruck, 1874). (Ficker, *Forschungen*.)

Filippini, F. and Luzzatto, G., 'Archivi Marchigiani', *AMSM*, N.S., VII (1911–1912).

Finke, H., *Acta Aragonensia* (Berlin-Leipzig, 1908–23).

Foglietti, R., *Statuto del comune di Macerata del sec. XIII* (Macerata, 1885).

Foglietti, R., *Il catasto di Macerata dell'anno 1268* (Macerata, 1881).

Fumi, L., *Codice Diplomatico della Città d'Orvieto* (Florence, 1884). (Fumi, *Orvieto*.)

Gazzera, E., *Sanginesio e lo suo antiquo Archivio* (Tolentino, 1915). (Gazzera, *Sanginesio*.)

Ghirardacci, C., *Historia di Bologna* (Bologna, 1605). (Ghirardacci, *Bologna*.)

Gianandrea, A., *Carte Diplomatiche Iesine* (Ancona, 1884). (Gianandrea, *Iesi*.)

Gianandrea, A., 'Le pergamene del Comune di Staffolo', *Archivio Storico per le Marche e per l'Umbria*, III (1886).

Grimaldi, G., 'Le pergamene di Matelica, I', *Fonti della R. Deputazione Marchigiana di Storia Patria* (Ancona, 1915). (Grimaldi, *Matelica*.)

Grimaldi, G., 'Il nonno di Petrarca nelle Marche' in *Miscellanea di Storia e Filologia. Miscellanea per Nozze Crocioni-Ruscelloni* (Rome, 1908).

Hagemann, W., 'Kaiserurkunden und Reichssachen im Archivio Storico von Gubbio', *QFIA*, XXVIII–XXIX (1937–9) and XXXIV (1954).

Hagemann, W., 'Le lettere originali dei dogi Ranieri Zeno (1253–68) e Lorenzo Tiepolo (1268–75) conservate nell'Archivio Diplomatico di Fermo', *Studia Picena*, XXV (1957).

Hagemann, W., 'Un trattato del 1225 tra Fermo e Termoli finora sconosciuto', in *Studi in Onore, di R. Filangieri*, vol. I (Naples, 1959).

Hampe, K., 'Eine unbekannte Konstitution Gregors IX. zur Verwaltung und Finanzordnung des Kirchenstaates', *Zeitschrift für Kirchengeschichte*, XLV (1926).

Hampe, K., 'Aus verlorenen Registerbänden der Päpste Innozenz III. und Innozenz IV.', *MIÖG*, XXIII–XXIV (1902–3).

Huillard-Bréholles, J. L. A., *Historia diplomatica Friderici secundi* (Paris, 1852–1861). (Huillard-Bréholles.)

Kaltenbrunner, F., *Actenstücke zur Geschichte des deutschen Reiches unter den Königen Rudolf I. und Albrecht I.* (Vienna, 1889.)

Kehr, P., *Italia Pontificia* (Berlin, 1906 ff.). (Kehr, *It. Pont.*)

Kehr, P., 'Papsturkunden in der Romagna und den Marken', *Nachrichten v. d.K. Gesellschaft d. Wissenschaften zu Göttingen, Phil.-Hist. Klasse*, V (1898).

Lanzi, L., 'Un lodo d'Innocenzo III ai Narnesi, specialmente per la terra di Stroncone', *BDSPU*, I (1895).

Leopardi, M., *Annali di Recanati* (ed. Vuoli, Varese, 1945). (Leopardi, *Recanati*.)

Liber Censuum, ed. P. Fabre and L. Duchesne (Paris, 1889 ff). (*Lib. Cens.*)

Lilii, C., *Historia di Camerino* (Rome, 1719). (Lilii, *Camerino*.)

Loevinson, E., 'Sunti delle pergamene marchigiane conservate nell'archivio di stato di Roma', *AMSM*, s.2, X; s.3, I–IV; s.4, VI (1916–29).

Luca, G. de, 'Un formulario della cancelleria francescana e altri formulari tra il XIII e XIV secolo', *Archivio per la Storia della Pietà*, I (1951).

Marangoni, G., *Delle memorie sagre e civili de Civita Nova* (Rome, 1743). (Marangoni, *Civitanova*.)

Martène, E. and Durand, U., *Thesaurus novus anecdotorum* (Paris, 1717). (Martène and Durand.)

Martorelli, L., *Memorie historiche dell'antichissima città d'Osimo* (Venice, 1705). (Martorelli, *Osimo*.)

Massèra, A. F., 'Il serventese romagnolo del 1277', *ASI*, LXXII (1914).

Mazzatinti, G., *Gli archivi della storia d'Italia* (Rocca S. Casciano, 1899 ff). (Mazzatinti.)

Mei, G., *Catalogo delle pergamene originali degli archivi di Cagli dell'anno 1285 al 1292* (Cagli, 1889). (Mei, *Cagli*.)

Michaeli, M., *Memorie storiche della città di Rieti* (Rieti, 1897–9). (Michaeli, *Rieti*.)

Monumenta Germaniae Historica, *Constitutiones et acta publica imperatorum et regum* (1893 ff).

Monumenta Germaniae Historica, *Epistolae saec. XIII a regestis pontificum Romanorum selectae* (1883–94).

Monumenta Germaniae Historica, *Scriptores* (1826 ff).

Morini, A., *Le pergamene dell' archivio comunale di Cascia* (Norcia, 1941). (Morini, *Cascia*.)

Muzi, G., *Memorie ecclesiastiche e civili di Città di Castello* (Città di Castello, 1842–4). (Muzi, *Città di Castello*.)

Pacifici, V., *Codice Diplomatico di Tivoli* (Tivoli, 1929).

Palmieri, G., *Introiti ed Esiti di papa Niccolò III, 1279–80* (Rome, 1889). (Palmieri.)

Pantanelli, P., *Notizie Istoriche appartenenti alla terra di Sermoneta* (Rome, 1911). (Pantanelli, *Sermoneta*.)

Pflugk-Harrtung, J. von, *Iter Italicum* (Stuttgart, 1883). (Pflugk-Harttung.)

Poesie provenzali storiche relative all' Italia, ed. V. De Bartholomaeis (Rome, 1931).

Potthast, A., *Regesta Pontificum Romanorum* (Berlin, 1874–5). (Potthast.)

Regesta Innocentii III, P.L. vols. 214–217. (*Reg. Inn. III.*)

Regesta Honorii papae III, ed. P. Pressutti (Rome, 1888–95). (*Reg. Hon. III.*)

'Regesta Reformationum Comunis Perusii, 1256–60', *BDSPU*, XXV–XXVII (1922–6) (and separately, Perugia, 1935).

'Regesto e documenti di Storia Perugina', *ASI*, XVI, 2 (1851).

Regestum Innocentii III papae super negotio romani imperii, ed. F. Kempf (Rome 1947). (*R.N.I.*)

Regestum Clementis Papae V (Rome, 1885). (*Reg. Cl. V.*)

Registres de Grégoire IX, ed. Auvray (Paris, 1896 ff). (*Reg. G. IX.*)

Registres d'Innocent IV, ed. Berger (Paris, 1884 ff). (*Reg. Inn. IV.*)

Registres d'Alexandre IV, ed. Bourel de la Roncière and others (Paris, 1902 ff). (*Reg. Alex. IV.*)

Registres d'Urbain IV, ed. Guiraud (Paris, 1901 ff). (*Reg. Urb. IV.*)

Registres de Clément IV, ed. Jordan (Paris, 1893 ff). (*Reg. Cl. IV.*)

Registres de Grégoire X, ed. Guiraud (Paris, 1892 ff). (*Reg. G. X.*)

Registres de Nicolas III, ed. Gay and Vitte (Paris, 1898 ff). (*Reg. N. III.*)

Registres de Martin IV, various editors (Paris, 1901 ff). (*Reg. M. IV.*)

Registres d'Honorius IV, ed. Prou (Paris, 1898 ff). (*Reg. Hon. IV.*)

Registres de Nicolas IV, ed. Langlois (Paris, 1886 ff). (*Reg. N. IV.*)

Registres de Boniface VIII, ed. Digard and others (introduction by R. Fawtier) (Paris, 1890 ff). (*Reg. B. VIII.*)

Registres de Benoît XI, ed. Grandjean (Paris, 1883 ff). (*Reg. B. XI.*)

Richard de Bury, *Liber Epistolaris*, ed. N. Denholm-Young (London, 1950).

Sansi, A., *Documenti Storici inediti in sussidio allo studio delle Memorie Umbre* (Foligno, 1879). (Sansi, *Spoleto*.)

Santoni, M., 'Il libro rosso del comune di Camerino, 1207–1336', *Archivio Storico per le Marche e per l'Umbria*, II (1885). (Santoni, 'Camerino'.)

Sarti, M., *De Episcopis eugubinis* (Pesaro, 1755). (Sarti, *Gubbio*.)

Schneider, F., 'Untersuchungen zur italienischen Verfassungsgeschichte. II. Staufisches aus der Formelsammlung des Petrus de Boateriis', *QFIA*, XVIII (1926).

Schneider, F., 'Beiträge zur Geschichte Friedrichs II. und Manfreds', *QFIA*, XV (1913).

Sella, P., 'Costituzioni promulgate nel Parlamento di Macerata dell'anno 1272', *RSDI*, II (1929).

Sella, P., 'Costituzioni per la Romagna pubblicate nel parlamento di Cesena dell'anno 1289', *ASI*, LXXXIII (1925).

Sonetti Burleschi e Realistici dei primi due secoli, ed. A. F. Massèra (ed. 2, Bari, 1940).

Tanursi, F. M., *Memorie istoriche della città di Ripatransone* (Fermo, 1793: vol. XVIII of Colucci, *Ant. Pic.*, *q.v.*). (Tanursi, *Ripatransone*.)

Theiner, A., *Codex Diplomaticus dominii temporalis S. Sedis* (Rome, 1861–2). (Theiner = vol. I.)

Theiner, A., *Vetera Monumenta Slavorum Meridionalium* (Rome, 1863). (Theiner, *Vet. Mon. Slav. Merid.*)

Tonini, L., *Storia civile e sacra riminese* (Rimini, 1848–88). (Tonini, *Rimini*.)

Turchi, O., *De Ecclesiae Camerinensis Pontificibus* (Rome, 1762). (Turchi, *Camerino*.)

Valeri, G., 'L'Archivio Segreto di Serrasanquirico', *Archivio Storico per le Marche e per l'Umbria*, I–II (1884–5).

Vogel, J. A., *De Eclesiis Recanatensi et Lauretana Commentarius Historicus* (Recanati, 1859). (Vogel, *Recanati*.)

Waley, D. P. and Holtzmann, W., 'La legazione papale in Umbria del 1210 in un documento inedito di Amelia', *Rivista di Storia della Chiesa in Italia*, XII (1958).

Waley, D. P., 'Constitutions of the Cardinal-legate Peter Capocci, July 1249', *EHR*, LXXV (1960).

Winkelmann, E., *Acta Imperii Inedita saec. XIII* (Innsbruck, 1880–5).

Zonghi, A., *Carte Diplomatiche Fabrianesi* (Ancona, 1872). (Zonghi, *Fabriano*.)

II. Secondary Works

Alberti, F., *Notizie antiche e moderne riguardanti Bevagna città dell'Umbria* (Venice, ? 1791). (Alberti, *Bevagna*.)

Aloisi, U., 'Sulla formazione storica del "Liber Constitutionum Sancte Matris Ecclesie"', *AMSM*, N.S., I–V (1904–8).

Arduini, C., *Memorie storiche della città di Offida* (Fermo, 1844). (Arduini, *Offida*.)

Baethgen, F., 'Beiträge zur Geschichte Cölestins V.', *Königsberger Gelehrten Gesellschaft, Geisteswissenschaftliche Klasse*, Jahr. 10, Heft 4 (1934).

Baethgen, F., *Der Engelpapst* (Leipzig, 1943).

Baethgen, F., 'Quellen und Untersuchungen zur Geschichte der päpstlichen Hof- und Finanzverwaltung unter Bonifaz VIII.', *QFIA*, XX (1928–9).

Bartoloni, F., 'Per la storia del Senato Romano nei sec. XII e XIII', *BISI*, LX (1946).

Bartoloni, F., 'Un Trattato d'Alleanza del sec. XIII tra Roma e Alatri', *BISI*, LXI (1949).

Batzer, E., *Zur Kenntnis der Formularsammlung des Richard v. Pofi* (Heidelberg, 1910).

Boase, T. S. R., *Boniface VIII* (London, 1933). (Boase.)

Bock, F., 'Il Registrum super senatoria Urbis di papa Nicolò III', *BISI*, LXVI (1954).

Bock, F., 'Le trattative per la Senatoria di Roma e Carlo d'Angiò', *ASRSP*, LXXVIII (1955).

Böhm, L., *Johann von Brienne, König von Jerusalem, Kaiser von Konstantinopel*, (Heidelberg, 1938). (Böhm.)

Bonoli, P., *Istorie della Città di Forlì* (Forlì, 1661). (Bonoli, *Forlì*.)

Brezzi, P., *Roma e l'impero medioevale (774–1252)* (Bologna, 1947). (Brezzi.)

Bricchi, F., *Annali di Cagli* (Urbino, 1641). (Bricchi, *Cagli*.)

Caetani, G., *Domus Caietana* (Sancasciano Val di Pesa, 1927–33).

Calisse, C., 'I Prefetti di Vico', *ASRSP*, X (1887): also published separately.

Calisse, C., *Storia di Civita Vecchia* (Florence, 1898).

Cameli, U., 'Un episodio di storia Fermana dei tempi di Manfredi e Corradino', *Studia Picena*, XI (1935).

Campanari, S., *Tuscania e i suoi monumenti* (Montefiascone, 1856). (Campanari, *Toscanella*.)

Cantèra, B., *Cenni storici-biografici riguardanti s. Pier Celestino* (Naples, 1892).

Caperna, V., *Storia di Veroli* (Veroli, 1907). (Caperna, *Veroli*.)

Cecchelli, E., *I Crescenzi, i Savelli, i Cenci* (Rome, 1942).

Ceci, G., *Todi nel Medio Evo* (Todi, 1897). (Ceci, *Todi*.)

Clausen, J., *Papst Honorius III.* (Rome, 1895).

Codignola, T., 'Ricerche storico-giuridiche sulla Massa Trabaria nel XIII secolo', *ASI*, XCVII–XCVIII (1939–40).

Colini-Baldeschi, L., 'Vita pubblica e privata maceratese nel duecento e tre-cento', *AMSM*, VI (1903). (Colini-Baldeschi, 'Macerata'.)

Contelori, F., *Memorie Historiche della terra di Cesi* (Rome, 1675). (Contelori, *Cesi*.)

Cristofani, A., *Delle Storie di Assisi* (ed. 3, Assisi, 1902). (Cristofani, *Assisi*.)

Davidsohn, R., *Forschungen zur älteren Geschichte von Florenz* (Berlin, 1896–1908).

De Boüard, A., *Le régime politique et les institutions de Rome au moyen-âge, 1251–1347* (Paris, 1920). (De Boüard).

De Vergottini, G., 'Il papato e la comitatinanza nello stato della Chiesa, sec. XIII–XIV', *AMSR*, N.S., III (1951–2).

De Vergottini, G., 'Contributo alla storia della comitatinanza nello Stato della Chiesa', *RSDI*, XXVI–XXVII (1953–4).

De Vergottini, G., 'Concezione papale e concezione comunale dei rapporti di comitatinanza in conflitto in Romagna al principio del sec. XIV', *AMSR*, N.S., V (1953–4).

Dictionnaire de Droit Canonique, (Paris, 1935 ff), art. 'Guilielmus Durantis', (vol. V, cols. 1014–1075).

Digard, G., *Philippe le Bel et le Saint-Siège* (Paris, 1936). (Digard.)

Dupré-Theseider, E., *Roma dal comune di popolo alla signoria pontificia (1252–1377)* (Bologna, 1952). (Dupré-Theseider.)

Dupré-Theseider, E., 'L'eresia a Bologna nell'età di Dante', in *Scritti in onore di G. Volpe*, vol. I (Florence, 1958).

Elkan, H., *Die Gesta Innocentii III. im Verhaltniss zu den Regesten desselben Papstes* (Heidelberg, 1876).

Ermini, G., 'Caratteri della sovranità temporale dei papi nei sec. XIII e XIV', *ZSSR*, Kanon. Abt., XXVII (1938). (Ermini, 'Caratteri'.)

Ermini, G., 'Aspetti giuridici della sovranità pontificia nell' Umbria nel sec. XIII', *BDSPU*, XXXIV (1937). (Ermini, 'Aspetti giuridici'.)

Ermini, G., 'La libertà comunale nello Stato della Chiesa, I', *ASRSP*, XLIX (1926). (Ermini, 'La libertà comunale'.)

Ermini, G., *La libertà comunale nello Stato della Chiesa, II* (Rome, 1927). (Ermini, *La libertà comunale, II*.)

Ermini, G., 'I rettori provinciali della Stato della Chiesa da Innocenzo III all' Albornoz', *RSDI*, IV (1931).

Ermini, G., *I Parlamenti dello Stato della Chiesa dalle Origini al periodo Albornoziano* (Rome, 1930). (Ermini, *Parlamenti*.)

Ermini, G., 'Stato e Chiesa nella monarchia pontificia dei sec. XIII e XIV', *RSDI*, V (1932).

Ermini, G., 'I giudici provinciali della monarchia pontificia nel medioevo', in *Studi economico-giuridici pubbl. per cura della Facoltà di Giurisprudenza della R. Università di Cagliari*, XVIII (1931).

Eubel, C., *Hierarchia Catholica Medii Aevi*, vol. I (Münster, 1913). (Eubel.)

Fabre, P., *Étude sur le Liber Censuum de l'Église Romaine* (Paris, 1892).

Falco, G., 'Il comune di Velletri nel Medio Evo', *ASRSP*, XXXVI–XXXIX (1913–16).

Falco, G., 'I comuni della Campagna e Marittima nel Medio Evo', *ASRSP*, XLII (1919) and XLVII–XLIX (1924–6).

Falco, G., 'Sulla formazione e la costituzione della Signoria dei Caetani, 1283–1303', *Rivista Storica Italiana*, N.S., VI (1928).

Fasoli, G., 'La pace del 1279 tra i partiti bolognesi', *ASI*, XCI (1933).

Fasoli, G., 'Guelfi e Ghibellini di Romagna nel 1280–81', *ASI*, XCIV (1936).

Faure, C., *Étude sur l'administration et l'histoire du Comtat Venaissin du XIII au XV siècles* (Paris, 1907). (Faure.)

Fawtier, R., 'L'attentat d'Anagni', *MAH*, LX (1948).

Fehling, F., *Kaiser Friedrich II. und die römischen Cardinäle in den Jahren 1227 bis 1239* (Berlin, 1901). (Fehling.)

Felten, J., *Papst Gregor IX.* (Fribourg im Breisgau, 1886).

Ficker, J. F., *Forschungen zur Reichs- und Rechtsgeschichte Italiens*, vols. I–III (Innsbruck, 1868 ff). (Ficker, *Forschungen*.)

Ficker, J. F., 'Der Einfall Reinalds von Spoleto in den Kirchenstaat', *MIÖG*, IV (1883).

Ficker, J. F., 'Ueber das Testament Kaiser Heinrichs VI.', *Sitzungsberichte der Phil.-Hist. Classe d. K. Akad. d. Wissenschaften* (Vienna), LXVII (1871).

Fortini, A., *Assisi nel Medio Evo* (Rome, 1940). (Fortini, *Assisi*.)

Franceschini, G., 'La signoria dei conti di Montefeltro a Cesena (1275–1301)', *Studi Romagnoli*, V (1954).

Franceschini, G., 'Un caduto del "sanguinoso mucchio". Il conte Taddeo di Montefeltro (1230 ?–1284) e la sua discendenza', *Studi Romagnoli*, VII (1956).

Franceschini, G., 'Vescovi e prelati della famiglia dei conti di Montefeltro', *Studia Picena*, XXIV (1956).

Göller, E., 'Handschriftliches aus dem Vat. Archiv zur Geschichte des 14 Jahrhunderts. VII. Die Beamten der Kirchenstaatlichen Gebiete und deren Gehälter under Benedikt XI., *Römische Quartalschrift*, XVIII (1904).

Gorreta, A., *La lotta fra il comune bolognese e la signoria estense, 1293–1303* (Bologna, 1906).

Gregorovius, F., *History of the City of Rome in the Middle Ages* (London, 1894–1902). (Gregorovius.)

Gross, W., *Die Revolutionen in der Stadt Rom, 1219–1254* (Berlin, 1934). (Gross.)

Grundmann, H., Review of *R.N.I.* (ed. Kempf) in *ZSSR*, Kanon. Abt., XXXVII (1951).

Guerrieri, R., *Storia civile ed ecclesiastica del comune di Gualdo Tadino* (Gubbio, 1933). (Guerrieri, *Gualdo Tadino.*)

Hagemann, W., 'Fabriano im Kampf zwischen Kaisertum und Papsttum', *QFIA*, XXX (1940) and XXXII (1942).

Hagemann, W., 'Jesi im Zeitalter Friedrichs II.', *QFIA*, XXXVI (1956).

Hagemann, W., 'Studien und Dokumente zur Geschichte der Marken im Zeitalter der Staufer. I. Corridonia', *QFIA*, XXXVII (1957).

Haller, J., 'Heinrich VI. und die römische Kurie', *MIÖG*, XXXV (1914).

Haller, J., *Das Papsttum. Idee und Wirklichkeit* (ed. 2, Basle, 1951–3). (Haller, *Papsttum.*)

Halphen, L., *Études sur l'Administration de Rome au Moyen-Age* (Paris, 1907).

Hampe, K., *Deutsche Kaisergeschichte in der Zeit der Salier und Staufer*, ed. F. Baethgen (ed. 9, Leipzig, 1945).

Hampe, K., *Urban IV. und Manfred* (Heidelberg, 1905).

Hessel, A., *Geschichte der Stadt Bologna von 1116 bis 1280* (Berlin, 1910).

Heywood, W., *A History of Perugia* (London, 1910). (Heywood, *Perugia.*)

Hofmann, A. von, *Das Land Italien und seine Geschichte* (Stuttgart-Berlin, 1921).

Honig, R., *Guido da Montefeltro* (Bologna, 1901).

Jones, P. J., 'The Vicariate of the Malatesta of Rimini', *EHR*, LXVII (1952).

Jones, P. J., 'The Malatesta of Rimini'. Unpublished D.Phil. thesis, Oxford, 1950.

Jordan, E., *L'Allemagne et l'Italie aux XIIe et XIII siècles* (Paris, 1939). (Jordan, *L'Allemagne et l'Italie.*)

Jordan, E., *De mercatoribus camerae apostolicae saeculo XIII* (Rennes, 1909). (Jordan, *De mercatoribus.*)

Jordan, E., *Les Origines de la domination angevine en Italie* (Paris, 1909). (Jordan, *Origines.*)

Jordan, K., 'Das Eindringen des Lehnswesen in das Rechtsleben der römischen Kurie', *Archiv für Urkundenforschung*, XII (1932).

Kantorowicz, E., *Kaiser Friedrich der Zweite* (Berlin, 1927–31).

Kempf, F., 'Die zwei Versprechen Ottos IV. an die römische Kirche' in *Festschrift E. Stengel* (Münster, 1952).

Kirsch, J. P., *Die Finanzverwaltung des Kardinalkollegiums im XIII. und XIV. Jahrhundert* (Münster, 1895).

Laurent, M.-H., *Le Bienheureux Innocent V* (Vatican City, 1947).

Lefèvre, Y., 'Innocent III et son temps vus de Rome. Étude sur la biographie de ce pape', *MAH*, LXI (1949).

Léonard, E. G., *Les Angevins de Naples* (Paris, 1954). (Léonard.)

Leopardi, M., *Series Rectorum Anconitane Marchiae* (Recanati, 1824).

Lombardini, F., *Storia di Sezze* (Velletri, 1909). (Lombardini, *Sezze.*)

Luchaire, A., *Innocent III: Rome et l'Italie* (Paris, 1905).

Luchaire, A., 'Innocent III et le peuple romain', *Revue Historique*, LXXI (1903).

Lunt, W. E., *Papal Revenues in the Middle Ages* (New York, 1934).

Luzzatto, G., 'I più antichi trattati tra Venezia e le città marchigiane', *Nuovo Archivio Veneto*, N.S., XI (1906).

Luzatto, G., 'Le sottomissioni dei feudatari e le classi sociali in alcuni comuni marchigiani (sec. XII e XIII)', *Le Marche*, VI (1906).

Luzzatto, G., 'I prestiti comunali e gli Ebrei a Matelica nel sec. XIII', *Le Marche*, VII (1907).

Luzzatto, G., 'Le finanze di un castello (Matelica) nel secolo XIII', *VSWG*, XI (1912).

Maccarone, M., 'Innocenzo III prima del pontificato', *ASRSP*, LXVI (1942).

Maccarone, M., 'Innocenzo III e la famiglia di S. Tommaso d'Aquino', *Rivista di Storia della Chiesa in Italia*, X (1956).

Main, A., 'Il cardinale di Monselice Simone Paltanieri nella storia del secolo XIII', *Nuovo Archivio Veneto*, N.S., XXII (1920).

Marchetti-Longhe, G., 'La carta feudale del Lazio nella mostra permanente del Lazio meridionale in Anagni', *QFIA*, XXXVI (1956).

Marchetti-Longhi, G., 'Ricerche sulla famiglia di Gregorio IX, *ASRSP*, LXVII (1949).

Marcucci, F. A., *Saggio delle cose Ascolane* (Teramo, 1766). (Marcucci, *Ascoli*.)

Martin-Chabot, E., 'Contribution à l'histoire de la famille Colonna de Rome dans ses rapports avec la France', *Annuaire-Bulletin de la Societé de l'Histoire de France*, LVII (1920).

Mira, G., 'Il fabbisogno di cereali in Perugia e nel suo contado nei sec. XIII–XIV', in *Studi in onore di A. Sapori*, vol. I (Milan, 1957).

Mira, G., 'L'estimo di Perugia dell'anno 1285', *Annali della Facoltà di Scienze politiche ed economiche e commerciali dell'Università degli studi di Perugia*, N.S., IV (1955–6).

Mollat, G., 'La diplomatie pontificale au XIVe siècle' in *Mélanges L. Halphen* (Paris, 1951).

Mollat, G., *Les papes d'Avignon* (ed. 9, Paris, 1949).

Morghen, R., 'Il cardinale Matteo Rosso Orsini', *ASRSP*, XLVI (1923).

Morghen, R., 'Una legazione di Benedetto Caetani nell'Umbria e la guerra tra Perugia e Foligno del 1288', *ASRSP*, LII (1929).

Muratori, L. A., *Delle Antichità Estensi ed Italiane* (Modena, 1717–40).

Neumann, R., *Die Colonna und ihre Politik, 1288–1328* (Langensalza, 1916). (Neumann.)

Nitschke, A., 'Untersuchungen zu Saba Malaspina', *Deutsches Archiv*, XII (1956).

Pagliacci, G., 'Fonti archivistiche per una storia economica di Assisi', *Annali della Facoltà di Scienze politiche ed economiche e commerciali dell'Università degli studi di Perugia*, N.S., IV (1955–6).

Partner, P., *The Papal State under Martin V* (London, 1958). (Partner.)

Pellini, P., *Dell' Historia di Perugia* (Venice, 1664). (Pellini, *Perugia*.)

Perrin, C.-E., 'Les négociations de 1196 entre l'empereur Henri VI et le pape Célestin III' in *Mélanges L. Halphen* (Paris, 1951).

Peruzzi, A., *Storia d'Ancona* (Pesaro, 1835). (Peruzzi, *Ancona*.)

Petit, J., *Charles de Valois* (Paris, 1900).

Peyer, H. C., *Zur Getreidepolitik Oberitalienischer Städte im 13. Jahrhundert* (Vienna, 1950).

Pfaff, V., 'Die Einnahmen der römischen Kurie am Ende des 12. Jahrhunderts', *VSWG*, XL (1953).

Pinzi, C., *Storia di Viterbo* (Rome, 1887–1913). (Pinzi, *Viterbo*.)

Raynaldus, O., *Annales Ecclesiastici* (Lucca, 1738 ff). (Raynaldus.)

Reh, F., *Kardinal Peter Capocci* (Berlin, 1933). (Reh.)

Roth, C., *The History of the Jews of Italy* (Philadelphia, 1946).

Roth F., 'Cardinal Richard Annibaldi, first protector of the Augustinian Order', *Augustiniana*, II–IV (1952–4).

Runciman, S., *The Sicilian Vespers* (Cambridge, 1958).

Rusch, B., *Die Behörden und Hofbeamten der päpstlich–Kurie des 13. Jahrhunderts* (Königsberg, 1936).

Sabatier, P., *Vie de Saint François d'Assise* (ed. 35, Paris, n.d.).

Sägmuller, J. B., *Die Thätigkeit und Stellung der Cardinäle bis Papst Bonifaz VIII.* (Freiburg, 1896).

Salvemini, G., *Studi Storici* (Florence, 1901).

Salzer, E., *Über die Anfänge der Signorie in Oberitalien* (Berlin, 1900).

Sansi, A., *Storia del Comune di Spoleto* (Foligno, 1879). (Sansi, *Storia*.)

Saracini, G., *Notitie historiche della città d'Ancona* (Rome, 1675). (Saracini, *Ancona*.)

Savio, F., 'Gli Annibaldi di Roma nel sec. XIII', *Studi e Documenti di Storia e Diritto*, XVII (1896).

Seeger, H., *Die Reorganisation des Kirchenstaates unter Innocenz III.* (Kiel, 1937).

Seidlmayer, R., 'Bonifaz VIII. und der Kirchenstaat', *Historisches Jahrbuch*, LX (1940).

Sella, P., 'Le Costituzioni dello Stato della Chiesa anteriori alla riformazione Albornoziana', *ASI*, LXXXV (1927).

Signorelli, G., *Viterbo nella storia della Chiesa* (Viterbo, 1907 ff). (Signorelli, *Viterbo*.)

Smith, A. L., *Church and State in the Middle Ages* (Oxford, 1913).

Sora, V., 'I Conti di Anguillara', *ASRSP*, XXIX (1906).

Sperandio, F. P., *Sabina Sagra e Profana Antica e Moderna* (Rome, 1790).

Suetterlin, B., *Die Politik Kaiser Friedrichs II. und die römischen Kardinäle in den Jahren 1239 bis 1250* (Heidelberg, 1929.)

Sugenheim, S., *Geschichte der Entstehung und Ausbildung des Kirchenstaates* (Leipzig, 1854).

Tenckhoff, F., *Der Kampf der Hohenstaufen um die Mark Ancona und das Herzogtum Spoleto von der zweiten Exkommunikation Friedrichs II. bis zum Tode Konradins* (Paderborn, 1893). (Tenckhoff.)

Tenckhoff, F., *Papst Alexander IV.* (Paderborn, 1907).

Tillmann, H., *Papst Innocenz III.* (Bonn, 1954).

Tillmann, H., 'Das Schicksal der päpstlichen Rekuperationen nach dem Friedensabkommen zwischen Philipp von Schwaben und der römischen Kirche', *Historiches Jahrbuch*, LI (1931).

Tomassetti, G., 'Feudalesimo Romano', *Rivista Internazionale di scienze sociali e discipline ausiliarie*, VI–VII (1894–5).

Tomassetti, G., *La Campagna Romana antica, medioevale e moderna* (Rome, 1910–1926).

Tonduzzi, G. C., *Historie di Faenza* (Faenza, 1675). (Tonduzzi, *Faenza*.)

Torre, A., 'Le controversie fra l'arcivescovo di Ravenna e Rimini nel sec. XIII', *Studi Romagnoli*, II (1951).

Vehse, O., 'Benevent als Territorium des Kirchenstaates bis zum Beginn der Avignonischen Epoche', *QFIA*, XXII–XXIII (1930–2).

Vernarecci, A., *Fossombrone dai tempi antichissimi ai nostri* (Fossombrone, 1903–1914). (Vernarecci, *Fossombrone*.)

Volpe, G., *Medio Evo Italiano* (ed. 2, Florence, 1928).

Waley, D. P., 'Pope Boniface VIII and the commune of Orvieto', *TRHS*, 4th s., XXXII (1950).

Waley, D. P., *Medieval Orvieto* (Cambridge, 1952). (Waley, *Orvieto*.)

Waley, D. P., 'An Account-Book of the Patrimony of St. Peter in Tuscany, 1304–1306', *J Eccl H*, VI (1955).

Waley, D. P., 'A Register of Boniface VIII's Chamberlain, Theoderic of Orvieto', *J Eccl H*, VIII (1957).

Waley, D. P., 'Papal Armies in the Thirteenth Century', *EHR*, LXXII (1957).

Wenck, K., 'Die römischen Päpste zwischen Alexander III. und Innocenz III. und der Designationsversuch Weihnachten 1197' in *Papsttum und Kaisertum, Festschrift P. Kehr* (Munich, 1926).

Westenholz, E. von, *Kardinal Rainer von Viterbo* (Heidelberg, 1912). (Westenholz.)

Willemsen, C. A., *Kardinal Napoleon Orsini* (Berlin, 1927).

Winkelmann, E., *Philipp von Schwaben und Otto IV. von Braunschweig (Jahrbücher)* (Leipzig, 1873–8).

Winkelmann, E., *Kaiser Friedrich II. (Jahrbücher)* (Leipzig, 1889–99).

Winkelmann, E., 'Kaiser Friedrichs II. Kampf um Viterbo' in *Historische Aussätze dem Andenkenen G. Waitz gewidmet* (Hanover, 1886).

Zaccagnini, G., 'Maghinardo da Susinana e il comune di Bologna', *AMSR*, s. IV, VIII (1918). (Zaccagnini, 'Maghinardo'.)

Zerbi, P., *Papato, impero e 'respublica christiana' dal 1187 al 1198* (Milan, 1955).

Zimmermann, H., *Die päpstliche Legation in der ersten Halfte des XIII. Jahrhunderts* (Paderborn, 1913). (Zimmermann, *Legation*.)

INDEX

ABRUZZI, the, 27, 135, 136, 225
ACERRA, Count of, *see* SCHWEINSPUNT,
 Dipold of
ACQUAPENDENTE, 5, 14, 36, 60, 66, 69 n. 2,
 70, 83, 92, 132 n. 3, 157, 167, 169, 226,
 255, 257, 270
ACQUAPUZZA, 69 n. 2, 184
ACQUASPARTA, 167
 Cardinal Matthew of, 224, 225, 226,
 247, 318
ADRIAN IV, Pope, 4–5, 11–14, 20
ADRIAN V, Pope, 185, 188 n. 3
ADRIATIC, 28, 87, 88, 92, 93, 94, 184, 193
ALATRI, 54, 55 n. 3, 82, 91, 148, 245, 272,
 Richard of, 318
'ALATRINUS', papal chaplain, 104, 137,
 312, 319
ALBAN hills, 20 n. 4, 45 n. 3, 55, 81, 200,
 209, 213
ALBANO, 209, 320
ALDOBRANDESCHI
 Countess Margherita degli, 225, 246,
 247 n. 3, 248
 Counts of, 52, 59 n. 2, 84
 family of, 59
 territory of, 157, 243, 247
 Aldobrandeschine war, 248
ALDOBRANDINO da Romena, bishop of
 Arezzo, 117, 218–9, 318
ALEXANDER, papal chaplain, 312
ALEXANDER III, Pope, 13–16, 17, 18, 19
ALEXANDER IV, Pope, 82, 95, 103, 104,
 110, 147, 153, 158, 159, 163, 164, 167,
 169, 170, 220, 251, 260, 285, 290,
 294
ALIDOSI, family of, 194, 228
ALMAINE, Henry of, 197
AMANDOLA, 75 n. 2, 118 n. 2, 205, 216,
 220 n. 2, 264, 278
AMELIA, 25, 31, 37, 60, 65, 83, 92, 137 n. 4,
 138 n. 4, 142, 226, 256, 283
 fights Todi and Orvieto, 225, 226
 granted Rocca di Foce, 158 n. 2
 Bishop of, 104
 Walter, bishop of, 319
 Brother Bartholomew of, (inquisitor),
 319
ANAGNI, 14, 16, 18, 45, 55, 81, 82, 100, 134,
 142, 143, 161, 163, 169, 189, 233, 240,
 247
 Amatus of, 104, 239, 311, 316
 Blaise of, canon of Cambrai, 313
 Geoffrey of, 195, 274, 315

 Guarnazonus of, 309
 John of, 237–8
 Matthew of, 170
 Nicholas 'Guarcini' of, 322, 323
 Papareschi family of, 82 (*see also*
 GREGORY IX, Pope)
 Rainald of, 170
 the outrage of, 247, 248, 250, 251
ANCONA, 34, 41, 42, 48, 63, 64, 87, 88, 89,
 133 n. 2, 140, 144, 145, 149, 150, 162,
 179, 184, 205, 227, 231, 232, 246
 port of, 87, 88, attacked by Venice, 186
 bishop of, 4, 146 n. 2
 granted trading privilege, 151 n. 1
ANCONA, March of, 28, 31, 33, 37–8, 40,
 42, 51, 56, 59, 60, 62, 71, 77, 91, 96,
 104, 106, 109, 126, 127, 128, 133, 148,
 150, 153, 158, 159, 162, 165, 176, 184,
 187, 199–200, 202, 205, 210–11, 213,
 222–3, 258, 265, 276, 286
 area of, 92–3, fiscal fertility of, 268–9, 274
 the 'fickle' March, 182, 186
 Boniface VIII's Constitution for
 (*Celestis patrisfamilias*), 122, 234–5,
 247 n. 1, 250, 291
 account book of, 252, 261–3
ANDALÒ
 Brancaleone degli, 157, 160, 161, 180
 Castellano degli, 163
 family of, 172
ANDREW *dictus* Vetulus, 316
ANGELO 'de Malliano', 319
ANGOULT, Amiel d', 202, 208, 315
ANGUILLARA
 Counts of, 11, 27, 83, 294
 Leo of, 24
ANJOU, house of
 Charles of Anjou, 172, 173–5, 176,
 189 n. 1, 201, 228, 288, 289, 298, 300,
 301
 his Byzantine ambitions, 182
 offered Senatorship of Rome, 172, 202
 Angevin-papal alliance, 102, 103, 172,
 173 ff, 181–182, 186, 201, 208, 297
 Angevin conquest, 86, 298
 Angevin vicars, 202, 207
ANNIBALDI
 family of, 46, 55, 82, 103, 161, 182, 200,
 214, 225, 240, 243, 244, 246
 Annibaldo, 142, 207, 286
 Peter, 51
 Richard, 104 n. 1, 163, 170
 Cardinal Richard, 187, 200–1, 313

ANWEILER, see MARKWARD of
APENNINES, 4, 80, 82, 83, 84, 85, 87, 92, 93, 109, 125, 152, 193, 216, 274
  Passes, 22, 89, 169
AQUILA, Count of, 67, 131
AQUINO, lords of, 54, 66
ARAGON
  Constance of, 54
  Peter III of, 172, 207
ARBITRATION, 18, 22, 41, 44, 47, 49, 70, 74, 86, 111, 132, 198, 210, 211, 224, 242, 244
ARCE, 53, 54, 55
AREZZO, 93, 117, 283 n. 3, 287
  Bishops of, 96 n. 5, 146, 147
  See ALDOBRANDINO and MARCELLINUS
ARICCIA, 9 n. 4, 20 n. 4, 69 n. 2, 209
ARMIES, see also MILITARY OPERATIONS, WARFARE etc.
  feudal armies, 288, and see FEUDALISM
  Army of the Keys, 138
  Papal armies, 13, 40, 46–7, 48–9, 54, 135, 197–8, 206, 217, 244, 279 ff, 299
  Pope's bodyguard, 289
  Angevin forces, 196, 197, 295
  Mercenaries, 9, 40, 102, 173, 203, 241, 261 n. 3, 266, 287, 288, 289, 290, 293, 294, 295
  the posse, 277 ff
  numbers, 289, 295 n. 1
  standing army, 289
  recruiting agents, 208, 285, 289 n. 5, 290 n. 1, 295
  soldiers' pay, 203, 204 n. 3, 259, 261, 266, 280, 283, 289, 290–1, 293, 295 n. 1, 299
  Scutage, 235, 264, 290–1, 292
ARRONE, 216, 244 n. 2
ASCOLI PICENO, 31, 37, 40, 47, 64, 70, 83, 87, 89, 92, 120, 121 n. 3, 130 n. 3, 141 n. 2, 149, 155, 186, 210, 216, 231, 236, 239, 246, 263, 265, 286 n. 2
  Bishop of, 134 n. 1, 163 n. 5
  podestà of, 19 n. 2, 127 n. 3, 221
  Jerome of, see NICHOLAS IV, Pope
  secures privileges, 75, 156, 159–60, 212–213, 232
  claims appellate jurisdiction, 205
  troops ambushed by militia of Fermo, 159, 286 n. 2
  at war with Macerata, 200
ASSISI, 31, 33 n. 4, 36–7, 94, 110 n. 2, 140, 141, 148, 149, 156, 157, 180, 187, 206, 210, 216, 250 n. 3, 255
  Castle of, 33, 36–7, 85, 86
  granted privileges, 48, 49, 156
  quarrels with Perugia (q.v.), 48
  at war with Bettona, 181–2
  appoints excommunicate as Podestà, 48, populat on, 86
  71

Bishop of, 4, 92
Count of, 85
Matthew, canon of, 321
Moricus, canon of, 320
ASTURA, 82, 246
AVERSA, Odonisius of, 311
AVIGNON
  papal residence at, 230, 248, 251, 252, 302, 303
  Zoen, bishop of, 310

BAGNACAVALLO, 119, 217 n. 7, 271, 293 n. 2
  appeals against Rector of Romagna, 119 n. 3
  pays tallia, 293 n. 1
BAGNOREA, 4, 92, 226 n. 1
  Simon, bishop of, 319
BANKERS, 80–1, 86, 107, 157, 176, 178, 251, 266, 275
BARTHOLOMEI, Altovitus, of Siena, 323
BARTHOLOMEW 'de Palatio', 312
BASSIANO, 243
BATTLES, See BENEVENTO etc., also under MILITARY OPERATIONS
BAUCO, 53, 245, 272
BEAUVAIS, Bishops of, see also CHATILLON, MILO of, 95, 96, 102, 188
BECKET, Archbishop, 15
BELVOIR, Matthew, 160
BENEDICT, Cardinal of S. Susanna, 60
BENEDICT, papal chamberlain, 308
BENEDICT 'Carushomo', 26
BENEDICT VIII, Pope, 7
BENEDICT XI, Pope, 105, 107, 112, 123, 249–51, 271, 303
BENEVENTO, xiii n. 3, 8, 15, 102 n. 3, 135, 223
  Battle of, 98, 174, 176, 177, 188, 261, 264, 266
BERNARD, Archdeacon of Narbonne, (Archbishop-elect of Genoa), 321
'BERNARD', Treasurer of the Tuscan Patrimony, 322
BERNARD 'de Podio', 316
BERTINORO, 18, 35, 43, 94, 212, 219
BERTO 'de Scivinictis', 226–7, 322, 323
BETTONA, 83, 181–2, 250 n. 3, 255, 257
BEVAGNA, 83, 100, 110, 112, 132, 206 n. 1, 278 n. 3
  parliaments at, 111–12, 115, 119, 226, 304
BIEDA, 169
BISENZIO
  Castle of, 170
  Lords of, 169, 170
  Nicholas of, 170 n. 1
BOCCAMAZZI, Nicholas dei, 308
BOCCASINI, Nicholas: see BENEDICT XI, Pope

BOLOGNA, 1, 85, 93, 112 n. 2, 117, 118, 157,
185, 192, 193, 194, 195, 196–9, 203,
212, 217, 218–19, 224, 229, 250, 268,
271, 286, 288, 289 n. 2
factions in, 197, 211 n. 5, *see also*
GEREMEI, family of, LAMBERTAZZI
etc.
merchants of, 245, 255 n. 7, 274 n. 3
heretics in, 300
attitude to Papacy, 227–8 and *passim*
war with League of Ghibelline tyrants,
240, 242, 245
hires mercenaries, 289
refuses to pay *tallia*, 218–19
podestà of, 78
Jobensius 'de Azoguidis', D.C.L. noble
of, 313
Fra Ranier of, 247
BOLSENA: *see also under* ORVIETO, 69 n. 2,
83, 243, 246
Lake of, 84, 100, 167, 169, 225–6
Val del Lago di, 69 n. 2, 74, 120, 135 n.
1, 141 n. 2, 144, 157, 167, 180, 286
BONACOLTI, Ranuccinus, 324
BONIFACE VIII, Pope: *see also* ANAGNI,
outrage of, 71, 73, 76, 80, 82, 93, 95,
103, 104, 111, 121, 122, 123, 189, 213,
222, 223, 289, 291, 294, 295, 298, 300,
303
Death of, 230 ff, 248–9, 269, 308, 313
BORGO S. SEPOLCRO, 93
BRACCIANO, Lake, 32, 83
BRANCALEONE, *see* ANDALÒ
BRESCIA, 250
Arnold of, 11–12, 299
BRIBERY, 20, 31, 32 n. 3, 98, 146, 157, 193,
258
BRIE, Simon de: *see* MARTIN IV, Pope
BRUNFORTE
Lords of, 216, 220
Ottaviano da, 220 n. 2, 308
Rainald of, 186, 220 n. 2
BRUNSWICK, Otto of, 43, 47, 49
See OTTO IV, Emperor
BRUSCIATI, Tebaldo, 250, 318
BURY, Richard of, 98, 102 n. 1, 237 n. 5

CAETANI, family of, 82, 104, 224, 225,
243–4, 249
Benedict, 238, 246
Cardinal Benedict, 215, 224, 311, 313,
see also under BONIFACE VIII, Pope
Francis, 247
James, 238, 239 n. 2, 309
Nicholas, of Pisa, 309
Peter 238, 239, 243, 246, 247, 311, 316
Count Roffred, 238, 243, 246, 308, 311
CAGLI, xv, 40, 47 n. 4, 71 n. 5, 92, 139, 144,
149, 152, 166–7, 170, 205 n. 6, 210,
216, 221, 242, 246, 279, 292
owes military service, 280–2

CALBOLI, family of, 228
CALIXTUS II, Pope, 9
CALVI, 243
CAMERINO, 38, 40, 41, 42, 47, 59, 76, 89, 92,
101, 108, 139, 149, 152, 159, 210, 216,
220, 226, 227, 246, 249, 261, 263, 265
burned by Doria (q.v.), 162
owes military service, 277, 287 n. 5
Philip, bishop of, 310, 312
CAMPAGNA, the, 3, 40, 91, 96, 135, 142,
169, 177, 206–7 etc.
CAMPAGNA-MARITTIMA, province of, 51,
54, 81, 91, 95, 107, 121, 129, 142, 145,
150, 182, 202, 213, 214–15
area of, 91–2, 297
Boniface VIII's constitution for, 76, 122,
233–4, 235
finances of, 272
CANACOSIA
Parliament at, 306
CANINO, 170
CANNARIA, 216
CAPOCCI
Angelo, 180
Cardinal Peter, 95, 96, 99, 111, 147–8,
149–50, 151, 152, 153–4, 259 n. 4,
260 n. 2
CAPOCCIO, John, 26, 32 n. 2, 38, 39, 46
CAPUA, 135
Richard of, 8
Cardinal Thomas of, 139
CARDINALS, *see also* under proper names,
esp. COLONNA family
College of, 122–4, 224, 269
constitutional rights of, 122–3
status of, 123–4, 223, 224
as rectors, 96 ff
as protectors of towns, 224
revenues of, 223–4, 269
attempt to raise force against Orvieto,
285–6
CARPINETO, 244
CARZOLUS, Stephen, Rector of the Tuscan
Patrimony (q.v.), 51, 309
CASCIA, 206 n. 1, 216, 271
CASTEL GANDOLFO, 209
CASTELFICARDO, 63, 64, 133 n. 2
CASTILE, Henry of, 180, 194
See also under FERDINAND III, King of, etc.
CASTLES, *see also* MILITARY OPERATIONS,
and under proper names, NARNI, etc.,
9, 24, 36, 87, 151, 212, 213, 249
castle-building, 121, 144 n. 3
unauthorised, 121, 154 n. 6, 236
destruction of, 41, 74, 212 n. 2
defence of, 289
castellans, 53, 66, 69, 115, 167, 187 n. 4,
240, 245, 262
castellania, 254, 270
CASTRO, 169, 212 n. 2
CASTRO DEI VOLSCI, 246

CASTROCHIARO
  Castle of, 219
  Lords of, 204
Castrum Arsi, 169
CECCANO
  Lords of, 7, 9, 15, 42, 81, 214
  John of, 54, 55, 67, 131, 244, 247
CELANO
  Count of, 63
  Thomas of, 86 n. 6
CELESTINE III, Pope, 23, 26, 31, 44, 92, 189
CELESTINE V, Pope, 103, 209, 228–9, 237 n. 1
CENCI? G., noble of Rome, 309
CENCIUS, papal chamberlain, *see* HONORIUS III, Pope
census, 1, 2, 41, 70, 72, 73, 74, 93, 205, 256, 261, 263, 268, 269
  Liber Censuum, 3 n. 3, 29 n. 2, 125, 136, 252, 253, 256
CEPRANO, 5 n. 1, 14, 43, 54, 55, 62, 94
  Peter of, 10
CERCHI, family of, 107
CERRETO, 119
CERVIA, 57, 87, 93, 204, 212
CESENA, 114, 193, 194, 204, 212, 218, 219, 229, 248
  parliaments at, 115, 198, 241, 305, 306
  right to elect podestà, 231 n. 2
CESI, 33, 69 n. 2, 85, 94, 167, 187 n. 4
  castellan of, 187 n. 4
  Andrew of, 313
CHATILLON, Milo of, Bishop of Beauvais, 138–9, 145, 312, 314
CHIANA, river, 82
CHIARENTI, family of, 107
CHIENTI, Val di, 85
CIBO, William, of Genoa, 311
CINGOLI, 47, 64, 80 n. 2, 128, 133 n. 2, 150, 151, 162, 242
  Parliament at, 305
CINTHIUS, Cardinal of S. Lorenzo in Lucina, 48, 314
CISTERNA, 69 n. 2
CITTÀ DI CASTELLO, 4, 33 n. 4, 37, 42, 66, 70, 85, 86 n. 1, 2, 92, 93, 95, 122, 126 n. 1, 134, 136, 145 n. 5, 180, 283 n. 3, 285 n. 4
  Bishop of, 4
CITTÀ PAPALE: *see* PALESTRINA, 244, 277
  Theoderic, Cardinal-bishop of, 311
CITTADINO 'Episcopi', 308
CIVITA CASTELLANA, 4, 37, 42 n. 3, 70, 92, 142, 276 n. 2
CIVITANOVA, 149, 156, 159, 205 n. 3, 227, 245 n. 2, 260
CIVITAVECCHIA, 69, 77 n. 1, 83, 84, 92, 169, 221
CIVITELLA, 214 n. 1
  James of, 309
CLEMENT III, Pope, 23, 24, 25, 26

CLEMENT IV, Pope, 95, 98, 100, 103, 171, 172, 174, 177–81, 184, 188, 266–7, 294
CLEMENT V, Pope, 192, 239, 251, 302
CLERMONT-FERRAND, Bishop of, 138
CLERECATTIUS 'de Monte', 315
COCONATO, Cardinal Uberto de, 187
COLLALTO, Rambaldo of, Count of Treviso, 250, 316
COLLEMEZZO, 244
COLLUS, canon of Pieve S. Lazzaro (dioc. Florence), 322
COLONNA, family of, 9, 11, 15, 81, 103, 131, 148, 213–14, 215, 224, 249
  property of, 15, 16, 213–14, 244
  quarrels with Boniface VIII (q.v.), 230 ff
  the Colonna war, 243–4, 245 n. 2, 248, 251, 269, 281, 294, 295
  Agapito Colonna, 214 n. 1, 316
  Cardinal James, 214, 215, 224 n. 2
  John, 131, 135, 136, 137, 145, 147, 191, 214, 215, 217, 223 n. 2, 295, 316
  Landulf, 104 n. 1, 214, 232 n. 5, 313
  Pandulf, 214
  Cardinal Peter, 224 n. 2, 243
  Stephen, 104 n. 1, 116, 213 n. 1, 214, 217, 218, 243, 318
COMMUNES, *see also* JURISDICTION, LEAGUES, OATHS of fealty, TOWNS etc.
  of the papal State, 35 ff, 65, 69, 287, 294, and *passim. See also under* names of towns
  terms of submission to the papacy, 69–70
  relations with Pope Boniface VIII, 230 ff
  and the cardinals, 224, 286
  refractory, 65, 75, 239, and *passim, see also* NARNI, PERUGIA etc.
  status of, 37–8, 68, 121, 138, 220, 221
  early communes, 86, 88, 89, new communes, 75 n. 2, (*and see under* TOWNS)
  pro-Este, 64
  number of, 89–90
  compound for unpaid fines etc., 265–6
  make loans to the papal chamber, 258, 259
CONCA, river, 92, 94
CONDOTTIERI, 219
  (*See also* ARMIES: Mercenaries, SIGNORI etc.)
CONRAD 'of Antioch', 172, 178 n. 5, 207
CONRAD, Emperor, 17
CONRAD IV, 153, 155, 158
CONRADIN, King of the Romans, 177, 179–81, 194, 288
CONSTANCE, Empress, 22 n. 3, 28, 40, 49
CONSTANTINOPLE, 88
CONSTANTINUS, canon of Adria, 321
CONSTITUTIONS, *see also* DECREES and under names of Provinces.
  publication of, 112, 233

promulgated by parliaments, 116–17, 119
of Cardinal Napoleon Orsini, 101–2
Constitutio Romana, 2
{ for the March of Ancona, 111 n. 5, 122, 234–5 etc.
{ *Celestis patrisfamilias*, 124, 234–5
Constitutio super electione senatoris Urbis, 190 (*see also* ROME)
Romana mater ecclesia, see CAMPAGNA-MARITTIMA
Licet merum, see TUSCANY
CONTI
family of, 44, 51, 158, 170
lands, 55, 67
Adenulf dei, 247
Cardinal Lothair dei, 31, *see* INNOCENT III, Pope
Nicholas dei, 247, *see* ALEXANDER IV, Pope
Rainald 'Rosso' of Genna, 169
Richard dei, 39, 45, 46, 47, 50, 51, 54, 55, 66, 131
CORI, 15, 69 n. 2
CORNAY, Robert de, 229, 240 n. 5, 241, 318
CORNETO, 15, 25, 51, 71, 83 n. 2, 84, 92, 113, 142, 161, 207 n. 3, 215, 245 n. 1, 270
Peter, provost of S. Fortunato in, 311
CORNWALL, Richard of, 163, 172
CORRIDONIA: *see* MONTOLMO
COURBAN, lords of, 202, 315
COXADOCA, Gerard, papal chaplain, 315
CRESCENTII, family of, 7, 8, 9, 10, 14, 81, 125, 209
Crescentius, 309
CRUSADES, 27, 84, 117, 134, 148, 173, 182, 208, 293–4, 295
Fifth crusade, 88
crusading tenth, 202, 203, 268
crusading privileges, 293
CURRENCY
Roman, 56
right to a mint, 12, 130
gold coins at Perugia, 86
currency of Ravenna, 98, 261, 272 n. 2

DAIFER, Count, 7
DANTE, 189, 192, 193, 299
DASSEL, Rainald of, 14
DECREES, Papal, *see also under names of* POPES, PROVINCES, ROME etc., 121, 122, 139
Celestis altitudo, 123, 223, 224, (*see also under* NICHOLAS IV)
Clericis laicos, 240
DONATI, Corso, 238, 317
DONATIONS, 2, 3, 13, 31, 184–5
of Constantine, 3, 8, 299, 301 n. 2
of Charlemagne, 1, 4, 16, 29, 30, 34, 126 n. 2

Carolingian, 1, 5, 16, 29, 30, 34, 126 n. 2
by Otto I, 2, and Otto III, 3
'privilege' of Henry II, 3
of Frederick II (q.v.), 125, 127
DUBOIS, Pierre (Petrus de Bosco), 301–3
DURAND, William, 75, 77, 95, 195, 202, 208, 211, 241, 242, 295, 308, 311, 316, 318, 321, 322

EDMUND (son of King Henry III of England), 153
EGER, the promise of, 61–2
EMPERORS, *see under* HOHENSTAUFEN etc. *and under* proper names
coronation of, 3 n. 7, 4, 16, 21, 25, 57, 58–9, 130–1
disputed successions, 21, 30, 43, 49–50
ENGLAND, 223
See HENRY II King of, etc.
English clergy, 20, 294, 299 and ADRIAN IV, Pope
parliamentary institutions in, 112
ENZO, King, 145, 148, 152 n. 5
EPPE, Jean d', 202, 203–4, 208–11, 289, 317
ESINO, river, 108
valley, 89
ESTE, family of, 66, 90, 96, 136, 138, 139, 242, 256, 258, 314
Marquis Azzo VII of, 58, 59, 60, 61, 62, 63, 64, 123, 127–8, 138
Aldobrandino, 62, 63, 127
ESTENDART, William, de Beynes, 198, 207
EUGENIUS III, Pope, 11

FABRIANO, xv, 59, 63, 72, 80 n. 1, 92, 105 n. 3, 149, 150, 187 n. 1, 199, 205, 216, 249, 251, 264, 265, 279, 293
neutrality of, 64
receives privileges from Dipold of Acerra (q.v.), 63
wars, 227 n. 1, 251 *see also* S. GINESIO
extends rule, 38, 89
claims *merum et mixtum imperium*, 75, 211
podestà at, 121, 222
residence of rector, 100
pays fines to papacy, 156 n. 3, 158 n. 2, 182 n. 1, 193 n. 1, 260, 265, 266, 290, 291–2
owes military service, 277, 280, 282–3, 290 n. 4, 291 n. 4
FAENZA, 40, 114, 193, 194, 198, 203, 212, 218, 229, 241, 242, 245, 248, 271
Bishop of, 290
Parliament at, 112 n. 2, 117, 199, 305
falls to Mainardo of Susinana (q.v.), 211
FAGGIUOLA, Uguccione della, 236, 245, 248
FALVATERRA, 20 n. 4, 55
FANO, xv, 41, 42, 48, 63, 64, 139, 144, 148, 149, 246, 251, 260, 264, 278, 285
parliament at, 111, 149–50, 304, 305
expansion of, 88, 133

FANO (*cont.*)
  owes military service, 276
  fights Fossombrone, 133, 159, 178
  quarrel with Pope HONORIUS III (q.v.),
    133–4
  Thomas, provost of, 321
FARFA, Abbey of, 6, 7, 8, 9, 10, 13, 20 n. 4,
  31, 92, 108
FERDINAND III, King of Castile, 180
FERENTINO, 45, 55, 74 n. 2, 81, 82, 100,
  134, 170, 214, 219, 247
  David 'Paparone' of, 104, 316
  Richard of, 236–7, 241, 242
  Roland of, 209 n. 4, 312, 313, 320
FERMO, 34, 40, 41, 42, 48, 59, 63, 89, 120,
  126 n. 1, 130, 133, 140, 149, 150, 159,
  179, 180–1, 186, 188, 199, 200, 205,
  210, 216, 220, 227, 242, 246, 263, 285,
  292
  expansionism of, 159, 245, 262, 286 n. 2
  right to a mint, 130
  attacked by S. Ginesio, 249 n. 1, war
    with Ascoli, 263
  privileged by Manfred, 162
  Bishop of, 4, 31, 69, 128, 259
FERRARA, 4, 5, 22, 59, 87, 93, 128
  Castle at, 61
  Bernard, canon of, 321
FEUDALISM, *see also* OATHS etc., 81, 114,
  288
  feudal compacts, 12–13, 62
  feudatories, 8, 9, 10, 52, 54, 68, 89, 90,
  103, 110, 111, 112, 132, 220, etc.
  feudal obligations, 9, 12–13, 68, 73
FIESOLE, Anthony, Bishop of, 251, 313, 316
FILANGIERI, Count Richard, 173
FILETTINO, 244
FLORENCE, 87, 93, 107, 192, 194, 197, 226,
  238, 239, 245
  Florentine merchants, 89, 274
  'Bertus Simonicti' of, 322, 323
  Buonconte of, 324
  Clarus 'Sagine' of, 323
  Dinus of, 322
  Francis 'Bernardi' of, 324
  Henry of, 323
  Maynectus 'de Puliti' of, 322
  Philip 'Hugonis Spine' of, 323
  Rainald 'Campane' of, 323
  Roger of, 262 n. 1, 323
  Thomas 'Lapi Diedi' of, 324
Fodrum, *see also* HOSPITALITY, 6, 12, 13, 22,
  57, 152, 254 n. 5, 256, 258
FOGLIANO
  Boniface of, 158, 312
  Thomas of, 184
FOLIGNO, 33 n. 4, 42, 59, 74 n. 6, 80 n. 2,
  83, 85, 87, 110 n. 2, 126, 132, 134, 135,
  149, 151, 155, 156, 205–6, 216, 219,
  243, 250 n. 3, 255, 257, 267
  Bishops of, 4, 92

merchants of, 86, 226–7 and n. 5
  podestà at, 86, 132
  Benvenuto of, 106–7
  James of, 321
FONDI, 3 n. 1, 127, 246
  Count of, 66
FORLÌ, 114, 116, 117, 119, 193, 194, 196,
  198, 199, 203–4, 211, 212, 218, 248,
  250, 271, 292, 294
  Parliament at, 219, 305
  factions in, 228
FORLIMPOPOLI, 212
FORTIFICATIONS, *see also* CASTLES and
  MILITARY OPERATIONS, 16, 36, 121,
  151, 160, 167, 179
FOSSOMBRONE, 41, 133, 159, 178, 242, 250
FOURRIER, Adam, 202, 311
FRANCE, *see also under* ANJOU, NORMANS,
  and names of kings, 9, 14, 201, 301–2
  anti-French feeling, 208
FRANCIS, S. of Assisi, 86, 298
FRANGIPANI, family of, 9, 11, 14, 15, 27,
  46, 82, 246
FREDERICK I, Emperor (Barbarossa), 5, 12,
  14, 16, 17, 18, 19, 21, 22, 23, 56, 297
FREDERICK II, Emperor
  Ward of Pope Innocent III, 40, 44, 50,
    53, 55, 66, 127
  betrothal to Constance of Aragon (q.v.),
    22 n. 3, 54
  imperial candidature, 56, 61–2
  coronation, 131
  claims right to military service, 287
  relations with papacy, 95, 122, 126–7,
    136, 142, 143, 146, 152–3, 258, 259,
    286, 288, 294, 297
  excommunication, 134, 136, 145
  death, 145, 150, 153, 157, 176, 194, 259
FRIARS, *see also under* proper names, esp.
  NICHOLAS IV, Pope, 104–5, 299
  Franciscan movement, 52, 300
  Fraticelli, 300
  Friars Minor, 192, 212, 213
  Dominicans, 195, 245
FROSINONE, 55 n. 3, 81, 100, 170, 207, 257
FUMONE, 69 n. 2, 246

GABRIEL 'de Patientibus' D.C.L., 321
GALLICANO, 81
GANTEAULME
  James, 186–7
  Rostand de, 238, 240 n. 1, 308
GASPAR 'de Montasia', canon of Cumae,
  319
GENEZZANO, 213, 214
GENNA, Rainald 'Rosso' of, 169
GENOA, 15, 83 n. 2, 84, 87, 88
  Archbishop of, 321
  Walter, archbishop of, 314
GENTILE 'de Popleto', 314

GERARD, *plebanus* of S. John 'de Penna', 321

GEREMEI, family of, *see also* BOLOGNA, 194, 199

GERMANY, *see also* HOHENSTAUFEN etc., 39, 47, 49, 58, 60
German clergy, 60, 61, 299
German princes, 58, 125, 185, 195
anti-German feeling, 30
and propaganda, 33

GHERARDI, Avogadus, of Florence, 322, 324

GHIAGGIOLO, 218

GHIBELLINES, *see also* LEAGUES, 179, 180, 194, 198, 199, 200, 203, 204, 207 n. 2, 211, 239, 240, 242, 245, 247

GRANTS, *see also* DONATIONS, *merum et mixtum imperium* etc., 150–2
of privileges, 20, *see under* TOWNS, proper names of
fiscal exemptions, 150
papal, 69 n. 4, 124, 130, 147, 150, 222–3, 240, 257 etc.
imperial, 86, 129 etc.

GRECA, Neri della, 208

GREGORY, cardinal-deacon of S. George *ad Velum Aureum*, 309, 312

GREGORY, Cardinal-deacon of S. Maria in Aquiro, 37

GREGORY, Cardinal of S. Maria in Porticu, 31

GREGORY 'de Romania', 97 n. 1, 102, 137, 146, 307, 310, 312

GREGORY VII, Pope, 3, 8, 9, 189, 297

GREGORY VIII, Pope, 24, 297

GREGORY IX, Pope, 70, 102, 108, 110, 122, 123, 134, 136, 138–9, 140, 142, 143, 144, 148–9, 150, 158, 181, 284, 288, 293

GREGORY X, Pope, 97, 100, 102, 103, 106, 181, 182–5, 188 n. 3, 301

GROSSETO, Bishops of, 105, 322

GUALA, Cardinal, 60

GUALDO TADINO, 33, 69 n. 2, 75 n. 5, 85, 137, 183, 206 n. 1, 210, 216, 255
podestà of, 183 n. 3

GUARCINO, John of, canon of Albano, 320

GUBBIO, 4, 31, 33 n. 4, 47 n. 4, 59, 70, 77 n. 2, 80 n. 2, 85, 120, 126, 130 n. 3, 132, 141 n. 2, 144, 148, 149, 152, 158, 167, 170 n. 5, 183, 187, 200, 210, 222, 226, 239, 242, 249, 260, 284
Bishops of, 4, 92
contado, 120 n. 1, 158, 160
independence threatened, 160, 162, 251
(*see under* PERUGIA)
captured by Uguccione della Faggiuola (q.v.), 245
enmity with Cagli (q.v.), 144, 284
granted privileges by Urban IV, 170
grievances of, 120 n. 1
Andrew of, 319, 320, 321

GUELFS, 194, 197, 203, 212, 229, 242

'GUENZOLUS de Pusio', 317

GUIDI, family, of Romena
Counts of, 218
Count Alexander, 218
See also ALDOBRANDINO, Bishop of Arezzo

GUY, papal chaplain, 320

GUY, archpriest of Sasso, 315

GUY 'Codeporcus', 308

GUY 'de Pileo', archdeacon of Soissons, 180, 309, 310

HAGENAU, agreement of, 24–5

HAPSBURG, Rudolf of, *see* RUDOLF, King of the Romans

HENRY, imperial marshal, 66

HENRY 'Manentis', canon of Spoleto, 320

HENRY, *plebanus* of S. Stephen *de Campis* (dioc. Florence), 320

HENRY V, Emperor, 3 n. 7, 4, 10

HENRY VI, Emperor, 16, 21, 23, 26, 27, 30, 32, 35, 48, 56, 58, 60, 84, 85, 86, 92, 297
will of, 28

HENRY II, King of England, 15, 20

HENRY III, King of England, 145 n. 5, 153

HERESY, *see also* BOLOGNA, VITERBO etc., 65, 76 n. 3, 234 n. 2, 300
repression of, 52, 53, 73, 110
heretics, 36, 192, 300
Catharism, 52

HILDEBRAND, *see* GREGORY VII, Pope

HOHENSTAUFEN, *see also* FREDERICK II, Emperor, etc.
family of, 56, 95, 100, 150, 155, 162, 163, 173, 297, 303
influence of, 47, 70, 71, 84, 87, 126, 157, 159, 176, 186, 188, 249, 251, 261, 298
policy of, 67, 86, 87, 152–3
officials, 148

HOLLAND, William of, 184

HOLY LAND, 127, 182

HONORIUS III, Pope, 70, 96, 102, 109, 121, 126 ff, 150, 158, 162, 209, 285

HONORIUS IV, Pope, *see also under* SAVELLI, Cardinal James, 103, 209–12

HOSPITALITY, *see also* Fodrum, 41, 69, 70, 73, 245, 248 n. 6, 254, 258
procuratio, 254

HOVEDEN, Roger of, 32 n. 3

HUGH 'the Red', provost of Rheims, 315

IESI, xv, 40, 41, 42, 64, 89, 128, 139, 144, 145, 149, 150, 151, 155, 161, 162, 186, 187 n. 1, 199, 200, 219, 227, 242, 246, 257, 260, 263, 264, 265, 276 n. 1, 286, 291–2
Parliament at, 305
buys privileges, 231–2
war with Cagli, 205 n. 6, and Fabriano, 251
dispute with Montalboddo, 156

IESI (*cont.*)
military service, 280–2, 286
throws out podestà, 210
takes outlaw as, 265 n. 2
Manente, citizen of, 231, 232 n. 1
IMOLA, 58, 112 n. 2, 114, 117, 193, 194, 198, 199, 203, 211, 212, 242, 248
Parliaments at, 112 n. 2, 118, 119, 204, 212 n. 1, 218, 219, 229, 240 n. 5, 292, 305
claims to elect podestà, 121
subject to Bologna, 228
Gerard of, 251
INGERAMUS 'de Savolis', 309
INNOCENT II, Pope, 9, 17
INNOCENT III, Pope, 1, 2, 16, 28, 30, 36, 91–2, 94, 96, 102, 103, 121, 134, 184, 256, 263
election of, 31
his Italian policy, 31–2, 33, 36, 38, 40–1, 43, 53, 67, 122
relations with Rome, 31–2, 38, 39, 46–7, 80, 131
relations with the Empire (*see also* FREDERICK II), 49–50, 56–7, 58, 60
his wars, 41, 46–7, 283 n. 3, and armies, 288, 293
relations with the communes, 31, 32, 35, 37, 38, 70
excommunicates opponents, 63, 70
achievements of, 42, 47, 53, 67, 258
realism of, 56, 80
death of, 67
INNOCENT IV, Pope, 71, 77 n. 4, 103, 122, 124, 149, 153, 156, 157, 167, 184, 220, 259, 288, 293, 299
INNOCENT V, Pope, 185, 186, 187, 188 n. 3, 288
ISOLA URBANA (formerly Isola Bisentina), 169
IVREA, Frederick bishop-elect of, 274, 308, 316

JAMES, papal marshal, 43, 51, 64, 65, 66, 67, 309
JAMES 'de Bargiaco', sacrist of Evreux, 319
JAMES 'Confarenarius', 308
JAMES 'Johannis', clerk of S. Apostoli, Orvieto, 319
JAMES 'de Porclano' clerk of S. Angelo (dioc. Anagni), 319
JAMES 'de Ranzano', 308, 316
JAQUINTUS, papal chaplain, 317
JERUSALEM, 88
King of, *see* JOHN of Brienne
JEWS, 89
JoJewish communities, 88, 89 n. 6, 274
HN, Cardinal-priest of S. Praxed, 103, 307, 312, 314
JOHN 'Compater', papal chaplain, 312
JOHN 'Guallati', canon of S. Theodore's, Rome, 320

JOHN, King, of Brienne, 95, 103, 104, 129 n. 4, 135, 137, 138, 139, 141, 309
JOHN 'Judicis', 307
JOHN XXI, Pope, 185, 186, 187, 188 n. 3, 189
JORDAN, papal notary, 308
JORDAN 'di Labbro', 320
JUBILEE of 1300, *see also under* ROME, 240
JURISDICTION, *see also* LAW, PROVINCIAL GOVERNMENT, RECTORS etc.
Jurisdiction of Rectors' Courts, 78–80, 105 and n. 3
jurisdictional privileges, 41, 59, 156, 213, 244, 245
appellate jurisdiction, 37, 41, 77 n. 4, 78, 166, 205, 228, 230 n. 3, 234, 249
usurped, 180
rival jurisdictions, 76 ff
judicial exemptions, 77, 111, 120, 206, 210–11, 213, 240, 244, 250
judicial profits, 253, 256–7, 258, 262, 268
judges, 6, 12, 77, 108, 139, 155, 158, 211, 221, 222 n. 1, 257, 262

LAMBERTAZZI, family of, 194, 197, 198, 199, 204
LANCIA, family of
Galvano, 172
Manfred, 157
LAND, *see also* DONATION, GRANTS, JURISDICTION
agriculture, 80, 82, 83, 87, 88, 193, 254, 255, 257, 274
landed families, 80, 82, 88, 89, 113, 124, 189, 243
See also under ORSINI etc.
great landowners, 54 etc.
LANFRANC, Master, 120
LARIANO, 20 n. 4, 69 n. 2, 246
LATIUM, 14, 15, 81
LAURI, 13
LAVÈNE, Robert de, 209 n. 4
LAWLESSNESS, 40, 209, 212, 225, 251
LAWSUITS, 10, 39, 79, 104, 108, 124, 132, 251, 258
LEAGUES, 122, 211
of Ghibelline tyrants, 240, 242, 245
of towns, 133, 139, 144, 145, 219 n. 2
Manfredian, 162
anti-papal, 110, pro-papal, 150, 164
neutralist, 40, 147
unauthorised, 122, 179
Tuscan League, 31, 35, 36, 39
against Markward of Anweiler (q.v.), 33–4, 37
LEO VIII, Pope, 4
LEO 'de Romania', Canon of Bayeux, 309, 310
LIUPOLD, Bishop of Worms, 47, 48–9
LOIANO, Deoteclericus of, 313
LOMBARDY, 56, 87, 289, 294

LOTHAIR III, Emperor, 3 n. 7, 17
LOTTUS 'Falconieri', 324
LOUIS the Pious, Emperor, 1, 3, 43
LUCCA, 107, 194, 217
  'Cecius Dentis' of, 323
  Ptolemy of, 192
  Roland 'Paganelli' of, 323
LUCIUS II, Pope, 11
LUCIUS III, Pope, 19, 20, 21, 22
LUGNANO, 60
LÜTZELHARD, Margrave Conrad of, 18
LYONS, papal residence at, 146, 149, 153,
  157, 158, 182, 188 n. 3, 277

MACERATA, xv, 59, 72, 78 n. 4, 87, 128,
  135, 149, 150, 159, 161 n. 1, 199, 210
  n. 6, 216, 260, 265, 292
  expansion of, 274
  diocese of, 89
  seat of provincial government, 281
  parliament at, 117, 305
  account book of, 199
  statutes of, 171, 223 n. 2
  privileges to, 223, 245 n. 3
  right to appoint own podestà, 205, 211
  builds Pal. del Comune, 211
  university of, 89
  Jewish community in, 89 n. 6
  call to arms, 278, 280–2, 284
  at war with Ascoli, 200
MAGLIANO, 93
MAINZ, Archbishops of, 47, 49, 82, 170 n. 3
  Christian, 14–15, 18, 19
MALABRANCA
  John, 207
  Cardinal Latino, 191, 192, 195
MALASPINA's chronicle, 207 n. 2, 208
MALATESTA
  family of, 193, 217, 241, 250–1
  of Rimini, 117, 119, 194, 212, 217, 218,
    219, 228, 242
  of Verucchio, 184
MALAVOLTI, Rinaldo, Bishop of Siena,
  113, 252–3
MANFRED, 95, 98, 110, 121, 153, 155, 157,
  159, 162–5, 169, 173, 177, 186, 194,
  220, 261, 266, 288, 289, 295
MANFRED, Bishop, see ROBERTI
MANFREDI, family of, 193, 194, 211, 218
MARCELLINUS, Bishop of Arezzo, 314
MARKWARD of Anweiler, 27, 28, 30, 31,
  33–4, 37, 38, 40, 41, 42 n. 1, 2, 44, 49,
  60, 63, 67, 87, 134, 288, 293, 297
MARLEI, Conrad of, 53–4, 55
MARTA, 167, 169, 256 n. 3
MARTIN IV, Pope, 103, 122 n. 1, 201–4,
  206, 207, 208, 266, 277, 288, 292,
  297
MASSA TRABARIA, province of, 91, 94, 95,
  96, 106, 113 n. 1, 125, 129, 202, 223,
  238, 283 n. 3, 287, 316–7, 322

extent of, 93
  Bocca Trabaria, 93
MATELICA, xv, 47, 57 n. 2, 59, 89, 92, 149
  n. 3, 179, 205, 222, 223 n. 5, 226, 227,
  244 n. 4, 250 n. 3, 260, 289 n. 5
  Jews and Florentines in, 89 n. 6
  military service, 280–2, 287
MATILDINE LANDS, xiii n. 3, 5, 12, 17, 18,
  22, 28, 34, 35, 43, 50 n. 3, 57, 59, 62,
  64, 134
MATTHEW Cardinal of S. Maria in Porticu,
  165, 310
MAYROLLES (or MEYROLLES) Jean de, 202,
  313
MEDICINA, 228
MELDOLA, 204
MERCATELLO, 93
Merum et mixtum imperium, see also
  JURISDICTION, 75, 76, 211, 230, 234
MILAN
  Hubert 'de Notis' of, 322
  John 'Bellus' of, 321
  Lanterius of, 20
MILITARY OPERATIONS, see also: ARMIES,
  TAXATION
  Military problems, 87, 112, 200
  Military service, 7, 9, 13, 33, 127, 171, 193,
    227, 276
    summons to, 127, 161, 165, 276, 277–8,
      279–85, 287, 289, 293
    evasion of, 79, 257, 279–83, 285
    exemption from, 227, 276, 286
  strongholds, 8, 12, 13, 16, 36, 53, 86,
    132, 137, 160, 200, 246, 249, 256, 268,
    and see NINFA etc.
  commanders, 138, 147, 198, 203, 218,
    294–5, and under proper names
  cavalry, 81, 198, 226, 276, 277, 278, 280,
    281, 283, 286, 287, 288, 289, 292, 294
MIRANDA, 69 n. 2, 137, 167, 168, 188, 256
Missi, 2, 6, 7, 31, 60, 120, 137, 236–7, 240
MODENA, 93
MODIGLIANA, Bandino of, 219
MONALDESCHI
  Conrad, 180
  Ermanno, 217, 318
MONOPOLIES, 225, 255 n. 7, *see also* Salt tax
  (under TAXATION)
MONREALE
  Archbishop of, 241, 242, 318
MONTALBODDO, 156
MONTALTO, 69 n. 2, 84, 142, 143, 270 n. 3
MONTASOLA, 93, 149
MONTE CALVO, 198 n. 1, 216
MONTE S. ANGELO, 188
MONTE S. MARTINO, 118 n. 2, 212, 216
MONTE S. PIETRO, 120
MONTEBELLO, 270
MONTECCHIO, 38, 127 n. 2, 133 n. 2, 161
  n. 1, 172, 205 n. 3, 242
MONTEFALCO, 110 n. 2, 132, 149 n. 3

MONTEFELTRO, 93
  bishop of, 4
  counts of, 89, 104 n. 1, 114
  Conrad of, 242
  Galasso of, 218
  Guy of, 192, 193, 194, 199, 200, 203–4, 211, 228, 229, 287, 289 n. 3
  Taddeo of, 100, 150 n. 1, 194, 205 n. 4, 310
MONTEFIASCONE, 27 n. 2, 30, 36, 51, 60, 69 n. 2, 83, 92, 100, 113, 170, 251, 255, 276 n. 2
  parliament at, 113–14, 115, 304
  seat of Patrimony, 251
MONTEFORTINO, 220 n. 2
MONTEGIORGIO, 145 n. 3
MONTELPARO, 291 n. 3
MONTELUNGO
  family of, 82, 170 n. 3
  Lando di, 51, 307
  Roland of, 74 n. 2, 170
MONTEMEZZANO, Hugh Marquis of, 112, 187, 313, 317
MONTEMILONE, 108, 205 n. 3, 216
MONTEVECCHIO, 214 n. 1, 245 n. 2
MONTFERRAT, Conrad of, 15 n. 1, 18
MONTFORT
  Guy of, 197, 204
  John de, 197
  Simon, Earl of, 197
MONTMAJOUR, Bernard Abbot of, 262 n. 1, 274, 315
MONTOLMO, 89 n. 6, 118 n. 2, 135, 149 n. 3, 151, 159 n. 4, 205 n. 3, 209 n. 3, 251 n. 3
MORESCO, 262
MURRO 'Magister Raynucinus de', 311

NAPLES, 2, 153
  Kingdom of, 30, 53, 55, 60, 188
  Philip of, papal chaplain, 313
NARBONNE, Bernard archdeacon of, 321
NARNI, 3, 4, 8, 25, 33, 36, 42 n. 5, 74 n. 6, 83, 84, 92, 93, 110 n. 2, 137 n. 4, 138 n. 4, 142, 148, 149, 158 n. 2, 209, 256
  fortress of, 8–9, 188
  heresy in, 65
  capture by Henry VI, 24
  struggle with Popes Innocent III, 65
  and Urban IV, 167, 168, 171
  Bishop and citizens excommunicated, 65
  buys privilege, 231
  right to elect podestà, 231 n. 2
  alliance with Perugia, 210, 226
  claims Stroncone, 65, 74, 130, 167, 171, 225–6
  and Otricoli, 74
  war with Terni, 84, 132, 160
  John 'Angeli' canon of, 320

Martin Mayoxen canon of, 321
  prior of, 104
NEPI, 83, 92, 142, 214 n. 1, 243–4
  Lituardus, Bishop of, 319
NEPOTISM, *see under* PAPAL RELATIVES
NERA, river, 84, 168, 173
NEUSS, 'promise of', 43, 53, 57, 59, 67
NICHOLAS 'Falconis', papal chaplain, 317
NICHOLAS III, Pope, 72, 91, 92, 99, 103, 111, 121, 186, 189 ff, 288
NICHOLAS IV, Pope, 74, 76, 77, 94 n. 1, 103, 121, 122, 123, 212 ff, 227, 303
NICOLINO 'de Camilla', 308, 311
NINFA, fortress of, 9 n. 4, 43, 55 n. 3, 67, 69 n. 2, 81, 100, 132, 214 n. 1, 243, 244
NOCERA UMBRA, 33 n. 4, 83, 85, 92, 94, 110 n. 2, 129, 152, 183, 187, 206 n. 1, 216, 250
  Count of, 109, 251
NOGARET [William of], 247
  See also ANAGNI, outrage of
NORCIA, 87, 92, 109, 135, 206 n. 1, 212, 216, 286 n. 1
NORMA, 15, 243
NORMANNI, family of, 83
NORMANS, *see also under* proper names
  invasions of, 3, 12
  power of, 8, 26, 188–9
  support for Papacy, 8, 9, 13, 14, 15
NUMANA, 64, 88, 133 n. 2, 151, 249
  Bishop of, 152, 223 n. 5

OATHS
  Coronation, 3 n. 7
  of fidelity, 12, 13, 31, 37, 52, 54, 70, 163, 185, 195, 196
  of obedience, 25, 52, 68, 99–100, 141, 142, 176; *see also* COMMUNES, TOWNS
  sworn by Rectors, 97
OCTAVIANI, family of, 7, 8
OFFIDA, 159, 286 n. 2
  Walter of, 308
OFFREDUCCIO, 168
OLEVANO, 81
ORCHIA, 13, 69 n. 2, 270
ORDELAFFI, family of, 228, 248
ORSINI, family of, *see also* CELESTINE III, Pope, 44, 45, 83, 103, 148, 149, 189, 192, 197, 200–1, 202, 224, 238, 240, 244, 246, 247, 249, 250
  enmity with COLONNA (q.v.), 214, 217, 225
  and ANNIBALDI (q.v.), 200–1, 214, 225
  driven from Rome, 207
  Bertold, 99, 104 n. 1, 112 n. 2, 117, 191, 192, 196–9, 224, 238, 313, 317
  Gentile, 198, 246
  John Gaetan, 309, *see* NICHOLAS III, Pope
  Cardinal Matthew 'Rosso', 187, 191, 196, 215, 224, 239 n. 2

Cardinal Napoleon, 77, 95, 96, 224, 232 n. 3, 235, 238, 239, 244, 309, 313, 316

Orsello, 246 n. 3

Orso, 104 n. 2, 191, 200, 238, 246, 311

ORTE, 25, 37, 60, 83, 142, 283, 286

ORVIETO, 1, 13, 14, 24, 25, 36, 60, 65, 83 n. 2, 84, 92, 100, 132, 138, 148, 149, 156–7,, 160, 169, 182, 186, 202, 207, 215, 224, 225, 247, 248, 284, 286
  heretics in, 36
  parliament at, 107 n. 2, 304
  owes military service, 277 n. 1
  Pope resides in, 172–3, 203, 206, 208, 213, 214 n. 4, 295
  Martin IV as podestà, 222
  oath of fealty to Pope, 13
  Capitano del popolo of, 208, 247 n. 3
  riots in, 207, 208
  war with Todi, 144, 156, 160, 284 n. 4
  claims Acquapendente, 36, 157, 167, 169 170, 226, 246
  and Val del Lago (*see under* BOLSENA), 74, 120, 141 n. 2, 144, 157, 167, 180, 225–6, 231, 243, 246, 286

OSIMO, 34, 40, 41, 42, 47, 59, 64, 89, 126, 135, 144, 145, 149, 151, 171, 227, 246
  called to arms, 278 n. 4, 279
  lends money to Azzo of Este, 63
  Bishop Benvenuto of, 315
  Gonzolino of, 206

OSTIA, 69 n. 2, 147
  Rainald, Bishop of, 176; *see also* ALEXANDER IV, Pope

OTRICOLI, 36, 65, 69 n. 2, 74, 83, 137, 167, 171, 257 n. 1, 268

OTTO I, Emperor, 2, 3, 4

OTTO IV, Emperor, 43–4, 47, 49, 56 ff, 89, 125, 134

OUTLAWS, 79, 112, 161, 224, 265 n. 2, 283

PAGANELLI, Nellus, of Florence, 324

PAGANI, Mainardo dei, 193, 194

PAGLIA, river, 82, 84

PALESTRINA, 81, 213, 244
  Bishop of, 311, *see also* NICHOLAS IV, Pope

PALIANO, 69 n. 2, 256

PALTINIERI, Cardinal Simon, 178, 179, 181 n. 2, 184 n. 4

PANDULF, papal notary, 96, 110, 128 n. 3, 129–30, 132, 135

PAPACY, *see also* DECREES, JURISDICTION, PROVINCIAL GOVERNMENT, RECTORS, ROME etc.
  Papal legislation, 122, *see also* CONSTITU-TIONS
  Papal prestige, 8, 16, 104, 297, 298, 299–300; (*and see* ANAGNI, outrage of)
  papal chamber and chamberlain, 120–1, 163 n. 5, 237–8

papal-imperial struggle, *see also* HOHENSTAUFEN, 5, 9, 12, 14, 16, 17, 21, 125 ff, 294

papal provinces, 91 ff, 94, *see under* ANCONA, March of, etc.

revenues, 8, 41, 106, 122, 205, 252 ff and *passim*

papal residence, *see* ANAGNI, AVIGNON, PERUGIA etc.

territorial rights, 2, 5, 66, 69, also DONATIONS

purchase of lands, 2, 13, 69, 136–7, 184–5, 256, 298

papal vacancies, 77, 149, 165, 173, 181, 188, 200–1, 210, 211, 212, 225, 227

weakness of papacy, 4, 6, 9, 19, 20, 22, 23, 25, 39, 40, 47, 56, 66, 70, 130, 134, 136, 139, 143, 156, 176, 180, 215, 247, 248

papal registers, xv n. 1, 98, 231

papal officials; *see* Missi etc.

Papal chaplains under proper names

PAPAL RELATIVES, *see also* under proper names, 45, 50–1, 55, 82, 102, 103–4, 134, 138, 141, 142, 158, 159, 161, 163, 169, 170, 176, 182–3, 184, 190–2, 209 n. 3, 238, 239, 273, 298, 301

PAPARONUS doctor of laws, 311

PARCITADI, family of, 193

PARENZO
  Andrew, 132
  Parenzo, 131, 132

PARIS, MATTHEW, 141 n. 3, 145 n. 5, 147 n. 4, 294, 295 n. 1, 299

PARLIAMENTS, Provincial, *see also* CON-STITUTIONS, PROVINCIAL GOVT., TAXA-TION etc., 67, 90, 99, 100, 105, 110 ff (and under names of towns)
  (for meeting places *see under* towns)
  composition of, 113–14, 119
  frequency, 112, 115
  length of session, 115
  business, 110–20
  powers, 73, 115–17
  disputes, 118–19
  open-air, 115 n. 3
  non-attendance at, 114, 118
  lists of, 112, 304–6
  the Viterbo parliament of 1207, 52–3, 110

PARMA, 1, 149, 185 n. 3, 250
  James of, 319
  Thomasinus 'de Inzola' of, 308

PASCHAL II, Pope, 4, 9

PAVIA, Bishop of, 236, 237, 241–2

PEACE NEGOTIATIONS; *see also* TREATIES, NEUSS, promise of, etc., 27–8, 41–2, 47, 74

PEGLIO, 101

PENNA S. GIOVANNI, 219 n. 3

PENTAPOLIS, 3, 42, 185, *and see under* ROMAGNA

PEREGRINUS, papal chaplain, 320
PEROCCHIO, 168
PERUGIA, xv, 1, 4, 31, 33 n. 4, 36, 70, 80
    n. 2, 83, 85, 86, 137 n. 4, 138, 142 n. 4,
    148, 149, 156, 158, 162, 180, 182, 186,
    187, 216, 242–3, 249, 255, 260, 271,
    283
  granted a charter, 24
  and judicial rights, 37, 76, 206
  Parliament at, 110, 304
  Bishops of, 4, 92
  podestà of, 86, 222, 284
  submits to papacy, 31, 60
  Pope resides in, 66, 135, 141, 173, 203,
    206, 208, 258
  riots in, 64, 86 n. 2
  burns Pope and Cardinals in effigy, 206,
    300
  gives them Christmas present, 255 n. 2
  military service with papal armies, 276–
    277, 280–1, 283–4
  fined, 267–8, 272, 274
  and excommunicated, 183, 206, 285
  financial and commercial character,
    86
  population of, 85 n. 3
  territorial claims, 183, 187, 210
  enmity with Assisi, 48
  with Foligno, 80 n. 2, 156, 205–6, 210,
    215–16, 219, 243, 285
  and Gubbio, 160, 162, 245, 249, 251
  archpriest of, 310, 312
PESARO, 41, 42, 88, 92, 93, 144, 212, 228,
    242, 251, 276 n. 1, 278
PETER, cardinal-deacon of S. George *ad
    velum Aureum*, 42, 308, 309, 310,
    314
PETER, prior of S. Ippolito, 319
PETER 'Alafredi', spiritual vicar of the
    March of Ancona, 315, 321
PETER 'de Buclano' archpriest (dioc.
    Chieti), 322
PETER 'Iudicis' canon of S. Peter's, 316
PETER 'de Manganella', 311
PETER 'Saraceni' Bishop of Vicenza, 322
PETER *de Saxo*, Cardinal, 54, 307
PHILIP de SARTINANO, 308
PHILIP-AUGUSTUS, King of France, 56, 60
PHILIP III, King of FRANCE, 203, 301
PHILIP IV 'the Fair', King of France, 247,
    289, 302
PIACENZA, 106, 107, 120, 182, 320
  Roger, provost of S. Anthony's in, 120,
    237
PIERLEONE
  family of, 9, 10
  John, 26, 38, 39, 46 n. 2
PIETRARUBBIA, Taddeo of, 194
PIETRASANTA
  Guiscard of, 104, 165, 168, 170, 310
  Pipio of, 165, 310

PIPERNO, 55 n. 3, 81, 82, 132, 184, 191
  Maximus of, 242, 318
  Cardinal Peter of, 2, 242 n. 3, 311, 318
PISA, 88 and n. 8, 274, 309
  Council of, 4
  armed forces, 228
  and galleys, 84
  Ranier of, papal notary, 309, 313
PISTOIA
  Clarus 'Montalti' of, 107, 324
  Nicholas 'Giandonati' of, 323
  Simon 'q. Bonaccursi' of, 323
PO, river, 5, 62, 87, 138
PODESTÀ, *see* mainly under towns
  office of, 41, 68, 70, 75, 78, 82, 110, 133,
    167, 220, 240
  appointment of, 70, 71, 130, 132, 141,
    161, 200, 205 n. 4, 221, 230
  by the Pope, 70–2, 166–7, 213 n. 1, 222
  for life, 233, 240
  the Pope as podestà, 214, 221–2, 233, 240
  outlaw as, 265 n. 2
  right of election of, 70, 71, 72, 119, 120,
    121, 150, 211, 222, 234, 252, 260
  excommunication of, 48, 70, 187
  potesteria, 254, 270
POLENTA family (of Ravenna), 112 n. 2,
    117, 119, 193
  Guy da, 194, 195, 211, 218, 219
POLI
  lords of, 13, 45–6
  lands, 47, 50, 55, 91
  castles, 55
POLVERIGI, 42
PORTO S. GIORGIO, 89
PORTS, *see also under* ANCONA, GENOA etc.,
    88–9
POTENZA, river, 89, 284
POPES, *see under* ADRIAN IV etc.
  character of papal rule, 68 ff
  burned in effigy, 206, 300
  said to have been excommunicated, 48
  anti-Popes, 9–10, 14
PREFETTI, Godfrey dei, papal chaplain, 310
PROCENO, 13, 66, 69 n. 2, 132 n. 2
PROVINCES, *see under* proper names, also
    ARMIES, JURISDICTION, RECTORS etc.
PROVINCIAL GOVERNMENT, *see also* JURIS-
    DICTION, RECTORS, TAXATION etc.
  Revenues, (see also *Liber Censuum*, under
    Census), 260 ff, esp. 272–3
  Provincial courts, 77, 78, 101, 106, and
    passim
  peripatetic character of, 100, 101
  duties of vicars, 103–4 (*and see under*
    RECTORS)
  archives, xiv–xv, 79, 98, 188, 266
  relations with communes, *passim*, and,
    p. 303
PULCI, family of, 107
PUYRICARD, Fulk of, 182, 183, 186, 274, 315

RADICOFANI, 13, 36, 43, 60, 62, 66, 69 n. 2, 70, 92, 94, 95, 132 n. 3, 149, 206
RAINALD, papal chaplain, 317
RAINALD 'de Basciano', 322
RAINALD, bishop of Valencia, 316
RAINIERI, Ranier de, of Lucca, 323
RAINUZIO, Manfredo di, of Siena, 323
RAMBONA, Philip, Abbot of, 314
'RANCERUS' de Robertis, 317
RANIER, papal chaplain, 310
RANIER, Cardinal, of Viterbo, 95, 96, 97, 132, 137, 146, 147, 149, 151, 153, 167, 259, 277, 295, 310, 312, 314
'RANNUS RAYNALDI', 320
RAVENNA, *see also* POLENTA, Guy of, xv, 87, 93, 94, 115, 117, 118, 119, 193, 198, 211–12, 217, 218, 228, 229, 242, 292
  duchy of, 5, 27, 28, 33, 34, 57, 62
  exarchate of, 1, 2 n. 4, 3, 43, 127, 185
  parliament at, 112 n. 2, 242, 306
  residence of Rector of Romagna, 101 n. 4
  Archbishop of, 35, 40, 59, 197, 199 n. 1, 251
RAYMOND 'Caprarii', canon of Lerida, 316
RAYMOND 'de Nogeriis', 310
RECANATI, 64, 89, 128, 133 n. 2, 135, 144, 147 n. 3, 151, 152, 162, 171, 172, 227, 242, 245 n. 4, 246, 249
  Bishop of, 105 n. 3
RECTORS of PROVINCES (q.v.). *See also* under proper names, 6, 9, 10, 51, 52, 73, 91 ff, 115, 154–5, 158, 165–6, 234 ff
  list of, 307–318
  spiritual rectors, 104, 105–6, 319–22
  titular, 103–4, 239
  appoint vicars as deputies, 103–5
  status of, 52, 95 ff, 154–5, 196, 210, 234–5
  duties of, 103–4, 196–8
  appointment of, 97, 102, 158, 165, *see also* PAPAL RELATIVES
  salary, 98, 104, 105–6, 251
  legatine powers, 96
  Cardinals as, 102–3, 126, 139
  Frenchmen as, 208
  laymen as, 102, 103–4, 105, 158–9, 165
  of two adjoining provinces, 95
REGGIO (Emilia), 1, 164
REGNO, the, 40, 48, 49, 50, 54, 55, 59, 60, 66, 81, 87, 87–9, 91, 92, 103, 108, 135, 149, 153, 177, 178, 200–2, 288
RICCIARDI, family of, 107
RICHARD, cardinal-deacon of S. Angelo, 96, 146, 307
RICHEVILLE, Robert de, 202 n. 1
RIETI, 33 n. 4, 37, 60, 83, 94, 95, 126 n. 1, 134, 141, 142, 149, 166, 177, 255, 256, 257, 261, 267

  builds unauthorized castle, 236
  bishops of, 92, 239, 247–8, 309, 318
  James, Bishop of, 239, 318
  Angelo of, 313
  Matthew of, 321
  Offreduccio podestà of, 168
RIMBERTINI, family of, 107
RIMBERTINUS 'Piovanelli', 323
RIMINI, *see also under* MALATESTA, xv, 34, 87, 92, 119, 193, 198, 203, 212, 241, 242, 292
  Bishop of, 4
  podestà of, 217
RIPATRANSONE, 40, 69, 112 n. 2, 159 n. 4, 181, 210, 216, 219, 222, 265
  parliament at, 112 n. 2
  James of, 308
RIPESENA, 13
ROADS
  Highways, 36, 45, 74
  from Rome, 10, 36, 81, 82, 213
  Via Amerina, 83, 85
    Appia, 81, 243
    Cassia, 83
    Emilia, 58, 93, 193
    Flaminia, 58, 83, 85, 137
    Labicana, 81, 82
    Latina, 55, 243
    Prenestina, 81, 213
    Salaria, 83, 92
    Tiburtino-Valeria, 83, 243, 244
ROBERT, papal chaplain, 317
ROBERTI, Manfred de', Bishop of Verona, 164, 165, 172, 261, 310, 312, 315
ROCCA D'ARCE, 55
ROCCA CIRCEA, 246
ROCCA DI FOCE, 154 n. 4, 158 n. 2
ROCCA DI PAPA, 19
ROLAND 'de Campania', 159, 315
ROMAGNA, province of, 40, 56, 59, 87, 91, 92, 94, 100, 106, 112, 114, 115, 116, 119, 184–5, 196–9, 202, 211–12, 294, 297
  character of, 93, 193–5, 274
  war in, 203–5, 217–18, 239, 245, 265, 267, 268, 286–7, 291, 292
  finances of, 271
  Romagnol poets, 300
ROMAN families, *see also* COLONNA, FRANGIPANI etc., 9, 14, 44–5, 80, 83, 147, 190–1, 200, 202 n. 3, 214, 225, 240, 297, 303
ROMANI de Scotta, family of, 44
ROMANUS, cardinal-deacon of S. Angelo, cardinal-bishop of Porto, 307, 309, 312
ROME, *passim, see also* PAPACY etc., *also* ROADS
  claim to suzerainty, 10–11, 15, 157, 160, 215

ROME (*cont.*)
expansionism, 74, 142–3, 157, imperialism, 131
economic life, 81–2
famine in, 47
disorder in, 9, 45–7, 207
papal residence in, 15, 19, 23, 49, 80–1,
  131, 143, 157–8, 192, 195 n. 1, 209
Pope driven from, 9, 16, 19, 24, 131, 140,
  160–1
quarrels with Papacy, 10–11 ff, 19–20,
  38–9, 55, 131, 142–3
with Empire, 10, 18–19, *and see under*
  EMPERORS
Roman alliance with Papacy, 36, 215
Prefecture of, 7, 17, 18, 32, *and under*
  VICO
Senators, *see also under* ANDALÒ, CAPOCCIO
  etc., 32, 55, 131, 157, 174, 181, 190–1,
  209, 240, 301
Constitutio super electione senatoris Urbis,
  190
Deodatus of, 308
ROSSI, family of, 82
RUDOLF, King of the Romans, 3, 184–6,
  194, 195

SABINA, province of, 1, 3, 4, 6, 20 n. 4,
  69 n. 2, 83, 84, 91, 92, 107, 121, 142,
  177, 308–9, 319
extent of, 93, 297
county of, 81, 92, 93, 94, 100, 209, 256,
  271
bishop of, 93, 247, 309, 320
Sabine hills, 213
SACCO, river, 55, 213
SALERNO, 2, 3
Romuald of, 16 n. 1
SALIMBENE, 137, 187, 206 n. 2, 299 n. 3
SALINGUERRA, 59, 62, 64, 128
SALINO, river, 108
SALISBURY, John of, 15 n. 3, 20
SANGRO, Gentile da, 316
S. AGATA, 93
'Terra S. Agathae', 94
S. ALBERTO
Lorenzo of, 318
Matthew of, 315
S. ANGELO in Vado, 93
S. ANGELO PAPALE, 221
See under CAGLI
S. DONATO, 243
S. ELPIDIO, 205 n. 3
S. ERCOLANO, 242
S. FELICE, 246
S. FIORA, Guy of, 246
S. GEMINI, 69 n. 2, 74 n. 6, 137 n. 4, 149
  n. 2, 167, 168, 171, 239, 283
Fra Bartholomew of, 192
S. GERMANO, 54

Richard of, 127 n. 2, 136, 141 n. 3, 288
  n. 4
Treaty of, 134, 138
S. GINESIO, 77 n. 4, 149 n. 3, 155, 159 n. 4,
  227, 249 n. 1, 285
S. LEO, 204
S. LORENZO in Campo, 108
S. PROCOLO, 194
S. SEVERINO, 161, 227
Count Thomas of, 229
S. VITTORIA, 145 n. 3, 149 n. 3, 263, 264
SASSOFERRATO, 216
SAVELLI, *see also* Popes HONORIUS III & IV
family of, 83, 125, 131, 147, 209, 213,
  214, 240, 250
Cardinal James, 187, 209
Luca, 180, 209, 311
Cardinal Ottobuono, 187
Pandulf, 191, 207, 209
Peter, 239 n. 2
Cardinal William, 187
SCHWEINSPUNT, Dipold of, 59–60, 61, 63,
  64, 65
SCOTTI, family of, 107
SCOTTUS 'Paparonis', Roman senator, 31
SEGNI, 15, 55, 82, 132, 134, 142, 283 n. 2
Counts of, 9, 20 n. 4, 21 n. 1, 81
SELVAMOLLE, 243
SENIGALLIA, 34, 42, 63 n. 4, 64, 88, 89, 126
  n. 1, 200, 219, 242, 251, 279
Count of, 40, 41, 42 n. 2
SERMONETA, 20 n. 2, 132, 243
SERRAVALLE, 69 n. 2
SERRONE, 69 n. 2, 246, 256
SEZZE, 20 n. 4, 55 n. 3, 81, 82, 160, 184, 191
SGURGOLA, 244, 246 n. 5, 247
SICILY, *see also* the REGNO, and under
  ANJOU and HOHENSTAUFEN, 2, 51, 198,
  223
Sicilian Kingdom, 16, 26, 27, 28, 40, 48,
  50, 55, 67, 112, 153, 228
Tancred of, 21, 26
War of the Sicilian Vespers, 207, 208,
  209, 238, 288, 289, 295
SIENA, 36, 66, 157, 173–4, 194
bankers of, 266
bishops of, 113, 244–5, 270, 311
Ranier, bishop of, 312
Bindus 'Deotavive' of, 323
Bonsignore 'Gregorii' of, 322
SIGNORI, 219–20, 222, 228, 233, 244, 245
SIGNORIA, 74, 219, 220, 223, 242, 243 n. 4
SIMON, Cardinal of S. Martin, 103, 106,
  111 n. 5, 165, 178, 186, 312, 315
SINIBALD, Cardinal, 146, 149, 314
See under INNOCENT IV, Pope
SOMMERSOT, Geoffrey de, 202, 208, 308
SORA, 53, 54, 55, 66, 67, 131
SORELLA, 53, 54, 55
SORIANO, 192, 201
SPELLO, 31, 130, 149, 187, 206 n. 1, 215–16

SPEYER, 57
promise of, 57, 58, 59
SPILIATI
family of, 107
Andrew, subdeacon and papal chaplain, 308, 315
SPINI, family of, 107
SPLIT, 88
SPOLETO, 3, 33 n. 4, 37, 63, 76, 78 n. 2, 83, 85, 86–7, 94, 118, 132, 141, 148, 151, 171, 173, 187 n. 4, 206, 210, 216, 226, 244, 245, 267, 271, 277, 285
bishop of, 4, 92
castle of, 86
granted privileges, 151, 230–1, 245
relations with Popes Urban IV, 167–9
and Boniface VIII, 230–1
Valle Spoletana, 85, 206
SPOLETO, Duchy of, *see also* URSLINGEN, Dukes of, 1, 3, 4,7, 19, 27, 31, 33, 36–7, 42, 43, 51, 56, 59, 62, 64, 66, 91, 94, 106, 109, 125–6, 127, 129, 144, 148, 149, 155, 158, 173, 176, 183, 202, 210, 215–16, 233–4, 247, 304, 312–13, 320, 322
extent of, 92
revenues of, 271, 274
STEFANESCHI, Peter, 119, 318
STEPHEN, Cardinal-priest of S. Maria in Trastevere, 146–7, 307, 308
STEPHEN the papal chamberlain, 54, 60, 64, 307
STEPHEN, Canon of S. Peter's, 321
STRADILIANO, Ruffino da, 106, 107, 323
STRONCONE, 65, 69 n. 2, 74, 130, 137 n. 4, 149 n. 2, 171, 225, 226, 256
SUBIACO, Abbots of, 169
Cardinal Simon, 14
SUBURRA, Pandulf of, 46
SUPINO
Lords of, 82, 131, 214
Adinulf of, 244
Rainald of, 247, 312
Thomas of, 81
SUSINANA, Mainardo da, 114, 211, 212 n. 1, 217, 218, 219, 239, 241, 242, 248
SUTRI, 24, 43, 83, 92, 142, 172, 255, 277 n. 1
SWABIA, Philip of, 27, 30, 35, 38, 43, 44, 47, 48, 49–50, 54, 55 n. 1, 56, 57, 84, 86

TAGLIACOZZO [battle of], 181, 194, 288
TARANO, 100
TAVERNA, Roland, Bishop of Spoleto, 320
TAXATION, *see also* ARMIES (Scutage), *Census, fodrum* etc., 6, 99, 199, 253 ff
farming of taxes, 253, 255
of clergy, 65, 105, 134, 143
of towns, 59, 70, 79, 94, 111, 162, 174, 179, 199–200, 253
tallia militum, 112, 115–16, 117, 119, 186,

199, 205, 211, 212, 217, 218, 254–5, 262, 264–5, 266, 269, 270, 273, 287, 291–2 ,293
fictus, 258, 262, 263, 264
tolls, 30, 59, 73, 150, 156, 255, 256, 268
dues in kind, 254, 256
corvées, 255
tax-gatherers, 82
exemptions, 260
hearth tax, 73, 186, 228 n. 3, 234, 234 n. 3, 254, 270
salt tax, 224, 255
TEDALDINI, Malabranca dei, 311
TENNA, river, 108
TENNACULA, river, 108
TERNI, 3, 59, 83, 84, 94, 110 n. 2, 132, 137, 148, 155, 159 n. 2, 160, 173, 206, 210, 224, 255, 256, 260, 268, 271
fined 10,000*l*, 156
'TERRA ARNULFORUM', 85 n. 2, 94, 151, 167, 168, 187 n. 4, 223, 255, 256
TERRA DEL LAVORO, 40, 54, 135
TERRACINA, 7, 14, 15, 25, 69 n. 2, 131–2, 157, 163, 184, 191, 210 n. 1, 214, 215, 220 n. 2, 222, 244, 283 n. 2
claims exemption from military service, 276
merchants of, 82
THEODERIC, papal chamberlain, (afterwards Card. bishop of Città Papale), 224, 237, 238, 244, 246, 311
THEOPHYLACT, papal *vestiarius*, 6, 7
TIBER, river, 13, 36, 60, 61, 83, 84, 92, 93, 94, 95, 132, 139, 142, 173, 256
flooding of, 141–2
TIEPOLO, LORENZO, 179
TINTINANNO, 277 n. 1
TIVOLI, 3, 5 n. 1, 10, 13, 25, 55, 64, 83, 91, 134, 148, 149, 160, 163, 168, 173
comitatus of, 3, 170
clergy, 240
TODI, 4, 33 n. 4, 42, 52, 60, 65, 76, 83, 84, 92, 93, 95, 111, 121, 132, 137 n. 4, 138 n. 4, 156, 180, 183, 210, 215–16, 224, 225, 226, 235, 236, 252, 283, 289 n. 5
Bishops of, 4 (Nicholas), 313
claims exemption from Tuscan Patrimony, 95, 111, 183, 200, 243
lawsuits with Gubbio, 200
war with Orvieto, 144, 156, 160, 281
visited by Pope Innocent IV, 37
ordered to send ambassadors to Boniface VIII, 236
Gerardinus of, 317
Giles of, 317
Mathiolus of, 317
James, son of John of, 317
'Salcius Grappavingie' of, 317

TOLENTINO, 42, 112 n. 2, 159 n. 4, 205 n. 3, 227, 281 n. 2
  Parliament at, 111 n. 4, 112 n. 2, 304, 305
  Lambertinus of, 319
TOLFA, 240 n. 2
TORGIANO, 187, 242
TORRE DI PALMA, 69 n. 2, 243
TORRE PIOMBINARA, 55
TOSCANELLA, 51, 83 n. 2, 84, 92, 142, 174, 182 n. 3, 212 n. 2, 240
TOWNS, *see also* COMMUNES, JURISDICTION, PODESTÀ, TRADE
  castra, 59; *see also* CASTLES
  relations with Papacy, *passim*
  rivalry, 47, 48, 87, 89, 210
  attempts to dominate smaller towns, 47, 74; *and see* NARNI, ORVIETO etc.
  foundation of new towns, 12, 13, 221, 244, 277
  population, 85 n. 3, 86, 88
  imperial grants to, 59, 60, 75, 86, *and see under* proper names
  for *tallia militum* etc., *see under* TAXATION
TRADE, 80–1, 83, 86, 88, 89
  with Egypt, 88
  encouragement of, 65
  trading centres, 80, 82, 84, 86–8
  trading privileges, 15, 151, *and see under* names of towns
  merchants, 81 n. 3, 86, 88, 89, 165, 193, 226–7, 245, 275, *see also under* BOLOGNA etc.
  salt trade at Ravenna, (q.v.), 57
TRASMONDO, Annibaldo di, 103, 158–9, 193 n. 1, 315
TREASURERS, 106–8, 183, 189
  list of, 322–4
TREATIES, *see* HAGENAU, S. GERMANO etc.
TREVI (Campagna), 91, 169, 244
TREVI (Umbria), 64, 74 n. 6, 83, 151, 284 n. 3
  Nicholas of, 237, 273
TREVISO, 250
  Counts of, 250, 316
  podestà of, 250
TROGIR, 88
TRONTO, river, 83, 92, 94
TUSCAN PATRIMONY
  geographical character of, 82–3, 274
  Tuscan Maremma, 142, 274
  Tuscan patrimony, 14, 15, 36, 58, 64, 65, 82, 83, 89, 91, 94, 95, 100, 103, 126, 129, 130, 137, 142, 144, 146, 148, 150, 159, 169, 176, 177, 187, 195, 202, 225, 238, 246, 252, 255, 270, 289, 293, 304, 309–11, 319–20, 322
  Boniface VIII's constitution for, 234
TUSCULUM, 10, 15, 19, 25, 26, 213
  proximity to Rome, 7, 8, 15
  Counts of, 7, 8, 9, 20 n. 4, 213

  Jonathan of, 13
  Count Ptolemy of, 10
  Raino of, 15–16
TYRANTS, *see also* SIGNORI, LEAGUES etc., 114, 296
TYRRHENIAN, 1, 36, 53, 55, 82, 91

UBERTUS, papal chaplain, 317
UGOLINO, Treasurer of the Duchy of Spoleto, 107 n. 2, 322
UGOLINO 'Rainerii', 314
UMBRIA, 4, 67, 84, 157, 158, 203, 210, 276, 295, 300
  Umbrian towns as papal summer residences, 214 (*see also* PERUGIA etc.)
URBAN II, Pope, 9
URBAN III, Pope, 20, 23–4
URBAN IV, Pope, 71, 95, 103, 110, 121, 123, 164 n. 1, 165–72, 173, 174, 178, 183, 192, 194, 221, 261, 275, 284, 294, 295
URBINO, 87. 89, 92, 106, 179, 193, 204, 213, 217, 228, 277, 281, 287, 291, 292
  bishops of, 4
  province of, 93–4, 317
URSLINGEN, *see also* SPOLETO, Duchy of
  family of, 126, 127, 135, 136, 141
  Bertold of, 126–7, 129, 130, 132, 133
  Conrad of, 19, 27, 30, 33, 37, 60, 85, 86, 92, 110, 125, 129, 132, 297
  Rainald of, 127, 129, 134–5, 138, 144, 145

VALENCIA, bishop of, 227
VALENTANO, 100, 169
VALLEPIETRA, 244
VALMONTONE, 55, 81
VALOIS, Charles of, 104, 239, 247, 269–70, 302 n. 1, 313, 316, 318
VALTOPINO *see under* SPOLETO
VARANO
  lords of, 89, 219 n. 3
  Berard da, of Camerino, 317
  Gentile da, 162
VAUCOULEURS, Thierri of, xv, 168
VELLETRI, 7, 9 n. 2, 45, 74, 82, 111 n. 2, 142, 207, 231 n. 2, 240
  James of, 309
VENAISSIN, the Comtat, xiii n. 3, 102 n. 3, 223
VENICE, 1, 87, 144, 179, 250
  assault on Ancona (q.v.), 186
  commercial undertakings, 87, 88, 89, 135, 184, 274
  Treaty of, 17, 18, 19, 20, 21
  Venetia, 1, 87
  James 'Quirini' of, 311
VENTIMIGLIA, Henry of, 162, 172
VEROLI, 15, 20 n. 4, 76 n. 1, 82, 91, 126
  John of, 6
  Roffred of, 6
  Roffred II of, 6
VERONA, 24, 87, 180

bishop of, 95, 103, 164, 165, 261, 310
peace negotiations at, 22–3
VESPERS, Sicilian, *see under* SICILY
VETRALLA, 25, 27, 83
VICENZA
bishops of, 117, 248
VICO
lands, 83, 167, 169, 173
lords of, 11, 83, 286
prefects of Rome, 14, 32, 42 n. 4
Peter di, 32, 167, 169, 173, 309, 312
Peter III, 169
VICOVARO, 44, 189
VICTOR II, Pope, 7, 8
VICTOR IV, Pope, 14
VILLANI, Giovanni, 82
VISCONTI
Henry, 183, 315
Tebaldo (of Piacenza) *see* GREGORY X, Pope
Uberto, 182, 308
Ubertino, 313
Visconte (of Piacenza), 182, 310
William, 182, 313
VISSO, 109
VITERBO, *see also* Cardinal RANIER of, xv, 10, 15, 25, 60, 74, 83, 84, 92, 126, 127, 134, 144, 146, 149, 157, 164, 169, 177, 182, 186, 192, 200, 270 n. 2, 276, 285, 286, 294
falls to Henry VI, 24
parliament in, 52–3, 54, 56, 110–11, 121, 304
bishops of, 105 n. 2
Pope at, 51, 58, 143, 161, 163, 181, 190
Curia at, 19, 188, 189, 195, 200
war with Rome, 39, 42, 44, 74, 131, 132, 141, 142, 149, 258

class struggles, 84
and violence, 200
heresy in, 52, 53, 238 n. 1
awarded fiscal privileges, 65
deprived of right to appoint podestà, 72, 221
relations with papacy, 39, 65, 142 n. 4, 201, 210, 215
John of, 195, 196
VITORCHIANO, 38
VOLSCIAN hills, *see also* CASTRO DEI VOLSCI, 213

WALES, Gerald of, 27 n. 4
WALTER, Marquis, 40
WARDSHIP, *see under* FREDERICK II, Emperor
WARFARE, *see also* ARMIES, MILITARY OPERATIONS, COLONNA War etc., 20, 42, 47, 212
Wars, 88 n. 5, 89, 131, 132, 133, 144, 156, 159, 160, 181–2, 188, 200, 201, 203, 205–6, 214, 215–16, 226, 241, 242, 246, 263, 265 (*see also under* names of towns)
weapons, 46, 277, 278, 281, and notes, 1, 2, 3
increased cost of war, 290
WILLIAM, Cardinal of S. Eustace, 295
WILLIAM 'de Alba', 318
WILLIAM of S. Lorenzo, papal chaplain, 320
WILLIAM 'Paganus', 55
WOLFENBÜTTEL, Gunzelin von, 126, 130, 132, 134
WOLFGER, Patriarch of Aquileia, 56, 57

ZADAR, 88
ZAGAROLO, 244

PRINTED IN GREAT BRITAIN BY ROBERT MACLEHOSE AND CO. LTD
THE UNIVERSITY PRESS, GLASGOW